D1720641

TREES OF SOUTHERN AFRICA

VOLUME TWO

Trees of Southern Africa

covering all known indigenous species

in the

Republic of South Africa, South-West Africa,

Botswana, Lesotho & Swaziland

by EVE PALMER and NORAH PITMAN

With the co-operation of the Director

DR L.E.W.CODD

and the staff of the Botanical Research Institute

VOLUME TWO

A.A.Balkema / Cape Town / 1972

Volume 2 first published 1973

Unsigned drawings are by Norah Pitman; those signed
R.C. are by Rhona Collett.

Text (c) Eve Palmer 1972
Monochrome photographs (c) Eve Palmer 1972
Colour photographs (c) Geoffrey Jenkins 1972
Unsigned line illustrations (c) Norah Pitman 1972
Line illustrations signed RC (c) A.A. Balkema 1972
ISBN 0 86961 033 3

Contents

Colour plates

42 The Legume Family (Leguminosae)

The family Leguminosae, with its hundreds of genera and some 12,000 species, is one of the largest and most cosmopolitan of all the plant families. Trees, shrubs, and herbs are scattered throughout the world, usually in tropical and subtropical regions, and are very well represented in South Africa.

Plants of the family have been cultivated since early times, and are widely used for various purposes. Peas and beans provide food; senna is used medicinally; certain plants yield indigo; the bark of others is used in tanning; still others yield an edible gum. Lucerne, clover, and the pods of such trees as the honey-locust, mesquite and carob, and of many of our wild trees, are good fodder. The lovely laburnum and wisteria are legumes, as are some of our own beautiful flowering plants and trees.

The Judas tree (*Cercis siliquastrum* L.) of Mediterranean regions and western Asia is one of the most famous members of the family for by tradition it is the tree on which Judas Iscariot hanged himself.

In South and South West Africa just over 100 species of trees belong to Leguminosae, that is, nearly one ninth of the total number found in these territories. They occur mainly in open forest, in parkland, and in the arid regions of the country. Among them are some of our most familiar, characteristic, and best-loved trees such as the sweet-thorn, *Acacia karroo* Hayne. On the other hand, some of the rarest trees in South Africa such as *Xylia torreana* Brenan and *Xeroderris stuhlmannii* (Taub.) Mendonça & E.P. Sousa also belong to Leguminosae. These are tropical species which penetrate into the north eastern Transvaal. Other species, possibly the well-known Rhodesian msasa, *Brachystegia spici-formis* Benth., may one day be discovered in this remote region of deep Kalahari sand.

Some trees of the family, such as the kiaat, *Pterocarpus angolensis* DC., and the Rhodesian teak, *Baikiaea plurijuga* Harms, yield a handsome and popular wood; others such as the knoppies-doring, *Acacia nigrescens* Oliv., give durable fence poles and mine props, and the sekelbos, *Dichrostachys cinerea* (L.) Wight & Arn., is splendid fuel. The bark of many species was once used for tanning, and sometimes still is.

In the early days trees of the family gave colonists timber for almost everything they needed — for houses, floors, furniture, wagons, fencing, hoe and axe handles, and fuel, while the bark of acacias in particular was used in tanning, and for rope and string, and their gum for glue.

They were used medicinally by Europeans, Africans, and Hottentots for everything from toothache to snake-bite.

Members of the family have given food to primitive man, and to animals, from immemorial times. The foliage and pods of many species are first-class fodder. Seeds, such as those of the boerboon, *Schotia afra* (L.) Thunb., were roasted and eaten. The seed and tubers of *Bau-*

hinia esculenta Burch. are still staple foods of Kalahari Bushmen, while seeds of *Bauhinia macrantha* Oliv. and *Guibourtia coleosperma* (Benth.) J.Léon. are also eaten. The big leaves of *Piliostigma thonningii* (K.Schum.) Milne-Redh. are chewed to relieve thirst. The seeds of the lemoendoring, *Parkinsonia africana* Sond., are sometimes used for coffee, while the gums exuded by many species are often eaten by men, domestic and wild animals, and birds. They are said to be a sustaining food. The fruits of a species such as *Dialium schlechteri* Harms are much sought by African children. Some species, such as *Erythrophleum africanum* Harms, and the mopane, *Colophospermum mopane* (Kirk ex Benth.) Kirk ex J.Léon., are hosts to caterpillars which are eaten by Africans and which are a valuable protein-rich food.

One small thorn tree of the Kalahari and western and north western Transvaal is noteworthy for an unusual reason — it apparently acts as a "host" to the South African species of truffles. The tree is *Acacia hebeclada* DC., the trassiebos, often forming a low impenetrable thicket, and sometimes making a small upright tree. It can be identified by its straight hard pods carried stiffly erect. Truffles are underground edible fungi which grow in association with certain species of trees, in Europe usually oaks and beeches. There they have since early times been regarded as the choicest delicacies, and today high prices are paid for them. Little is known of the South African truffles, species of *Terfezia,* but they are eaten and enjoyed by the peoples of the desert areas of South Africa.

Such foods as these, while they may generally be considered unattractive, have great value to an unsophisticated and rural people.

Many trees of the family have poisonous principles, and these, too, have been used by man. They are utilized as fish, crocodile, and animal poisons, for arrow poisons, and in witchcraft. *Erythrophleum lasianthum* Corb., for instance, is a notorious tree which grows from Natal and Zululand to tropical Africa, with poisonous bark, leaves, and seeds, which have been used from ancient times in trials by ordeal.

Many species give outstanding shade and shelter to a variety of wild animals and stock. Our thorn trees — species of *Acacia* — are common in the dry parts of the country where blazing hot summers and bitter winter nights are the rule, and the value of these trees to people, stock, and game cannot be over-estimated. Early travellers, crossing the glowing plains of the Karoo and north-west Cape, wrote with almost passionate gratitude of the clumps of sweet-thorn, "as grateful to the traveller as the oases in the sandy desert".

Some of our most beautiful trees belong to this family. In a setting of hot red Kalahari sand, there is little to equal the beauty of the drooping silver-grey foliage of a vaalkameeldoring, *Acacia haematoxylon* Willd.

"Mimosa. . . . Last of our phoenix-trees to light its pyre", wrote Roy Campbell of the sweet-thorn.

A sweet-thorn, smothered in yellow perfumed flowers, is not easily surpassed by the choicest flowering trees of Europe. In beauty of shape a well-grown apiesdoring, *Acacia galpinii* Burtt Davy; an anaboom, *Acacia albida* Del.; a sweet-thorn, or a giant *Newtonia hildebrandtii* (Vatke) Torre, is almost unequalled. The thorn trees of the bushveld and lowveld with their unique umbrella-shaped crowns add much to the fascination of the northern areas of South Africa.

The brilliance of the various kafferbooms (*Erythrina* species) in bloom, or the richness of a pink keurboom (*Virgilia* species) is known to many. Less common are trees such as the boerboons (*Schotia*

706

species), the long-tail cassia, *Cassia abbreviata* Oliv. subsp. *beareana* (Holmes) Brenan; the *Calpurnia* species; the Vanwykshout, *Bolusanthus speciosus* (H.Bol.) Harms; the huilboom, *Peltophorum africanum* Sond., and many others. Their blooming is usually brief but gorgeous.

Particularly eye-catching are several climbers or monkey ropes of the family which occur on forest fringes, in bush, and along streams. The pale yellow flower spikes and large, flat, maroon, papery pods of *Entada spicata* (E.Mey.) Druce with its hooked thorns — the "skunk's trap" of the Zulus — are familiar from the Eastern Province to the northern Transvaal. In Natal and Swaziland the green and red flower spikes of its relative, *Entaba wahlbergii* Harv., are common and distinctive.

One of the best known and most widely spread climbers or shrubs through the Transkei, Natal, Zululand, Swaziland, and the Transvaal is not indigenous at all. It is the Mauritius Thorn or Devil Thorn, *Caesalpinia decapetala* (Roth.) Alston, a spiny species with yellow flowers, used as live fences around kraals wherever it grows in Southern Africa. It is reputed to have been introduced by missionaries as protection against lions, and a fine, thorny protection it must have made, impenetrable to everything but rhinos.

Nearly all the leguminous trees have compound leaves, that is, they are divided into leaflets. These may be arranged along a common midrib, when they are known as pinnate, or divided up still further when the common midrib bears secondary branches on which the leaflets are produced. These are known as bipinnate. The big *Acacia* genus, to which our common thorn trees belong, is characterized by these feathery, bipinnate leaves.

A few trees — of the genera *Bauhinia*, *Piliostigma*, and *Adenolobus* — have simple lobed leaves, while simple leaves are also found in the genera *Baphia*, *Podalyria*, *Indigofera* and *Lonchocarpus*. Trees of the genera *Colophospermum* and *Guibourtia* have "butterfly" leaves with two leaflets.

The family is divided up into three distinct groups — often considered three separate families — on the structure of the flowers. Here these groups are treated as three sub-families.

Mimoseae includes all the albizias, the acacias, and the sekelbos, *Dichrostachys cinerea* Wight & Arn.; the beautiful *Newtonia hildebrandtii* from Zululand, the rare *Xylia torreana* from the north east Transvaal, and the *Elephantorrhiza* species. All these have tiny flowers in heads or spikes with protruding stamens.

Caesalpinieae includes trees often with large showy flowers, usually with 5 petals arranged symmetrically. The boerboons, cassias, huilboom, mopane, and others belong here.

The third sub-family, Papilionaceae, is composed of plants with flowers somewhat like those of a sweetpea, with a broad erect upper petal, the "standard"; two narrower petals — the "wings" — on either side of this, and two lower united petals, the "keel". Many trees with brilliant flowers, such as the Vanwykshout, and the kafferbooms, *Erythrina* species, belong to this group.

The fruits of nearly all members of the family are the well-known pods. Four interesting exceptions are *Dialium schlechteri* Harms from Zululand, *Dialium engleranum* Henriques from the Caprivi Strip, *Cordyla africana* Lour. from the eastern Transvaal and Zululand, and the nyala tree, *Xanthocercis zambesiaca* (Bak.) Dumaz-le-Grand, which grows from the Transvaal lowveld northwards into tropical Africa. The first three bear edible and pleasant-tasting fruits, while the nyala tree has rather insipid, plum-like fruits which are eaten by Africans in times of famine.

Key to Genera (Sub-family Mimoseae)

Trees with feathery foliage

Spineless trees; the foliage often feathery, the flowers in heads or spikes the stamens long, numerous, joined at the base and sometimes the whole length into a tube making an often fluffy flower-head; the pods sometimes bursting open; the seeds not winged.

1. *Albizia*

Spiny trees or shrubs; the spines usually hardened stipules; the flowers in balls or spikes with the stamens free or joined at the base into a shallow disc; the pods often bursting open; the seeds not winged.

2. *Acacia*

A small tree or shrub; the spines hardened branchlets; the flower spikes in 2 colours, pink-mauve and yellow; the pods much twisted, not bursting open; the seeds not winged.

3. *Dichrostachys*

A large spineless tree; the flowers in spikes; the pods flat, much-veined, red when mature, bursting along one side; the seeds winged.

4. *Newtonia*

Small spineless trees or shrubs; the flowers in racemes; the pods long, woody, bursting open, the valves separating from the rims; the seeds not winged.

7. *Elephantorrhiza*

Trees with the foliage not feathery

The pinnae in usually 1-6 pairs; the leaflets up to 6.5 cm long; the flowers in roundish, usually fluffy heads; the pods often oblong, flat, with bumps showing the position of the seeds, sometimes bursting open.

1. *Albizia*

The pinnae in 2-5 pairs; the leaflets up to 1.9 x 1.3 cm; the flowers in spikes; the pods thick, woody, with 4 distinct blunt angles, not bursting open.

5. *Amblygonocarpus*

The pinnae in 1 pair; the leaflets 2.5 − 10 cm long; the flowers in round heads; the pods large, woody, broadly sickle-shaped, bursting open along 2 valves.

6. *Xylia*

Sub-Family Mimoseae

1. *Albizia* Dur.

Over 100 species from the warm parts of Africa, Asia, and Australia belong to this genus, named after an Italian nobleman of the family Albizzi who over 200 years ago first introduced a species into Europe from Constantinople. Today the name of the genus is usually spelt with one "z" – *Albizia*.

As a genus *Albizia* much resembles *Acacia*, and its members are often mistaken for acacias, for many of them have similar feathery foliage made up of fine compound leaves, twice-divided (or bipinnate). These usually have a conspicuous gland on the leaf stalk, and sometimes on the side branches.

In South African *Acacia* species the stipules become hard and pointed – these are the "spines" or "thorns" of the layman – but in *Albizia* species the stipules fall off early so that, except in those cases where the ends of the shoots are hard and pointed, albizias have no spines at all. The flowers are usually bisexual, sometimes with unisexual flowers in the inflorescence. The calyx is 5-toothed and the corolla tube 5-lobed. The pods are oblong, sometimes narrowly so, flat, and papery or somewhat leathery, usually with several flat seeds.

In flower it is easy to distinguish between the genera *Acacia* and *Albizia* for the flowers of albizias usually have longer stamens, giving the flower heads a fragile, fluffy appearance. Botanists note that these are joined at the base, or sometimes for more than half their length, into a tube, whereas those of acacias are free or joined at the base in a shallow saucer.

About 11 tree species are known to be indigenous to South Africa and South West Africa. Two introduced species have become naturalized. These are *Albizia lebbeck* (L.) Benth., a native of tropical Africa and Asia, which grows in a semi-wild state in Zululand, and *Albizia lophantha* (Willd.) Benth., an Australian species, that grows from southern Natal to the Cape Peninsula, often on river banks.

The albizias are not as widespread as the acacias, nor – with a few exceptions – as well-known, for they are usually tender to frost and confined to the warmer parts of the country. Some have no English or Afrikaans common names at all.

Most of them make fine, shapely trees, striking in flower or covered with young pods.

Several species of butterflies, including the Common Hairtail, *Anthene definita*, the Mirza Blue, *Azanus mirza*, and several *Charaxes* species, breed on albizias.

The genus has recently been revised by Dr. L.E. Codd, on whose work many of these descriptions are based.

Key to species

Leaves with small leaflets (under 1.3 cm long)

Pinnae 6-10 pairs; the leaflets 10-20 pairs, up to 5mm long, with the

Above
Albizia flowers (*A. anthel-mintica*)

Left
Albizia brevifolia north of Wyllie's Poort, northern Transvaal

Below
Albizia brevifolia flowers

upper part of the leaflet straight and the tip round; the mature leaves and twigs smooth. (Transvaal, Botswana, Kaokoveld, Rhodesia, Mozambique)

a. *A. brevifolia*

Pinnae 8-18 pairs; the leaflets 12-24 pairs, up to 6 mm long, with *the tips curved and pointed*; dark green above, paler below; the mature leaves smooth but the main stalk rough. (Swaziland, Transvaal, Botswana, Caprivi Strip).

b. *A. harveyi*

Pinnae 15-35 pairs; the leaflets 25-42 pairs, up to 4 mm long; the mature leaves and twigs hairy. (North eastern Transvaal, Botswana, northwards to Eritrea).

c. *A. amara* subsp. *sericocephala*

Pinnae 2-7 pairs; the leaflets 6-14 pairs, about 7mm long, the margins inrolled. (Eastern Transvaal, Zululand, Mozambique)

d. *A. forbesii*

Leaves with medium leaflets (1-2.5 cm long)

Pinnae 2-4, the leaflets 2-5 pairs, the leaflets about 0.8-2.5 cm long, the uppermost the largest; dark green and smooth above, paler and sometimes hairy below; *the branches often spine-tipped*. (Zululand, Swaziland, Transvaal, Botswana, S.W.A., northwards to Ethiopia).

i. *A. anthelmintica*

Pinnae 2-4 pairs, the leaflets 2-5 pairs, about 1.2 cm long, dark above, light below, rough. (North eastern and eastern Transvaal, northern Zululand, Mozambique)

j. *A. petersiana* subsp. *evansii*

Pinnae 4-7, the leaflets 6-12 pairs, 1-1.8 cm long, with a diagonal midrib, rough below. (Transkei, Natal, Zululand, Transvaal).

k. *A. adianthifolia*

Leaves with large leaflets (1.9 – 6.5 cm long)

Pinnae 1-3 pairs; the leaflets 3-5 pairs, about 3-6 cm long; the mature leaflets *hairy*. (Zululand, Swaziland, Transvaal, Botswana, S.W.A., Angola, Rhodesia, Mozambique).

e. *A. versicolor*

Pinnae 1-3 pairs; the leaflets 5-9 pairs, 2.5-6 cm long, smooth, dark above, lighter below. (North and north eastern S.W.A., northwards to the Congo).

f. *A, antunesiana*

Above
Albizia harveyi in pod alongside the Rushton road, northern Transvaal

Left
Albizia harveyi bark

Below
Albizia brevifolia: A flowering twig (70%)

712

Pinnae 2-5 pairs; the leaflets 5-12 pairs, 2-4 cm long, smooth or slightly hairy. The bark pale *brown to orange, papery, peeling.* (Transvaal, Botswana, northwards to Tanzania).

g. *A. tanganyicensis*

Pinnae 2-4 pairs; the leaflets 5-9 pairs, up to about 2.5 cm long, *the margins crisped*; dark green above, paler below. (Northern Zululand).

h. *A. suluensis*

(152)   a. *Albizia brevifolia* Schinz

= *Albizia rogersii* Burtt Davy; = *Albizia parvifolia* Burtt Davy

Mola albizia; mmola (Tsw – Mang), molalakgaka (Tsw – Taw); mosala kgwale (NS)

Albizia brevifolia, "the short-leaved albizia", first described from Mozambique, grows also in the northern Transvaal, Botswana, the Kaokoveld, and in Rhodesia. In South Africa it is usually found on the dry rocky slopes of hills, and fine specimens grow on the low hills north of Wyllie's Poort near the Great North Road.

This deciduous species may be a shrub or a many-stemmed tree, often large, wide-spreading, and handsome. The bark is grey, the young twigs hairy becoming quite smooth with age. The compound leaves, often with a bluish tinge, up to about 10 cm long and 6 cm wide, are composed of up to 10 pairs of pinnae, each with 10-20 pairs of small narrow leaflets, up to 5 mm long. The shape of these leaflets helps to separate the tree from a similar species, *Albizia harveyi* Fourn. The upper part of the leaflets of *Albizia brevifolia* are straight with a round tip; those of *Albizia harveyi* have a somewhat curved tip with a sharp point.

The creamy-white flowers in puff-like heads bloom from about October to November.

They develop into large, flat, red-brown pods, with a thickened margin, and well defined bumps indicating the position of the seeds.

Branches and leaves are eaten by elephant.

The wood is said to be hard and strong, and the termite-proof bark is made into rope to tie the rafters of huts.

The North Sotho name means "francolins' roost".

Above
Albizia brevifolia pinnae, showing the round-tipped leaflets

Below
Albizia harveyi leaflets with sharply pointed tips

(155)   b. *Albizia harveyi* Fourn.

= *Albizia pallida* Harv.; = *Albizia hypoleuca* Oliv.

Bleekblaarboom; umThololwane (Sw); mmolela (Tso); molalakgaka (Tsw)

The bleekblaarboom has a wide distribution in Africa, through Portuguese East Africa, Swaziland, the northern Transvaal and Botswana, and northern South West Africa, northwards to tropical Africa. It is fairly common north of the Soutpansberg in the flat bush country of the northern Transvaal, and is widespread in the Kruger National Park, where it grows in several of the rest camps.

It may be a shrub, or a tree, seldom very wide-spreading, usually with a single main trunk, up to about 11 m high in South Africa, but reported

Above
Albizia amara subsp. *sericocephala,* near Sibasa in the north-eastern Transvaal

Left
The house among *Albizia forbesii,* Mt. Edgecombe, Natal

Below left
Albizia forbesii, Mkuze, Zululand

Below right
Albizia amara subsp. *sericocephala:* A leaf and pods (45%)

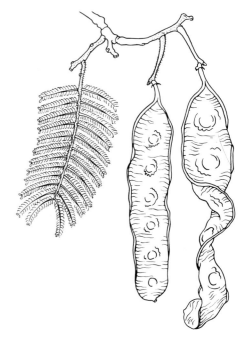

714

up to 18 m high in northern South West Africa. The bark is grey to dark brown, and in old trees is rough, seamed longitudinally, and often flaky. The twigs are hairy.

The compound leaves, 6-11 cm long, have up to 18 pairs of pinnae, and 12-24 pairs of tiny narrow leaflets. The tips of these are slightly curved and pointed while those of *Albizia brevifolia*, which they resemble, are straight with a round apex. In youth they are hairy and a tawny colour. Mature leaves are smooth — although the leaf stalk is hairy — green above, paler below. C.A. Smith says when blown by the wind they appear pallid, due to the pale under-surface, hence the name bleek-blaarboom.

The creamy-white or greenish, fragrant flowers in fluffy heads on long stalks, appear in late spring and develop into large, flat, thin pods, with slightly thickened margins, usually constricted between the seeds, ripening in the late autumn.

The pods, bark and roots are eaten by elephant, and the leaves by elephant, giraffe, kudu, and eland.

The timber is reddish and tough.

The specific name honours W.H. Harvey, appointed Colonial Treasurer at the Cape in 1835, and collaborator with Sonder in the first three volumes of *Flora Capensis*. The Tswana name molalakgaka means "guineafowl roost".

(149)   c. *Albizia amara* (Roxb.) Boiv.
            subsp. *sericocephala* (Benth.) Brenan

= *Albizia sericocephala* Benth.; = *A. struthiophylla* Milne-Redh.

Muvola: muvhola (V)

Like the bleekblaarboom, this has a big distribution in Africa, occurring from the Sudan and Ethiopia southwards to Rhodesia, Botswana, and the Transvaal. It is a somewhat rare species here, growing mainly in the sandy woodland between Sibasa and Punda Milia in the north eastern Transvaal.

It grows to a height of about 12 m. The bark is grey and is rough or smooth. The leaves are larger than those of *Albizia harveyi*, up to 18 cm long and 5 cm wide, with more numerous pinnae and leaflets, 15-35 pairs of pinnae and up to 42 pairs of tiny, narrow, oblong leaflets. They are softly hairy and tawny when young, becoming rough and red-brown to grey with age. The common midrib is densely hairy.

The tawny velvety buds open into white flowers in a puff-like head about 2.5 cm wide, with a golden, velvety calyx.

The long, narrow, oblong pods, purplish when young, pale brown when mature, are longer than those of *Albizia harveyi*, from 10-28 cm long, flat, thin, with the margin slightly thickened, and with several bumps indicating the position of the seeds. They ripen in late summer and early autumn.

The specific name *amara* is probably the Latin word meaning "bitter", although the allusion is not clear: *seriocephala* is based on Greek words meaning "silky head", and refers to the silky appearance of the flower-head.

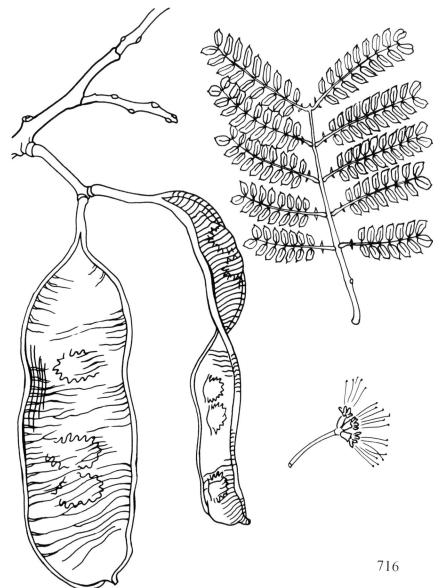

Above
Albizia forbesii flowers

Left
Albizia forbesii: A leaf,
flower and pods (80%)

Opposite
Albizia forbesii trunk

716

(154)   d. *Albizia forbesii* Benth.

Umnala albizia; umNala (Z); rinyani (Tso)

Visitors to Mkuze Game Reserve in Zululand may remember this tree, which is common and conspicuous in the Reserve. It grows in forest, thornveld scrub, often along rivers, from Zululand northwards to Portuguese East Africa, and in the northern and eastern Transvaal, a limited distribution compared with that of most albizias. It sometimes occurs in groups together.

This is often a tall tree, sometimes up to 18 m high, with a single trunk, or branched from near the base; thick, dark bark, and spreading, rather drooping, branches.

The somewhat rough leaves are up to 10 cm long and 6.5 cm wide, frequently — according to Dr. Codd — folded along the midrib. There are 2-7 pairs of pinnae and 6-14 pairs of small, oblong, tightly-packed leaflets, with the midrib to one side of the leaflets, and the margins inrolled.

The blond velvety buds open into powder-puff-like flower-heads, white, cream or yellow, blooming November and December. These develop into flat, fibrous, rather oblong pods up to 15 cm long and 5 cm wide, marked crosswise with many fine lines, and with thickened margins, but with no bumps apparent indicating the position of the seeds. In the autumn these russet pods, hanging in great numbers, are handsome among the feathery green leaves.

Zulus use the roots with those of an *Acacia* species and a small piece of *Spirostachys* root, to rid themselves of a tokoloshi. Tongas put the tree to a more mundane use — the four corner posts and the door posts of a hut are often of *Albizia forbesii*.

The tree was called after John Forbes, naturalist and botanical collector, who was sent out to South Africa in 1822 by the Horticultural Society of London, and who collected the type specimen in Portuguese East Africa.

(158)   e. *Albizia versicolor* Welw. ex Oliv.

= *A. mossambicensis* Sim

Umpiso albizia; umPhiso, umBhangazi, umVangazi (Z); siVangatsane, umVangatana (Sw); mbheswi (Tso); muvhamba-ngoma, mutamba-pfunda (V); linko (Sub); kakomo (Yei); mokongotshi (Mbuk)

This beautiful, sturdy, spreading tree grows from tropical Africa southwards to South West Africa in the west, the north and eastern Transvaal, and northern Natal, Swaziland, and Mozambique in the east. It is a common lowveld tree, often growing in parkland, in sand, along ridges, or on stream banks.

The tree photographed on a low hill in the woodland near Sibasa in the north eastern Transvaal was a big specimen, at least 12 m tall, with a spread more than twice as great.

This is one of the finest of the albizias. It often has a single main trunk — occasionally up to 1.5 m in diameter — with a very rough, dark grey, corky bark, the segments, in an old trunk, cracked and almost 2.5 cm deep. The young branches are buff-coloured, the older ones a dark colour, and hairy.

The round or flattish crown is made up of large compound leaves,

Above
Albizia versicolor north east of Sibasa

Left
In pod in northern Zululand

Below left
The flowers

Below right
Albizia versicolor leaves

718

Right
Albizia versicolor: The
leaves, pod and seeds
(65%)

Below
Albizia versicolor trunk

often covered with reddish hairs, up to 30 cm long and 20 cm broad,
carried on fairly long stalks. The leaves have few pinnae or side-branches — 1-3 pairs — and only 3-5 pairs of leaflets. These are large, 2.5-5 cm
long, oblong, egg-shaped or almost round, the top pair the largest,
velvety above, the undersides covered thickly with rust-coloured hairs.
They are borne on very short velvety stalks. The midrib — slightly to
one side — and the veins, are raised and conspicuous below. Young
foliage is particularly beautiful, the leaflets being a soft silky-velvet.

Leaves and young shoots are eaten by kudu.

The large powder-puff-like heads of flowers are a creamy-white or
yellow, often with a reddish tinge, blooming in abundance from August
to November. The young pods, which vary from pale green to brilliant
red, are often borne in great numbers, and then the tree is a wonderfully
rich and lively colour.

The pods are up to 23 cm long and 6.3 cm wide, flat, with raised
bumps showing the position of the seeds, and with thickened margins.
They are reported to have poisoned cattle.

The bark is used for tanning, and for fibre. This, and the roots, have a
lathering quality and are used by Africans as soap. The roots are also

719

used medicinally as an enema and purgative, or mixed with *Terminalia* roots, as an emetic, and the leaves in a headache remedy.

The gum is reputed to be poisonous.

The wood is hard with a dark, sometimes almost black heart and a good grain, termite resistant, and valued for building and cabinet-making. It resembles kiaat. In Tongaland mortars for stamping mealies are sometimes made of it.

In parts the tree is judged an indicator of underground water.

The name *versicolor* means "changing colour" or "variously coloured", but in this case the allusion is not clear. Perhaps the name refers to the brightly coloured pods.

Codd says that the popular name "umvanghaas" is sometimes applied to this tree in the eastern Transvaal, or to its timber, but that this name is more usually given by Africans to the kiaat, *Pterocarpus angolensis* DC. A Swazi name for this albizia is siVangatsane, meaning "the little kiaat". The similarity of the wood of the two species has probably given rise to these names. The Vendas call this by a name meaning "stretch drum head".

(151)   f. *Albizia antunesiana* Harms

Albizia antunesiana has not been recorded at all in South Africa. It grows in northern South West Africa — in the Okavango Native Territory and the Caprivi Strip — northwards into Angola, Rhodesia, and central Africa, usually in dry open woodland on sandy soil at medium elevations.

This is most often a fairly small or medium sized tree up to about 9 m (although in Zambia it reaches a height of 23 m), and is much branched and spreading, with rough grey bark.

The deciduous leaves are large and feathery, 11 cm — 25 cm long and up to 20 cm broad, slightly hairy when young, but becoming smooth, and are carried on long smooth stalks. They have 1-3 pairs of pinnae or side-branches, which bear 5-9 pairs of widely spaced large leaflets. These are egg-shaped to oblong, or irregularly 4-sided, with the apex sharp, blunt, rounded, or notched, 2.5 to nearly 6.5 cm long and up to just over 2.5 cm wide, and lopsided, one side being more rounded than the other. They are green above, paler below, and are often slightly purple-tinged.

The creamy-white or yellowish-green flowers are in fluffy heads and have stamens up to 2.5 cm long. The calyx is rusty-coloured or greenish, and hairy. They bloom September to November, often with the new leaves.

The flat, oblong, brown pods are usually 10-15 cm long, occasionally up to 22 cm, and about 2.5-5 cm wide, with slightly thickened margins, and conspicuous bumps marking the position of the seeds. They split open when mature, the valves curving backwards.

The tree yields a valuable termite-resistant timber with a brown, fairly hard, heavy heartwood, rather like kiaat wood.

It is used medicinally in many parts. Keith Coates Palgrave says that most Africans know the roots, pounded, boiled, and the steam inhaled, as a remedy for a cold in the head.

The specific name *antunesiana* honours P.J.M. Antunes, a botanical collector at Huila in Angola from 1889-1903.

This species is closely related to the tropical *Albizia coriaria* Welw.

720

See colour plate facing
page 762

Above left
Albizia tanganyicensis
in the Waterberg

Above right
Its peeling bark

(157)　　g. *Albizia tanganyicensis* Bak.f.

= *Albizia rhodesica* Burtt Davy; = *Albizia lebbeck* var. *australis* Burtt
Davy.

Paper-bark albizia, fever tree; koorsboom; dzuvudzuvu (Tso); sipumbula
matako (Sub)

A paper-like, orange-yellow bark peeling off a pale smooth trunk and
branches, sets the paper-bark albizia apart from the surrounding trees
on the rocky granite or quartzite hill slopes it inhabits from Warmbaths
northwards to the Soutpansberg. Some particularly fine specimens grow
in the Waterberg and may be seen close to the Great North Road north
of Warmbaths, and near other roads through these mountains. It grows,
more sparingly, on rocky ridges in the north east Transvaal, westwards
to Botswana, and northwards to Rhodesia and tropical Africa.

It was first collected in Tanganyika — now Tanzania — hence the
specific name.

This is a small to medium sized tree, 3-9 m tall, of unusual grace and
colouring. The thin, translucent, orange, "paper" bark and the light
satiny trunk below are conspicuous for they are usually clearly
visible through the rather sparse crown of rich green, feathery foliage.

The tree may have a single trunk, when it is at its finest, or several
branching from near the base. The branches, usually rather few in
number, grow upwards rather than outwards and are soft and brittle.
Young twigs are slightly hairy, becoming smooth later.

The leaves are up to 40 cm long and 28 cm broad, borne on stalks
from 5-10 cm long, with a gland or small bump towards the base. They
have 2-6 pairs of side-branches or pinnae and where these join the
common midrib there are conspicuous swellings. The pinnae bear from
about 5-13 pairs of opposite leaflets. These are oval, oblong, or widely

721

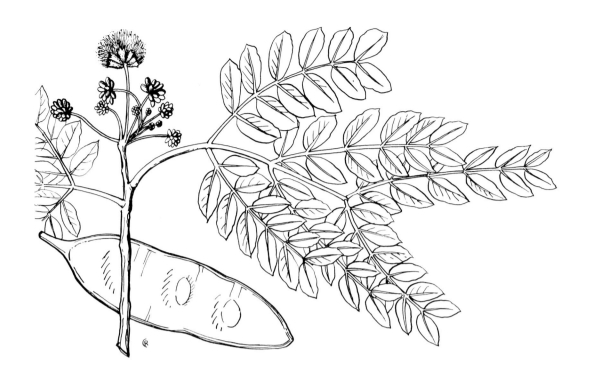

Above
Albizia suluensis: Flowers, leaves and pod (70%)

Below left
Albizia tanganyicensis leaves (45%)

Below right
The pod (45%)

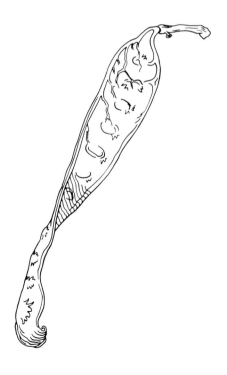

lance-shaped, and slightly uneven in shape for the midrib is a little to one side, with a pointed, blunt, or rounded apex, 1.9-4 cm long and up to 2.5 cm wide. The midrib, secondary veins, and network of smaller veins are clearly visible on the upper surface, less so below. They are smooth or slightly hairy, and deciduous. Young leaves are rosy-red, turning a light and later a darker green.

The rough, rust-coloured buds open into creamy-white to yellow, sweet-scented flowers in fluffy heads, which bloom before the leaves, from September to November. These flower-heads have fairly long stalks and are borne in tufts, several grouped together.

The large, flat, woody pods are up to 25 cm long and 5 cm wide, light brown, with several hard, dark, oval seeds. They differ from those of most other albizias in that the margins are hardly thickened and lack the bulges indicating the position of the seeds.

The wood is white, soft, coarse-grained, and light. When worked, the wood-dust is said to cause irritation to nose and throat.

Paper-bark seed germinates easily; and the tree can also be grown from truncheons.

Codd says that leaves and flowers of this species are easily confused with those of the imported *Albizia lebbeck*, which, however, has fewer leaflets – from 3-9 – and stalked flowers, whereas the individual flowers of the paper-bark are without stalks. In the field it is not likely to be confused with any other species, although it bears a superficial resemblance to the fever tree, *Acacia xanthophloea* Benth., and because of this is sometimes called "fever tree". The true fever tree is a species of hot, low, swampy country and lowveld river banks.

(156)   h. *Albizia suluensis* Gerstn.

Zulu albizia; uNyazangoma, iNgwebu enkulu (Z)

"The Zulu albizia" is a fine species with a limited distribution, for up to date it has been recorded from only a few districts of northern Zululand, growing in savanna bushveld and forest, and in bush along rivers.

It grows up to about 12 m high and has a round or flat, spreading crown, and grey fissured bark. The young twigs are hairy, becoming smooth with age.

The dark green leaves are up to 20 cm long and 20 cm broad, and are borne on stalks up to 5 cm long. The 2-4 pairs of pinnae or side-branches bear 5-9 pairs of large leaflets, roughly 2.5 cm long and 1.3 cm wide, oblong, oval, or egg-shaped, with a round or flat apex, sometimes with a sharp point, lopsided at the base, and with crisped margins, an unusual feature in albizia leaflets. They are dark green above, paler below. Samango monkeys eat them.

The golden, velvety buds open into creamy-white flowers.

The pods are about 7-15 cm long and about 2.5 cm wide, a narrow oblong, light brown, flat, with slightly thickened margins, and the position of the seeds marked by small swellings. Codd says this can be distinguished from *Albizia lebbeck* by the crisped margin of the leaflets, and by the golden hairy calyx (the calyx of *A. lebbeck* has short, pale brown hairs).

The Zululand missionary, Jacob Gerstner, who collected and described this tree, called it "iNgwebu enkulu", meaning "the great foam",

Left
Albizia anthelmintica in the
Khomas Hochland, South
West Africa

Centre
The pods

Below left
Albizia anthelmintica flowers
(60%)

Below right
Albizia anthelmintica bark

because the bark, pounded with water, foams abundantly. Zulus use it as an enema in the treatment of fever.

The wood is hard and durable, of outstanding quality, and has been used to make beautiful furniture. The sawdust is said to be an irritant, causing sneezing.

(150)   i. *Albizia anthelmintica* (A.Rich.) Brongn.

= *Besenna anthelmintica* A.Rich; = *Acacia marlothii* Engl.; = *Albizia umbalusiana* Sim

Monoga, kersieblomboom, bonthout; umNalahanga (Z); shivulanguva (Tso); monoga (Tsw); uchundwe (Sub); omuuama (Her); arúb (Nama)

One of the first trees to flower in early spring, this species when in bloom is one of Africa's most conspicuous trees or shrubs. It has an enormous distribution from Zululand, Swaziland, the eastern and northern Transvaal, the northern Cape, Botswana, to South West Africa — where it is fairly widely distributed — northwards through Angola and Portuguese East Africa to Rhodesia, and tropical Africa as far north as Ethiopia.

It is not limited to one type of habitat, for while it grows in bushveld, in woodland, and in scrub in Zululand and the Transvaal, it is equally at home in the deep, loose, red sand of the dunes in the Kalahari Gemsbok National Park, or on dry wooded slopes or sandy grassland in South West Africa.

In South Africa it is usually a shrub or small tree. In South West Africa it may grow up to 9 m tall, while in tropical Africa it is reported to become a large tree. It is many-branched. The bark is fairly smooth, dark grey, brown, or reddish. The young twigs are slightly hairy, becoming smooth, and the branchlets are often spine-tipped.

The leaves are up to about 7.6 cm long and 5 cm wide, borne on shortish stalks, with 2-4 pairs of pinnae or side-branches, bearing 2-5 pairs of opposite leaflets. These are egg-shaped to almost round, often irregularly formed, and, like those of many albizias, the two sides often do not match one another in shape. They are up to 2.5 cm long and 1.3 cm wide, but usually smaller, the uppermost usually the largest, dark green and smooth above, below paler, smooth, or slightly hairy. They turn shades of yellow and gold in winter before they fall.

This is usually the first albizia to bloom in early spring, when the trees are covered with tufts of round, compact, green buds which open into delicate, fluffy, creamy flowers with a heavy, sweet, lily scent that is spread for yards around. In the Kruger National Park, and in parts of Zululand as at Mkuze, these airy, blossom-covered shrubs or trees are one of the spring sights, and when around them hover butterflies, or a Purple-banded Sunbird, they are unforgettable.

The flat, narrow, oblong pods are up to 12 cm long and 2.5 cm broad, yellow to light brown, with slightly thickened margins, and raised bumps showing the position of the seeds.

The timber is variously described as soft or hard, and is used for wood carving. The bark is an African remedy for worms in people and animals and appears to be remarkably effective. Dr. G.H.Teichler, writing on the tree in Botswana Notes and Records, vol. 3, says that the medicine made from the bark is but one of the many good drugs obtained from African plants and urges the collection of the old herbalists' knowledge before it finally disappears.

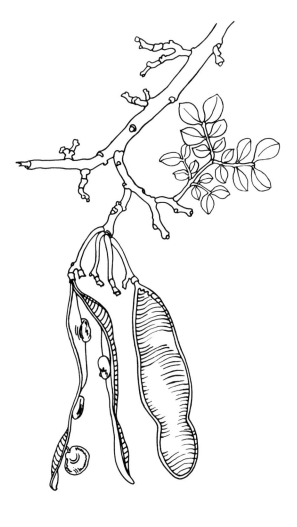

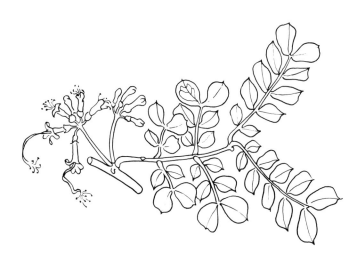

Above left
Albizia petersiana subsp. *evansii,* Ndumu, Zululand

Above right
Albizia petersiana subsp. *evansii:* a fruiting branchlet (65%)

Left
Portion of a flowering twig (80%)

A traditional doctor in Botswana — "one of the proud ones who has a sign of a hand on his roof with the five fingers outstretched to show that nobody should come to consult him unless he is prepared to put five pounds on the table at the start" — told him the uses of the tree — for stomach troubles (a decoction of the boiled root), a body wash to reduce fever and for worms (when the bark is stamped with red mealies and the leaves of the mokokwele and swallowed raw). In South West Africa the powdered bark is used successfully as a worm remedy.

Animals, including cattle, writes Dr. Teichler, seem to know the action of the bark and eat it when infested with worms.

These anthelmintic properties are recorded in the specific name. Dr. Teichler notes that the Tswana name, monoga, means "snake tree", probably not in reference to snakes at all but to worms, which are called dinoga.

Africans sometimes clean their teeth with the twigs, and the Hereros place the bark in milk to thicken it.

In parts — as in the country round Gobabis in South West Africa — the tree is considered good fodder. The pollen is supposed to irritate the eyes and there the sheep sometimes get inflamed eyes when the tree flowers.

The common name kersieblomboom or cherry-blossom tree is a misnomer, for the flowers do not much resemble those of a cherry tree. The abundance of creamy flowers perhaps reminded some early admirer of a cherry tree mantled in spring bloom, and was the basis of the name. A better common name — and indigenous — might be the Tswana "monoga", simple and short enough to be remembered by all.

(153)   j. *Albizia petersiana* (Bolle) Oliv.
          subsp. *evansii* (Burtt Davy) Brenan

= *Albizia evansii* Burtt Davy

Nala albizia; umNala (Z); nnala (Tso)

The often rather V-shaped form of growth of the nala albizia — branched from the base, or from near ground level,with upward-growing branches — helps to distinguish it from the other species in the areas where it grows, the eastern and north eastern Transvaal, Tongaland (where it is common in the sand forest), and in the country from Portuguese East Africa to tropical Africa.

Codd says it is of a gregarious nature and tends to grow in groups on brackish, sandy flats, as near the Lion Pan in the southern Kruger National Park. It is a fairly common tree at Ndumu in northern Zululand in arid, low-lying veld.

It grows from about 3.5-7.6 m tall, and has a grey trunk and hairy twigs. Unlike *Albizia anthelmintica*, the shoots are not spine-tipped.

The leaves are up to about 7.6 cm long and 6 cm wide with 2-4 pairs of pinnae and 2-5 pairs of medium sized leaflets, 8-16 mm long and about 8 mm broad, egg-shaped to an angled oblong, with a blunt apex, often with a short sharp point, and with a lopsided base. They are dark green and slightly rough above, lighter and covered with rough hairs below, and this roughness helps to distinguish the leaves from those of *Albizia anthelmintica*, which in South Africa are usually smooth or with only a few hairs on the nerves.

Leaves and shoots are eaten by elephants.

The leaves and flowers appear together in early summer. The pinkish

The flat-crown, *Albizia adianthifolia*, at Ifafa Lagoon, on the south coast of Natal

flowers, unlike those of most albizias, are not fluffy because the stamens are not united merely at the base but are joined in a long raspberry-red tube, and this tube is a character shared by the flat-crown, *Albizia adianthifolia* (Schumach.) W.F.Wight. They are borne densely and are delicate and airy.

The smooth, flat, red- or yellow-brown pods are up to 13 cm long and nearly 2.5 cm wide, somewhat woody, and with the seeds not forming conspicuous bulges.

Until recently this tree was considered in South Africa to be a distinct species, *Albizia evansii* Burtt Davy, named after Dr. I.B. Pole Evans, former Chief of the Division of Plant Industry, who discovered it in what is now the Kruger National Park. Now, however, it is judged to be a subspecies of the tropical *Albizia petersiana*, the specific name of which honours Professor Wilhelm Peters of Berlin, who collected plants in Mozambique in the 19th century.

(148)   k. *Albizia adianthifolia* (Schumach.) W.F.Wight

= *Mimosa adianthifolia* Schumach.; = *Zygia fastigiata* E.Mey.;
= *Albizia fastigiata* (E.Mey.) Oliv.; = *Albizia gummifera* of many authors

Flat-crown; platkroon; umHlandlothi (X); umHlandlothi, uSolo, umNalahanga, iGowane, umNebelele (Z); muomba-ngoma, muvhada-ngoma, muelela (V)

The flat-crown is a conspicuous, and at its best a noble tree, common along the east coast, often on forest margins or in open forest, from Port St. John's in the south through Natal and Zululand to the eastern Transvaal, and north through tropical Africa to Ethiopia. Wherever it grows its flat wide-spreading crown and horizontally growing leaves distinguish it from surrounding trees, although when not in bloom it is sometimes confused with the imported flamboyant.

It grows from 6-15 m high. Even in winter its singular shape and white-coloured twigs make it conspicuous. The trunk is tall and straight, the bark grey and fairly smooth, the young twigs reddish and hairy. The large, feathery, fern-like leaves (*adianthifolia* means "with leaves like a maidenhair fern") are up to about 23 cm long and 15 cm wide, carried on sturdy stalks covered with reddish hairs, which are swollen at the base. They are composed of about 4-7 pairs of side-branches or pinnae and 6-12 pairs of leaflets.

The leaflets are irregularly angled with the midrib running diagonally across them. They are up to about 1.9 cm long, dark green above, paler and rough below. On the upper surface of each leaf stalk near the base is usually a gland — a round, pitted swelling — and similar ones are found at the base of the last couple of pairs of pinnae. After picking, the leaflets close up to face one another.

The pale yellow-green spring foliage usually makes the flat-crown easily distinguishable from the trees about it.

The flower-heads are individually less showy than in the albizias with the fluffy flowers, for the stamens are united into a long tube. They are unusual and curious, however, the short outer flowers in the head being bisexual, with a few large male flowers protruding in the centre, giving the head a spidery and delicate appearance. They are borne on long stout stalks and stand up well above the leaves, turning the

Above left
Albizia adianthifolia:
pods and a flowering
twig (50%)

Above right
Flat-crown bark

whole flat top of the tree a creamy green. They have a strong, sweet smell, and according to Medley Wood the central flower of the head is usually filled to the brim with nectar. Masses of butterflies flutter around a tree in bloom. The young leaves, folded together and a rich red colour, often appear at the same time as the flowers, from August to November.

The pale brown pods are smaller than those of *Albizia versicolor*, usually no more than 18 cm long and 2.5 cm wide, flat, papery, hairy, straight or wavy, with thickened margins and bumps upon the valves indicating the position of the seeds.

The wood is described by M.H. Scott as "clean, light, useful, soft, straight-grained, used largely for naves and suitable for many other general purposes; works well and easily with a good finish". The colour is a light golden yellow, sometimes with a greenish tinge. It makes an attractive coloured parquet floor.

The bark is poisonous, but is used medicinally by the Zulus, who make a "love-charm emetic" from it.

This is a beautifully shaped tree and could be used with advantage in gardens and streets. In South Africa it does not appear to be as easy or fast-growing as most acacias. In Rhodesia it is considered to be very fast-growing indeed, strongly fire resistant, and only slightly sensitive to frost. Keith Coates Palgrave says that in Malawi planters often use this species as shade trees among their tea bushes.

In a Pretoria garden a tree grew fast, but the leaves were continually stripped off by weaver birds which hung their nests at the end of the bare branches.

At least two handsome butterflies with blue markings, the Blue Spotted Charaxes and the Satyr Charaxes, *Charaxes cithaeron* and *Charaxes ethalion*, common along the Natal coast, breed on this species. Their large spineless larvae with horned heads are often to be seen on the tree. The larvae of the little Mirza Blue, *Azanus mirza* fairly common in the lowveld of the eastern Transvaal, feed on the flowers.

Zulu herbalists call this tree "umGadankawu". The Venda name "mu-vhaḓa-ngoma" means "material for drums".

730

2. *Acacia* Willd.

The name *Acacia* is derived from the Greek word "acantha", meaning "thorn", and refers to the outstanding characteristic of this genus in Africa — its thorns — straight, hooked; in pairs, in 3's, or scattered. These are usually the stipules — the leafy outgrowths at the base of the leaves — which in acacias become hard and spiny.

From early times they have been noted. Thomas Baines, in his *Explorations in South West Africa*, classified the thorn trees he saw in a manner that is still appreciated today.

"Class one", he wrote, "for tearing clothes; class two, for tearing flesh; class three — the largest — for tearing flesh and clothes both together".

Some of the thorns are enormous, as in *Acacia karroo*, growing up to 18 cm long, and these long brilliant white blades have always been used by country people and early travellers for needles, pins, pegs, and — who knows? — for daggers. Hooked thorns, among some African tribes, are believed to ward off evil influences, so that many of the acacias have a special significance for them.

Today they are considered by laymen in particular as a valuable aid in identifying the many members of this bewildering and fascinating genus.

Most of the acacias have a fine feathery foliage, composed of twice-divided compound leaves. The leaflets are usually very small and often fold up against each other in sun or heat, or at night. The leaf stalks usually carry glands like knobs or saucer-shaped structures on the upper side, and sometimes where the pinnae join the rachis.

The tiny fluffy flowers, bisexual or male and bisexual, are borne in round balls or in spikes, usually with a heavy sweet scent. It is noteworthy that acacias with flower spikes usually have hooked thorns, while those with round flower heads usually have straight thorns. The calyx mostly has 4-5 teeth and the corolla 4-5 lobes. The stamens, giving the blooms their fluffy appearance, are many and most often free, and the ovary may be with or without a stalk. The pods, straight, sickle-shaped, or twisted, are generally browsed by stock and wild animals. In certain species these may be toxic.

This is a vast genus with about 900 species, concentrated mainly in Africa and Australia. About 40 species are native to South and South West Africa, Botswana, and Swaziland. Some Australian species, such as the aggressive and fast-spreading Port Jackson willow, *Acacia cyanophylla* Lindl., are cultivated in South Africa.

Ecologically, this is an important group, tightly woven into the lives of people and animals.

Countless insect species are associated with it, amongst them handsome butterflies of the genus *Charaxes*; and several Playboys, *Deudorix* species, the larvae of which feed upon the pods.

The little butterflies of the genus *Azanus*, blue, mauve, lilac, pink, and sometimes marked with brown, or speckled, inhabit thornveld because their larvae feed on parts of the acacias, in particular on the flowers. (Clark and Dickson say that the caterpillars have the ability to elongate their necks, permitting them to burrow deeply into the buds!)

The Topaz Blue, *Azanus jesous* — occurring from the Cape to Arabia; the Thorn Tree Blue, *Azanus moriqua;* the Mirza Blue, *Azanus mirza;* the Natal Blue, *Azanus natalensis,* and the Velvet Spotted Blue, *Azanus ubaldus,* are all dwellers in thornveld, breeding on the flowers, buds, leaves or sometimes the galls. Swanepoel describes the Velvet Spotted Blue among the thorn trees of the northern Transvaal in December when the trees were blooming, the males sipping the nectar and the females meticulously searching out the young flower buds on which to lay their eggs.

The Hairtails of the genus *Anthene* (they have tail-like tufts of hair on their hind wings) are also associated with acacias — like *Azanus,* this is a widespread genus, some species breeding on thorn trees from Southern to Tropical Africa. Two familiar species, the Common Hairtail, *Anthene definita,* and the Mashuna Hairtail, *Anthene otacilia,* have been noted breeding on *Acacia karroo,* the Common Hairtail laying its eggs on the flowers. (It also uses the flower buds of well known species as the Kaffir Plum, *Harpephyllum caffrum; Pappea capensis,* and *Schotia, Allophylus* and *Bersama* species).

In the northern Cape and Botswana as well as in the thornveld of the Transvaal and Natal the inconspicuous little Ella's Bar, *Spindasis ella,* occurs, breeding on the leaves and galls of thorn trees, while the beautiful bright Common Scarlet, *Axiocerses bambana,* of thorn veld, occurs from the eastern Cape and Natal to Botswana, the eggs often being laid on the juvenile shoots of the thorn trees.

The young thorns and shoots of species such as *Acacia karroo* are the food of the widespread Silver Studded Grey, *Crudaria leroma,* a greyish, medium-sized butterfly — at its most plentiful, according to Swanepoel, in the thornveld of the Springbok Flats.

The wattle bagworm, *Kotochalia junodii,* the larva of a moth of the family Psychidae, breeds upon members of the genus, and in particular upon *Acacia karroo.* There are many more.

Acacias are, on the whole, easy to grow, frost being the principal limiting factor in many cases. Their shiny brown seeds are tough and need to be soaked in hot or boiling water before planting. Thereafter they grow easily with a minimum of care.

The ease with which acacias grow has facilitated their growth in parts, where they have ousted less hardy plants, resulting in some areas in a dense impenetrable mass of thorn bush, useless to men or animals. Thorn bush encroachment in modern times has thus become a serious farming problem.

Dr. J.H.Ross, of the Botanical Research Institute, is at present revising the genus *Acacia* in Southern Africa. His work will bring clarity to an exceedingly difficult and complicated group.

Key to *Acacia* species

The acacias are divided here into groups according to the nature of their thorns. Botanists sometimes tend to regard these as a minor feature, but for the layman they are a character that is easily distinguished. Great care, however, should be taken to examine the spines on the tree *as a whole*, and not only those on a twig, as in the few instances where a *tree* bears both straight and hooked thorns, a *twig* may bear spines of only one kind. The range in the numbers of pinnae and leaflets may well be expanded when the revision of the genus is completed, so that the numbers listed here should be considered a rough guide only.

Thorns straight or slightly curved

A large tree; the trunk light-coloured, the twigs creamy; the thorns paired, straight; the leaves often bluish, the pinnae about 2-12 pairs (usually plus-minus 6), the leaflets 6-23 pairs; the flowers in creamy spikes; *the pods orange to reddish-brown*, about 10 cm long, *very twisted*. (Northern Zululand, northern Transvaal, Botswana, S.W.A.)

1. *A. albida*

A medium-sized, spreading tree; the bark dark, rough; the young twigs angled; the thorns straight, paired, *brown, often much swollen*, 0.6-5 cm long; the leaves with pinnae usually 1-4 pairs, the leaflets 10-18 pairs; the flowers in round yellow balls; *the pods large, thick, half-moon shaped, grey, velvety*. (Transvaal, O.F.S., north west Cape, Botswana, S.W.A.)

17. *A. giraffae*

A shrub to medium-sized tree; the branches *drooping*; the thorns paired, straight, *often slender*; the leaves small, the pinnae 6-25, the leaflets *tiny, numerous, grey, woolly, closely packed*; the flowers in round yellow heads; the pods long, narrow, woody, furry grey. (North west Cape, S.W.A.)

18. *A. haematoxylon*

A *suckering bush or medium-sized tree*; the twigs velvety; the thorns paired, *stout, straight or with the tips down-curved*; the pinnae 3-8 pairs, the leaflets up to about 15 pairs; the flowers white to gold in round balls; the pods *grey, furry, often grooved, straight, oblong, woody*, usually 6.5-12 cm long and 1.3-2 cm wide, carried *upright*. (Transvaal, north west Cape, Botswana, S.W.A.)

19. *A. hebeclada*
subsp. *hebeclada*

Similar to subsp. *hebeclada* but a *dome-shaped tree* with the branches touching the ground; the pods larger, up to 16.5 cm long and nearly 5 cm wide. (S.W.A.)

19b. *A. hebeclada*
subsp. *chobiensis*

Similar to subsp. *hebeclada* but the mature pods *pendulous*; the pods 10-16 cm long and up to about 1.3 cm wide. (S.W.A.)

19c. *A. hebeclada*
subsp. *tristis*

A tall, flat-topped tree; *the bark light, corky, flaking*; the thorns paired, straight, 2.5-5 cm long; the leaves 7.6-10 cm long, the pinnae about 11-20 pairs, the leaflets about 17-40 pairs; the common midrib spine-tipped; the twigs and young leaves *densely yellow-hairy*; the flowers white or pale yellow in balls in the axils of the leaves; the pods *hard, woody, thick*, 10-25 cm long and about 2.5 cm wide, velvety when young. (Natal, Zululand, Swaziland, Transvaal, Botswana, S.W.A.)

20. *A. sieberana*
var. *woodii*

A shrub to 9 m, flat-topped tree; *the bark blackish, furrowed, not peeling*; the thorns paired, straight, the leaves slender, the pinnae about 25-40 pairs, the leaflets very fine, about 40-50 pairs; the twigs and undersurface of the leaves *velvety, bright yellow*; the flowers in greenish-white balls; the pods *flat, leathery, much-veined*, up to 10 x 2.5 cm (Natal, Transvaal)

21. *A. rehmanniana*

A many-stemmed shrub to 9 m tree; the branches slender, ascending; the bark grey to yellow, *papery, flaking*; the thorns paired, straight, white, up to 7.6 cm long; the leaves up to 8 cm long, the common midrib with a hard point, the pinnae 6-14 pairs, the leaflets many, fine, softly hairy; the flowers in white or pink balls; the pods *shortish, broad, constricted, with a knobbly boss over each seed.* (S.W.A.)

23. *A. kirkii*

A small to medium, round to flat-topped tree; the bark dark, rough; the twigs hairy; the thorns paired, 1.3-3.8 cm long, straight, or slightly curved when young; the leaves up to 5 cm long, the pinnae 2-11 pairs, the leaflets about 12-25 pairs; the flowers in yellow balls; the pods *narrow, pendulous*, 7.6-15 cm long, *constricted, black when mature with a strong fruity scent.* (Natal, Transvaal, Botswana)

24a. *A. nilotica*
subsp. *kraussiana*

Similar to the above but the pinnae 3-6 pairs, the leaflets 10-24 pairs. (S.W.A.)

24b. *A. nilotica*
subsp. *subalata*

A many-stemmed shrub or small slender tree; the branches ascending; the whole twig *sticky*; the thorns paired, straight, slender, white; the pinnae 6-8 pairs; the leaflets 8-12 pairs, *glandular, with the outline irregular*; the flowers in round yellow heads in the axils of the leaves; the pods *slender, often sickle-shaped, beaded, reddish, sticky, shiny.* (Zululand, Swaziland)

25. *A. borleae*

A many-stemmed shrub to slender tree; branched towards the top; the trunk and branches with thin peeling skin; the thorns long, paired, straight, white; the pinnae 1-6 pairs, the leaflets 3-6 pairs; the flowers in yellow balls; the pods *curved, beaded*, up to 6.3 cm long. (Eastern and northern Transvaal)

26. *A. exuvialis*

A bush or small tree; the bark rough; the branches few, weak, ascending; the twigs reddish, densely hairy; the thorns paired, long, straight, white; the leaves up to 4 cm long; the pinnae 2-4, the leaflets up to 8 pairs with thornlike points, sometimes fringed with hairs; the flowers in yellow balls; the pods *short, flat*, up to 4 cm long and 1.3 cm wide, straight to slightly curved, *covered with brown glandular dots*. (Transvaal)

27. *A. permixta*

A small tree, sometimes making thickets; the bark dark, smoothish; the thorns straight, paired; *the pinnae usually 1 pair*, the leaflets 3-4 pairs, oval or round; the flowers axillary, in golden balls, shortly stalked; the pods *short, curved, red-brown, glandular*. (Swaziland, Transvaal, Botswana, S.W.A.)

28. *A. nebrownii*

A small tree; the thorns paired, straight, white, slender; the leaves up to 5 cm long; the pinnae 1-3 pairs; the leaflets about 3-6 pairs, pointed; the leaf stalk and common midrib often with *glandular dots*; the flowers in orange-yellow balls; the pods up to 4 cm long, *flat, curved, yellow-brown to red-brown*, with *sticky brown glandular dots*. (Swaziland, northern Zululand, Transvaal)

29. *A. swazica*

A small to large tree, rounded, spreading; the bark typically rough, brown, sometimes (in Natal) light, smooth; the thorns paired, straight, white, 1.3-17 cm long; the leaves up to 11.5 cm long; the pinnae 2-7, the leaflets about 8-20 pairs, smooth or slightly hairy; the flowers in golden balls, *sweet-scented, in a long terminal inflorescence* and in the axils of *the upper leaves; the pods dark, narrow, flattish, sickle-shaped, dehiscent*. (Widespread in South and S.W.Africa)

30. *A. karroo*

A medium-sized, sparse tree; the branches ascending; the bark reddish-brown, fissured; the thorns paired, straight (slightly hooked when short), about 2.5 cm long, softly hairy; the twigs *hairy*; the leaves up to 9 cm long; the pinnae about 5-10 pairs, the leaflets 15-20 pairs, hairy; the flowers in creamy balls in groups *in the axils of the leaves; the pods narrow, sickle-shaped, hairy*. (Zululand, Swaziland, Transvaal)

31. *A. gerrardii*

A shrub to small tree; the bark light-coloured, corky; the thorns paired, straight, (when short, slightly hooked); the leaves up to 16 cm long; the pinnae 12-22 pairs; the leaflets up to 36 pairs; the twigs and leaves smooth; the flowers in yellow balls, terminally and in the axils of the upper leaves, *without scent*; the pods *narrow, straight,* or slightly curved, sometimes *constricted, smooth*, up to 10 cm long. (Zululand, Swaziland, Transvaal)

32. *A. davyi*

A many-stemmed shrub or small tree; the bark grey; the thorns paired, straight, about 4 cm long; the twigs zigzag, often hairy; the leaves up to 21 cm long; the pinnae about 30-40 pairs; the leaflets about 25 pairs, small, closely packed; the flowers in *pink* balls; the pods dark brown, *long, narrow, slightly curved*, up to about 15 cm long. (S.W.A., Botswana)

33. *A. arenaria*

A small to medium tree, spreading or flat-topped; the bark ashy-grey to black, furrowed; the thorns paired, straight, white, up to 8 cm long, sometimes *inflated and fused at the base*; the leaves in tufts; the pinnae about 3 pairs, the leaflets 8-15 pairs, slightly hairy; the flowers in white balls in groups in the axils of the leaves; the pods brown, *curved, woody, veined*, up to 7.6 cm long. (Zululand, Swaziland, Transvaal, Botswana)

34. *A. grandicornuta*

A small to large tree; the bark rough, black; the twigs and branches often noticeably *thick*; the thorns paired, straight; the pinnae 2-6 pairs, the leaflets up to 15 pairs; the flowers in creamy to yellow balls *before the leaves, in groups on cushions above the spines*; the pods *almost straight, rather woody*, usually up to 13 cm long. (Natal, Zululand, Swaziland, northern Cape, Transvaal, Botswana)

35. *A. robusta*

A medium to large tree; the branches ascending; the trunk and branches *bright yellow-green, powdery*; the thorns paired, straight, white; the leaves 2.5-10 cm long, the pinnae 4-7 pairs, the leaflets 10-17 pairs; the flowers in golden balls; the pods 5-12 cm long, *straight, pale brown, flat, papery*. (Zululand, Swaziland, Transvaal, Botswana)

39. *A. xanthophloea*

Thorns hooked — paired

A tree, medium to large; *the trunk and branches often with spine-tipped knobs*; the thorns paired, small, hooked; the leaves *with pinnae 1-4 pairs, the leaflets usually 1 pair, large*, 1.3 to nearly 2.5 cm long; the flowers in *creamy spikes*; the pods dark, narrowed both ends, up to 10 cm x 2.5 cm. (Zululand, Swaziland, Transvaal, Botswana, S.W.A.)

5. *A. nigrescens*

A very thorny shrub or small tree; the thorns paired, small, hooked; the flowers in *creamy balls*; the pods, *flat, papery, oval, narrowing both ends.* The trunk usually *reddish*; the leaves with pinnae usually in *2 pairs*, the leaflets 1 pair, fairly large, *up to 1.5 cm long* (S.W.A.)

6a. *Acacia mellifera* subsp. *mellifera*

The trunk *smooth greeny-yellow to grey*; the leaves with pinnae usually *in about 3 pairs*, the leaflets 1 pair, *usually under 1 cm long*. (Transvaal, O.F.S., northern Cape, Botswana, S.W.A., northwards)

6b. *A. mellifera* subsp. *detinens*

A medium to tall tree; the bark corky, yellow to black, *sometimes with thorn-tipped knobs*; the thorns paired, dark, hooked; *the pinnae 1-10 pairs, (usually over 4 pairs)* the leaflets about 1-16 pairs (often 5 pairs), hairy on the under-surface; *the twigs, common midrib, and stalks hairy*; the flowers in creamy spikes; the pods 7-10 cm long, flat, thin, pointed, red to black. (Natal, Zululand, Swaziland, Transvaal, Botswana)

7. *A. burkei*

Resembling the above, but the *leaves, leaf stalks, and twigs without hairs*. (Eastern Transvaal and Swaziland)

8. *Acacia welwitschii* subsp. *delagoensis*

736

A medium-sized tree, when young slender, with age spreading; the trunk *shiny red-brown with a yellow peeling skin*; the thorns paired, small, hooked; the *pinnae 3-5 pairs*, the leaflets up to 13 pairs; the flowers pale yellow in spikes; the pods *hard, woody* up to 15 x 2.5 cm, tapering to the base. (S.W.A.)

9. *A. montis-usti*

A shrub to medium-sized tree; the bark *light coloured, corky or papery*; the twigs light-coloured, often with a papery bark; the thorns paired, short, hooked; the leaves 3.8-5 cm long, *the pinnae about 5 pairs*, the leaflets about 20 pairs; the flowers in pale yellow spikes, before the leaves; the pods 5-10 cm long, about 1.3 cm wide, *straight, flat, papery, much veined*. (Transvaal, Botswana, S.W.A.)

10. *A. erubescens*

One or more slender stems up to 4.5 m *arising from a low shrubby growth*; the thorns paired, hooked; *the mature leaves in tufts, pinnae usually 1*, the leaflets usually 6-8, smooth; the flowers white, in spikes; the pods *red-brown, flat, papery, oval, oblong or egg-shaped*. (S.W.A.)

11. *A. robynsiana*

A shrub to a bushy tree; the bark light, peeling; the thorns paired, hooked, abundant (*sometimes scattered*) often with a *swollen base*; the leaves 5-8 cm long, the *pinnae 6-14 pairs*, the leaflets 10-30 pairs, hairy, greyish; the flowers white to pale yellow in spikes; *the pods flat, papery, with thickened margins*. (Transvaal, Botswana, S.W.A.)

12. *A. fleckii*

A small to medium-sized tree; the *bark dark, smooth to rough*; the thorns paired, small, hooked, reddish; the leaves 2.5-5 cm long, the *pinnae 8-26 pairs*, the leaflets 16-48 pairs, *the rachis with small prickles*; the flowers in creamy spikes; the pods *flat, papery*, 5-10 cm long and under 2.5 cm wide, red-brown. (Transvaal, O.F.S., Botswana, S.W.A.)

13. *Acacia hereroensis*

A medium-sized tree; the trunk often crooked; the bark dark, rough; the thorns paired, hooked, not numerous; the leaves large, the pinnae *5-38 pairs*, the leaflets 15-60 pairs, smooth or hairy; the flowers pale yellow, in spikes; the pods 8-13 cm long, *narrow, straight, flat, dark*. (Widespread in South Africa and Swaziland)

14. *A. caffra*

A tall, erect, flat-topped tree; the bark light, rough, corky, flaking; the branches light, *often with cushioned hooked thorns*; the thorns hooked, in pairs (or singly); the leaves 10-18 cm long, the pinnae *12-26 pairs*, the leaflets *up to 70 pairs*, small, hairy; the leaf stalk with a *large gland at the base*; the flowers creamy, in spikes; the pods *straight, light brown*, up to 18 x 1.3 cm, *much lined*. (Transvaal, Botswana)

15. *A. polyacantha*
subsp. *campylacantha*

A large, wide-spreading tree; *the bark light, corky, flaky, with hooked thorns*; the thorns paired, short, hooked, shiny brown; the leaves up to 15 cm long, the *pinnae 6-10 pairs*, the leaflets 17-40 pairs, small, smooth; the flowers in creamy-yellow spikes; the pods *woody*, 7.6-20 cm long, 2-5 cm broad, *flat, light brown*. (Transvaal, Botswana)

16. *A. galpinii*

A small tree, branched from the base, the *crown low, spreading;* the thorns paired, hooked, small, *usually with a few inflated ones which are then almost straight;* the young parts densely hairy, the pinnae about 2-12 pairs; the flowers in white or yellow balls; the pods *straight, leathery, up to 3 cm wide but often narrower*. (Zululand, Swaziland, Transvaal)

37b. *A. luederitzii*
var. *retinens*

Thorns straight and hooked

A small to medium-sized tree, *flat-topped to rounded*, the bark reddish-brown, seamed; the thorns hooked, in pairs, *a few* long, straight, white, *never inflated*; the pinnae up to 12 or sometimes more pairs; the leaflets with *long spreading hairs*; the flowers in whitish balls; the pods *straight, flat, reddish, up to about 3 cm wide*. (Northern Cape, Botswana, S.W.A.)

37a. *A. luederitzii*
var. *luederitzii*

A small, spreading tree; the bark reddish-brown, fissured; the thorns in small hooked pairs together with some that are long, straight and white; the pinnae about 2-9 pairs, the leaflets about 5-11 pairs, tiny, *almost smooth*; the flowers in yellow balls; the pods flat, narrow, reddish or buff, straight or *slightly curved, up to 1.3 cm wide*. (Botswana, S.W.A.)

36. *A. reficiens*

A medium-sized tree; the bark dark, fissured; the thorns of 2 kinds, long, straight and white, and small, hooked and brownish; the leaves *small*, usually up to 2.5 cm long, the pinnae 4-10 pairs; the leaflets about 15 pairs, *minute*; the flowers white to yellow in round balls; *the pods much twisted and curled, smooth*. (Widespread)

22. *A. tortilis*
subsp. *heteracantha*

Thorns hooked, in 3's

A slender, upright tree; the bark corky; the thorns small, hooked, in 3's; the pinnae about 5 pairs, the leaflets small, 8-14 pairs; *the midrib smooth*; the flowers in creamy spikes; the pods *flat, papery, usually round-tipped*, up to 8 cm long. (Eastern and northern Transvaal)

2. *A. senegal*
var. *leiorachis*

A small flat-topped tree branching from the base; the thorns small, hooked, in 3's; the *leaves with a hairy midrib*; the flowers creamy, in spikes; the pods broad, flat, papery, veined, *usually with sharp slender points*. (Zululand, Swaziland, Transvaal, Botswana, S.W.A.)

3. *A. senegal*
var. *rostrata*

Thorns hooked and scattered

A thorny creeper, shrub, or spreading, bushy tree; the thorns scattered, short, stout, hooked; the leaves up to about 13 cm long, the pinnae about 7-17 pairs, the leaflets 20-45 pairs; the stipules large; the flowers *in creamy spikes*; the pods *long, narrow*, up to 8 cm, in terminal bunches, *bright red* when ripe. (Zululand, Natal, Swaziland, Transvaal, Botswana, S.W.A.)

4. *A. ataxacantha*

A woody climber, only very occasionally a small tree; the thorns hooked, scattered; the leaves large, the pinnae 4-20 pairs, the leaflets about 30 pairs, smooth; the flowers *in creamy balls*; the pods up to 18 cm long, *flat, brown, much veined*. (Natal, Zululand, Swaziland, Transvaal, Botswana)

38. *A. schweinfurthii*

Species with flowers in round balls

Acacia giraffae (yellow flowers)
Acacia haematoxylon (yellow)
Acacia hebeclada – all forms – (white to gold)
Acacia sieberana var. *woodii* (white or pale yellow)
Acacia rehmanniana (greenish-white)
Acacia kirkii (white to pink)
Acacia nilotica subsp. *kraussiana* (yellow)
Acacia borleae (yellow)
Acacia exuvialis (yellow)
Acacia permixta (yellow)
Acacia nebrownii (yellow)
Acacia swazica (orange-yellow)
Acacia karroo (golden)
Acacia gerrardii (cream-coloured)
Acacia davyi (yellow)
Acacia arenaria (pinkish)
Acacia grandicornuta (whitish to yellowish)
Acacia robusta (cream-coloured to yellow)
Acacia xanthophloea (golden)
Acacia mellifera subsp. *mellifera* and subsp. *detinens* (creamy)
Acacia luederitzii var. *luederitzii* (whitish)
Acacia luederitzii var. *retinens* (white to yellow)
Acacia schweinfurthii (creamy)
Acacia tortilis subsp. *heteracantha* (white to yellow)
Acacia reficiens (yellow)

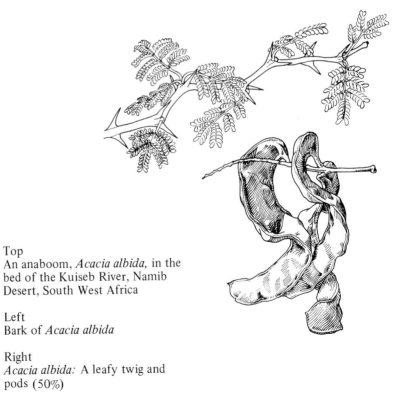

Top
An anaboom, *Acacia albida,* in the
bed of the Kuiseb River, Namib
Desert, South West Africa

Left
Bark of *Acacia albida*

Right
Acacia albida: A leafy twig and
pods (50%)

740

Flowers in spikes

Acacia albida (creamy flowers)
Acacia nigrescens (creamy)
Acacia burkei (creamy)
Acacia welwitschii subsp. *delagoensis* (creamy)
Acacia montis-usti (pale yellow)
Acacia hereroensis (creamy)
Acacia erubescens (pale yellow)
Acacia robynsiana (white)
Acacia fleckii (white to pale yellow)
Acacia caffra (pale yellow)
Acacia galpinii (creamy-yellow)
Acacia polyacantha subsp. *campylacantha* (creamy)
Acacia ataxacantha (creamy)
Acacia senegal var. *leiorachis* and var. *rostrata* (creamy)

(159)   1. *Acacia albida* Del.

Ana tree, anaboom, white-thorn, winter-thorn, apiesdoring; umHla-lankwazi, umKhaya wemfula (Z); mmolela (Tso); mokosho
(Tsw — Máng); mogabọ, mogôhlô (NS); muhotọ (V); omue (Her); aná-heis, anás (Nama)

The ana tree or anaboom is the largest acacia of South and South West Africa, a spreading giant, one of the noblest of the great acacia race. It grows, usually on river banks, alluvial flats, or in woodland, often in deep, pure sand, from Mozambique, northern Tongaland and the northern Transvaal, through Botswana to South West Africa, and northwards to tropical Africa, where it is widespread. Ross says that it has also been recorded from Syria, Israel, and Cyprus.

Some botanists see two geographical types or races of this acacia, one generally smooth and the other hairy, with intermediate forms. The hairy form is typical of South and South West Africa.

Young trees are often spindly but spread with age. Mature trees are sometimes beautifully rounded, growing, in South Africa, up to 20 m high with a trunk circumference of up to 4.6 m, while in northern South West Africa they are reported up to 31 m high.

The fine, often drooping foliage is sometimes a light green, sometimes grey, but most often a soft blue-green. The trunk in adult trees is light brown to greenish-grey, in young ones creamy. The twigs are white and smooth. Typically this is a large tree with a round crown and with the white twigs shining through the rather drooping, bluish, feathery leaves.

The thorns are straight, up to about 4 cm long, white at the base and reddish-brown at the tips, and in pairs. They distinguish it from two other acacias, *Acacia galpinii* Burtt Davy and *Acacia burkei* Benth., which have small hooked thorns, and which are also — and more commonly — known as apiesdoring. Old branches of mature trees often have few and small thorns.

Each leaf usually has about 4-8 — occasionally 2-12 — pairs of pinnae or side-branches, which carry about 6-23 pairs of medium-sized to small, oblong leaflets. The leaf stalks are without glands, although there is usually a conspicuous gland between each pair of pinnae.

Above left
Acacia senegal var.
leiorhachis in the northern Transvaal

Above right
Its stem and bark

Left
Acacia senegal var.
rostrata near Sorris
Sorris, South West
Africa

The foliage in Southern Africa is usually deciduous, although the times at which the trees lose their leaves often vary. In parts they lose their leaves in summer, coming into leaf again at the beginning of winter.

The flowers of the anaboom grow in long creamy spikes. This tree, alone among the acacias of South Africa, has the combination of straight thorns and flowers in spikes, balls of flowers being most often associated with straight thorns. Giant anabooms along the Kunene River are a sight in bloom, their creamy-yellow flowers mingling with the white flowers of a jasmine that drapes the trees.

The pods are large, about 10 cm by 2.5 cm, a rich red- or orange-brown when mature, and very twisted, sometimes curled almost into a ring. They do not burst open. A large tree in a good year bears about 1 metric ton of pods, and as these are eaten by stock and wild animals from elephants to antelope and baboons, the anaboom is a valuable fodder tree.

The gum, pods, and leaves are used medicinally.

The pods contain several hard, shiny seeds with a fairly high protein content, and in times of scarcity these are eaten by Africans after having been boiled and reboiled and the skins removed. The pods themselves have a high starch content and are sometimes eaten.

The anaboom, and its relative the camelthorn, are the basis of the life of a primitive group of people, the Topnaar Hottentots, who live in the dry bed of the Kuiseb River in the Namib Desert of South West Africa. The bark of the anaboom builds their huts, the pods form a large part of their food, while the camelthorn is almost their only source of income. They burn its wood and sell the charcoal in the coastal towns.

Anaboom wood is coarse-grained, light in weight, and a whitish colour. Although not particularly suitable for building or furniture it was used for both by the early colonists of South West Africa, and today drinking troughs are sometimes made of it.

A group of anaboom on the road from Potgietersrust to Saaiplaats in the Transvaal has been proclaimed a national monument. They bear the name of "Livingstone's Trees", although there seems little connection with Livingstone himself. An historic tree near Pietersburg is said to have been planted by Louis Trichardt on a visit to Sekukuni.

Galpin says that on the Springbok Flats the anaboom is held sacred by the Africans.

This is one of the fastest-growing of all indigenous trees, under good conditions reaching a height of 7 m in three years. It is slightly tender to frost.

The anaboom is not closely related to any other of the acacias. Indeed, on the basis of its differences – such as the glandless leaf stalks and the unusual pod – it was once removed to a separate genus when it was known as *Faidherbia albida* (Del.) A.Chev. Botanists today, however, do not consider its differences warrant its separation from the genus *Acacia*.

The specific name *albida* means "white". The common name "ana" is a Nama name, Zulus call the tree umHlalankwazi or "the tree where the fish eagle sits", indicating its size for the fish eagle is usually seen perching on the largest tree in the neighbourhood.

Above right
Acacia senegal var. *rostrata* leaves and thorns

Above left
Its stem and bark

Below left
Acacia senegal var. *rostrata* flowering
twig (60%)

Below right
Acacia senegal var. *leiorhachis* twig
with pod and spines in threes (60%)

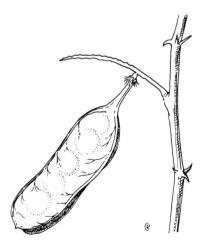

744

2. *Acacia senegal* (L.) Willd.

(185)   var. *leiorhachis* Brenan

Gomdoring

(185.1)   3. var. *rostrata* Brenan

= *Acacia volkii* Susseng

Geelhaak, three-thorned acacia, drievingerdoring; umKhaya omhloshana, isiKhambophane, umKhala (Z); umHlahlalinye (Sw); Shin'ayi (Tso)

Acacia senegal in its typical form does not enter South or South West Africa. Two varieties, however, are found here, the gomdoring, *Acacia senegal* (L.) Willd. var. *leiorhachis* Brenan, and the geelhaak, var. *rostrata* Brenan. Some botanists see the two varieties as completely distinct species, and possibly in the future they will be separated. Certainly in form they are very unlike one another.

The gomdoring var. *leiorhachis*, belongs to East and South Africa, growing in this country in dry bush in the eastern and northern Transvaal, while the geelhaak or three-thorned acacia, var. *rostrata*, grows widely in scrub and bush from Mozambique, Swaziland and Zululand, westwards to South West Africa, and north to Rhodesia. It is fairly common in the eastern, northern, and central Transvaal, and in parts of the Waterberg is encroaching rapidly and becoming a problem to farmers.

The leaves, thorns, and flowers of the two varieties resemble one another, the main distinction between them being the habit of growth, for whereas the gomdoring (var. *leiorhachis*) is a slender upright tree up to about 6 m tall with a few erect branches and an orange-brown, corky bark, the geelhaak (var. *rostrata*) is entirely different, a small tree, seldom more than 3.6 m high, usually branching from the base, with a flat spreading crown, numerous, light-coloured, interlacing branches, and a greyish trunk becoming somewhat flaky with age.

Both varieties have fairly small leaves about 4 cm long, made up of about 5 pairs of side-branches and 8-14 pairs of very small leaflets. In the case of the geelhaak the main midrib of these is hairy, in the case of the gomdoring it is smooth — the name *leiorhachis* means "with a smooth rachis".

They both have small, sharply hooked thorns usually in 3's (occasionally borne singly), the middle one hooked downwards, the side ones upwards, and yellow or cream-coloured flowers in long, dense, sweet-smelling spikes. The axis of these is slightly or very hairy in the geelhaak, and smooth or nearly smooth in the gomdoring.

The pods are broad, flat, up to about 8 cm long, papery, buff-coloured and veined, borne on short leaf stalks. Those of var. *rostrata* usually have a sharp slender beaked point and are the reason for the name *rostrata*, meaning "with a beaked or slender tip". Those of var. *leiorhachis* usually have round tips.

The pods of var. *rostrata* sometimes cover the tree in numbers, making it making it conspicuous. Visitors travelling the road between Outjo and Welwitschia in South West Africa in winter may remember the geelhaaks, small, dense, fan-like trees, festooned with pale papery pods, which are such a feature of the countryside.

Both forms of the tree yield a good gum.

Top
Acacia ataxacantha growing on the Soutpansberg in the northern Transvaal

Centre
Baskets made of *Acacia ataxacantha* wood

Below left
Acacia ataxacantha flower spikes

Below right
Acacia nigrescens: pods and a leaf (50%)

Opposite
Acacia ataxacantha: A twig showing the scattered thorns

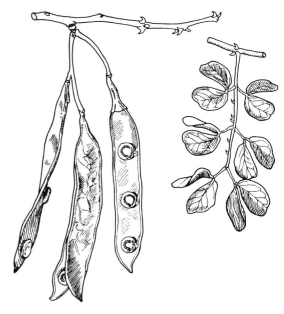

746

(160)   4. *Acacia ataxacantha* DC.

= *Acacia eriadenia* Benth.; = *A. lugardae* N.E.Br.; = *A. ataxacantha* DC. var. *australis* Burtt Davy

Flame thorn, rank wag-'n-bietjie, tierbos; uThathawe (Z); luGagane (Sw); mooka-tau (Tsw), mokgwa (Tsw-Kwena), and mokuku (Tsw — Taw); mologa (NS); muluwa (V); mogotau (Sub); mokona (Kol)

The flame thorn is variable in habit, growing as a thorny climber, a many-stemmed shrub, a large, spreading, shrub-like tree up to 12 m high which usually supports itself on other trees, and occasionally as a large, single-stemmed tree, and in these guises it grows from Zululand and Natal, through Swaziland and the Transvaal, to Botswana and South West Africa, and northwards·to tropical Africa.

It grows along rivers, in valleys, and on forest margins where it often makes dense thickets, on flats, and on hill and mountain sides. On the slopes of the Soutpansberg it is common as a large, bushy, rounded tree with long trailing branches. It is common in bushveld, and in the bushveld country of South West Africa it frequently grows as a small dense bush.

The small, stout, hooked thorns help to identify the tree for they are not in pairs but scattered along the stems. They give the tree its specific name for *ataxacantha* is based on Greek words meaning "irregular thorns". These thorns are not stipules for in the case of this tree the stipules are leaf-like but soon fall off.

The bark is light coloured, smooth when young but becoming longitudinally ribbed with age.

The leaves are up to about 13 cm long and often have small prickles on the common leaf stalk. Each leaf has 7-17 pairs of pinnae, which bear 20-45 pairs of tiny, hairy or smooth, slightly curved leaflets. Small stalked glands on the leaf stalk near the base of the leaf are often conspicuous.

The creamy-white or yellow flowers are borne in abundance in the summer in spikes up to 10 cm long. They develop into long, narrow pods up to about 8 cm long and 1.3 cm wide, tapering both ends and sharply pointed, with thin brittle valves. They hold 2-5 seeds. The pods are borne in clusters at the ends of the branches and when mature are purple or a beautiful strong clear red, giving the tree its common name of flame thorn. Some fine specimens grow alongside the road over the Soutpansberg between Louis Trichardt and Wyllie's Poort, and from March to May when the pods are red, they make brilliant patches of colour. The pods become brown with age.

In the eastern and northern Transvaal this tree is used to make baskets. The wood can be split to the thickness of paper without cracking and this — red, white or white with a dark streak — is the weaving material.

Until recently two varieties of this acacia were recognized, *Acacia ataxacantha* DC. var. *ataxacantha*, a smooth-leaved form from South West Africa and tropical Africa, and var. *australis* Burtt Davy, with hairy leaves. These are now regarded as not worthy of separate rank.

Above
The well-known knoppiesdoring, *Acacia nigrescens*

Left
The stem of the knoppiesdoring

(178)   5. *Acacia nigrescens* Oliv.

= *Acacia pallens* (Benth.) Rolfe

Knobthorn, knoppiesdoring; umKhaya, umBhebhe, isiBambampala (Z); umkhaya (Sw); nkayi (Tso); mokala, mokôba, more o mabele (Tsw); mokgalô, moku, mongana-mabêlê (NS); mudhaya (V); ungandu (Mbuk)

The well-known knob-thorn, or knoppiesdoring as it is widely known, is an upright tree up to 18 m tall — although usually smaller — with a somewhat spreading crown and a stem diameter of 20-76 cm. It is common in the lowveld of the drier parts of the Transvaal, Zululand, and Swaziland, and in Botswana, northern South West Africa, Rhodesia, southern Portuguese East Africa — where it occurs as pure open forest — and in parts of Zambia, Malawi, and Tanzania.

It is a familiar tree to visitors to the Kruger National Park where, according to Codd, it avoids moist sites, occurring on the turfy flats between the Olifants River and Satara as the dominant large tree, while in the south between Skukuza and Pretorius Kop it is associated with black turfy soil derived from dolerite dykes.

Farmers consider knoppiesdoring veld good ranching country.

The most obvious characteristic, and one that distinguishes it from most other acacias, is its knob-studded grey or yellow trunk and branches, each knob being tipped with a hooked thorn. These are obvious and highly dramatic on the trunks of young trees, and on their branches, but in older trees the knobs are usually absent on the rough trunks and must be looked for high up on the branches. Occasionally they are altogether absent. The knobs give the tree its English and Afrikaans common names.

The knoppiesdoring is completely deciduous and remains bare for several months in winter and in early spring, when, however, it can often be identified by the knobs. In leaf, it is again easily identified for the leaf, although compound, is not finely feathery as in most acacias. There are only 2-4 pairs of pinnae and these bear only one pair of large leaflets, 1.3 cm to nearly 2.5 cm long, grey-green with lopsided bases. The common midrib is usually studded with small recurved spines.

The branchlets are armed with pairs of small, hooked thorns. Colonel Stevenson-Hamilton, famous warden of the Kruger National Park, wrote that of all those coming under the collective title of "wait-a-bit" the worst to his mind was this species. It was so fresh and innocent looking, he wrote, with its little round leaves of tender green, that the unwary stranger was apt to brush against it, "to be firmly grasped by the frightful hook thorns, which are set back-to-back in pairs, much like those at the tail of a spoon bait. So tightly do they grip him, indeed, that disentanglement can seldom be effected save with the loss of some part of the garments, and possibly of the person as well".

The sweet-scented flowers, which bloom from August to November before the leaves appear, grow in a spike up to 10 cm long. In the bud stage, the spikes are a reddish-brown and from the distance the tree appears covered in autumn-coloured foliage. These buds open into creamy blossom giving the knoppiesdoring for a brief while an air of fragile loveliness. Anyone who has been to the Kruger National Park in early spring will remember the knoppiesdoring blooming luxuriantly for miles on end.

The thin, dark pods, narrowed at both ends, grow to about 10 cm long by 1.3-2.5 cm broad. They enclose 5 to 7 flattish brown seeds. The pods are eaten by wild animals including giraffe.

Elephant eat the branches, leaves and shoots, kudu browse the leaves and shoots, and monkeys and baboons eat the flowers.

The tree offers excellent nesting sites to hole-nesting birds, which are therefore common in *Acacia nigrescens* veld.

It is strongly fire-resistant.

The sapwood is a pale creamy colour, the heartwood a dark brown. The wood is exceptionally hard to saw, even when green; is strong, close-grained, termite-resistant, durable underground, and makes good fencing posts, mine props, and jukskeis. Africans use it to make fighting sticks. The bark is sometimes used for tanning.

In the eastern Transvaal Africans smear stakes of the wood with a specially prepared medicine, and hammer these into the ground round a kraal to protect it from evil influences and from lightning.

This is not a very quick-growing acacia, seldom even under the best conditions growing 0.6 m in a year, and far outstripped in speed of growth by acacias such as *A. albida, A. galpinii,* or *A. karroo.* It is drought resistant, but sensitive to frost.

The name *nigrescens* means "becoming black", and probably refers to the blackish pods.

This was the *Acacia mellifera* of Henkel in his *Woody Plants of Natal and Zululand.*

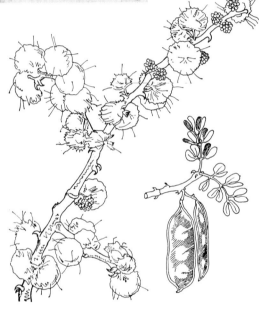

(176)   6. *Acacia mellifera* (Vahl) Benth.
         a. subsp. *mellifera*
         b. subsp. *detinens* (Burch.) Brenan

= *Acacia detinens* Burch.

Swarthaak, blackthorn, hookthorn, haakdoring, blouhaak, wynruit, hakiesdoring; mongana (Tsw), monka (Tsw – Kgat), monyaka (Tsw – Kwena); monganga-tau, mongana-moswana (NS); moga (Kal); omusaona (Her); / nóës (Nama)

Two forms of this thorny shrub or small tree grow in South and South West Africa, *Acacia mellifera* (Vahl.) Benth. subsp. *mellifera* which occurs from northern South West Africa to tropical Africa, and subsp. *detinens* (Burch.) Brenan which grows in the northern Transvaal, the western Orange Free State, the northern and north western Cape, Botswana, South West Africa, Angola, Rhodesia and Zambia. This is a common small tree in parts of the Transvaal bushveld, on koppies and in dry bush in the northern Cape and in South West Africa, and on the red dunes of the Kalahari Desert, growing in sand, in clayey soils, or among stones.

It is one of the few species seen when travelling the long desert roads through Bushmanland, and near Upington is conspicuous as a thorny shrub on stony koppies in company with the gifboom, or poison tree, *Euphorbia virosa* Willd.; the driedoring, *Rhigozum trichotomum* Burch., and the stinkboom, *Boscia foetida* Schinz subsp. *foetida.*

The South African form has – particularly in the Vryburg, Mafeking, and Kuruman districts – become a problem for, spreading by coppice and seed, it can cover the veld, forming an absolutely impenetrable, tangled, thorny growth. In tree form, however, it is valuable for fodder and shade.

The two subspecies resemble one another closely, the most obvious differences being in the appearance of the trunks and the leaves. *Acacia mellifera* subsp. *mellifera* usually has a reddish trunk, and subsp. *detinens* a smooth greeny-yellow trunk becoming grey with age. The foliage of both is blue- or greyish-green, the leaves differing from those of most acacias as the compound leaves have few pinnae or side-branches – usually about 2 pairs in the case of subsp. *mellifera*, and about 3 pairs in subsp. *detinens*, and these usually bear only one pair of fairly large leaflets. The pinnae in subsp. *mellifera* are noticeably larger than those of subsp. *detinens* – up to 1.5 cm long compared with the small, leaflets under 1 cm long of subsp. *detinens*, and smooth.

The common and widespread subsp. *detinens* is known in South Africa by a variety of names, swarthaak, blackthorn, blouhaak, hakiesdoring, hookthorn, and others. Its leaves are usually shed after the first frost and the tree remains bare until September or October when it bursts into a mass of flowers in fragrant, fluffy, cream-coloured balls very attractive to bees. Their perfume is strongest at night.

This is one of the few acacias to have the combination of flowers in balls and hooked thorns.

The thorns, which are in small, hooked pairs, are inconspicuous and innocent looking. They are, on the contrary, some of the most wicked of all the many acacia thorns. Burchell, who named subsp. *detinens* after an encounter with them, wrote:

"I was preparing to cut some specimens of it, which the Hottentots observing, warned me to be very careful in doing, otherwise I should

OPPOSITE

Above
The swarthaak, *Acacia mellifera* subsp. *detinens*, near Kimberley

Centre left
Swarthaak bark

Centre right
Acacia mellifera subsp. *detinens:* Flowering and fruiting twigs (50%)

Below
A hill near Upington with a plant community typical of the area – *Acacia mellifera* subsp. *detinens* in the foreground, with *Euphorbia virosa, Boscia foetida,* and the driedoring, *Rhigozum trichotomum*

Left
Acacia burkei near Hartebeestpoort Dam in the Transvaal
bushveld

Above
A form of *Acacia burkei* at Mkuze, Zululand

Below left
Acacia burkei flower spikes

Below right
Acacia burkei: A flowering twig (50%)

Opposite
The stem of an *Acacia burkei* in the Transvaal bushveld

752

certainly be caught fast in its branches. In consequence of this advice I proceeded with the utmost caution, but, with all my care, a small twig caught hold of one sleeve. While thinking to disengage it quietly with the other hand, both arms were seized by these rapacious thorns and the more I tried to extricate myself the more entangled I became; till at last it seized hold of the hat also; and convinced me that there was no possibility for me to free myself but by main force, and at the expense of tearing all my clothes. I therefore called out for help, and two of my men came and released me by cutting off the branches by which I was held. In revenge for this ill-treatment, I determined to give the tree a name which should serve to caution future travellers against allowing themselves to venture within its clutches".

And so the tree became *Acacia detinens* Burch., the specific name being based on the Latin "detinere" meaning "to detain" or "to hold". The tree has now been renamed *Acacia mellifera* subsp. *detinens*, which freely translated means, "the honey-bearing acacia that holds one fast".

Swarthaak pods, which develop quickly and in abundance, are papery, flat, and oval-shaped, narrowing slightly at both ends, and enclosing 2 to 3 seeds. The pods, young twigs, leaves, and flowers are nutritious and greedily eaten by stock, and sheep and goats in particular. Kudu are also very fond of them.

In the 1966 drought, farmers in the Orange Free State ground up small branches of the tree in hammermills, mixed this with molasses, and fed the mixture to their stock.

The wood is used extensively for fuel. The sapwood is thick and whitish. The heartwood is dark brown to greenish-black, and when oiled turns almost black and takes a high polish. Galpin says it is very tough and elastic, does not split, and is unsurpassed for axe and pick handles. He states that the heartwood is termite- and borer-proof, and that larger stems make excellent fencing posts.

The tree produces an edible gum which is sometimes mixed with clay to make floors.

In Botswana a decoction of the roots is a medicine for stomach pains. The poison with which Bushmen tip their arrows is often made from a powdered grub mixed with the sap of the swarthaak.

In Griqualand West the Africans believe that this tree, like the camelthorn, attracts lightning. The hooked thorns are thought by them to have the power of enticing rain.

(161)   7. *Acacia burkei* Benth.

Black monkey thorn, black apiesdoring, swart apiesdoring, bruinapiesdoring, geelapiesdoring, apiesdoring, haakdoring; umKhaya, umuNga (Z); mokotokoto (Tsw), mokgwa (Tsw – Kwena & Ngwak), mokoba (Tsw – Mang & Taw); mokgwaripa (NS)

The black apiesdoring is a tree of bushveld and lowveld savannah, of river banks and sandy flats, from Natal, Zululand, Swaziland, the eastern, northern and central Transvaal, to Botswana in the west.

It is a medium-sized to large tree up to 24 m high with a spreading crown and single trunk with bark which is corky, yellow and flaking when young, and dark brown or blackish and rough when old. Sometimes knobs tipped with hooked thorns grow on the trunk, and the tree is then easily confused with the knoppiesdoring, *Acacia nigrescens*, to

Acacia montis-usti in the Brandberg valley

which it is closely related.

The leaves are 5-8 cm long with 1-10 pairs of pinnae — 4 to 5 pairs are most typical — and these bear about 5 pairs (occasionally 1-16 pairs) of often medium-sized leaflets. The common midrib is hairy and the leaflets on their under surface usually bear a tuft of hairs at their base. Sometimes these can be seen with the naked eye, at others only with a microscope, but they are important for these hairy tufts, and the hairy twigs and stalks, separate this species from the Delagoa thorn, *Acacia welwitschii* Oliv. subsp. *delagoensis* (Harms) Ross & Brenan, which has entirely smooth leaves, twigs, and leaf stalks, and a more eastern distribution.

The thorns, dark and hooked like a parrot's beak, are in pairs. The flowers are in narrow creamy spikes up to 5 cm long, and the pods are 8-10 cm long, flat, thin, pointed, and reddish to black. They remain on the tree for many months.

Leaves and pods are eaten by giraffe and the gum by monkeys.

The wood is dark brown, heavy, tough, and works well. It was once used for furniture, for when polished it has a good grain, and for wagons and fence posts.

Africans believe the tree attracts lightning.

This is not a clear-cut species. Some botanists consider that it may not be separable from the Delagoa thorn. Others see it as a possible hybrid between *Acacia nigrescens* and *Acacia galpinii*. In the eastern parts of the country trees occur that are not typical *Acacia burkei* although they appear to grade into it. From the Pongola River near Jozini comes a tree with large leaflets in 3 to 5 pairs, much larger than those usually borne by this species; while again on the eastern side of the Lebombo mountains a type grows with a flat crown, twisted gnarled trunk, flaking bark, and with smaller and more numerous leaflets than in the typical form. Ross says that in Natal trees are often referred to as the "small leaflet" *Acacia burkei* and the "big leaflet" *Acacia burkei*, the former with leaflets less than 3 mm wide and a typically flattened crown favouring sandy soil, and the latter with leaflets more than 3 mm wide, and a more rounded crown, often growing on hard loam.

The specific name of the tree honours Joseph Burke, who collected the tree in the Magaliesberg in the 1840's.

(163)   8. *Acacia welwitschii* Oliv.
          subsp. *delagoensis* (Harms) Ross & Brenan

= *A. delagoensis* Harms

Delagoa thorn

The Delagoa thorn is primarily a species of Mozambique, reaching into the eastern Transvaal and Swaziland lowveld. It closely resembles *Acacia burkei*, but the leaves, leaf stalks, and twigs are without hairs.

The tree was named after F.M.F. Welwitsch, Austrian botanist and medical doctor, who collected in Angola from 1853-1861 and after whom the genus *Welwitschia* was named.

Above
Acacia montis-usti: Leaves, pod and
flower spike (80%)

Right
Acacia erubescens: Portion of a
fruiting twig (80%)

Below
Acacia erubescens in the north eastern Transvaal

OPPOSITE

Above
Acacia montis-usti bark

Below
Acacia erubescens stem

(177)   9. *Acacia montis-usti* Merxm. & Schreib.

Brandberg acacia, ysterhout

Acacia montis-usti — "the acacia of the Burnt Mountain" — is well named. It grows in numbers in the valley leading to "the White Lady", the famous prehistoric painting in the South West African mountain known as the Brandberg, of which *montis-usti* is the Latin translation. It also grows in the country to the north west.

This is a remarkable acacia and one only recently described. Old trees are wide-spreading, with rough grey trunks, but young ones are often tall and slender, like a cypress in form, sometimes with a single stem for many feet and then branching upwards with many slender reddish branches and a feathery crown, sometimes branching from the base. Stem and branches are a shiny red-brown, with thick, crisp, yellow skin that flakes off in the manner of a commiphora.

The small, stout, paired thorns are hooked. The leaves have 3-5 pairs of pinnae and up to 10 pairs of leaflets about 8 mm long — fairly large for acacia leaflets — with rounded tips and with the margin to one side.

The pale yellow flowers grow in long spikes which develop into hard woody pods up to 15 cm long and nearly 2.5 cm broad, with thickened margins.

The Brandberg valley — the Tsisab Ravine — has a wild beauty, and against its piled rocks and kranses these delicate trees show up magnificently. One cypress-like tree grows out of black polished rock at the entrance to the valley, shedding its yellow skin on the jet-black stones below. It is probably the most-photographed tree of the species.

(164)   10. *Acacia erubescens* Welw. ex Oliv.

= *Acacia dulcis* Marloth & Engl.; = *A. kwebensis* N.E.Br.

Blouhaak, geelhaak, withaak, katnael; moloto (Tsw); moremgambo (Mbuk); omungongomui (Her)

The blouhaak, a semi-deciduous tree with yellowish-green or grey-green foliage, and a pale peeling trunk, is widespread in the eastern, northern and central Transvaal, reaching across Botswana to South West Africa, and northwards to Angola and tropical Africa.

It grows in mixed tree veld, often with the haak-en-steek, in brak or stony soil, favouring — in particular — deep sand. It may be a shrub, or a medium-sized tree up to 6 m high, sometimes with a single trunk when it is often graceful and spreading, often with many stems from the base. The bark is distinctive, corky or papery, yellow, white, or bluish, and flaking. In parts of South West Africa this thin, white, paper-like bark has given rise to the name, "birthtree bark". The branchlets and twigs are often grey or white, sometimes with an orange tinge, somewhat papery and peeling, and gleam among the foliage.

The thorns are short, paired, hooked, and extremely sharp. They are sometimes bluish in colour. The leaves, 4-5 cm long, have about 5 pairs of pinnae which bear up to 20 pairs of leaflets. These are somewhat larger than those of *Acacia hereroensis*, but smaller and more numerous than the leaflets of *Acacia burkei* with which the tree is sometimes confused.

The flowers appear about September and October before the leaves in fat, pale yellow, sweet-scented spikes. The pods, in bunches, are 4-10 cm long and about 1.3 cm wide, straight, flat, pointed, papery, dark reddish-brown, criss-crossed with a network of veins, and with thickened margins. They are browsed by cattle and wild animals and are nutritious.

The wood is hard and durable and is said to provide a very "hot" fuel. It is also used for yoke-skeys and for fencing poles.

The blouhaak produces an extremely good gum, yellow and very sweet, much sought after by country children.

The name *erubescens* means "blush red", but the allusion is not clear. Nor is that of the name "blouhaak", used by farmers in the north western Transvaal. It may refer to the colour of the trunk, to that of the thorns, or to that of the leaves.

(184)   11. *Acacia robynsiana* Merxm. & Schreib.

Radio tree

This little known and strangely formed acacia from South West Africa has been recorded from the Outjo and Welwitschia districts, and from the Kaokoveld, growing on stony koppies and on mountain slopes.

It makes a low, dense, shrubby growth about 1 m high, sending up from this either 1 or several slender stems up to 4.5 m high which bear at the top a few thin drooping branches. Farmers use this tree for putting up their aerials, hence the common name "radio tree".

The thorns are paired and hooked.

The mature leaves are in tufts and usually unijugate, that is with 1 pinna with about 6-8 pairs of smooth leaflets. When young they are alternate with up to 2 pinnae.

The white flowers are in spikes. The pods are red-brown, oval, oblong or egg-shaped, flat, papery, with thickened margins.

This tree was named after Professor W. Robyns, former director of the State Botanic Gardens in Brussels.

(165)   12. *Acacia fleckii* Schinz

= *A. cinerea* Schinz

Bladdoring; mhahu (Sub); mokoka (Kol)

Acacia fleckii, which somewhat resembles the blouhaak, *Acacia erubescens*, occurs in the western and north western Transvaal, spreading through Botswana — where it is common in parts — to the eastern and northern areas of South West Africa, and to Angola.

It may be a several-stemmed, semi-deciduous shrub up to about 2.5 m tall, or a shrubby tree up to 6 m, with a round or spreading crown, a trunk with rather thin, grey, buff, or creamy peeling bark, and light coloured branches peeling in small papery pieces.

This is a thorny little tree with abundant, vicious, hooked thorns in pairs, or sometimes scattered, and these have a somewhat swollen base and give the tree its common name.

The leaves — about 5-8 cm long — have a gland, a flat, raised knob, at their base. The 6-14 pairs of pinnae bear from about 10 to 30 pairs of hairy, grey leaflets, usually finer and more numerous than those of the blouhaak.

Above
Acacia fleckii near
Thabazimbi in the west-
ern Transvaal

Right
Acacia fleckii: A fruiting twig (70%)

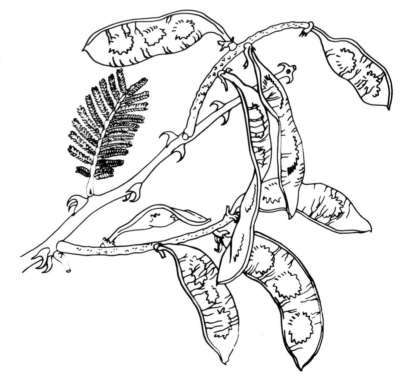

The white to pale yellow flowers are in spikes up to about 8 cm long and bloom about December.

The flat, papery pods, up to about 9 cm long, are pale grey or brown, covered with many tiny glands which appear as small red or black, raised spots. These are not always clearly visible.

The bladdoring produces an edible gum.

This species was named after Dr. E. Fleck, geologist and plant collector in South West Africa in the last century.

759

(171)   13. *Acacia hereroensis* Engl.

= *Acacia mellei* Verdoorn

Bergdoring, rooihaak

Formerly the bergdoring, *Acacia hereroensis* Engl., from South West Africa, and *Acacia mellei* Verdoorn from the central and western Transvaal, northern Cape and Botswana, were thought to be two separate species. Now *Acacia mellei* is considered inseparable from *Acacia hereoensis* and included in it. The species thus has a big distribution, from the Pretoria district and the western Orange Free State in the east to South West Africa, where it is spread fairly widely, growing in bushveld, in savannah, and on hills, usually on dolomitic soils.

It is a common small tree in the hills and in the scrub around Windhoek where it is often no more than a small bushy tree. It can, however, grow to a height of 9 m, either single-trunked or branching from the base.

The bark is dark and smooth when young, and in old trees rough and peeling. It is deciduous and bare of foliage from late winter to late spring. The leaves are very fine, often about 2.5-5 cm long, composed of about 8-26 pairs of pinnae or side-branches, with 16-48 pairs of fine, closely packed leaflets, which — according to Ross — tend to stand erect, whereas those of *Acacia caffra*, which it resembles, droop.

The small, reddish, hooked thorns are in pairs. C.A. Smith says that in older plants the thorns are easily broken off and can cause a wound which festers readily. The flowers, borne in summer, are in pale yellow or cream, pendulous spikes and are scented. In South West Africa they are used in a cough medicine.

The narrow, flat, papery pods, ripening in the autumn, are up to 10 cm long and under 1.3 cm wide, sometimes with wavy edges, and with thickened margins. When held against the light they are transparent. They hang in bright, red-brown bunches.

In the western Transvaal around Klerksdorp and Ventersdorp where the trees are common, they are conspicuous when the leaves have fallen because of the nests of the sparrow-weavers decorating the bare branches.

The wood is used for yoke-skeys.

The specific name is based on the place name "Hereroland" in South West Africa, where the tree is abundant.

OPPOSITE

Above
Acacia hereroensis between Ventersdorp and Wolmaransstad, where it is a common species

Centre left
Acacia hereroensis stem

Centre right
Acacia hereroensis: A fruiting branchlet (60%)

Below
A sparrow weaver's nest in *Acacia hereroensis*

(162)   14. *Acacia caffra* (Thunb.) Willd.

= *Mimosa caffra* Thunb.; = *Acacia fallax* E.Mey.; = *A. multijuga* Meisn.

Cat thorn, Kaffer-wag-'n-bietjie, water thorn, katdoring; umNyamanzi, umTholo (X); umTholo, umThole (Z); mositsane (Tsw), morutlhware (Tsw — Kwena), morutlhare (Tsw — Mal). morutlhatshana, morunlhatana (Tsw — Ngwak); mošitšane, mothôlô (NS); muvuṇḍa-mbaḍo (V)

The cat thorn, or kaffer-wag-'n-bietjie as it is commonly known in many parts, is a graceful deciduous tree widely distributed over the eastern part of South Africa from the eastern Cape to Zululand, ranging widely over the Transvaal, and entering Botswana to the west and tropical Africa to the far north.

It is an adaptable species growing from coastal scrub to moun-

Kaffer-wag-'n-bietjie trees, *Acacia caffra*, near Pienaar's River Dam close to Pretoria

Albizia tanganyicensis in the Waterberg

See text page 721

tain slopes at an altitude of roughly 1520 m, along rivers — and in the eastern Cape it is particularly common along stream banks — on hill slopes where it is often associated with dolerite, in bushveld and savannah. It is the commonest acacia in parts of the Transvaal, as around Pretoria, Rustenburg, and Krugersdorp.

Along the Natal coast and in the eastern Cape it is sometimes a shrub. Normally, however, it is tree-like, growing to a height of about 8 m and occasionally 10 m. Its graceful shape and feathery foliage make it one of the most ornamental of trees. It has a characteristic, crooked stem, rough bark — dark brown, grey, or almost black — and reddish twigs. It is deciduous and in spring the new leaves clothe the tree in bright green, airy foliage. This is composed of large compound leaves made up of from 5-38 pairs of pinnae, and up to roughly 60 pairs of small leaflets on each pinna. The typical *Acacia caffra* has smooth leaves but a form with very hairy leaves, formerly described as var. *tomentosa,* grows in the northern and eastern Transvaal, Zululand, Natal, and the eastern Cape.

The flowers — in bloom from September to November — are borne in clustered spikes, 5-8 cm long and a pale yellow in colour with a reddish tinge, turning darker with age, so that light and dark yellow flowers are seen in the same bunch. They have a heavy perfume and are much frequented by bees. In flower the tree is easily distinguished from *Acacia hereroensis* which it resembles, for *Acacia hereroensis* has flower spikes borne singly and not in bunches.

The pods are 7-10 cm long, dark brown, narrow, straight, and flat.

This is one of the least thorny acacias for its small hooked thorns are few in number, although very sharp.

The tree has many uses. Sound wood is beautiful. It is heavy and close-grained — the heartwood is dark, very hard, and termite - and - borer-proof — the sapwood whitish and not termite-proof. It makes good fence posts, and fuel which is said to be good for brick-burning. Xhosas use the rootwood to make long-stemmed tobacco pipes, that from trees growing at the edge of water reputed to be the best. The long whippy twigs are used for making baskets. When the head of a Zulu family dies, mourning bands are made of the inner bark.

The bark of the tree has medicinal uses, and is prized by African medicine men. In Botswana the boiled roots which are red (like blood) are used to treat blood disorders.

In parts the foliage is valued as fodder and farmers claim that it is often eaten by cattle in preference to lucerne. Gerstner notes that in Zululand it is the earliest acacia to sprout, often blooming in July. "Then", he says, "the soft, juicy tops are a most delicious winter-feed for stock, lacking other green fodder." Reedbuck are said to be particularly fond of it. BlackRhino and antelope browse the foliage and rhino eat stems and bark.

According to African magical beliefs, this is a lucky tree, its hooked thorns holding sorcerers at bay. For this reason, says Ferreira, the Transvaal Sothos plant pegs of the wood around their cultivated fields to protect them from harm. The Zulus make a love charm emetic from the root.

Like most acacias, this tree is easily cultivated, although many gardeners find it slow-growing. It is hardy and drought resistant. Many gardens in Pretoria have been planned around old trees carefully left standing when the ground was cleared. They are a lovely feature of the spring gardens in some of the eastern suburbs in particular.

Above left
Acacia caffra bark

Above right
Acacia caffra blooming abundantly
in September

Left
Acacia caffra: A flowering and
fruiting twig (50%)

Below left
The best Xhosa pipes are carved
from *Acacia caffra* roots and are
much sought after

Below right
A mature leaf (50%)

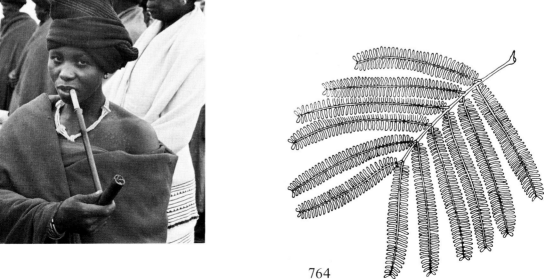

764

The specific name *caffra* means "kaffir". Different common names are given by Europeans to the tree in various parts of the country. In the eastern Cape and Natal, it is most often known as "cat thorn", but over most of the Transvaal "kaffer-wag-'n-bietjie" is used. The name "wag-'n-bietjie" is given not only to this but to other plants with "wait-a-bit" thorns which so easily hook and detain the passer-by.

Miller says that in the Transkei the name for the bushy form growing near streams is "umNyamanzi" meaning "water thorn", and for the larger, erect form "umToli" (umTholo). The Venda name for the tree means "the axe-breaker".

Acacia caffra is closely related to *Acacia herercensis*, and also to *Acacia polyacantha* Willd. subsp. *campylacantha* (Hochst. ex A.Rich.) Brenan, with which it is often confused.

(180)   15. *Acacia polyacantha* Willd.
          subsp. *campylacantha* (Hochst. ex A.Rich.) Brenan

= *Acacia campylacantha* Hochst.

White thorn, witdoring; nkowakowa (Tso); tshikwalo (V)

This "large, strikingly handsome tree", as Burtt Davy described it, is an Indian and tropical African species reaching southwards into the northern and eastern Transvaal and into Botswana. It grows in open parkland, in thornveld, and in deep soil near rivers.

It is a tall, erect, often flat-topped tree up to about 12 m high with a trunk diameter of roughly 0.6 m. The thick rough bark is light-coloured, yellow or grey, and flakes off in corky pieces. This light-coloured trunk, and the light branches, give the tree its common name for they are conspicuous, particularly when the tree is bare of leaves. The branches often bear large, cushioned, hooked spines.

The strong hooked thorns are paired or sometimes single. The leaves, from 10-18 cm long, have about 12-26 pairs of pinnae and up to 70 pairs of tiny, very narrow, hairy leaflets, pinnae and leaflets looking like slender feathers. A conspicuous feature of the leaf is a gland, a large, flat, oval knob, on the common leaf stalk just above its junction with the stem.

The cream-coloured flowers, blooming about December, are in long thin spikes. The pods are straight — up to 10 cm long and 1.3 cm wide — thin, light brown, and covered with a network of fine lines.

The heartwood is dark brown, and the wood generally is rather coarse-grained and little used.

A large, green, spiny caterpillar, the larva of the moth *Gynanisa maia*, breeds on this species, and this — and the bristly pupas of the moth *Gonometa postica*, also found on the tree — are edible and a favourite food of Africans.

The white thorn and the kaffer-wag-'n-bietjie are sometimes confused for their fine foliage is somewhat similar. The white thorn, however, has even more, and finer, leaflets than *Acacia caffra*, with much larger glands on the leaf stalk. The pods are also broader. Under the microscope the leaflets are seen to be a different shape.

The specific name *polyacantha* is based on Greek words meaning "many thorns", while *campylacantha* is the Greek for "curved thorns".

A giant apiesdoring, *Acacia galpinii*, near Thabazimbi in the western Transvaal

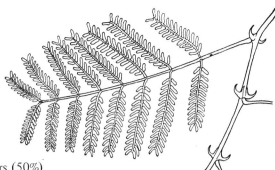

Above left
Acacia galpinii: the flowers (50%)

Above right
Acacia galpinii: a leaf (50%)

Below
The stem of an apiesdoring

(166) 16. *Acacia galpinii* Burtt Davy

Apiesdoring, monkey-thorn; mokala (Tsw); mologa, mokgapa (NS)

A giant of possibly 25 m in height with wide-spreading branches, full rounded lines, and light-green, luxuriant foliage, the apiesdoring is a magnificent sight in the Transvaal bushveld, often spreading over a stream where its thick roots may be seen covering a big area of bank. It occurs as far east as about the Steelpoort valley in Sekukuniland in the Transvaal, west into Botswana, and north into tropical Africa.

It is typically a symmetrical tree with a single straight trunk up to nearly 5 m in circumference — sometimes fluted — branching fairly high up or close to the ground. In young trees the bark is whitish-yellow, cork-like, and very flaky, the outside becoming darker with age. It is often covered with strong hooked thorns.

The compound leaves, up to 16 cm long, have about 6-10 pairs of pinnae which bear about 17-40 pairs of small smooth leaflets. There is a small gland about the middle of the leaf stalk. At the base of the leaves are the thorns, which are short, strongly hooked like a parrot's beak, and a shiny brown.

The flowers bloom from October to January in clustered spikes which in bud are a purplish brown, becoming creamy-yellow as the flowers open, and with a honey scent. A big tree in full bloom is said to be "too bright to look at". In the spring the drone of bees about a giant apiesdoring in flower can be heard from a distance away.

The large woody pods grow from 8-20 cm long and 2.5 cm broad, and are flat and light brown, sometimes with a purple tinge. They are eaten by animals but not as readily as are those of other species.

Apiesdoring wood is hard, heavy, and coarse-grained, the sapwood pale brown, the heartwood darker. It is generally useful and was once used for wagons. Good furniture is made from it, although it is difficult to work. Galpin says that Africans on the Springbok Flats make their winnowing dishes from the inner bark and that these are light, strong, and durable. (The North Sotho name for this, "mologa" means "plaiting tree", a name also given to *Acacia ataxacantha*).

Apiesdoring seed germinates readily when soaked, and grows easily. If given compost or manure and sufficient moisture, the tree thrives even in poor soil, and is fast-growing. A fine avenue of graceful,

A camelthorn and a kokerboom — two of the great desert trees of the north west Cape — shading a cemetery near Keimoes.

light-stemmed apiesdoring trees 6 m high can be grown in under 10 years. Coming as it does from the bushveld with its cold winter nights, it can resist a fair amount of frost. Some splendid trees have been grown in Pretoria.

The name *galpinii* honours Dr. E.E. Galpin, banker, botanist, and plant collector from the late 19th century until almost the mid 20th century, who collected the tree near Naboomspruit. The common name, "apiesdoring", was given the tree because monkeys take cover among the wide leafy branches. (Possibly they also eat the pods and seeds).

(168)　　17. *Acacia giraffae* Willd.

Camelthorn, kameeldoring, swartkameel; mokala (Tsw), mogôtlhô (Tsw — Kwena), mogotho (Tsw — Taw); mpatsaka (NS); mosu (Mbuk); omumbonde (Her); // gànab, // ganas (Nama)

The camelthorn is the great tree of the desert regions of Southern Africa. It grows, it is true, in parts of the central and western Transvaal and western Orange Free State, in Rhodesia and in Angola, where the rainfall is average, but it is in the arid regions of South and South West Africa and Botswana that it is most conspicuous.

In parts of the Kalahari it is the dominant tree, and visitors to the Kalahari Gemsbok National Park will remember the sight of the wild animals sheltering in the shade of the camelthorns that stud the sandy slopes of the river valleys. It is one of the few trees common in the Richtersveld, the desert area of northern Namaqualand, and in the Namib Desert in western South West Africa the dark line of trees fringing the river beds is composed largely of camelthorns.

In the Transvaal a few trees grow on the outskirts of Pretoria. They occur in numbers close to the Great North Road from about Warmbaths to Potgietersrust, and are conspicuous in flower or in pod when they are much admired by travellers along the road. The most eastern specimens are probably those in the Steelpoort valley in Sekukuniland.

The camelthorn is the royal tree of southern Botswana.

In parts of the Kalahari and north west Cape the camelthorn crosses with the vaalkameeldoring, *Acacia haematoxylon* Willd. These hybrids have the habit of the camelthorn and the beautiful silver-grey colouring of the vaalkameeldoring.

The camelthorn rarely grows to more than 9 m in height in South Africa, while in parts of Botswana it is no more than a 2 m shrub. It usually has a wide-spreading crown made up of dense, yet delicate foliage, and a sturdy, usually upright trunk with rough dark bark. In old trees this is often cracked into long, narrow, corky strips looking like a rough block floor.

The young twigs are noticeably angled between each pair of thorns. The leaves are made up of several pairs of pinnae, usually 3-4, and these bear from 10-18 pairs of leaflets from 6-13 mm long. There is a small gland at the junction of each pair of pinnae.

The sweet-smelling flowers appear from August to November in round yellow balls, and are very like the flowers of the sweet-thorn but are borne in a different manner, in tufts in the axils of the leaves and not in panicles at the ends of the branches. They are followed by the dense spring foliage.

The thorns, 1-5 cm long, are brown, straight or slightly curved,

Above
A camelthorn, *Acacia giraffae*, growing alongside the Great North Road in the Transvaal

Below left
Two old camelthorns preserved as national monuments alongside the Great North Road between Potgietersrust and Nylstroom

Below right
An ancient camelthorn on the farm "Oasis", South West Africa

Above left
Acacia giraffae: A fruiting
twig (60%)

Above right
The trunk of an old
camelthorn

strong, and often inflated at the base. They sometimes strongly resemble a pair of miniature buffalo horns. Robert Moffat, the missionary, in his *Missionary Labours*, told a story of the strength of these spines. A lion, springing upwards onto the neck of a giraffe that was browsing on a camelthorn, missed his grasp and falling on his back in the centre of the mass of thorns, was there impaled.

"I still found some of his bones under the tree and hair on its branches to convince me of what I scarcely could have credited", he wrote.

The most distinctive feature of the camelthorn is its huge, thick, curiously shaped pods, sometimes up to 10 or 13 cm long and 4 to 6.5 cm wide, often half-moon-shaped, hard when mature and covered with thick, grey, velvety felt. These pods are 1.3 to 2.5 cm thick, spongy within, and contain hard brown seeds which lie in several rows. The pods are often attacked by insects. Unlike those of many acacias, the pods do not burst open to set free the seeds.

These seeds are used as a coffee substitute by the Koranas.

The flowers, together with the foliage, were a favourite food of the giraffe which was one of the few wild animals able to browse them with ease, using its long flexible lips to pull off the fine leaves and flowers between the thorns. One of the early travellers who feasted off giraffe flesh in spring when the camelthorns were in bloom found that the meat was strongly flower-scented.

The pods are eagerly eaten by stock and are highly nutritious, their feeding value approximating to that of legume hay. In drought time cattle will rush towards any camelthorns over which a whirlwind has passed to pick up the fallen pods. On such a day cows are said to have an increased milk yield! Elephant, giraffe, rhino, gemsbok and eland are also fond of them, and baboons eat the young ones.

It has been found that prussic acid is sometimes present in the pods and in the foliage and farmers have complained that they have at times poisoned their animals. Tests made at Onderstepoort of samples of green foliage, mature and fresh green pods, revealed "dangerous quantities of prussic acid", the foliage containing the greatest amount and the mature pods the least. When eaten *slowly*, they are usually harmless. (See the chapter on poison trees in volume one).

The astringent gum is of good quality and eaten by people, and — it is said — by the giant bustard, the "gompou", which is supposed to have been given its name because of its liking for acacia gum. The tree rat, *Thallomys paedulcus*, which lives in the camelthorn trees in the Kalahari, feeds almost entirely on the gum, leaves and seeds.

In Botswana the powdered burnt bark is used for headaches, and — according to Dr. Teichler — the crushed and powdered pods are put into discharging ears.

The shade and shelter given by the tree in desert areas is great, and is made use of by all manner of creatures from men to butterflies. The association best known is that with the Sociable Weavers which often choose to build their big communal nests in the branches of the tree.

The camelthorn is not today regarded as a valuable timber tree, its heartwood alone being of use. Burchell, however, noted that the wood was excessively hard and heavy, of a dark or reddish-brown colour, and used by the Bechuanas for their smaller domestic utensils such as spoons and knife-handles. Burtt Davy says that in the early days of mining in Kimberley the heartwood was used to make bearings for machinery shafts, and that old residents stated that for this purpose, if kept well oiled, it would outlast brass fittings. In the past it was used to make wagons and mine props. Its chief use since European settlement has been for fuel, and tens of thousands of trees, particularly in the country round Kimberley, have been felled in the past 90 years. Even before the arrival of the Europeans many camelthorns had been destroyed by the Bantu, and Moffat, more than 140 years ago, wrote of "the remains of ancient forests of the camelthorn".

The roots, which have been known to penetrate 24 m into the soil, are said to smell of cinnamon, or sometimes to have an unpleasant odour. The Namas use them to make flutes when reeds are not available. The Bushmen of Botswana use the skin of the root, carefully chosen from an isolated tree with straight roots and slipped off a heated section of root, to make the quivers for their poisoned arrows.

Africans believe that this species attracts lightning. It certainly appears to be particularly susceptible to fire.

The camelthorn is a very slow-growing tree and it is possible that the oldest ones standing today are hundreds of years old. Moffat, meeting with trunks of enormous size, concluded, somewhat picturesquely, that the trees had sprung up immediately after the flood, if not before it. Whatever the history of the camelthorn in the past, farmers say that few seedlings appear to be establishing themselves today, although seeds are freely distributed by animals that eat the pods. The tree, however, coppices and suckers fairly readily.

The Department of Forestry has established a reserve, Kathu, about 65 km from Kuruman, and here a number of camelthorns are protected.

Nursery work is not always straightforward. Even when seeds are soaked in boiling water, sown and covered lightly with soil, germination is often poor. Farmers find that best germination is secured by "planting" a pat of dung from cattle which have been feeding on the pods. They say that the seeds germinate with a definite hiss! Seedlings should be planted out when some 46 cm or more in height and should be watered for the first few months, after which they are drought resistant. The young plants like plenty of light. Under all circumstances, the young trees seem to be slow-growing.

It is noteworthy that even seedlings soon develop very long tap roots.

It is rare to see a camelthorn as a street tree, but there are some beautiful specimens in Potgietersrust.

Between Potgietersrust and Nylstroom in the veld stand two old camelthorn trees which will be remembered by travellers on the Great North Road. These are now protected as national monuments — in memory of 33 Voortrekkers who were murdered there by Makapan in 1854.

One of the best known camelthorns was a solitary tree that stood for many generations on the farm "Anthorn" in the Barkly West district. It was the boundary between two tribes and under this tree erring boys were thrashed with switches made of rosyntjiebos.

Until not long ago a magnificent camelthorn grew in the garden of number 16, Belgrave Road, Kimberley. This was once on the edge of the diamond diggings and under this tree Cecil Rhodes was supposed to have sorted his first parcel of diamonds. The tree was chopped down recently to make room for a block of flats.

The most surprisingly located tree is the one that grows outside Graaff-Reinet close to the national road (far from its home country). It dates from the days of transport riding to the Kimberley diamond mines.

The origin of both common and botanical names is of special interest. It is generally believed that the name camelthorn was first recorded by Burchell. In actual fact it was Jacobus Coetsé — the first European officially to have crossed the Orange River — who gave the tree this name in 1760 some 50 years before Burchell, because he saw the giraffes eating the tops of the trees. This was recorded by Hendrik Jacob Wikar, the soldier who deserted from the Company's service in 1775 and left a fascinating journal of the time he spent along the Orange River. The early colonists often called the giraffe "kameel", short for kameelperd — the Afrikaans for giraffe — hence the name "kameeldoring". The English "camelthorn", instead of the more correct "giraffe-thorn", is a literal translation.

In Colonel Robert Gordon's map of the Orange River and north west Cape, done in 1779, there is a beautiful little drawing of a giraffe browsing the top of what is presumably a camelthorn.

Burchell was not — as was formerly thought by many botanists — the first to describe the tree. Willdenow's description — based on a specimen collected by Lichtenstein — antedates Burchell's by a number of years. The botanical name, freely translated, means "the acacia of the giraffe".

See colour plate facing page 779

(169)   18. *Acacia haematoxylon* Willd.

= *Acacia atomiphylla* Burch.

Vaalkameeldoring, basterkameel, volstruiskameel, kaboom; mokholo (Tsw)

One of the finest of all acacias, the vaalkameeldoring is confined largely to the sandy desert in the north western Cape and in southern South West Africa, so that it is a comparatively little-known species.

In these parts it is a common tree, growing singly or — as on the great plain east of the Langeberg — in stunted forest many kilometres

Above
A vaalkameeldoring, *Acacia haematoxylon,* and driedoring bushes on the great plain east of the Langeberg in the north west Cape

Left
A vaalkameel trunk

Below right
Acacia haematoxylon: A fruiting twig, showing the slender spines and minute leaflets (50%)

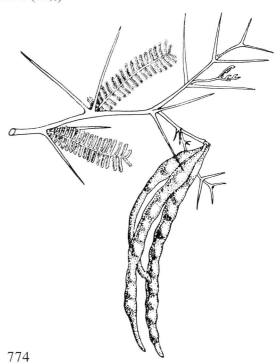

774

in area. Visitors to Upington or to the Kalahari Gemsbok National Park know its silver-grey, drooping, feathery foliage outlined against the red sand. In the Kalahari it grows in the dry river beds and sometimes in the flat valleys between the red dunes.

It is usually a shrub or a fairly small tree up to 5 m high, but it is also occasionally a larger tree rivalling the camelthorn in size. It usually has drooping branches and branchlets.

The spines are long, slender, and straight, and grow in pairs. The grey, woolly, compound leaves have 6-25 pairs of pinnae and numerous pairs of very tiny leaflets, which are the basis of the name *Acacia atomiphylla* which Burchell gave the tree. He described it as a beautiful species of acacia of a hoary complexion, "the technical name (atomiphylla) of which is taken from its curious and singular leaves, consisting of very minute leaflets, resembling seeds or atoms, squeezed laterally so close together as to seem united".

The flowers are in round yellow balls. The long, rather narrow pods are thick and woody, spongy within, and covered with a thick grey fur without. Parts of them, possibly the spongy inside, are eaten by Hottentots.

The heartwood is hard and a fine red, a fact noted by Jacobus Coetsé, the first white man officially known to have crossed the Orange River, who described vaalkameel trees in southern South West Africa as large with "heart or innermost wood of an unusually beautiful bright red colour." A later traveller, Henry Lichtenstein, who called the tree the red ebony, wrote, some 160 years ago, that the wood was remarkably good for making wind instruments, and that a German musical-instrument maker had made from it a flute with a particularly fine, full tone.

Burchell several times mentions the beauty of this tree. Gardeners who see it invariably long to plant it, with its "soft masses of pale foliage" and its "hoary appearance and soft tufted shape", but its cultivation away from deep sand and desert climate appears difficult.

The specific name *haematoxylon* is based on Greek words meaning "blood-red wood". The name "vaalkameel" or "grey camelthorn" is self-explanatory. C.A. Smith gives a South West African common name as "haaikoos", stating that the name survives in the place name Haaikoos Hill.

(170)   19a. *Acacia hebeclada* DC.

subsp. *hebeclada*

= *Acacia stolonifera* Burch.

Trassiedoring, trassiebos, terassiedoring; sekhi, setsi (Tsw), setshe (Tsw − Ngwak); mokgwaripa (NS); otjimbuku (Her);!gos (Nama)

(170.1)   19b. subsp. *chobiensis* (O.B.Miller) Schreib.

= *Acacia stolonifera* var. *chobiensis* O.B.Miller

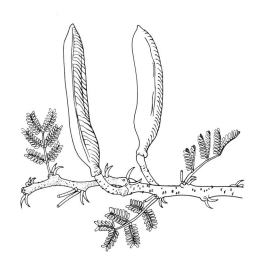

776

(170.2)   19c. subsp. *tristis* (Welw. ex Oliv.) Schreib.

= *Acacia tristis* Welw.

Burchell in 1812 recorded that a grove of these trees — the typical form of *Acacia hebeclada* — and other acacias stood on the original site of Litakun, famous in South African missionary history and exploration. Today this species still grows around Kuruman, near the old Litakun, and observers note instantly, as Burchell did, that here it makes a thicket because of the stems running just beneath the surface of the soil from which arise "a multitude of shoots and branches". Burchell named it aptly *Acacia stolonifera. Acacia hebeclada*, meaning "hairy branches", is, however, the older name, and this is what it bears today.

The trassiebos grows in a number of forms, and several subspecies are recognized. The typical form, *Acacia hebeclada* DC. subsp. *hebeclada*, is the form found in South Africa and which is common in Botswana. This subspecies may grow as a suckering bush or as a medium-sized tree and although some botanists see two varieties or subspecies in these, an erect tree may sometimes grow out of a thicket, and the tendency is to regard these forms as inseparable.

The subspecies *hebeclada* occurs from the central, northern, and western Transvaal, the dry north western Cape and the Kalahari to South West Africa, where it is widespread, sometimes as a shrub no more than 1 m high, or as a tree 6 m tall with a single stem.

It is most conspicuous in its thicket form and travellers in the western Transvaal, along the Kuruman river, and in the Gemsbok National Park in the Kalahari always note the low, dense, dark clumps, stretching 15 m or more in the sandy soil, embroidered with stiff, upright pods which appear like a crop of large pale thumbs sticking into the air.

The upright growth of these pods is the characteristic by which most people identify the tree for, whatever the size, they are — in this subspecies — always upright and persist on the tree for several seasons. They are usually straight, and oblong in shape — sometimes slightly curved — hard, strong, woody, grey, and slightly furry, and often distinctly grooved, and they are carried on stout stalks. There are about 10 seeds within which rattle when ripe.

The stout branchlets are velvety when young. The leaves are typically bipinnate and feathery, with 5-8 pairs of pinnae and about 15 pairs of leaflets. The thorns, often in opposite pairs, look like a pair of miniature, wide-spreading ox horns with the tips slightly down-curved, or occasionally straight. They are sometimes brown, or white and red-tipped, and always stout and sharp. The flowers, which bloom about September, are in round heads, white or golden, and are scented.

The gum is edible.

Leaves and pods are eaten by stock, although the leaves are occasionally poisonous. In a thicket, the pods on the outside are invariably stripped off by animals, only those in the impenetrable centre remaining.

Root wood, ground to a powder and mixed with fat, is used by Africans in South West Africa to dress their hair.

The wood is strong and used for hoe and axe handles.

It is not surprising that the trassiebos can live in desert. In the files of the Botanical Research Institute is a remarkable letter from a Botswana trader describing the fitness of this species to survive. He dug a well and found trassiebos roots thick and very moist at 35 m below the surface of the soil. They had advanced tenaciously downwards "in a

OPPOSITE

Above
A trassiedoring, *Acacia hebeclada* subsp. *hebeclada*, near Warmbaths, Transvaal

Centre left
A trassiedoring near Usakos, South West Africa

Centre right
Acacia hebeclada subsp. *hebeclada:* A portion of a branchlet showing the upright pods (40%)

Below
The trassiedoring growing in thicket form in the bed of the Kuruman River

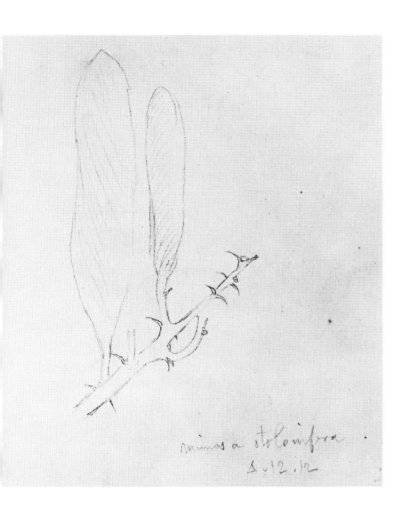

mimosa stolonifera
△.12.12

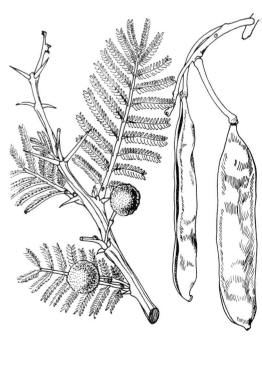

778

A vaalkameeldoring, *Acacia haematoxylon*, growing in Kalahari sand in the north west Cape

See text page 773

OPPOSITE

Above left
Burchell's drawing in his
field sketch book of the
trassiedoring pods

Above right
A trassiedoring stem

Below left
A paperbark thorn,
Acacia sieberana var.
woodii, in the Transvaal
bushveld near Groblers-
dal

Below right
Acacia sieberana var.
woodii: A flowering
twig and pods (90%)

Below
Paperbark thorn bark

sort of tube of soil which goes down the side of the well like a pipe".
He added that these roots were from young trees!

The trassiebos is unusual for yet another reason — it is thought to be
one of the host plants to the desert truffles which grow under the
ground in association with certain species of plants and which are
relished by the desert dwellers.

Two further subspecies occur in South West Africa. *Acacia hebeclada*
DC. subsp. *chobiensis* (O.B.Miller) Schreib., taking its name from the
Chobe River, comes from the Okavango and Caprivi Strip and from
Botswana. It is a dome-shaped tree with the lowest branches touching
the ground (and with larger pods than the typical trassiebos) holding
about 30 seeds.

Acacia hebeclada DC. subsp. *tristis* (Welw. ex Oliv.) Schreib. grows
in Angola and northern South West Africa. In this form the mature
pods, smaller than those of subsp. *chobiensis* hang downwards and give
the tree the imaginative name of *tristis* or "sad".

The common name trassiebos is — according to C.A. Smith — a corruption of "terassiebos", derived from the Hottentot "taras", meaning
"hermaphrodite", and applied to the plant in a figurative sense because
its thorns are sometimes straight and sometimes hooked. Galpin says
on the Springbok Flats the tree is called the pendoring — the name
usually given to *Maytenus heterophylla* (Eckl. & Zeyh.) N.Robson — or
sometimes blouhaak. C.A. Smith includes several other names, such as
muisdoring (because field mice shelter in its dense growth), Siki-
doring — which is obviously based on the Tswana name — and Ghobos.

(187)   20. *Acacia sieberana* DC.
         1. var. *woodii* (Burtt Davy) Keay & Brenan

= *Acacia woodii* Burtt Davy

Paperbark-thorn, Natal camelthorn, papierbasdoring, platkroonsoet-
doring; umKhamba, umKhambathi, umKhaya (Z); umNganduzi (Sw);
more-o-mosetlha (Tsw); mošibitlha mokgaba (NS); musaunga, muunga-
luselo (V)

(187.1)   2. var. *vermoesenii* (De Wild.) Keay & Brenan

= *Acacia amboensis* Schinz

The paperbark-thorn of South Africa, *Acacia sieberana* var. *woodii,* is
one of the most striking of all indigenous acacias, usually with a flat-
topped crown so characteristically shaped that this and the light corky
bark often serve to identify the tree at a glance.

It grows in Natal from the coast to the Drakensberg — it is particularly
conspicuous in the grasslands of the central districts where magnificent
stands occur around Estcourt, Ladysmith and Colenso — from Zululand
and Swaziland to the eastern and northern Transvaal, northwards to
Rhodesia and westwards to Botswana and northern South West Africa.
Some botanists see the South West African form as a distinct variety
vermoesenii. It is a tree of rather dry bushveld and grassveld, according
to Ross favouring deep soils, or shallow soils over-lying shale. The South
West African form often grows along river banks, and is fairly common
along the Okavango River.

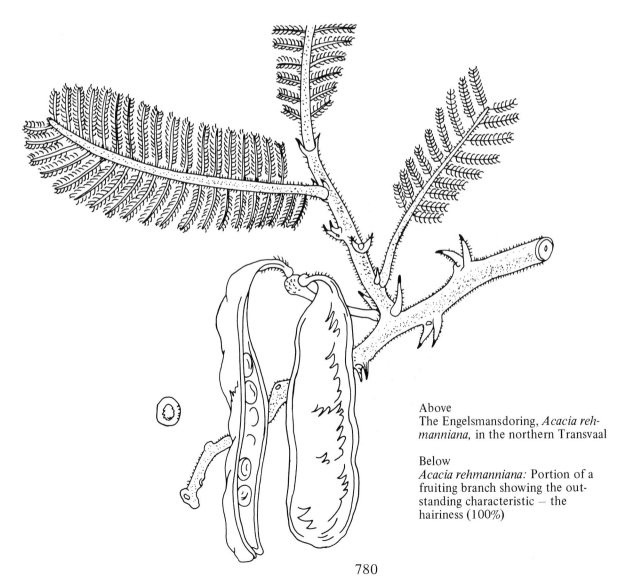

Above
The Engelsmansdoring, *Acacia rehmanniana*, in the northern Transvaal

Below
Acacia rehmanniana: Portion of a fruiting branch showing the outstanding characteristic — the hairiness (100%)

780

It grows up to 12 m high, sometimes with a rounded but usually with a flat, spreading crown of feathery green, deciduous foliage. It may be single-stemmed or with several stems from the base, and these are conspicuous because of the corky bark, usually grey or yellow but sometimes darker, that flakes off in strips. This bark is very inflammable.

The paired thorns are short and straight, about 2.5-5 cm long. The leaves are up to about 8-10 cm in length, occasionally longer, with the common midrib — the rachis — ending in a small, short, sturdy spine, a feature that is noticeable on the under surface of the leaf. The pinnae or side-branches are in 11-20 pairs, and these each bear about 17-40 pairs of small, narrow, oblong leaflets about 3 mm long. Near the base of each leaf, on the upper surface, is a gland like a small knob. The branchlets and sometimes the leaves — especially when young — are covered with thick yellowish hairs, the degree of hairiness varying a good deal. In this hairiness it resembles *Acacia rehmanniana*, which, however, usually has more numerous pinnae and more, and smaller, leaflets, smaller and less woody, much veined pods, which — unlike those of the paperbark-thorn — usually burst open on the tree, and a brown cracked trunk.

The flowers, blooming from September to March, are in small white or pale yellow balls, borne singly or clustered in the axils of the leaves on slender stalks.

Below
Bark of *Acacia rehmanniana*

The stout, hard, woody pods, ripening late summer to early winter, are 10-25 cm long, about 2.5 cm wide, and sometimes nearly 1.3 cm thick, velvety when young, and with a heavy sweet scent. They do not open on the tree but usually where they fall upon the ground. The fallen pods are eaten by cattle and antelope, and are believed to give an unpleasant taste to the milk of cows that have eaten them.

It is noteworthy that the foliage, especially when wilted, contains a large amount of prussic acid and can be dangerous to stock. Many cases of poisoning are known.

The gum produced is edible.

Galpin says that the wood is soft and easily destroyed by termites and boring beetles unless seasoned under water, but that when seasoned for 6 months thus, it makes good wagon wood.

The species was named after Franz Wilhelm Sieber, Bohemian botanist, plant collector, and traveller, in the early 18th century. The specific name has up to date been spelt *sieberiana* but *sieberana* is the correct spelling. The variety *woodii* was named after Dr John Medley Wood, noted Natal botanist, and the variety *vermoesenii* after the plant collector, F. Vermoesen, who collected this form at Boma in the Congo in 1919.

Once the South African paperbark-thorn was known as *Acacia lasiopetala* Oliv. but this was an incorrect identification.

The Venda name for the tree is "muunga-luselo" because the crown resembles a luselo — a shallow winnowing basket — turned upside down. The Zulus call it "umKhambathi", and Table Mountain near Pietermaritzburg "emKhambathini", "at the umKhambathi". Doke and Vilakazi in their Zulu dictionary suggest that the Zulu and English common names for the mountain are based on the resemblance of the flat-topped mountain to the flat crown of the tree, but the names may suggest merely the abundance of the species near the mountain.

The haak-en-steek, *Acacia tortilis* subsp. *heteracantha*, has many forms. This flat-topped tree, backed by *Euphorbia ingens*, grew in Zululand.

(182)   21. *Acacia rehmanniana* Schinz

Engelsmansdoring, Engelsedoring; musivhiṭha(V); mgaba (Kal)

A bright yellow-green colour characterizes this deciduous species, which is common in the central and northern Transvaal. It is the dominant acacia in the open bushveld in parts of the northern Transvaal near Pietersburg and Louis Trichardt.

It is a shrub, or a somewhat flat-topped tree up to 9 m high, with reddish twigs, occasionally slightly peeling; red-brown, smooth branch bark, and a trunk which when old does not peel as does that of the paperbark-thorn which it resembles.

The spines are paired and straight, the young ones yellow, the older brown, and while these are conspicuous on young twigs, the old wood is often spineless.

The yellow-green foliage is distinctive with long, neat, slender leaves composed of about 25-40 pairs of slender pinnae, and some 40-50 pairs of very small leaflets, with the common midrib ending, as in the paperbark-thorn, in a sharp point. There is a gland on the petiole.

The outstanding characteristic of this species is its hairiness, like bright, mustard-yellow velvet, on the young twigs and the under-surface of the young leaves and common midrib.

The flowers in round greenish-white, fragrant balls, appearing in summer, are borne in clusters at the nodes. The pods are flat, leathery, and much-veined, up to 10 cm long (although often shorter) and nearly 2.5 cm wide, unlike the woody pods of the paperbark-thorn which are up to 25 cm long.

This species was named after Anton Rehmann of Cracow, a botanist and collector who visited South Africa between 1875 and 1880.

(188)   22. *Acacia tortilis* (Forsk.) Hayne
          subsp. *heteracantha* (Burch.) Brenan

= *Acacia heteracantha* Burch.; = *A. litakunensis* Burch.; = *A. spirocarpoides* Engl.; = *A. maras* Engl.

Umbrella thorn, haak-en-steek, haakdoring, withaak, basterkameeldoring, tafelboom; umSasane, isiThwethwe (Z); isiThwethwe (Sw); nsasane (Tso); moku, musu (Tsw), mosunyane (Tsw – Kgat), mosu (Tsw – Kwena and Taw), moshu (Tsw-Mang); mošwana, mošu (NS); muswu (V); orusu, orupungiuja (Her); / naras, / narab (Nama)

The umbrella thorn, or the haak-en-steek as it is probably most commonly known, is one of the most widespread of the acacias for it is found in the northern parts of Natal, the Orange Free State, the Cape and Transvaal, in Swaziland, in Botswana and South West Africa, and northwards into tropical Africa.

It is noteworthy that Brenan, who has revised many of the acacias, recognizes six forms of this in Africa. The South African form, subsp. *heteracantha*, is a common bushveld tree, usually growing in deep loam. Bushveld farmers consider it a good "index" tree, growing in association with sweet grasses likely to provide good winter grazing.

In the northern Cape and South West Africa it is a characteristic tree of red Kalahari sand. What is probably the first mention of a haak-en-steek was made of trees along the Orange River in the northern Cape, for Wikar in the 1770's described how the Hottentots used them here to make trapping pits.

OPPOSITE

Above
A graceful, spreading
haak-en-steek, *Acacia
tortilis* subsp. *heteracantha* near Kimberley

Centre left
An upward-growing
form in the dry bush-
veld near Kimberley

Centre right
A flowering twig and
pods (50%)

Below
A haak-en-steek familiar
to tourists, growing out-
side Fort Namutoni in
the Etosha Game Reserve,
South West Africa

Below
Haak-en-steek bark

Although it is a typical tree of the dry west, some of the loveliest specimens grow in the dry thornveld of the east, as at Mkuze in Zulu-land.

It is a common tree around Pretoria and until recently a specimen with historical associations stood at the corner of Beatrix Street and the Soutpansberg Road. It is believed that a toll gate once stood in the shade of this tree, and here people arriving by wagon or cart had to pay toll for the upkeep of the roads.

The haak-en-steek rarely grows into a large tree, although in some areas in South Africa it reaches a height of 12 m and in South West Africa 15 m. It is common, sometimes as a small tree 3-4.5 m in height with a clean trunk and a flat crown that gives good shade, sometimes with rounded lines and branches almost at ground level.

The foliage is very fine, even for an acacia, and is composed of 4-10 pairs of pinnae, each of which have about 15 pairs of minute leaf-lets. The whole leaf is rarely more than 2.5 cm long.

The foliage is browsed by cattle, antelope, and giraffe.

The thorns are a distinguishing feature of the tree. There are two kinds — long, straight, and white, and small, brownish and hooked — some times borne in more or less equal numbers, sometimes with one kind in the majority. These differently shaped thorns serve to identify the tree but must be looked for carefully, not only on one branch but on the tree as a whole. They give the tree its most graphic popular name, "haak-en-steek" meaning "hook-and-prick".

Several other South African and South West African species have both hooked and straight thorns, but these have very different pods, which are straight and not twisted as in the haak-en-steek.

The flowers appear in masses all over the tree in spring or after rain in small, round, sweet-scented balls which vary from almost white to sulphur yellow in colour. They develop into flat pods which are usually hairless — some of the tropical forms have densely hairy pods — and are curled or twisted into spirals, and these, like the thorns, are distinctive.

They are rich in protein — according to Professor J.C. Bonsma, an analysis of the pods revealed a protein content of 18.83 per cent and cattle usually eat them in preference to any other pods. Like those of many acacias, they are not only browsed on the tree, but eaten from the ground where they fall. Not only do wild animals such as antelope relish them, but giraffe, monkeys and baboons.

Africans use them to string into necklaces.

The sapwood is whitish and soft, the heartwood red. Galpin says it warps on drying and is often riddled by borers, but if cut when the sap is down and then water-seasoned, makes good disselbooms and yokes. It is used for firewood, and the gum is edible.

It is easily raised from seed and is extremely hardy and drought resistant but rather slow-growing.

Since it has been known to botany the haak-en-steek has borne several scientific names, *Acacia heteracantha* Burch., *Acacia litaku-nensis* Burch., *Acacia spirocarpoides* Engl., and *Acacia maras* Engl. Recently it was found to be a form of *Acacia tortilis* (Forsk.) Hayne from Egypt and Arabia, described almost 200 years ago. The name *tortilis* means "twisted" and refers to the pods, and the subspecific name *heteracantha* means "different thorns".

786

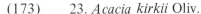

OPPOSITE

Above
Acacia kirkii: Leaves,
pods and flowers (100%)

Below
Acacia kirkii in the
Caprivi Strip

Below
Acacia kirkii stem

(173)   23. *Acacia kirkii* Oliv.

Moralo: moralo (Tsw − Taw); ijwairi (Sub)

The moralo is a species of northern South West Africa − of the eastern and central Kaokoveld and Caprivi − of Botswana (where it often occurs in country subject to flooding), and of Zambia. It grows as a many-stemmed shrub or as a tree up to 9 m high, frequently branching low down, with slender upward-growing branches, sometimes spreading to make a flattish crown, and with whippy twigs.

The brown, grey, or yellow bark is papery, flaking off in irregular patches.

The thorns are straight, up to 8 cm long, paired, and white. The leaves grow in their axils. These are up to 8 cm long, with the midrib ending in a sharp point, softly hairy, and composed of about 8-12 pairs of pinnae, each bearing about 10-15 pairs of fine leaflets.

The flowers − which appear about November − are in round, white, or pinkish heads on long stalks, and these are borne singly or in clusters at the nodes.

The shortish, broad pods, in clusters − ripening in the autumn − are constricted between the 4-6 seeds, with a characteristic knobbly boss over each seed. They have a small jutting point and often narrow at the base into a long "neck".

Brenan has divided this species into varieties, but these are of doubtful value.

The species was named after Sir John Kirk, explorer, naturalist, and companion of Dr David Livingstone.

(179)   24a. *Acacia nilotica* (L.) Willd. ex Del.
    1. subsp. *kraussiana* (Benth.) Brenan

= *Acacia arabica* (Lam.) Willd. var *kraussiana* Benth.; = *Acacia benthami* Rochebr.

Ruikpeul, lekkerruikpeul, stinkpeul, redheart, gum acacia, kudu-pod; umNqawe, uBobe, uBombo, umQawe (Z); isiThwethwe, umNcawe (Sw); nxangwa (Tso); motabakgosi (Tsw), motsha (Tsw − Kgat), motshi (Tsw − Mang), moshu (Tsw − Ngwak), motlhabakgosi (Tsw − Taw); moku, mŏgòhlô motšhê, motshê, (NS); sinzi (Kol)

    b. subsp. *subalata* (Vatke) Brenan

Acacia nilotica is one of the most widely distributed of the acacias for it extends in one form or another throughout Africa and south east Asia. Brenan recognizes seven subspecies, one of which, subsp. *kraussiana*, occurs in South Africa.

The South African form, commonly known as the ruikpeul or lekkerruikpeul, or sometimes as the red-heart, grows in Natal, in the eastern, northern, and central Transvaal, westwards into Botswana, in dry thornveld and bushveld, usually in company with sweet grasses.

It is one of the trees encroaching in bush form on the Springbok Flats, where − with its vigour and wide-ranging roots − it has become a serious problem, ousting other plants.

This is usually a small tree with a round or flat crown, up to 9 m high but usually smaller, with thick, rough, deeply fissured brown or

Above
The ruikpeul, *Acacia nilotica* subsp. *kraussiana,*
in the Transvaal bushveld

Left
Acacia nilotica subsp. *kraussiana:* the pods,
leaves and flowrs (50%)

Below
Acacia permixta: A flowering and fruiting twig
(100%)

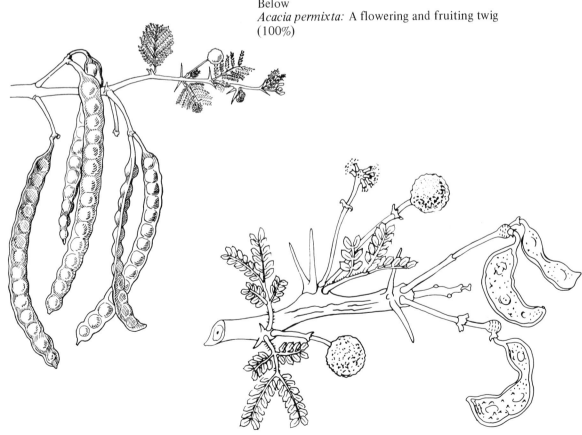

black bark and brownish branchlets usually covered with short grey hairs.

The paired spines are from 1.3 to 8 cm long, brownish-white, often with white tips, almost straight but tending to curve backwards very slightly when young, unlike those of *Acacia karroo* which are completely straight. When young they are often hairy, as are the twigs.

The leaves are small, up to about 5 cm long, and hairy, made up of about 4-8 pairs of pinnae and about 15 pairs of small, narrow leaflets. They are eaten by Black Rhino, nyala, kudu and impala, and the young shoots by baboons. The flowers are in small, round, yellow balls, very like those of the sweet-thorn but not so sweetly scented. They bloom about October.

When in pod the ruikpeul is easily identified for the long pendulous pods, borne singly or in pairs at the end of sturdy stalks, look like dangling necklaces. They are 8-15 cm long and up to 1.9 cm wide, constricted between the seeds, the shape of each round seed being plainly seen. The young green pods are covered with fine red hairs, and on maturity — March to April — turn almost black. They usually contain from 10-15 seeds. As the pods mature they develop a strong, sweet, fruity scent, and are eaten by stock, baboons, rhino, and antelopes, nyala in particular being fond of them. They do not burst open but disintegrate on the ground.

The Voortrekkers used these to make ink.

The wood is hard, durable, reddish, and termite-proof, and is used for fuel, mining props, and fence posts. (Large parts of the Springbok Flats are fenced with ruikpeul). The tree has other minor uses. The pods are used for tanning and the gum is edible, of good quality, and suitable for confectionery.

The tree is used medicinally by the Zulus, a decoction of the bark being taken for coughs. In the Sudan it is used to treat leprosy.

The typical *Acacia nilotica* is native to the Nile countries, hence the specific name. The South African subspecies is named after Dr Ferdinand Krauss, Director of the Stuttgart Museum, who visited South Africa between 1838 and 1840, and who collected plants in Natal.

According to Brenan, the subspecies found in northern South West Africa is subsp. *subalata* (Vatke) Brenan, a form widely distributed in eastern Africa. This sometimes has fewer pinnae — 3 to 6 pairs — and about 10 to 24 pairs of leaflets.

The name *subalata* means "slightly winged".

The common name "red-heart" refers to the reddish colour of the wood, and the names "ruikpeul" and "lekkerruikpeul" to the sweet fruity smell of the pods.

(160.1)　25. *Acacia borleae* Burtt Davy

= *Acacia barbertonensis* Schweick.

Sticky acacia, gomdoring; uSaku, uBhidi (Z); luBibi (Sw)

The sticky acacia, *Acacia borleae*, belongs to a small group of five acacias which have sticky, glandular pods, the glands often appearing as small, reddish, conspicuous dots. The others in the group are *Acacia exuvialis* Verdoorn, *Acacia nebrownii* Burtt Davy, *Acacia tenuispina* Verdoorn, and *Acacia swazica* Burtt Davy.

These are shrubs or small trees, with the exception of *Acacia tenui-*

Above
Ruikpeul bark

Below
A ruikpeul pod

Above
Acacia borleae in the
dry Zululand bushveld

Left
A flowering and fruiting
twig

Below
A flowering branch

spina, the fyndoring, which appears to occur usually as a low-growing shrub.

Acacia borleae, named after Madame J. Borle, a botanical collector who found the species in Portuguese East Africa in the 1920's, grows in the dry bushveld of northern Zululand, Portuguese East Africa, Swaziland, and the eastern and northern Transvaal, sometimes as a shrub branching from the base and often forming thickets, sometimes as a small, slender tree with upward-growing branches. It favours heavy and often somewhat poorly drained soil.

The spines are straight, very slender, paired, and white. The leaves have up to 6 and occasionally 8 pairs of short pinnae, and these bear about 8-12 pairs of small leaflets, which have glands on the lower surface and margin, giving them an irregular outline. The glands help to distinguish this species from *Acacia karroo* which shares many features with it.

The flowers are in round, yellow heads on long slender stalks, and are borne in the axils of the leaves at the ends of the branchlets.

The slender, sickle-shaped, beaded pods are reddish-brown, and although the glands are not conspicuous, the pods are sticky and shiny. There are about 4-6 oval seeds.

The stickiness of this species — in a fresh twig the whole surface is covered with a sticky liquid — is its outstanding characteristic.

(164.1)   26. *Acacia exuvialis* Verdoorn

Scaly acacia; risavana (Tso)

The scaly acacia, a species of the eastern and northern Transvaal, is often more of a distinct tree than *Acacia borleae*, for — although it can grow as a shrub in many-stemmed groups — it is more typically a slender tree up to 4.5 m tall. It becomes, according to Dr Inez Verdoorn, more and more branched towards the top, broomlike, frequently seeming "too heavy for the slender stem, the whole tree eventually falling over".

The trunk and branches are shiny and sticky with a thin peeling skin, which gives the tree its specific name meaning "to shed scales".

The thorns are straight, white, and paired. The leaves have 1-6 pairs of pinnae with about 3-6 pairs of leaflets, which are larger than those of *Acacia borleae* and which have a small, thorn-like point.

The flowers are in yellow balls on long slender stalks. The pods are strongly curved and somewhat beaded, without obvious glands, and up to 6.5 cm long — much longer than those of *Acacia borleae* which they resemble.

27. *Acacia permixta* Burtt Davy

Slapdoring; luBibi (Sw)

The slapdoring is a bush or small tree with a rough trunk and a few weak, upward-growing branches, often found in the central and northern Transvaal on gritty, sandy hillsides and flats where the soil is derived from granite.

Like others in this group, the adult thorns are long, straight, white, and paired. They are reddish and hairy when young.

Above
Acacia nebrownii pods

Left
Acacia nebrownii in South West
Africa

Below
Acacia swazica: A flowering twig
and the glandular pods (90%)

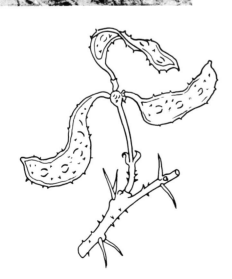

The leaves are short, seldom more than 4 cm long, composed of 2-4 pairs of short pinnae and up to 8 pairs of small leaflets with a distinct, thorn-like point. They grow in the axils of the thorns.

The outstanding character of the species is the thick hairiness of the stout chestnut-brown branchlets and twigs.

Leaf stalks and the common midribs are also slightly hairy, and the leaflets are sometimes fringed with hairs. Twigs of the slapdoring could easily be mistaken for those of *Acacia tenuispina* if it were not for this hairiness. (The habit of growth of the two species is, however, quite different).

The flowers are in round yellow balls on slender stalks. The short flat pods, up to about 4 cm long and just over 1.3 cm wide, are straight or slightly curved and covered with brown glandular dots.

Burtt Davy named this species *permixta*, meaning "confused", because, he said, it was easily confused with *Acacia glandulifera* Schinz, now known as *Acacia nebrownii* Burtt Davy.

28. *Acacia nebrownii* Burtt Davy

= *Acacia rogersii* Burtt Davy; = *Acacia glandulifera* Schinz

Waterdoring, gomdoring, kalkdoring, taaidoring; luBibi (Sw); lerwana (Tsw — Kgat)

Acacia nebrownii, often confused with *Acacia permixta*, has a much wider distribution, from Swaziland in the east, through the eastern, central, and northern Transvaal, to Botswana, and to South West Africa where it is widespread. (It is the dominant species around Gobabis). It favours low-lying, sandy, or limestone flats, the silt of river banks, and dry river beds in bushveld.

In South West Africa it is commonly called the waterdoring, and C.A. Smith says it is there considered as an indicator of underground water.

Although it often forms low dense thickets, it sometimes grows as a small slender tree up to 4.5 m high with dark, smoothish bark, purplish-brown twigs, straight paired thorns, and small dark green leaves which usually have only 1 pair of pinnae, each one with 3-4 pairs of oval or sometimes almost round leaflets.

The flowers, blooming irregularly, are in round, golden, sweet-smelling heads and are borne on short stalks, in contrast to the long stalks of the other species in the group.

In Botswana it is said that when the waterdoring blooms rain will fall within a month.

The short curved pods are covered with red-brown glandular dots.

This species was named after Dr N.E. Brown, noted Kew botanist, who worked extensively on African flora.

(187.2)   29. *Acacia swazica* Burtt Davy

Swazi acacia; uKhalimele, uKhamele (Z); kaimela, kalimela (Sw)

The Swazi acacia is the last of the group with glandular pods. As the name suggests this little tree — sturdy in comparison with the others in the group — occurs in Swaziland, in northern Zululand on the foothills

Above
Acacia swazica on a dry
hillside near the Abel
Erasmus Pass in the
eastern Transvaal

Left
Acacia swazica bark

Below
Acacia swazica flowers

of the Lebombo mountains, and in the eastern Transvaal on dry, rocky, bushy slopes.

It may be single or several-stemmed, and reaches about 4.5 m in height. The straight, slender, white thorns are in pairs, often with brownish tips, and the leaves are up to about 5 cm long, arranged in tufts arising from swellings in the axils of the thorns. The pinnae or side-branches number only 1 or 2 pairs, each bearing about 4-6 pairs of leaflets. In Swaziland these leaflets may be nearly 1.3 cm long, and conspicuously veined, but in the Transvaal they are smaller. They have a small point at the end. The leaf stalk and common midrib often have glandular dots.

The flowers are in round, orange-yellow heads on long stalks. They grow singly or in pairs in the axils of the leaves. The pods are up to 4 cm long, flat, curved, yellow to red-brown, and covered with sticky, raised, brown dots.

This is sometimes confused with *Acacia karroo*, but the glandular leaf stalk and glandular pods are distinctive.

(172)   30. *Acacia karroo* Hayne

= *Acacia hirtella* E.Mey.; = *A. natalitia* E.Mey.; = *A. inconflagrabilis* Gerst. [Erroneously known in the past as *Acacia horrida* (L.) Willd.]

Sweet-thorn, mimosa, Cape thorn tree, karoo-thorn, white-thorn, doringboom, soetdoring, karoodoring, witdoring; umNga (X); umNga, isiKhombe (Z); umDongolo, isiNga (Sw); leoka (SS); mooka, mookana (Tsw); mooka, mopkana (NS); muumga, muunga-ludzi (V); gaba (Kal); orusu (Her); // khub, // khus (Nama)

The sweet-thorn or mimosa may be termed the "great" tree of South Africa, not because of its stature — it is seldom more than 12 m high — but because it is the commonest tree of the country, the most widely distributed, and the most generally useful.

Ecologically it is of great importance. It attracts countless insects, and therefore birds, which in their turn attract lizards, snakes, and mammals, so that in an indirect way it provides food for many creatures. It has always offered to the people of South and South West Africa shelter, shade, protection, and fuel. Men, birds, baboons and monkeys, and probably many other wild animals, have eaten its gum, and stock and antelope its flowers, pods, and foliage. Its wood made the furniture of early colonists, their fence posts, sometimes their wagon wheels, and doubtless their coffins; its branches were their kraals; its bark was used to tan their leather and to make string and rope. Its medicinal uses have been many and varied. It is an indicator of surface and underground water, and as a guide to water in an arid land it has had no equal. It is, and has been, the background to the lives of countless South Africans, white, brown, and yellow, from immemorial times.

It occurs, and widely, in every province of South Africa, although — in spite of reaching further south than any other acacia — it does not enter the Cape Peninsula. It is common in South West Africa, in Botswana, and grows northwards to Rhodesia and Zambia. It is very adaptable, growing under many differing conditions of soil, climate, and altitude, its limiting factors appearing to be intense cold and lack of moisture, for it is seldom found on the higher slopes of mountains, while in the arid areas it is associated with sub-soil moisture or stream banks.

The sweet-thorn, *Acacia karroo*, growing in the Karoo near Middelburg

Farmers in bushveld consider it an indicator of sweet veld.

History has probably been made many times beneath its branches. An historic tree once stood in High Street, Grahamstown. On a June day in 1812 Colonel Graham and Captain Stockenstrom are said to have rested here, hanging their swords in the branches, and here planned and decided upon the present site of the city of Grahamstown. The tree was a favourite meeting place in the early days of Grahamstown, until blown down in a gale in 1844.

At its most striking the sweet-thorn is a large spreading tree growing up to 12 m high, and even higher in Rhodesia, with a branch span greater than its height, full rounded lines, and a trunk some 0.6 m in diameter. Usually it grows from 3-7.6 m high, occasionally with a flattish crown, only on river banks or in other favourable situations becoming a very large tree.

The typical sweet-thorn in most parts of the country has a rough dark bark, longitudinally fissured, but occasionally a tree with orange-yellow or creamy coloured bark is found, as in parts of Natal and Zululand. In the woodland fringing the coastal forest of Mapelane in Zululand and in other such situations, trees up to at least 12 m grow together. They are very different from the trees of inland areas — slim, with delicate airy crowns and bark that is pale and smooth; and seeing them, it is difficult to believe that they are *Acacia karroo* at all.

In the Hluhluwe and Umfolozi Game Reserves a form occurs which Ross refers to as the "spindle" *Acacia karroo*, and these trees are slender with few branches, with — he says — bright reddish-brown bark flaking minutely.

The most outstanding character of the typical *Acacia karroo* is its paired, straight, shining white thorns, from 1.3 cm to the enormous length of 15 cm. A tree covered in these straight white spikes is an arresting sight.

Marloth draws attention to the protective function of the thorns which are more numerous on the lower branches that are within reach of roaming animals. "It is", he says, "a remarkable adaptation of the plant to its environment that it produces numerous and full-sized spines only on the lower branches of trees while the higher parts of larger trees are always so little armed that it is often difficult to find flowering twigs with spines on them".

It is noteworthy that the trees of the dry areas tend to have longer and more conspicuous thorns than those from parts with a high rainfall.

The branches are dark, the twigs often reddish and smooth. The feathery leaves, rich green and borne in tufts on small knobs in the axils of the thorns, are up to 12 cm long and about 5 cm broad, and have 2-7 pairs of pinnae and about 8-20 pairs of small oblong leaflets. These may be smooth or slightly hairy. The foliage, although dense, is usually so fine that it throws a light, dappled shadow.

The tree is sometimes evergreen but in drought time or in very dry or cold localities it often loses its leaves and the autumn colours are then often fine. Sim says the tree may be continuously leafless for years in succession and is then enormously spiny and colours the veld white instead of green.

The sweet-thorn is usually the last of the common acacias to bloom and it flowers off and on during most of the summer — whenever it smells rain, say the farmers. The flowers are in small, yellow, fluffy balls, on slender stalks, borne in long, loose or tightly packed terminal sprays (racemes or panicles), and in the axils of the upper leaves. They

Above
The luxuriant rounded crown of *Acacia karroo* is a feature of many a Karoo landscape

Left
A typical Karoo dam, ringed with sweet-thorns

Below left
Acacia karroo: A flowering twig and pods (50%)

Below right
Acacia karroo in the coastal woodland of Zululand

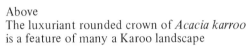

798

fill the air for far around with their delicious fragrance, and, like all acacia flowers, they attract masses of bees and other insects. Sweet-thorn blossom provides a particularly good bee feed. The early Hottentots had a saying:

"When the doringboom blossoms the honey is fat".

The traveller and ornithologist, Francois le Vaillant, some 170 years ago noted the infinite number of insects and therefore of birds attracted to the mimosa in bloom.

Monkeys eat the flowers, as do Meyer's Parrots.

The flowers develop into dark, narrow, flattish pods, 5-13 cm long and not more than 1.3 cm wide, and usually sickle-shaped. They split open on the tree to release small, shiny, brown seeds.

The sweet-thorn is an important fodder tree for the young foliage, the pods and old flowers are all eaten by stock. At intervals all these have been tested and have been found to be poison free. Occasionally in the winter a farmer will cut a tree or a few leafy branches for fodder; or for the sake of the heavy bunches of mistletoe that are often found in the branches and which are readily eaten by stock. Farmers differentiate between "sweet" and "sour" thorn trees, the latter seldom being eaten by stock. Botanically, however, there appears to be no difference between the two. Twigs are said to be the favourite food of the Black Rhinoceros.

One of the many insects associated with the tree is the big flat cream-coloured scale insect, *Lecanodiaspis mimosae*, which is often seen upon it.

Growing as it does in regions often otherwise bare of trees, as in the Karoo and the highveld, it provides valuable shade and shelter. In the early days it was used extensively to make kraals for stock and even today is often used for this purpose. In all parts of the country sweet-thorn provides valuable fuel, and it has many uses on the farm. Farmers use the branches, packed into dongas, to gather silt and so build up the bed of the donga, or to protect young seedlings where no natural cover is afforded.

It is difficult today to realize how valuable the sweet-thorn was in the early days of colonization. Not only was it used for fuel, fodder, shade, shelter, and protection, but for a variety of other purposes as well. Pappe says of it:

"Wood hard and tough, extensively employed in the interior for building purposes; looks well when varnished and therefore adopted for all kinds of common furniture".

It was used for wheels, poles, yokes, rural implements, turners' work, and the thorny branches for protection against savage ostriches.

In Natal this was once the wood used to fence the quarters of the royal Zulu women.

The thick dark bark was used extensively for tanning leather, to which it gave a reddish colour. Sheep leather tanned with this was used even for women's gowns and petticoats.

Hottentots used the bark for making cord and mats. Burchell's raft with which he crossed the Orange River was made of logs of dead willow wood bound together with long strips of green sweet-thorn bark, the green bark being preferred to leather thongs as it did not stretch when wet. Probably all traffic to and fro across the river where baggage was carried was once accomplished thus. Zulus still make a bark cord from the tree which they use in building huts.

The tree has a picturesque use. A well-shaped branch covered with

The dark rought bark of the typical sweet-thorn

A picnic spot under a sweet-thorn near Ventersdorp, western Transvaal

Sweet-thorn pods which are borne terminally and burst open on the tree

A Karoo store-room — pumpkins piled underneath a big sweet-thorn

thorns and often with yellow blossom makes many a Karoo Christmas tree!

In parts of Southern Africa the Africans make needles of the thorns and they have always been valued by country people as pegs or pins. The early naturalists sometimes used them to pin their specimens.

The sweet-thorn is used medicinally in many ways. A mould growing on the tree makes a poultice to draw abscesses or needles broken in the flesh. A decoction of the bark is sometimes given to cattle suffering from tulp poisoning, and the bark makes a famous country gargle. Bark was once used to make splints, and probably still is in cases of emergency.

The gum exuding from the trunk and branches is widely popular with Africans and with children of all races (and also with Vervet Monkeys). It is clear and transparent with a pleasant, slightly sour taste, and has been used, although never extensively, for confectionery and adhesive gum. From early days this gum attracted the attention of travellers who always considered it a rarity. Dried and powdered, it is the best first-aid for those with the fine prickly pear thorns in their eyes. Once it was exported under the name Gomme du Cap.

The culture of the sweet-thorn is simple. Seeds should be soaked in boiling water, sown, and covered lightly with soil. They germinate easily, transplant well, and the trees are usually quick-growing. An early colonist planted an avenue of sweet-thorns in a street in Pearston in the Karoo. These trees reached a great height and met in an arch over the road before they were felled. Old inhabitants still remember and talk of the beautiful avenue. In a garden this is a satisfactory tree, bare in winter and casting light shade in summer. Indigenous bulbs such as freesias and ixias grow — and look — particularly well below it.

It is doubtful to what age a sweet-thorn lives, but an old thorn tree that used to stand in Parliament House grounds in Cape Town and was blown down in the 1890's was judged to be over 300 years old. The tree interested botanists who did not believe it was indigenous to the Peninsula. They thought that seed had probably been left there by wandering Hottentots or their cattle.

This species is sometimes confusing even to botanists. In parts of the Eastern Province the tree sometimes assumes shrub form, very unlike the typical tree, coppicing when chopped, and encroaching on valuable farming land. The tree has smooth and hairy forms, and Burtt Davy divided the species into varieties on the basis of these characters, calling the hairy forms var. *transvaalensis*.

A Natal and Swaziland form, previously known as *Acacia natalitia* E.Mey., is somewhat lanky and has a light, almost white bark and narrower, more numerous pinnae and leaflets, than the typical form. A shrubby form in the midlands of Natal and Zululand has a dark smooth trunk, horizontally fissured, and a remarkable ability to resist grass fires. This was given a separate name *Acacia inconflagrabilis* Gerst. — "the acacia that does not burn".

The modern tendency is to regard these merely as forms of the very variable *Acacia karroo*.

The specific name *karroo* does not signify that this is a species of the Karoo alone, but that it is the principal and most conspicuous tree of this semi-desert, noted and welcomed here from early times. A common name often given it is that of "mimosa". It is not entitled to this name, however, for *Mimosa* is the botanical name of another genus of the legume family. Once it was known as *Acacia horrida* (L.) Willd. but this was an

The pale smooth bark of the sweet-thorn growing in the coastal woodland of Zululand

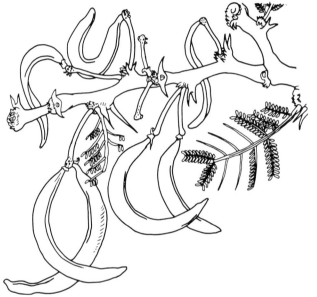

Above left
Acacia gerrardii in the
north eastern Transvaal

Above right
Acacia gerrardii bark

Centre left
Acacia gerrardii: A twig
with leaves and pods
(50%)

Below left
Acacia davyi on a stream
bank in Zululand

incorrect identification, *Acacia horrida* being an Indian species and not belonging to South Africa at all.

Acacia karroo is closely related to the northern species, *Acacia seyal* Del., which takes its place in tropical Africa.

(167)   31. *Acacia gerrardii* Benth.

Red thorn, rooidoring ,rooibas, rooihaak, aapkop; umPhuze, umNgampunzi (Z); siNga (Sw); moki (Tsw — Mang); mooka (NS); muunga (V)

The red thorn, typically a rather sparse acacia with few upward-growing branches, occurs from northern Zululand and Swaziland, through the eastern Orange Free State (but sparingly here), the eastern, central, and northern Transvaal, to Rhodesia and Zambia, often growing in black turf or on sandy flats in open tree savannah.

The bark on young trees is fairly smooth and grey, seamed crosswise, and on older trees reddish-brown, rough, and deeply fissured, often "wrinkled like an elephant's trunk" in the words of one collector.

The thorns are paired and straight, although occasionally when short they are slightly hooked. They are usually about 2.5 cm long but sometimes longer, and are covered with soft hairs.

The leaves are crowded at the nodes. They are up to about 9 cm long, with 5-10 pairs of pinnae or side-branches, and about 15-20 pairs of small, oblong leaflets. These, the young twigs, and pods are covered with thick grey hairs.

The flowers are in round, creamy, sweet-scented heads crowded at the nodes in the axils of the leaves, and usually bloom from December to March. They develop into narrow sickle-shaped, hairy pods. These mature from autumn to winter.

The pods and young shoots are eaten by baboons, the bark and leaves by Black Rhino, and the foliage by domestic stock, giraffe, duiker and steenbok. Farmers consider the tree a good winter feed.

The wood is sometimes described as soft and at others as tough and strong, but all the authorities agree that it is subject to borer attack and is of little value. Africans sometimes make string of the bark.

The red thorn can easily be confused with the sweet-thorn, which, however, is usually more spreading and better shaped and without the hairiness typical of the young twigs, the thorns, and pods of the red thorn. The sweet-thorn usually has slightly larger leaflets than the red thorn, and flowers in long terminal racemes or panicles, whereas those of the red thorn are in groups in the axils of the leaves.

The species is named after William T. Gerrard, English botanical collector in Natal, who collected the tree in the middle 19th century. The common names "red thorn" and "rooidoring" refer to the colour of the bark. "Aapkop" is used in a derogatory sense because the wood is good for nothing.

(163.1)   32. *Acacia davyi* N.E.Br.

Isikwishi; isiKhwishi, iPhuthwa (Z); umGamba (Sw); mologa-tshêlô (NS)

Acacia davyi, a shrub or tree occasionally reaching 5 m or more in

Above
Acacia grandicornuta in thorn scrub in Zululand

Left
Acacia grandicornuta stem

Below
Acacia grandicornuta thorns

height, occurs in the bushveld and grassveld of Zululand, Swaziland, and the eastern, central, and northern Transvaal.

In the field the most obvious difference between this and the sweet-thorn, *Acacia karroo*, and the rooidoring, *Acacia gerrardii*, is its usually corky, yellow or light brown bark.

The twigs are light coloured. The spines are paired and straight or, when they are very short, slightly hooked. The bright green leaves, larger than those of the sweet-thorn and somewhat resembling those of *Acacia caffra*, are up to 15 cm long with generally up to 18 pairs (12-22 pairs) of pinnae and up to 36 pairs of leaflets to a pinna. Twigs, leaves, and pods are smooth, unlike those of *Acacia gerrardii*.

The flowers in round, deep yellow heads resemble those of *Acacia karroo*, and — like those of this species — they are borne terminally and in the axils of the upper leaves. They lack, however, the deep rich fragrance of sweet-thorn flowers. They bloom summer to autumn.

The pods, in bunches, are long and narrow, up to 10 cm long, straight or slightly curved, with thickened margins, and are sometimes constricted between the seeds.

Bark and leaves are eaten by Black Rhino.

The wood is soft and brittle.

This species was named after the noted botanist, Joseph Burtt Davy. There appears to be no English or Afrikaans common name beyond "Burtt Davy's acacia", or "papierdoring", the latter being easily confused with paperbark-thorn, *Acacia sieberana* var. *woodii*. The Zulu name "isiKwishi" or the Swazi "umGamba" might with profit be adopted as the general common name.

(186)   33. *Acacia arenaria* Schinz

= *Acacia hermannii* Bak.f.

Sand acacia

This — the acacia of sandy places, as the botanical name suggests — grows as a many-stemmed shrub or as a small, very thorny tree up to 4.5 m tall with zig-zag branches, in sandy parts of northern South West Africa, Botswana, and in country northwards to Tanzania.

The bark is grey, the thorns straight, white or light brown, about 4 cm long, and paired. The twigs are often hairy. The long slender leaves are up to 20 cm long with about 30-40 pairs of pinnae, and these each bear plus-minus 25 pairs of small closely packed leaflets. The common midrib is smooth or hairy.

The flowers are in round balls, usually a pink colour, and are borne in bunches in the axils of the leaves. These develop into long, narrow, slightly curved pods, up to 15 cm long, dark brown and veined.

(168.1)   34. *Acacia grandicornuta* Gerstn.

Horned acacia, horingdoring; umDongole, umNgampondo (Z)

A tree of thorn scrub and dry, often hilly bushveld, *Acacia grandicornuta* grows in Zululand and the lowveld of Swaziland, the eastern and northern Transvaal, and in Botswana.

It is frequently small, in northern Zululand often forming dense

Acacia robusta subsp. *clavigera*, a larger tree than subsp. *robusta*, near Lake Sibayi, Zululand

thickets, but it can grow into a fairly big tree up to 15 m in height, round-topped or spreading, much like the sweet-thorn, *Acacia karroo*, in habit. Gerstner, the Zululand missionary-botanist, who described it, said it resembled a pear tree, and was related to *Acacia robusta*. (Ross says it could almost be regarded as a dryland form of *Acacia robusta*, differing from it in having fewer pinna pairs, smaller leaflets, and smaller, less woody pods).

The bark is variable, ash grey to almost black, becoming furrowed with age. The straight, white, paired thorns are sturdy, up to 8 cm long, and sometimes inflated and fused at the base. The leaves are borne in bunches of 3 to 5 on small cushions in the axils of the spines and are up to about 8 cm long, usually with about 3 pairs of pinnae, and about 8-15 pairs of slightly hairy leaflets.

The flowers, blooming in early spring, are in white balls, about 4 to 12 being borne in tufts in the axils of the leaves. The brown curved pods are somewhat woody, and up to about 8 cm long with conspicuous longitudinal veins, and enclose smooth, dark, oval seeds.

The timber is used only for fuel.

The Zulu name for this tree is umNgampondo, meaning "resembling horns", in reference to the thorns, and the botanical name, meaning "big thorns", is based on this.

(183)   35. *Acacia robusta* Burch.
         1. subsp. *robusta*
(183.1) 2. subsp. *clavigera* (E.Mey.) Brenan

= *Acacia clavigera* E.Mey.

Enkeldoring, Engelsedoring, oudoring, brosdoring, brakdoring; umNga-manzi (Z); munga, mungamazi (Tso); moga (Tsw — Kwena), moku (Tsw — Ngwak); moku (NS)

This fine acacia — in flower one of the loveliest of all the wild thorn trees — offers some difficulty to botanists, some of whom regard it as a very variable species widely distributed in the central and eastern parts of the country and in the northern Transvaal, while others see the eastern — the coastal form — as a separate species, *Acacia clavigera* E.Mey., or a separate subspecies, *Acacia robusta* subsp. *clavigera* (E.Mey.) Brenan. The tendency in South Africa is to regard the tree as one species with two subspecies, and the differences between the forms as climatic and geographical only.

Regarded as a single species, *Acacia robusta* is distributed from the eastern Cape, northwards through Natal, Zululand, and Swaziland, to the Transvaal — where it is widespread — and westwards to the northern Cape and Botswana. It occurs, although rarely, in the Orange Free State, and is found north of South Africa in Rhodesia and Mozambique.

In their extremes, the two forms of *Acacia robusta* are distinct. In the Natal interior, the Transvaal, and Botswana the trees are medium-sized, up to about 10.5 m tall, and nearly always distinguished by thick branches and twigs, a character that is often very noticeable indeed. It was on this feature that Burchell named the tree, which he first collected near Kuruman, "the robust acacia".

In the coastal districts of the Cape, Natal, and Zululand a much larger form, subsp. *clavigera*, is found, and this grows up to 18 m in height and has a shapely spreading crown. The branches and twigs of such trees are

Above left
Acacia robusta – the typical form – in the Transvaal bushveld

Above right
Acacia robusta pods

Below left
Acacia robusta: a flowering and fruiting twig (50%)

Below right
Acacia reficiens: the leaves, flowers and pod (80%)

OPPOSITE
Acacia robusta stem

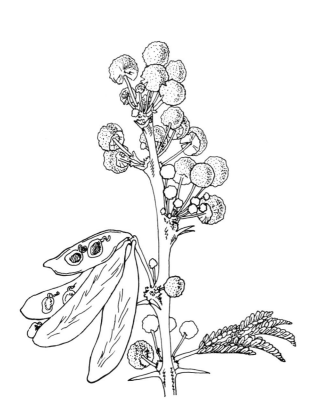

far more slender than in the typical *Acacia robusta*.

Both forms have rough, black, fissured bark, straight paired thorns, feathery dark green leaves in clusters on cushions above the thorns, and flowers borne in spring in round heads in bunches on these cushions. The flower-heads are from off-white to a rich butter yellow in colour and have a delicious scent which is spread for a long way around the trees. They burst into blossom before the leaves appear, or when there are only young green shoots, and the blossom covering the dark bare branches is an unusual and lovely sight.

The pods are straight or slightly curved, and covered with faint, rib-like marks. They split open on the tree to release small, hard, flattish, shiny seeds. The pods are usually damaged by small insects. Old pods often hang on the trees together with the fresh spring blossom.

Within this broad framework certain differences are noticeable. The typical *Acacia robusta* has longer and stouter spines, up to 10 cm in length, while those of subsp. *clavigera* are usually shorter. Its leaves often have fewer pinnae — usually 2 to 4 pairs — and fewer and larger leaflets, generally up to 15 pairs, and the midribs of these are smooth, while subsp. *clavigera* has up to 6 pairs of pinnae and more numerous and smaller leaflets, with the common midrib hairy. Pods of the typical form are shorter and broader than are those of subsp. *clavigera*.

These forms tend to grade into one another.

The wood is light coloured with a dark heart and tough, and does not split readily. Galpin says it warps easily and is often attacked by borers unless water-seasoned, while old trees are usually affected with dry rot and riddled by borers. He says it makes good yokes. Generally, it is considered of little value as timber or fuel, hence was named by the early Dutch settlers "Engelsdoring" or "English thorn", meaning good-for-nothing!

The foliage and pods are sometimes browsed by stock, and as far as is known these are not poisonous. Rhino eat the bark, baboons the young shoots, and monkeys the leaves, roots, and gum. In Zululand the ground bark, mixed with water, is said to dispatch snakes.

Little is known of the cultivation of the enkeldoring. It seems slower-growing than the sweet-thorn, for example, and is hardy and drought-resistant.

This species is sometimes confused with *Acacia karroo*. In flower or pod it is easy to distinguish between them for the sweet-thorn bears its smaller, bright golden flowers at the ends of the branches and not on cushions above the spines, while the pods are narrow and usually much curved, unlike the almost straight, woody pods of the enkeldoring.

(181)   36. *Acacia reficiens* Wawra & Peyr.

Deurmekaardoring; omungondo (Her); gŏs (Nama)

Acacia reficiens, a widespread acacia from South West Africa, Angola, and Botswana, belongs to a small group of acacias which usually has spines that are both hooked and straight. Only one other species besides those in this group has such spines, the common haak-en-steek, *Acacia tortilis* subsp. *heteracantha*, but this has pods that are much twisted and not straight like those of the other species.

The group itself is very complex, for at one time or another it has been divided into 6 separate species, *Acacia reficiens* Wawra & Peyr.,

PHOTOS

Above
Acacia reficiens trunk

Right
Acacia reficiens near the
Petrified Forest, South
West Africa

810

DIAGRAMS
OPPOSITE

Above
Acacia luederitzii var.
luederitzii: a portion of
a fruiting branch (80%)

Below
Acacia luederitzii var.
luederitzii: A flowering
twig and pod (40%)

BELOW
Acacia luederitzii var.
retinens: A twig with
the typically swollen
spines, a pod, and a
flowering twig (60%)

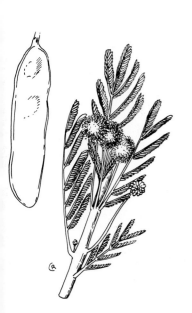

Acacia luederitzii Engl., *Acacia uncinata* Engl., *Acacia goeringii* Schinz, *Acacia retinens* Sim, and *Acacia gillettiae* Burtt Davy, the various species often being confused.

Even modern botanists are not in agreement about them, some seeing them all as but variants of one species, *Acacia reficiens*. Others consider the 5 remaining species differ from it in several small details and they place them all under *Acacia luederitzii*, the oldest name among them. This is the grouping followed here.

Acacia reficiens occurs in central and northern South West Africa and in Angola as a many-stemmed shrub, or as a small spreading tree with a reddish-brown fissured bark. The thorns are small, hooked, and in pairs. Long straight white spines are also present but usually they are much fewer in number. The foliage is very fine. The leaves are made up of about 2-9 pairs of pinnae or side-branches, which bear up to about 5-11 pairs of tiny leaflets. Under the microscope these are seen to be almost smooth, or to have very short hairs, with smooth margins, a feature that separates it from *Acacia luederitzii* which has leaflets covered with long spreading hairs and hairy margins. *Acacia luederitzii* also has more numerous long straight spines than has *Acacia reficiens*.

The flowers are borne in round yellow heads and develop into flat, narrow, reddish or buff pods, straight or slightly curved, often marked with many fine lines, about 5 cm long and seldom more than 1.3 cm wide. Those of *Acacia luederitzii* are often almost twice as wide.

The tree is said to yield an edible gum.

(174)   37. *Acacia luederitzii* Engl.

a. var. *luederitzii*

= *Acacia uncinata* Engl.; = *A. goeringii* Schinz

Mooku; mooku, moku (Tsw — Rolong); kangarangana (Tsw — Mbuk); omungondo (Her); gòs (Nama)

(174.1)   b. var. *retinens* (Sim) Ross & Brenan

= *Acacia retinens* Sim; = *A. gillettiae* Burtt Davy

Swollen-spine acacia, blinkhaakdoring; umBambampala, umNgampondo, uGagu, umKhaya — omnyamana, umKhays omnyama, umShangwe (Z)

Acacia luederitzii var. *luederitzii* is widely distributed from the northern Cape, through Botswana, to South West Africa, Rhodesia and Zambia, growing as a small to medium-sized tree, rounded or flat-topped, with a reddish-brown bark that is longitudinally seamed.

The thorns are of two kinds, short and hooked, and long and almost straight, and this has more straight thorns than has *Acacia reficiens* with which it is often confused. (These are never inflated as are those of *Acacia luederitzii* var. *retinens*). It is a far hairier species than *Acacia reficiens*, the leaflets having long spreading hairs and hair-fringed margins. There are about 2-12 pairs of pinnae.

The flowers, blooming in summer and autumn, are in round whitish balls and sweetly scented. The straight, flat, reddish-brown pods on long stalks, are in bunches. They are up to nearly 2.5 cm wide, both longer and wider than those of *Acacia reficiens*.

Fever trees, Acacia xanthophloea, growing in a pan, Weipe farm, near the Limpopo River

It is not clear whether this tree was named after the enterprising Bremen merchant, F.A.E. Luederitz, who did so much to build up South West Africa in the early days, or after his brother, A. Luederitz, a botanical collector in the territory.

Is this species the tree seen by Burchell near Douglas and named by him *Acacia heteracantha*, a tree that has puzzled botanists for over a century? Probably this will never now be known for sure, and is of little interest to the layman. To the botanist interested in the history of plants and their names it is a fascinating point.

Burchell described a tree with straight and hooked spines and straight pods as *Acacia heteracantha*, and later at Litakun near the present site of Kuruman another with similar thorns but with twisted pods, which he called *Acacia litakunensis*. Most botanists today think he mistook the straight pods and that he named the same tree — now *Acacia tortilis* subsp. *heteracantha* — twice over. A few believe it is more likely that his specimen was incorrect and his description correct, and that this is Burchell's tree, entitled to the name *heteracantha*.

Acacia luederitzii var. *retinens* has a more easterly distribution, occurring in thornveld in Portuguese East Africa, Swaziland, Zululand, and the central Transvaal.

It is a smaller tree than var. *luederitzii*, often no more than 4 m high and usually shorter, many-branched from low down, and with a low spreading crown, often making dense thickets.

It has hooked spines only, a curious feature being that these often become large and inflated and then almost straight. Ants or other small insects, entering through a small hole near the tips of the spines, occupy these, so that they are often known as "ant-galls". These swollen spines are a characteristic of the variety.

All the young parts of the tree are densely hairy. The leaves are variable, those in the Transvaal usually having fewer pairs of pinnae than those from Natal and Swaziland which have up to 13 pairs.

The flowers, appearing in summer, are in white, scented balls, and the pods are straight and leathery.

The heartwood is dark, heavy, and tough. Galpin says it stands up excellently to moisture and is the best timber for lining wells. It is fire resistant and makes particularly good fence poles.

The name *retinens* means "detaining", probably in reference to the thorns. The Zulu name "umBambampala" means "the impala's trap".

(184.1)   38. *Acacia schweinfurthii* Brenan & Exell

Wrongly identified in the past as *Acacia pennata* (L.) Willd. Ubobe; uBobhe, uGagane, uThathawe (Z)

This woody climber from Natal, Swaziland, the eastern and northern Transvaal and Botswana and the country northwards to tropical Africa, much resembles *Acacia ataxacantha,* but unlike it, it is only seldom tree-like. It is a common climber or sprawling shrub, often making impenetrable thickets, along river banks in particular. Occasionally it grows into a small flat-topped tree.

It has scattered hooked thorns, and large, bright green, feathery leaves with 4-20 pairs of pinnae, and about 30 pairs of smooth leaflets. A knobbed gland above the base of the leaf stalk is conspicuous. The flowers are in creamy-white, round heads borne in early summer to-

Above
Acacia luederitzii var. *retinens,* Mkuze, Zululand

Below left
The trunk of a fever tree, *Acacia
xanthophloea*

Below right
A fever tree twig and pod (50%)

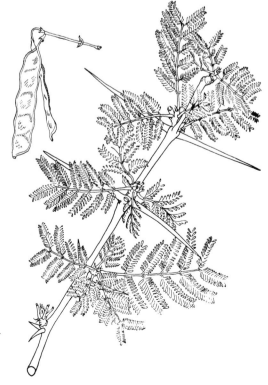

814

wards the ends of the branches, and the pods are large – up to 18 cm long – flat, brown, smoothish, and much-veined, with thickened margins.

The species was named after Dr Georg Schweinfurth, traveller and collector in east and north Africa in the mid 19th century.

Acacia schweinfurthii is sometimes confused with the shrub or climber, *Acacia brevispica* Harms subsp. *dregeana* (Benth.) Brenan which, however, has a yellow tinge to the foliage, hairier leaflets, and pods which burst open readily.

(189)   39. *Acacia xanthophloea* Benth.

Fever tree, koorsboom, sulphur bark; umHlosinga, umHlofunga, umKhanyakude, umDlovune (Z); umHlafunga (Sw); nkelenga (Tso); more o mosetlha (Tsw – Taw, Mang); munzhelenga (V)

This is not a widely distributed species in South Africa, for it grows only near rivers, swamps, and pans in the lowveld of Zululand, Swaziland, the Transvaal and Botswana, and in Rhodesia and Portuguese East Africa. Yet by name it is known to a vast number of people – and to children the world over – who have loved Rudyard Kipling's *Just so Stories* and the adventures of the Elephant Child.

He, it will be remembered, went from Graham's Town to Kimberley, and from Kimberley to Khama's Country, and from Khama's country he went east by north, eating melons all the time, "till at last he came to the banks of the great grey-green, greasy Limpopo River, all set about with fever trees".

It is fitting that it should be widely known if only by name, for it is one of South Africa's strangest trees. It is remarkable, not so much for its grace and shape, but for the colour of its trunk and branches which are yellow-green and smooth, covered with a powdery bloom. A fever tree in winter, spreading bare yellow branches against a background of dark-foliaged trees and tropical river, is never forgotten.

It grows up to about 15 m high and has, as a rule, rather few and upward-growing branches. The foliage is typically acacia-like with feathery leaves up to 10 cm long, (but usually about 4 cm), with a hairy midrib. There are 4-7 pairs of pinnae and about 10-17 pairs of small leaflets. The thorns are long, straight, white, paired, and often slender.

The sweetly scented flowers are in round, golden balls on slender stalks, very like those of the sweet-thorn. Several are borne together, with a tuft of leaves, in the axils of the thorns.

The pods are 5-10 cm long, pale brown, straight, flat, rather papery, usually borne in small clusters.

Elephant eat the young branches, leaves and roots, giraffe the leaves and pods, and Vervet Monkeys eat the young leaves, flowers, the pods just forming, and the seeds.

The wood is hard, heavy, and generally useful. The best fever trees in Zululand have been felled in recent years for timber.

The fever tree is scarce in cultivation, although many gardeners wish to grow it. The main difficulty is lack of seed as few pods are produced, while monkeys eat the ones that have formed while they are still young. The trees are easy, fast-growing, and – surprisingly – tolerate several degrees of frost.

Above
Dichrostachys cinerea subsp. *africana* in the
Transvaal bushveld

Below left
Dichrostachys stems

Below right
Dichrostachys cinerea subsp. *africana* pod,
leaves and flowers (50%)

The specific name *xanthophloea* is based on Greek words meaning
"yellow bark". The common name "fever tree" is an old one, given because the tree grows where malaria is prevalent. In parts people believe
that the tree itself has the power of conveying malaria. Colonel Stevenson-Hamilton wrote that he knew of men so convinced of this that
they would hold their noses when passing it.

Various other trees are known as fever trees because of their medicinal
use in cases of fever, or because they grow where malaria is rife. This,
however, is the tree most commonly known as fever tree.

3. *Dichrostachys* Wight & Arn.

Dichrostachys, a fairly small and mainly tropical genus of the Old
World, is represented in South and South West Africa by one variable
species, formerly split up into several species, *Dichrostachys cinerea*
(L.) Wight & Arn.

The species may be spiny or unarmed. All have bipinnate leaves with
leaflets that are often small and numerous; flowers 5-numerous, in
cylindric spikes borne singly or in clusters in the axils of the leaves,
those in the upper part yellow and bisexual, in the lower purple or pink
and sterile; the pods long, narrow, often twisted and curled; the
seeds — in the African species — flat and smooth.

The generic name *Dichrostachys* is based on Greek words meaning
"two-coloured flowers".

(190)   *Dichrostachys cinerea* (L.) Wight & Arn.

1. subsp. *africana* Brenan & Brummitt

= *Dichrostachys glomerata* (Forsk.) Chiov.; = *D. nutans* (Pers.) Benth.

(190.1)   2. subsp. *nyassana* (Taub.) Brenan

= *Dichrostachys nyassana* Taub.

Sekelbos, sicklebush, Kalahari Christmas tree, Chinese lantern tree;
uGagane, umThezane, umZilazembe, uSegwane (Z); umSilazembe (Sw);
ndzenga (Tso); mosêlêsêlê (Tsw); morêtshê (NS); murenzhe (V);
keye (Sub)

This is a widespread species reaching from the dry parts of Natal and
the Transvaal, Botswana and South West Africa, northwards to tropical
Africa, and eastwards to India and Australia. Over so vast an area it
naturally shows many variations and was at one time divided into
various species.

While botanists today consider it a single variable species, they differ
as to its division, botanists such as Brenan and Brummitt subdividing it
into a great many subspecies and varieties on small features such as the
number of pinnae, the size and hairiness of the leaflets, the smoothness
or hairiness of the flower stalks, and sometimes the width and curliness
of the pods.

The Botanical Research Institute in Pretoria recognizes only two of
these subspecies in Southern Africa, subsp. *africana* with one or two

varieties — var. *africana* and possibly var. *pubescens* — and subsp. *nyassana*.

The tree grows on flats, or sometimes on low hills and along stream banks, in thornveld and mixed woodland, often in a loamy soil.

Generally it is a shrub or small tree, easily mistaken for an acacia, with a grey or red-brown, twisted, deeply fissured stem, and an often umbrella-shaped crown. The branches usually intertwine and give the crown a thick, matted appearance, very noticeable in winter when the tree is bare of leaves. At other times it is not sturdy but slender and straggling in growth.

The foliage is very fine, resembling that of an acacia, the compound leaves being made up of about 4 to 13 pairs of pinnae, composed of numerous pairs of tiny leaflets. These close up together almost as soon as a leaf is picked so that, for examination, they must be observed on the tree itself.

The subspecies *nyassana*, common in the eastern parts of the country, is a robuster form with larger and smoother leaves than in subsp. *africana*, and larger leaflets.

The most obvious difference between *Dichrostachys* and *Acacia* species lies in the fluffy flower spikes which are in two distinct sections, the basal half a pinky-mauve, composed of sterile flowers, and the tip yellow and composed of bisexual flowers. These are gay and gaudy, and are scented like a cheap synthetic perfume.

The flowers usually appear in late spring or early summer and so the tree is sometimes known as the Kalahari Christmas tree. One African name, according to Keith Coates Palgrave — means "the tree which provides tassels for the Chief's hat".

Dichrostachys further differs from *Acacia* in that the spines are not stipules but hardened branchlets ending in a straight, sharp point.

The pods are curled and twisted together, and are borne on the end of a fairly long stalk, each pod containing several seeds. Young pods are curved like sickles. The pods are eagerly eaten by stock, antelope, giraffe, rhino, monkeys, and bush pigs, and the leaves are browsed by a variety of animals.

The stem is seldom more than 23 cm in diameter and usually smaller, too small to be much used, although when big enough it makes excellent fence posts, borer and termite-proof and said to be almost imperishable. The wood is very hard and dark, and is the best bushveld fuel, burning steadily and with an intense heat for a long while. The inner layers of the bark yield a fibre which the Africans make into cordage.

It is believed that the old Bantu iron and copper smelters in the western Transvaal worked with bored stone tools with handles made of sekelbos.

Wherever it grows, the sekelbos is used medicinally to treat the most diverse diseases; and it is interesting that in all parts of Africa it is used to treat snake bite, both medicinally and magically. Coates Palgrave says that the Africans believe the leaves produce local anaesthesia. Chewed leaves are placed on scorpion stings and snake bites, and leaves and roots are supposed to relieve toothache. These pain-killing properties are valued by Zulus who drink a decoction of the roots, mixed with those of *Vangueria infausta* Burch. and *Bridelia micrantha* (Hochst.) Baill. to ease pain, or rub them into incisions in the skin over the painful area. In Botswana parts of the tree are a tapeworm cure.

The sekelbos has a picturesque use for it lends itself to Bonsai, the Japanese art of dwarfing trees. At the Republic Festival floral exhibition

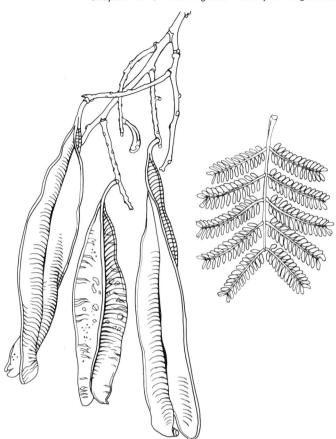

Newtonia hildebrandtii:
pods and leaf (60%)

in Pretoria in 1966 a dwarf tree some 30 cm high, a perfect miniature sekelbos with flat crown, ribbed trunk, and tight clusters of curled pods, delighted thousands of visitors.

The specific name *cinerea* means "ashy".

4. *Newtonia* Baill.

Newtonia is a genus of roughly 14 species of trees occurring in tropical Africa and South America, the majority being African. In South Africa one species is recorded from Zululand.

The species are all large, unarmed trees with bipinnate leaves, the common midrib with a gland between each pair of opposite pinnae, and 5-numerous flowers in long spikes or racemes. The pods are flat, straight or very slightly curved, and the seeds are oblong to egg-shaped, flat, and winged.

The name *Newtonia* honours a Portuguese collector of English descent, Francisco Newton, who worked in West Africa.

(191)   *Newtonia hildebrandtii* (Vatke) Torre

= *Piptadenia hildebrandtii* Vatke

Umfomoti; umFomothi, uDongolokamadilika (Z)

The umfomoti, up to 18 m high, with a branch span as large and a straight trunk up to 1 m in diameter, is one of the noblest of all the

OPPOSITE

Above
The umfomoti tree,
Newtonia hildebrandtii,
in full leaf in the Tongaland sand forest

Below
Newtonia hildebrandtii
– leafless – at Mkuze in
winter

Below
Newtonia hildebrandtii
trunk and bark

trees of Zululand. It is a tropical species reaching south into central and northern Zululand, growing in sandy country in high forest, in savanna woodland and dry bushveld. It is common at False Bay – where it is dominant in parts in the short sand forest – and in the Mkuze Game Reserve where its size makes it conspicuous even in this well wooded area.

Recently it has been reported from the eastern Transvaal.

It has a wide crown, formed of many spreading branches and fine twigs which make a beautiful pattern in winter when the tree is bare of leaves. The young branches are smooth or slightly hairy, a mottled dark and light grey, and the older bark is dark grey, deeply cracked into segments and flaking longitudinally.

The tree lacks spines, but the fine, feathery leaves resemble those of an acacia, bearing 4-7 pairs of pinnae, each generally with about 6-19 – or sometimes more – pairs of narrow or oblong leaflets with the veins sometimes raised on the under-surface. There is often an oval gland between each pair of pinnae.

The flowers are in delicate, creamy spikes up to about 9 cm long. The pods, reported up to 30 cm long but usually 10-18 cm, and up to 2.5 cm wide, are slightly curved, much-veined, with thickened margins. They are a light, glossy, glowing red and are often borne in great numbers when the tree with its dark emerald foliage and bright pods is striking. They hold large, flat, winged seeds.

The timber is described by Gerstner as "like hard chocolate-brown ebony", and "a fine royal timber".

Zulus make a decoction of the roasted ground bark, mixed with water and elephant dung. They lick a few drops of this off their hands to drive away "starts" while sleeping.

When a boy baby is born in Zululand he is often washed in water heated on a fire made of dry umFomothi sticks, for it is thought the tree's masculine qualities of toughness and hardness will then be conferred upon the baby.

The name *hildebrandtii* honours the famous German collector, J.M. Hildebrandt, 1847-1881, who worked in central and north Africa and in Madagascar. The tree is widely known in Zululand as "um-Fomothi".

5. *Amblygonocarpus* Harms

The rather awe-inspiring name of this genus is descriptive. It is based on Greek words meaning "blunt-angled fruit", referring to the distinctive shape of the pods.

This is a genus of 1 species only. It is a spineless tree with bipinnate leaves; bisexual flowers in racemes, solitary or in pairs, in the axils of the leaves, 5-numerous, and pods that are oblong, bluntly angled, hard, woody, indehiscent – that is, not splitting open – the seeds brown, hard, and wingless.

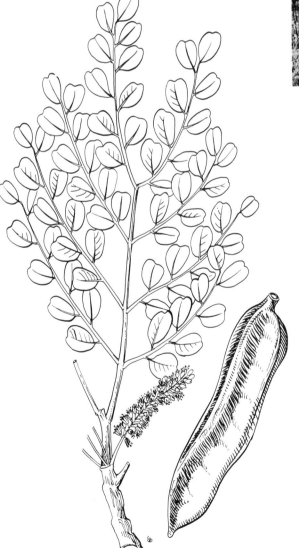

Above left
Amblygonocarpus trunk

Above right
Amblygonocarpus andongensis

Below left
Amblygonocarpus andongensis: A flowering branch-let and fruit (50%)

822

(190.2)   *Amblygonocarpus andongensis* (Welw. ex Oliv.) Exell & Torre

= *Tetrapleura obtusangula* Welw. ex Oliv.; = *Amblygonocarpus obtusangulus* (Welw. ex Oliv.) Harms; = *Amblygonocarpus schweinfurthii* Harms

Scotsman's rattle; mbaimbai (Tsw)

This fine and — in South Africa — little known tree of the sub-family Mimoseae occurs in the Caprivi Strip, in Botswana, Rhodesia, Mozambique, Angola, and in tropical Africa, usually growing on Kalahari sand. Miller says that a fine specimen stands on the Victoria Falls railway station.

It grows up to some 12 m high, and has a rough dark stem up to about 30 cm in diameter and a somewhat rounded or spreading crown of fine blue-green leaves. These are bipinnate, 20-30 cm long, with 2-5 pairs of pinnae, usually widely spaced, and 4-7 pairs of oblong, oval, or egg-shaped leaflets about 19 by 13 mm long, typically with a round notched tip.

The flowers, blooming about October, are in long, yellow, somewhat lax racemes. The large woody pods are conspicuous and when in fruit the tree is easily identified. They are from 7-20 cm long and almost 2.5 cm thick, with four distinct blunt angles, dark shiny brown, borne on stout stalks. They contain a number of seeds embedded in a thick woody pulp. When dry they rattle, and this has given rise to the common name "Scotsman's rattle".

The tree yields a pleasing useful timber.

Welwitsch collected the tree in Lower Guinea at Pungo Andongo, hence the specific name.

6. *Xylia* Benth.

About 13 species found mainly in the tropics of Africa and in Madagascar belong to this genus, noted for its good timber trees and therefore given a name based on the Greek "xylon" meaning "wood".

All the species are unarmed, with bipinnate leaves bearing only 1 pair of pinnae, the leaf stalk with a gland at its junction with these pinnae; the flowers — male and female or bisexual, 5-numerous — in round heads; and the pods egg-shaped, oblong or hatchet-shaped, lopsided, hard and woody, and splitting along 2 valves; the seeds lying crosswise, flat, smooth and unwinged.

(192)   *Xylia torreana* Brenan

Xylia

One species of the genus *Xylia, X. torreana* Brenan, grows in the north eastern Transvaal near the Portuguese border, in Portuguese East Africa itself, and in Rhodesia, usually on sandy soils in open woodland.

It is a small to medium-sized tree from 6-12 m high, with an oval or spreading crown, and a straight, wrinkled, grey trunk.

The twigs are densely hairy, the leaves bipinnate, but not feathery as in most other members of the sub-family Mimoseae. They have only 1 pair of pinnae or side-branches, about 7.6 to 10 cm long, the stalks of these having a slight swelling — a gland — at the base. Each side branch

Above
The basboontjie, *Elephantorrhiza burkei,* on a hillside near Pretoria

Left
The basboontjie stem

Below
Xylia torreana: Leaves, flowers and pod (60%)

824

carries 3-6 pairs of large, rather leathery leaflets, 2.5-10 cm long and 1.3-5 cm wide, egg-shaped, oblong or widely lance-shaped, usually bluntly pointed, and with a rounded and sometimes notched base. They have about 7-11 pairs of side veins and these are often conspicuous. The leaflets are borne on short stalks.

The small flowers are in round, cream-coloured heads, on hairy stalks, often several in a cluster, in the axils of the leaves. They bloom in early summer.

The greenish-brown pods can be confused with those of no other species for they are large, flat, and woody, broadly sickle-shaped, about 7.6 cm long, and nearly 5 cm wide, narrowing to the base, and briefly pointed at the apex. The large oval seeds within lie in a semi-circle to one side of the pod. The pods ripen in late summer and autumn, bursting open along 2 valves.

The leaves are browsed by kudu.

The species was named after A.R. da Torre, a Portuguese botanist at present working on the flora of Angola and Portuguese East Africa.

7. *Elephantorrhiza* Benth.

This small, purely African genus is represented in South and South West Africa by several species, the exact number uncertain, for several described species resemble one another closely and may, in fact, prove to be inseparable.

The best-known member of the genus is the low-growing elands-boontjie, *Elephantorrhiza elephantina* (Burch.) Skeels — the species on which the genus was founded — with roots up to 7 m long, used since early times for food and medicine, and for tanning.

All the species are unarmed small trees or shrubs, sometimes with thick underground parts; the leaves bipinnate, the leaflets numerous and small, often with the midrib oblique, the leaf stalks without glands; the flowers — usually bisexual — 5-numerous in spikes or racemes which are borne singly or in clusters, in the axils of the leaves; the pods often large, straight or curved, flat, not splitting along the edges but the valves separating from the rims, often peeling in layers; the seeds flattish.

The generic name *Elephantorrhiza* means "elephant root" and is based, most descriptively, on the large underground stem common to some members of the genus.

(193)   *Elephantorrhiza burkei* Benth.

Basboontjie, looibas; mositsane (Tsw); tshisesevhafa (V); namba (Sarwa)

The basboontjie is a deciduous shrub or small tree up to 3.6 m high growing on the Magaliesberg — it is fairly common in the hills round Pretoria and near Johannesburg — in the Waterberg, and in the Soutpansberg in the northern Transvaal, most often occurring on rocky slopes. It also grows westwards into Botswana.

It is usually several-stemmed, the trunks arising from a swollen underground stem, the young wood grey or almost black, and smooth, the older dark, rough, and peeling.

It has feathery, acacia-like leaves up to about 23 cm long, with 3-7

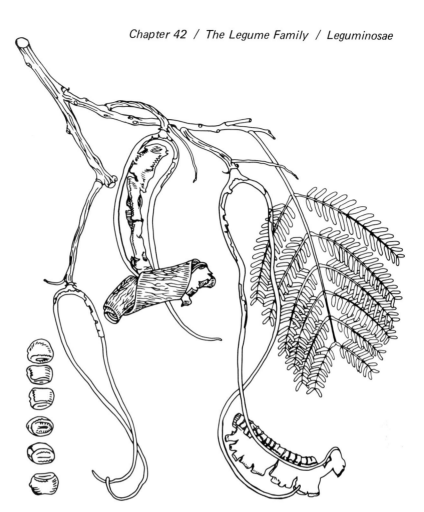

Above
A basboontjie *(Ele-
phantorrhiza burkei)*
twig, showing the rims
of the old pods clinging
to the branchlet, a leaf,
and the angled seeds (45%)

OPPOSITE

Above left
Elephantorrhiza goetzei
stem and bark

Above right
Elephantorrhiza goetzei
in the hills near the
Bundu Inn, close to
Groblersdal

Below left
Elephantorrhiza goetzei
inflorescence

Below right
Basboontjie flower
spikes

pairs of side-branches up to about 10 cm long, each bearing numerous leaflets, a long oval in shape, and often with a small jutting point at the apex. The midrib is distinct below and in the centre of the leaflet. It is without thorns.

The flowers are in cream-coloured and yellow, fragrant spikes up to 10 cm long borne in the axils of the leaves, often towards the base of the leafy branches, so that they are not easily seen. They bloom from about September to October, and are attractive to insects.

The pods are large, sometimes over 30 cm long and up to 4 cm broad, flat and brown. They remain on the tree for a long time and in winter are very characteristic, the rims of the pods remaining intact and the brown and gold valves curling up between them − while underneath the tree lies a harvest of curled pods and large, fat, dark, smoothly angled seeds.

The specific name honours Joseph Burke, botanical and zoological collector in the 19th century. The common Afrikaans names are based on the use of this species in tanning.

Elephantorrhiza goetzei (Harms) Harms

= *Piptadenis goetzei* Harms; = *Elephantorrhiza elongata* Burtt Davy

Goetze's elephantorrhiza

Elephantorrhiza goetzei, a small, deciduous tree or shrub, is a tropical species growing from Tanzania southwards to the central, eastern and northern Transvaal, in stony bushveld and on dry, wooded hillsides.

It is usually many-stemmed with brown or reddish bark and smooth dark twigs. The large leaves – up to about 40 cm long – have about 4-30 pairs of pinnae and up to 48 pairs of usually small, narrow, oblong leaflets with the midribs near the centre.

The cream-coloured flowers are in long, spike-like racemes, towards the ends of the branches, blooming about November, and the pods are long – up to 40 cm – flat, narrowly oblong, with thickened margins, the seeds showing as slightly raised bumps.

The tree is used medicinally. The powdered root, mixed with the powdered red seed of the Kaffir watermelon, and the powdered C.M.R. beetle, is considered by Africans in the Transvaal to be cleanser and purifier after a wild party. (Large doses have proved fatal!)

Porcupines eat the roots.

The specific name honours Walter Goetze, who collected for the Berlin Botanic Gardens in East Africa and died there in 1899.

Two species from South West Africa sometimes grow as small trees but whether these are distinct from *E. goetzei* is not certain. They are *E. rangei* Harms, named after Dr Paul Range, a German geologist and plant collector in South West Africa from 1906 to 1913, which grows in central South West Africa, and *E. suffruticosa* Schinz which is widespread in the territory. These differ from *E. goetzei* principally in the position of the midribs of the leaflets, which are near the margin and not in the centre of the blades.

Sub-Family Caesalpinieae

Although trees of the sub-family Mimoseae are more numerous and widespread in South and South West Africa than are members of Caesalpinieae, north of the Limpopo trees of this sub-family become of great importance – White describes them as "the most important woody group in Zambia". Even in the northern parts of South Africa they become a typical and often beautiful part of the tree population.

A genus such as *Schotia* is widespread from the Cape to the Transvaal and South West Africa, while genera such as *Guibourtia* and *Cordyla* have, in South Africa, a limited distribution, being confined to parts of the northern and eastern Transvaal or to Zululand. Other tropical genera, such as *Baikiaea* and *Swartzia*, occur in the Caprivi Strip but have never been collected in South Africa. Nor has the great tree of Central Africa, the msasa, *Brachystegia spiciformis* Benth., yet it is possible that these, and other such species, do enter northern South Africa and may one day be collected in the botanically little-explored country north east of Sibasa, where a tongue of deep Kalahari sand carries a vegetation often associated with these species.

A genus such as *Umtiza* is unique. It is composed of a single species which occurs only round East London and in a few other isolated places in the eastern Cape.

The trees of this sub-family sometimes have twice-divided (or bi-pinnate) leaves, sometimes leaves consisting of 2 leaflets only, and occasionally simple leaves. The flowers are often large and beautiful with a calyx that is conspicuous or insignificant, composed of 5 sepals, with 5 petals – which are sometimes reduced to a single petal – or without petals at all. There are usually up to 10 stamens. The fruits are mostly the typical pods, but 3 species have pulpy fruits that are edible and pleasant-tasting and are therefore a curiosity in this group. They are *Dialium engleranum* Harms, *Dialium schlechteri* Harms, and *Cordyla africana* Lour.

Key to Genera
Sub-family Caesalpinieae

LEAVES SIMPLE

Shrubs or small trees; the leaves 2-lobed, small to medium-sized; the flowers *bisexual*, the flower tube *long*, the sepals *divided*; the pods long, narrow, *bursting open*.

k. Bauhinia

A small to medium tree; the leaves 2-lobed, large; the flowers *male or female borne separately*, the sepals *united into a tube*; the pods large, woody, heavy, *not* bursting open.

l. Piliostigma

A many-stemmed shrub or small tree; the leaves 2-lobed, small, folded, blue-green; the flowers *small, cup-shaped, without a long flower tube*, the *calyx bell-like*; the pods short, broad, flat, curved, pointed, smooth or with glandular dots.

m. Adenolobus

LEAVES COMPOUND

Leaves with 2 leaflets

Shrubs to medium-sized trees; the leaves with butterfly leaflets, finely gland-dotted; the leaflets *shortly stalked; no point between the leaflets;* the pods *bursting open*; the seeds *without resinous dots*.

c. Guibourtia

A shrub to medium-sized tree; the leaves with butterfly leaflets, *without stalks*, 7-12 nerves from the base, gland-dotted; *a small pointed growth between the leaflets*; the pods *not* bursting open; the seeds yellowish with small *glandular, resinous dots*.

d. Colophospermum

Leaves imparipinnate (once divided, terminated by 1 leaflet)

Small to large trees; the leaflets 2-6 pairs and a terminal one, 1-4 cm long; the flowers inconspicuous, the petals often absent; the fruit oval, about 2.5 cm long, *with a brown velvety "rind" and within a layer of dry pulp*.

n. Dialium

A large tree; the leaflets 9-12 pairs and a terminal one, 2.5-7 cm long; the flowers without petals, the stamens conspicuous; the fruit *fleshy, succulent, oval,* 2.5-5 cm long *with a leathery yellow skin, the flesh glutinous.*

r. *Cordyla*

A small to medium-sized tree; the leaflets usually 1-3 pairs and a terminal one, 2.5-7 cm long; *the flowers with 1 petal only, large, crisped, white with a yellow spot,* conspicuous; the pods long, narrow, up to 30 x 1.3 cm, *cylindrical or bluntly 4-sided,* dark red-brown, hard, shiny.

s. *Swartzia*

Leaves paripinnate (once divided, terminated by 2 leaflets)

Medium to large trees; the leaflets few to many; the leaflet stalks short *with a swelling at the base,* or absent; the flowers small, the calyx *green.*

e. *Brachystegia*

A medium to large tree; the leaflets in 4-7 pairs, the stalks short, *without a swelling at the base,* the flowers with more or less reduced petals, the calyx *dark brown, furry, conspicuous.*

j. *Julbernardia*

Small to medium-sized trees, unarmed, often deciduous; the leaflets small to large, few to many; the flowers *red, cup-shaped, facing upwards,* in short panicles; the pods *smooth, woody;* the seeds *often with a conspicuous aril.*

f. *Schotia*

A small spiny tree; evergreen; the trunk with twisted buttresses; the leaflets 7-12 pairs; the flowers *small, star-shaped, whitish,* in short panicles at the ends of the twigs on the top branches; the pods *long, narrow, flat, pointed.*

g. *Umtiza*

A medium to tall tree, unarmed; the leaflets 4-5 pairs, oblong, thickish; the twigs and leaf stalks *velvety brown;* the flowers large, *white to purple in long upright sprays* (racemes or panicles); the pods *brown, velvety, pear-shaped, flat.*

h. *Baikiaea*

A large tree, unarmed; the leaflets 4-7 pairs, oval, shiny, with wavy edges; the flowers with *1 large clawed reddish petal;* the pods *dark, smooth, oblong, thick, woody;* the seeds oblong, shiny, *black with a conspicuous red aril.*

i. *Afzelia*

Shrubs or small trees, unarmed; the leaves large, graceful, *the stipules often conspicuous;* the leaflets usually 5-12 pairs; the flowers *bright yellow,* often conspicuous, in a dense inflorescence terminally or in the axils of the leaves; *the pods long, narrow, sausage-like or flat,* pendulous, many-seeded.

o. *Cassia*

A small tree or shrub, the branches *smooth, thin, flexible, yellow-green, with horizontal spines*; the leaves *usually without leaflets, only the mid-ribs most often remaining*; the leaflets when present minute, in 8-10 pairs; the flowers yellow, inconspicuous; in the axils of the leaves; the *pods oblong, shiny, compressed between the seeds*.

p. *Parkinsonia*

Leaves bipinnate (twice-divided)

Medium to large trees; the twigs slender; the pinnae 2-4 pairs; the leaflets 5-14 pairs, arranged alternately; the flowers *small, in racemes*; the *pods large*, up to 20 cm long, *splitting open*.

a. *Erythrophleum*

A small to medium tree; the twigs robust; the young shoots *dense red-velvety*; the pinnae usually 2-3 pairs, the leaflets 5-11 arranged alternately; the flowers small *in string-like pendent spikes*; the pods 4-8 cm long, flat, hard, *not splitting open*.

b. *Burkea*

A small to large tree; the leaves *feathery*; the pinnae 4-7 pairs, the leaflets 10-20 pairs; the twigs, midribs and stalks *with rusty hairs*; the flowers *bright yellow*, conspicuous in axillary or terminal racemes; the pods about 5 x 1.3 cm, *narrowed both ends, flat, hairy, red-brown, winged slightly both margins*.

q. *Peltophorum*

a. *Erythrophleum* Afzel.

About 17 species native to Africa, the Seychelles Islands, Asia and Australia, belong to this genus. One species occurs in South Africa and one in South West Africa.

All the species are spineless trees with bipinnate leaves, the leaflets often large, and alternate; the flowers bisexual, individually small, in racemes in a panicle at the end of the branches, the calyx lobes and petals 5, the stamens 10; the pods often large, flat, woody, 2-valved; the seeds flattish.

Members of the genus are often poisonous, containing a powerful alkaloid, erythrophleine. They are widely used by African doctors in medicine and magic.

The name *Erythrophleum* is based on Greek words meaning "red bark". Trees of the genus are often called "redwater trees" because a red sap is exuded when the bark is cut and this colours water red.

(194)   *Erythrophleum africanum* (Welw.) Harms

= *Gleditschia africanum* Welw.

Ununza tree; ununza (Sub); umkonkotsi (Mbuk)

Erythrophleum africanum has not, as yet, been collected in South Africa but grows from northern South West Africa, Botswana, and

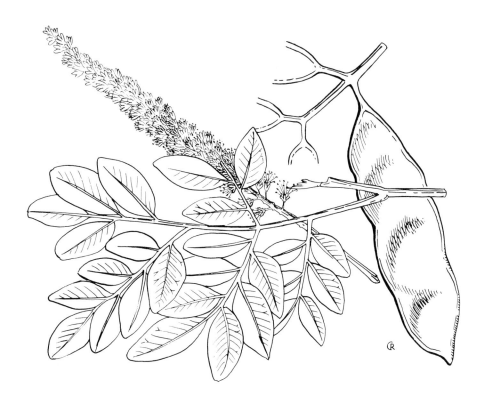

Above right
*Erythrophleum africa-
num* stem

Above left
*Erythrophleum africa-
num* in the Caprivi
Strip

Left
*Erythrophleum africa-
num:* the leaves, flowers
and pod (70%)

Portuguese East Africa, northwards to tropical Africa, usually in Kalahari sand.

It is a medium-sized to large tree up to 15 m high, with bark that is grey and smooth in young trees, with age becoming red-brown, rough, and fissured.

The leaves are alternate and twice divided (or bipinnate), with 3-4 pairs of pinnae and about 11-14 pairs of alternate, egg-shaped to oblong leaflets, 2.5 cm to nearly 5 cm long, with the under-surface hairy. These often have the tips notched, and the unequal-sided bases narrowed, with prominent veins on the lower surface. They are carried on very short stalks.

In autumn these turn a fine bright yellow.

The flowers are borne from September to October in short, dense, greenish-yellow racemes about 6.5 cm long, to which the anthers give a reddish tinge.

The pods are 8-20 cm long and up to 4 cm wide, oblong with a narrowed base, flat, hard, bursting open to show up to about 6 hard brown seeds which are said to be edible.

The timber is red-brown, heavy and hard, difficult to work but resistant to termites and borers. White says it makes beautiful furniture and is valuable for pit props. A glue is made from the roots, and the poles are used by Africans for building. It is burnt to make charcoal.

The tree yields an amber-coloured gum.

In some areas the bark, roots, and leaves are looked upon as poisonous. The leaves are known to be toxic to stock. Watt and Brankwijk say that the tree is still reported to be used in the Victoria Falls — Livingstone area in trials by ordeal.

(196)   *Erythrophleum lasianthum* Corb.

Ordeal tree, rooihout; umKhwangu, umKhangu, umBhemise (Z); umKhanku (Sw)

Until recently this species was confused in South Africa with *Erythrophleum suaveolens* (Guill. & Perr.) Brenan, a tropical species which, according to the recent study by Dr J.H. Ross, does not occur at all in the Republic.

Both of these trees, because of their poisonous properties, are unusual, but it is no longer clear which facts apply to which species. It is probable that the two have much in common.

Erythrophleum lasianthum, which is usually a smaller tree than *Erythrophleum suaveolens* — most often from 7-11 m high — grows in Natal, Zululand and Swaziland, in Portuguese East Africa, and northwards, usually in short open forest, on forest margins and on stream banks, most frequently on sandy soil.

It has a much-branched crown and large, alternate, bipinnate leaves, growing from a slight swelling on the branches. The leaves have about 2-3 pairs of opposite pinnae, up to about 15 cm long, each bearing about 5-6 pairs of oval or egg-shaped leaflets from 1.9 — 5 cm long, arranged alternately. They are smooth, glossy and leathery, sometimes with slightly undulating margins, with lopsided bases, with the midrib conspicuous below, and with the margins untoothed.

The leaf stalk is grooved.

The tiny, yellow-green flowers with orange anthers are borne in honey-

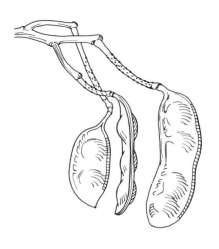

Left
Erythrophleum lasianthum in
north eastern Zululand (35%)

Above
Erythrophleum lasianthum
pods

Below
Flowering twig(50%)

834

scented racemes in terminal sprays about October. They give the tree its specific name meaning "with woolly flowers". A tree in full bloom is both handsome and deliciously perfumed.

The pods are large and robust, oblong, often slightly curved, with a round apex, narrowing to the base, up to about 13 cm long, enclosing about 5-7 dark, fat seeds.

The bark and seeds of this species – like those of *Erythrophleum suaveolens* – contain a powerful alkaloid, erythrophleine. This has a triple action. It is a poison reacting on the heart with much the same action as digitalis, a convulsive poison, and it has at the same time local anaesthetic properties. The two species have been used, wherever they occur in Africa, in trials by ordeal since time immemorial. Such an authority as Professor Watt states that it is impossible to estimate the number of people who have been disposed of by means of the bark of *Erythrophleum suaveolens* – and this probably applies equally to the South African species.

The Medicinal and Poisonous Plants of Southern and Eastern Africa devotes four pages to *Erythrophleum suaveolens*, largely to its use in trials by ordeal, when – generally speaking – an accused person is given a brew of bark, seeds, or leaves (which have a weaker action) to drink. If he vomits, his innocence is held to be proved. If he does not vomit, he dies from the brew! It is considered probable that a larger dose is required to produce vomiting than is necessary to cause death, the size of the dose depending on the wishes of the witchdoctor.

The bark is thought to be an ingredient of an arrow poison used in tropical Africa. It is also used as a fish poison, to kill rats, and to poison water where game drinks. The leaves are known to have killed stock. In South Africa sheep have died after eating the leaves of *Erythrophleum lasianthum*.

As with many poisons, this has its beneficences. It is widely used in Africa in medicines and magic, to heal as well as to kill. In Zululand the bark of *Erythrophleum lasianthum*, ground and sniffed, is used to cure headaches and colds and to drive off both hallucinations and spells. A little ground bark is mixed with water as an emetic, or as an enema – referred to as a Zulu injection. The bark is also used as a remedy for lung sickness in cattle. In other parts it has other medicinal uses, notably in the treatment of snake bite and as an anthelmintic. It is also used as a charm against magic influences, and to increase the potency of palm wine! The leaves are placed with grain to keep insects away.

Burtt Davy says that in Swaziland a dried bean ground into powder is given to a hunting dog before the chase, to make him vomit instantly and violently and clear his stomach, so that "it runs light and of strong wind".

Because of its potency, the bark has a great market value. It is interesting to note that snuff to relieve colds, made from the powdered bark, is sold in Durban itself.

The sapwood is light-coloured, the heartwood dark, hard, heavy, and said to be termite-proof.

b. *Burkea* Benth.

This small African genus of only 2 species was named after James Burke, 19th century botanist and collector.

The species are spineless trees or shrubs, the young twigs covered

Above
The wild seringa, *Burkea africana,*
in the Transvaal bushveld

Centre left
Burkea africana bark

Below left
Burkea africana in bud

Below right
Burkea africana: A young leaf,
flowers and pods (90%)

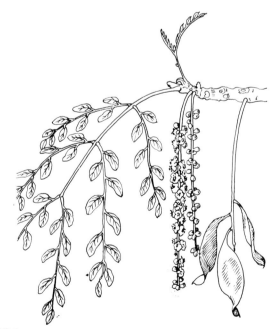

with rust-coloured hairs; the leaves twice-divided; the flowers bisexual, in spikes; the calyx lobes and petals 5, the stamens 10; the pods oblong, flat, woody to leathery; the seeds flattened.

(197)   *Burkea africana* Hook.

Wild seringa, Rhodesian ash, wildesering, kafferseringboom; mpulu (Tso); monato, mosheshe (Tsw); monatô (NS); mufhulu (V); mkalati (Kal); omuparara (Her)

The wild seringa is a tree with an extensive distribution for it grows from the bushveld and lowveld of Portuguese East Africa and the Transvaal, westwards through Botswana to northern South West Africa, and northwards to Ethiopia and Nigeria. It is common in the sandy areas of dry open bushveld at altitudes between 600 and 1370 m. This is one of the best-known trees on the hills around Pretoria.

It is often a small tree 4.5-8 m high — in Malawi it is reported up to 21 m — often flat-crowned, sometimes rounded, but always graceful. In northern Botswana it is described, surprisingly, as growing straight and slender like a Lombardy poplar.

The bark is dark, rough, fissured, and often flaking, and the twigs are robust, ending in a stubby tip, a character noticeable in winter when the tree is bare. The buds and the young growing tips of the branches are covered with thick, velvety, chestnut-red hairs and these are a bright contrast among the blue-green leaves.

The drooping leaves, up to 38 cm long, are clustered at the ends of the branches and are bipinnate or twice-branched, with about 2-4 pairs of pinnae, and the leaflets — about 5-11 — are arranged alternately. The end leaflet is not terminal, although it often appears to be so, but slightly to one side of the midrib. The leaflets are oval, usually about 2.5 cm long and 1.9 cm broad, silvery when young, becoming a darker greeny-blue with age. They are often marked with brown spots.

The tree blooms in October and November when the small, greeny-yellow buds in long pendulous tassels or strings at the ends of the branches open into tightly packed, pale yellow, starry flowers with a sweet scent. These are usually conspicuous and even when driving past the trees at speed, the long, thin, dangling strings are very noticeable in silhouette.

The pods are about 3-8 cm long and 1.9-2.5 cm wide, flat, brown, woody, holding usually only 1 seed. A tree often bears an enormous number of pods which sometimes remain on the tree even when the new leaves have appeared. The tree is reputed to fruit every other year only.

Elephants eat the branches and leaves, and monkeys the flowers and pods. The gum is said to be edible.

The wood varies in colour from whitish-yellow to pink, deep mahogany-red, and red-brown, sometimes with black and gold markings, and both sapwood and heartwood have a lovely lustre. It is hard and tough with a marked cross-grain which makes it difficult to plane. While the sapwood is subject to borers, the heartwood is borer-proof. The heartwood is used for fence posts and makes good parquet flooring and lovely furniture. Galpin considered it one of the most valuable timbers for furniture, wagon-wood, and for general purposes. Wagon-makers claim it makes "the best hubs in the world" because it does not shrink or split; and they once travelled from the Cape to the Transvaal

Above
Guibourtia coleosperma

Below left
Guibourtia coleosperma stem

Below right
Guibourtia conjugata leaves (60%)
and pod (100%)

838

to buy the wood. It also makes good firewood and charcoal.

In parts of Africa the pods and bark are used for tanning.

The authors of *The Medicinal and Poisonous Plants of Southern Africa* say that Africans use the pounded bark and fruit of the tree as a fish poison by simply throwing these into the streams.

The tree is used medicinally in many ways.

It is often infested by caterpillars, the larvae of the moth *Cirina forda,* which strip the leaves. Africans boil these, roast them lightly, or dry them in the sun, and store them, as they keep well for several months. Dr R. Story describes them as "slightly oily but crisp in texture, with the smell and flavour of kippers".

The widespread little violet blue butterfly known as the Common Blue, *Syntarucus telicanus,* lays its eggs on the flower buds of this species and of *Mundulea sericea.*

Wild seringas often grow together in numbers or in company with the vaalboom, *Terminalia sericea* Burch. ex DC.; the Transvaal boekenhout, *Faurea saligna* Harv.; the marula, *Sclerocarya caffra* Sond., and various kinds of combretums. Farmers find that veld where large numbers of wild seringas, vaalboom, and lekkerbreek trees (*Ochna pulchra* Hook.) grow together, is also often characterized by gifblaar, *Dichapetalum cymosum* Engl., the plant that has poisoned so many cattle.

This might prove a good garden tree when grown in sandy soil for it is graceful in shape and has beautiful red and copper autumn foliage. In heavy soil, it is usually slow-growing. The seed often proves difficult to germinate.

The tree has a superficial resemblance to the common seringa of gardens, *Melia azedarach* L., hence the name wild seringa. The specific name means "African".

c. *Guibourtia* J.J.Benn.

Guibourtia is principally a tropical African genus of about 7 species, with a few occurring in the West Indies and in South America. One species grows in the north-eastern Transvaal and 1 species in northern South West Africa, including the Caprivi Strip.

All are thornless, evergreen trees with leaves usually composed of a pair of leaflets, the leaflets opposite, lopsided, and usually with transparent gland dots. The flowers — with 4 to 5 calyx segments or lobes, without petals and with usually up to 12 stamens — are in loose sprays (panicles); the pods flat, often bursting open; the seeds large.

The genus was named after a learned French pharmacologist, N.J.B. Guibourt, 1790-1861, who wrote a history of drug plants.

(200)   *Guibourtia conjugata* (Bolle) J.Léon.

= *Gorskia conjugata* Bolle; = *Copaifera conjugata* (Bolle) Milne-Redhead

Tsotso tree; ntsotso (Tso)

This species was collected for the first time in South Africa fairly recently in hot, dry bush country near Punda Milia in the north-eastern Transvaal close to the borders of Portuguese East Africa and Rhodesia. It is well known in these territories where it is fairly widespread between the Limpopo and Zambezi Rivers, and to the north in Zambia. It grows on

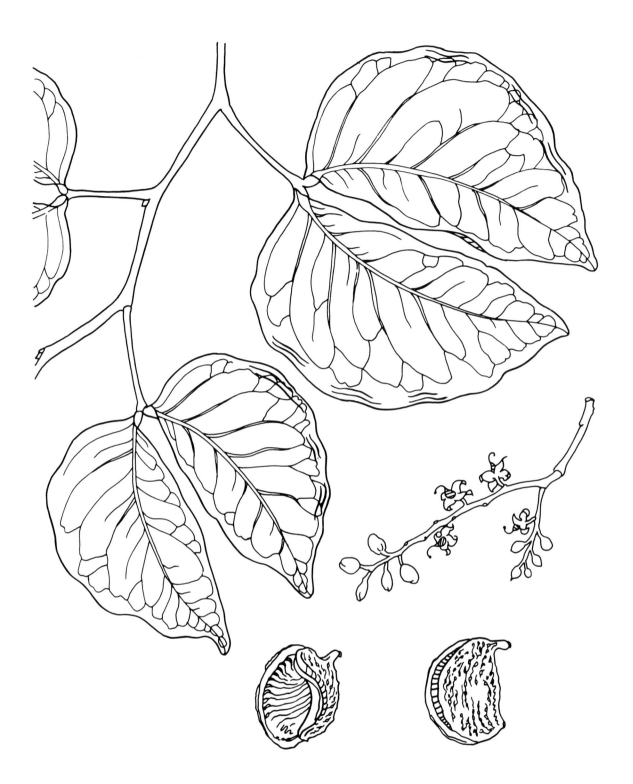

Guibourtia coleosperma: The leaves, a spray of buds and flowers, and fruits (100%)

sandy soils, in the Transvaal at the foot of quartzite ridges, often in groups together.

Usually it is a slender tree up to 9 m high, sometimes single and straight-stemmed, sometimes many-stemmed, with a smooth pinkish-grey to grey bark, often mottled, and with upward-growing branches.

Like its relative the mopane, the leaves consist of 2 leaflets resembling wings, on very short stalks, and they are shorter and wider in proportion than mopane leaves, sometimes egg-shaped with rounded, or occasionally bluntly pointed tips, the base irregularly shaped, and with distinctive veins looping along the margin. They grow up to 5 cm long and about 4 cm wide, and are smooth with minute transparent dots and slightly undulating margins.

The small white flowers are in loose bunches borne terminally or in the axils of the leaves about December. The pods, about 4 cm long and 2.5 cm broad, are oval or roundish, and taper to the stalk end. They are flat, leathery, much-veined, and 1-seeded, and burst open when ripe.

The leaves are browsed by kudu, nyala and eland, and the branches are eaten by elephants.

The wood is hard and heavy with light sapwood and almost black heartwood with a fine grain. It is difficult to work but is durable and termite-resistant, making good fence posts.

This species, mainly on account of its butterfly leaflets, is easily confused with the mopane. The leaflets, however, are a different shape and are shortly stalked, whereas the mopane leaflets have no stalks but are "hinged" together; they lack the tiny point between the leaflets that the mopane has, the pods are a different shape, and they burst open, whereas those of the mopane remain closed, and the trunk is smooth, contrasting with the much fissured, peeling trunk of the mopane.

The specific name *conjugata* is Latin meaning "joined", and refers to the paired leaflets.

(199)   *Guibourtia coleosperma* (Benth.) J.Léon.

= *Copaifera coleosperma* Benth.

Bastard mopane, bastard teak, Rhodesian mahogany; motsaodi (Tsw — Taw); nsibi (Sub); motsaodi, munzauri (Kol); oshi (Mbuk); ushivi (Samb)

Guibourtia coleosperma does not grow at all in South Africa but is a species of Botswana and northern South West Africa, Rhodesia, Zambia and Angola, where it is almost entirely confined to Kalahari sand formations, often occurring on sand dunes.

This is a fine, shady, in parts almost evergreen tree, up to 19 m high, with a large crown of many somewhat pendulous branches. The trunk is sometimes slightly buttressed. The bark is grey to red-brown or black in colour, smooth when young, becoming rougher with age.

The leaves are composed of 2 wing-like leaflets up to 10 cm long and 4 cm wide (but usually smaller), slightly curved, each with one main vein, smooth, glossy, covered with fine transparent dots, each leaflet on a very short stalk and not "hinged" together as are those of the mopane. The whole leaf is carried on a stalk about 1.9 cm long.

The tree is seldom leafless and sometimes almost evergreen. New leaves appear in the spring. From December to February loose sprays of small oval buds appear in the axils of the leaves or terminally, and these open into small white flowers. The pods, ripe from June to August, are small, shiny, roundish or the shape of a half-circle, dark, with the stalk to one side, and each contains one brown seed which is enveloped in a scarlet skin — an aril. When the fruit ripens the pod opens and these bright seeds protrude and remain hanging below the pods.

This is a tree much used by the indigenous peoples. The red arils enclosing the seeds are edible. They are oily and said to be nourishing, and are eaten raw, mixed in porridge, or made into a drink which is claimed to have saved lives in time of famine. The seeds themselves are roasted and ground, and are a staple food of both Bushmen and African tribes. The red dye from the aril is used to stain furniture red.

The seeds are much relished by birds.

Both the leaves and roots are used medicinally, the roots being applied to wounds and the leaves used for coughs.

The bark is used to cure skins.

The wood, sometimes known as Rhodesian mahogany, is hard and heavy, the heartwood handsome — reddish-pink, often with dark and light veins — of fairly fine testure, and durable. It is used for railway sleepers, building, joinery, furniture, parquet flooring, and for canoes. It is sweetly scented when newly cut.

The name *coleosperma* is based on Greek words meaning "sheathed seed", and refers to the aril-coated beans.

d. *Colophospermum* Kirk ex Benth.

The name of this tropical and subtropical genus of 1 species is based on Greek words meaning "oily seed" — Colophon in Ionia was celebrated for its rosin — and refers to the very pronounced turpentine-smelling oil contained in the seeds. Colophon was the birthplace of Homer so that in a most unlikely way the name links this African genus with some of the world's great heroic stories.

The single species is a spineless tree or shrub, the leaves alternate, with 2 opposite leaflets, the nerves arising from the base, without a midrib, with stipules; the flowers small, in racemes, arranged in panicles, the calyx segments 4-5, the petals absent, the stamens up to 25; the pods leathery, oval to half-moon-shaped; the seed single, wrinkled, with resinous dots.

(198)   *Colophospermum mopane* (Kirk ex Benth.) Kirk ex J.Léon.

= *Copaifera mopane* Kirk ex Benth.

Mopane, butterfly tree, turpentine tree, Rhodesian ironwood, Rhodesian mahogany, ironwood; nxanatsi (Tso); mophane (Tsw); mupani, mutanari (V); omutati (Her); omufiadi (Ov)

The mopane is the dominant tree of large parts of northern South and and South West Africa where great stretches of hot, arid country — from about 300 — 600 m above sea level — are covered with it, often to the exclusion of any other trees. It is a common species beyond the borders of South Africa, in Portuguese East Africa, Botswana, Angola, Rhodesia, and Zambia.

In South Africa it occurs mainly in the hot dry country north of the Soutpansberg, and in the eastern Transvaal north of the Letaba River, its southernmost limit in the Kruger National Park appearing to be some

842

65 km south of the Olifants River. It is noteworthy that while in South Africa it is often shrub-like — and then mopane country is usually sandy, hot, shadeless and of intense monotony — it tends to grow higher to the north and west. Visitors to the Etosha Game Reserve in South West Africa will remember the wonderful mopane woodland, the tall graceful trees turning bright autumn colours in June and July.

The reason for the different growth forms is not clear. Botanists suggest that they are probably governed by temperature and by type of soil. What is clear is that the tree is adapted to a wide variety of soils, and that it is extending its area of domination.

The mopane — when a tree — is usually slender with one or more stems from the base, and a few upward-growing branches, sparse but graceful. The trunk in large specimens has a diameter of up to 1 m but is usually less; the bark is grey or brown, very rough, deeply fissured and flaking, and so conspicuous that it helps to identify the tree even when it is leafless.

When in leaf the mopane is not readily confused with any other tree. The butterfly leaves are made up of 2 stiff, separate leaflets "hinged" together at the base. They are roughly a narrow triangle in shape, with 7-12 nerves radiating from the base, up to about 8 cm long, yellowish-green, shiny, gland-dotted, and smelling strongly of turpentine. Between the leaflets is a small point, a much reduced terminal leaflet. In hot dry weather, or at midday, the leaflets fold up together so that the only shade they throw is the shadow of their thin edges. The traveller passing at midday through the "large monotonous shadeless forests" of mopane may search in vain for a patch of deep shade in which to rest.

The flowers are small, pale green, and borne in slender drooping sprays. The pod is flat and kidney-shaped, up to 5 cm long and 2.5 cm broad, enclosing a single seed which is kidney-shaped, much-wrinkled, yellowish, and covered with small red dots — sticky resinous oil glands. The pods do not burst open.

As a fodder tree the mopane plays a vitally important role in the areas of low rainfall. Cattle, elephant, giraffe, buffalo, and antelope browse the foliage eagerly and sometimes eat the dry leaves and seeds on the ground. Farmers in mopane veld look upon the tree as providing valuable fodder, even in winter when the leaves are dry. Analyses have shown that the portions of the mopane eaten by stock have an average monthly crude protein content of 12.6 per cent, which is high. The leaves and seeds smell strongly of turpentine. It is an interesting fact that although the breath of animals feeding on green mopane leaves, and even the kraals in which they live, smell strongly of onions, the meat and milk of these animals is in no way tainted.

The mopane is a favourite food of the elephant, and in the Kruger National Park numbers of elephants are seen in the mopane country. Visitors are frequently nonplussed at the way the vast animals merge into the low mopane scrub so that even a few feet away they are often completely camouflaged.

Hole-nesting birds, too, are common in such country for the trees offer them good nesting sites.

Large, dark, spotted caterpillars, the larvae of the moth *Gonimbrasia belina* — 5 to 8 cm long and fat as a finger — feed upon the mopane leaves and are used by Africans and Bushmen as food. They dry and store them for months, or roast them and eat them with their food. Mopane worms are much valued by rural Africans and are often their richest source of protein. The current price for them is about R12.50 per 70 lb bag (roughly 32 kg).

Colophospermum mopane leaves and pods (50%

844

Mopane bark

Brachystegia boehmii trunk

OPPOSITE

Above
Tall shapely mopane trees, *Colophospermum mopane*

Below
Prince of Wales feather trees, *Brachystegia boehmii*

The sapwood of the mopane is yellow but the heartwood is dark red, sometimes "with a purple sheen", fine-textured, very hard, durable, and termite-resistant. It is one of the heaviest of indigenous woods, according to C.P. Kromhout, weighing 76 lbs (34.5 kg) per cubic foot air dry. He says that trees as a rule have poor form, contain large knots, and are often spoilt by heart rot.

Because of its hardness, mopane wood is difficult to work. Only occasionally is furniture made from it, but it is used for mining props, poles for house-building, disselbooms, felloes, and parquet flooring, and it makes excellent durable fence posts. In Rhodesia it is used for making toys. The bark is, in parts, used to make twine.

It is reputed to make splendid wooden legs. A Botswana official in Singapore recently injured his leg but postponed the necessary amputation until his return to his native country when he could get a leg of mopane wood!

It is an excellent firewood and yields a good charcoal. The ash from dry timber contains 15.5 per cent of lime.

Mopane burns even when green, and in mopane country there is therefore a danger of fire throughout the year. Africans believe it is more frequently struck by lightning than any other tree. Livingstone remarked that Africans cautioned travellers never to linger near a mopane when a thunderstorm was brewing. "Lightning hates it", they would say.

In parts of South West Africa the tree is sacred, signifying life and strength. This is one of the plants strewed before the entrance to a new kraal, and over these the people must walk.

In the Transvaal an extract of the wood is used medicinally. In South West Africa the gum which exudes from heated wood is believed to heal the most stubborn wounds.

Mopane seed germinates well but young plants damp off easily. The trees are sensitive to frost.

The distribution of the mopane sometimes overlaps that of its relatives, *Guibourtia conjugata* and *Guibourtia coleosperma*, and then the species may possibly be confused. The mopane, however, has a rough fissured trunk in contrast to the smoother trunks of the guibourtias; its leaflets have no stalks at all but are "hinged" together, and between them is a small point – about 3 mm long – which the leaves of the guibourtias lack. The mopane pods do not split open; those of the two guibourtias do; the mopane seeds are covered with red resinous dots – those of the guibourtias are not. Botanists note that the mopane flowers have 20-25 stamens, all of an equal length, while the guibourtias have a maximum of 12 stamens, of which some are long and some short.

The specific name *mopane* is derived from a Bantu common name for the tree.

e. *Brachystegia* Benth.

This large and often dominant genus of about 70 species is confined to tropical Africa, where it occurs abundantly in dry savannah forest on the great plateau from Angola in the west to Mozambique in the east, and from Rhodesia northwards to Malawi and Kenya. Up to date no species have been collected in South Africa, although they may occur in the belt of deep Kalahari sand in the northern Transvaal, the vegetation of which remains relatively unexplored. The genus is reported from the Caprivi Strip, although the species are not known and two species, the msasa — *Brachystegia spiciformis* Benth. — and *Brachystegia boehmii* Taub., have been collected in Botswana.

Over a very large area of Africa this is the most abundant and important genus of all, playing an important part in the economic life of Africans wherever it occurs. The ash is used as fertilizer in shifting cultivation. The bark of many species is made into cloth, rope, sacks, fishing and game nets, baskets, and mats, and is used for roofing, and the timber is used in building, for poles, and as fuel and charcoal.

All the species are without thorns. They have alternate, once-compound leaves, with from 2-60 pairs of leaflets. These are paripinnate, that is, terminated by *a pair* of leaflets. Stipules are present, and these may be deciduous or persistent. The rather small flowers are borne in panicles or racemes at the ends of the branches. In bud they are often enclosed in 2 bracteoles. The calyx may have 5 small sepals, sometimes reduced to 1, or none at all. The petals are absent or present only in the form of small scales, and the stamens are joined at the base only, or in a fairly long tube. The fruit is a hard, woody, oblong pod, with a flattish tip, which explodes when ripe, the valves twisting into a spiral, and the seeds being thrown out with considerable force. They are roundish, flat and hard.

Brachystegia species generally are slender and graceful with a clean bole and a crown of handsome delicate leaves. Many species have a remarkable characteristic — new spring foliage that is pink, red, scarlet, purple and copper, traditional autumn colours — mixed with fawn and green, and these fill the savannah forest with brilliance. They are one of the great spring sights of central Africa.

The generic name is based on Greek words meaning "short" or "flattened", and "roof" or "cover", but the allusion is not clear.

Brachystegia boehmii Taub.

Prince of Wales' feathers tree; umvombo (Wankie)

Brachystegia boehmii is one of the most widely distributed members of the genus, growing from Malawi southwards to Rhodesia, often on hill slopes or in shallow gravelly soil. It occurs in Botswana.

It is usually a fairly small, flat-topped tree, 6-9 m high, with a trunk 30-60 cm in diameter, rough grey or brownish bark, and rather few, upright branches. It is more or less hairy. The compound leaves, on short, robust stalks, grow up to about 22 cm long and are composed of 13-24 pairs of narrow almost stalkless leaflets that are crowded together, often overlapping, and giving the leaf a feather-like appearance. They are 3-6 cm long and often less than 1.3 cm wide, a slender oblong, with rounded tips and a lopsided base, in spring yellow, pink, and salmon, becoming green as they age. The stipules are long — up to 5 cm in length — much flattened at the base, appearing collar-like, sheathing the stem, and falling early.

The flowers are borne from September to December in a compact inflorescence — a raceme — at the end of the branches.

The fruits are woody, pinky-brown pods with a dull, scurfy surface, up to 16 cm long and 4.5 cm wide, oblong or widest at the tip, slightly

Brachystegia spiciformis: A fruiting twig and flowers (60%)

beaked, and splitting spirally. They are borne well above the leaves. The seeds, ejected with force, are roundish, hard and shiny.

The bark is used for tanning and is said to yield the best of all bark-cloth and rope. The wood is subject to decay and borer-attack when not treated. It is used for making small articles, and for fuel.

The specific name honours Richard Böhm, 1854-1884, a German botanical collector in East Africa from 1881-1882.

Brachystegia spiciformis Benth.

= *Brachystegia randii* Bak.f.

Msasa

The msasa is one of the few trees, growing beyond the borders of the Republic, that is well-known to South Africans.

It is the dominant tree in most of the savannah forest of Rhodesia, reaching northwards to Zambia and Malawi, and is famous for the gorgeous pink, wine red, copper and bronze colours of its spring foliage. It has been reported from Botswana, and possibly grows in the Caprivi Strip.

It is a medium-sized to large tree, 9-18 m high — occasionally up to 28 m — with a trunk up to 1 m in diameter, bark that is smooth and light coloured when young, becoming rough and darker with age, and with spreading branches and a round or flat crown of delicate foliage.

The leaves are 5-20 cm long, each bearing 3-6 — usually 4 — pairs of

Above
The msasa, *Brachystegia spiciformis,* one of the great trees of Central Africa

Left
Msasa bark

Below
To the right of this old Karoo boerboon on the farm "Cranemere" lay an ancient Stone Age grinding stone

opposite or nearly opposite leaflets, the terminal pair the largest (2.5-9 cm long) and the bottom the smallest. These are oblong to egg-shaped, the tips pointed, blunt or round, the base narrowed or round, and lop-sided, the margins untoothed, shiny above and below smooth or slightly hairy, the common midrib hairy; the short leaflet stalks hairy with a swelling at the base.

The flowers, with bracteoles, are small, inconspicuous, sweet-scented, and popular with bees. They are borne in dense and often stubby heads — racemes — at the ends of the branches in spring. White says that after flowering the axis is closely scarred spirally and resembles a rat's tail.

The fruits are yellow or red-brown woody pods up to 13 cm in length, the base narrow, broadening towards the apex, the tips strongly beaked. The explode with a sharp crack, the valves twisting and the round, flat, brown seeds scattering far and wide. The pods are usually hidden in the foliage.

The gum is deep red.

The bark contains tannin and is used to tan leather, and to make rope, cloth, sacks, corn-bins and beehives. The wood, brown and rather coarse, is subject to termite attack, but when treated is used for a variety of purposes. Keith Coates Palgrave says it is not a satisfactory wood for it seasons slowly and tends to twist, split and warp. It makes good fuel and charcoal.

Over 20 species of butterflies breed on this species.

The msasa is a wonderfully decorative tree, but grows slowly and is tender to frost.

In Rhodesia this is easily confused with *Julbernardia globiflora* (Benth.) Troupin, formerly known as *Isoberlinia globiflora* (Benth.) Hutch & Greenway, a tree that is widespread in Rhodesia and which enters the Caprivi Strip. It has 5-7 pairs of leaflets which are oval and hairy with the terminal pair the smallest — in the msasa they are the largest — and with the pods carried *above* the leaves.

The specific name *spiciformis* means "spike-like" and refers to the shape of the inflorescence.

f. *Schotia* Jacq.

Schotia, a Southern African genus, has in the past offered many difficult-ies to botanists for wherever the members occur — in Portuguese East Africa, Rhodesia, and South and South West Africa — they are variable and hybridize easily, causing confusion. The genus has now been re-vised by Dr L.E. Codd and the position clarified — the 15 specific names published in the past are reduced to 4, and the existence of several hybrid forms recognized.

The genus is widely scattered in South and South West Africa, and wherever trees of the genus grow they are most commonly known as boerboons. This is said to be due to the fact that the seeds are edible, and were used not only by Hottentots and Africans but by the early farmers, or it may be because the seeds resemble the domestic broad beans. A suggestion that the name is a corruption of "bourbon" — in reference to the colour of the flowers — and was so called for the first time by the 1820 Settlers has no foundation. The name boerboon had then been in use for over 50 years.

The trees have no great economic value. The wood was often in the past used for furniture, and sometimes still is. The leaves of one species, *Schotia afra* (L.) Thunb., are valuable fodder. The seeds today have only a limited value as food.

While the trees may be of small importance to modern man, they are of the greatest value to the bird life of the countryside where they grow, their crimson cups of flowers, brimming with nectar, attracting insects by the million, and both nectar- and insect-eating birds.

In their early flowering period when such species as *Schotia afra* (L.) Thunb. and *Schotia brachypetala* Sond. literally weep nectar at the touch of a branch, they are alive with birds. C.J. Skead in his *Sunbirds of Southern Africa* says that so noisy can such a tree become with its sunbird inmates, that the position of the tree can be pinpointed in the bush even before it is seen. Even in city gardens a tree in bloom is visited by the occasional sunbird and many other species, including nearly always a number of little white-eyes attracted not only by the nectar, but by the aphids that attack trees in young leaf or in bloom.

Trees of all species tend to have irregular flowering times, so that while one tree is in bloom, another of the same species, a few feet away from it, may be without a flower. According to Skead, this irregularity is of great value to nectar-eating birds, ensuring a long and well-spaced supply of nectar through the year.

Did primitive man once value the boerboon nectar as do the sunbirds of today? It is a fascinating fact that in parts of the Karoo, Late Stone Age implements for cutting, scraping, digging, and especially for grinding, are often — too often for coincidence — found strewn on the ground close to an ancient boerboon. For some reason, if not for nectar then for its beans (which the Hottentots were known to grind), for its shade, or for the food value of the many birds around its flowering crown, it was once a focal point of life in an arid countryside.

One of the numerous insects associated with trees of this genus is the brightly coloured butterfly, the Apricot Playboy, *Deudorix dinochares dinochares,* the larvae of which live within the pods, feeding on the seeds.

The boerboons are as a rule characterized by bunches of cup-shaped flowers, held upwards so that their nectar is unspilt. These are usually a rich red and handsome, but in some species in which they are borne on the old wood they are hidden by new growth. When they bloom before, or with the very young leaves, the trees have a brilliance and richness not easily matched by any other species. A boerboon, covered with red blossom and green Malachite Sunbirds, is one of the most beautiful sights the Karoo has to offer.

Boerboons are wonderful in the bush and veld, or in a garden, and although usually slow-growing they are reasonably fast where winters are mild and ordinary garden conditions are suitable.

The species have compound leaves, once divided, and terminated not by one leaflet but by a pair; the calyx with 4 segments, the petals usually 5, the stamens 10; the pods large, smooth, woody, the seeds roundish and flat, often with a conspicuous fleshy aril.

The genus was named in honour of Richard van der Schot, a travelling companion and friend of Jacquin.

(201)   *Schotia afra* (L.) Thunb.

1. var *afra*

= *Schotia speciosa* Jacq.; = *Schotia tamarindifolia* Afz. ex Sims

(201.1)   2. var. *angustifolia* (E.Mey.) Harv.

= *Schotia parvifolia* Jacq.; = *Schotia angustifolia* E.Mey.; = *Schotia venusta* Mason

Karoo boerboon; umGxam, umQaqoba, umQonci (X); umGxamu (Z)

Schotia afra, the "African schotia" — the species on which the genus was founded — has a wide distribution from the eastern Cape, where it grows in abundance in the scrub of the catchment of the Fish and Sundays Rivers, in the Little Karoo, in Namaqualand, and in southern South West Africa. The variety *afra* tends to grow in the coastal districts, while var. *angustifolia* grows further west and more inland. It is the form found in Namaqualand and South West Africa.

It is a shrub or small many-branched dense tree up to 6 m high, more shrub-like in habit than the other species of boerboon, and often with several stout, thick, sometimes twisted stems. Along the coast, within range of the salt sea winds, it may grow as a spreading bush some 1 m high and 1.5 m across, making — in bloom — a mound of brilliant colour.

The foliage is usually a dark green, and among it the smooth grey twigs are conspicuous. The leaves are paripinnate, or once divided and terminated by a pair of leaflets, and they tend to fold up along the midrib, which is sometimes slightly winged. They have stipules at their base.

The two varieties are separated largely on the leaflets, those of var. *afra* having 6-18 pairs, varying from a slender shape to egg-shaped and usually about 13 mm long, but sometimes from 6-25 mm. The inland variety *angustifolia* — meaning "narrow-leaved" — usually has more leaflets, 12-18 pairs, and these are smaller and narrower, roughly 6-12 mm long and often only just over 1 mm wide.

It is noteworthy that var. *angustifolia* growing in Bushmanland and Namaqualand has whiter twigs and an indefinably different look from the same form growing in the Karoo.

Both varieties have bright red, or very occasionally pink, flowers borne in bunches on short woody side twigs or sometimes terminally, and these have 5 petals.

The pods are 5-13 cm long and up to 4 cm broad, hard and woody, containing several roundish tan-coloured seeds without an aril or with a very small one. They have been eaten by men since early times. Wikar, in the 1770's, noted that near the Augrabies Falls the Hottentots cooked them so that the outer astringent skin peeled off; roasted them under the coals, and pounded them into meal, or ate them while still green. Stone Age Man ate them before the Hottentots — in the Late Stone Age middens in the Gamtoos Valley the litter holds many empty boerboon pods, the seeds of which archaeologists believe were eaten.

A tree covered with young pods is almost as striking a sight as a tree in blossom for the pods are all shades of green, rust and pink, or a combination of them all.

The bark is astringent and was once used medicinally and in tanning. The red-brown wood is hard, tough, and durable, and is used for yokes, felloes, and for fuel.

The foliage is browsed by stock. Thunberg thought that it was poisonous, but he was wrong.

As with other species of boerboon, this is of more value to birds than to men, for its flowers are a source of nectar in what are often hot arid parts of the country where little else blooms lavishly. Skead says that at its best each flower holds 0.5 cc of sweet clear nectar, the peak of the flow weakening fairly rapidly as the peak pollinating period ends.

This is of great value as a shade tree, casting, unlike the acacias, a dense cool shade. It is irregularly deciduous.

The Karoo boerboon is occasionally cultivated and germinates well, if erratically, and transplants easily. It is generally reputed to be tender to frost, but this is by no means always true for it flourishes in the bitter winters of the Karoo. It is drought-resistant and usually slow-growing.

This species is known to hybridize with *Schotia latifolia* in the country between Port Elizabeth and East London, where both species occur, the hybrids having some of the characters of both species.

(203)   *Schotia capitata* Bolle

= *Schotia transvaalensis* Rolfe

Dwarf boerboon, Transvaal boerboon; umGxamu, uVovovwana (Z)

The dwarf boerboon of Natal, Zululand, the eastern Transvaal, Portuguese East Africa and Swaziland, is a shrub, or slender tree up to about 6 m high with several slender, upward-growing branches, single or sometimes several-stemmed, often growing among, and partially supported by low trees in the tangled thorny scrub it favours.

The bark is grey. The leaves are once compound, up to about 8 cm long, with a common midrib that is slightly winged, along which they fold slightly. There are usually 3-5 pairs of leaflets which are opposite, roundish or egg-shaped, usually 1.3-2.5 cm long, with a sharply pointed tip, and without stalks. They are eaten by Burchell's zebra.

The bright scarlet, cup-shaped flowers are in dense round bunches borne terminally or on short side branches, usually in the summer. The sepals, like the petals, are deep red. The flowers hold copious nectar which is often drunk by Africans. The pods are large and woody, the edges outlined with a broad rim, containing several pale brown seeds with a large yellow aril.

The wood is said to be like that of walnut and to make good furniture.

This species is easily confused with youthful specimens of *Schotia brachypetala*. The latter, however, is a taller and more robust tree, usually with a single dark trunk up to 46 cm in diameter, and a round crown, and often with larger leaves. The flowers of the dwarf boerboon have petals; those of *Schotia brachypetala* usually have none.

The name *capitata* means "growing in a head" and refers to the flowers.

OPPOSITE

Above
A Karoo boerboon, *Schotia afra,* near Ann's Villa, Eastern Province

Below left
The stem of an old Karoo boerboon

Below right
Schotia afra A. var. *angustifolia:* Leaves and flowers B. var. *afra:* showing the larger leaflets (50%)

Top left
The forest boerboon, *Schotia latifolia,* at the foot of t
Suurberg, Eastern Province

Above right
The weeping boerboon, *Schotia brachypetala,* in the n
ern Transvaal

Centre left
Schotia brachypetala: leaves, flower and pod (50%)

Below left
Schotia latifolia: a flowering twig (50%)

Below right
A spreading *Schotia brachypetala* growing in the dry
veld between the Soutpansberg and Messina

854

The bark of a young
Schotia brachypetala

The bark of an old tree

(204)   *Schotia latifolia* Jacq.

= *Schotia diversifolia* Walp.; = *Schotia cuneifolia* Gand.

Forest boerboon, bosboerboon; umGxam, umXamo (X); umGxamu (Z)

The forest boerboon occurs mainly on the margins of forests or in dry scrub in the Eastern Province. It does not appear to grow very far north of the Kei River, further inland than Stutterheim, or west of George, although more research is needed to determine its exact distribution.

In the dry bush of Sekukuniland in the Transvaal a shrubby, pink-flowered boerboon is found. Surprisingly, this seems botanically the same as *Schotia latifolia*, although both habit and habitat are different.

When it grows in scrub this is usually a medium-sized, round-topped tree, but in forest — as in those on the lower slopes of the Suurberg — it makes a tall graceful tree up to 12 or 15 m high.

The bark is fairly smooth, and grey to reddish-brown. The leaves are up to about 10 cm long and 8 cm broad, smooth or hairy, borne on stalks up to nearly 2.5 cm long. In the young leaves the midrib is some-times slightly winged. There are 3-5 pairs of large oblong to egg-shaped leaflets up to nearly 6.5 cm long and 4 cm broad (the upper leaflets the largest) with rounded or pointed tips, and a narrowed or rounded, lop-sided base.

Unlike those of most boerboons the flowers are pale pink or flesh-coloured, usually with 5 petals, and a reddish-brown calyx, and are borne in rather open bunches at the ends of the branches.

The mature pods are up to 15 cm long, woody, hard, roundish or oblong, and hold several light brown seeds with a yellow aril.

The ripe pods sometimes burst open, leaving hanging on the tree only the thin hard rims of the pods to which the seeds are attached by the fleshy arils. These arils are rich and fatty and act as a bait to birds which find them more attractive than the beans. The Hottentots used to roast the green pods and eat the seeds within, a practice learned later by Europeans and Bantu. Monkeys open the pods — which are astrin-gent and which they spit out — and eat the seeds.

This species, although it has not as plentiful a supply of nectar as *Schotia afra*, is popular with birds, and insects such as beetles, flies, wasps and ants.

The foliage is browsed by animals.

The timber is white, tough, and heavy, and makes good fence posts, but is little used. A greenish dye is sometimes made from the bark. This was once also used as a tanning material.

When it is without flowers *Schotia latifolia* is easily confused with *Schotia brachypetala* which grows to the north and north west. In bloom they are easily separated for the flowers of *Schotia brachypetala* are deep red and usually have no petals.

Its distribution overlaps that of *Schotia afra*, and where this happens hybrids between the two species are known.

The name *latifolia* means "broad-leaved".

(202)   *Schotia brachypetala* Sond.

= *Schotia rogersii* Burtt Davy; = *Schotia semireducta* Merxm.

Weeping boerboon, huilboerboon, tree fuchsia, African walnut; uVovovo, umGxamu (Z); uVovovo (Sw); n'wavilombe (Tso); molope (NS); muṋunzwa (V)

The weeping boerboon is a fine tree of dry savannah and scrub forest from Rhodesia and Portuguese East Africa southwards through the Transvaal, Natal and Swaziland. It is recorded as far south as Umtata. Whether its distribution in the south overlaps that of the forest boer-- boon, *Schotia latifolia*, is still not clear. Where their areas of distribution are near one another the two species are often confused when they are not in flower.

This is one of the most beautiful of the boerboons, a wide-spreading, leafy tree up to 15 m high with a trunk up to 0.6 m in diameter and bark that in young trees is fairly smooth and reddish-brown, often lined or lightly seamed crosswise, and in older trees is rough and darker.

The leaves are smooth or hairy, up to 17 cm long and 8 cm wide, and have stipules at the base. They are composed of 4-7 pairs of oblong or egg-shaped leaflets (there is no single terminal leaflet) with lopsided bases. As in *Schotia latifolia*, which has similar leaves, the upper leaflets are the largest.

In warm frost-free areas, as in the extreme northern Transvaal, the tree is almost evergreen; in colder parts it loses its leaves for a short while, usually just before or during flowering time. The young spring foliage is of great beauty, all shades of rose and ruby red, turning gradually to copper and fresh light green. For a brief period it is probably unexcelled as a foliage tree.

It usually blooms in spring, with the rich crimson, cup-like flowers in clusters. Each flower faces upwards and is filled with abundant nectar, attracting children of all races, baboons, monkeys, a host of birds, and bees and other insects.

These flowers are unique among the boerboons, for the petals are partly or completely reduced to linear filaments and inconspicuous and the beauty lies in the showy sepals and stamens. The flowers are usually borne on the old wood.

The big brown pods are up to 12 cm long and 5 cm broad and contain 6 or more light brown seeds with a conspicuous lime green aril covering one end. Like the pods of *Schotia latifolia*, they often burst open leaving only the rims hanging on the twig, and to these the seeds are attached at the aril end.

The seeds are edible after roasting. It is said the Voortrekkers in Natal used them as food.

In Zululand a decoction of the bark is taken for heartburn and as a hangover cure. Zulus also use the water in which bark and roots have been soaked as a medicine to strengthen the body and purify the blood.

The foliage is eaten by baboons, presumably when young, by giraffe, kudu, impala, and Black Rhino which also eat the bark. Vervet Monkeys eat the buds and Burchell's and Cape Glossy Starlings eat the whole flower.

The wood contains tannin and the wood dust is said to irritate the eyes. The sapwood is pink when newly sawn, changing to yellow-brown. It is not durable unless treated. The heartwood is dark brown to black with a pronounced green tinge, hard, fairly heavy, termite resistant, and with a dense fine texture. It makes handsome furniture and flooring blocks.

This is a particularly shapely and beautiful tree for a garden, germinating and transplanting well. On heavy soils it is very slow-growing indeed, but in deep sandy soil, protected from frost and cold wind, it can be surprisingly fast. A magnificent tree planted in a Messina garden from a truncheon grew up to 12 m in 17 years with a spread of well over 12 m. It can, after the early stages, stand at least 6 degrees of frost, but needs protection in a very cold garden.

Schotia brachypetala is one of the rain trees of the Transvaal, Natal, and Zululand, for on occasions its branches appear to rain water. This is caused by a small insect — a species of froghopper or spittle bug — which sucks up the sap and ejects it as a froth that collects and drips down the branches like water. This, or the nectar-filled flowers that overflow and "weep" may be the origin of the common name, the weeping boerboon. The specific name *brachypetala* means "short petals" and refers to the petals which are characteristically reduced.

g. *Umtiza* Sim

Umtiza, a genus of 1 species only, occurring in parts of the eastern Cape, is the only South African genus of trees to bear a Bantu name. Locally the tree is known to Africans as "umThiza".

It is a small, spiny, evergreen tree, the leaves paripinnate, without stipules; the flowers in panicles at the ends of the twigs on the top branches, the calyx lobes and petals 5, the stamens 10; the pods long, narrow, flat, bursting open; the seeds oval and flattish.

(205)   *Umtiza listerana* Sim

This small, spiny, evergreen tree, somewhat resembling *Schotia afra* when not in flower, is of particular interest; it is the only species in the genus and its distribution is extraordinary for it grows — and abundantly — only in forested kloofs near East London, and in a few other isolated spots in the eastern Cape, as in the Kentani district, and as far as is known nowhere else at all. It seeds profusely yet does not appear to increase its area of distribution.

When standing on its own it is usually a bushy shrub, but in deep forested kloofs it is slender and upright, up to about 8 m high, spiny, many-branched, and with a trunk, or trunks, which are much buttressed, in particular towards the base, the buttresses very twisted and jumbled. The bark is dark, rusty brown, rough and fissured.

The branchlets are often modified into spines, 2.5-10 cm long, straight, sturdy, tough, and sharp, and these sometimes bear leaves on them. They are reminiscent of the spines of *Maytenus heterophylla* (Eckl. & Zeyh.) N. Robson.

The leaves are alternate and compound, bearing 7-12 pairs of small oblong to oval leaflets, about 1.3 cm long, bluntly pointed, smooth, glossy, and without stalks. They resemble those of *Schotia afra*.

The flowers are small, white to yellow-green, star-shaped, and massed abundantly at the ends of the twigs on the top branches. In the blooming seasons — and they often bloom twice, in late summer and early winter — the forest canopy is creamy-white. The trees can then be easily identified and are well known to motorists through Buffalo Pass near East London.

The pods are long, narrow, flat, and pointed, usually ripening in autumn.

Above
Umtiza listerana near East London

Below left
Umtiza stem

Below right
Umtiza listerana: A section of a trunk (40%)

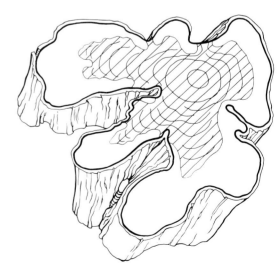

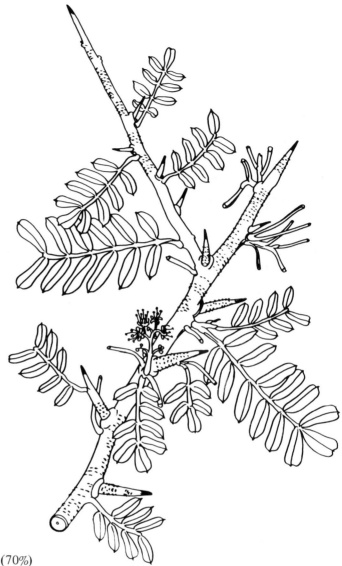

Umtiza listerana: A flowering twig (70%)

The sapwood is a pale yellow, the heartwood small, red to purple-black, fine-grained, very hard, heavy, and oily. It was once used to house propellor shafts in small boats because its oiliness provided a constant lubrication.

The tree is much respected among Africans who regard it as sacred and hang a piece of the bark in their huts to guard against both evil spirits and lightning. Such bark is collected on special expeditions. In times of trouble, Xhosas make pilgrimages to a particular tree near East London.

Witchdoctors use sticks of the tree as healing wands.

Efforts are being made to protect this tree. According to Mr C.J. Skead, biologist at the King William's Town Museum, "the future of the umtiza trees is in the lap of — not the gods — but of East Londoners". It is one of the very rare trees of the world and worthy of a future.

The generic name *Umtiza* is Xhosa. The specific name honours a former Conservator of Forests in the Cape, Joseph Storr Lister.

Above left
A Rhodesian teak tree, *Baikiaea plurijuga*

Above right
A Rhodesian teak tree, 20 m high

Below left
Baikiaea plurijuga: A leaf, fruits and seed (50%)

Below right
Rhodesian teak bark

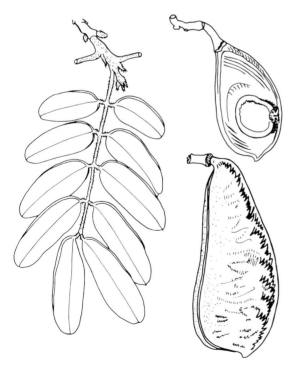

860

h. *Baikiaea* Benth.

Baikiaea is a purely African genus with about 6 members, one of which enters South West Africa and Botswana. It was named in honour of William Balfour Baikie, commander of the Niger Expedition in 1858.

All the species are unarmed trees, the leaves paripinnate, the flowers large and often handsome, in racemes or panicles, in the axils of the leaves or terminally; the calyx lobes 4, the petals 5, the stamens 10; the pods often pear-shaped with a little stalk (or stipe) between them and the calyx, woody, velvety, brown; the seeds large and flat.

(206) *Baikiaea plurijuga* Harms

Rhodesian teak, Rhodesian chestnut, Zambezi redwood; mokusi (Tsw); ukusi (Mbuk)

The Rhodesian teak is a fine, semi-evergreen, thornless tree, entirely confined to areas of Kalahari sand — where it is the main timber tree — in Botswana, north and north east South West Africa, Rhodesia and Zambia. It is a common tree in the Caprivi Strip, growing in woodland.

It is tall and well-shaped, 8-18 m high, with a spreading, much-branched crown, and a trunk up to 0.6-1 m in diameter. The bark varies from smoothish and cream-coloured or grey-blue in young trees to a rough grey or dark brown in older ones.

The leaves are once compound, up to about 10 cm long, and bear 4-5 pairs of rather thick leaflets, oblong to oval, and up to 7 cm long. The under-surface is slightly velvety with the rusty midrib conspicuous. The twigs and leaf stalks are velvety-brown.

The plump, oval, velvety buds are borne in sprays which can grow over 30 cm long and which are held upright. They open into large flowers, attractive to bees, with 5 crisped petals, white, mauvy-pink, or purple-red, the dark brown velvety calyx contrasting handsomely. They bloom over a long period in summer from about January to March.

The red-brown velvety pods, ripening June-July, are flat, woody, beaked, up to about 13 x 5 cm, and often pear-shaped. After they open, the valves twist spirally. They contain large, flat, often roundish seeds.

The wood is considered the most valuable product of the Kalahari sands. The broad heartwood is brownish when newly cut, becoming dark red on exposure. It is fine and even-textured, hard, strong, durable, termite-resistant, somewhat difficult to work, and is used for railway sleepers, flooring blocks, poles, mine props, and sometimes for furniture. Keith Coates Palgrave says the parquet block floor laid down in 1952 in the Corn Exchange in London is of this wood. It is a grooved floor to take the grain thrown down by the merchants.

Africans use the wood to make dug-out canoes, pestles for stamping corn, and for hoe handles and rakes. They drink a decoction of the bark to cure syphilis, and for eye diseases.

The specific name *plurijuga* means "many-jugate".

Above
A giant pod mahogany, *Afzelia quanzensis* in the north eastern Transvaal

Below left
Julbernardia globiflora: A flowering branch and pod (50%)

Below right
Afzelia quanzensis A leaf and pod split to show the distinctive seeds within (50%)

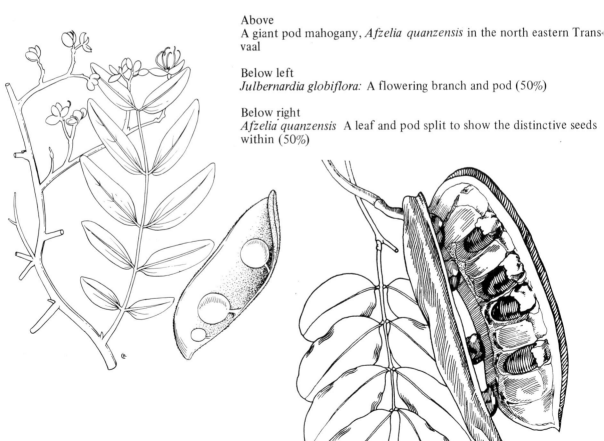

862

i. *Afzelia* Smith

Over 40 species of trees belong to this genus of the tropical regions of the Old World. One species occurs in South and South West Africa and Botswana.

All are unarmed trees, the leaves paripinnate; the calyx lobes 4, the petals 1, clawed and often conspicuous, the stamens 3-8, the flowers in racemes at the ends of the branches; the pods (in the South African species) large, oblong, thick, hard, sometimes bursting open; the seeds large, usually with a conspicuous red aril.

The genus was named after Adam Afzelius of Upsala, 1750-1837, who once lived in Sierra Leone.

The straight sturdy trunk of the pod mahogany

Its distinctive bark

(207)   *Afzelia quanzensis* Welw.

Pod mahogany, Rhodesian mahogany, mahogany bean, chemnen, lucky bean; inKehli, umHlavusi, umShamfuthi (Z); umKholikholi (Sw); nxenhe – pronounced nshenhe – (Tso); muṭokoṭa (V); muwande (Sub); mukamba (Sarwa)

The pod mahogany, as *Afzelia quanzensis* is commonly called, is somewhat unfamiliar to most South Africans for although it occurs in the lowveld woodland of the northern and eastern Transvaal, in Zululand and Swaziland, it is not abundant in South Africa. Across the Limpopo in Rhodesia and Mozambique, and further north, it is far more common and it grows in numbers in parts of Angola, as on the Cuanza River, from which it takes its specific name. It also occurs in northern South West Africa and in Botswana.

It is a fine tree, at its best up to 20 m high, with a huge spreading crown, and a straight trunk up to 1 m in diameter, or occasionally more. The tree photographed near Sibasa in the north-eastern Transvaal was some 19 m high with a span of at least 23 m.

The smoothish, creamy-brown to pale grey bark is seamed crosswise, or patterned with raised rings, giving a beautiful effect. It flakes off irregularly.

The tree is deciduous. In spring the new foliage is copper-coloured and glossy, becoming dark green with age. The leaves are alternate and once-divided, made up of 4-7 pairs of oval leaflets, usually about 5 x 3 cm but sometimes larger, shiny and smooth, with wavy edges, borne on very short stalks. The leaf stalk is noticeably twisted, and is swollen at its junction with the twig.

The leaves are eaten by duiker, and by elephant, which also devour shoots and bark.

· When in bloom, October to November, the pod mahogany cannot be confused with any other tree for the flowers are unique. The long, green, well-shaped buds, in a rather short terminal raceme, open into flowers that have 4 green, boat-shaped sepals, from which protrudes a single flaring, reddish petal, and these, with the puff of long white stamens, are individually handsome. The flowers stand upright and the leaves – looking as if polished – droop, the effect being both bright and graceful. A tree in full bloom is never, however, a sheet of colour for only one flower in the head opens at a time.

The flowers are strongly scented and attractive to insects. When they fall they are relished by stock and antelope.

The flowers are surpassed in interest by the fruit, a large, thick, hard, smooth, woody pod, usually up to about 15 cm long but sometimes up to 30 cm, and some 5 cm wide and 1.9 cm thick, which contains 6 or more hard, shiny, oblong black beans with a red aril. Most people have seen these for they are sold as curios and are sometimes strung into necklaces.

The Zulu name for these beans is inKehli, meaning "betrothed girl", the black seed with the red aril suggesting the head of a Zulu girl with the ochred topknot which she wears when betrothed.

Several handsome butterflies, *Charaxes* species, breed on the tree.

The heartwood of the pod mahogany is hard, durable, and termite resistant, ornamental, working and polishing well. It is used for general carpentry, wagons, railway sleepers, bridges and canoes, and in Tongaland for planks for the punts used on the shallow pans. In Rhodesia, Africans make musical instruments, and in particular, ornamental drums from it. It is useful where wood with a small shrinkage is required.

The tree is used medicinally in Zululand, and specially to treat eczema. The affected spots are rubbed with python fat, and then with powder made of the ground bark.

j. *Julbernardia* Pellegr.

Julbernardia — a genus dedicated to and named after a former governor of Gabon, M. Jules Bernard — is not, as far as is known, represented at all in South Africa. One member, *Julbernardia globiflora* (Benth.) Troupin, does occur in the Caprivi Strip in north eastern South West Africa.

The members of the genus are unarmed trees; the leaves paripinnate with opposite leaflets and stipules that fall early; the flowers with petals that are more or less reduced, the calyx with 5 sepals, the stamens 9-10; the fruit a flat, oblong pod with thickened margins.

Julbernardia globiflora (Benth.) Troupin

= *Brachystegia globiflora* Benth.; = *Berlinia globiflora* (Benth.) Harms.; = *Berlinia eminii* Taub.; = *Westia eminii* (Taub.) MacBride; = *Isoberlinia globiflora* (Benth.) Hutch. ex Greenway; = *Pseudoberlinia globiflora* (Benth.) Duvign.

Mnondo; mutondo (Mashonaland)

The mnondo, as the tree is often known in Rhodesia, is a common and handsome species of sandy woodland in Central Africa, often growing in company with *Brachystegia* species. It does not, as far as is known, occur at all in South Africa, but it is found in the Caprivi Strip where it was recently — and possibly for the first time — collected (by a young amateur botanist, Peter Croesér.)

It is usually recorded as a small to medium-sized tree but it can grow up to 18 m in height, with a trunk up to 0.9 m in diameter, and thick, fire-resistant bark that is smooth and light-coloured when young, becoming rougher and darker with age.

The crown is rounded, spreading and many-branched, and the leaves are alternate and compound. They are usually 10-16 cm long and are made up of 4-7 pairs of opposite dark green leaflets borne on very short, densely hairy stalks. They are oval or oblong, 2.5-8 cm in length and up to 2.5 cm in width, those towards the centre usually the largest, the tips pointed or rounded, the base lopsided, the surface softly hairy, the margins untoothed and with a distinct fringe of hairs, the midrib raised above. Three or four veins arise from the base and the remainder are normal lateral veins and loop along the margin.

The young leaves are a beautiful pink colour.

In summer and autumn the small, round, velvety-brown buds appear. They split to reveal white, sweet-scented flowers with small petals that fall early, and long, showy stamens, giving the trees, in Pardy's words, "a brown flecked with white appearance". They are borne at the tops of the trees, giving rise to brown pods, mature usually in winter time, massed together and held well above the foliage. They are 5-13 cm long, rectangular, with square tips, bearing at one corner a sharp point, and are woody, covered with velvety hairs. They split, the valves curling into a spiral, and scatter small, roundish, flat seeds.

The wood is hard and tough with a heartwood — although not sapwood — resistant to borers. It is used as mining timber, door and window frames, wagon shafts, axe-handles, and, when treated, as fence posts.

Africans make a rope from the bark, which is fairly good although of poorer quality than that of the brachystegias. Fish nets are woven from the root bark.

Every description of this tree mentions its likeness to the msasa, *Brachystegia spiciformis*. They can, however, be told apart by the size of the leaflets for in the msasa the terminal pair of leaflets is the largest, while in the julbernardia the largest are usually the middle pairs. The leaflets of the julbernardia are also more oblong in shape than are those of the msasa, the flowers bloom in summer and not spring, while the pods are velvety and held well above the foliage, and those of the msasa are smooth and borne among the leaves.

The specific name *globiflora* is based on Latin words meaning "round" and "flower", in reference to the round flower head.

Until recently, this tree was widely known as *Isoberlinia globiflora* (Benth.) Hutch. ex Greenway.

k. *Bauhinia* L.

Until recently a large group of mainly tropical plants, characterized by "butterfly" or 2-lobed leaves, or sometimes by leaves with 2 leaflets, were included in the genus *Bauhinia*. Botanists in the past, although realizing thàt the flowers of some species differed, felt that the plants formed — in the words of *Flora Capensis* — "so truly natural an assemblage, agreeing in general habit and in their very peculiar foliage" that the group was kept as one.

Their paired leaves were the basis of the generic name. *Bauhinia* honours two 16th century herbalist brothers, John and Caspar Bauhin, the paired leaves — most fancifully — being held to reflect their relationship.

Some modern botanists separate the 500 or more species formerly belonging to *Bauhinia* into different genera, basing the division mainly on the flowers, and in South and South West Africa two tree species which were until recently considered as bauhinias are now placed in *Piliostigma* and *Adenolobus*. Other botanists, such as Dr John

Top
Bauhinia tomentosa leaves

Centre
Bauhinia macrantha: A pod. leaves
and flower (70%)

Left
Bauhinia tomentosa flower

866

Hutchinson, consider this — pending a world-wide examination of the group — as one genus.

Bauhinia flowers are usually large and showy with a long flower tube and 5 often slender sepals which are clearly divided or bract-like. The flowers, with 5 petals, are bisexual, and the pods usually burst open.

Adenolobus flowers are not nearly as showy. They are cup-shaped, without the long flower tube of a *Bauhinia* species, and with a bell-like calyx.

In *Piliostigma* flowers, the sepals are joined together in a tube. They are not bisexual but male or female borne separately. The pods do not burst open.

(208.1) *Bauhinia tomentosa* L.

Hairy bauhinia; isiThibathibana (Z)

This, "the hairy bauhinia", is a cosmopolitan species growing in South Africa from Natal and Zululand to the eastern Transvaal, northwards to tropical Africa, and eastwards to Ceylon and India. In this country it grows in forest, bushveld, and in coastal dune bush.

While usually a rambling many-stemmed shrub it can be a small tree with many slender twigs. The 2-lobed leaves, like butterfly wings, are joined at the base. They are from 0.8-8 cm long, the lobes rounded at the tips, and hairy or smooth.

The flowers are large, pendulous, solitary, and a pure lemon yellow with a red or maroon blotch. The pods are thin, narrow, velvety, pointed, up to 10 cm long, and enclose 6-12 seeds. They ripen in the autumn.

The butterfly popularly called the Orange Barred Playboy, *Deudorix diocles* breeds in the pods.

The wood makes rafters for huts, and the dried leaves and flowers are used by African doctors.

Bauhinia bowkeri Harv.

Bowker's bauhinia

Bowker's bauhinia is an evergreen, spreading shrub or small tree of the Transkei with deeply-lobed leaves, 1.3-5 cm long, with the leaflets rounded; usually smooth and shiny, and 4-veined from the base.

The long, slender buds open into sweetly scented flowers, 2.5-4 cm long, with smooth, white, wavy petals in terminal bunches. The pods are long, straight, narrow, and borne in numbers.

The plant is named after Colonel James Henry Bowker, 1822-1900, soldier and noted naturalist, who collected it on the Bashee River near Fort Bowker.

(208.2) *Bauhinia galpinii* N.E.Br.

= *Bauhinia punctata* Bolle

Pride of De Kaap, lowveld bauhinia; umDlandlovu (Z); liSololo (Sw); tswiriri (Tso); mutswiriri (V)

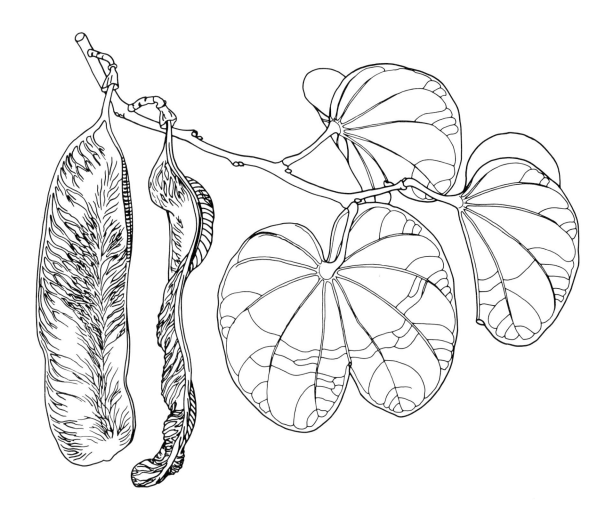

Above
Piliostigma thonningii, pods
and leaves (50%)

Left
Buds of the wild coffee bean,
Bauhinia macrantha

868

This beautiful rambling shrub or climber is only very occasionally tree-like, although when growing on its own it can be a shrubby rambling tree up to 4.5 m high. It is common in the eastern and northern Transvaal and Swaziland, and grows northwards to Rhodesia, wherever it occurs providing almost throughout the summer particularly fine, bright red bloom.

The long whippy branches (used in parts to make baskets) bear simple, alternate, lobed leaves up to 6.5 cm long, with about 7 yellowish veins from the base, and with slender stipules.

The flowers, with 5 brick-red, wavy-edged petals, are large — 5 cm or more across — borne in racemes, often in great abundance, from November to February.

The pods are 8-10 cm long, slender, pointed, hard and woody, enclosing several hard oval seeds.

Two butterflies of the genus *Deudorix,* the Brown Playboy and the Orange Barred Playboy, breed within the pods, the larvae feeding on the seeds. The small holes often apparent in old pods are their work, and through these the young butterflies emerge.

This is rightly a popular garden plant, germinating well, drought-resistant, growing in poor soils, and surviving neglect. It tolerates mild frosts.

The specific name honours Dr E.E. Galpin, noted Transvaal botanist and botanical collector in the late 19th and early 20th century.

Bauhinia macrantha Oliv.

Wild coffee beans; mugutswe, mupondopondo (Tsw), motwakidja (Tsw-Kwena), mokoshi (Tsw-Ngwak); motsope (Sub); mochope (Mbuk); omuti uakatjipera (Her)

Bauhinia macrantha, "the large-flowered bauhinia", grows from the central Transvaal and northern Cape through Botswana to South West Africa, usually in Kalahari sand and often in communities. It is usually a shrub or a semi-climber, but can grow into a 6 m tree, when it closely resembles *Bauhinia petersiana* Bolle.

This has the typical *Bauhinia* 2-lobed leaves, usually 1.3-8 cm in diameter, velvety, with a rounded or notched base, the lobes joined for perhaps half the length of the leaf. There are about 7 veins from the base, which are red-brown and prominent below.

The twigs are hairy.

The large, white, fragrant flowers are about 6.5 cm long with broad, crisped petals. They appear irregularly throughout the year, with a main blooming season in spring and often another in late summer.

The pods are long and narrow, up to 20 cm long and 4 cm wide, dark coloured, smooth, often velvety, or sometimes rough, with several shiny brown seeds within. These are sometimes called "wild coffee beans" and are edible. Thomas Baines used these, or the ground seeds of *Bauhinia petersiana*, as a coffee substitute in 1863 on his trip to the Zambesi. Farmers today still use them for coffee, and Bushmen and African peoples eat the roasted beans, pounded into a meal, which is nourishing, palatable, and one of their staple foods.

Story says that the importance of this species as a food plant may be gauged by the heaps of empty pods found near Bushman shelters and Bakalahari villages. The meal-making, he adds, is a laborious business be-

Above
Piliostigma thonningii, the Rhodesian bauhinia, photographed in Modjadji's Location in the northern Transvaal

Left
Rhodesian bauhinia bark

Below
Rhodesian bauhinia flower and buds photographed in February

cause about 1500 beans are needed to produce a pound (.45 kg) of dry meal.

In times of famine even the roots, baked and pounded, are eaten.

The leaves, pounded, mixed with salt, and boiled, are used as a dressing for wounds.

When not in flower, this species may easily be mistaken for *Bauhinia peterisana* which, however, is more consistently a tree and which grows from Botswana northwards to tropical Africa. In flower the species are easily distinguished, for *Bauhinia petersiana* most often has very narrow petals, whereas those of *Bauhinia macrantha* are broad.

Bauhinia urbaneana Schinz

Urban's bauhinia

Although *Bauhinia urbaniana* is most often a shrub, it can grow into a small bushy tree, 3-3.5 m high. It is a tropical species which extends southwards in mixed woodland and usually on sandy soils to north eastern South West Africa, including the Caprivi Strip.

It is most often a many-stemmed shrub. The leaves, 1.3-5 cm long, have the typically bauhinia form, 2-lobed and cleft, in this case to about half their length. They are smooth above and below velvety, with the veins — springing from the base — reddish and hairy.

The rather club-shaped, furry buds open into flowers about 1.9 cm long with white or pink, crinkled petals. They are crowded in short clusters and bloom from autumn to early spring.

The pods are up to about 16 cm long, narrowed to the base, the tips with a distinct "tail", and are a velvety brown.

The specific name commemorates Dr Ignatz Urban, 1848-1930, Assistant Director of the Botanical Gardens and Museums at Berlin-Dahlem.

1. *Piliostigma* Hochst.

Three species of deciduous trees, African, Asian and Australian, belong to this genus. One occurs in South and South West Africa.

They have simple, lobed leaves arranged alternately, and flowers, usually with the sepals joined together in a tube, the petals 5, male and female flowers usually being borne in racemes on separate trees. The pods are oblong, sometimes narrow, leathery or woody, many-seeded, and do not burst open. The seeds are embedded in a floury pith. The generic name means "cap-like stigma".

(209)   *Piliostigma thonningii* (K.Schum.) Milne-Redh.

= *Bauhinia thonningii* K.Schum.

Wild bauhinia, Rhodesian bauhinia, camel-foot; kolokotso (Tso); mokgôrôpô (NS); mukolokote, mukalakata (V); mutukutu (Sub); nsekese (Kal); musekese, mubaba (Kol); mupapama (Mbuk)

Piliostigma thonningii is usually known as the wild or Rhodesian bauhinia — a name to which it is no longer strictly entitled for it has

Above
Adenolobus garipensis on the plains
near Sorris Sorris, South West
Africa

Below left
Adenolobus garipensis stem

Below right
A twig with leaves, flowers and pod (100%)

872

now been removed from the genus *Bauhinia* to *Piliostigma*. It is, however, called this, or by a number of African names, from northern Zululand, the eastern and northern Transvaal, and northern South West Africa, through tropical Africa as far as Ethiopia.

It grows, usually in open woodland and often on river banks, as a leafy shrub or as a spreading tree up to 12 m high, conspicuous because of its large lobed leaves, and often because of the abundance of its flowers and pods.

It is deciduous, with rough brown bark, longitudinally fissured. The leaves are simple, alternate, large, with a diameter up to 20 cm, and a length slightly less, a deeply lobed apex, and a notched base with veins radiating from it. The upper surface is green, the lower lighter in colour, velvety, with the reddish veins boldly and beautifully outlined. There are small stipules that soon fall off. The leaves are borne on thick stalks.

They are browsed by kudu.

The flowers are male or female, borne separately — one of the main reasons why *Piliostigma* was separated from the genus *Bauhinia*, which has bisexual flowers. The male heads are fewer-flowered than the female.

The fat, oval, red-brown, velvety buds on sturdy stalks are borne in string-like racemes in great abundance during the summer and when in bud the trees have a warm red-brown tinge. The flowers, although not spectacular, are individually pretty, about 2.5 cm wide, with crisped white petals which contrast well with the velvety brown calyx. Only 1 or 2 open at one time in a bunch. They hang downwards and drop at a touch.

The pods are large — up to 23 cm long and 8 cm wide — woody, heavy, green becoming bright chestnut brown, and are covered with tiny raised lines. When in full fruit in winter and spring, the branches are weighed down by the weight of the massed pods.

These do not burst open but fall to the ground where they decay, break up, or are eaten by cattle and wild animals such as kudu. Cattle are sometimes seen running eagerly from tree to tree to pick up every fallen pod. Farmers sometimes grind these into meal.

In times of famine Africans eat the pods and seeds, while herdboys chew the young leaves to relieve thirst. Baboons and monkeys are known to eat the seed coats. The leaves, bark, and pods are used medicinally in many ways to cure many different illnesses. They are widely used in Africa to cure coughs.

The green pods are used by Africans in place of soap, and the bark is used for string, and rubbed on the lips in place of lipstick. The tree yields three different dyes, the bark a red one, the roots red-brown, and the pods and seeds a blue-black. The timber is generally useful.

The specific name of the tree honours Peter Thonning, a Danish botanist, who travelled and collected in Guinea from 1799-1803.

m. *Adenolobus* (Harv.) Torre & Hillcoat

This genus of 2 species, 1 tropical and 1 from South and South West Africa, differs from *Bauhinia* mainly in the structure of the flowers, which are cup-shaped without the long flower tube of a *Bauhinia*, and with a bell-like calyx. They are borne singly. The leaves are deeply notched rather than lobed.

The generic name means "glandular lobes".

Left
Dialium engleranum

Below left
The bark

Below right
Dialium engleranum:
Flowers, leaves and
fruits (70%)

874

Lebeckia sericea in the Namaqualand hills in springtime

See text page 910

(208)   *Adenolobus garipensis* (E.Mey.) Torre & Hillcoat

= *Bauhinia garipensis* E.Mey.

Orange River bauhinia

The botanical name of this species means "the adenolobus of the Orange River", Gariep being the old name of the river. It is indeed a common species along parts of the river in the west – in Namaqualand, Bushman-land and Gordonia – but it also ranges far to the north being widespread in South West Africa.

It grows on stony or gravelly soil, rocky hills, or in coarse sand, and is equally at home on the plateau of the Namib Desert and on the islands and the banks of the Orange River. Visitors to the Augrabies Falls may remember it growing among the tumbled rocks.

This is most often a many-stemmed, spreading shrub, but sometimes a small erect tree up to 3.6 m tall with long wands of branches, covered with a silver-grey bloom, bearing small, neat, blue-green folded leaves on long slender stalks. These are broadly rounded, 2-lobed, 0.8-2.5 cm long, 3-5-nerved from the base, sometimes wider than long, and arranged alternately or sometimes in tufts.

The cup-like flowers, about 0.8-2.5 cm long, are yellow striped with red – "elegantly veiny" according to *Flora Capensis* – and are borne singly or a few together on slender stalks on short side branches. They are not showy, as are those of a true bauhinia. Nevertheless, decorating a little blue-green tree on a wide South West African plain, they are surprisingly distinctive.

The pods are red-brown, short, broad, flat, curved, with rounded tips, one margin extending as a slender point, smooth or covered with small dark, glandular dots.

The tree is well grazed by stock.

n. *Dialium* L.

Over 50 species make up this mainly African genus, 1 species occurring in South Africa and 1 in South West Africa and Botswana.

They are unarmed trees, the leaves imparipinnate, with small sti-pules; the flowers small, in clusters – panicled cymes – in the axils of the leaves or terminally, the calyx with 5-7 lobes, the petals absent or up to 5, the stamens 2-10; the fruits often round or oval and pulpy, and indehiscent, an unusual form for a member of the legume family.

The origin of the generic name is not known. J.E. Smith, noted 18th century English botanist, sought it and could not discover it – nor have modern botanists.

(210)   *Dialium engleranum* Henriques

= *Dialium simii* Phillips

Usimba: usimba (Mbuk)

Dialium engleranum is not a South African species but grows in north-ern and north eastern South West Africa – where it is a common and often dominant tree in the north eastern districts – and in Botswana, northwards into Angola, Rhodesia and Zambia, in forest and woodland on Kalahari sand.

A thiba tree, typically several-stemmed

It is a small to large tree 6-18 m high, with a dark green, much-branched, rounded crown, a trunk with rough, grey, furrowed bark, and with shortly velvety twigs that peel in small flakes.

The compound leaves, up to about 15 cm long, are made up of several pairs of opposite leaflets and a terminal leaflet, sometimes narrow, sometimes egg-shaped, bluntly pointed, or with a sharp and rigid point, smooth and leathery, 2.5-8 cm long and 2.5-5 cm wide. The stipules are small and inconspicuous.

Small oval, greenish buds in short sprays open into small creamy flowers, favourites with bees.

The fruits, usually ripening in late spring or summer, are most un-legume-like. They are oval, 2.5 cm or more long, with a dry pulp and an outer skin which is velvety, and brown when ripe. They are edible and an important food of the Kalahari Bushmen, the Okavango tribes, and of other African people, who devour them in quantities, soaking them and eating them fresh, often with milk, or boiling them with meal. They deteriorate when stored for over a month.

The trunks of the trees are made into dug-out canoes. The crushed wood is widely used as a disinfectant and the bark in an eye lotion. The leaves are used either fresh or made into a medicine to cure coughs, and the shredded, boiled root as a dysentry remedy.

The specific name of the tree commemorates H.G. Adolf Engler (1844-1930) distinguished German botanist, traveller, and author, Professor of Botany and Director of the Botanic Garden at Berlin-Dahlem.

(211)   *Dialium schlechteri* Harms

= *Andradia arborea* Sim

Thiba tree, sherbet tree; umThiba (Z)

This common tree of bush and open forest in Natal, Zululand, and Portuguese East Africa grows from 6-15 m high. In the open it has a spreading crown and a short stem, or several stems, which are white mottled with grey, handsome and distinctive. The smooth branches, a bright whitish-grey, often mottled, and the many dense twigs make a fine and characteristic tracery in winter and early spring when the tree is without leaves.

The leaves are alternate, up to about 15 cm long, with 3-6 pairs of leaflets and a terminal one, 0.8-1.9 cm long and up to about 1.9 cm wide, unequal-sided, with the midrib to one side, green and shiny. The leaves have slender petioles; the leaflets have no stalks.

The foliage turns yellow before it falls.

In spring dense sprays of round, brown, hairy buds, borne in the axils of the leaves, open into small greenish, scented flowers. These develop into oval fruits about 2.5 cm long, red-brown and velvety, with a crisp shell enclosing a thin layer of reddish flesh — tasting like dried apricots — and small, shiny, irregularly shaped seeds.

These fruits are sometimes borne in enormous quantities, and from autumn onwards the crowns of the trees are often massed with the brown fruit, held rigidly in sturdy bunches.

The fruits are edible and are very popular with Zulu children who may be seen in the bush and on the roads, carrying sprays of fruit which they nibble as they walk. The pulp is sometimes mixed with

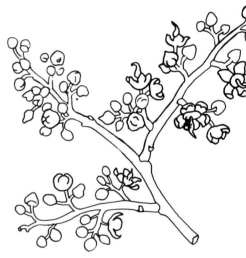

Dialium schlechteri: Leaves, fruits, and a dissected fruit showing the seed (70%)

OPPOSITE

Top
The thiba tree, *Dialium schlechteri,* Mkuze

Centre left
The abundant fruits of the thiba tree

Centre right
Dialium schlechteri: Buds and flowers (100%)

Below
The thiba tree – leafless – as it appears in winter and in early spring

water and milk to make a refreshing drink.

Elephants are especially fond of the fruits, and in country where the thiba tree grows elephants may often be found.

Sim, in his *Forest Flora of Portuguese East Africa*, describes the wood as "the best hardwood seen", with a beautiful close grain, good surface and fine colour, reddish towards the centre, lighter outward, but without sapwood. It is hard and heavy, and insect-proof. Zulus grind the bark to powder and apply this to burns.

The specific name honours Rudolf Schlechter, a German botanist who collected widely in South Africa between 1891 and 1893, and 1896 and 1898.

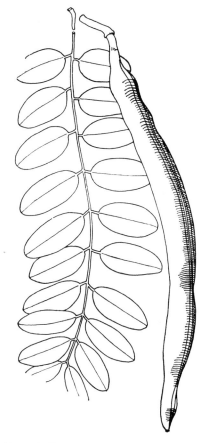

Above left
A long-tailed cassia, *Cassia abbreviata* subsp. *beareana,* in the northern Transvaal

Above right
Cassia abbreviata subsp. *beareana:*
A leaf, and pod which is shorter than the typical (50%)

Below left
Long-tail cassia bark

o. *Cassia* L.

Cassia is a very large genus numbering some 700 species of trees, shrubs and herbs found in all the warm parts of the world. About 13 species grow in South and South West Africa, some 3 of which are trees or sometimes tree-like. They are all characterized by graceful, once-compound leaves, and showy yellow or orange flowers, the calyx lobes and petals 5, the stamens 10, the pods sometimes long and narrow, 2-valved or not bursting open; the seeds flattish.

Plants of the genus are used medicinally, several species yielding senna. In South Africa their medicinal and magic uses are many and varied.

Cassia is an ancient Greek name, derived in its turn from the Hebrew.

(213)   *Cassia petersiana* Bolle

= *Cassia delagoensis* Harv.

Eared cassia, dwarf cassia, liJoyi (Sw); nnembenembe (Tso); munembe-nembe (V)

Although this is sometimes known as the dwarf cassia, it grows not only as a low bush but as a dense bushy tree or as a graceful slender little tree up to about 6 m high, and occasionally higher. It is fairly common in bushveld, damp valleys, on moist hill sides, and along streams in the northern and eastern Transvaal, Zululand and Swaziland. It grows northwards into tropical Africa.

The slender stem, or stems, are grey, the leaves alternate, up to about 26 cm long, with leafy stipules — kidney-shaped or roundish with a pointed wisp — at their base. These are conspicuous and characteristic and give rise to the name "eared cassia". There are about 6-11 pairs of slender or oblong, pointed leaflets, from 2.5-6.5 cm long, arranged opposite one another, and these are dark green and glossy, or slightly hairy below. There is a gland between each pair of leaflets.

The tree is deciduous.

Dense sprays of canary yellow, scented flowers are borne in autumn. The scent is variously described as "like Sunlight soap", or "like peaches".

The pendulous pods, ripening in spring, are long — up to 20 cm — slender, rough and woody, often outlined with a white or dark brown rim, and holding many seeds. These are edible, and are used in making a fermented drink. They are popular with children and birds, baboons and monkeys.

In Swaziland the roots are used in a medicine to treat sick goats. The leaves are used as a purgative and in treating fever, for gonorrhoea and skin diseases. In tropical Africa they have even wider uses.

The butterfly known as the African Vagrant or Cabbage White, *Catopsilia florella*, widespread and sometimes migrating in numbers, is one of several species that breeds on this tree.

The specific name honours Professor W. Peters, a German 19th century botanist, who collected many plants in Portuguese East Africa.

The little desert tree, *Parkinsonia africana*, growing between Upington and Pofadder – the only tree for many miles

882

(212)   *Cassia abbreviata* Oliv.
         subsp. *beareana* (Holmes) Brenan

= *Cassia beareana* Holmes; = *Cassia granitica* Bak.f.; = *Cassia abbreviata* Oliv. var. *granitica* (Bak.f.) Bak.f.

Long-tail cassia, cloth-of-gold, peulbos, kersboom; nnumanyama (Tso); monêpênêpê (Tsw − Mang), monêpênêpê (NS); muluma-ṇama, munembe-nembe (V); nshashanyana, nlembelembe (Kal); mokwankusha, sifonkola (Kol)

This tree was previously known as *Cassia granitica*, but is now considered only a form of the widespread tropical species, *Cassia abbreviata*, which reaches as far south as the northern and eastern Transvaal and northern South West Africa, growing in bushveld and open woodland, sometimes on river banks, at an altitude of between 600 and 900 m.

The long-tail cassia is seldom more than 6 m high, and usually has a rounded crown, somewhat drooping branches, and a slender trunk, dark, fissured, and flaking. The leaves are once-compound, drooping, about 30 cm long, clustered at the ends of the branches. They have 2 stipules at their base which fall off early. The leaves are composed of about 8-12 pairs of oblong or oval leaflets with round tips, 2.5-6 cm long (the topmost the smallest), with untoothed margins. They are thin, dull green, softly hairy at first, becoming smooth, arranged opposite to one another or alternately.

These, and the young branches, are eaten by elephants.

The reddish buds are in terminal bunches on slender stalks. They open into flowers which are creamy-yellow to bright yellow, 2.5-4 cm across, the petals encircling a puff of stamens, 3 of which are long, curved, and graceful, the rest shorter, and these stamens are conspicuous and add much to the beauty of the flowers. They are borne in masses and are very sweet-scented. Sometimes they bloom with the young leaves, sometimes before.

They are followed by unique and distinctive pods, dark coloured, cylindrical in shape, about 1.9 cm thick, and up to 60 cm or more long, the outer woody rind enclosing a pithy layer divided crosswise into compartments, each holding 1 seed. The young pods are velvety, the mature pods smooth. The seeds are flat, roundish, red-brown or black tinged with lime green, and shiny.

This is an easy tree to identify at certain seasons. In the northern Transvaal it is often the only tree in leaf in spring before the rains come and its bright leafy crown may be noted at a distance. In bloom it is unmistakable. In the recent drought years in the northern Transvaal this tree bloomed unaffected, its gay and apparently fragile bloom sometimes only dimly seen through swirling red dust. In pod − and the pods often hang on the tree throughout the year − the tree can be confused with no other. It appears to be weeping tails or long thin sausages.

The wood is light brown, marked with darker streaks, rather coarse-grained, and little used. Shangaans believe the bark has magic properties and that if they eat meat, cooked together with the bark, they will be successful in hunting. The bark is widely used in diarrhoea and dysentry medicine.

In warm areas the long-tail cassia makes a good garden tree. It germinates well and takes up little room, but is tender to frost, particularly when young.

The name *abbreviata* means "shortened" but the allusion is not clear.

Above
A large parkinsonia between Keetmanshoop and Aroab, South West Africa

Below left
Parkinsonia africana stem

Below right
Parkinsonia africana: A flowering twig, a pod, a twig showing the midribs resembling needle-like leaves, and the minute true leaflets (60%)

The name of the subspecies was given by Edward Morell Holmes, a well known pharmaceutical botanist, in honour of Dr O'Sullivan Beare who collected the tree in Tanzania at the beginning of the century. The common name "long-tail cassia" refers to the long, tail-like pods.

Cassia singueana Del.

Wild cassia

Cassia singueana is a tropical species with a wide range, stretching southwards from Ethiopia – where it was first collected – through Tanzania, Zambia, Rhodesia and Mozambique, to the north eastern parts of South West Africa. It does not grow in communities but singly and scattered.

It is a shrub or slender tree up to about 6 m tall, with a trunk up to 15 cm in diameter, and a rough, dark brown or grey, flaky bark.

The leaves are borne on stalks which are distinctly swollen at the base. They are from about 12-30 cm long and are composed of 4-10 pairs of leaflets. These are opposite or alternate, with glands at the base of their short stalks, and are 2.5-5 cm long, oval or egg-shaped, the tips round and usually notched, the base roundish and lopsided, the midrib, nerves and net veins conspicuous above. The upper surface is hairy becoming smooth with age, and below they are hairy, particularly along the midrib and lateral veins. Stipules are present but fall early.

The bright golden flowers are borne in short clusters at the ends of the branches from late autumn to late spring – usually when the tree is leafless. Trees may flower several times in a year. The flowers are up to 5 cm long, with much-veined petals, and are fragrant and ornamental.

The pods are up to 20 cm in length, slightly rounded, regularly constricted, smooth, and yellow when ripe.

Keith Coates Palgrave says that in Rhodesia the bark is used by African doctors to "chase devils out".

The origin of the specific name is not clear. Delile described a number of plants collected by the early 19th century traveller in Ethiopia, Caillinand, and it is possible that he based the name on the place where Caillinand found the plant: or it may be derived from the Latin "singularis", meaning "unique" or "distinguished".

p. *Parkinsonia* L.

Parkinsonia is mainly a tropical genus of about 3 species, with *Parkinsonia africana* Sond. – of South West Africa and the north west Cape – the only African representative. *Parkinsonia aculeata* L., a Mexican species, is commonly cultivated in South Africa, and is a conspicuous feature along the roadside approaching Lourenco Marques.

The trees or shrubs of the genus are usually spiny, the leaves pinnate, the leaflets tiny or often absent; the flowers small, in short racemes in the axils of the leaves, the calyx lobes and petals 5, the stamens up to 10; the pods narrow, sometimes twisted or compressed between the seeds; the seeds oblong.

The genus was named after John Parkinson, the London apothecary who lived three and a half centuries ago and wrote *Paradisus Terrestris*. Our desert tree is thus linked with one of the matchless garden books of the world.

A huilboom, *Peltophorum africanum*, in the Transvaal bushveld

(214)   *Parkinsonia africana* Sond.

Lemoendoring, lemoenboom, lemoenhout, wildelemoenhout;! khas
(Nama)

The green-hair tree is a name sometimes given to trees and shrubs of
this genus, and this is a descriptive name for the ones that are usually
leafless, such as our indigenous species, *Parkinsonia africana*. Growing,
often on sandy plains, in the bare arid north-west, and in South West
Africa — in the Namib Desert itself — this tree has a freak quality about
it suited to its wild setting. It is one of the few trees growing on the
great desert plain near the Orange River west of Pofadder where it
stands, gaunt and straggling, shaped by wind and drought.

Although it is usually small, it can grow up to 6 m high. The branches
are many, smooth and flexible, the old ones grey, the young ones
bright yellow-green, armed with horizontal spines.

Usually the tree has not a single leaf upon it, only the slender bare
midribs of the compound leaves clinging to the branches and often
enough streaming in the wind like a mop of yellow-green hair.

The leaflets, when present, are minute, narrow and arranged in about
8-10 opposite pairs. Many observers have never seen any at all. The
spines are stout and vary in length; the small yellow flowers bloom in
lax bunches, borne in the axils of the leaves and at the ends of the
branches. The pods, 10-15 cm long, are reddish-brown and compressed
between the seeds, which number about 8 to a pod and are oblong and
shiny.

The tree is browsed by animals, and coffee is sometimes made of the
beans.

There are people who believe that they can tell the type of tree and
foliage from the sound of the wind through the crown; and that the
wind in this tree makes a sound of its own with a high, shrill, keening
note.

The specific name *africana* means "African". C.A. Smith says that it
is commonly called lemoenhout because the branches are pale yellow
("lemoen" in Afrikaans).

q. *Peltophorum* Walp.

About 16 species, spread throughout the tropics and subtropics of the
world, belong to the genus *Peltophorum*. One species occurs in South
and South West Africa and in Botswana.

They are all tall, unarmed trees; the leaves bipinnate and acacia-like,
the stipules small; the flowers with 5 calyx lobes and petals, the stamens
10, often showy; the pods flat, oblong to lance-shaped, with usually
1-2 flattish seeds. They do not burst open.

The generic name is derived from Greek words meaning "shield-
bearing" and refers to the shield-like shape of the stigma.

(215)   *Peltophorum africanum* Sond.

Huilboom, huilbos, African wattle, Rhodesian black wattle, dopperkiaat; umSehle, umThobo, isiKhaba-mkhombe (Z); isiKhabakhombe
(Sw); nhlanhlanhu, ndzedze (Tso); mosêtlha (Tsw); mosêhla (NS);
musese (V); mosiru (Sub); nzeze (Kal); movevi (Mbuk); omuparara (Her)

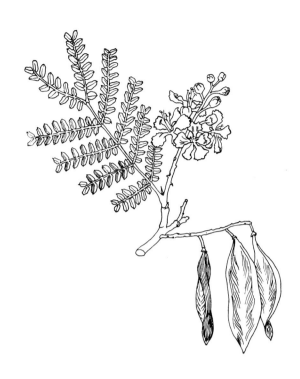

Above left
Huilboom bark

Above right
Peltophorum africanum:
A twig with leaf,
flowers and fruits (50%)

The huilboom, a beautiful, deciduous, thornless tree, grows — often in sandy soil — in the dry bush and open savannah country of Zululand, Natal, Swaziland, and of the northern and eastern Transvaal, northwards to central tropical Africa, and west to Botswana, South West Africa, and Angola. It is one of the commonest trees of the Transvaal bushveld and is conspicuous when flowering or fruiting along the Great North Road between Pretoria and Messina.

It is a spreading tree up to 9 m and occasionally 15 m high, with a trunk that is often crooked or forked close to the ground, and rough brown bark.

The acacia-like, feathery leaves are alternate, silvery-grey, and twice-divided, with small stipules that usually fall off as the leaves mature. The leaves are about 10 cm long with 4-7 pairs of side-branches and 10-20 pairs of small oblong, hairy leaflets. These and the shoots are eaten by elephant, giraffe, kudu, and by Black Rhino which also take the bark.

The twigs, midribs, and leaf stalks are covered with rust-coloured hairs.

The flowers, blooming from September to December, are up to 1.9 cm wide, with bright yellow crinkled petals, and a rusty-coloured, hairy calyx, and are borne in upright sprays (racemes arranged in panicles) terminally or in the axils of the leaves. They are ornamental and sweet-scented.

The pods are flat, red-brown, hairy, winged, about 5 cm long and 1.3-1.9 cm wide, narrowing both ends, ripening summer and autumn and hanging on the tree in great numbers. They are favourites with cattle.

The gum is reputed to be poisonous.

When not in flower the huilboom can easily be confused with an acacia, except for the fact that it is completely without thorns.

The heartwood is reddish, close-grained, of medium weight, fairly hard and tough, but needing seasoning against borer attack. It takes a good polish and works easily. Sim did not consider it of much use, but Galpin thought it one of the most valuable and generally useful timbers of the Springbok Flats. It is used for furniture, wagons, axe-handles, buckets, and native ornaments, and is good fuel. In South West Africa the wood, ground and mixed with fat, is rubbed into the hair.

Africans use the tree medicinally. The Zulus boil the roots with those of *Bridelia cathartica* Bertol.f. and of a species of *Ochna* and drink the mixture to cure infertility. The roots boiled in water are used as an enema.

J.G. Frazer in *The Golden Bough* says: "When Ovambo women go out to sow corn they take with them in the basket of seed two green branches of a particular kind of tree (*Peltophorum africanum*), one of which they plant in the field with the first seed sown. The branch is believed to have the power of attracting rain, hence in one of the native dialects the tree goes by the name of 'rain bush' ".

This, and the common name huilboom (weeping tree) probably indicate one of the most interesting features of *Peltophorum*. It is one of the rain trees of Africa. In late spring, water drips from the branches of some trees often making pools on the ground below. This is a characteristic well known to country people, and even to some townsmen who grow the tree in gardens. The raining or weeping is probably in all cases caused by the small insect known as froghopper or spittle bug.

The huilboom is a most satisfactory garden tree. Seed is obtainable easily; it germinates well; the young plant transplants easily, is fairly fast-growing, and stands some frost. It is a good shade tree and lovely when in brilliant yellow bloom. It is said to have all the requirements of a perfect avenue tree.

In Zululand it is never planted near a kraal for it is thought "a bad tree" in such a position, probably on account of the poisonous gum.

r. *Cordyla* Lour.

Cordyla is a small genus of 5 or 6 deciduous, unarmed trees, all African except for 1 species from Madagascar. They all have alternate, imparipinnate leaves, leaflets that are usually alternate, with many transparent dots, and small stipules; flowers that are bisexual or male in racemes, the calyx lobes 3, the petals absent, the stamens many and conspicuous; and fruits that are roundish to oval, fleshy drupes, containing 1-6 large seeds.

The generic name, according to Joaŏ de Loureiro, the Portuguese botanist-missionary who collected and described the tree in Portuguese East Africa, is based on a Greek word meaning "club-shaped" or "thickened towards the apex", in allusion to the shape of the bud and fruit.

(216)   *Cordyla africana* Lour.

Sunbird tree, wild mango

Cordyla africana is a rare tree in South Africa for it is a species of tropical African forests and river banks, occurring as far south as Zululand, and the eastern Transvaal (where it has been collected near Komatipoort).

It can grow into a big tree up to 22 m high, with a trunk diameter at

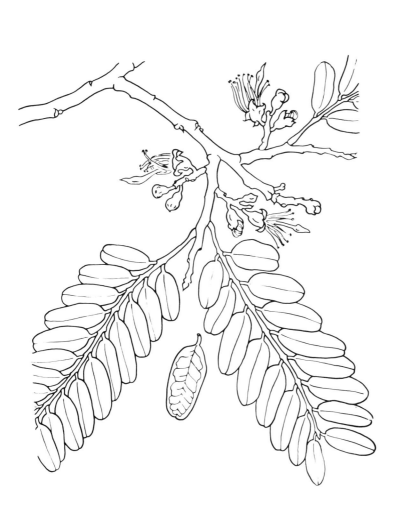

Above
Cordyla africana

Centre right
The fruit (50%)

Left
Cordyla africana: A
flowering branchlet
(60%)

Ekebergia pterophylla, Blyde River Canyon, north eastern Transvaal

See text page 1068

breast height of up to 1.2 m, and a great spread of branches.

The bark is greyish-brown and furrowed longitudinally. The leaves are alternate and once compound, up to about 25 cm long, with small stipules that fall off early. There are about 9-12 pairs of oblong leaflets and a terminal one, 2.5-4 cm long, arranged opposite one another or alternately, dark green and smooth above, paler and slightly hairy below, with translucent dots scattered across the surface of the blades.

The flowers are borne in short sprays in the axils of the leaves, all facing upwards and filled with nectar. They usually bloom in September and October, together with the new leaves. Although they are without petals, they are very showy with their puff of feathery golden stamens protruding from the cup-shaped calyx, and when flowering abundantly the tree is a splendid sight.

The fruit, like that of the dialiums, is unusual in a legume for it is not the usual pod but a yellow, fleshy, succulent fruit up to about 4 cm long — sometimes reported as big as a lemon — roundish to oval, with a rather leathery skin, containing 1-8 seeds embedded in the glutinous flesh. It ripens December to January.

The fruits are eaten by Africans, either fresh or cooked, and animals such as monkeys. They are a favourite elephant food.

Sim described the wood as light and soft, Sousa as fairly heavy, oily, yellowish with specks, and ornamental. It is used in particular to make African drums, a whole trunk being hollowed out, and such a drum is said to be sonorous and heard a great distance away.

The specific name means "African". The tree is sometimes called the Sunbird Tree because of the sunbirds attracted to it when in flower — there is a record of an observer counting over 100 in a tree growing on the banks of the Usutu River near Ndumu.

s. *Swartzia* Schreb.

Over 100 species of trees or shrubs, mainly in tropical America, belong to this genus. Two species are African, one of which occurs in northern South Africa.

All the species are thornless with compound leaves which are imparipinnate, or with 3 leaflets or sometimes only 1, without transparent dots, and with small stipules; flowers that are bisexual and 1-petalled, with numerous stamens, and pods that are stipitate — that is, with a special stalk or stipe — leathery or woody, often cylindrical, sometimes splitting into 2 valves, and with 1 to several seeds.

The genus was named after Olof Peter Swartz, 1760-1818, Professor of Botany at Stockholm.

(217)　　*Swartzia madagascariensis* Desv.

Snake bean tree, ironheart tree; moshakashela (Mbuk)

The snake bean is fairly widely scattered at medium and low altitudes in open woodland, often on sandy soils, in central Africa, and extends south to the north and north eastern parts of South West Africa, and to Rhodesia and Portuguese East Africa.

This is usually a small to medium-sized tree, 4-8 m high, occasionally taller, with a spreading, much-branched crown, either bushy or with a

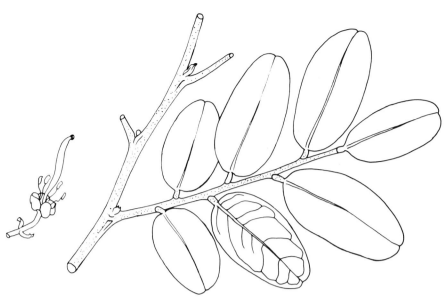

Swartzia madagascariensis: A leaf and flower (80%)

short clean stem up to 40 cm in diameter, with grey or brown, deeply fissured bark.

The twigs and leaf stalks are velvety.

The leaves are alternate and once-divided, with 2-7 shortly stalked, oval leaflets, 2.5-5 cm long, usually with round notched tips and rounded or narrowed bases, the terminal leaflet being much the largest. The upper surface of these is dull green, the lower covered with short, dense, red-brown hairs.

The sweet-scented flowers, blooming September to November, are borne singly on long stalks or a few in a bunch with the new leaves, about October. They have one petal only, which is large, white, and crinkly with a yellow spot at the base, and conspicuous yellow stamens, growing from a cup-shaped velvety-brown calyx. They are attractive but fall soon.

The pods give the tree its common name for they are snake-like, up to 30 cm long and 1.3 cm in diameter, cylindrical or bluntly 4-sided, when mature dark red-brown, hard and shiny, containing many small brown seeds that rattle in the pod. They do not split open but hang on the tree during the winter when they are conspicuous.

Strangely enough, cattle and game eat these with impunity although the pith of the pods is widely used to kill rats, mice, fish, and bilharzia snails. (The milk and butter from cows which have eaten these is tainted). The pith of mature pods, roasted, ground, and mixed with *Diamphidia* larvae, make an arrow poison. The leaves are also used to stupify fish. The pod is an antidote for poisons, causing vomiting. Bark, roots, and sometimes leaves are used medicinally to cure coughs, leprosy, and eye diseases. African doctors use them to treat cataract. The powdered pods are said to keep termites from stored grain.

When the tree is large enough it yields good timber which is dark red-brown or sometimes almost purple-black, close-grained, hard, durable, termite-resistant, generally useful where a hard wood is needed, and which makes attractive furniture. Sim says it is excellent for piano manufacture, and Palgrave states that Africans in Rhodesia call it Mpingo and rank it second only to *Dalbergia melanoxylon* for making curios and small ornaments. Many of the small wooden articles they sell at the Victoria Falls are of this wood.

The specific name indicates that the tree was originally collected in Madagascar.

Sub-Family Papilionaceae

This is an important and widespread group of about 12,000 species, with members growing all over South Africa under varying conditions. Although many species are herbs a number of beautiful flowering trees, such as the kafferbooms, *Erythrina* species; the keurbooms, *Virgilia* species; *Calpurnia* species; the Vanwykshout, *Bolusanthus speciosus* (H.Bol.) Harms, and the olifantsoor, *Lonchocarpus capassa* (Klotzsch) Rolfe, belong here.

Papilionaceae includes one of South Africa's most famous timber trees, the kiaat, *Pterocarpus angolensis* DC.

The trees have leaves that are usually pinnate or sometimes with 3 leaflets, (rarely one), occasionally with simple leaves. All the members have flowers like those of the familiar sweetpea with a broad upper petal called the standard, two narrower — the wings — on either side, and the two bottom petals joined to form the keel. The stamens are usually united in a sheath within the keel. The structure is both complicated and beautiful, and is thought to facilitate cross pollination. Flowers, such as those of the kafferbooms, are filled with nectar and much sought by birds and insects.

The fruits are usually pods, with the exception of those of *Xanthocercis zambesiaca* (Bak.) Dumaz-le-Grand, which are like small plums in shape with a dry fleshy pulp.

Key to Genera
Sub-Family Papillionaceae

LEAVES SIMPLE

Trees or shrubs; the leaves often pear-shaped, velvety; the flowers white marked with yellow, strongly scented; the pods up to 8 cm long, wide-tipped, narrowing to the base, hard, smooth.

e. *Baphia*

Silky-haired shrubs or small trees; the leaves silky-haired; the buds covered by *cap-like bracts*, lifted as the flower opens; the flowers white to pink; the pods flat, furry, widest at the top, up to 4 cm long.

f. *Podalyria*

LEAVES COMPOUND

Leaves reduced to 1 leaflet

Medium-sized trees, the leaves sometimes reduced to 1 leaflet (see also imparipinnate leaves), up to 13 x 10 cm, densely velvety when young, the flowers violet, the pods up to 7 cm long, flat, papery, not bursting open.

s. *Lonchocarpus*

Leaves with 3 leaflets

Shrubs or shrub-like trees; sometimes spiny and silky; the leaves usually with 3 narrow leaflets, the stipules usually absent; the flowers often *yellow*, small or large; *the stamens united*; the pods usually narrow, *flat or cylindric, tipped with the persistent style.*

g. *Lebeckia*

Shrubs or small trees, often spiny; the leaves with 3 often narrow leaflets arranged digitately; the stipules small or absent; the flowers *yellow, often in a one-sided raceme*; the pods stalked, flat, *conspicuously winged on the upper side.*

h. *Wiborgia*

Herbs, shrubs, or occasionally small trees, usually unarmed; the leaves with 1-5 leaflets (usually 3), digitately arranged, with stipules; the *keel petal beaked*; the pods *inflated*, the seeds within rattling.

i. *Crotalaria*

Medium-sized to tall trees; sometimes with prickles on the trunk and branches; the leaves stipulate with glands at the base; the flowers large, usually *bright red or crimson*; the pods *long, narrow, constricted like a bead necklace*; the seeds red, shiny.

v. *Erythrina*

Leaves imparipinnate (once-divided, terminated by 1 leaflet)

A small tree or shrub with *silvery-white*, hairy branches and twigs; the leaflets 3-8 pairs and a terminal one, *densely silky*, silvery-grey; the flowers *yellow*; the pods *long, thin, constricted*, with 1-3 (sometimes 6) seeds.

a. *Sophora*

Small trees or shrubs; the leaves drooping; the leaflets 3-12 pairs and a terminal one, pale green, oblong; the flowers *bright yellow*; the pods 5-8 cm x 1.3-1.9 cm, *narrowly winged on one side, papery*.

b. *Calpurnia*

A small tree; the leaves drooping, shiny; the leaflets 5-6 pairs and a terminal one, on yellow stalks, pointed, unequal-sided, the margins minutely scolloped; the flowers *blue-mauve*; the pods *flat, narrow, pointed*, up to 10 cm long, *unwinged*.

c. *Bolusanthus*

Trees, sometimes bushy; the leaves feathery with 3-13 pairs of leaflets and a terminal one; the leaflets small, oblong; the young parts reddish-velvety; the flowers *white, pink, mauve,* massed; the pods *narrow, oblong, hairy, splitting*.

d. *Virgilia*

Herbs or shrubs, occasionally small trees; the leaves (in the South African tree species) imparipinnate; stipules present; the flowers often small, *the keel spurred*; the pods usually *small, narrow, often cylindrical, bursting open.*

j. *Indigofera*

Herbs, shrubs, occasionally small trees; *aromatic*; the leaves *with gland dots*, the species listed with imparipinnate leaves, the leaflets usually very narrow, with stipules; the flowers *purple, blue, or white; the pod enclosed in the calyx, not bursting open.*

k. *Psoralea*

A small tree or shrub *with silky hairs*; the leaflets 4-10 and a terminal one, grey-green, *densely silky*; the flowers *violet; the pods long, narrow, velvety.*.

l. *Mundulea*

Medium to tall trees; the leaflets 3-7 pairs (opposite) and a terminal one; with often conspicuous stipels (secondary stipules) at the base; the flowers *purple*, borne at the ends of the branches; the pods up to 15 x 4 cm, *woody, red-brown, upright or pendulous.*

m. *Millettia*

A medium to large tree; the leaflets 1-2 pairs, alternate, and a terminal leaflet; the flowers *white*; the pods *smooth, widest at the middle, tapering both ends*, up to 5 cm long.

n. *Craibia*

A small tree or shrub, sometimes spiny; the leaflets small, oblong, usually 4-6 pairs and a terminal one, with a thorn-like point; the flowers *blue, pink, grey, veined in blue*; the pods *cylindrical, golden-brown, with bristly hairs.*

p. *Ormocarpum*

Climbers, shrubs or small trees, sometimes spiny; the leaflets few to many, small to large; the flowers *small*, white to pink; *the pods flat, papery*, 2.5-8 cm long, *not bursting open.*

q. *Dalbergia*

A small to medium tree, without spines; *a slash oozing thick red sap*; the leaflets few to many, small to large, often with very distinct veining; the flowers *yellow to orange*; the pods *sometimes saucer-like; thickened in the middle with a bulge that is often bristly; winged, not bursting open.*

r. *Pterocarpus*

Small to medium-sized trees; the leaflets usually 1-3 pairs and a terminal leaflet — the terminal the largest — (or reduced to 1 leaflet); the flowers *small, violet*; the pods *flat, pointed, unwinged or with a very narrow rim-like wing.*

s. *Lonchocarpus*

A medium to tall tree; the leaves large; the leaflets 6-9 pairs and a terminal one, without stipules; the flowers *white*; the pods up to 15 x 2.5 cm, *flat, narrowly winged along both margins.*

t. *Xeroderris*

A large wide-spreading tree; the leaflets 5-15 pairs, the terminal the largest, and a terminal one; the flowers small, *mauvy-white*; the fruit *plum-shaped*, 2.5 x 1.3 cm, the rind brown, *enclosing a thin layer of fleshy pulp and 1 seed*.

u. *Xanthocercis*

Leaves paripinnate (once-divided, terminated by 2 leaflets)

Small, soft-wooded trees or shrubs; the leaves with *many* slender leaflets; the flowers yellow or blue; the pods *very long and narrow with partitions between the seeds*, usually borne abundantly.

o. *Sesbania*

a. *Sophora* L.

Sophora is a genus of over 70 species, centred in Asia and America, but found in most of the warm parts of the world. One species, *Sophora inhambanensis* Klotzsch, grows on the sandy shores of Zululand and in Portuguese East Africa, northwards to Kenya, and a second species, *Sophora tomentosa* L., has a more northern distribution and a wider one, for it grows on shores fringing the Indian, Pacific, and Atlantic Oceans.

It is thought by some botanists that these species are not native to South Africa or to the continent of Africa, but that the seeds were sea-borne from the East in ancient times. Today in Africa they grow only on the sandy beaches of the east coast, above the high-water mark. Their seeds, which are buoyant, are known to float for months.

Until recently these were considered the only members of the genus in Africa. In 1960, however, a third species was collected not far from the Zimbabwe ruins in Rhodesia, giving the genus in Africa an entirely new interest and fascination.

On examination at Kew it proved to be closely related to a species from India, China, and Indonesia, *Sophora velutina* Lindl., and was eventually described as a subspecies of this. If the Asian species is the parent, as is thought likely, how and when did it come over sea, and above all, over land, to Zimbabwe, to evolve into the Rhodesian form with its small botanical differences? Possibly the Chinese porcelain — fragments of which have been found in the ruins — and the *Sophora* travelled together.

The early Chinese sailors carried plants with them across the seas which they exchanged for those of foreign lands, and this was a well-known commercial practice. Perhaps all three sophoras of Africa came, not by accident, but by design. Plants of the genus, it is known, had a special significance for the Chinese. It is recorded in one of the ancient travel books of China, *The Travels of Emperor Mu* — who lived 1001-945 BC. — that the Emperor travelled westward to the domain of "the Royal Mother of the West" (possibly the Queen of Sheba), where he planted a memorial tree of sophora.

Sophora species are usually trees or shrubs, the leaves imparipinnate and often densely velvety, the flowers bisexual in a terminal raceme or panicle, pea-like in form; the pod flattened, constricted like a bead necklace, often beaked; usually not bursting open.

Sophora is based on an Arabic name "sophera".

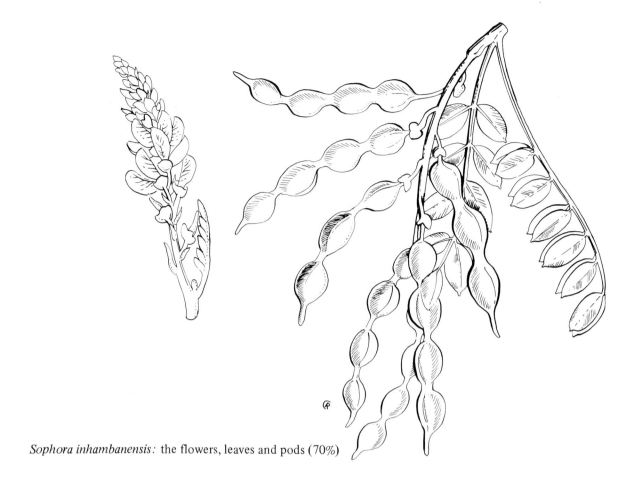

Sophora inhambanensis: the flowers, leaves and pods (70%)

(218)   *Sophora inhambanensis* Klotzsch

Sophora

The silver, silky-velvety foliage of this strikingly beautiful little tree or shrub of Zululand beaches and dunes sets it apart from all other plants. The colour resembles that of the silver tree, but the leaves are compound and softer to the touch.

It often grows as a spreading shrub but may be a tree up to 4.5 m high with silvery-white branches, and bright, silvery, compound leaves up to about 13 cm long and 10 cm wide. These have about 3-8 pairs of opposite or alternate leaflets, and a terminal one which is much the biggest. They are 1.9-4 cm long, widely lance-shaped or oblong, and covered on both sides with a soft mat of silver-grey silky hairs.

The yellow pea-like flowers are in terminal sprays up to 13 cm long. The pods are long and thin, up to about 10 cm in length, holding generally 1-3, but sometimes up to 6 seeds, deeply constricted and looking like a bead necklace.

Until recently it was thought that the Zululand species was *Sophora tomentosa*. This, however, grows further to the north.

The specific name *inhambanensis* indicates that the plant was collected first near Inhambane, between Lourenco Marques and Beira in Portuguese East Africa.

897

Right
Calpurnia aurea subsp. *sylvatica:* A leaf, flowers and pods (60%)

Below
Calpurnia intrusa, Giants Castle, Natal

b. *Calpurnia* E.Mey

The genus *Calpurnia* is a small one with about 7 species, and is widely distributed from Uitenhage in the Cape Province to Ethiopia in the north.

In South Africa the species grow in the eastern parts of the country, usually as shrubs, but one species, *Calpurnia aurea* (Ait.) Benth., can become a 6 m tree. This, in its typical form, is the only *Calpurnia* to grow out of South Africa and is widespread in tropical Africa. The plant on which the original description was based was introduced into England from Ethiopia in 1777. Since then this little tree has been widely cultivated in Europe, Africa, and in India for its golden, laburnum-like flowers, and it is said to have been planted as a shade tree in tea and coffee plantations.

Its southern-most form was until very recently known as *Calpurnia sylvatica* (Burch.) E.Mey. This is now regarded as a subspecies of *Calpurnia aurea*.

Various other and smaller species are distributed mainly over eastern South Africa. *Calpurnia villosa* Harv., with silky-hairy leaves, grows in the Riversdale and Oudtshoorn districts; *Calpurnia woodii* Schinz in Natal; *Calpurnia floribunda* Harv. from the eastern Cape to the eastern Transvaal; *Calpurnia intrusa* E.Mey. from the Transkei and Pondoland to the eastern Orange Free State, Lesotho, Natal and the Transvaal on forest edges and on river banks at fairly high altitudes; *Calpurnia robinioides* E.Mey. in the Orange Free State and Lesotho.

Recently a new species of *Calpurnia* from the eastern Transvaal and parts of Swaziland adjoining it was described. This is *Calpurnia glabrata* Brummitt. Formerly it was confused with *Calpurnia floribunda* which, like it, has flowers that are smaller than those of the other species, but they differ on the point of hairiness, *Calpurnia glabrata* being, as the name suggests, smooth, and *Calpurnia floribunda* being hairy in every part.

In its smooth leaflets and ovary it resembles *Calpurnia aurea* subsp. *sylvaticus* which, however, occurs to the south. Its distribution and that of the typical *Calpurnia aurea* overlap but it is separated from the latter by its smaller flowers and smooth ovary.

The species have leaves that are imparipinnate, with 3 to many pairs of leaflets that are often softly hairy; yellow flowers — very bright and beautiful — in racemes in the axils of the leaves or terminally, and somewhat slender pods, often narrowly winged on one side.

The leaves have vermin-killing properties.

The origin of the name *Calpurnia* is singular. The plants of the genus somewhat resemble those of *Virgilia*, named after the poet Virgil, so that they bear the name of a man whose work was considered an imitation of Virgil's — Calpurnius.

(219)   *Calpurnia aurea* (Ait.) Benth.
         subsp. *aurea*

= *Calpurnia subdecandra* (L'Herit.) Schweick.; = *Calpurnia lasiogyne* E.Mey.

Natal laburnum, geelkeurboom; umHlahlambedu, inSiphane, isiKhiphampethu (Z)

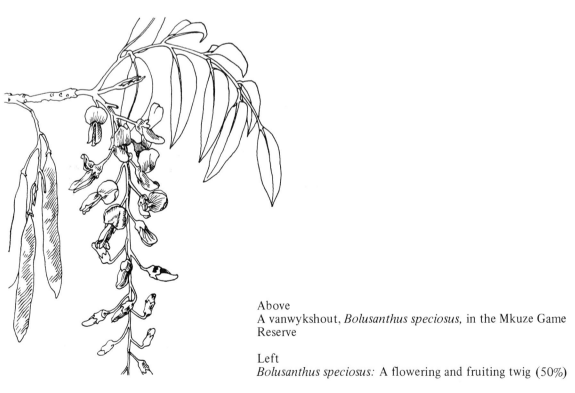

Above
A vanwykshout, *Bolusanthus speciosus,* in the Mkuze Game
Reserve

Left
Bolusanthus speciosus: A flowering and fruiting twig (50%)

900

(220)   subsp. *sylvatica* (Burch.) Brummitt

= *Sophora sylvatica* Burch.; = *Calpurnia sylvatica* (Burch.) E.Mey.

Cape laburnum, geelkeurboom; inDloli, umSitshana (X); umKhiphampethu (Z)

The two forms of this elegant, gay little tree grow from Somerset East and Uitenhage in the south, through the eastern Cape to Natal and the Transvaal. Subsp. *sylvatica* is common in the eastern Cape and subsp. *aurea* further to the north in Natal and the Transvaal.

The tree is often found in forests, on their margins, on hill sides, or on the edges of woody kloofs — Burchell collected subsp. *sylvatica* on the Bosberg near Somerset East — a 9 m tall tree in forests, a shrub or small tree when standing on its own. Wherever it grows it is lovely in bloom, its often slender and graceful form transformed into a fountain of gold and glowing against its background.

The evergreen, alternate, compound leaves up to 20 cm long are graceful and drooping. They have 3-12 pairs of pale green leaflets and a terminal one, which are oblong, 2.5-5 cm long, with a lopsided base and a rounded or notched apex.

The brilliant yellow pea flowers about 2.5 cm long are in pendulous sprays in the axils of the leaves, appearing irregularly. The main difference between the two forms of the tree is seen in the flowers, in subsp. *aurea* the ovary being silky, in subsp. *sylvatica* smooth.

The fruit is a brown papery pod, 5-8 cm long and 1.3-1.9 cm wide, narrowly winged on one side, growing in bunches. It holds several dark oval seeds.

The wood is yellowish with a dark brown heartwood which is heavy and hard, and — according to Sim — not much used. Zulus treat sores on cattle which are infested with maggots with parts of this plant, and the crushed roots in a wash to destroy lice.

This is a good garden tree. Seed is usually available, it germinates well, and the tree is fast-growing and flowers when small.

The name *aurea* is Latin and means "golden" and *sylvaticus* means "growing among trees". The Zulu herbalist's name for this is umKhiphampethu, meaning "maggot-extracter". Miller gives umSitshana as the name for this in the Transkei, although apparently this is applied to *Diospyros natalensis* in other areas.

c. *Bolusanthus* Harms

One species only comprises this Southern African genus, named after Dr Harry Bolus, businessman and botanist, and founder of the Bolus Herbarium in Cape Town.

It is a tree with leaves that are imparipinnate, the leaflets in 5-6 pairs, opposite or sub-opposite, silky when young; the flowers blue, pea-like, in a drooping terminal raceme, the pod narrow and flat, the seeds 1-4, flat and shiny.

(222)   *Bolusanthus speciosus* (H.Bol.) Harms

= *Lonchocarpus speciosus* H.Bol.

Vanwykshout, tree wistaria, South African wistaria, Rhodesian wistaria,

anwykshout stem and
rk

wild wistaria, elephantwood, olifantshout; umHohlo (Z); umHohlo
(Sw); mpfimbahongonyi (Tso); motsokophala, nsukungaphala
(Tsw – Mang); kgomo-nahlabana (NS); mukamba, muswinga-phala (V);
nsungamola (Kal)

The Vanwykshout is one of the loveliest of our wild trees with its
slender shape, light green leaves drooping at the ends of the branches,
and its long tresses of violet coloured blooms.

It grows along the northern foothills of the Soutpansberg and in the
bushveld or in the open parkland of the Transvaal, in Swaziland, Zululand, Natal, in Rhodesia, Portuguese East Africa, and Angola, tolerating
a variety of soils.

Although it is commonly a small tree 3-6 m high, it can reach 12 m
in height with a trunk diameter of 38 cm.

The bark is light to dark brown, in old trees deeply corrugated; the
branches are brownish green and are marked with the scars of the old
leaf stalks. The shining, drooping leaves are deciduous, falling in late
spring just before flowering time. Young leaves appear again within a
few weeks, occasionally at the same time as the flowers.

The leaves are compound with a long, flexible, yellowish-green
midrib bearing about 5-6 pairs of opposite or nearly opposite leaflets
and a terminal leaflet, on yellowish stalks. The leaflets are from 4-8 cm
long and 1.3-1.9 cm broad, tapering to a sharp point, with the base often
so unequal-sided and with the yellow midrib so much to one side,
that the leaf is slightly curved. If the margins are closely studied, they
are seen to be minutely scolloped.

The flowers are pea-like in form, scentless, violet blue, and borne in
drooping sprays at the end of the branches in spring. (In the bud stage,
they are eaten by Vervet Monkeys). They develop into flat, narrow,
greyish, pointed pods, somewhat veined, up to 10 cm long, holding
3-8 small, flat, shiny seeds.

The wood is white with a reddish heartwood that is hard, durable,
and termite- and borer-proof. Farmers consider it a valuable wood,
using it for wagons, spokes, yokes, axe-handles, fence poles, and for
furniture, and Africans use it medicinally.

This is one of the finest garden trees, in flower more delicate
and lovely than a jacaranda. On heavy soils it is very slow-growing, but
it is decorative from the early stages, its light, graceful, pendulous
foliage shining as if polished. The seed germinates well, but should be
sown in pots as gardeners sometimes find difficulty in transplanting it.
It does not thrive in shade and should always be planted in the open,
and if possible in sandy soil when it often grows up to 3 m in about 4 or
5 years. It is said to benefit from an application of lime.

This little tree deserves far more attention from gardeners than it
ever receives, considering its beauty, and the fact that it stands fairly
dry conditions and several degrees of frost. It may be seen in Pretoria
gardens and as a street tree in Salisbury.

It is sometimes infested with a big scale insect, *Aspidoproctus*
species, white when young, hard and brown when mature, and this
secretes so much honey-dew that lumps of crystallized sugar pile up
below it.

In the veld the Vanwykshout can often be identified at a distance
because of the glinting and shine of the leaves in the sun. It sometimes
grows in association with the huilboom and when the two flower together, as they sometimes do, the violet and yellow are a wonderful
sight.

The specific name *speciosus* is the Latin for "beautiful". The origin of the name Vanwykshout is unknown. This is by far the commonest name for the tree in South Africa, although tree wistaria would seem more fitting. The Venda name muswinga-phala means "impala-blinder".

d. *Virgilia* Lam.

Virgilia is a small genus of 1 or possibly 2 tree species, native to the Cape. The trees have leaves that are imparipinnate, with narrow leaflets, crowned with a short thorn-like point, with stipules; pea-like flowers that are pink or mauve in racemes massed in the axils of the leaves and terminally, borne in great abundance; pods that are narrow, leathery, 2-valved and hairy, and seeds that are oval and black.

The generic name honours the poet Virgil.

(221)   *Virgilia oroboides* (Berg.) Salter

= *Sophora oroboides* Berg.; = *Virgilia capensis* Lam.

(221.1)   *Virgilia divaricata* Adamson

Keurboom

Botanists, foresters, and gardeners have not decided to their mutual satisfaction whether the genus *Virgilia* is composed of one, two, or three different species of keurboom.

Phillips in his *Genera of South African Flowering Plants* lists only one species. This is *Virgilia oroboides* (Berg.) Salter. Many botanists feel, as did Phillips, that this one species embraces the various forms of *Virgilia* found along the Cape coast. Others see at least two species, *Virgilia oroboides*, native to the Cape Peninsula, which has rather sparse leaves and which bears its pale mauvish flowers intermittently from Christmas to April: and *Virgilia divaricata* Adamson, growing to the east, which bears rich, soft pink flowers in profusion in spring. Others recognize yet a third form that flowers from April to spring and which has flowers from white to deep pink.

The genus has an unusual distribution, for although keurbooms have been successfully introduced into various parts of the country, they are native to a small area only, a narrow coastal strip from Van Staden's Pass near Port Elizabeth westwards to the Cape Peninsula, being most abundant in the George and Knysna forests and on the lower foothills of the mountains. When they are in bloom they splash the fringes of these forests with pink, rose and mauve.

The keurbooms do not as a rule grow much over 9 m high, and in the open often have a bushy type of growth with branches growing close to the ground. Among other trees, they have a more upward form of growth. A mature trunk may reach 0.6 m in diameter and is then dark grey and rough, but in young trees the stem is slender, and the bark is silver-grey and smooth.

The stipulate feathery leaves are once compound, from 8-20 cm long and up to 7 cm wide, with about 3-13 pairs of narrowly oblong leaflets, and a terminal leaflet, 1.3-2.5 cm long and 6-8 mm wide. They are bluntly

A young keurboom, *Virgilia* species, growing in the Montagu Pass near George, where it is common

904

pointed with a small thorn-like point at the tip, and the midrib prominent below. Young leaves, stalks, and twigs are reddish and velvety. The
leaves become dark green and smooth above with the undersurface
paler, duller, and slightly hairy.

The flowers, varying in colour from white to deep rose, are shaped
like those of the pea, about 1.3 cm long, borne in dense bunches in the
axils of the leaves and at the ends of the branches. They are sweetly
scented, rich in nectar, and visited by birds and insects.

The pods are 5-8 cm long, brown, softly hairy, and split into 2
valves, releasing the 2-6 seeds. These are very hard but, mixed with
other food, are often eaten by stock, wild pigs, and elephants, and are
passed out in the manure of animals in a softened state in which they
germinate readily. They are further dispersed by rainwater and
streams.

The seeds of the keurboom are amazingly fertile. After exhaustive
examination and tests it has been established that a very large proportion of the seeds are fertile and that the seed germination of no other
native tree at Knysna even approaches its record. The seeds are so hard
that some form of stimulation is necessary before they germinate
successfully. In nursery work the seeds are soaked in hot water before
sowing; or their skins are cracked artificially; or they are sown 1.9 cm
deep, the soil covered with light brushwood which is set alight and
burnt, and the seeds then watered. Seeds can remain alive for many
years after they have fallen and after even as many as 30 years they will
germinate if conditions become favourable. A forest fire is often followed by a dense growth of keurboom seedlings.

The keurboom needs a fair supply of moisture and cannot stand
severe frost. It is more light demanding than most forest trees and is
found on the outskirts of forests, on hillsides, along open watercourses or in open glades. Even young seedlings flourish best in sunlight. It is one of the most virile forest trees. The rate of growth in a
young plant – often 8 m in 6 years – is exceptional. The tree is short-
lived, the life of the average keurboom being from 12 to 20 years.

Both keurbooms are evergreen and make good garden trees, but the
pink-flowered *Virgilia divaricata* is preferable for in spring it is a
gloriously decorative tree, mantled in pink, and its growth is somewhat
more compact than that of *Virgilia oroboides*. Both species are so fast-
growing that after two years they are a conspicuous feature of a garden.
Young trees should be given good soil and plenty of moisture in parts
with dry winters. They need protection while young, but thereafter
will stand a good deal of frost.

In a garden they have one drawback – their strong spreading
roots – and it is as well to plant them on their own or with bulbs or
annuals.

Keurbooms should be planted far more widely than they are. In
Australia, for example, they are very popular; and in England they were
cultivated as long ago as 1767, a sobering thought for South Africans,
who often cannot even identify a tree.

The wood is light and soft, handsome when polished but said to be
subject to worm attack. It is used for yokes, rafters, and for fuel. The
transparent gum that exudes from the bark was once used as a substitute for starch.

Many insects are probably associated with keurbooms. Among them
are the little blue butterfly known as the Lucerne Blue, *Lampides
boeticus*, which breeds not only on lucerne but on keurboom species;

Opposite inset
Virgilia oroboides: A
flowering and fruiting
twig, and the pods split
open (50%)

Below
Keurboom stem and
bark

Above
Baphia massaiensis subsp.
obovata leaves, flowers, pod
and seed (80%)

Below right
Baphia racemosa pods and
seeds (80%)

906

and the large handsome ghost moth, *Leto venus*. The latter is a forest beauty, laying its eggs at the foot of a keurboom, into the wood of which the caterpillars bore.

The specific name *oroboides* means "resembling *Orobus*", a genus of plants with pea flowers which is now included in *Lathyrus*, the sweet-pea genus. The name *divaricata* means "divergent" and alludes to the widely spreading branches. Keur means "choice", or "pick", so that the common name means "pick of the trees". See them in their home country in the spring and the reason is obvious.

e. *Baphia* DC.

Two species of this African and Madagascan genus of just over 70 species grow in South and South West Africa.

The genus has an unusual feature — its members have simple leaves whereas the leaves of most leguminous plants are compound. The flowers are pea-like and are borne in racemes or sometimes in clusters in the leaf axils, and the pods are narrow, flat and 2-valved. A butterfly commonly known as the Orange Barred Playboy, *Deudorix diocles*, breeds on these.

The generic name is based on the Greek word "baphe", meaning "dye", which was based in its turn on the brilliant red dye given by the heartwood of a tropical African species, *Baphia nitida* Lodd., known as camwood. The dye was used locally as a cosmetic and commercially to colour the English bandana handkerchiefs.

(223)   *Baphia massaiensis* Taub.
          subsp. *obovata* (Schinz) Brummitt

= *Baphia obovata* Schinz

Isunde; isunde (Tsw)

This is a rare species in South Africa, growing only in sandy soil in the north-eastern Kruger National Park near the Portuguese border. It occurs westwards on Kalahari sand — often in abundance — through Botswana to South West Africa, and northwards to Angola, Rhodesia, and Zambia. It grows on the dunes of the sandveld and is a common small tree in the woodland of the Caprivi Strip.

Although in northern South West Africa this grows up to 8 m high, as a rule it is no more than 3-5 m and is sometimes only a low bush. It has branches which frequently droop, and a light-coloured bark.

The simple, dull-coloured leaves are oval, egg-shaped, or pear-shaped, and arranged alternately. They are 2.5-8 cm long and up to 5 cm wide, usually broadest at the upper end, with a fine point at the apex or with the apex notched, narrowing to the base, finely velvety, and with neat, conspicuous, parallel veins, prominent below, running outwards and curving upwards abruptly at the margin. They are carried on short, furry stalks.

The flowers are borne in clusters in the axils of the leaves from October to January. They are the typical pea flowers in shape, white marked within with a yellow spot, and scented like jasmine.

The pods are up to 8 cm long, widest towards the tip and narrowing to the base, with a point often slightly curled. They are hard, brown,

Baphia racemosa: Leaves and flowers (100%)

smooth, and much lined. Within are 1-2 seeds.

Leaves and flowers are eaten by cattle and antelope — in the Transvaal notably Livingstone's Antelope. The wood makes good walking sticks.

The tree was called after the Masai people of Kenya and the name *obovata* refers to the shape of the leaves.

(224)   *Baphia racemosa* (Hochst.) Bak.

= *Bracteolaria racemosa* Hochst.

Violet pea; isiFithi, uTshupu (X); isiPhithi (Z)

The violet pea of Natal and Zululand grows from the coast to an altitude of 600 m or more, in forest or in dense bush. It was first described in 1841 from a plant collected by Dr F. Krauss "in the forests of Natal".

It is a shrub or small tree up to 6 m tall, sometimes rather lax-growing, sometimes well-shaped, with a grey or dark brown, fairly smooth bark.

The leaves are simple, alternate, and untoothed, 5-9 cm long and up to 5 cm broad, widely lance-shaped to egg-shaped, tapering to the 1.3 stalk, smooth above and slightly velvety below, with veins looping along the margin. Where the leaf meets the stalk there is a small swelling or "knee" and this is characteristic and helps to identify the tree.

Baphia racemosa stem and bark

The white pea-like flowers with a yellow throat, appearing from spring to early summer, grow in short sprays in the axils of the leaves and at the ends of the branches. They are strongly violet-scented and give the tree its common name of violet pea. A tree in flower is ornamental.

The flat, pointed pods resemble those of *Baphia massaiensis* subsp. *obovata*, and are widest in the upper portion, narrowing to the base. They split open to release the smooth brown seeds.

The butterfly known as the Blue Spotted Charaxes breeds on this species as does the widespread Brown Playboy, *Deudorix antalas*.

The wood is yellowish, and is subject to borer attack unless carefully seasoned. It is not as a rule used in building huts as it is thought to bring bad luck. Young wood is supple and was once used to make wagon and cart tents, and for other purposes where an easily bent wood was required. It makes good hoe handles and sticks when cut in the winter, the bark removed, and seasoned.

The name *racemosa* refers to the showy racemes of flowers.

f. *Podalyria* Lam.

The genus *Podalyria* — named after Podalyrius, a physician in the Greek camp at Troy and a son of Aesculapius, the Greek god of healing — is centred in the south west Cape.

It has about 25 members, nearly all of which are notable for their silky, silvery, simple leaves, arranged alternately, and for their pink or purple pea-like flowers borne singly or in small groups in the axils of the leaves. The pods are oval or oblong and usually crowned with shaggy hairs.

Above
The ystervarkbos, *Lebeckia macrantha*, near Witsand in the north west Cape

Below
Lebeckia sericea on a rocky hill in Namaqualand

(225)   *Podalyria calyptrata* Willd.

Keur, keurtjie, ertjiebos

Podalyria calyptrata, the best known member of the genus, is a fairly common, and in spring beautiful little evergreen tree or shrub growing along the banks of mountain streams and on forest edges in the western Cape.

"The plant that appealed to me most . . . " wrote Dr John Hutchinson, noted Kew botanist, when he first visited the Cape, "was the beautiful mauve-pink *Podalyria calyptrata* which is abundant in the woods" Marloth, too, admired it and its flowers which, he wrote, filled the air of whole valleys with their sweet scent.

The keur is a sturdy, rounded, much-branched little tree up to about 4 m high. The young branches are velvety, the leaves simple, alternate, oval or egg-shaped, narrowing to the base, 1.3-4.5 cm long and up to 2.5 cm wide. They are greeny-grey and lack the dense silky hairs common to so many of the podalyrias for the silky white hairs on both sides of the leaves are sparse. The midrib, and sometimes the veins, are prominent on the under-surface of mature leaves.

The flowers, in bloom from July to September, are pea-shaped, pink or occasionally white, 2.5 cm or more across, borne on short twigs between the leaves. When in bud they are covered by bracts which are joined together to make a silken cap, which is lifted and thrown off as the flower opens. This gives the tree its specific name, *calyptratus* being a Latin word meaning "bearing a cap-like covering".

The flat, furry, brown pods are usually widest in the top portion, narrowing to the base, and measure up to 4 cm in length.

In bloom, perhaps grouped with Cape bulbs, the keur is wonderful. It is easily cultivated in the winter-rainfall districts, and even in the summer-rainfall area if given a light acid soil with plenty of compost, and well watered in the winter.

See colour plate facing
page 874

g. *Lebeckia* Thunb.

Lebeckia is a purely South African genus confined — with the exception of about 2 species — to the Cape Province. Here it is widespread from the Richtersveld in northern Namaqualand to the south west Cape, extending in the north east to Kuruman and Gordonia and in the south east as far as Cradock, Albany and Port Elizabeth.

Most of the species are woody shrubs but occasionally they may become small trees in stature. The ystervarkbos, *Lebeckia macrantha* Harv. of the north west Cape, with its bare stems reaching to 2 m or over in height, is such a one. Its spine-tipped almost leafless branches are reminiscent of those of *Cadaba aphylla*, and are a familiar sight on arid hillsides.

The best known species is probably *Lebeckia sericea* Thunb., a common bush in Namaqualand broken veld, which in favourable positions grows into a small tree.

The species are sometimes spiny; smooth or with silky hairs; the leaves with 3 leaflets (or with only 1 developed), occasionally almost absent — as in *Lebeckia macrantha* — the leaflets often narrow or thread-like, the stipules usually absent; the flowers varying in size and number, borne in a terminal raceme, sweetpea-like in structure, all the petals clawed and usually smooth, the standard petal reflexed, the pods usually narrow, often a slender oblong, flat or cylindric, usually tipped with the remains of the persistent style.

The genus was named in memory of Lebeck, 'an obscure botanist'.

Lebeckia sericea Thunb.

Silver pea, vaalertjiebos

The silver pea is one of the very common species of Namaqualand, growing on hill slopes, on coastal dunes and on sandy flats from the northern parts of the territory southwards to about Saldanha Bay. It has been collected as far east as Pofadder.

Although usually a sturdy shrub it can, under favourable conditions, grow into a little tree. Its rounded lines and silvery foliage, and in spring its bright yellow flowers, are a common sight alongside the roads enlivening, together with the bright daisy flowers, the somewhat sombre hills.

The leaves, borne on long stalks, are composed of 3 leaflets. These vary from 3 mm to 38 mm in length and are slender, sometimes needle-like, at others up to 6 mm wide, covered with silky-grey hairs. The "pea" flowers, all facing the same way, are crowded in racemes. They are a fine clear yellow and silky, and are shown off splendidly by the silver foliage. Occasionally purple or cream-flowered forms are found.

The pod is cylindric, when young with a wispy point, covered with silky grey hairs, when mature often without the point, and smoother.

The plant is described as "well eaten by sheep".

The specific name *sericea* means "silky" and describes one of the outstanding characteristics of the plant — its covering of silky hairs.

h. *Wiborgia* Thunb.

Wiborgia is a small genus of about 10 species of shrubs — occasionally tree-like — which occur from Namaqualand southwards to the south west Cape and eastwards to about the George district.

They are stiff and often spiny species with smooth or softly hairy leaves; the leaves with 3 leaflets arranged digitately; the leaflets often narrow; the stipules small or none; the flowers in a terminal and often one-sided raceme; the bracts and bracteoles small; the flowers yellow, pea-like, the calyx bell-shaped, all the petals clawed, the standard petal standing away from the other petals; the ovary with few ovules; the pod stalked, flat, and winged on one or two sides.

The genus was named after a Danish botanist, Eric Viborg.

(225.1)   *Wiborgia sericea* Thunb.

Wiborgia

This is not a common tree, occurring only on the dry rocky slopes of the Cedarberg and the mountains to the north. *Flora Capensis* does not record it as a tree at all, but travellers descending the steep road into the lovely Bidouw valley — in spring time jewelled with flowers — note it as a decorative little tree on the steep stony valley sides. Here it grows

Above left
Wiborgia sericea stem

Above right
Wiborgia sericea on the
slopes of the Bidouw
Valley near Wupperthal
in the western Cape

up to 3.6 m tall, with a stem diameter up to 15 cm.

The bark is light brown and deeply ribbed, the branches spreading, stiff, and sometimes spiny. The leaves, composed of 3 leaflets digitately arranged, are crowded along the hairy twigs. The leaflets are small, up to 8 mm long, oblong or somewhat triangular, with blunt, notched or slightly pointed tips, and densely covered with silky-grey hairs. They dry a pale silvery colour.

The yellow pea flowers are borne in short racemes.

The pods are stalked, flat and winged, broadly so on one side, with small, hair-like wisps at the tips.

The specific name is based on the Latin "sericeus" meaning "silky", in allusion to the silky hairs covering most parts of the tree.

i. *Crotalaria* L.

Crotalaria is a large genus of over 500 species, widespread in the tropical and subtropical parts of the southern hemisphere and to a lesser degree in the northern.

Over 100 species occur in South Africa. Many of these are important economically, either because they are good fodder — or because they are poisonous to stock.

One of the commonest of all butterflies, the little Lucerne Blue, *Lampides boeticus,* breeds on members of the genus. It is associated with many other species of legumes, and is a familiar butterfly in lucerne lands.

They are herbs or shrubs, or in the case of *Crotalaria capensis* Jacq., sometimes tree-like, upright or trailing, and usually unarmed. The leaves have 1-5 leaflets (usually 3) digitately arranged, and stipules that may be large or small. The inflorescence is a raceme or a head borne at the end of the branch or opposite the leaves, or occasionally the flowers are solitary. These may be large or small and are sweetpea-like in form, with the standard usually clawed, the keel often L-shaped ending in a beak, and the wings shorter than the keel, the stamens united in a tube, the ovary with 2 to many ovules; and the pods with or without stalks, and inflated.

The generic name *Crotalaria* is based on the Greek word for castinet, "because the seeds rattle in the inflated pods when shaken".

(224.1) *Crotalaria capensis* Jacq.

Yellow pea, geelkeurtjie, Cape laburnum, wilde ertjie

The yellow pea is a widespread species occurring from the Cape Penin-sula northwards through the eastern Cape, Natal, Zululand, Swaziland and the eastern and northern Transvaal to Portuguese East Africa, grow-ing in forest, on forest margins, in lowveld bush and in thornveld, on dunes, on stream banks, and on old lands. It occurs occasionally in the Orange Free State.

This is a shrub or small tree up to 6 m high with a light-coloured, fissured stem and a crown of many slender drooping branches. The twigs are covered with soft felty hairs. The leaves are compound and alternate, and are carried on long slender stalks. They are composed of 3 leaflets of variable shape and size, 0.5-5 cm long, the middle the big-gest, usually oval or egg-shaped, narrowing to the base, with round or bluntly pointed tips with short, thorn-like points. They are thin, a light green and hairy above, and below blue-green with the veins conspicuous. The stipules at the base of the leaf stalk are conspicuous and resemble a small pair of leaves. (They are a character that helps to identify the species).

The flowers measure up to 2.5 cm in length. The standard may be yellow lined with red and the keel pale green; or the colours may vary from red to orange or pink. The calyx is softly hairy. The flowers are borne in racemes at the end of the branches or opposite the leaves and bloom in summer and autumn. The stalk bearing the flowers has small, narrow growths — bracts — along it.

The flowers are pollinated by bees.

The pods, up to about 5 cm long, have a stipe and are tipped with a slender wisp. They are yellowish, ridged, inflated, and pendulous, and when ripe rattle in the wind.

Although this species is heavily browsed in parts, in others it is reported to be poisonous to stock.

In the Cape it is sometimes planted as a hedge — in the flowering season a very colourful one. This was one of the early South African species to be known to European gardeners and was cultivated in Vienna over 200 years ago.

The specific name means "of the Cape".

j. *Indigofera* L.

Indigofera is a genus old in the history of trade. One of the species on which the genus was founded, *Indigofera tinctoria* L., and a number of allied species, yield indigo which was valued in ancient Egypt, the Medi-terranean countries, and Western Asia, as a dye and medicine. It was one of the very early exports from India to Europe.

Marco Polo knew it. "It is made of a certain herb, which is gather-ed" . . . he wrote, "put into great vessels upon which they pour water and lave it until the whole of the plant is decomposed. They then put this liquid in the sun, which is tremendously hot there, so that it boils

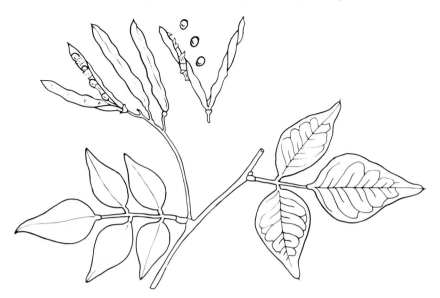

Indigofera natalensis:
Leaves, pods and seeds
(60%)

and coagulates, and becomes such as we see it. They then divide it into pieces of four ounces each, and in that form it is exported to our ports".

Pliny wrote of its "wondrous combination of purple and deep azure" and of its use in treating ague and other ailments.

Several South African species, such as *Indigo arrecta* Hochst. ex A.Rich., contain indigo, but its exploitation on any scale has proved impractical. Africans, however, use the blue dye, and so, sometimes, did the early colonists. Many of the species are used medicinally by country people, while others are poisonous – or suspected of being so.

It is a large genus of over 800 species, mostly herbs and undershrubs found in all tropical and subtropical countries, with over 200 species in South Africa alone, and well represented in South West Africa. At least two species are sometimes tree-like.

Several species of butterflies, including the common Lucerne Blue, *Lampides boeticus*, and the Drakensberg Blue, *Lepidochrysops niobe*, breed on members of the genus.

The species are characterized by leaves that, while sometimes simple, are usually compound, with 3 leaflets, or imparipinnate – that is, with several or a number of pairs of leaflets, terminated by a single leaflet – with stipules; the flowers in a raceme or spike at the ends of the branches; the flowers sweetpea-like, the keel petal spurred; the pods usually small, narrow, and cylindrical, bursting open.

The generic name is based on the word "indigo" and the Latin "fero", meaning "to bear".

(225.3) *Indigofera natalensis* H.Bol.

inSiphane encane (Z)

"The Natal indigofera" occurs in forest and on its fringes from Zululand southwards to Pondoland. It is fairly common along the coast and inland in forests such as Ngome, as an undershrub in deep shade, or growing thickly along the forest paths.

It is a shrub or small tree with a slender, whitish stem, and a crown

Right
Indigofera cylindrica:
flowering and fruiting
twigs (80%)

Below
Indigofera cylindrica
growing alongside a
Pondoland country road

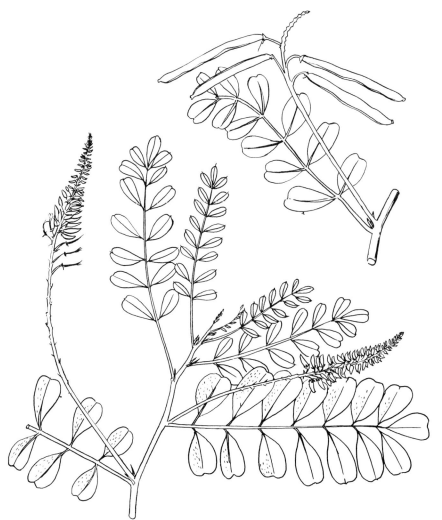

of delicate, compound leaves which tend to spread horizontally. They
are composed of one or two pairs of leaflets and a terminal one, thin,
dark green and glossy, 1.3-5 cm long, egg-shaped, the tips narrowed into
blunt, jutting points, the base round or somewhat narrowed.

The tiny white flowers are borne in a delicate, terminal, spike-like
inflorescence.

The fruits are narrow pods up to 5 cm long — remarkably worm-
like — light-coloured, often mottled with red, turning brown with age
and rattling. They are borne on slender stalks.

The wood is used for fuel.

The specific name means "of Natal".

(225.2)   *Indigofera cylindrica* DC.

Tree indigofera

Indigofera cylindrica, usually considered the most tree-like of the genus
in South Africa, grows from about East London through Pondoland
and Natal to Zululand, in scrub and on forest margins, often on river
banks. There is one doubtful report from Clanwilliam.

916

The fair-sized specimen in the photograph grew on a forest edge in Pondoland alongside the road to the mouth of the Umgazi River.

It is a small, handsome tree up to 4.5 m in height, with a stem up to 13 cm or more in diameter. The compound leaves — usually from 5-10 cm long — consist of 4-7 pairs of fairly widely spaced leaflets and a terminal leaflet. These are 0.8-2.5 cm long, egg-shaped, the tips round and often notched, the base narrowed, and smooth. Small stipules are present. The common leaf stalk is up to 10 cm long.

The small flowers grow in spike-like inflorescences — botanically racemes — on slender stalks in the axils of the leaves. They are white, pink or purple and bloom usually in summer.

The pods are straight, slender, cylindrical, and smooth, with about 8-10 seeds. Presumably they are the basis of the specific name *cylindrica*.

Occasionally this species is cultivated. It domesticates happily and is showy in flower.

k. *Psoralea* L.

Psoralea is a fairly large genus of over 100 small trees, shrubs or herbs, common in the tropics and subtropics. It is well represented in South Africa where roughly 50 species occur — mainly in the south west Cape.

One species, *Psoralea pinnata* L., grows as a small tree and it is possible, although apparently not recorded, that others may also become tree-like.

The outstanding character of the genus is its strong scent, and the resinous, dark or transparent dots that cover the leaves. The latter are usually pinnate or with 3 leaflets, occasionally with 1, with stipules clasping the branches; the flowers blue, purple or white, pea-like, the calyx bell-shaped, the standard petal broad with the sides curved backwards, the wings clawed, the keel curved and clawed, the stamens in two groups, borne in spikes, racemes, heads, the bracts 2-3; the pod enclosed in the calyx; 1-seeded (a distinctive character of the genus) and indehiscent.

The generic name is based on the Greek word "psoraleos" meaning "warted" or "scurfy", in reference to the dots or warts characteristic of the genus.

(225.4) *Psoralea pinnata* L.

Fountain tree, fonteinbos, fonteinhout, bloukeur, penwortel; umHlonishwa (Z)

The fountain tree, the most widely distributed member of the genus *Psoralea*, is a common species on stream banks, near vleis and spring heads, on forest margins and on mountain slopes, at altitudes up to at least 1524 m in many areas of the country. It grows from about Clanwilliam southwards to the Cape Peninsula — it is recorded from Table Mountain itself — eastwards and northwards through the George and Knysna districts to the eastern Cape, Natal, Zululand, Swaziland, and the eastern and northern Transvaal. It occurs, although less frequently, in the mountains of the eastern Orange Free State.

The trees illustrated grew on a stream bank high in the Outeniqua Mountains.

Psoralea pinnata growing in the Outeniqua Mountains

918

Psoralea pinnata: a flowering twig (90%)

Below
Psoralea pinnata stem and bark

This is usually a shrub or a small tree up to 4 m high, although it is recorded up to 6 m in height. It may be many-branched but is often a slender, graceful tree with a trunk up to 15 cm in diameter, which is smooth and a light brown colour marked with white. Branches and twigs are angular.

The leaves are compound, composed of several pairs of leaflets and a terminal one (often 7 in all). The leaflets measure up to 5 cm in length and 3 mm in breadth although forms with narrower, needle-like leaves are common. The tips are pointed and sometimes curled and the whole blade dotted with dark glands which are conspicuous in dried material. The leaves are aromatic when crushed.

The tree blooms off and on throughout the year. The pea flowers, rich blue, purple or white and often finely striped, are borne at the ends of the branches or in the axils of the upper leaves and although seldom very showy are delicate and charming on the slender branches. The flower stalks are up to 2.5 cm long and in the upper part, just below the calyx, is a tiny cup formed by the united bracts. The flower stalks, bracts and calyx are often, but not always, covered with black hairs.

The fruit is a small pod concealed in the calyx and is 1-seeded. It does not burst open.

This is one of the earliest South African plants to be cultivated for in 1690 it was growing in England from seed collected at the Cape. Linnaeus named it and Burchell collected it "at Sylvan Station" in the Cape in September 1814. (One of the specimens he collected there is today in the National Herbarium in Pretoria).

It would be interesting to know if this little tree exists anywhere today in a private garden. Records on herbarium sheets state that it persists even under pines and wattles, and with these staying powers it might well be worthy of gardeners' notice. C.A. Smith notes that Thunberg considered the plant a weed in gardens, and says the reason for the common name "penwortel", or "taproot" is that the deep firm roots make eradication difficult.

The name "fountain tree" refers to its liking for spring heads. The specific name *pinnata* is based on the pinnate leaves.

L. *Mundulea* Benth.

About 17 species of shrubs and trees, ranging from Africa and Madagascar to Ceylon and east India, belong to this genus.

They all have leaves that are imparipinnate, covered with silky hairs, pea-like flowers — often showy — in terminal or axillary racemes, and flat, hairy pods containing kidney-shaped seeds.

The origin of the generic name *Mundulea* is not known.

(226)   *Mundulea sericea* (Willd.) A.Chev.

= *Cytisus sericeus* Willd.; = *Mundulea suberosa* Benth.

Silver bush, cork bush, Rhodesia silver-leaf, blou-ertjieboom, olifantshout, visboontjie, visgif; umHlalantethe, umSindandlovu (Z); umSindandlovana (Sw); mosita-tlou (Tsw-Hebron); mukunda-nḍou (V)

"That which resists the Elephants" is the meaning of several African names for this sturdy little tree with its tough stem and young branches

Above
Burchell's sketch of *Psoralea pinnata*

Below
Mundulea sericea growing on a hillside on the outskirts of Pretoria

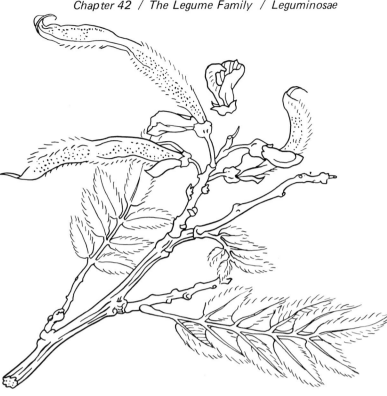

Above left
Stem and bark of *Mundulea sericea*

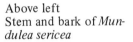

Above right
Mundulea sericea: A twig with leaves, flowers and pods (80%)

that bend like a leather whip; and anyone who has ever tried to break a live branch will know just how good this name is.

The only South African member of its genus, this little tree is widespread, not only in Africa, where it grows from Zululand and the Transvaal bushveld westwards into South West Africa and Angola, eastwards in Madagascar, and northwards into tropical Africa, but in India and Ceylon as well. It favours savannah woodland, wooded hills, scrub-covered koppies, and even dry bare flats. Not only should the people of Pretoria and Johannesburg know it well — for it is scattered on the hills about the cities — but equally the tourists to the Kruger Park in the east and to the Etosha Pan in the west.

It is a small graceful tree seldom above 3 m high, with a bushy, much-branched crown. The bark on the stem and branches is pale, corky, and deeply furrowed, a fine contrast to the delicate silver foliage.

The leaves vary a good deal, although they are most often 8-10 cm long, composed of about 4-10 pairs of leaflets and a terminal leaflet, typically about 1.3 cm long, which vary from oval to lance-shaped. They are a pale grey-green and covered densely with silver hairs. A form with much larger leaflets is occasionally found.

The pea-flowers are a rich violet or mauve and bloom in small terminal sprays in spring and early summer, when the tree — silver and violet — is charming. These develop into clusters of long narrow pods, up to 10 cm in length, yellow-brown, brown, or grey, and velvety, and these remain on the tree for months, sometimes in winter looking rather forlorn and untidy.

The wood is light yellow with a rather unpleasant smell when worked, tough, hard, and strong.

In some parts of the world — as in India, Ceylon and tropical Africa — this tree has an unusual interest, the seeds, the bark, and the roots are used for poisoning fish. The leaves are commonly stripped, pounded, and put into bags which are thrown into the water, which

921

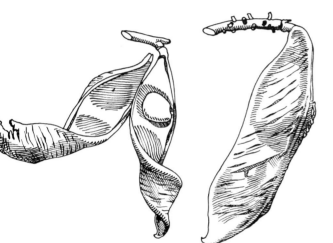

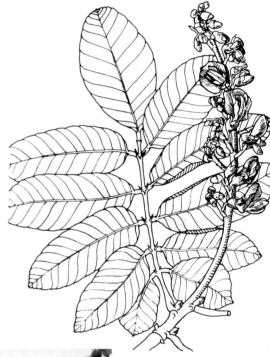

OPPOSITE

Above
A small umzimbeet,
Millettia grandis, grow-
ing on the edge of the
Egossa Forest, Pondo-
land

Centre
Millettia grandis: A leaf,
flowers, and pods which
through age have lost
their characteristic hairs
(50%)

Below
Leaves and pods of the
umzimbeet

kill and not merely stupefy the fish. In East Africa the bark is said to
kill even small crocodiles! In the Transvaal, too, Africans sometimes
know the tree as a fish poison. In view of this it is surprising to find the
leaves and bark are eaten, and apparently with no ill effects, by cattle,
goats, elephant, and antelope.

Zulus use the bark as an emetic to treat poisoning.

Two species of common and well known butterflies breed on this
tree. They are the Natal Barred Blue, *Spindasis natalensis,* and the
Common Blue, *Syntarucus telicanus.*

The silver bush has one surprising use in South Africa. Watt and
Brandwijk in *The Medicinal and Poisonous Plants of Southern
Africa* say that the Venda use the powdered root to "doctor" a man
and his wife when the latter has had a miscarriage, "the couple being
tied with their backs to opposite sides of a *Mundulea sericea* tree during
the treatment".

This is a decorative little tree in the garden and easily grown on well-
drained soil. The seeds, like so many legume seeds, should be soaked in
warm water before planting. It is very slow-growing but, considered as a
decorative shrub in its youth rather than a tree, it is satisfactory for it
blooms when perhaps only 40 cm high and the silver foliage is lovely.
It is sometimes deciduous, sometimes almost evergreen, hardy, and
uncomplaining.

The specific name *sericea* is the Latin for "silky".

m. *Millettia* Wight & Arn.

Below
Umzimbeet bark

About 150 tropical and subtropical species of the Old World belong
to the genus *Millettia,* named after Charles Millet of Canton, China, who
was in the service of the British East India Company in the 1830's.
Two species grow in South Africa.

All have leaves that are alternate and imparipinnate, with small stipules and pea-like flowers — often showy — in racemes or panicles at
the ends of the branches. The pods vary from narrow to egg-shaped, and
are 2-valved, leathery, or woody, smooth or hairy, and the seeds are
round or kidney-shaped.

(227)   *Millettia grandis* (E.Mey.) Skeels

= *Virgilia grandis* E.Mey.; = *Millettia caffra* Meisn.

Umzimbeet, Kaffir ironwood, kafferysterhout; umSimbithi,
umKunye (X); umSimbithi (Z)

The umzimbeet is a medium to large tree of the coastal forests north-
east of the Kei River, and a common and beautiful species of the Transkei, Natal and Zululand, usually growing at an altitude of under 600 m.

Sim describes it as most often a gnarled tree on shale, but in forest, at
forest margins, or under suitable conditions, it is a fine tree up to 12 m
high. In forest the trunk is light brown, flaky and often covered with
moss. Sometimes it is deeply scarred for baboons strip and eat the bark.
The leaves are stipulate, once divided, and up to about 15 cm long and
10-13 cm wide, consisting of about 5 or 6 pairs — sometimes 7 — of
opposite leaflets and a terminal leaflet. These are broadly lance-shaped
or oblong, pointed, with a rounded base, smooth above, sparsely silky-

924

OPPOSITE

Above left
Millettia sutherlandii
growing alongside the
road to the Umgazi
River mouth near Port
St. John's.

Above right
A typical trunk of *Mil-
lettia sutherlandii* in
deep forest

Below left
Millettia sutherlandii
pods hang downwards in
contrast to those of *Millettia grandis*. These
were photographed in
May.

Below right
Millettia sutherlandii: A
flowering twig and pod
(60%)

Below
Millettia sutherlandii
bark

haired below, up to about 7 cm long and 1.9 cm wide, with the midrib and close secondary veins conspicuous below. The common midrib is channelled. At the base of the leaflet stalk is a pair of stipels, or very small fine leafy growths. Young leaf stalks are reddish and velvety as is the veining on the under-surface of the leaves.

The tree may be evergreen or deciduous.

The sprays of rusty-brown buds borne at the ends of the branches in spring open into purple pea-flowers, handsome and colourful. These develop into woody pods up to 15 cm long and 4 cm wide, red-brown, furry, and borne upright, giving the tree a reddish tinge. They split to release the flat, oblong seeds. A common butterfly of the Natal coastal forests, the Orange Barred Playboy, *Deudorix diocles,* breeds in the pods of this species and sometimes those of *Millettia sutherlandii.* The whole larval and pupal stage, according to Clark & Dickson, is spent inside the pod, the larvae boring an "escape" hole through the hard surface of the pod before pupation. Certain trees in Durban parks, are on occasion favoured by the butterfly.

The wood of the umzimbeet is extremely heavy, hard, and strong. It polishes well and is used for furniture, for wagon wheel spokes, for axles, and for sticks. The heartwood is dark brown and the sapwood yellow. Sim remarks that the dividing line between heartwood and sapwood is very sharply defined and that the Africans when making knob-kerries usually manage to have one side of the stick white and the other black. These piebald sticks may be found in many Pondoland shops catering for tourists.

The ground beans in milk are used as a cure for round worms, but the beans are poisonous if taken in quantity. Zulus use the roots in a truly remarkable tranquillizer. They grind them together with those of a croton — in equal quantities — and mix this with 1 part of lion fat and a little ground lion bone, plus 1 portion of python fat. A pinch of this is burnt in a hut to dispel worries. Mr Ian Garland of Zululand, who supplied this Zulu doctor's recipe, added a special note from Mrs Beeton — "First catch your lion and python! "

The roasted ground roots are also mixed with water, the mixture left to evaporate, and the residue licked off the fingers, to induce sleep.

This makes a good, shady, decorative garden tree with glossy mature foliage, and new foliage in shades of rosy-brown. It is well-shaped, fairly fast, and withstands several degrees of frost. A warm·sunny spot in deep soil is ideal for it, and it responds well to copious watering.

The name *grandis* means "large". The common name, "ironwood", is a direct translation of the Xhosa name "umSimbithi".

(228)   *Millettia sutherlandii* Harv.

Giant umzimbeet, bastard umzimbeet, basteroemzimbiet; umQunye, umGunye (X); umKhunye, umSimbatshani (Z)

The giant umzimbeet is a noble tree — an evergreen of high forest and forest edges from Pondoland to Zululand — growing up to 30 m high, with a dense crown and a trunk up to 1.2 m in diameter. It is one of the common trees in forests such as Ngoye in Zululand, and the Egossa in Pondoland where huge specimens occur, and is one of the familiar species around Port St. John's. Driving along the river road to this little

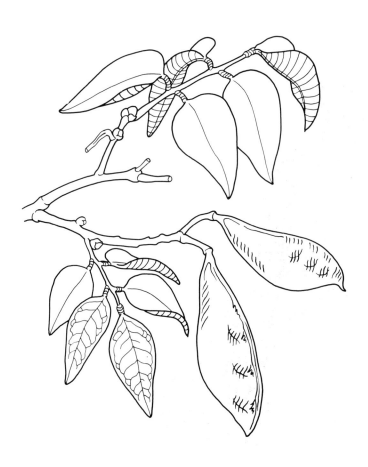

926

OPPOSITE

Above
Craibia zimmermannii
growing at Lake Sibayi

Below left
Craibia stem and bark

Below right
Craibia zimmermannii:
Leaves and pods (60%)

Below
Craibia stem and bark
— another form

village, the numerous straight grey trunks appear almost white against their forest backdrop.

Most often the trunk is this light bright grey, but in forest it may be olive-grey, mottled with lichens, and frequently is cracked into tiny squares. Forest forms are typically buttressed, often with several stems from the base, and suckering.

The branches are smooth and grey. The dark green leaves are once compound, usually composed of about 3 pairs of opposite leaflets — occasionally more — and a terminal leaflet. These are about 4 cm long, somewhat oblong or broadly lance-shaped, very rarely egg-shaped, smooth when mature, borne on short, stout, hairy stalks. They resemble the leaves of the umzimbeet but usually have fewer leaflets and these are more widely spaced with veins looping along the margin, unlike the neat parallel veins of the umzimbeet leaflets which reach to the very edge of the margin and are not looped.

Young twigs and stalks are covered with rust-coloured hairs.

The brownish, hairy buds in dense terminal sprays open into pink, mauve, or purple pea-flowers with a silky brown calyx. The pods are 4-10 cm long, usually somewhat oblong with a short jutting point, outlined with a fine rim, and holding flat, shiny, oval or rather kidney-shaped seeds. The pods hang downwards and in late autumn when they are light green and brown, they are conspicuous.

At least 4 species of butterflies breed on this tree, including *Coeliades forestan*, which is popularly called the Striped Policeman because, in its bush and forest home, it flits constantly to and fro suggesting a policeman on his beat.

Sim thought the timber of the giant umzimbeet was useless because it flakes off in rings. He described it as "one of the largest, most abundant, and most useless trees in the Egossa Forest, East Pondoland". It is, however, beautiful and might be of use for shade and decoration.

The specific name honours Dr Peter Cormack Sutherland, 1822-1900, medical doctor, geologist, and former Surveyor-General of Natal.

n. *Craibia* Harms & Dunn

About 9 species belong to this tropical genus which shows affinities with *Millettia*.

The species are trees usually with gold or black hairs, with alternate, imparipinnate leaves and thickened petioles; pea-like flowers in panicles or racemes, and pods that are egg-shaped to oval, and flat, with 1-4 seeds.

The genus was named after W.G. Craib, who was Assistant for India at Kew, and later Professor of Botany at Aberdeen.

(229)   *Craibia zimmermannii* (Harms) Harms ex Dunn

= *Lonchocarpus zimmermannii* Harms; = *Craibia gazensis* Bak.f.; = *Craibia filipes* Dunn

Craibia; uBambo-livenyoka (Z)

One species of the tropical genus *Craibia*, *Craibia zimmermannii*, grows both in high and short forest and on forest margins in Zululand and Swaziland. Members of the genus much resemble those of *Millettia*

Above
Sesbania sesban subsp. *sesban* var. *nubica*, Pongola Poort

Left
Sesbania sesban var. *nubica:* A flowering twig and pods (80%)

928

but the leaflets of the compound leaves are usually arranged alternately, and are not opposite as in *Millettia*.

Craibia zimmermannii occurs from Tanzania southwards to Zululand and Swaziland. It is common in the bush around False Bay and at the camping site there, and northwards in the sandy woodland of Tongaland, while in the forest round Lake Sibayi it grows up to 15 m high.

It is often many-stemmed, with a silvery, slightly flaky bark. The dense foliage is composed of shiny compound leaves 10-13 cm long, with about 2 pairs of leaflets, alternately arranged, and a terminal leaflet. These are 2.5-7 cm long and up to 4 cm wide, egg-shaped to widely lance-shaped, usually widest in the lower half, with a rounded or narrowed base and a pointed apex, both leaf and leaflets being borne on hairy brown stalks. The midrib is raised below, and the veins, running outward and branching along the margin, are conspicuous.

The fragrant white pea-flowers are about 1.9 cm long, and are.borne in terminal bunches about November. They develop into smooth brown pods about 6.5 cm long, slightly curved, widest in the middle, and tapering both ends. They enclose 1-2 oval, shiny, brown seeds about 1.3 cm long.

The blue and black butterfly of Natal, the Blue-Spotted Charaxes, *Charaxes cithaeron*, breeds on this species.

Zulus and Tongas often use the wood to build grain stores.

The specific name honours Professor A. Zimmerman, Director of the Biological-Agricultural Institute at Amani in Tanzania, who made large plant collections.

o. *Sesbania* Scop.

Sesbania, a genus of about 70 species of the warm parts of the world, is centred in tropical Africa. Its members are herbs, shrubs, or rather short-lived little trees, with graceful compound, paripinnate leaves made up of many often narrow oblong leaflets. The pea flowers are usually in racemes or panicles, and the pods are most often narrow, and flat, round, angled or winged.

The genus takes its name from the Arabic "sesban" – the name given to a member of the genus.

Several species grow in South and South West Africa, of which 3 are sometimes small trees. These are forms of *Sesbania sesban* (L.) Merr. subsp. *sesban* which occur widely in South and South West Africa; *Sesbania cinerascens* Welw. ex Bak. and *Sesbania coerulescens* Harms.

Sesbania cinerascens, "the ashy-grey sesbania", is a rather sparse, blue-grey shrub or small tree occurring from northern and eastern South West Africa northwards. It has leaves up to about 15 cm long made up of 15-60 pairs of narrow oblong leaflets, spotted above, grey-green below; showy yellow flowers in long racemes in the autumn; and very long narrow dark brown pods up to 40 cm long and about 6 mm wide which ripen from autumn to early winter.

Sesbania coerulescens Harms, "the blue sesbania", grows in eastern South West Africa and resembles *Sesbania cinerascens* closely. It differs from it in the colour of the flowers which are blue, as the Latin name *coerulescens* indicates.

Left
Ormocarpum trichocarpum
near Potgietersrust in the
Transvaal

Below
Ormocarpum trichocarpum
leaves, flowers, and pods
(80%)

Opposite
Ormocarpum stem

930

(229.1) *Sesbania sesban* (L.) Merr. subsp. *sesban*
        1. var. *nubica* Chiov.

Frother, rivierboontjie; umSokosoko, umQambuqweqwe (Z); mpupunwa (V)

        2. var. *zambesiaca* Gillett

Two varieties of *Sesbania sesban* (L.) Merr. subsp. *sesban* occur in South
and South West Africa, the variety *nubica* in the eastern and northern
Transvaal, Zululand, Natal, and Swaziland, and var. *zambesiaca* Gillett
in northern South West Africa, Botswana, and Angola. Both grow along
rivers and are graceful small trees, var. *nubica* reaching a height of 8 m
along streams in Swaziland.

   Both forms are somewhat sparse with thin branches and blue-green
compound leaves made up of numerous narrow, oblong leaflets under
2.5 cm long, which close up in the evening. Both stems and leaf stalks
are hairy in varying degrees, var. *zambesiaca* being most hairy.
   They both have yellow pea flowers on slender stalks towards the ends
of the twigs, and long narrow pods up to 30 cm or more long, and
these often hang on the trees in great profusion.
   Zulus use the leaves as a soap substitute by rubbing them between
the hands and producing a foam. (The Venda name "mpupunwa" means
"frother").
   The shoots and leaves are eaten by elephants.
   The various forms of the tree, widely spread over Asia and Africa,
are used to treat a variety of ailments, including feverish conditions.

        p. *Ormocarpum* Beauv.

Ormocarpum is mainly a tropical genus of the Old World composed of
some 27 shrubs or small trees. One species is recorded from South and
South West Africa.
   The leaves are imparipinnate or sometimes with 1 leaflet, and stipulate; the pea-like flowers are borne singly or in racemes in the axils
of the leaves, and the pods are narrow, flat, compressed, rough or
hairy, and divided into two or more parts.
   The generic name is based on Greek words meaning "necklace" and
"fruit", and refers to the shape of the pods.

(230)   *Ormocarpum trichocarpum* (Taub.) Engl.

= *Diphaca trichocarpa* Taub.

Ormocarpum; umSindandlovana, isiThibane (Z); isiTsibane, isiTibane
(Sw)

Strangely enough, this little tree or bush, common in bushveld from
Zululand, the Transvaal, Botswana, and northern South West Africa to
tropical Africa, does not seem to be known to Europeans by any popular name.
   This is surprising for its fruits alone would entitle it to such names as
"the caterpillar tree", or "the jackal-tail tree", and perhaps in country
districts such names do exist but have never been recorded.

It is a short tree, sometimes spiny, at others not, usually 2.5-3 m high, of stony shallow soil, of valleys, ridges, and flats. It has a small crown of rigid, arching branches and a rough, deeply fissured, corky brown trunk.

The young twigs are purplish, becoming creamy with age. The compound leaves are small, usually 1.3-4 cm long, and are borne in tufts on small knobs up the twigs, or on the short side branches which sometimes end in a stout spiny point. They are composed of from 4-6 pairs of small oblong leaflets — occasionally more — and a terminal one, 4-12 mm long, with a tiny sharp point at the end. The common midrib is distinctly hairy.

The flowers, about 1.3 cm long, are borne in the axils of the leaves on hairy stalks and are sweetpea-like, a violet blue, pink, or grey veined with blue. They develop into pods 2.5-4 cm long, cylindrical, golden-brown, and covered with stiff hairs so that they look like furry tails in miniature, or like caterpillars. They are sometimes borne in numbers, occasionally at the same time as the flowers, so that the branches are both purple and brown. The trees flower and fruit irregularly.

When it grows as a bush the ormocarpum is undistinguished but as a small tree, with its clean, corky, fissured trunk and fine foliage, it can have character; and when its branches are crowded with flowers and pods, it cannot be mistaken for any other species.

The leaves are eaten by Black Rhino, giraffe and kudu, the young branches by giraffe, and the bark by rhino.

The wood is white, tough, and fine-textured with very little heart. It is little used. Occasionally the leaves are browsed by. cattle.

The name *trichocarpum* is Greek meaning "bristly fruit" or "hairy fruit". Both generic and specific names thus refer to the most outstanding feature of this little tree — its curious pods.

Gerstner says that the Zulus give the tree the same name as *Mundulea sericea*, umSindandlovu (umSindandlovana), meaning "even an elephant will recover", because the bark of both are used as an emetic to treat poisoning.

Below
Dalbergia armata thorny stem

q. *Dalbergia* L.f.

Dalbergia is a large genus of over 100 species of trees, shrubs, and climbers, widely distributed through the tropics and subtropics of both hemispheres. Many species are noted for their fine dark heartwood which varies from purple to black.

Five species which are trees, or which under certain conditions can grow as trees, occur in South and South West Africa. Some of these, such as *Dalbergia obovata* E.Mey., *Dalbergia armata* E.Mey. and *Dalbergia multijuga* E.Mey., are commonly woody twiners or monkey ropes in forests, while all of them, at some time or another, grow as twiners.

Plants of the genus usually have imparipinnate leaves, small pea flowers in cymes or panicles, and pods that are oblong and usually flat and that do not burst open.

(231)   *Dalbergia armata* E.Mey.

Hluhluwe climber, monkey-rope, bobbejaantou, uBobo (X); umHluhluwe (Z); umGcophe (Sw)

932

Although this may be a 4 m tall shrub or small tree, it is more commonly a monkey-rope or a rampant climber up to 15 m high, growing in coastal bush, in forests, in wooded kloofs and on river banks from the eastern Cape, northwards through the Transkei to Natal, Zululand, Swaziland, and the northern and eastern Transvaal.

As the name suggests it is usually armed, the stem and branches bearing long, sharp, stout spines 5-10 cm long. Sim called it "a dangerous monkey-rope", and it often is.

The leaves are composed of 6-20 small oval or oblong leaflets, usually bluntly pointed or rounded both ends, dark above, paler below, when young slightly velvety but becoming completely smooth with age.

In spring the small, fragrant, creamy flowers bloom in dense clusters in the axils of the upper leaves or at the ends of the twigs. The pods are flat, papery, oblong, with a small jutting point, tapering to the base, 2.5-5 cm long, much veined, borne on slender stalks.

The bark and leaves are eaten by Black Rhino.

The Zulus use this to make a muzzle to fix round the noses of calves to keep them from stealing milk from the cows.

In the Transkei the plant is used as a love charm. Here it is often called inTozane, a name given also to other thorny shrubs.

(233)   *Dalbergia multijuga* E.Mey.

Hairy dalbergia

Unlike *Dalbergia armata*, this species has no spines. It is a low bush, a small tree, or a shrubby creeper, which grows in the eastern parts of the country from the eastern Cape, northwards through Natal to Portuguese East Africa, on the edge of coastal bush and in forest.

It has slender velvety branches and delicate foliage. The compound leaves are 10-13 cm long with about 10-16 pairs of small oblong leaflets, and a terminal leaflet, and these are densely velvety below. Twigs and leaf stalks are covered with dense tawny hairs.

The orange-yellow flowers bloom abundantly in short bunches in the axils of the leaves and at the ends of the branches. The flat pods are about 5 cm long, narrowed at both ends, and covered with rust-coloured hairs.

(235)   *Dalbergia obovata* E.Mey.

Umzungulu; umZungulu, uDukuduku, uMangcina, iZimbandlovu, uPhandlazi, uPhondlana (Z)

This species grows from East London northwards to Natal, Zululand, the eastern Transvaal, and Portuguese East Africa, in forest, on their fringes, on wooded hill slopes, and in dune bush.

It is commonest as a climber or monkey-rope, with young branches rambling among surrounding growth and often killing the trees it covers. Sim knew it in this form only, describing it as a "noxious weed with no redeeming quality". It can, however, be a much browsed shrub (so that it is not without use), or a wide-spreading tree from 2.5-6 m high, with greyish bark — smooth or cracked into sections — many stout or slender branches, and a leafy crown.

933

Above
Dalbergia obovata, growing as
a small tree, Ngoye Forest

Right
Dalbergia obovata: A flowering branch (50%)

Below left
Dalbergia obovata bark

Below right
Dalbergia melanoxylon bark

The leaves are alternate and compound, and can easily be distinguished from most others of the genus because the leaflets are larger and fewer. There are only 2-4 pairs of alternate leaflets and a terminal leaflet, which is borne on a long stalk swollen at the upper end. These are 1.9-7 cm long and up to 2.5 cm wide, usually oblong to egg-shaped, with a round or pointed tip and a round or narrow, sometimes unequal-sided base. They are smooth both sides, deep green above, lighter below, with the midrib prominent below and about 12 or more pairs of neat outward- and upward-pointing veins.

The common leaf stalk is brown and velvety.

The small, white to yellow, scented flowers are borne in much-branched bunches in the axils of the leaves and terminally.

The pods are 2.5-8 cm long, oblong to broadly lance-shaped, usually narrowing both ends, flat, with swellings marking the seeds, greenish-yellow, becoming red or yellow when ripe, and later brown. They enclose 1-2 seeds.

The timber is heavy, red, and handsome. The stems are used to make the framework of fishing baskets in Tongaland and Zulus make rope from the bark, and sticks and stools from the wood. They mix the ashes of the bark with their snuff, and use it medicinally to treat sore mouths in babies. Zulu youths use the roots in a love potion emetic, and a love charm seems to be the most general and picturesque use of the plant in Zululand.

The name *obovata* refers to the obovate leaflets.

(232)   *Dalbergia melanoxylon* Guill. & Perr.

Zebra-wood, ebony, African blackwood, swartdriedoring, driedoring ebbehout; umPhingo (Z); shilutsi, shipalatsi (Tso); mokelete (Tsw); muhuluri (V)

The zebra-wood has a wide distribution in Africa, extending from the eastern and northern Transvaal and northern Zululand, Portuguese East Africa, and Botswana, northwards through tropical Africa to Ethiopia, growing usually in bushveld, and often on gravelly soils. It is a common and widespread tree in Rhodesia.

It may be a semi-twiner, but is most often a much-branched, several-stemmed, spiny shrub, or a small tree up to 3 m or 4 m high and occasionally up to 9 m.

The bark is light grey and smooth, sometimes peeling off in strips and spiny. The branches bear thick spines at the nodes which are modified shoots, and these may bear both leaves and flowers.

The dark green, once-compound leaves are composed of from 7-13 shortly stalked leaflets, 0.8-4 cm long, oblong to egg-shaped, occasionally almost round, often with notched tips, and arranged alternately.

The small white or pale pink, scented flowers in slender bunches, borne in the axils of the leaves or at the ends of the branches, bloom in late spring or early summer covering the bare branches, and it is then that this little tree is conspicuous.

The pods are about 4 cm long, flat, narrow, papery, each holding 1-2 seeds. They do not burst open.

The leaves are eaten by elephant, giraffe, impala and kudu, the roots by elephant, and the pods by kudu.

The sapwood is narrow and a yellowish-white, the heartwood dark

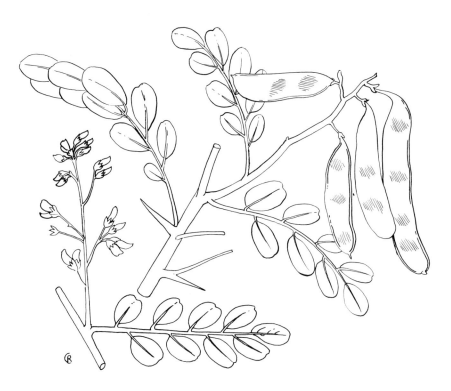

Dalbergia melanoxylon:
flowering and fruiting
twigs (80%)

purple, becoming almost black on exposure, and scented. It is said to
be borer-proof and resistant to weather extremes. In Britain this is
known as Mozambique ebony and in France as Senegal ebony. Sousa
says that in Portuguese East Africa the tree has been so much exploited
for its timber that it has become rare.

Pardy says the heartwood is particularly good for musical wind
instruments and is one of the best turnery woods. It is used for rafters,
hammers, arrow-tips, and for small articles such as chessmen and ornamental boxes. Africans in Rhodesia use this more than any other local
wood for the small ornaments they sell to tourists.

In parts the root is used as a toothache remedy.

The name *melanoxylon* is Greek and means "dark wood".

(234)   *Dalbergia nitidula* Welw. ex Bak.

Shiny dalbergia

Dalbergia nitidula, "the shiny dalbergia", is a slender shrub or small
tree from 2.7-7.5 m tall which grows from Natal and the eastern and
northern Transvaal, westwards to northern South West Africa, and
north to tropical Africa.

It is usually small with several slender stems covered with rough dark
grey or silver bark. The twigs are hairy, the leaves once compound with
4-7 pairs of leaflets and a terminal leaflet, varying in shape from a wide
oval to oblong, occasionally almost round, 1.3-5 cm long, hairy below
and shiny above. The many neat parallel veins are usually distinct.

The buds are in velvety yellow clusters in the axils of the fallen
leaves and open into small white flowers, sometimes — although not
always — sweetly scented, and usually much visited by bees. The pods
are up to about 4 cm long, widely oval, narrowing to the base, flat,
papery, and pendulous.

When dry the heartwood is violet-coloured. Fine walking sticks are made from it. In parts the bark is used in a dressing for wounds.

r. *Pterocarpus* L.

About 30 species of this genus are scattered through the tropics of the world, with 3 species extending southwards into South and South West Africa and Botswana.

The trees are often large and yield good timber, and are frequently and widely known for their blood-red sap, which is used commercially. The red dyewood from India known as "Red Saunders" and once exported in quantities, came from a species of this genus. In parts of Africa pieces of the fresh wood are sold in the African markets for dyes and cosmetics. In pharmacology the sap is known as "false dragon's blood".

The leaves of many species are good fodder.

All the members of the genus have once compound leaves, made up of several or many pairs of leaves and a terminal leaflet, often with beautifully distinct veining; pea flowers in racemes or panicles; and with winged or ridged pods that give the genus its name, for *Pterocarpus* is based on the Greek words "pteran" meaning "a wing", and "karpos" meaning "fruit".

(236)   *Pterocarpus angolensis* DC.

Kiaat, bloodwood, African teak, Transvaal teak, Rhodesian teak, sealing-wax tree, Matabeleland deal, kehatenhout, greinhout, lakboom. (In Rhodesia it is commonly known as mukwa, and in parts of Portuguese East Africa, where it is extensively worked, it is called ambila, umbila, and gulomnila); umBilo, inGozina, umVangazi, inDlandlovu (Z); um-Vangatsi, umVangati (Sw); mokwa (Tsw); morotomadi (Tsw); morôtô (NS); mutondo (V); mulombe (Sub); uguva, muguva (Deiriku); moowa (Mbuk); ugruva (Samb)

The kiaat is a medium-sized deciduous tree of northern Natal, Swaziland, the northern and eastern Transvaal, Botswana, the Caprivi Strip, and northern South West Africa, Portuguese East Africa, Rhodesia, and tropical Africa generally. In South Africa it is usually found in the low-veld in woodland and bushveld in deep sandy soil, and sometimes on hillsides.

It is a graceful tree growing up to about 12 m in height — up to 36 m in Portuguese East Africa — with a spreading crown and a single trunk up to 0.6 m in diameter, and rough dark bark cracked into sections. When this is slashed, a blood-red juice oozes out and congeals, and for this reason the kiaat is sometimes called the bloodwood tree.

The foliage is composed of graceful, drooping leaves up to about 38 cm long, arranged alternately. They have about 4-12 pairs of leaflets, usually alternate, and a terminal one, egg-shaped to oblong, usually with a short jutting point and a rounded base, about 2.5-5 cm long and 1.9 cm wide, or occasionally larger. These are finely hairy at first, later smooth above and often velvety below, with many conspicuous fine, parallel veins sloping upwards, which cover the whole surface of the leaf. They are browsed by elephant and kudu.

Above
A kiaat, *Pterocarpus angolensis*, in the north eastern Transvaal

Below left
Kiaat carvings from the Okavango, South West Africa

Below right
Pterocarpus angolensis: A leaf and the large disc-like pods (50%)

938

The pea-like flowers are abundant, orange-yellow, very sweetly scented and borne in sprays at the ends of the branches. They open in spring — from September to November — at the same time the leaf buds are shooting. The dark branches of a kiaat covered with orange flowers are a striking sight, but unfortunately the flowering time is short — no more than 2 weeks.

The tree bears disc-shaped pods with a diameter of 8-10 cm, composed of a thick bristly centre portion almost surrounded by a light wing, which adds to its buoyancy. There are usually 1-2 small seeds in the pod. As the kiaat grows mostly in malarial country many people only see it in winter when there is less danger of fever. It is then easily identified, for although it is leafless, its mature pods usually hang in profusion, the light coffee-coloured wings around the dark centres looking like large flowers on the tree. These are eaten by baboons and monkeys and by Yellow-footed Squirrels.

The kiaat yields a strong, durable, and beautiful wood, very suitable for furniture, closely following stinkwood in popularity. It varies greatly in colour and in weight. The sapwood is yellow. The heartwood ranges from light brown to dark reddish brown with purplish or golden wavy streaks, and these are often blended in the same piece of wood.

The heartwood is extremely durable, although the sapwood is susceptible to borer attack and should be treated with an insecticide. It works and turn well, takes glue easily, and shrinks and swells very little, so that it is used for canoes and for bathroom floors. It makes most handsome furniture and shelving, floors, panels, doors, and window frames. When worked it has a pleasant pungent smell but can cause irritation and asthma.

Kiaat wood from Rhodesia and South West Africa is lighter and softer than that from South Africa. In South West Africa Africans use it a good deal for carving.

A minor trade in kiaat, dependent strangely enough on ranching operations, existed years ago in the Transvaal. Kiaat timber was sawn into planks in the winter, and in the spring when cattle, which had been grazing the sweet winter lowveld grass, were driven back to the high-veld, the kiaat planks were taken with them. On the whole, however, the timber was not then valued for its beauty and was used mainly for rough work.

Kiaat bark

The sap from the wood makes a permanent red stain on clothing and in parts is used by Africans as a dye. In Ovamboland in northern South West Africa the red inner bark of the roots is sold in bundles. This is powdered, mixed with fat, and used by both men and women to anoint their bodies and faces. The sap is reputed to heal sores, including ringworm sores, and to cure stabbing pains, and has various other medicinal uses. Because it is the colour of blood, Africans believe it has magical powers to cure blood disorders. The Mbukushu name (used in the Okavango swamps and the western Caprivi) is "morotomadi" meaning "exudes blood".

In Botswana, according to Dr. Teichler, the tree is used in a cure for a swelling and discharging eye, a decoction of the boiled roots being drunk, and also bandaged over the eyes with a string of ostrich leather ("because the ostrich sees very far").

The pod of the kiaat does not split open, and for nursery work it must be broken open. Both foresters and nurserymen have experienced great difficulty in germinating seed. Seed which has been filed germinates more readily than untreated seed, but even this is not satisfactory.

939

Above
Pterocarpus antunesii: A flowering
twig and fruits (90%)

Right
Pterocarpus antunesii stems

One imaginative forester placed seed in a termite heap, planting it only after it had been well nibbled by termites. Good germination followed!

The kiaat grows well from truncheons but, according to Palgrave, these must be planted in October when the sap is rising or they will not strike.

It is a curious thing that while in South Africa the kiaat is considered an extremely slow-growing tree, in Rhodesia it is fairly fast.

It is tender to frost.

The specific name means "of Angola". The common name kiaat is derived from "kajaten", the old Dutch name for teak, because the wood of the South African tree was held to resemble teak. Sometimes the tree is known as African, Transvaal, or Rhodesian teak.

(236.1) *Pterocarpus antunesii* (Taub.) Harms

= *Calpurnia antunesii* Taub.; = *Pterocarpus stevensonii* Burtt Davy

Antune's kiaat

Antune's kiaat is a 3.6-12 m tree growing on Kalahari sand from the northern Transvaal to northern South West Africa, and northwards to Rhodesia and Zambia. In South Africa small trees east of Punda Milia in the northern Kruger Park are believed to be this species, and up to date this is the only area in South Africa where it has been collected.

It is often a many-branched tree, several-stemmed, sometimes with dark rough bark, sometimes with bark smooth, mottled, and flaking, which when cut exudes a red-brown sap.

The foliage is light green and drooping. The leaves are alternate, compound, with the leaflets arranged alternately or nearly opposite one another. They are egg-shaped to oblong, sometimes with a rounded or notched apex but usually with a pointed one, 2.5-8 cm long, smooth above and shortly velvety below. The secondary veins are many, fine, close together, and run upwards and outwards, looping along the margin.

The pea flowers are bright lemon yellow and sweet-scented. They are borne in long slender sprays in the axils of the leaves or, according to White, from below the leaves from near the base of the current year's growth, in late spring and in summer.

The flat, buff-coloured pods are 4-5 cm long and about 2.5 cm wide, roughly oval in shape, with a round apex and tapered base, and a slight swelling in the centre — without the bristles so characteristic of the kiaat pod. They ripen in late summer.

The tree yields a light yellow hard wood which does not split. It is used for axe handles and felloes.

The specific name honours a Portuguese priest, José Maria Antunes, 1856-1928, who collected plants in Angola.

(237) *Pterocarpus rotundifolius* (Sond.) Druce
        1. subsp. *rotundifolius*

= *Dalbergia rotundifolia* Sond.; = *Pterocarpus sericeus* Benth.

Round leaf kiaat; dopperkiaat, blinkblaarboom; inDlandlovu (Z); inDlebezindlovu (Sw); miyataha, nshelela (Tso); mushusha-phombwe, muataha (V); mpanda (Kal); modianzovu (northern Botswana); mulianzoha (southern Zambia)

Above
The round leaf kiaat, *Pterocarpus rotundifolius,* growing on the slopes of the Soutpansberg

Left
Pterocarpus rotundifolius leaf (50%)

Below right
Pterocarpus rotundifolius pods (60%)

Opposite above
Round leaf kiaat flower

Opposite below
Round leaf kiaat trunk

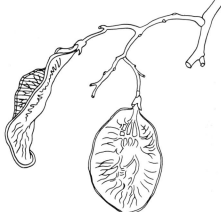

(237.1)   2. subsp. *polyanthus* (Harms) Mendonça & E.P.Sousa var.
martinii (Dunkley) Mendonça & E.P. Sousa

= *Pterocarpus martinii* Dunkley

Pterocarpus rotundifolius has a wide distribution from Zululand in the east, through Swaziland, the eastern, central, and northern Transvaal, and Botswana, to northern South West Africa and the Caprivi Strip, Portuguese East Africa, Rhodesia, Angola, Zambia and Malawi.

It is common in woodland and bushveld, often on sandy soil, as a shrub or as a small to medium-sized tree 4.5-12 m high, at its best wide-spreading, shapely, with a crown of dark-green, wonderfully glossy foliage.

It is often many-stemmed with bark that is pale grey to light brown, cracked, and slightly rough, and branches that are a mottled grey and smooth. The twigs are noticeably velvety.

The typical form, var. *rotundifolius*, is a tree of open woodland. It has few leaflets, sometimes no more than 1 pair with a terminal leaflet, sometimes up to 3 pairs, and these are often large but vary from 1.3-15 cm in length, and up to 11.5 cm in width. They are usually almost round, or egg-shaped, the terminal leaflet being the largest. They have a neat herringbone pattern of veining, with about 9-11 pairs of veins running upward and outward, parallel to one another, and these are most conspicuous on the lower surface. The upper surface is usually shiny, but is occasionally hairy, and below densely velvety. The young leaflets are folded together and are soft and silvery.

The leaves are borne on short, thick, velvety stalks.

The tree is deciduous and often completely bare from June to October.

The flowers are borne in sprays terminally and in the axils of the upper leaves. They are like brilliant yellow sweetpeas with crinkled petals, and protrude from a bright green calyx, and together with their slender green stalks and the bright green twigs, they make a singularly gay and beautiful combination. They have a sweet scent and are popular with bees.

They usually bloom in the rainy season, from January to about April, and appear to delay their blooming until rain falls.

The pods are somewhat oval with a small point to one side of the apex, lopsided, flat, somewhat leathery, with a swelling in the centre where the seeds lie – and this is not bristly as in kiaat pods. They are usually about 3.5 cm long and contain about 2 seeds.

The leaves and young shoots are browsed by cattle and elephants. R.H. Compton says that this is a common tree on the bush-covered hills of Swaziland but that many are so heavily browsed by cattle that they never reach the flowering stage.

The wood is sometimes described as durable and insect-proof, and used for wagon wheels and furniture, at others as of poor quality and too thin for cutting.

To the north and north west in the Zambezi valley in the Caprivi Strip, Botswana, Zambia and Rhodesia a form occurs in the hot dry Kalahari sand which has consistently more – and usually smaller – leaflets than has subsp. *rotundifolius*, and these are characteristically covered with tawny hairs. This used to be known as *Pterocarpus martinii* Dunkley, but it is connected with *Pterocarpus rotundifolius* by intermediate forms and is now included in it as subsp. *polyanthus* (Harms)

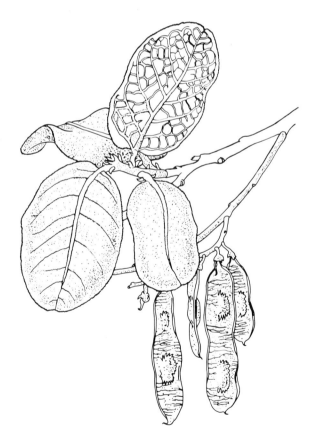

Above
The appelblaar, *Lonchocarpus nelsii,*
outside Namutoni Camp, Etosha
Pan, South West Africa

Left
Lonchocarpus nelsii: Young leaves
and pods (50%)

Below right
Lonchocarpus nelsii flowers in
branching sprays (60%)

Opposite
Stem of the appelblaar

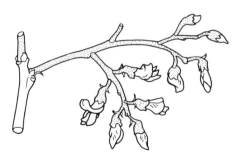

944

Mendonça & E.P.Sousa var. *martinii* (Dunkley) Mendonça & E.P.Sousa

The name *rotundifolius* means "round-leaved". C.A. Smith says that the name "blinkblaar" is one of the very few recorded common names for plants given by the early Afrikaner settlers in Rhodesia. It was prompted by the sheen of the leaves in sunlight. The Venda name for this, mushusha-phombwe, based on the rustling of the leaves, means "startles the adulterer".

s. *Lonchocarpus* H.B. & K.

About 100 trees or tall climbing shrubs from the tropics of Africa, America, and Australia, belong to this genus. One species grows in northern South Africa and 2 in South West Africa.

The members have leaves that are imparipinnate, or sometimes with 3 leaflets (or reduced to 1), the leaflets usually large and distinctly veined; the flowers pea-like, white, mauve or purple and showy in racemes, panicles or clusters. The pods are flat, papery or leathery, and do not burst open. These give the genus its name, *Lonchocarpus*, derived from Greek words meaning "lance-shaped fruit".

(239)   *Lonchocarpus nelsii* (Schinz) Schinz ex Heering & Grimme

= *Dalbergia nelsii* Schinz

Appelblaar

Lonchocarpus nelsii grows widely in woodland — and usually on Kalahari sand — in northern South West Africa and in the Caprivi Strip. It occurs also in Botswana, Angola, Rhodesia, and Zambia.

It is usually a small tree, 4.5-8 m high, graceful and leafy. In winter its foliage turns a deep clear yellow, and it is then conspicuous in the woodlands of the north. The bark is yellowish and flaky.

It is very like its more widely distributed relative, *Lonchocarpus capassa*, in general appearance, the most obvious difference being in the leaves. *Lonchocarpus capassa* has compound leaves made up of 3-7 leaflets; *Lonchocarpus nelsii* has leaves usually reduced to 1 leaflet although occasionally forms are found with 3 or 5 leaflets.

The leaflets — apparently simple leaves — are oblong, egg-shaped or oval, with a flat or slightly notched base, densely velvety when young (under the microscope they are seen to be covered with curly white hairs), becoming less so with age, up to 13 cm long and 10 cm wide, with the buff-coloured midrib and veins clearly marked. They are carried on velvety grey stalks 0.8-1.6 cm long.

The violet pea flowers, about 1.3 cm long, are in large branched sprays, flowering about September before the leaves, and cover the trees in a mantle of colour. Trees in bloom are surrounded by bees and a cloud of other insects.

The pods are about 4-7 cm long and about 1.3 cm wide, flat, papery, without any wing, but with the edges inrolled. They are finely hairy.

This is an excellent fodder tree browsed by many animals, including horses.

The specific name commemorates a young man, Nels, who was a plant collector in South West Africa in the 1880's, and assistant to Dr Heinrich Goering (father of Field Marshal Goering) when he was "Reichs Commissioner for the Protectorate of Luederitzland".

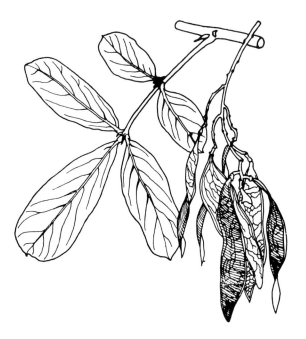

Above
The olifantsoor, *Lonchocarpus capassa,* Pafuri, Kruger National Park

Left
Lonchocarpus capassa: a leaf and pods (50%)

Below right
Lonchocarpus capassa flowers in unbranched sprays (80%)

Opposite
Olifantsoor bark

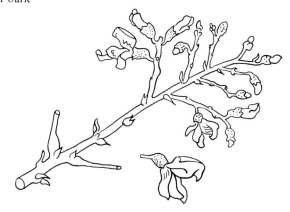

946

(238)   *Lonchocarpus capassa* (Klotzsch) Rolfe

= *Capassa violacea* Klotzsch

Olifantsoor, lance tree, rain tree, panda tree, appelblaar, raasboom stamperhout; umBandu, umPhanda, isiHomohomo (Z); isiHomuhomu (Sw); mbhandzu, mbhandu (Tso); mopororo (Tsw), mohata (Tsw-Mang); mufhanda (V); mukololo (Sub); mopanda (Kol); upanda (Mbuk)

The olifantsoor, with its greyish blotchy stem and pale green drooping foliage, is common in parts of the bushveld and lowveld of Zululand, Swaziland, and the eastern and northern Transvaal. It grows, too, in the woodland of north eastern South West Africa, in the Caprivi Strip, in Botswana, northwards into tropical Africa. This is a common tree in the Kruger National Park, in particular near Pafuri, where it is abundant and often a backdrop for the numerous elephants there which eat the leaves and branches.

It is a small to medium-sized tree, 4.5-12 m high, round-topped or slender, with the branches, or sometimes only the ends of the branches, drooping. The often hollow trunk is usually unbranched for many feet. The bark is variable, smooth, and blotched white and grey, sometimes flaking in strips, or cracking to show a creamy-yellow colour below, occasionally cracking in circles. When slashed, a red gummy sap exudes.

The pale grey-green foliage is distinctive. The widely spaced compound leaves on long stalks are composed of 1-2 pairs of opposite stalked leaflets and a terminal leaflet which is by far the largest. The side leaflets are about 4-10 cm long and 2.5-5 cm wide, egg-shaped, oval, or oblong, the terminal one 6.5-15 cm long and up to nearly 10 cm wide, often with a rounder or flatter apex than the side leaflets. The veins are clearly marked.

Young leaves are densely velvety, but with age the upper surface becomes leathery and rough although the lower remains more or less velvety. There are small leafy growths — stipules and secondary stipules — at the base of the leaves and leaflets.

The small, fragrant, pea-like flowers are blue or violet with a velvety-grey calyx, and bloom in large unbranched sprays towards the ends of the branches, usually in October and November. This is a graceful tree and in flower, with its grey leaves and soft violet bloom, it is unusually lovely.

The pods are flat and greyish, up to 12 cm long and just over 2.5 cm wide, tapering both ends, with a narrow flat rim, sometimes described as a narrow wing, along one side. This is the only species in the genus with a winged pod, and some botanists feel it should therefore be removed from *Lonchocarpus* and transferred back to the genus in which it was first placed in 1861, becoming again *Capassa violacea* Klotzsch. The Botanical Research Institute in Pretoria, however, upholds its present status.

The pods contain several flat seeds. They ripen from December to May, often hanging on the trees in quantities, and this is how they are best known to tourists.

The wood is yellowish, streaked with blue, close-grained, fairly hard, but very liable to borer attack. Pardy says that when the wood is cut with a sharp knife it is readily recognized in cross section by a regular series of fine wavy lines.

Africans use it for poles for building and for stamps for pounding grain, for pots, and for axe-handles. The green wood is said to be used

Left
Xeroderris stuhlmannii leaf (60%)

Below
Ostryoderris stuhlmannii pods (50%)

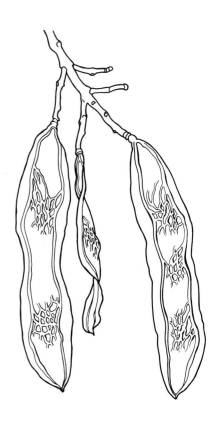

948

for making canoes in the Okavango Swamps.

Africans consider the tree of medicinal value. They burn the roots and inhale the smoke to relieve colds, and sometimes use it to treat snakebite. The bark and root are reported to be highly toxic and in parts are used as a fish poison. The leaves are apparently harmless and are much browsed by stock and game, which also relish the fallen leaves.

This should make a good garden tree, for it is graceful in habit, the grey-green foliage is pleasing and the bloom charming, if brief. It is reasonably quick growing and stands several degrees of frost.

It is a rain tree, raining in the same way as does *Schotia brachypetala*. A small froghopper, *Ptyelus grossus*, pierces the wood and sucks the sap which it excretes as apparently pure water, and which not only drips down the branches but forms large pools below the tree. In Rhodesia the common name of this *Lonchocarpus* is the "rain tree".

In South West Africa, where both species grow, *Lonchocarpus capassa* and *Lonchocarpus nelsii* may be confused. *Lonchocarpus capassa*, however, has compound leaves, flowers in unbranched sprays together with the leaves, and pods with very narrow wings. *Lonchocarpus nelsii* usually has simple leaves, flowers in large branched sprays without any leaves, and wingless pods.

The name *capassa* is based on the African name for the tree in Portuguese East Africa. The common name "appelblaar" is due to the supposed similarity of its leaves to that of the apple tree, but both this and "olifantsoor" seem highly fanciful. The name "panda tree" is based on the African "umPhanda" and is probably the best common name of all.

t. *Xeroderris* Roberty

The only member of this genus, *Xeroderris stuhlmannii* (Taub.) Mendonça & E.P.Sousa, has had a varied history, having in the past been placed in four different genera. Until recently it was included in the tropical *Ostryoderris*. Today the tendency is to place it in the genus *Xeroderris*, botanists separating it from *Ostryoderris* on a few characters including the exstipulate leaves and the lateral panicles (in contrast to the stipulate leaves and terminal panicles of *Ostryoderris*).

The leaves are alternate, imparipinnate and without stipules; the flowers sweetpea-like in structure borne in lateral panicles; the pods flat and conspicuously winged along the margins; and the seeds oblong and thick.

(240)   *Xeroderris stuhlmannii* (Taub.) Mendonça & E.P.Sousa

= *Deguelia stuhlmannii* Taub.; = *Derris stuhlmannii* (Taub.) Harms; = *Ostryoderris stuhlmannii* (Taub.) Dunn ex Harms; = *Xeroderris chevalier* (Dunn) Roberty

Muzamalowa: muzamalowa (Kol)

This fine, deciduous, tropical species was first collected in Zambia, and occurs also in the Republic, in the Caprivi Strip, Rhodesia, and Portuguese East Africa. It was discovered in the Kruger National Park in 1953 and since then has been found in the hot, dry, sandy country between Chipise and the western boundary of the Park, but not — as

Above left
Xeroderris stuhlmannii
trunk

Above right
Xeroderris stuhlmannii
near the Mutali River,
north eastern Transvaal

yet — anywhere else in the Republic.

It is a medium to large tree, 7-15 m high, with robust grey branches and a rounded crown of blue-green compound leaves crowded at the ends of the branches. The trunk, 30 cm or more in diameter, is sturdy, the bark is grey and rough, tending to flake off in longitudinal strips. When injured, it exudes a red sticky sap.

The leaves — up to 30 cm or more long — usually have 6-9 pairs of opposite or alternate leaflets, and a terminal leaflet, oblong, egg-shaped or almost round, with a notched or a flat base which is sometimes slightly lopsided. They are 2.5-7 cm long and 2.5-4 cm wide, fairly smooth to hairy, with the midrib raised below and about 4-5 pairs of veins clearly marked. They are borne on short stout stalks.

Young foliage has a soft bronzy tint and is covered with short gold hairs.

The sprays of red-brown hairy buds open into white flowers before or with the new leaves, about October.

The pods, up to 15 cm long and 2.5 cm broad, are flat, with 1-4 seeds making a very obvious bulge, covered with a network of lines, and with a characteristic raised line running slightly within the margin. This border is sometimes spoken of as a wing. The pods, light green in February, turning light brown later, hang in masses, and then the trees are conspicuous.

The wood is hard, yellow to orange in colour, and used for planks and canoes, and in Tanzania for railway sleepers. The resin is used in parts for tanning leather.

The seeds are reported to be poisonous, yet in parts the pods are eaten by stock, as are the leaves. The tree is used medicinally in many ways. In South Africa, where the tree is rare, little is known of these uses.

The specific name honours Franz Ernest Stuhlmann, a German colonial senior official — at one time Acting-Governor — in Tanzania, who collected plants widely in East Africa between 1883 and 1894.

u. *Xanthocercis* Baill.

This genus of 2 species is represented in South Africa by one magnificent tree occurring in the northern Transvaal. The remaining species is in Madagascar.

The species have imparipinnate leaves, the leaflets alternate; small, pea-like flowers; and fruit that is unusual in the legume family — plum-shaped, with a fleshy covering that is sometimes edible and with a stipe or false stalk.

The origin of the generic name is far from clear. "Xanthos" is the Greek for "yellow", and *Cercis* is a genus of the legume family, so that this could be "the yellow Cercis".

(241)   *Xanthocercis zambesiaca* (Bak.) Dumaz-le-Grand

= *Sophora zambesiaca* Bak.; = *Pseudocadia zambesiaca* (Bak.) Harms

Nyala tree, hoenderspoor; nhlahu (Tso); motha (Tsw — Mang)

The nyala tree, or nhlaru as it is commonly known in the Kruger National Park, is one of the least known — and the most magnificent — of all the lowveld giants. It grows in numbers on the wooded flats and in deep sandy soil along rivers, in the hot dry country between the Soutpansberg and the Limpopo River, in the northern part of the Kruger National Park, in northern Botswana, and in Rhodesia and Zambia.

Particularly beautiful specimens of these fine, leafy trees are found along the Limpopo, at Chipise Hot Springs near Messina, and in the Kruger National Park around Pafuri.

The nyala tree is evergreen, up to 18 m high with a spread as great, or greater, a single, or more often several trunks which are sometimes some 46 cm in diameter but often up to 2.4 m, much fluted, brown or light grey tinged with yellow, rough and cracked into small squares.

The branches droop at the ends. The once-compound leaves are alternate with about 5-15 alternate or nearly opposite leaflets, the terminal one being the largest. These are oval or oblong, usually with a notched tip, up to 7 cm long and 4 cm wide, but mostly smaller, a dark shiny green and conspicuously veined above, the lower paler and often slightly hairy. The leaflets are borne on hairy stalks. Elephants, giraffe and nyala feed upon them.

The small mauvy-white flowers with a greyish-velvety calyx are borne from about October onwards to December in small bunches towards the ends of the branches, and have a strong sweet perfume. The fruit is unusual for that of a legume, being plum-shaped, about 2.5 cm long and 1.3 cm broad, with a smooth brown skin, enclosing one shiny black seed in a thin fleshy pulp. In some parts the pulp is eaten by Africans in time of famine, and the fruit is generally a great favourite with birds, monkeys, baboons, elephant and buck, and the nyala in particular, and when ripe is one of the main sources of food along the rivers.

Mr Howard Kirk of White River once saw the Grey, Trumpeter and Yellow-billed Hornbills, Green Pigeons and Brown-headed Parrots all feeding on the fruit at the same time. These birds, he noted, together with monkeys and baboons, knocked down and dropped as many fruits as they ate, and the fallen fruit in their turn attracted nyala, bushbuck, impala, francolin and guineafowl which picked them up from the ground, while the birds and monkeys fed above them.

951

Above
The nyala tree, *Xanthocercis zambesiaca,* in the north
eastern Transvaal

Right
Xanthocercis zambesiaca: A leaf, fruits and seeds (100%)

Below
A nyala tree trunk

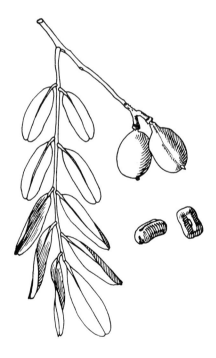

The wood is white, hard, heavy, and handsome. It is said to irritate the nose and throat when being worked. It is not for its timber, however, that the nyala tree is most valued but for its deep cool shade in which animals of all kinds, including elephant and antelope, take refuge from the lowveld heat. It is a favourite with monkeys which may often be seen by the hundred swarming about a tree, swinging from the branches, and peering through the fine foliage.

The tree is easily raised from seed but is tender to frost and appears to damp off easily. It probably needs deep sandy well-drained soil, but little is known of its cultivation and every effort should be made to propagate this exceptionally fine species.

At present the nyala tree is protected in the Soutpansberg district "within 300 yards of all streams that carry water in the rainy season".

v. *Erythrina* L.

This is the "red" genus, the kafferboom genus, known, lauded and loved for its bright bloom since the early days of South African history.

Men, black and white, have always planted the trees of this genus for their beauty and for their ease in cultivation — a twig or branch planted in the ground will root. Thus they have been royal trees, planted on the graves of Zulu chiefs; living palisades round the homes of early settlers; fences round kraals and water holes; and probably the first wild trees to be planted in numbers in the gardens of the eastern Cape.

A solitary kafferboom near the present site of Port St. John's figured in one of the very early Cape journals, that of Jacob van Reenen, whose party journeyed into the then unknown east in search of the wreck of the Grosvenor. The leader, Jan Andries Holtshausen, who died of lockjaw, was buried under the tree on November 24, 1790. His friends carved their names upon its trunk.

Although they have been associated with men for so long, it is not in the lives of men but in those of birds that the erythrinas are all-important. Several species, such as *Erythrina caffra* and *Erythrina lysistemon*, produce abundant nectar and in full bloom are alive with birds — sunbirds, Yellow Weavers, starlings, orioles, bulbuls, and many others. C.J. Skead, in his *Sunbirds of Southern Africa*, describes how even when *Erythrina caffra* trees grow in streets and gardens of the eastern Cape, flocks of birds wheel and swirl from kafferboom to kafferboom throughout the flowering period, while even such a forest-shy bird as the Black Sunbird will fly over the forest canopy to feed on the red blossom of the tall trees.

All the kafferbooms have soft wood which, when dead, is the ideal nesting-place for birds such as barbets and woodpeckers, while the hollow trunks are often inhabited by swarms of bees.

The erythrinas yield a poison with a curare-like, and paralyzing, action, which is used medicinally to relax the muscles in treating nervous diseases. The seeds of all are said to be poisonous and the leaves of *Erythrina caffra* are known to have poisoned cattle. In parts an infusion of the boiled bark and roots is used for earache, tooth-ache, and eye-washes, and a paste made of the leaves is used medicinally in many ways.

The genus is a tropical and subtropical one with just over 170 species. Six species grow wild in South Africa, of which 4 are trees, and 2 grow in South West Africa, one of which is a small tree. A Brazilian species, *Erythrina crista-galli* L., is often cultivated in South Africa but is not indigenous.

953

Above
The Cape kafferboom, *Erythrina caffra,* growing round a water hole in the Peddie district

Left
A leaf and pods (50%)

Right
Erythrina caffra flowers (50%)

Above
The stem of a young
Erythrina caffra

Below
A mature trunk

Until recently the kafferbooms of the Transvaal and the eastern Cape were considered one variable species, *Erythrina caffra* Thunb. Now they are recognized as two distinct species, *Erythrina caffra* growing near the coast from Humansdorp in the south to Port Shepstone in the north, and strangely enough appearing again in Zululand, and *Erythrina lysistemon* Hutch., which occurs in Rhodesia, Portuguese East Africa, Botswana, Swaziland, and in South Africa in the Transvaal and Natal, and in parts of the eastern Cape. Its distribution in the south overlaps that of *Erythrina caffra* and it extends further inland than does this species.

Erythrina latissima E.Mey. is a big-leaved species growing in the Cape, Natal, Swaziland, and the eastern Transvaal. It was once thought to be identical to the Rhodesian and tropical species, *Erythrina abyssinica* Lam. (*E. tomentosa* R.Br. ex A.Rich.) but the two are now recognized as distinct. This species is known in parts to cross with *Erythrina caffra* and *Erythrina lysistemon*.

Erythrina humeana Spreng. is a shrub or small tree with long slender spikes of flowers, that grows in grassveld, thornveld, dry scrub, or on rocky mountain sides from the eastern Cape, through Natal, Zululand and Swaziland, to the eastern Transvaal.

Erythrina decora Harms is a small tree occurring in rocky places from Swakopmund to the Kaokoveld in northern South West Africa. In many ways it resembles *Erythrina baumii* Harms from the Okavango territory and the eastern Caprivi but in the field they can be separated easily for *Erythrina baumii* is never more than a low shrublet.

All the species are notable for their heads of bright, beautiful flowers; all have stipulate leaves composed of 3 leaflets, and some have short, broad-based thorns on the twigs and trunk. The pods are usually sickle-shaped and narrow, and constricted between the seeds.

The generic name *Erythrina* is based on the Greek "erythros" meaning "red".

(242)   *Erythrina caffra* Thunb.

Cape kafferboom, coral tree, lucky bean tree, koraalboom. The seeds are known as kaffir beans, cocky-doodles, kafferboontjie, kafferkrale, dopkrale; umSintsi (X); umSintsi (Z)

The Cape kafferboom grows in the coastal districts from Port Shepstone to the Humansdorp district, the wild tree seen farthest from the coast being – according to Dr Codd – about 53 km inland in the Albany district. It appears again in the north in the Hlabisa and Lake Sibayi areas in Zululand, jumping over 400 km of country in which it is unknown in the wild, a surprising and interesting distribution.

It is a tree of coastal forests and wooded stream banks, usually some 9-12 m high, but in forest up to 21 m. Some of the largest and most beautiful specimens grow in the Alexandria forest where, next to the yellowwoods, they are the tallest trees.

The trunk and branches are grey, sometimes set with short prickles. The leaves have the typical 3 leaflets, the centre one being the largest. They are usually somewhat heart-shaped, broader in the lower half and tapering to a point, the terminal one up to 17 cm long and 18 cm broad (although usually smaller), the lateral ones slightly less, smooth, and borne on short stalks. The whole leaf is carried on a long stalk, sometimes with a few small prickles. The leaves resemble those of *Erythrina lysistemon*, and when the trees are not in flower it is difficult to tell them apart.

The flowers are produced before the leaves in large clusters at the ends of thick stalks. They have a short broad standard petal; the lower half of which curves upward to expose the stamens, and these give the flower spikes (botanically racemes) a bewhiskered appearance. *Erythrina lysistemon* has a longer and narrower standard petal which folds to enclose the stamens. A difference in colour has been noted too for *Erythrina caffra* usually has flowers of an orange-scarlet with a tinge of terra cotta, in contrast to the clear scarlet of those of the northern species. The colour of the Cape kafferboom is, however, known to vary, and a cream-flowered form is occasionally seen.

Black-eyed Bulbuls have been seen eating the flowers.

When the trees bloom in spring, the Africans of the eastern Cape know that it is the time to start planting their crops.

The narrow dark pods are up to 6.5 cm long, deeply constricted between the seeds, with the constrictions often long and narrow. They split to show small, shiny, coral-red seeds, marked on one side with a black spot. These are made into necklaces by African women, and children collect them as "lucky beans". On weathering they are inclined to lose their brilliancy and become a rich red-brown. Small yellowish eggs of a type of beetle may sometimes be seen on the seeds, and these hatch into larvae which develop in the seed.

The seeds are poisonous.

The wood is white or grey-blue and is very soft, light, and spongy. Pappe states that canoes and troughs are made from the hollowed trunks, that the wood is used for floats for fishing nets, and that when tarred it makes good roofing shingles.

Thomas Baines, experimenting with a species of kafferboom some 90 years ago, wrote: "The wood seems very tough and fibrous — I shot one branch about as thick as my thumb with four bullets in the same place and only shattered it to fibre instead of cutting if off." Its most common use today is for brake-blocks.

It is believed to have magic properties and in parts of the eastern Cape Africans will not burn the wood for fear of attracting lightning.

This is a great nectar-bearer, each floret in a flower-head — according to Skead — holding from 7-10 drops, four to six florets producing a cubic centimetre of liquid. One flower head may hold up to 80 florets, so that the abundance of nectar contained in the flowers of one large tree in bloom and its importance to bird life may be imagined.

This, like *Erythrina lysistemon*, is an easy tree to cultivate for it grows readily from seed, cuttings, and truncheons. Branches cut and planted in spring and early summer quickly shoot and have been known to flower within a year. It is fairly drought resistant and will stand several degrees of frost. Where frosts are heavy it may grow but will seldom flower well.

Sometimes the trees are attacked by borers that destroy young plants in particular.

Naturally enough, these trees are used to make live fences round kraals, and in the Peddie district there are several instances of kafferbooms having been closely planted by Africans round water holes, to keep stock from the water or to guide them to the entrance.

They are much-prized garden trees, and especially fine specimens have been cultivated in Grahamstown and Graaff-Reinet. An avenue of them near Port St. John's in full spring flower and alive with birds is a splendid sight.

Right
The Transvaal kaffer-
boom, *Erythrina lysis-
temon,* in bloom in the
Transvaal lowveld

Below
The stem

Thunberg in the 1770's gave the tree both its specific and common name which have an identical meaning – "kaffir". The name "gif-boom" is occasionally used and this is derived from the supposed poisonous properties of the leaves.

In the United States of America and in Europe this species was cultivated under the name *Erythrina constantiana* Mich.

(245)   *Erythrina lysistemon* Hutch.

Transvaal kafferboom, coral tree, lucky bean tree, kanniedood; um-Sintsi (X); umSinsi (Z); umSisi (Sw); muvale, nsisimbane (Tso); mophete (Tsw); mmalê, mokhungwane (NS); muvhale (V)

Erythrina lysistemon grows under drier conditions than *Erythrina caffra*, in scrub forest, wooded kloofs, in dry savannah, on koppie slopes, or on coastal sand dunes, and is a shorter tree, seldom above 12 m high, and often stocky. It occurs from the central, northern and eastern Transvaal, through Swaziland and Natal, to about the Bashee Mouth, at the southern range of its distribution overlapping that of *Erythrina caffra*. It also occurs in Botswana, Angola, and Portuguese East Africa, and to the north.

This species is known at least indirectly to most South Africans for this was the kafferboom figured on one of the first stamps issued after South Africa became a republic. It is the kafferboom, often stocky, robust, and brilliant with colour, familiar in spring to visitors to the Transvaal lowveld and Kruger National Park.

The trunk often branches low down. The thorny branches and foliage are similar to those of the Cape kafferboom, and it has the same habit of flowering before the leaves appear, sometimes with the very young leaves. The flower of *Erythrina lysistemon*, however, has a longer and narrower standard petal which encloses the stamens, so that the spike does not have the whiskery look of the Cape species given by

957

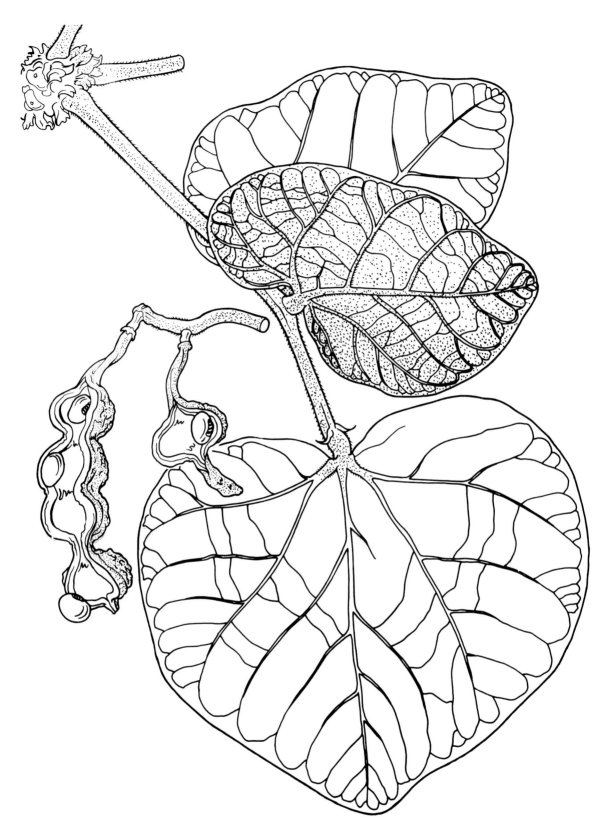

Erythrina latissima leaf and pod (60%)

the protruding stamens. Dr Codd describes the flower spike as having the appearance of an epaulette, and this is a good description. The colour is usually a bright clear scarlet, whereas that of the Cape kafferboom has a tinge of orange or terra cotta.

The long narrow black pods, constricted as in *Erythrina caffra,* burst open to show the brilliant red seeds attached within.

In the lowveld of the eastern Transvaal a branch from a tree growing near a man's hut is often planted on his grave. In this part, the tree is considered to have magical properties. A pregnant woman, whose time is near, is given an infusion of herbs to make the birth easier, and in the preparation of these, a sliver of bark, taken from each of the four sides of the tree, is tied round the bundle of herbs before boiling.

The bark is soaked in water which is used by chiefs for washing; and this is believed to make them respected by their people. Medicinally (and magically) such water, mixed with the root of a *Cussonia* species, is used as a purifying emetic. Crushed leaves placed on a maggot-infested wound are said to clear the maggots.

The leaves are eaten by kudu, Black Rhino, baboons and klipspringer, the bark by baboons, Black Rhino and elephant, the roots by bushpig, and the seeds are eaten by the Brown-headed Parrot. The nectar in the flowers is sought by many birds. Ian Garland of Zululand saw, one July day, the trees alive with Olive, Scarlet-chested, and Grey Sunbirds, and with Yellow Weavers which were nipping off the petals and eating some substance at their base.

The wood resembles that of the Cape *Erythrina* and is used for the same purposes. Like that tree, it is easily cultivated, and fine trees grow in towns such as Pretoria, Pietersburg and Rustenburg. An avenue of kafferbooms, interplanted with wild pear trees — *Dombeya rotundifolia* (Hochst.) Planch. — at Nelspruit in the lowveld is both imaginative and decorative. This is a colour combination of scarlet and white copied from the bush where the two species often grow together.

The specific name, *lysistemon*, is based on Greek words meaning "free stamen" and refers to the "vexillary" stamen which is free from the staminal tube.

(244)   *Erythrina latissima* E.Mey.

(In the past confused with *E. abyssinica* Lam.)

Broad-leaf kafferboom, hairy kafferboom, cork tree, royal kafferboom, breëblaarkafferboom, grootkafferboom; umNqwane (X); umKhakhasi, umGqwabagqwaba (Z); mofhupe, monabete (Tsw); mphapha (NS)

The broad-leaf kafferboom is common in frost-free parts of Natal; and grows, although more rarely, in the Transkei, Swaziland, and the eastern Transvaal. In the Hlabisa and Port Shepstone districts, where it grows together with *Erythrina caffra* and *Erythrina lysistemon*, it is known to hybridize with them.

It is often a sturdy tree with spreading branches, 3-9 m high, with a thick rough brown trunk and branches covered with formidable prickles. The branches, thickly hairy at first, become smooth with age.

The leaves distinguish this kafferboom from the other South African species, for they are very large and rounded, the terminal leaflet 6-30 cm long and slightly broader, and the side leaflets 5-21 cm long and unequal-sided. When young these are a fine velvety grey, soft to the

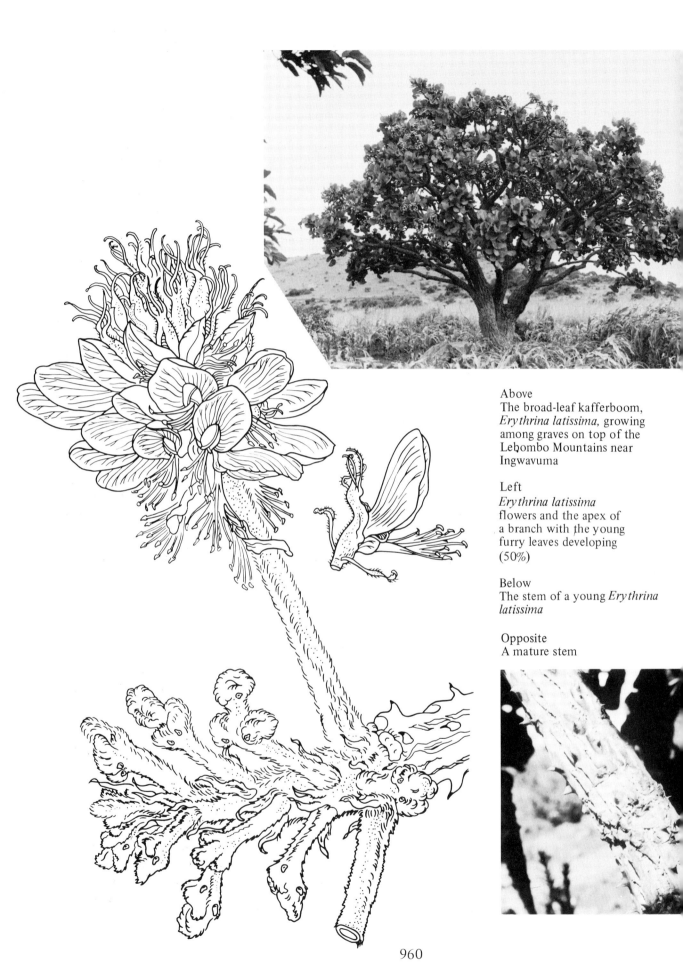

Above
The broad-leaf kafferboom,
Erythrina latissima, growing
among graves on top of the
Lebombo Mountains near
Ingwavuma

Left
Erythrina latissima
flowers and the apex of
a branch with the young
furry leaves developing
(50%)

Below
The stem of a young *Erythrina
latissima*

Opposite
A mature stem

touch, but become smoother and more leathery with age. The midrib, secondary and netted veins are raised on the under-surface. The veins are occasionally armed with prickles. The leaves are borne on sturdy, slightly furrowed stalks which when young are covered with dense white hairs but which become smooth with age.

The flowers, in dense, rather short heads are a full rich crimson, with a white woolly calyx. Although they are not as brilliant as those of the Cape and Transvaal kafferbooms, a tree in full bloom is a fine sight.

The pods are black, constricted, and contain several red seeds marked with a black spot.

Like the other erythrinas, this is an easy tree to grow. It is this species that is accounted a royal tree in parts of Natal and Zululand, being planted on the graves of chiefs, and this is the origin of the name "royal kafferboom". The tree photographed grew next to a grave high on the Lebombo mountains in Zululand.

The specific name, *latissima*, is Latin, meaning "very broad" in reference to the size of the leaves. The common name "cork tree" is derived from the thick corky bark. The Zulu name umQwabaqwaba is a general name given to this and other trees with broad leaves such as *Ficus hippopotami* and *Ficus quibeba*.

Until recently this tree was considered indistinguishable from the tropical *Erythrina abyssinica* Lam. They are now separated on the size of the flower petals, those of *Erythrina latissima* being much larger than those of *Erythrina abyssinica*. The terminal leaflet is larger and usually roundish and broader than long in the southern species, while in the tropical species the terminal leaflet is egg-shaped and longer than broad.

Erythrina humeana Spreng.

Dwarf kafferboom; umSintsane (X); umSinsana (Z)

Erythrina humeana has a wide distribution from the eastern Transvaal, Swaziland and Zululand through Natal and the Transkei to the Bathurst and King William's Town districts of the eastern Cape. It grows in dense dry valley scrub — as in the Muden valley — in thorn and grassveld, on stony koppies, rocky outcrops, and on wooded mountain sides. It is a common species on the slopes of the Drakensberg in Natal.

Although usually a shrub, it can grow into a small tree some 4 m high. The light grey stem and branches are armed with prickles. The leaves, as in others of the genus, are composed of 3 leaflets. The middle, the largest, measures from 5-13 cm in length and up to 12 cm in width, and is triangular with a long jutting point. The lateral leaflets are usually somewhat narrow in proportion to their length. Small spines are often present on the midrib and veins on the lower or on both sides, and on the stalk of the middle leaflet. The stipules are broad or narrow and are deciduous.

This is the only kafferboom to bloom in summer instead of in winter and spring. The showy pendulous flowers are crowded in slender racemes on long stalks at the ends of the branches. They give rise to black or purple pods up to 16 cm long, deeply constricted between the seeds, velvety when young but smooth later. The seeds number 2-5 and are oval, somewhat flattened, and red marked with a scar.

This species was known to gardeners in Europe over a century ago, and was figured in Curtis's *Botanical Magazine* in 1823.

The tree has left its name in history. The battle of Umsintsane, which was fought in a Transkeian valley on a December day some 90 years ago, took its name from the Xhosa word for this little species. The valley in which the battle was fought was blazing with its red blooms, and so the battle was known as "the little umSintsi" or "the little kafferboom".

The specific name honours Sir Abraham Hume, F.R.S., (1749-1838) who had a famous garden at his seat, Wormleybury, Herts, in which he cultivated many exotic plants.

The dwarf kafferboom is the emblem of Prince Alfred's Guard, the famous old Eastern Province regiment.

(243)   *Erythrina decora* Harms

Western kafferboom

This little kafferboom from rocky places in central and northern South West Africa — from the plateau of the Namib Desert itself — bears a botanical name meaning "the lovely erythrina".

It is a small to medium-sized shrubby tree — it is recorded up to 9 m in height — with prickly branches and twigs, the young ones covered with dense, silver-white, velvety hairs.

The leaves are sometimes large, the terminal leaflet being wider than long, with a flattish tip, up to 10-15 cm broad; the lateral leaflets rather egg-shaped, up to 10 cm long and 9 cm wide, with a narrowed or a flattish base. Both sides of the young leaves are densely velvety, the upper side becoming smoother with age.

The silver-velvety buds open into coral red flowers in a dense spike, up to about 9 cm long, broadest at the base and narrowing to a thick, blunt apex.

The woody pods are up to 10 cm long and 1.3 cm wide, constricted between the bulging seeds, like a string of large beads. They are slightly hairy and split to show the scarlet and black seeds.

43 The Erythroxylum Family (Erythroxylaceae)

Erythroxylaceae is a family of 4 genera of trees and shrubs, which belong to the warm parts of both hemispheres. One species, *Erythroxylum coca* Lam., is the source of cocaine.

About 5 species occur in South Africa. These were formerly all placed in the genus *Erythroxylum*, which is well represented in tropical Africa, but modern botanists place two of these in the small genus *Nectaropetalum*, basing the separation on a few botanical differences.

The two species of *Nectaropetalum* grow in the eastern and frequently in the coastal districts of the country, *Nectaropetalum capense* (H.Bol.)Stapf & Boodle in the Transkei — it is particularly frequent in the Manubi Forest — and *Nectaropetalum zuluense* (Schonl.) Corb. in Natal, and in Zululand where it is common in the Ngoye Forest.

The *Erythroxylum* species are spread from the eastern Cape through Natal and Swaziland to the Transvaal.

All the South African species of the family have simple, alternate, smooth, untoothed leaves, twigs which are usually flattened when young, small usually bisexual flowers, most often with scales (or small growths) attached to the inner face of the petals, and fruits that are nearly always 1-seeded fleshy drupes. The young flattened twigs are the most conspicuous feature of the family and a guide to identification in South Africa.

Key to Genera

The leaves with pointed tips, the styles 2, united.

1. *Nectaropetalum*

The leaves with round or blunt tips, often notched; the styles usually 3 and free or only partially united.

2. *Erythroxylum*

1. *Nectaropetalum* Engl.

Nectaropetalum is a small genus of about 6 species of shrubs or low to medium-sized trees occurring from tropical Africa to the Cape Province, mainly in coastal areas. Two species occur in South Africa.

The typical characteristic of the family in South Africa, the young flattened twigs, is represented here. The simple alternate leaves are smooth, untoothed, somewhat leathery, with dense net-veining, with stipules that often fall early; long slender bud sheaths; flowers that are borne singly or in small groups in the axils of the leaves, the sepals usually 5, the petals usually 5, the nectary pocket small, the stamens 10, the filaments united below to form a shallow saucer, the ovary with 2 chambers, each one with usually 1 ovule, the styles united, the stigmas free, the fruit a small drupe.

Formerly these species were placed in the genus *Erythroxylum*. They are separated now on a few botanical details — the number and form of the styles (2 and not 3), which are united and not free or semi-free as in *Erythroxylum*, and on the ovary which is 2-chambered and not 3-chambered as is common in *Erythroxylum*.

The most conspicuous difference between the genera in the field (in South Africa) is the shape of the leaves, which in *Nectaropetalum* have pointed tips and which in *Erythroxylum* have round or blunt and often notched tips. The *Nectaropetalum* species also have long slender growths, elongated leaf bud sheaths, at the ends of the twigs.

The growths on the petals, the nectary scales, give the genus its name meaning "petals with scales".

Key to Species

The veins clearly marked on the upper surface of the leaf; the flowers on short stalks; the petals without a pocket at the base.

a. *Nectaropetalum capense*

The veins not clearly marked on the upper surface; the flowers on long stalks; the petals with a pocket at the base.

b. *Nectaropetalum zuluense*

(246)   a. *Nectaropetalum capense* (H.Bol.) Stapf & Boodle

= *Peglera capensis* H.Bol. = *Erythroxylum capense* (H.Bol.) Stapf

Cape nectaropetalum

"The nectaropetalum of the Cape", frequent in parts of the Transkei, grows — often on the poorest soil — in forests or on forest fringes.

It is a small tree with smooth branches. The bright green simple leaves are alternate, untoothed, oval, oblong, or egg-shaped, usually with a jutting blunt tip, and with a narrowed or rounded base, 5-9 cm long and up to 5 cm wide, smooth, with many fine secondary veins, conspicuous on the upper surface, running outwards and branching along the margin. The stipules are small.

The flowers, about 8-12 mm in diameter, have 5 narrow petals, usually without a pocket at the base, and a conspicuous puff of stamens. They are borne singly or in pairs in the leaf axils on short stalks. The fruit is probably a small drupe like that of the *Erythroxylum* species.

The tree was originally called *Peglera capensis* after Miss Alice Pegler, an early botanical collector in the Kentani area.

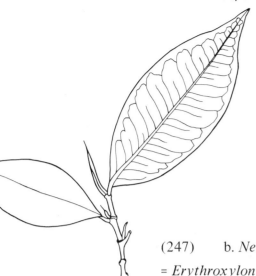

Above
Nectaropetalum zuluense leaves
(50%)

Below
Nectaropetalum zuluense stem

(247)   b. *Nectaropetalum zuluense* (Schonl.) Corb.

= *Erythroxylon zuluense* Schonl.

Zulu nectaropetalum; iDweleba, isiGqalaba, iXweleba (Z)

As the specific name suggests, this is a Zululand tree, where it is particularly common in the Ngoye forest. It extends southwards to roughly Port Shepstone, usually (according to E.P. Phillips) in rocky places and on granitic dry soil where it grows in numbers together. It can grow and reproduce itself in deep forest shade.

This is usually a small tree, 12 m in height being its maximum, and 4.5-6 m its normal height. It has a clean trunk up to about 30 cm in diameter, the outer bark smooth and thin, the inner red, and branches that are smooth. The twigs are also smooth, with the young growths somewhat flattened.

The leaves are oblong or sometimes slender, up to about 8 cm long and about 3 cm wide, narrowing slightly to a pointed tip, with veins that are not as clearly marked on the upper surface as are normally those of *Nectaropetalum capense*. The young leaves are pinkish red, the mature ones dark green and shiny.

The small flowers, with usually 5 oblong petals, are borne on longer stalks than are those of the Cape species, singly or in small groups in the axils of the leaves. There are pockets at the base of the petals. The fruit is small, oblong to oval, and fleshy.

The tough, reddish, elastic wood is used by farmers for yoke skeys and disselbooms, and by Africans to make excellent sticks.

Erythroxylum P.Br.

Erythroxylum is a far bigger and more widespread genus than *Nectaropetalum* for it comprises some 200 species which are spread throughout the warm parts of the world, being particularly abundant in America and Madagascar. Three species occur in South Africa.

The members are trees or shrubs with simple, alternate, smooth leaves, with stipules: The flowers are borne singly or in groups in the axils of the leaves. They are bisexual. The sepals and petals number 5, and the nectary scales attached to the petals are large, the stamens are 10, the styles usually 3, free or partially joined (in which the genus differs from *Nectaropetalum*) and the ovary usually has 3 chambers

Erythroxylum delagoense growing on a rocky slope of the Lebombo Mountains in Zululand

with usually 1 ovule per chamber. The fruit is a small 1-seeded drupe.

Erythroxylum takes its name from the Greek words for "red" and "wood", in allusion to the red wood of several exotic species.

Key to Species

A shrub or small tree; the leaves small, usually under 4 cm long, broader in the upper half, sharply narrowed to the base; the venation indistinct; the leaf stalks short, up to 2 mm long; the ovary normally 3-chambered.

a. *E. delagoense*

A tree; the leaves up to 8 cm long, most often narrowed in the lower one third, the venation most often indistinct, the leaf stalks up to 8 mm long; the ovary normally 3-chambered.

c. *E. pictum*

A shrub or small tree; the leaves up to 9 cm long, the tips *always* notched; the venation usually *prominent*; the ovary normally 2-chambered.

b. *E. emarginatum*

(248)   a. *Erythroxylum delagoense* Schinz

= *E. brownianum* Burtt Davy

Stone-digger, small leaf erythroxylum; umMbamatsheni (Z)

The stone-digger is a low tree or shrub growing from Natal, Zululand, Swaziland, and the eastern Transvaal to Portuguese East Africa, on forest margins, in savannah woodland, or in scrub, sometimes in sandy soil and very often among stones. (The common name "stone-digger" is a free translation of the Zulu name which means literally "digger among stones").

966

Above left
*Erythroxylum emargina-
tum:* The leaves, show-
ing the notched tips and
prominent venation
(60%)

Above right
*Erythroxylum emargina-
tum,* Fraser's Falls,
Pondoland

The bark is dark grey and apt to be warty, the upward-growing branches smooth, and young twigs flattened.

The pale green, stipulate leaves are alternate, untoothed, and vary in shape from oval and oblong to egg-shaped, typically with a rounded notched tip, broad in the upper half and with a narrowed base, but occasionally slender and pointed, about 1.3-8 cm long (usually under 4 cm long) and up to 1.3 cm wide, with the midrib slightly prominent below but the remaining venation indistinct. They are carried on short grooved stalks usually no more than 2 mm long.

The small green to creamy flowers are usually borne singly or in pairs or occasionally in bunches of up to 4, on slender stalks, in the axils of the old leaves. The small oblong or roundish fruits are succulent and bright red when fully ripe.

The specific name indicates that this species was first collected near Delagoa Bay in Portuguese East Africa.

(249)   b. *Erythroxylum emarginatum* Thonn.

= *Erythroxylum caffrum* Sond.; = *Erythroxylum emarginatum* var. *caffrum* (Sond.) O.E.Schulz; = *Erythroxylum emarginatum* var. *angusti-folium* O.E.Schulz

Notched erythroxylum; uQadansube, iTimani (X); umMbamatsheni, umBulatsheni-wangaphandle, iKhanda lempaka, umPhephane (Z)

This little evergreen is the most widespread *Erythroxylum* species in South Africa, occurring from the eastern Cape through the Transkei, Natal, Zululand, and Swaziland, to the eastern, central, and northern Transvaal, and northwards into tropical Africa.

It grows under very varying conditions, in evergreen forest as an understory tree or shrub, on forest margins, on rocky hillsides, in bush-veld and in scrub, in coastal forest, and in dune bush where it thrives in deep sand.

Above
Erythroxylum pictum, Magwa Falls, Pondoland

Left
Erythroxylum pictum bark

Below
Erythroxylum pictum: A fruiting twig (60%)

968

Naturally enough, it is extremely variable, often a shrub, sometimes a small tree, well-formed or straggly, with a rough grey trunk and smooth branches. The young twigs are flattened and characteristically knobbly and rough with small raised lines running crosswise and small, stiff, triangular stipules that persist on the twigs.

The smooth alternate leaves vary greatly, at their extremes looking so dissimilar as to appear to belong to entirely different species. They are, however, always dark green above and lighter below with untoothed margins and tips with a small notch. It is this latter character that gives the tree its specific name. The midrib is raised below and slightly above, and the secondary veins branch out horizontally or slightly upwards, loop along the margin, and are usually prominent on both sides. The leaves may be very small, no more than 1.3 cm in length, or up to 10 cm long, and 0.8-6 cm wide, often oval or oblong with a round notched tip but sometimes slender and bluntly pointed, while the base may be narrowed, round or flat. They are borne on slender, grooved stalks.

Sometimes one twig bears both large and small leaves.

The small 5-petalled flowers are snow white or pale green with a faint sweet scent, and are usually borne in groups of several in the axils of the leaves crowded on short shoots or those with many nodes. Botanists note that the ovary is usually 2-chambered.

The fruits are small, 0.8 to just over 1.3 cm long, when ripe like tiny thin plums in shape and a bright red or orange-red.

(250)   c. *Erythroxylum pictum* E.Mey. ex Sond.

Kanferboom; umCaka, umBamatsheni (Z)

The kanferboom, which occurs from the eastern Cape to Zululand, grows under very different conditions from its relative *Erythroxylum emarginatum*. This is a tree of coastal and midland forest and forest margins, or river and stream banks, from sea level up to an altitude of about 1700 m.

While it is sometimes a shrub, it is usually a small to medium-sized tree up to 13 m high, occasionally up to 18 m, many-branched and spreading, with light grey bark fissured longitudinally or in sections, and with the young knobbly twigs so flattened that they appear to have been hammered out of shape.

The leaves are alternate, the upper surface a dark shiny green, the lower a contrasting light colour. They are smooth, oval, oblong or egg-shaped, with a rounded and usually notched apex, most often narrowing to the base in the lower one third, about 4-7.5 cm long, with the midrib slightly raised above and conspicuously raised below, and about 10 pairs of rather indistinct secondary veins looping along the margin. They are borne on stalks up to 8 mm long, and have pointed stipules that soon fall off.

The insignificant creamy flowers, blooming in spring, are often borne singly in the axils of the leaves. The fruit is small, oblong to oval, nearly 1.3 cm long, and bright red. It ripens in summer and is eaten by the Zulu people.

The timber is used for carving.

The specific name *pictum* is Latin, meaning "painted", and possibly refers to the bright coloured fruits.

Above
The torchwood, *Bala-nites maughamii,* at Mkuze

Left
A torchwood trunk, typically folded and buttressed.

Right
Balanites maughamii:
A portion of a branch showing the stout spines
(50%)

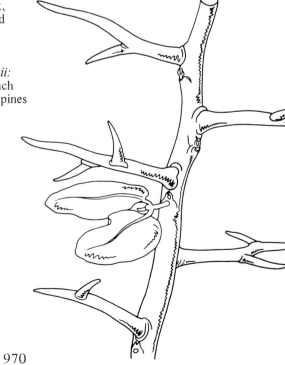

44 The Torchwood Family (Zygophyllaceae)

The family Zygophyllaceae, spread throughout the warm countries of the world, is composed of some 28 genera, 8 of which occur in South and South West Africa. The most noteworthy members are the various species of *Tribulus*, or dubbeltjiebossies (placed by some botanists in this family) which are common in dry, over-grazed, or cultivated country, known to farmers as the cause of the disease, geeldikkop, in sheep, and to all animals and bare-footed children because of their small, hard, spiky fruits which fall to the ground in numbers, causing acute pain and discomfort when trodden on. Dubbeltjies have been the best-known of all wild fruits to generations of country-born South Africans in arid parts.

Only 2 members of the family in South Africa grow as trees, and these belong to the genus *Balanites*. The family is characterized by leaves that have 2 leaflets, sometimes 1 or 3, or are pinnate, and most often opposite, with stipules that are often spiny; flowers that are usually bisexual, and fruit that is a capsule — or in the case of the South African tree members, a drupe.

Modern botanists tend to place the genus *Balanites* in a family on its own, Balanitaceae, an African and Asian group of trees and shrubs with spines that are simple or forked — an outstanding character — leaves composed of 2 leaflets, and fruit that is a drupe, and this arrangement may well be adopted in South Africa.

Balanites Del.

The genus *Balanites* is of interest historically for it has played a part in men's lives and religious beliefs since ancient times. Stones of *Balanites aegyptica* (L.) Del. have been found in Egyptian tombs of the 12th dynasty, placed there as votive offerings to the dead. The tree is said to have been cultivated in Egypt for its edible fruits for 4000 years.

About 28 species, mostly African, belong to the genus. The South African tree members are *Balanites maughamii* Sprague and *Balanites pedicellaris* Mildbr. & Schltr. *Balanites welwitschii* (Tieghem) Exell & Mendonça is a dense spiny bush found along watercourses in northern South West Africa.

The species are spiny trees or shrubs with alternate leaves composed of 2 leaflets; bisexual flowers in axillary cymes, the sepals and petals 5, the stamens 10, the ovary 5-chambered; the fruit a fleshy drupe, 1-celled and 1-seeded.

The name *Balanites* is of uncertain origin.

971

Above
A torchwood minor, *Balanites pedicellaris,* at Jobe's Kraal
in the Tongaland sand forest.

Below left
Balanites pedicellaris: The leaves and fruits (50%)

Below right
Balanites maughamii: The leaves and fruit (50%)

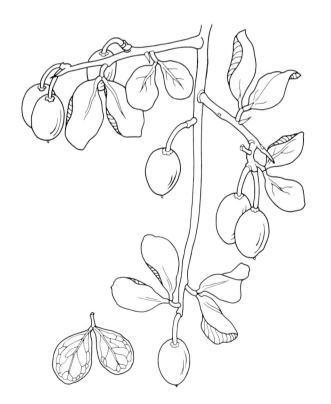

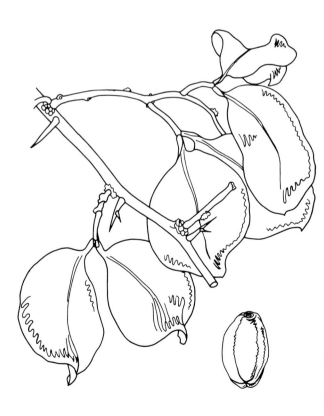

972

(251)   *Balanites maughamii* Sprague

= *Balanites dawei* Sprague

Torchwood, torch fruit tree; uGobandlovu, iPamu, umNulu (Z);
umNununu (Sw); nnulu (Tso)

The torchwood is a medium-sized to tall, deciduous tree of sand forest,
woodland, and bush, growing from Natal, Zululand, and Swaziland to
the eastern and northern Transvaal and Portuguese East Africa. Dr
Codd says that a large tree grows in the centre of Skukuza rest camp
in the Kruger National Park and is the nesting place of a large colony of
birds. It is a conspicuous feature of the sand forest in the Mkuze Game
Reserve in Zululand, and further north in Tongaland.

Typically it has a spreading crown, branching about 1.8 m above the
ground level, and a trunk up to 30 cm or more in diameter, which is
deeply folded and buttressed. This is so characteristic that a tree can be
identified from the trunk alone. Occasionally, however, as in the
country just north of the Soutpansberg in the northern Transvaal, trees
with unfolded trunks are sometimes seen.

The bark is usually light grey and smooth, or sometimes scarred and
torn by porcupines, and the young twigs are often zig-zag.

Balanites pedicellaris
stems

The branches are of two kinds, barren — when they usually bear
strong, robust, sharp spines up to 4 cm long — and fruit-bearing branches which either have no spines at all or only small ones. The spines are
usually forked whereas those of *Balanites pedicellaris* are single. The
branches are covered with short greyish-green hairs when young but
become smooth with age.

The leaves borne on the two different types of branches also vary
slightly. They are alternate and compound, made up of 2 leaflets on
very short furry stalks, but those on the barren branches are usually
longer than on the flowering branches, usually about 3.5-5 cm long but
occasionally up to 8 cm long and 6 cm wide, and although they are
roughly the same shape — egg-shaped or round with unequal bases — they
are often slightly pointed, whereas the leaflets on flowering branches
usually have rounded tips. They are more or less softly velvety,
becoming smoother as they age.

Elephants are known to browse the tips of the branches.

The small scented flowers have oblong, greenish-yellow petals, hairy
above and smooth below. They are borne in small bunches in early
summer.

The fruits are up to about 5 cm long, occasionally more, barrel-
shaped, usually with 5 grooves which are more distinct in the upper
half of the fruits. They have a brownish-yellow outer shell which encloses a large bony stone surrounded by a thin layer of flesh, and are
eaten by Africans and by a variety of wild animals from monkeys and
baboons to warthogs and antelope.

It was these fruits that first drew attention to the tree. In 1911
R.C.F. Maugham — after whom the tree was named — who was then
British consul at Lourenco Marques, sent specimens to Kew, stating that
the kernels yielded not less than 60 per cent of a fine oil. This oil, taste-
less and odourless, is said to equal the best olive oil, and to burn with a
bright flame. In parts the dry kernels are burnt as torches, hence the
common names "torchwood" and "torch fruit tree".

The tree is said to fruit after its fourth year.

Although harmless to people, the fruits have been found lethal to certain snails, tadpoles, and fish when placed in water, the poisonous principle being mainly in the kernel and pulp. It has been suggested that torchwood trees could be planted round dams used for watering stock and for bathing to kill bilharzia snails, although on a small scale, so as not to destroy fish and frogs and upset the balance of nature.

Africans use the tree in medicine and magic. A decoction of the bark makes an African emetic. Zulu witch-doctors use roots and bark, together with those of other plants, soaked in water and beaten to a froth, to ward off evil spirits. The froth is licked three times a day — without the use of the hands — and then thrown upon the roof to spill over the entrance. Zulus soak the bark in water for an exhilarating and refreshing bath.

The tree yields a valuable hard timber. In Zululand it is used to make handles for pangas and stocks for guns.

(252)   *Balanites pedicellaris* Mildbr. & Schltr.

= *Balanites australis* Brem.

Torchwood minor; uGobandlovana (Z)

Balanites pedicellaris, a much shorter and more shrubby tree than its relative the torchwood, grows in dry bushveld — often in dry acacia scrub — from Natal, Zululand, Swaziland, and the northern Transvaal to Rhodesia and tropical Africa. Both this and the torchwood sometimes grow in the same countryside, and both may be seen, for example, in the Mkuze Game Reserve in Zululand.

This may be a very dense shrub, or a little tree, straggling or bushy, with drooping, thin, rigid, or whippy branches armed with long unforked spines. The bark is light grey and often spiny. The leaves, grey-green or frequently yellow-green, are made up of 2 leaflets *without* stalks, oval or egg-shaped, up to about 4 cm long, with rounded tips, narrowing to the base. They are somewhat succulent, or hard and brittle, and they dry with conspicuous wrinkles. The branchlets end in spines and often leaves grow upon these.

Small triangular buds, borne in bunches in the axils of the leaves, open into greenish-yellow, smooth-petalled flowers on long, fairly stout stalks. These develop into plum-shaped fruits about 2.5 cm long, a brilliant orange-red when ripe, and said to be edible. A tree overhangs the path to the Bube Hide in the Mkuze Game Reserve and is noted by many visitors when its slender branches are weighed down with these bright fruits.

The name *pedicellaris* refers to the long pedicel or flower stalk.

The grey-green spiny *Balanites welwitschii* (Trieghem) Exell & Mendonça, a species of Angola and the Kaokoveld of South West Africa, much resembles this species. It is not recorded as anything but shrub-like in form.

45 The Citrus Family (Rutaceae)

Well over 100 genera with roughly 800 species belong to this family which is distributed through all the warm and temperate countries of the world. Its best known species — even in South Africa which has many common and widely spread wild trees and shrubs belonging to the family — are the various citrus species.

Nearly all the species share with the citrus one outstanding characteristic, gland-dotted leaves with a strong scent. Such leaves, held up to the light, usually have small translucent dots which are the oil glands, and these are an aid to identification.

The various species of buchu, *Barosma*, *Agathosma*, and *Diosma* species, famous for their aromatic dried leaves, belong here. The Hottentots and Bushmen used them medicinally and as a perfume, and today country people in the Cape still revere buchu brandy and buchu vinegar, which have a great reputation in the treatment of bladder diseases and as embrocations.

Trees occur in 8 genera in the family in South and South West Africa. *Fagara* is widespread, both in forest and bush, its species noteworthy for the strong lemon scent of their crushed leaves. As strong smelling, but not as pleasant, are the leaves of *Clausena anisata* (Willd.) Hook.f. ex Benth., popularly known as perdepis, or in the Transvaal by an African name meaning "stinks so that the hyena will not come near it".

Many of the species are widely used in African medicine. The perdepis, for example, is popular from the Cape to the Transvaal, and is one of the few indigenous trees to be bought by Africans to plant and cultivate. They use it to treat a multitude of ailments, and for such things as tooth brushes and deodorants.

Some of the trees of the family are hosts to the larvae of various Swallowtail butterflies, *Papilio* species.

The species have simple or compound leaves which may be opposite or alternate and are without stipules. Trees of several South African genera have leaves with 3 leaflets — *Oricia*, *Vepris*, *Toddaliopsis*, and *Teclea*. Three, *Fagara*, *Clausena*, and *Citropsis*, have once-compound leaves terminated by a single leaflet, and one species, *Calodendrum capense* (L.f.) Thunb., has simple leaves. The flowers may be bisexual or unisexual and are borne in heads, umbels, spikes, racemes, panicles, or sometimes singly. The petals usually number 4-5, the stamens as many or twice as the petals, a disc is usually present, and the gynaecium is usually composed of 4-5 carpels. *Calodendrum* is the only species in South Africa to have large flowers, and is a magnificent exception, its dense pink or mauve sprays of flowers in spring and summer touching kloofs, forests, and forest margins from the Cape to the Transvaal with rich colour.

The fruit is a drupe or capsule, or it may break up into 1-seeded parts or cocci.

LEAVES SIMPLE

A medium to large tree, unarmed; the flowers bisexual, showy, in terminal panicles; the fruit a large, dry, knobbly, 5-valved capsule.

2. *Calodendrum*

LEAVES COMPOUND

Leaves pinnate (with several pairs of leaflets)

Spiny trees or shrubs; the trunks with *spine-tipped knobs*; the leaflets several to 10 pairs and a terminal one, strongly *lemon-scented*; the flowers usually *unisexual*, in terminal or axillary panicles; the fruits small, round, gland-dotted.

1. *Fagara*

A small tree, *unarmed*; the leaves with 4-8 pairs of leaflets and a terminal one, with a *strong, usually unpleasant scent*; the leaflets often unequal-sided; the flowers *bisexual*, in axillary panicles; the fruits pea-sized, round, red, on longish stalks.

7. *Clausena*

A small spiny tree; the leaves with several pairs of leaflets and a terminal one, hairy; *the common midrib winged*; the flowers bisexual, *in clusters on the old wood*; the fruit resembling a tiny lemon, round, pitted.

8. *Citropsis*

Leaves usually with 3 leaflets

Small to medium trees; the ovary of 2-4 carpels, joined at the base but becoming separate in the fruit, 1-3 carpels usually failing to develop

3. *Oricia*

Shrubs to large trees; the leaflets usually 3, occasionally 4; the fruits small with 2-4 cells, leathery, slightly 4-lobed, not warted.

4. *Vepris*

A small tree; the fruits round, 1.3 cm diameter, usually only 1 cell developed, conspicuously *rough* and *warty*.

5. *Toddaliopsis*

Small to large trees; the fruit oval, 1-celled, smooth-skinned, often with small *smooth* knobs.

6. *Teclea*

976

1. *Fagara* L.

This is a fairly small African, East Indian, and American genus. Five described species occur in South and South West Africa of which 3 are trees – *Fagara capensis* Thunb., a tree of dry wooded country and rocky hill slopes from the Cape to the Transvaal; a species at present known as *Fagara thorncroftii* Verdoorn, which may prove to be inseparable from *Fagara capensis*; and *Fagara davyi* Verdoorn, a tree of forests.

Fagara humilis E.A.Bruce is a spiny shrub of the Transvaal, Rhodesia, and Portuguese East Africa, and *Fagara ovatifoliolata* Engl. is a shrub of northern South West Africa. A sixth species, apparently as yet undescribed, grows as a bushy tree on Kalahari sand in the well-wooded country between Sibasa and Punda Milia in the north eastern Transvaal, while a similar plant, probably the same species, has been collected in Zululand.

All these are characterized by spiny stems and branches, the larger trunks being studded with spine-tipped knobs up to 7.6 cm long, and alternate, once-compound, glandular leaves, made up of several to about 10 pairs of leaflets and a terminal leaflet, strongly lemon-scented; the flowers male or female in panicles sometimes borne on separate plants, the sepals and petals 4, the male flowers with 5 stamens, the female with a 1-chambered ovary; the fruits small, round and gland-dotted, in dense bunches, splitting to show black shiny seeds.

Fagara is a name of Arabic origin. In this, as in so many names, South Africa and the Middle East are linked.

Key to *Fagara* Species

Spines straight

The leaves with glandular dots along the margin only; the lateral veins in up to about 8 pairs; the inflorescence unisexual. (Widespread in forest, woodland and bush).

a. *F. capensis*

Spines sometimes hooked slightly upwards

The leaves with glandular dots along the margin only; the lateral veins numerous, 20 pairs or over. (Widespread in forests)

b. *F. davyi*

Spines sometimes hooked downward

The whole surface of the leaf with glandular dots. (Northern Transvaal and northern Zululand in sand forest)

c. *F.* sp.

Above left
Fagara capensis stem

Above right
Fagara capensis growing in scrub on
the Soutpansberg

Left
Fagara capensis: A portion of the
stem showing the knobs, and the
leaves (60%)

978

(253)   a. *Fagara capensis* Thunb.

= *Fagara armata* Thunb.; = *Fagara multifoliolata* Engl.; = *Fagara magalis-montana* Engl.; = *Xanthoxylum capense* (Thunb.) Harv.

Woodland knobwood, knophout, wild cardamon, wildekardamon, lemoenhout, lemoendoring; umNungumabele (X); umNungwane, umNungwane omncane, umNungumabele (Z); umNungwane (Sw); monoko-mabêlê (Tsw – Hebron); monokwane, senoko-maropa (NS); murandela, munungu (V)

The woodland knobwood grows in bush country, in dry forests, and on stony hillsides from Knysna in the Cape, through Natal, Zululand, Swaziland, and the Transvaal to Rhodesia and southern Portuguese East Africa. It is a very common little tree in bush groups on the Magaliesberg where the lemon scent of its small leaflets is known to hikers, farmers, and even to city dwellers in Pretoria where a stray plant has often survived in wild clumps in gardens.

It is a slender shrub or small tree, or sometimes a taller tree up to about 9 m high, the trunk in larger trees armed with corky, spine-tipped knobs, and in smaller ones with short, straight spines. The bark is light to dark grey, and the branches are usually smooth and spiny.

The leaves are about 5-13 cm long with about 4-10 pairs of opposite or alternate leaflets, and are borne on stalks that are channelled above. The common midrib is often spiny and sometimes raised on the upper surface. The leaflets, with slightly toothed, glandular margins are oval, oblong or lance-shaped, usually with bluntly pointed or rounded tips, from 0.6-8 cm long, the lower leaflets decreasing in size, with about 4, and sometimes up to 8 pairs of veins. They are a dark shiny green above, duller below, and are stalkless.

The small, creamy, sweet-smelling flowers are borne terminally or in the axils of the leaves in spring or early summer, male and female separately, or possibly sometimes together.

The fruits are small, roundish, red capsules smelling strongly of citrus, the outer shell splitting in two to show the small black shiny seed within. They are borne in dense sprays (botanically panicles) that are often held somewhat upright.

The Zulus use the seeds as perfume.

The wood is lemon yellow when freshly cut and makes excellent pick handles.

The leaves, bark, roots and fruit are widely used not only by Africans but by Europeans to treat a variety of illnesses. Watt and Brandwijk say that the bark is a widespread snakebite remedy, being swallowed at 15 minute intervals until the swelling subsides, and is also applied to the bites themselves, and is thus used by Europeans, Zulus, and Xhosas. The ground roots are a favourite Zulu toothache remedy, and a decoction and infusion of the leaves is used to treat fever. This is believed to cure a cold in the head and was very popular during the influenza epidemic in 1918.

The leaves are sometimes browsed.

Fagara capensis is a very variable species with both small- and large-leaved forms and some confusion still exists regarding it. The species known as *Fagara thorncroftii* Verdoorn, occurring in the eastern and possibly in the northern Transvaal, was formerly separated from *Fagara capensis* mainly on the grounds that a flower head held both male and female flowers and not flowers of one sex only as *Fagara capensis* was

Above left
Fagara davyi in Mboyti Forest, Pondoland

Above right
Fagara davyi trunk

Right
Fagara davyi: The horn-like knobs upon the trunk, and a leaf (70%)

once believed to have. It was also thought to have fewer and broader leaflets with the midrib raised below. It is possible that when the genus is revised in South Africa, *Fagara capensis* may be found to bear male and female flowers as well as flowers of one sex only in a head, and that *Fagara thorncroftii* will then be included in *Fagara capensis*.

The specific name *capensis* means "of the Cape".

(254) b. *Fagara davyi* Verdoorn

Forest knobwood, knophout, perdepramboom; umNungumabele (X); umNungwane, umNungwane omkhulu, umNungumabele (Z); mu-nungu (V)

Fagara davyi is a forest tree up to 24 m high, growing in deep forests and forest patches from Knysna northwards through Natal, Swaziland and the Transvaal to Rhodesia.

It is a fine tree, recognizable in forest — where its crown is often lost to view — by its knob-studded trunk, looking as if covered with small stout horns, an extraordinary and unforgettable sight. These knobs are part of the bark only and do not show as knots in the wood as might be expected; yet, like the trunk of a tree, they are said to have distinct annual layers. They are fairly easily broken off the trunk (which is left intact) and are light in weight. Traditionally they have been used by children as toys, and Africans make them into pipes.

The bark on old trees is dark brown, in young trees a light colour. The branches are smooth and armed with spines that usually curve slightly upwards (in contrast to those of *Fagara capensis* which are usually straight).

The large compound leaves, from about 8-30 cm long, usually have from 3-6 pairs of leaflets and a terminal leaflet, and are borne on a smooth stalk, channelled above. The leaflets are from 1.3-10 cm long and up to about 3 cm wide, becoming progressively larger from the bottom to the top, lance-shaped or sometimes oblong, tapering to the point, often slightly lopsided, with toothed and glandular margins, without stalks or with very short ones. They are a dark shiny green above, duller below, with the midrib prominent on the under-surface. They may be opposite or alternate.

The leaflets differ from those of *Fagara capensis* in size and veining — they are usually longer and thinner in texture, and the fine secondary veins are closely spaced and very numerous, usually numbering 20 pairs or over.

The flowers are greenish-yellow, small and inconspicuous, in rather short terminal sprays, male and female being borne apart.

The fruit, like that of *Fagara capensis*, is a small, round, reddish-brown capsule, gland-dotted, and smelling strongly of lemon. It splits to release a hard, shiny, black seed which does not seem to be generally eaten by birds or mammals.

The timber yielded by this species is a light colour with a fairly pronounced grain and a fine texture. It is hard, strong, elastic, polishes very well, and is used for handles of all kinds, walking sticks, and yokes. It is said to make good fishing rods. Scott says that it is one of the best of the local woods for bending and could be substituted for ash in many cases.

Like *Fagara capensis*, it is used medicinally in many ways, to treat

982

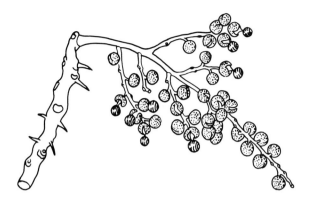

snake-bite, wounds, coughs and colds, while a decoction of the root is used as tonic.

The specific name *davyi* honours the noted botanist, Joseph Burtt Davy.

(255.1)c. *Fagara* sp.

Sand forest knobwood; umNungwane (Z)

A beautiful little species of *Fagara*, which appears to be undescribed, has several times been collected in the north eastern Transvaal growing in deep Kalahari sand. Unnamed specimens from the Tongaland sand forest may prove to be identical to this.

It has been seen as a shrubby, spiny tree up to 4.5 m high, dark green and glossy, with handsome compound leaves and pendulous bunches of bright red fruits.

The leaflets are in about 6-8 pairs with a terminal one, and are oval, sharpening to a pronounced jutting point, finely toothed, up to about 5 cm long and 2.5 cm wide, with the midrib raised above and below and with many numerous fine secondary veins. Unlike *Fagara capensis* and *Fagara davyi*, which have only the leaf margins glandular, the whole surface of the leaflets in this species is covered with translucent glandular spots.

The branch spines are small, sharp and straight, or hooked slightly downwards, and the fruit is the typical small capsule, in this case grooved, often a brilliant red, lemon-scented, and splitting to show the shiny black seed protruding.

The little tree photographed grew in the sandy woodland north east of Sibasa. In February the fruits, in long pendulous panicles, were mature, a pillar box red, bright and decorative among the glossy green leaves. Small trees, presumably the same species, seen — again in February — in the sand forest in northern Tongaland, bore fruits of a dull red-brown.

2. *Calodendrum* Thunb.

Calodendrum is a small African genus of 2 species, 1 of which is tropical while the other is widespread in Africa and occurs in most of the forests of South Africa.

Above
Fagara sp. The fruits (60%)

OPPOSITE

Above left
A probably undescribed *Fagara* species in the sand forest north east of Sibasa

Above right
The fruit of the Sibasa specimen, in February bright red and borne in abundance

Below left
The foliage of what is probably the same species, photographed in the Tongaland sand Forest

Below right
Fagara sp. A leaf (50%)

984

They have simple, opposite, glandular leaves; flowers that are bi-sexual, pink or mauve, in terminal panicles, the sepals 5, the petals 5, long and narrow, the stamens usually 10, 5 of which are petal-like staminodes, the ovary 5-chambered; the fruit a large, knobbly, 5-valved capsule containing shiny black angled seeds.

The generic name is based on Greek words meaning "beautiful tree".

(256)   *Calodendrum capense* (L.f.) Thunb.

= *Dictamnus capensis* L.f.

Wild chestnut, Cape chestnut, wildekastaiing, kastaiinghout; umBaba (X); umBaba, umBhaba (Z); mookêlêla, molalakgwedi (NS)

Seldom does a tree bear so appropriate a botanical name as this, for this literally is "the beautiful tree of the Cape". It is, however, more than a Cape tree but rather a tree of Africa, reaching from Swellendam to tropical Africa in forests, in kloofs, and sometimes in scrub, from sea level to the mountains of the interior, in full bloom one of the most glorious trees of Africa.

In forest it is tall, up to 18 or more metres in height, but in open country and on forest margins it is shorter and more spreading. The trunk is grey and smooth even in old trees, and often in forest buttressed and lichen-covered. The branches are opposite, the young ones hairy and flexible, soon becoming smooth and more rigid.

The leaves are simple, without stipules, opposite, untoothed, and borne on short stalks. They are usually fairly large, 5-22 cm long, and about 3 cm to about 10 cm wide (usually about 8-13 cm by 4-8 cm), oval or oblong with the tips pointed, bluntly pointed or round, and the bases slightly narrowed. The midrib is very conspicuous, as are the parallel veins which branch out almost at right angles from it to the edge of the leaves. The blades are studded with oil glands which appear as tiny light spots when a leaf is held to the light.

In inland forest the foliage is deciduous with rich yellow autumn colours but on the coast the trees are sometimes evergreen.

The flowers are borne in rather open terminal sprays — botanically panicles — and are bisexual. They have 5 long, narrow, hairy petals up to 4 cm long and 5 petal-like stamens or staminodes which are slender, graceful, longer than the petals and dotted with crimson or purple glandular dots. These tend to be upright, while the petals curl down-wards, the two together making a light airy flower in shades of rich pink or mauve, marked with purple or wine red. Occasionally white forms are seen.

The sprays are usually massed, lighting the tall tree tops in forest, and in the open studding the trees with colour. They have a faint sweet scent and butterflies are often seen feeding from them. The flowering season is usually early summer but is erratic for trees may be seen in full bloom as early as July and as late as March.

The fruit is a dry, knobbly, 5-valved woody capsule, 3.5-6 cm in diameter, containing several small, dark, angled, oily seeds. These are not generally popular with mammals or birds, but Samango Monkeys strip off the black outer skin to eat the nut within, and the Olive and Rameron Pigeons eat the seeds whole.

These smooth, jet-black seeds were once believed by Xhosa hunters

OPPOSITE

Above left
A wild chestnut, *Calodendrum capense,* in coastal forest near the mouth of the Umgazi River, Pondoland

Above right
The trunk of a wild chestnut.

Below
Calodendrum capense:
The leaves, flowers and fruit (50%)

to have magic properties. They tied them round their wrists when hunting to bring them skill and luck.

The kernel yields a lemon-yellow, rather bitter, fixed oil which is not considered edible but which can be used for soap making.

Although the fruit splits in autumn the shells sometimes hang on the tree during the winter, or fall to lie in heaps about the forest floor.

The timber of the wild chestnut is white or light yellow, sometimes with brown markings. It is fairly hard but bends well and is easily worked. It is used for tent bows, wagon-making, yokes, planking, shovel handles, and furniture, and is considered one of the most generally useful hard woods.

Strangely enough, the nectar-filled flowers do not seem favourites with birds, although butterflies feed from them. The larvae of several butterfly species, including the familiar Orange Dog or Christmas butterfly, *Papilo demodocus*, breed upon the foliage. This butterfly lays its eggs not only on the leaves of this species, but of citrus trees and those of other members of the family, unerringly recognizing their relationship.

The wild chestnut is probably most valued as a shade and decorative tree, and this has been so since early times. Thunberg, when he visited Grootvaderbosch in 1772, was so delighted with the blossom of the wild chestnut far above his head that he filled his gun with small shot and fired at the branches until he broke one and so secured the blooms he coveted. Burchell thought the tree "an elegant sample" of the Cape forests, noting that in flower and fruit it resembled the horse chestnut and so had received its common name.

It is still today greatly admired when in flower. Magnificent wild chestnuts grow in the forests of the eastern Cape, of which the local inhabitants are immensely proud: and in late February trees may still be seen blooming in Wyllie's Poort in the Transvaal Soutpansberg, delighting travellers along the Great North Road.

They are sometimes seen growing in gardens, and occasionally — as in Grahamstown — in streets, but, considering their beauty and the ease with which they grow, it is surprising they are so little planted. The seeds germinate quickly and young plants transplant easily. The trees like deep soil, compost, plenty of moisture, and a warm aspect, and when well established can stand some frost. When planted in tree or bush groups, which they favour, they will usually survive 8 degrees of frost, and have even been known to flower well in a Karoo garden. In areas with bitterly cold winters, where they do not flower regularly, they can often be grown as shade trees. A tree seldom flowers before it is 7 or 8 years old.

Africa's best known wild chestnut is in Kenya, for its branches grow through the famous Tree Tops Hotel. The hotel has a floor space 15 by 30 m, electric light, flush sanitation, hot and cold running water, and a bar. It stands near the old wild fig tree which housed the first Tree Tops Hotel and which was burned out by the Mau Mau many years ago.

3. *Oricia* Pierre

Oricia is a small African genus which includes several species of trees.

When the South African species were originally described by Dr Inez Verdoorn the material available was limited. Working with this, she described three species, separated largely on their degree of hairi-

986

Ilex mitis in the Royal Natal National Park

See text page 1269

ness, *Oricia bachmannii* (Engl.) Verdoorn, from Pondoland; *Oricia swynnertonii* (Bak.f.) Verdoorn, a tropical African species extending into the northern Transvaal, and *Oricia transvaalensis* Verdoorn, a species then believed to be confined to the mist-belt forests of the north eastern Transvaal.

Since then, a great deal more material has become available and on the basis of this Dr Verdoorn considers it probable that the tree forms of *Oricia* grade into one another, in which case their status as separate species cannot be upheld. *Oricia bachmannii*, the oldest name, thus stands.

The South African species has leaves made up of 3 leaflets, which are somewhat similar to those of its relatives in the genera *Vepris*, *Teclea*, and *Toddaliopsis*, and flowers which are usually either male or female. The sepals, petals and stamens number 4. Botanists note that the ovary is hairy and that the carpels are 2-4, united at the base, becoming free in the fruit, with 1-3 aborting. The fruit is thus often oval or roundish, about 1.3-1.9 cm long, often with the second lobe, or carpel – not fully developed – joined to it at the base.

The derivation of the generic name *Oricia* is not known.

(257)   *Oricia bachmannii* (Engl.) Verdoorn

= *Teclea bachmannii* Engl.; = *Teclea swynnertonii* Bak.f.; = *Oricia swynnertonii* (Bak.f.) Verdoorn; = *Oricia transvaalensis* Verdoorn

Oricia

This is probably not, as was originally supposed, merely a Pondoland tree but a very widespread species, embracing the forms previously known as *Oricia transvaalensis* Verdoorn from the mist belt forest of the north eastern and the northern Transvaal, and the tropical species, *Oricia swynnertonii* (Bak.f.) Verdoorn.

It may be a straggling forest shrub, or a small to large tree, with an evergreen, often dense crown, and softly hairy branches, often becoming smooth with age and covered with large corky spots.

The shiny, aromatic, leathery leaves are borne on fairly long stalks which are almost smooth to hairy. They are made up of 3 large leaflets, widely lance-shaped, oblong or egg-shaped, narrowing both ends, pointed or bluntly pointed, 5-15 cm long and 1.3-7 cm wide, dotted with transparent glands and with many fine parallel secondary veins, the surface usually smooth but with the midrib sometimes hairy. (The twigs and the leaf surface in the form known as *O. transvaalensis* are densely hairy). They are borne on short stalks.

The small creamy flowers are borne in big branching sprays towards the ends of the branches terminally and in the axils of the leaves, the flowers being either male or female, and probably borne on different trees. The flower stalks in the typical *Oricia bachmannii* are hairy, but in the form known as *Oricia swynnertonii* they are distinctly smooth.

The carpels of the ovary number 2-4, usually 2, of which 1 or more typically fails to develop properly or at all, so that the fruit is usually oval to round, shaped rather like a small plum or lemon, about 1.3-1.9 cm long, with an undeveloped lobe (a carpel) joined to it at the base like a small heel. It is yellow to orange when ripe.

The larvae of at least three Swallowtail butterflies breed upon this tree – the Orange Dog or Christmas butterfly, *Papilio demodocus*; the

Above left
Oricia bachmannii leaves and fruits

Above right
Oricia bachmannii flowers in the typical dense, terminal panicle

Left
Oricia bachmannii: A fruiting twig (60%)

988

Mocker Swallowtail, *Papilio dardanus*, of rain forests, and the beautiful blue and black butterfly of warm, moist, wooded places, the Green-banded Swallowtail, *Papilio nireus lyaeus.*

The specific name *bachmannii* honours Dr Franz Bachmann, a medical doctor who collected botanical specimens in Pondoland in the 1880's. The name *swynnertonii* – honouring C.F.M. Swynnerton, Director of Locust Research in Tanganyika (now Tanzania) towards the beginning of this century, and botanical collector in Gazaland – hitherto borne by the tropical form of the tree, seems a more appropriate name for a species that is widespread in central Africa. The name *bachmannii* is, however, older and is thus correct.

4. *Vepris* Comm.ex A.Juss.

Vepris is a small genus of about 15 species occurring mostly in Africa. A few grow in the Mascarene Islands and 1 species in India. Two or possibly 3 species are known from South Africa, one of them, *Vepris undulata* (Thunb.) Verdoorn & C.A.Sm. being widespread in forests from the Cape to the Transvaal.

Vepris zambesiaca S.Moore is a shrub or small tree from the Tati district of Botswana.

The compound glandular leaves with 3 leaflets much resemble those of *Teclea* and *Toddaliopsis*. The flowers are either male or female borne on separate trees, the calyx lobes and petals 4, in the male flowers the stamens 8, the female with a 2-4-celled ovary (sometimes 1-celled by abortion), and the fruit is small and furrowed, usually with 2-4 cells and 1 seed to a cell.

In fruit *Vepris* species can easily be separated from *Teclea* and *Toddaliopsis* for South African *Teclea* species have small, smooth, oval fruits with 1 cell and 1 seed, and *Toddaliopsis* has round, very rough and warty fruits, usually with only 1 cell and 1 seed.

The generic name *Vepris* literally means "bramble" or "spiny shrub", but as the genus is unarmed the reason for the name is not clear.

(261)   *Vepris undulata* (Thunb.) Verdoorn & C.A.Sm.

= *Boscia undulata* Thunb.; = *Toddalia lanceolata* Lam.; = *Vepris lanceolata* (Lam.) G.Don

White ironwood, witysterhout; umZane (X); umOzane (Z); iMotane (Sw); muhondwa (V)

The white ironwood, found in most forests of South Africa, coastal and inland, occurs as far north as tropical Africa and also in Mauritius and Reunion.

It is a tree adapted to a wide range of conditions, growing not only in deep forest but on their fringes, in scrub, and sometimes on dunes close to the sea. In high forest it grows up to 24 m in height and has a clean, fairly smooth grey or purple-grey trunk up to 1.5 m in diameter, sometimes shallowly striated lengthwise. In woodland or on forest margins it is typically somewhat triangular in shape with a slim trunk topped with a wide, gently-rounded crown, while on dunes it is often no more than a bush.

The branches, twigs, and leaves are smooth. The leaves are borne

OPPOSITE

Above right
Vepris undulata: The
leaves and fruits (50%)

Below left
A white ironwood,
Vepris undulata, near
Port St. John's, showing
the typical V shape of
young trees growing in
the open.

alternately on fairly long, slender, furrowed stalks and are composed of usually 3 stalkless leaflets, but occasionally 4. These are 5-10 cm long and 1.3-4 cm wide, usually lance-shaped but sometimes broader, with a sharply or bluntly pointed tip (occasionally rounded), narrowing to the base, gland-dotted, and usually with markedly undulate margins. When crushed, they smell like lemon leaves.

The small greenish, unisexual flowers are borne in dense, many-branched *terminal* heads. The small leathery fruit is usually slightly 4-lobed, 4-celled, and 4-seeded. The seeds are eaten by birds such as Red-wing Starlings and Layard's Bulbul.

At least 2 species of butterflies breed on this tree, *Papilio nireus lyaeus,* the Green-banded Swallowtail, and *Papilio echerioides,* the White-banded Swallowtail of rain forests.

White ironwood has fine, white, even wood which at the same time is hard, strong, and elastic, and is used for tent hoops, hammer and pick handles, spokes and beams.

The powdered root is used in parts as a remedy for influenza. Watt and Brandwijk say that in Zanzibar the fruit is used "to throw out the devil" by casting it on to a fire and making the "possessed" person breathe the smoke.

In parts of the eastern Cape the existence of the tree is threatened by porcupines which eat the bark, often over a period of years destroying the tree. In valleys near the Kei Road so many white ironwoods have been killed in this way that local farmers say the *Vepris* is doomed.

The specific name *undulata* refers to the undulate leaves.

Below
White ironwood bark

(260)   *Vepris reflexa* Verdoorn

Drooping-leaved vepris

Vepris reflexa, a tree with drooping leaves as the specific name suggests, is an aromatic evergreen shrub or small tree of dry woodland from Natal, Zululand, Swaziland, the eastern and northern Transvaal, and Botswana, Rhodesia and Portuguese East Africa.

It is usually a dense little tree with stiff, smooth, erect branches, and smooth, hard, drooping leaves that fold along the midrib. These have 3 usually stalkless leaflets, 3-8 cm long and up to 3.5 cm wide, varying from a narrow oblong to egg-shaped, with a more or less rounded tip and a narrowed base, the blade densely dotted with glands, the midrib much raised below, and with many fine secondary veins branching near the margin.

This may be confused with *Vepris undulata,* but in the latter the leaves are undulate and are not folded. In flower or fruit the species may be distinguished easily for whereas the white ironwood has terminal heads of flowers and fruit, *Vepris reflexa* bears short heads in the *axils* of the leaves. The flowers are small and yellowish, and unisexual, the fruits like small plums in shape, about 1.3 cm long, and 1-celled.

The branches and leaves are eaten by elephant.

Vepris carringtoniana Mendonça

A shrub or small tree identified tentatively as *Vepris carringtoniana* Mendonça — a Mozambique species — was recently collected on a hillside

Left
Vepris reflexa bark

Below
Vepris carringtoniana: leaves and
fruits (100%)

near Ndumu by Mrs Elsa Pooley, wife of a ranger at the camp.

If the identification is correct, this will be a first record for South Africa. At the time of writing, however, this little tree is something of a problem. Botanists are not certain whether it is separate from a shrub, *Teclea pilosa* (Engl.) Verdoorn, found previously in the Kruger National Park, and if the trees are identical, to which of the two genera — *Vepris* or *Teclea* — the species belongs, for it has characters of both. The ovary is 1-celled, and in this it inclines more to *Teclea* than *Vepris* (although the ovary of *Vepris* may be 1-celled by abortion) but the petals number 3 and the stamens 6, that is, there are twice as many stamens as petals, a character typical of *Vepris* but foreign to *Teclea*.

The little tree or shrub is deciduous, growing up to about 3 m tall, and has smooth branches, and alternate leaves composed of 3 stalkless leaflets. These are 1.5-5 cm long and up to 1.5 cm broad, oval, sometimes narrowly so, or egg-shaped, the tips bluntly pointed or notched, the base narrowed, the margins roundly toothed, and the blades densely covered with glandular dots. Numerous fine secondary veins branch near the margin, and these and the fine netted veins are conspicuous both sides. The leaf stalk is winged.

The small yellow flowers are borne in a short inflorescence — botanically a raceme or panicle — at the ends of the branches.

The fruits are up to 1 cm in length, pear-shaped, 1-celled, orange covered with small dots, and are borne on slender orange-green stalks. They ripened at Ndumu in November.

The specific name *carringtoniana* honours Prof Dr Joao S. Carrington da Costa, President of the Executive Commission, Dept of Ministry of the Portuguese Overseas Provinces.

5. *Toddaliopsis* Engl.

This is a genus of 2 species, 1 belonging to tropical Africa and 1 extending from Portuguese East Africa into South Africa. The generic name means "like *Toddalia*", a genus of woody scrambling plants which derives its name from a Malabar word for *Toddalia asiatica* (L.) Lam., the walking stick climber, a widely spread scrambler belonging to the citrus family and occurring from South and tropical Africa to Asia.

Both species have smooth, gland-dotted leaves composed of 3 leaflets; male or female flowers borne on separate trees in small panicles in the axils of the leaves, the sepals and petals 4, the stamens 8, the ovary usually 4-celled, the fruits round to oval, densely warted, usually 1-seeded.

(262)   *Toddaliopsis bremekampii* Verdoorn

Toddaliopsis: umOzane (Z)

Toddaliopsis bremekampii grows in dry bush, woodland, and scrub forest of Natal, Zululand, Swaziland, the northern Transvaal, and Portuguese East Africa. It occurs fairly frequently on the northern slopes of the Soutpansberg.

It is a small evergreen tree up to about 4.6 m high with smooth, reddish or grey branches and smooth, alternate, gland-dotted leaves carried on stout grooved stalks from about 1.3-4 cm long. They have 3 leaflets

Above left
*Toddaliopsis breme-
kampii:* The leaves and
fruits (80%)

Above right
Teclea gerrardii: A. The
leaves and fruits.
B. *Teclea natalensis:* A
flowering branch (50%)

4-8 cm long and 1.3-4 cm broad, widely lance-shaped to egg-shaped,
pointed or bluntly pointed, often with a somewhat jutting tip, narrowing to the base, with the margin untoothed but slightly wavy, the
midrib raised below, and with many fine parallel veins. They are a shiny
dark green above, yellowish below, and are without stalks or with very
short ones.

The small, pale green, unisexual flowers are borne in short sprays in
the axils of the leaves or at the ends of the branches. The fruits are
distinctive – round, about 1.3 cm in diameter, usually with 4 compartments, covered with small warts, green, turning reddish-brown when
mature. They ripen from February to March and are reputed to be
edible.

The tree yields a useful wood once popular for wagons.

The specific name honours Dr C.E.B. Bremekamp, formerly
Professor of Botany at the University of Pretoria.

994

6. *Teclea* Del.

Teclea is a genus of some 22 species, many of which are African and 2 or 3 South African. (Some doubt exists as to whether the shrub known as *Teclea pilosa* (Engl.) Verdoorn from the Kruger National Park is a *Teclea* or whether it should be included in the genus *Vepris*). The South African members of the genus grow from the forests of the eastern Cape to those of Natal and Zululand and may easily, when not in fruit, be mistaken for *Vepris* species.

They are evergreen, graceful, aromatic trees, with alternate, glandular leaves composed of 1-3 leaflets; flowers that are usually unisexual, the male and female borne on different trees in panicles, racemes, cymes or spikes in the axils of the leaves or terminally, the calyx lobes and petals 4-5, the male flowers with as many stamens as the petals, the female with the ovary 1-celled; the fruits 1-celled, oval, fleshy, smooth-skinned and often covered with small smooth swellings.

(263)   *Teclea gerrardii* Verdoorn

Umboza; umBoza, umBozane (Z)

The umboza is a tree of coastal forests, forest fringes, and dune bush from the Transkei to Zululand and Portuguese East Africa, sometimes a shrub or small tree, at others − as in the forests of Zululand − up to 15 m high.

It has a smoothish, grey, mottled trunk, sometimes flaking off in circular pieces or marked lengthwise with light lines, and when standing on its own or on forest margins, a beautiful, neat, spreading crown.

The twigs are grey with white dots. The leaves, carried on long, grooved, sometimes narrowly winged, smooth and often flattened stalks, are composed of 3 stalkless aromatic leaflets. These are 2.5-10 cm long and 1.3-4.5 cm wide, widely lance-shaped to egg-shaped, with a round or bluntly pointed, sometimes notched apex, narrowing to the base, with the midrib prominent below, and with parallel veins running outwards and branching and looping along the margin. They are a dark rather dull green above and paler below. The net veins are conspicuous both sides. The edges are slightly inrolled.

The small, yellow, unisexual flowers are in *short* clusters − botanically cymes − in the axils of the leaves, and they distinguish the species from *Teclea natalensis* which bears flowers in *elongated* branched sprays (panicles). The fruit is small, oval, fleshy, smooth, and 1-celled, holding 1 seed. When immature it is green with soft light hairs, when mature reddish and when fresh covered with small smooth knobs which often disappear with drying. It is borne on so short a stalk that it appears to "sit" on the branch.

This species was named after William T. Gerrard, famous plant collector, to whom Harvey in 1868 in *Flora Capensis* paid a tribute for his tireless exploration of the natural history of Zululand.

Teclea gerrardii, Kranskop

(264)   *Teclea natalensis* (Sond.) Engl.

= *Toddalia natalensis* Sond.

Umzane, bastard white ironwood, basterwitysterhout; umZane, um-Singomzane (X); umZane, iSutha (Z)

The umzane is a tree of coastal and inland forests or forest margins and of dune bush from the eastern Cape to Natal, Zululand, Swaziland, and the Transvaal.

It may be a shrub or rather rigid, medium-sized tree with smooth, light grey bark and smooth leathery leaves on fairly slender petioles. The leaves may have 1, 2, or 3 leaflets, usually 3, carried on very short stalks, and they are gland-dotted, smooth, drooping, sometimes folding inwards. They are widely lance-shaped to oval, 4.5-13 cm long and up to about 4 cm wide, narrowing to the stalk, typically pointed, with the midrib raised below, and with many fine secondary veins running outward to the margin, and these are fairly conspicuous on the upper side.

Teclea gerrardii trunk

The small creamy-yellow male or female flowers are in small spike-like branching heads — elongated panicles — in the axils of the leaves and occasionally terminally. The fruits are small, oval, 1-celled, aromatic, and red when ripe, and are carried on longer stalks than are those of *Teclea gerrardii*. These stalks, the usually more pointed and stalked leaflets, and the elongated inflorescence (in place of the short cluster) help to distinguish this species from *Teclea gerrardii*.

The Swallowtail butterflies, *Papilio dardanus cerea, Papilio demodocus*, and *Papilio nireus lyaeus*, are known to breed on the tree.

The timber is not considered of much value but is used for firewood.

The specific name means "of Natal", where the tree is common. Specimens originally believed to be this species, collected in the northern Transvaal, may possibly be the tropical species *Teclea nobilis* Del. It has further been suggested that the southern species may grade into the northern, and *if* this is proved to be correct the older name *Teclea nobilis* will stand and *Teclea natalensis* will fall away.

7. *Clausena* Burm.

About 46 species, distributed from Africa to India and Malaya, belong to this genus. Only 1 species, *Clausena anisata* (Willd.) Hook.f. ex Benth., occurs in South Africa, extending from the George and Knysna districts, through Natal and Zululand to the Transvaal, and thence northwards as far as Ethiopia.

The species are unarmed; the leaves imparipinnate, the leaflets often unequal-sided at the base, glandular, strong-smelling when crushed; the flowers in panicles or racemes at the end of the branches or axillary; the flowers bisexual, the calyx parts and petals 4-5, the stamens 6-10, the ovary usually 4-5-celled; the fruit oval to round, fleshy, 2-5-seeded.

The genus was named after P.Clauson, a 17th century Danish botanist.

Above
The perdepis, *Clausena anisata,* on the Natal slopes of the
Drakensberg

Right
Clausena anisata: The leaves.   A: flowers.   B: fruit (50%)

Below
Clausena anisata leaves

(265)   *Clausena anisata* (Willd.) Hook.f. ex Benth.

= *Amyris anisata* Willd.; = *Myaris inaequalis* Presl; = *Clausena inaequalis* (DC.) Benth.

Perdepis, perdebos; umNukambiba, umFuto, isiFutu (X); isiFuthu, umSanka, umNukambiba (Z); umNukelambiba (Sw); munukha-vhaloi, murandela (V)

This little tree or shrub, which reaches across Africa, is common in forests, on forest edges, in gully or in bush, in palm veld, sometimes on stream banks, from sea level to an altitude of 1520 m, in South Africa extending from George and Knysna northwards through the eastern Cape to Natal, Zululand, and Swaziland to the eastern and northern Transvaal.

It is often a pretty little tree up to about 7.6 m high, with a grey-brown, mottled, fairly smooth trunk and a spreading crown. When growing in forest, or among taller trees, it is often thin and straggly.

The leaves are alternate and compound, 6 cm to about 20 cm long, borne on rounded or slightly grooved stalks, 1.3-2.5 cm long. They are composed of about 4-8 pairs of leaflets and a terminal leaflet, borne on short stalks, the lateral leaflets alternate or nearly opposite and increasing in size from the bottom to the top. They are about 1.9-5 cm long and up to 2.5 cm broad, slender or egg-shaped, widest at the base and tapering towards the pointed apex, conspicuously unequal at the round or narrowed base, with toothed or untoothed margins, and with the blades densely dotted with glands. The young foliage is a dark purple-brown, the mature dark green.

The small, white, bisexual flowers are borne in loose sprays in the axils of the leaves in spring and although the individual sprays are rather few-flowered, the total number on a tree is often great. The fruits are small and round, about the size of peas, on longish stalks, bright red when mature in late summer, later black. They hold 1-2 seeds.

The tree is most noteworthy, not for its neat, pretty soft foliage or bright fruits, but for its smell. The common name "perdepis", is a most fitting one for the leaves, not only when crushed but even when touched, often smell strongly of horse urine. There is little suggestion of anise and the specific name is misleading. The smell alone could distinguish the perdepis from the knobwood, *Fagara capensis*, with which it is often confused.

The smell of the flowers is variable, sometimes pleasant, sometimes foetid.

The strong unpleasant smell of the tree as a whole is embodied not only in the name perdepis but in several African names with meanings such as "the smell of the striped fieldmouse", "stinks so that the hyaena will not come near it", or "to begin to stink".

The tree is, however, highly attractive to butterflies, at least 6 species of Swallowtails breeding on it. These include the Emperor Swallowtail, *Papilio ophidicephalus*, the largest butterfly in South Africa, termed by Swanepoel "the monarch of the rain forests".

The tree yields a hard, heavy, strong, and elastic timber.

This is one of the most widely used of all trees in African medicine, its strong smell believed to have great virtues. The smoke from a fire of perdepis wood is used to fumigate new-born Xhosa babies and steam from a decoction of leaves or twigs to strengthen them. It is supposed to strengthen the heart, cleanse the body internally, reduce fever, cure rheumatism, and kill tapeworms. Zulus use it as a deodorant, boiling the leaves in a pot of water over which they steam themselves. In parts the twigs are used as toothbrushes.

Not many creatures appear to eat the fruits. An exception is the Cape Glossy Starling, which regurgitates the pips.

The leaves are said to be very inflammable.

8. *Citropsis* (Engl.) Swingle & Kellerm.

This small and purely African genus of 3 or 4 species is not represented in South Africa. One species occurs in northern South West Africa and the Caprivi Strip.

The species are shrubs or small trees with spiny branches; the leaves imparipinnate or with 1 or 3 leaflets, gland-dotted, the common petiole winged, the flowers bisexual in axillary clusters, the sepals and petals usually 4, the stamens twice as many as the petals, the ovary usually 4-celled; the fruit roundish, gland-dotted and fleshy.

The name *Citropsis* means "like citrus", "citrus" in its turn being based on the Greek "kitron".

(266)   *Citropsis daweana* Swingle & Kellerm.

Citropsis

This is a spiny, often many-stemmed small tree up to about 4.5 m high, growing in the hot dry bushveld and woodland of northern South West Africa, the Caprivi Strip, Rhodesia, Zambia, and Portuguese East Africa.

Young twigs are hairy and older branches smooth, and grey or almost black in colour.

The soft aromatic leaves are compound, up to about 13 cm long, and arranged alternately. They have several pairs of opposite leaflets and a terminal one, growing – without stalks – on a much winged rachis or common midrib, and this, the leaves, and leaf and flower stalks are very hairy. The leaflets are widely lance-shaped to oblong or egg-shaped, 1.9-4.5 cm long and 0.6-2.5 cm wide, rounded or bluntly pointed, and narrowed to the base, the margin roundly notched, and the whole surface densely gland-dotted.

Sharp, straight, rather slender spines, 1.3-3 cm long, grow above each leaf.

The small cream-coloured to pale yellow flowers are bisexual and borne in clusters on the older wood, often on short side branches. They appear in late spring before the leaves. The fruit, like a dimunitive 1.3 cm lemon, is round, fleshy, and pitted with oil glands.

This species is much used for hut poles. It is closely related to the cultivated citrus and can be grafted onto citrus trees.

The specific name honours M.T.Dawe, formerly Director of the Botanical Gardens in Entebbe, who collected the tree in the Madande Forest in Portuguese East Africa.

Simarubaceae is a tropical family of some 30 genera and over 100 species distributed throughout most of the warm countries of the world. It is not a particularly well known family in South Africa although the exotic Tree of Heaven (*Ailanthus*) is sometimes cultivated. It is represented in South Africa by the genus *Kirkia*.

Members of the family have leaves that are usually alternate, simple or compound — imparipinnate in the Southern African species — and without stipules; the flowers are bisexual or unisexual; and the fruit is dry or fleshy, in the South and South West African species light, dry, woody capsules.

Kirkia Oliv.

Three tree species belonging to the African genus *Kirkia* are indigenous to South and South West Africa. They all have graceful compound leaves with many leaflets and a single terminal leaflet, crowded towards the ends of the branches; flowers that are bisexual or male or female borne in the same head, the calyx 4-parted, the petals and stamens 4, the ovary 4-celled; the fruits small and capsular which, when mature, split at the base from their central axis, remaining attached at the tip, and looking like miniature half-open umbrellas.

The generic name *Kirkia* was given in honour of Sir John Kirk, explorer, naturalist and companion for a time of Dr David Livingstone.

(267)   *Kirkia acuminata* Oliv.

= *Kirkia pubescens* Burtt Davy

White seringa, witsering; mvumayila (Tso); modumela (Tsw — Mang); mubvumela (V); ivomena (Sub)

The white seringa, in full foliage one of the most graceful of all indigenous trees, grows in the bushveld and lowveld of the Transvaal, in deep sandy soil or on rocky hills (where it favours northern slopes), in Botswana, and in South West Africa where it is common on the rocky hills of the central plateau, and in the north. It extends into tropical Africa and is a fairly common tree in the mopane country of Rhodesia. In South Africa it is probably at its best in the red sandy soil north of the Soutpansberg.

This is a straight-stemmed tree with a fine, round, leafy crown, up to 18 m high with a trunk diameter up to 0.8 m. The trunk is grey, varying from smooth to rough, young trees sometimes having grooved and corky bark with grooves nearly 2.5 cm deep. The older

The white seringa, *Kirkia acuminata*, growing in Van Coller's Pass on the northern slopes of the Soutpansberg

A sneezewood, *Ptaeroxylon obliquum,* on the slopes of the Suurberg in the Eastern Province

See text page 1373

branches are grey and smooth except for dark corky knobs with which they are often studded; the young flexible branchlets are grey and smooth, and marked with smooth circular or oval leaf scars.

The graceful leaves, from about 20-45 cm long, are without stipules and are bunched at the ends of the bluntly tipped branches, where they droop or spread out fan-wise. They are made up of 6-10 pairs of opposite or alternate leaflets and a terminal leaflet, which are roughly 2.5-6 cm long and up to 2.5 cm wide, usually slender and pointed, with notched edges and long sturdy midribs which are usually a rich plum colour on the upper side, and with short plum-coloured stalks. The young leaves are sticky.

The small whitish flowers are borne in loose branched sprays on long stalks at the ends of the branchlets. According to the authors of *Sixty-six Transvaal Trees* they are apparently bisexual but some are functionally male only and do not form fruits. Both male and bisexual flowers occur in the same flower head.

The fruits are light brown capsules, woody and 4-angled. When mature they split into 4 parts, joined at the tip of their central axis. Each part contains 1 seed.

This is a deciduous tree, losing its leaves early and coming into leaf fairly late in spring so that a slender young tree is often overlooked when bare of leaves. A large, well-formed tree, however, is conspicuous, its upward-growing branches and persistent fruits on stiff robust stems pointing upwards and making a characteristic silhouette. Particularly fine trees grow in central South West Africa and travellers to the Etosha Game Reserve cannot fail to notice them between Tsumeb and Namutoni, in winter time looking like great candelabras on the sides of the hills.

The sapwood, which is usually wide, is light grey to whitish, and the narrow heartwood is a dark coppery brown or greenish brown, with dark wavy markings. It is fairly light and works easily but is not durable. According to C.P. Kromhout, logs are not very straight and often have decayed hearts, and knots. He says the logs are easily sawn into boards but that due to the silica crystals in the ray cells they have an abrasive effect on the teeth of the saw and soon blunt them.

Beautiful and unusual furniture is made from the wood which has also been used for parquet flooring, for hoops, bowls, and spoons. The bark yields a fibre that African women in Rhodesia weave into material.

The white seringa has an uncommon and life-giving use. The swollen roots store liquid and in times of scarcity are used by Africans to quench thirst. In drought wild animals such as impala chew them.

In parts of Rhodesia this is regarded as a sacred tree.

The white seringa is a splendid tree for a warm garden, fast-growing, graceful, and exceptionally beautiful in light spring or golden autumn foliage. It is tender to frost and should always be protected when young. A warm sheltered position in sandy soil is ideal for it, although it tolerates a heavy soil. It grows fairly well in Pretoria, for example, in shale, surviving several degrees of frost. In suitable parts it makes an excellent street tree.

It is easily grown from seed or truncheons and in the Transvaal is often planted as a live fence round kraals as it possesses great vitality and is drought resistant.

Above
Kirkia acuminata near Tsumeb in South West Africa, showing the striking winter pattern of its branches.

Right
Kirkia acuminata: A portion of a branch, and fruits (50%)

Below
Kirkia acuminata bark

The specific name *acuminata* refers to the tapered or acuminate leaflets.

(269)   *Kirkia wilmsii* Engl.

Mountain seringa, wild peppertree, witsering, basterpeperboom, slaploot

This smaller relative of the white seringa grows only in the central, northern, and eastern Transvaal, usually on mountain slopes and on granite and dolomite formations. It is one of the common trees of the Waterberg, growing in numbers in the hills near Warmbaths and Potgietersrust, and on the slopes of the Drakensberg around the Abel Erasmus Pass.

It is a small tree, seldom more than 8 m high, usually with several grey, smooth stems from the base and a rounded crown of delicate feathery foliage from which it takes the common name of "wild peppertree". The branchlets are usually marked with the scars of old leaves and have noticeably stubby tips. The leaves are alternate, clustered at the ends of the branches, up to about 15 cm long, and with about 10-15 pairs of leaflets and a terminal leaflet. These are small and slender, usually no more than 1.5 cm long and 3 mm wide, pointed, smooth, and coarsely serrated. They have practically no stalks.

The small greenish-white flowers are borne in much branched heads on long stalks in the axils of the upper leaves, almost at the ends of the twigs.

The fruit is small, when mature about 8 mm long, smooth, some-what woody and — like that of the white seringa — splitting into 4 segments, joined at the tip to a central axis like a small, half-open umbrella.

The light, coarse-grained wood is a greyish colour and little used. A good strong fibre, however, is made from the bark of young shoots and roots. The large swollen tubers up to 30 cm long are eaten as food and drink in times of need.

This is a good garden tree, germinating easily when sown in spring, and growing from hard wood cuttings in the summer. It likes a well-drained soil in a warm sheltered garden where its red and gold autumn foliage is always an outstanding feature. It is a common belief that South Africa has no trees remarkable for their autumn tints; yet it is probable that no exotic trees can surpass this wild seringa in brilliant colour.

The specific name of the tree honours a German apothecary, Dr F. Wilms, 1848-1919, who worked in Lydenburg and made a large plant collection in the neighbourhood.

(268)   *Kirkia dewinteri* Merxm. & Heine

Kirkia dewinteri, a rare species from northern South West Africa, is of interest botanically for although its leaves are much like those of *Kirkia wilmsii* it has differences in the flowers and fruit which set it apart from the other members of the genus.

Dr B. de Winter, Assistant Chief of the Botanical Research Insti-

Bark of a young
Kirkia acuminata

Above
Kirkia wilmsii in the
Abel Erasmus Pass,
north eastern Transvaal

Below left
Kirkia wilmsii bark

Below right
Kirkia wilmsii: A flowering twig and fruits (50%)

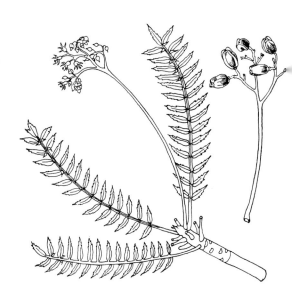

tute — after whom the tree was named — collected it in the Kaoko-veld and described it as a large tree with "yardbroom-like habit", a rounded or flattish crown, and yellow bark with small black spots — "like a leopard".

The slender graceful leaves are clustered at the ends of the branches, which — like those of the other South African kirkias — are marked with the scars of the old leaves. They are up to about 15 cm long and 2.5 cm wide, with many small narrow leaflets about 1.5 cm long and 1 cm wide, sharply pointed, with deeply toothed margins.

The male and female flowers are borne in the same head in the axils of the topmost leaves. They have small botanical differences which separate them from typical *Kirkia* flowers. The fruit splits not into 4 but into 8 parts.

Commiphora pyracanthoides subsp. *glandulosa* (*C. glandulosa*) near Tsumeb. Visitors to the Etosha Game Reserve in winter note its bare distinctive form close to the roads.

47 The Myrrh Family (Burseraceae)

This, like the fig family, links us with antiquity, with Biblical times and the very early days of civilization, for it is trees of two genera of this family, *Boswellia* and *Commiphora*, which yield two of the great commodities of early trade — frankincense and myrrh.

Around these precious resins history has been built. They have the most intimate connection with the beginning of the Christian religion, for these were among the gifts of the Three Wise Men. Historically they are much older for they were known and valued for many centuries before the birth of Christ. It is recorded that in the 15th century B.C. an expedition was sent by Queen Hatshepsut of Thebes "to the land of Punt" — probably the Somalia of today — to bring back myrrh trees to plant upon the terraces of the great temple she built near Thebes. Her ships were loaded along the shores of Somalia with "all goodly fragrant woods of God's Land, heaps of myrrh resin, of myrrh trees, with ebony and pure ivory, with green gold of Emu, with incense. . . ."

No trees belonging to *Boswellia*, the genus which yields frankincense, grow in Southern Africa, but many species of *Commiphora*, the myrrh-yielding genus, grow from South to South West Africa. None of these yield as precious a resin as do the famous *Commiphora* species of Arabia or Somaliland, such as *Commiphora myrrha* (Nees) Engl. or *Commiphora gileadensis* (L.) Christ., the Balm of Gilead, but some — such as *Commiphora woodii* Engl. — from the forests of Natal and the eastern Cape, do yield an aromatic gum that has been considered commercially (although not very seriously).

A fragrant resinous gum is sometimes found on other commiphora trees growing from the Transvaal to South West Africa, but little is known of it. Twigs, bark, and sometimes the leaves of various indigenous species are sometimes strongly and pleasantly aromatic.

The family is composed of 19 genera, mostly African, but with outliers in Madagascar, Arabia, and India. The species are all trees or shrubs, sometimes spiny, with alternate leaves that are usually compound; flowers that are bisexual or unisexual, and fruits that are drupes or capsules.

Commiphora Jacq.

The genus *Commiphora* is composed of over 200 species which occur mainly in Africa and Arabia, but also in Madagascar, Socotra, and in India. About 26 species in South and South West Africa grow as trees, or as dwarf trees for even when small in stature they often have a tree-like habit with robust trunk and branches. Although two of these, *Commiphora harveyi* (Engl.) Engl. and *Commiphora woodii*

Above
Commiphora angolensis near Usakos in South West Africa —
host to the poison grub from which Bushmen make arrow
poison

Below left
A kanniedood, or never-die tree — *Commiphora woodii* —
making a living fence post on top of the Lebombo Mountains in Zululand

Below right
When a commiphora fruit is broken open, the pseudaril and
seed are clearly seen, as in this *Commiphora woodii* fruit
with the seed projecting from the cup-like pseudaril. Botanists sometimes base an identification key on the type of
pseudaril.

Engl., are found in forest, the genus in these territories is primarily one of hot, dry bushveld and desert and semi-desert.

Commiphoras are especially abundant in the northern Transvaal, in particular in the hot dry country north of the Soutpansberg, and travellers along the Waterpoort road, or journeying to Chipisi and eastwards, will remember the commiphoras growing by the thousand, often to the exclusion of other species.

They are widely spread in South West Africa where they are frequently a feature of the countryside. Visitors to the Etosha Game Reserve in the winter season pass their bare distinctive forms in great numbers in the woodlands of the north.

This is a fascinating genus, worthy of study — not only for its historical associations — but for the bizarre characters of its many species. It is not on the whole outstanding for beauty but for the unusual appearance of its members, particularly when bare of leaves — and they are bare for the greater part of the year. It is then that they are most frequently seen by tourists.

They are usually small to medium-sized trees, often spiny and many-branched, with bark that in many cases is so outstanding and so characteristic that the species may often be recognized by this alone. While one has a smooth white bark, another has a bark marked with bold, black, corky strips, another a bark that peels in thick, yellow, crisp sheets, a fourth in thin, papery, yellowish flakes, and yet another has a silver-white bark peeling in creamy papery strips.

None of these trees has any great economic importance, yet their local uses are occasionally unusual and always interesting. *Commiphora africana* (A. Rich.) Engl. — widely distributed from the Transvaal and the open grassveld of South West Africa to tropical Africa — and *Commiphora angolensis* Engl., have the most uncommon uses of all. They act as hosts to the poison grubs, *Diamphidia* species, from which Bushmen make some of their arrow poisons. *Commiphora oblanceolata* Schinz is also the host of a caterpillar once used as arrow poison by the Bushmen of the north west Cape.

The sappy roots of several species are used to quench thirst, and a few have foliage that is browsed by stock and wild animals. The gum of at least one species is eaten. The fruits play an important part in bird life for many have the seed partly or wholly enveloped by an oily, often bright red covering — the pseudaril — which in some species is much sought by birds.

The wood is usually very light and soft, and used for such things as brake-blocks, dishes, and spoons.

Nearly all commiphoras have light corky wood and grow very easily from pole cuttings, so that as a group they are usually known as corkwood or kanniedood — "never die". Probably Queen Hatshepsut was aware of the vitality of the myrrh trees when she sent her expedition to bring trees from Somaliland to Egypt by ship — a lengthy business. The trees around a Transvaal kraal and those on the terraces of a temple in Thebes are not fancifully, but closely, connected.

Many of the species are spiny. The leaves of all are alternate and usually crowded towards the ends of the branches, sometimes reduced to 1 leaflet, but usually with 3 leaflets or with several pairs of leaflets and a terminal leaflet. The flowers are small, usually appearing before the leaves, in groups borne in the axils of the leaves or on very short side shoots. Male and female flowers are usually borne

1011

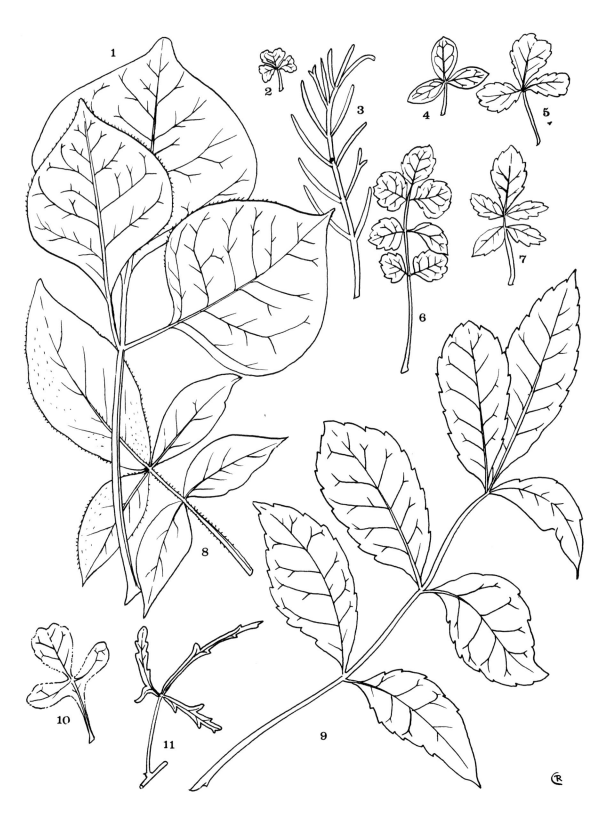

1. *Commiphora mos-sambicensis*
2. *Commiphora capen-sis*
3. *Commiphora kraeu-seliana*
4. *Commiphora vir-gata*
5. *Commiphora din-teri*
6. *Commiphora saxi-cola*
7. *Commiphora ango-lensis*
8. *Commiphora edulis*
9. *Commiphora schlechteri*
10. *Commiphora wildii* (This usually has 2-3 pairs of leaflets)
11. *Commiphora ob-lanceolata*

(100%)

separately and often on different trees. They have a 4-lobed calyx, 4 petals, and 8 stamens, and a disc that although inconspicuous is of importance to botanists in helping to determine the groups to which the species belong.

The fruit is resinous, oblong, egg-shaped or roundish, sometimes like a small cherry in shape and size, with a shell-like outer covering which — in all the species in Southern Africa — splits when mature into 2 halves exposing the single bony seed within, which in many species is "clasped" by the bright red or orange pseudaril.

All the species are deciduous, losing their leaves early in the year and putting out new foliage in late spring or early summer. This characteristic, combined with the fact that the flowers are usually borne before the leaves and that the trees are often in distant parts of the country and not easily accessible at flowering, fruiting, and leafing seasons, has given botanists in the past much trouble in relating leaves to flowers and fruit. One may drive mile upon mile through parts of the northern Transvaal, for example, in late spring and find flowers but not a single leaf, and in February or March trees in full leaf but often with scarcely a fruit to be seen.

The early keys to the genus were based on leaf characters. Modern botanists, however, tend to group the species according to fruit and flowers, which they consider more fundamental characters. The detailed botanical keys in Volume 2 of *Flora Zambesiaca* (1963-1966) — the most recent work on the species of Southern Africa — are based on H. Wild's classification. Wild divides the genus into sections, based on the number of disc-lobes together with the type of pseudaril, and uses the leaf characters only in the subsections of these. Anyone who has slipped off the outer shell of a ripe *Commiphora* fruit knows the striking colour and pattern of the pseudaril, and this seems a good basis for a key to distinguish trees in fruit. (In dried specimens it is not foolproof).

A key, based on Wild's classification, follows, but a simple leaf and bark guide has also been included as being of general use. It should be recognized that a key based only on leaves can lead to error. Even botanists in the past have confused genera such as *Lannea, Sclerocarya* and *Ekebergia* with *Commiphora* on the basis of leaf characters alone.

Unnamed *Commiphora* species may exist even in South Africa for in the Herbarium files at the Botanic Research Institute are several specimens that do not fit neatly into any category.

According to Wild's classification, South and South West African species fall into 4 sections. Several remain unclassed.

The generic name *Commiphora* is based on the Greek words "kommi" meaning "gum" and "phero" meaning "to bear". Many species were originally described in the genus *Balsamodendron*, a splendid name, which unfortunately must give place to the less picturesque but older name, *Commiphora*.

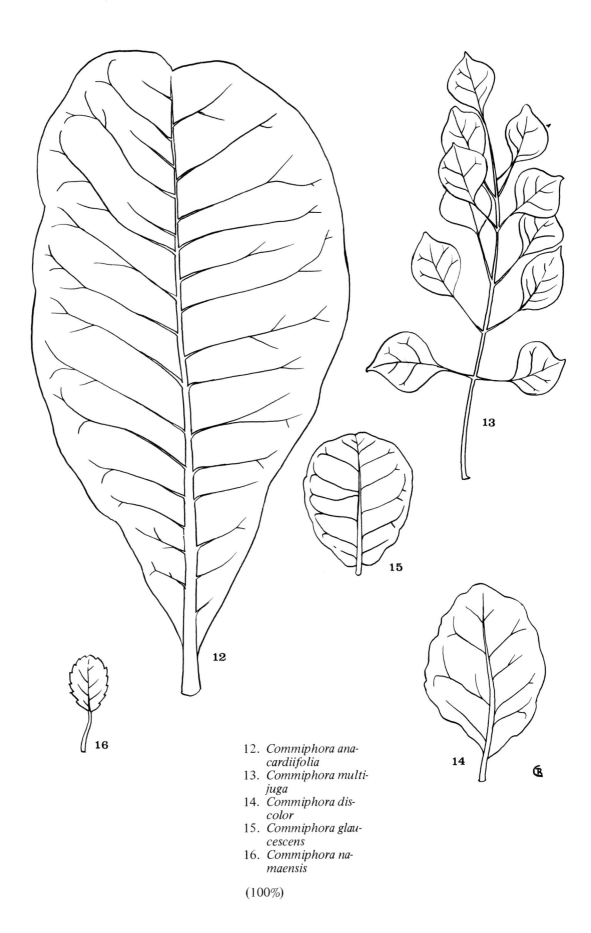

12. *Commiphora ana-cardiifolia*
13. *Commiphora multi-juga*
14. *Commiphora dis-color*
15. *Commiphora glau-cescens*
16. *Commiphora na-maensis*

(100%)

Flower and fruit key
(Based on that of H. Wild)

Section *Commiphora*

A widely distributed group with disc lobes usually 4; the seed with one markedly humped and convex side; the pseudaril usually with 4 arms at right angles to each other clasping the seed.

1. *C.pyracanthoides* subsp. *glandulosa (C. glandulosa)* (Northern Transvaal, Botswana, South West Africa)
2. *C. virgata* (Central and northern South West Africa)
3. *C. merkeri* (Northern Transvaal)
4. *C. mollis* (Northern Transvaal, Botswana, South West Africa)
5. *C. harveyi* (North eastern Cape, Natal, Zululand, Swaziland)
6. *C. neglecta* (Zululand, Swaziland, central and northern Transvaal)
7. *C. schlechteri* (Natal, Zululand, and possibly the Transvaal)
8. *C. multijuga* (Northern South West Africa)
9. *C. marlothii* (Central and northern Transvaal, Botswana)
10. *C. mossambicensis* (Botswana, Caprivi)

Section *Africanae* Engl.

A widely distributed group with disc lobes usually 4; the pseudaril in a fresh fruit completely enveloping the seed, but usually disappearing shortly after the fruit is picked.

11. *C. africana* (Central, eastern and northern Transvaal, Botswana, central and northern South West Africa)
12. *C. schimperi* (Zululand, central and northern Transvaal, northern Cape, Botswana)

Section *Coriaceae* Engl.

A group belonging to the semi-deserts of South West and north east Africa, with disc lobes 8, small or undeveloped; the pseudaril apparently absent.

13. *C. capensis* (Namaqualand, South West Africa)
14. *C. kraeuseliana* (Central and northern South West Africa)

Section *Spondioideae* Engl.

A section widely distributed from the forests of the eastern Cape and Zululand to the semi-deserts of South West Africa, with the disc 0, or with 8 small lobes; the pseudaril often fleshy when fresh, enclosing the lower part of the seed in a cup, or sometimes nearly enclosing the seed.

15. *C. edulis* (Northern Transvaal, Botswana, Caprivi)
16. *C. woodii* (Coastal districts of the eastern Cape, Natal, Zululand)
17. *C. glaucescens* (South West Africa)
18. *C. anacardiifolia* (Western South West Africa)
19. *C. saxicola* (South West Africa)
20. *C. dinteri* (South West Africa including the Namib Desert)
21. *C. namaensis* (South and south western South West Africa)
22. *C. crenato-serrata* (Western South West Africa)
23. *C. angolensis* (Transvaal, northern Cape, South West Africa)
24. *C. tenuipetiolata* (Northern Transvaal, Botswana, South West Africa)
25. *C. zanzibarica* (Northern Zululand)
    (It is interesting to note that *C. myrrha* belongs here)

Unclassed species

26. *C. oblanceolata* (Northern Cape, South West Africa)
27. *C. discolor* (Northern South West Africa)
28. *C. wildii* (Northern South West Africa)

Leaf and bark key

Leaves usually with a single leaflet

The bark grey or yellow-green, peeling in small papery flakes.

1. *C. pyracanthoides*
subsp. *glandulosa*
(C. glandulosa)

The bark greyish, patterned with horizontal black warty stripes.

3. *C. merkeri*

The bark pale, peeling in thin yellow papery strips.

17. *C. glaucescens*

The bark grey-green, peeling in papery strips.

18. *C. anacardiifolia*

The bark grey, not peeling.

21. *C. namaensis*

The bark papery

27. *C. discolor*

Leaves with usually 3 leaflets

The bark silver-grey to brown, peeling in horizontal strips.

2. *C. virgata*

The bark greenish, peeling in small papery flakes.

6. *C. neglecta*

The bark grey, smooth, or sometimes peeling

10. *C. mossambicensis*

The bark grey, usually not peeling.

11. *C. africana*

The bark greenish-yellow, mottled, smooth or peeling in small papery flakes.

12. *C. schimperi*

The bark smooth, grey.

13. *C. capensis*

The bark grey, sometimes mottled, not peeling.

20. *C. dinteri*

The bark silver-white peeling in strips.

24. *C. tenuipetiolata*

The bark blackish-grey, not peeling.

26. *C. oblanceolata*

The bark papery; (the leaves on the long shoots with 3 leaflets)

27. *C. discolor*

Leaves pinnate

The bark greyish-green, or brownish, mottled, cracking into circular flakes, not peeling.

4. *C. mollis*

The bark smooth, purplish-grey, furrowed with age, not peeling.

8. *C. multijuga*

The bark green, peeling in thin, chestnut-brown flakes.

5. *C. harveyi*

The bark greyish-green, peeling in papery flakes.

7. *C. schlechteri*

The bark green, smooth, with crisp, yellow skin peeling in large pieces

9. *C. marlothii*

The bark yellowish to purple, sometimes with orange-yellow peeling skin.

14. *C. kraeuseliana*

The bark grey, smooth or peeling.

10. *C. mossambicensis*

*Commiphora pyracan-
hoides* subsp. *glandulosa
(C. glandulosa)* near Chipisi in the northern
Transvaal — photograph-
ed in full leaf in February.

The same species —
completely leafless — as
it appears for the greater
part of the year. It was
photographed near Okau-
keujo, South West Africa

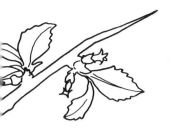

Commiphora pyracan-thoides subsp. *glandulosa (C. glandulosa):* A flow-ering twig (100%)

The bark silvery-white to grey, somewhat rough.

15. *C. edulis*

The bark greyish-white, sometimes peeling in papery strips

16. *C. woodii*

The bark yellow-grey, not peeling.

19. *C. saxicola*

The bark grey, papery.

22. *C. crenata-serrata*

The bark reddish-brown, grey or yellowish-green, peeling in thin hori-zontal papery strips.

23. *C. angolensis*

The bark silver-white peeling in strips.

24. *C. tenuipetiolata*

The bark grey with small raised dots, in South Africa not peeling.

25. *C. zanzibarica*

The bark grey-green, to brownish, sometimes peeling in small papery flakes.

28. *C. wildii*

The bark peeling in large flakes

Section *Commiphora*

(285)   1. *Commiphora pyracanthoides* Engl.

          a. subsp. *pyracanthoides*
(285.1)   b. subsp. *glandulosa* (Schinz) Wild

= *Commiphora glandulosa* Schinz

Kanniedood; shifati (Tso)

Two subspecies of *Commiphora pyracanthoides* are generally recog-nized, usually with a very different habit of growth, for whereas subsp. *pyracanthoides* is usually a sprawling, spiny, many-branched shrub, subsp. *glandulosa* is a tree, often with a fine umbrella-like crown. The low shrub form has a more southerly distribution than the tree form, growing from Zululand, Swaziland and the Transvaal to South West Africa and only just penetrating into Rhodesia, while the tree, subsp. *glandulosa*, grows from the northern Transvaal, Botswana, and South West Africa northwards through Rhodesia to Zambia.

In South West Africa this difference in habit of growth is not always constant, and the two subspecies are separated on a botanical de-tail — the calyx, which in the case of subsp. *pyracanthoides* is always smooth and in subsp. *glandulosa* always glandular. This difference is constant, and some botanists still consider it fundamental enough to separate the groups into two distinct species. Indeed, at the time of writing, the tendency is to regard subsp. *glandulosa* as a species in its

Above left
Commiphora pyracanthoides subsp. *glandulosa (C. glandulosa):* The bark peeling in tiny pieces

Above right
A fruiting twig and dissected fruit (100%)

Left
The flowers, blooming on the bare branches in November

own right, *Commiphora glandulosa* Schinz.

The subspecies *glandulosa (C. glandulosa)* is a fine, upright, spreading tree up about 6 m high with a grey, yellow or greenish trunk, sometimes marked with black, which when mature usually peels in small papery flakes. The branches are stiff and arching and the branchlets spine-tipped. The latter are sometimes dark in colour.

When bare of leaves the trunk and spiny branches, robust and shiny, make a striking outline.

Adult leaves always appear simple. They are, however, reduced to 1 leaflet, young leaves often having 3 leaflets, a large terminal one and 2 tiny lateral leaflets which drop off as the leaves mature. Adult leaves are up to 6 cm long and 3 cm wide, but usually smaller, almost without stalks, somewhat egg-shaped with sharply or bluntly pointed tips, narrowed to the base, with toothed margins, smooth, bright green above with conspicuous yellow midrib and veins, a paler green below. They are usually clustered on short side branchlets and sometimes on the branch spines.

Very young twigs are often crimson.

The small inconspicuous flowers — green or yellow, turning red with age — grow in bunches on the knob-like branchlets and bloom before the leaves appear. Botanists note that the calyx of these is glandular.

The small, almost stalkless, egg-shaped, sometimes pointed fruits, scarlet, reddish-green or brown when ripe, split when mature to show the brilliant seed within, black, clasped by the 3 or 4 long slender, bright red arms of the pseudaril.

The fruits of this species and of *Commiphora africana* are eaten by Yellow-billed Hornbills. The ornithologist, Alan Kemp, watched the birds pulling off the outer covering "like grape-skins" and eating the fruit (possibly the pseudaril) within.

The tree is sometimes planted as a living fence, and the wood made into cups or buckets. The foliage is often heavily browsed and the gum, which is said to be very bitter, eaten. The young shoots are eaten by duiker, and the bark by elephant. Subsp. *pyracanthoides* is called "a water plant" from the Transvaal to South West Africa, because its roots have thirst-quenching properties and are eaten by wild animals from elephants to porcupines, and by people who scrape and chew them. This virtue does not seem to be shared by subsp. *glandulosa,* and this is understandable if it is indeed a separate species.

The name *pyracanthoides* is based on Greek words meaning "fire thorn" while *glandulosa* refers to the glandular calyx.

(290)   2. *Commiphora virgata* Engl.

Twiggy commiphora

The twiggy commiphora is a small shrubby tree of desert regions of central and northern South West Africa, with a short thick trunk, often branching from the base, and with silver-grey to brown bark peeling in horizontal strips.

The branches are slender and smooth. The leaves have 3 small leaflets which are oval to egg-shaped, narrowing to the base, usually 0.6-1.3 cm long, the central the largest, smooth, untoothed, stalkless. The leaves are borne on slender, usually rather short petioles.

The small stalkless flowers are in clusters. The fruit is small, oval,

Above
The zebra commiphora, *Commiphora merkeri,* near Chipisi in the northern Transvaal

Below left
Bark of the zebra commiphora

Below right
Commiphora merkeri leaves (90%)

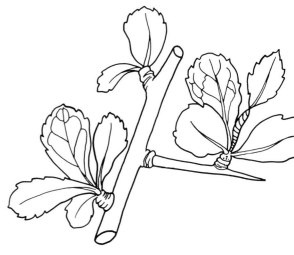

smooth, red when ripe, and the seed is black with a greenish aril reaching almost to the top of the seed.

The specific name *virgata* means "twiggy" or "wand-shaped".

(279)   3. *Commiphora merkeri* Engl.

= *Commiphora viminea* Burtt Davy

Zebra commiphora; shifati (Tso)

This little tree of the Transvaal north of the Soutpansberg, and of tropical Africa, may be instantly recognized because of its unusual trunk, in an adult tree grey and patterned horizontally with large warty black strips. Between these, the bark often flakes in pieces. In winter time these trees with their arresting zebra-patterned trunks are conspicuous in the woodland around Chipisi Hot Springs.

The trees are upright with straight clean stems. The branches are smooth and purplish. The smooth, simple, rather pear-shaped leaves, up to about 4 cm long, resemble those of *Commiphora pyracanthoides* but have a greyish bloom. They are borne in tufts on short leaf stalks on abbreviated, often spine-tipped side-shoots.

The small tubular flowers bloom before or with the young leaves, and the smooth, rather plum-shaped, pointed little fruits, about 1.3 cm long, split to show the seed, clasped by a 3- or 4-armed pseudaril.

The specific name honours a German botanical collector in East Africa, Moritz Merker, who died in 1908.

(280)   4. *Commiphora mollis* (Oliv.) Engl.

= *Balsamodendron molle* Oliv.; = *Commiphora welwitschii* Engl.; = *Commiphora cinerea* Engl.

Kuhuti; kuhuti, shisenga (Tso); mmetla-kgamêlô (NS)

Commiphora mollis, the "softly hairy commiphora", with its wide crown and soft compound leaves, is one of the most beautiful of the group — a widespread species growing in hot, sandy woodland and bushveld from the Kruger National Park, westwards through Botswana to northern South West Africa and into tropical Africa.

It reaches a height of about 7 m, and has a wide, many-branched, dark green crown, spineless branches which are hairy when young, and a brownish, grey or greenish-grey, smooth, shiny, sometimes fluted trunk. This — unlike that of most commiphoras — does not peel in papery flakes but is covered with a smooth mottled bark marked with a circular pattern that cracks into circular or oval flakes showing the green undersurface.

The twigs are brown, usually with small white dots, and are borne almost at right angles to the branches. The leaves are made up of several pairs of opposite leaflets —usually 1-3 pairs but occasionally more — and a terminal leaflet which is the largest. They are oval or oblong, 1.3-2.5 cm long, with a pointed or rounded tip and rounded base, except for the terminal leaflet that always narrows to the base, green above, whitish-green and densely and softly hairy below, with untoothed margins. These and the twigs have a strong aromatic smell.

From about the end of September onwards to November the tree

Above
Commiphora mollis alongside the Waterpoort road, northern Transvaal

Below left
The bark of *Commiphora mollis*

Below right
Commiphora mollis: A fruiting twig and individual fruit dissected (100%)

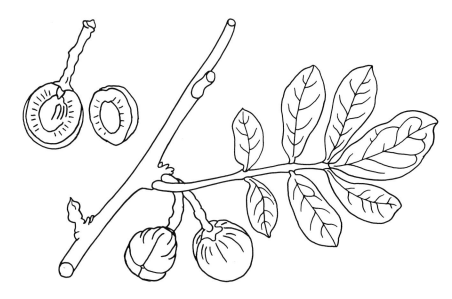

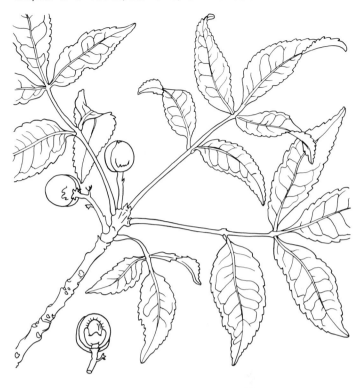

Left
Commiphora harveyi bark

Above
Commiphora harveyi: A fruiting
twig and a dissected fruit (60%)

flowers, the buds on long, red, slender stalks opening into small red and yellow, tube-shaped flowers in small slender sprays borne at the ends of the stubby twigs, sometimes with the first tufts of tender green leaves.

The pale grey or pinky-yellow, hairy fruit, like a small plum, on a stout stalk splits when mature to show the smooth oval seed within, clasped by a 4-armed pseudaril.

Kudu browse the leaves and young shoots.

The specific name *mollis* is the Latin for "soft" and refers to the soft, silky hairs on the leaves. The North Sotho name mmetla-kgamêlô, means "for carving milkpails".

(277)   5. *Commiphora harveyi* (Engl.) Engl.

= *Balsamea harveyi* Engl.; = *Protium africanum* Harv.

Harvey's cork tree; iMinyele, uSingankomo (Z)

Few commiphoras occur in the Cape Province, two in the eastern districts and several in the arid north west. *Commiphora harveyi* is one of the species with an eastern distribution and grows from hot rocky river slopes in the north eastern Cape, often on red dolerite soil, to the Natal and Zululand bushveld and the wooded ravines of the Lebombo mountains in Swaziland or the kloofs of the eastern Transvaal.

Top
A grove of *Commipho*
neglecta, Mkuze

Centre right
Commiphora neglecta
A fruiting twig and an
individual fruit dissec
to show the seed and
pseudaril (60%)

Centre left
Commiphora neglecta
fruits, photographed i
February in Tongalan

Left
Commiphora marloth
in Van Coller's Pass o
the northern slopes of
the Soutpansberg

1026

It is usually a small tree from 4-6 m high, with somewhat few, up-ward-growing branches and a smooth green trunk peeling off in thin, often bright chestnut, skin-like flakes. Observers have described this peeling bark as like "the skin of a new potato", or "thin sheets of brown paper".

The twigs are slender and white, marked by old leaf scars. The compound leaves are made up of usually two pairs of leaflets and a terminal leaflet which vary in shape from slender lance-shaped to egg-shaped. They are 5-8 cm long and up to 2.5 cm wide, tapering to the tip, the margins roundly toothed, borne on short stalks. They are thin in texture and turn a bright yellow before they fall.

The small cream-coloured flowers are carried in axillary sprays on long stalks on the young wood.

The fruits, on stout stalks, are oval or round, resembling a small cherry, mottled green turning red. When ripe the outer shell slips off if pressed between the fingers revealing the oval seed clasped at the base by the orange or bright red, 4-pronged pseudaril.

The tree has several uses. Klipspringer are known to eat the leaves and elephant the roots and bark. The very soft heartwood is eaten by Africans in lean times (in starvation times, one might guess). The soft white spoons and small beer stools sold in Pondoland stores — a tourist attraction — are made of the wood.

This species is often confused with *Commiphora woodii* which has roughly the same distribution, but is a larger tree with bigger leaves and fruit, and a bark that does not as a rule peel or flake off. Moreover the seed of *Commiphora woodii* has an unlobed pseudaril, unlike the lobed or pronged pseudaril of *Commiphora harveyi*.

The leaves and immature fruits sometimes resemble those of *Ekebergia capensis*.

The specific name honours W.H. Harvey, 1811-1866, distinguished Irish botanist and editor of the first three volumes of *Flora Capensis*.

Commiphora neglecta
stem

(283)   6. *Commiphora neglecta* Verdoorn

Neglected commiphora; iMinyela (Z); shisenga (Tso)

A thick greenish stem with resinous bark peeling in small, thin, papery flakes — rather like that of *Commiphora pyracanthoides* — helps to identify this commiphora. It normally grows in Zululand, Swaziland, in the Transvaal from the Waterberg northwards, and in Portuguese East Africa, in bushveld and savannah, on sandy flats, in sand forest, and among trees and rocks on steep hot slopes. The southernmost specimen known in the Transvaal is just outside Pretoria in a bush clump near the Pienaar's River Dam.

Visitors to Mkuze Game Reserve in Zululand may remember the groves of these trees, up to 5 m high and slender. Further north in the sand forest of Tongaland or on dry hillsides in the Transvaal they are small spiny trees, different in habit.

The often somewhat drooping branches, slightly hairy when young, are spine-tipped. The foliage is green. The leaves are composed of 3 leaf-lets, somewhat resembling those of a *Rhus*, and have a resinous smell when crushed. They are rather egg-shaped, variable in size, the terminal being the largest, with a rounded, pointed, or bluntly pointed apex, narrowing to the base, usually untoothed but sometimes serrated. They are smooth or with a very few hairs, bright green or grey-green, and shiny, with the yellow midrib raised below. In the Waterberg the leaves tend to be rather small, but the trees on the Makatini Flats in Zululand have leaves nearly 7.6 cm long and 5 cm wide. The leaflets are sessile but the leaves are borne on long slender stalks.

The small flowers are produced with the young leaves in spring in clusters on abbreviated side shoots.

The small egg-shaped or roundish fruits, about 1.3 cm in diameter, are green turning red, and split to show the seed within, embraced by the 4 rather wing-like arms of the pseudaril.

Zulus remove the skin of the roots and eat them like sugar cane.

The specific name was given by Dr Inez Verdoorn because — although fairly widely distributed and sometimes in well populated parts — this tree had for long been entirely overlooked as a separate species. She named it, therefore, "the neglected commiphora".

(288)   7. *Commiphora schlechteri* Engl.

The type specimen of this species was collected by the German botanist, Richard Rudolf Schlechter, in Mozambique in the late 19th century. It occurs, also, on the coastal dunes of Natal and Zululand, and according to *Flora Zambesiaca*, in the Transvaal. No specimen of it existed in either the Herbarium of the Botanical Research Institute or of the Forestry Institute at the time of writing.

It is described as a small tree with somewhat drooping branches; smooth, greyish-green bark peeling in papery flakes, and leaves which have 3 leaflets or 2-3 pairs of leaflets and a terminal leaflet, widely lance-shaped, narrowing both ends, up to about 6 cm long and nearly 4 cm wide, the margins with rounded teeth. They are borne on long stalks up to 5 cm long.

The flowers, blooming with the leaves, are in bunches in the axils of the leaves.

The fruits are up to 2.5 cm long, oval, narrowing to the tip and smooth. The seed is clasped by the 4 somewhat winged arms of the pseudaril.

(282)   8. *Commiphora multijuga* (Hiern) K.Schum.

= *Balsamea* (?) *multijuga* Hiern

This erect spreading tree from northern South West Africa grows up to some 6 m high.

The stem is smooth and purplish-grey, becoming furrowed with age, but does not peel. The graceful leaves, up to about 20 cm long, are composed of 3-7 pairs of neat, opposite, well-spaced leaflets, short, broad and pointed, with untoothed margins, borne on slender stalks. These and the twigs are strongly aromatic.

The fruits are small and pea-sized.

Commiphora marlothii
leaf (70%)

(278)   9. *Commiphora marlothii* Engl.

Papapa, paper tree; mopapama (Tsw — Mang)

Of all the commiphoras, this is one of the most outstanding, a rather compact, many-branched tree with a crown of graceful velvety yellow-ish-green leaves, and succulent stem and branches which are green and very smooth, covered with a crisp yellow skin that peels off in large pieces.

This is a tree of the central and northern Transvaal, Botswana, Rhodesia and Zambia, sometimes growing in open woodland but usually associated with rocky hills and gorges where its strange green and yellow trunk is shown off wonderfully against rocks and precipices. A tree stands at the northern entrance to Wyllie's Poort, and particularly beautiful specimens grow in Van Coller's Pass, on the northern slopes of the Soutpansberg.

Although the foliage is distinctive it is the trunk that sets this tree apart, for the trunk of no other species of tree peels in these large yellow sheets. These are hard, crisp and rather brittle, and may be used to write on. In Rhodesia, according to Keith Coates Palgrave, they give the tree the onomatopoeic name of Mpapapa, indicating the sound of paper flapping in the wind. The branches, too, are sometimes covered with the same peeling yellow skin. They are fragrant when newly cut.

The leaves are alternate, borne on densely hairy stalks, and crowded at the ends of the twigs. They are up to about 20 cm long and consist

Above left
The bark of *Commiphora marlothii*
peeling in large, crisp, yellow pieces

Above right
Commiphora africana stem

Left
Commiphora africana leaves (100%)

of 2-4 pairs of almost stalkless, widely spaced, opposite leaflets and a terminal leaflet. These are oblong to somewhat egg-shaped, often widest towards the tips with round bases, except in the terminal leaflet which sometimes has a narrowed base. The margins have coarse rounded teeth and both sides of the leaves are densely velvety. The midribs are prominent below.

The velvety buds open into small, greenish-white flowers in short velvety bunches borne on long stalks in the axils of the young leaves. The small roundish to oval, hairy fruits split to show the 4-armed yellowish pseudaril clasping the seed.

Unlike that of most commiphoras, the wood of this species is – according to Pardy – fairly hard, and the heartwood an attractive light brown colour.

The specific name honours Rudolf Marloth, famous South African botanist.

(281)   10. *Commiphora mossambicensis* (Oliv.) Engl.

= *Protium* (?) *mossambicense* Oliv.; = *Commiphora fischeri* Engl.;
= *C. stolzii* Engl.

Mozambique commiphora

This, as the name suggests, is not a South African species. It grows in the Caprivi Strip and Botswana, northwards to tropical Africa, and eastwards to Mozambique, in woodland and sometimes on rocky hills.

A small to medium-sized, many-branched tree, it has a smooth grey bark, sometimes peeling, with young branches densely hairy, and aromatic leaves, borne on long hairy stalks. They have as a rule 3 leaflets but sometimes about 2 pairs of leaflets and a terminal one. The leaflets are large and broad – up to 6 cm long and over 8 cm wide – egg-shaped, or almost round, sometimes flattened at both ends, with a short jutting point; sometimes notched, or narrowed at the base; untoothed, hairy, or – according to *Flora Zambesiaca* – almost smooth with tiny golden glands.

The small flowers, appearing about November, are in loose heads; the fruits on long stalks, are small, roundish, and the seed within clasped by the pseudaril which has 4 arms with a somewhat wavy outline.

The wood, which easily exudes a resin, is used by Africans to make dishes and bowls.

Section *Africanae* Engl.

(270)   11. *Commiphora africana* (A.Rich.) Engl.

= *Heudelotia africana* A.Rich.; = *Commiphora pilosa* (Engl.) Engl.;
= *Commiphora calcicola* Engl.

Although often a shrub, *Commiphora africana* can grow into a small well-shaped tree and in one form or the other is widely distributed from Swaziland, the central, eastern and northern Transvaal, through Botswana to the central and northern districts of South West Africa, north-

Commiphora africana in the bush-veld of the north eastern Transvaal

Centre
Commiphora schimperi,
Waterpoort road, northern Transvaal

Below
Commiphora schimperi
used as a living fence post on top of the Lebombo Mountains, Ingwavuma district

Opposite
Typical *Commiphora schimperi* bark

wards to tropical Africa. It favours low, dry woodland and bushveld, growing on sandy flats or rocky ridges.

This is a much-branched, spiny tree or shrub with a dense crown. It is one of the few commiphoras to have a commonplace grey trunk that usually does not peel, or peels in such small pieces as to appear not to peel at all, although at times the bark may be a dark green or yellowish when it may flake in strips. When injured it oozes a light-coloured gum.

The young branches are densely hairy and spine-tipped. The leaves, on long hairy stalks, are composed of 3 leaflets (occasionally 5) which are usually hairy and have margins with rounded teeth. The terminal leaflet, often egg-shaped, with a sharp or blunt point and narrowed base, is the largest, the lateral leaflets being smaller and often rounder, with a round or slightly narrowed base.

The small reddish flowers bloom in short axillary clusters, sometimes on the spines themselves, before the leaves appear. Botanists note that the 4 disc lobes are more or less bifid (twice cleft) at the tip.

The fruit is small and roundish. When completely fresh, the seed within is covered with a thin red pseudaril, but this usually disappears shortly after the fruit is picked. In dried specimens it is thus absent. Yellow-billed Hornbills eat the fruit within the shell.

This commiphora acts as a host to one of the "poison grubs", *Diamphidia* species, from which Bushmen make one of their arrow poisons. The adult beetle lays its eggs on the leaves and these hatch into larvae which feed on the leaves of this one species alone.

The pith of the roots is said to be eaten in times of need.

The specific name means "African".

(287)   12. *Commiphora schimperi* (O.Berg.) Engl.

= *Balsamodendron schimperi* O.Berg.; = *Commiphora betschuanica* Engl.

Seroka: seroka (Tsw)

A smooth greenish-yellow mottled bark, with the bark peeling irregularly, is characteristic of this small tree or shrub of northern Zululand, the central and northern parts of the Transvaal, the northern Cape, and of Botswana. It is one of the most widely distributed of the genus, growing from South Africa to Ethiopia in the north.

It is a tree of dry bush country, gritty flats, or stony wooded slopes. Visitors to the Mkuze Game Reserve may note it, or travellers along the Great North Road where — in the rather stunted bush near Bandolier Kop — it grows in numbers.

This is a spreading bush or small tree with drooping branches, the branchlets spine-tipped, the young twigs ruby red. The smooth leaves are composed of usually 3 leaflets, the terminal the biggest, up to about 2.5 cm long (although often smaller) somewhat egg-shaped with a narrowed base, the lateral ones smaller, pointed, and slightly narrowed to the base. They are all sometimes so deeply crenate as to appear lobed in the upper half, a character, together with their smoothness and shininess, that at once distinguishes them from those of *Commiphora africana*, a closely related species, or from those of *Commiphora neglecta*, which are almost untoothed or with very small serrations.

The small pale red flowers are borne in short clusters, often on the spines. The roundish or oval, pinky-red fruits are about 1.3 cm long.

Commiphora schimperi:
A fruiting twig (70%)

When pressed between the fingers, the outer covering slips off like a small pink shell, showing the 3-sided seed, completely enveloped in a red oily covering, the pseudaril. As in *Commiphora africana*, this disappears shortly after the fruit is picked, is usually absent in dried specimens, and often dissolves when the fruit is placed in spirits. Wild, in *Flora Zambesiaca*, grouped these two species together in a section which he called *Africanae* in which, he said, the pseudaril was usually not visible, probably being fused with the endocarp. He was probably dealing with dried material.

The roots and bark of *Commiphora schimperi* are eaten by elephant. Africans use the wood to make fire by friction.

The specific name honours Dr A.F.W. Schimper, Professor at the Bonn University and author of a standard work on plant geography, the English translation of which appeared in 1903.

Section *Coriaceae* Engl.

(273)   13. *Commiphora capensis* (Sond.) Engl.

= *Balsamodendron capense* Sond.; = *Balsamea capensis* (Sond.) Engl.;
= *Commiphora rangeana* Engl.

Cape commiphora

"The Commiphora of the Cape" is a shrub or small bushy tree up to about 3 m high growing from Namaqualand northwards to South West Africa.

It has a smooth grey or purplish-grey wrinkled bark and a crown of short, erect, smooth, somewhat purplish and spiny branches, and short side-shoots, at the tips of which the leaves are borne.

These are composed of 3 small, roundish leaflets, the terminal the largest, narrowed to the base, the lateral leaflets much smaller and without stalks, smooth, the margins with rounded teeth, and the whole leaf shortly stalked.

The flowers and fruit are borne at the top of the branchlets. The roundish fruit has a sharp point and is large for that of a commiphora, often over 1.3 cm long. It has no pseudaril, even when fresh.

Commiphora kraeuseliana near the foot of the Brandberg, South West Africa

14. *Commiphora kraeuseliana* Heine

Kraeusel's commiphora

This species of rocky hillsides and stony slopes of central and northern South West Africa seldom grows more than 1.5-2 m tall, yet its sturdy trunk and branches make it appear more of a dwarf tree than a shrub.

It is many-stemmed, with upward-growing branches that make a flattish top, like a big bushy fan. A small tree with this typical shape grows at the mouth of the valley leading to the famous prehistoric painting of the White Lady of the Brandberg, and must have been noted by hundreds of people.

Stems and branches are yellowish, red-brown or purplish, sometimes with an orange-yellow peeling skin, sometimes not peeling at all. Branches and the short side-shoots are very robust and somewhat sticky, with a strong resinous smell. The leaves grow in tufts at the ends of the side-branches and have about 6-8 pairs of leaflets and a terminal leaflet, up to about 1.9 cm long and so narrow that they appear like threads. The general effect, indeed, is of twigs crowned with finest hairs.

The small yellowish flowers (5-8 in a head), are clustered at the ends of long hairy stalks. The fruits are large, up to 1.9 cm long, like small plums in shape. The seed is without a pseudaril.

This species was named in honour of the distinguished German palaeobotanist, Professor Richard Kräusel, 1890-1966, of Frankfurt am Main who visited South West Africa during 1953-54 and contributed many valuable papers on fossil plants of that territory.

Above left
Commiphora woodii fruits are popular with
birds which — at the first sign of the outer shells
cracking — force the halves apart, eat the seeds
(which they later regurgitate) and the red
pseudarils.

Above right
Commiphora edulis in the Caprivi Strip

Below left
Commiphora woodii, Zululand

Below right
Commiphora woodii bark

Section *Spondioideae* Engl.

(275)   15. *Commiphora edulis* (Klotzch) Engl.

= *Hitzeria edulis* Klotzsch; = *Commiphora chlorocarpa* Engl.

Light-stemmed commiphora; shipondoti (Tso); moroka (Tsw)

Commiphora edulis is a shrub or small spreading tree of the northern Transvaal, Botswana, and the Caprivi, and of tropical Africa, growing in dry bush, on rocky hills, often at their foot.

This has a rough or smooth, grey or silvery-white stem, or several stems from the base, and branches that are light-coloured and hairy when young. It is conspicuous as soon as it sheds its foliage in early autumn for its light trunks then stand out among the surrounding bush and grass.

The leaves, borne on long stalks, have 2-4 pairs of side leaflets and a terminal leaflet, usually 4-5 cm long, widely lance-shaped to egg-shaped, pointed, with a rounded base, except in the terminal leaflet which narrows to the base. They are usually untoothed, hairy below, and are *rough* to the touch.

The small pale yellow flowers are in slender branched, very hairy heads, the individual flowers being almost without stalks. They usually appear with the young leaves.

The fruit, reddish when ripe, is up to 1.9 cm long, oval and hairy. The lower part of the seed within is covered with the fleshy cup-like pseudaril.

The name *edulis* means "edible", and suggests that the fruit is eaten. However, it seems to be favoured only by monkeys and baboons, and by elephant which also eat the bark and roots.

(291)   16. *Commiphora woodii* Engl.

= *Commiphora caryaefolia* Oliv.

Wood's cork tree; umHlunguthi (X); umuMbu, umuNde wasehlathini, umuNde wehlathi (Z); uMumbe (Sw)

Commiphora woodii is a tree of forest, dense valley bushveld and thorn-veld, occurring from the coastal districts of the eastern Cape northwards to Zululand. It is usually larger than the other eastern Cape species, *Commiphora harveyi*, and is recorded up to 15 m high, although is usually smaller.

The bark is often smooth, grey and white, not shed as obviously as many other commiphoras, but sometimes peeling in papery strips, showing a brown colour below, and often not peeling at all.

The compound leaves, crowded towards the ends of the branches, are large — up to 46 cm long — usually composed of 3-4 pairs of opposite leaflets and a terminal leaflet. These are a narrow oblong or oval, or narrowly egg-shaped, pointed, but rounded at the base, sometimes curved with the midrib slightly to one side, about 4-10 cm long and 1.3-6 cm wide, toothed, with very short stalks or none at all. The young leaves are red. The tree may lose its leaves entirely in winter, while in warm areas it is said to bear leaves twice in the year and to be almost evergreen.

Above
Commiphora glaucescens in full leaf in summer time near the foot of the
Brandberg in South West Africa

Below
Commiphora glaucescens photographed between Welwitschia and Sorris
Sorris in July

1038

The small cream flowers in short sprays bloom about December, sometimes with the young red leaves. The fruit, ripening towards the end of summer, is large for that of a commiphora, up to about 2.5 cm in diameter and roundish, rather like a large cherry in appearance. Within, the seed is based on a fleshy red pseudaril. This is a source of food to many birds, such as Crowned Hornbills, Redwinged Starlings, Cape Glossy Starlings, Black-headed Orioles, tits, white-eyes, and many others which devour it when the outer shell splits and the pseudaril becomes conspicuous.

According to Skead, the seeds themselves are eaten by parrots which do not wait for the fruits to split, but tear them apart.

The tree yields a resinous gum.

The species was named after John Medley Wood, noted Natal botanist.

(276)   17. *Commiphora glaucescens* Engl.

= *Commiphora pruinosa* Engl.

Sea-green commiphora

A bush or small tree up to roughly 6 m high, this South West African species grows from the Kaokoveld to Mariental in the south, and eastwards to the Grootfontein district, often on hills or mountain sides, or in red sandy soil.

The pale brown to bluish bark, occasionally with sunken depressions, peels all over in round flakes or in thin yellow papery strips. The young branches are greenish-yellow to purple and smooth. The leaves have only 1 leaflet and, as the botanical name suggests, they are a sea-green – green with shades of blue or grey – and are often covered with a waxy bloom. They are 2.5-5 cm long and 1.3-3 cm wide, egg-shaped or oval, with round, flat, notched, or bluntly pointed tips, the base narrowed or round, untoothed, the secondary veins and network of veins conspicuous. They are crowded at the ends of short branchlets or occasionally are alternate, and like most commiphoras turn yellow and sometimes red before they fall.

The flowers are small and yellowish-green, the fruits round or oval, about 1.3 cm long, and the seeds have a slightly fleshy pseudaril. They are reported to be edible.

(271)   18. *Commiphora anacardiifolia* Dinter & Engl.

Large-leaf commiphora

The botanical name of this South West African species means "the commiphora with leaves like those of the Anacardiaceae". It has, indeed, surprising leaves for a commiphora, with 1 very large leaflet (a simple leaf to observers), boldly marked with conspicuous veins.

It is a graceful tree, growing on the fringes of the Namib Desert, up to about 6 m high, with a round spreading crown, and a straight, clean trunk, grey-green or brown and peeling in papery strips.

The leaves are simple and large, egg-shaped, round at the apex, narrowed to the base, up to 15 cm long and 13 cm wide, without stalks, glossy dark green above and much paler below, with the broad midrib

Commiphora dinteri near Karibib in South West Africa

conspicuous, as are the secondary nerves running outwards parallel to one another and looping along the margin. They grow in a bunch towards the ends of the branches.

The flowers grow in a many-branched head. The fruit is oval, pointed, about 1.3 cm long. The seed is grey-brown with an orange-yellow pseudaril.

(286)   19. *Commiphora saxicola* Engl.

Rock commiphora

The botanical name of this species, meaning "growing among rocks", is descriptive for it is fairly widespread in South West Africa mainly on rocky hills and stony slopes along the fringes of the desert. It is one of the picturesque little commiphoras on the stony koppies fringing the great red plains near Sorris Sorris.

It is usually a spreading spineless dwarf tree, differing from many commiphoras because the smooth yellow-grey bark — often pitted and with a purple sheen — is not papery and does not peel. The thick branches are reddish when young, becoming grey when mature.

The leaves in bunches are crowded on short side-shoots, or are sometimes alternate. They are about 5-6 cm long, with 3-4 pairs of small leaflets and a terminal leaflet, and cannot be mistaken for those of any other species for they are almost round and smooth and shiny, and the margins have large round teeth. The twigs have a strong sweet smell when broken.

The flowers are small and stalkless, in heads. The fruits are egg-shaped, about 1.3 cm long, with pointed tips, and the seed within is black with a fine cup-like scarlet pseudaril.

20. *Commiphora dinteri* Engl.

Dinter's commiphora

Dinter's commiphora is a sprawling bush or small erect thick-stemmed tree up to about 3 m high growing from northern to southern South West Africa, in the Namib Desert itself or on its fringes, often on gravelly mountain sides and sandy slopes.

The short thick trunk is up to about 30 cm in diameter, and the bark is smooth and grey or yellow-grey, pitted and sometimes mottled, and does not flake.

The leaves, up to about 2.5 cm long, are composed of 3 tiny oval leaflets with roundly toothed margins, the middle being the largest, and narrowed to the base more than are the lateral leaflets. They are borne on slender stalks on knobs or short side-branches.

The small flowers are brownish-red, the fruits oval and reddish or greeny-brown. The seed is clasped by the red pseudaril which has 4 arms, 2 long and 2 short.

The species was named after Dr Moritz Kurt Dinter (1868-1945) botanist and botanical explorer in South West Africa for nearly 30 years, who was appointed first Government botanist in German South West Africa in 1900 and held this position until 1914.

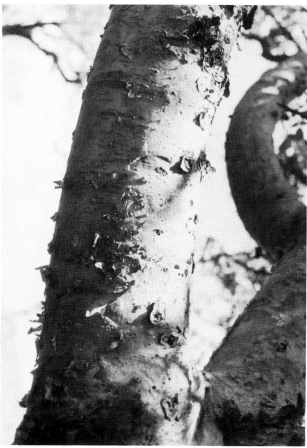

Above
Commiphora angolensis in the northern Transvaal

Left
Commiphora angolensis bark

21. *Commiphora namaensis* Schinz

= *Commiphora rotundifolia* Dinter & Engl.

This South West African species, occurring in the south and south west of the territory in desert country, is usually no more than a low, rounded, many-stemmed shrub, although it is recorded up to 3 m high.

It has a dark grey bark that does not peel. The leaves have 1 leaflet (they are apparently simple) and these are roundish to oval with a round or flat tip, usually 0.6-1.3 cm in diameter, smooth, blue-green, the margins with round teeth. They are borne on slender stalks in tufts on short side-branches.

The fruits are egg-shaped, and the seed has a shallow orange cup-shaped pseudaril.

The specific name means "of the Namas".

(274)   22. *Commiphora crenato-serrata* Engl.

A fine commiphora up to about 6 m high from the fringes of the Namib Desert in northern South West Africa, this species has a grey, papery, resinous bark which usually does not peel, and long graceful compound leaves.

The leaflets, with about 3 opposite pairs and a terminal leaflet, are up to about 5-8 cm long, lance-shaped, with long-drawn out, slender points, and margins with small round teeth. They are covered with thick red hairs when young, becoming smooth when mature.

The twigs are conspicuously rough and scarred.

The flowers bloom in spike-like heads. The fruit is oval, about 1.3 cm long, narrowed towards the tip.

(272)   23. *Commiphora angolensis* Engl.

= *Commiphora rehmannii* Engl.; = *C. oliveri* Engl.; = *C. kwebensis* N.E.Br.; = *C. nigrescens* Engl.

Angolan commiphora

This variable species now includes what were formerly held to be five different species. In its various forms it is widely distributed, ranging from Zambia, Rhodesia and Angola to the Transvaal, northern Cape Province, and South West Africa. It usually grows on sand and is fairly common on the pale red sandy flats round Monte Cristo in the north western Transvaal, or in the sandy bushveld on the dunes of South West Africa.

It may be a small, erect tree with a twiggy spreading crown or a bush which sometimes forms thickets. The stem bark varies from a reddish brown, very dark grey or green to yellow or almost white, peeling in thin horizontal, papery strips.

The leaves on long hairy stalks are composed of 1-5 pairs of opposite leaflets and a terminal leaflet, oval, egg-shaped to widely lance-shaped, narrowing both ends, sharply or bluntly pointed, toothed, 1.9-6 cm long and 0.8-2.5 cm wide. They are dark grey-green above, paler below, the common midrib red above, the veins yellow and more conspicuous above than below. They are rough to the touch.

Both leaves and young branches are often covered with hairs.

Commiphora tenuipetiolata: its silver-white, satin-smooth bark

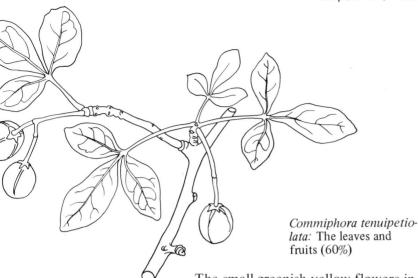

*Commiphora tenuipetio-
lata:* The leaves and
fruits (60%)

The small greenish-yellow flowers in long or short heads bloom with
the young light green leaves. The small, smooth plum-shaped fruits,
with tiny sharp points, split to show the seed, two-thirds covered by the
cup-like pseudaril.

The foliage is relished by stock.

The chief interest of this species is that it is the host of yet another
species of "poison grub" used for arrow poison. Entomologists claim
that the adult insects are fine botanists, unerringly selecting the right
species of plant on which to lay their eggs. When raised in captivity
the larvae prove difficult guests — they refuse to eat any plant but the
one particular species which in the wild acts as their host.

(289)   24. *Commiphora tenuipetiolata* Engl.

Satin-bark commiphora

The satin-bark commiphora is a widespread species distributed from the
northern Transvaal to South West Africa and northwards to Rhodesia,
often on sandy flats, sometimes in mixed mopane veld, and sometimes on stony slopes. Some of the finest specimens in South Africa
grow at the foot of Van Coller's Pass, on the northern slopes of the
Soutpansberg.

Of all the South African commiphoras this often has the most beautiful stem, covered with silver-white bark which peels in satiny strips to
show a smooth slate-blue, dark green or yellow below.

This may be a shrub or a 6 m tree with a fine rounded crown of light
green or blue-green foliage. The smooth leaves borne on very long,
slender, often twisted stalks usually have 3 leaflets but may have 2-3
pairs and a terminal leaflet. These are oval to egg-shaped with round or
bluntly pointed tips, and narrowed base, the terminal the largest, up to
about 6 cm long. Usually the margins are untoothed but they may have
a few round teeth near the tips.

The small flowers in slender branched groups, or 1-2 together, bloom
with the young leaves.

The small, red, roundish fruits, about 1.3 cm in diameter, split to
show the seed which is two thirds covered by the pseudaril.

The name *tenuipetiolata* means "with a thin petiole".

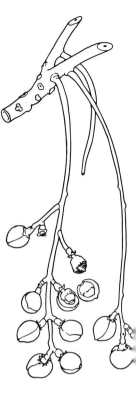

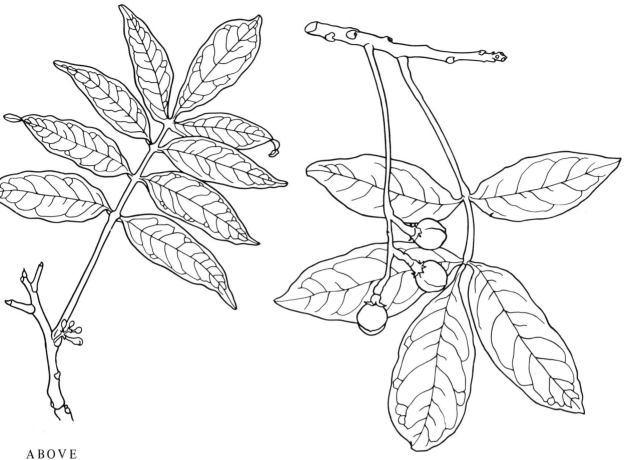

Left
*Commiphora zanzibar-
ica:* a leaf and flowers (50%)

Right
Portion of a fruiting
branch (50%)

OPPOSITE

Above left
A fine *Commiphora ten-
uipetiolata* growing in
Van Coller's pass

Above right
Commiphora zanzibarica
fruit (35%)

Below
*Commiphora tenuipetio-
lata* growing as a small
tree near the Gamsberg,
South West Africa

(291.1)   25. *Commiphora zanzibarica* (Baill.) Engl.
= *Balsamea zanzibarica* Baill.

Jobe's commiphora

The type specimen of this species came from Zanzibar, as the specific
name indicates. It also occurs in coastal Tanzania, in Rhodesia and
Mozambique, and was collected in South Africa for the first time by
Mr Ian Garland in December 1968. He found it at "Jobe's Kraal" near
Makane's Drift in northern Zululand growing in clumps in the dry sand
forest, and later in the taller forest round Lake Sibayi.

Although the tree is described as reaching a height of 12 m, in South
Africa it is not known more than 4 or 5 m high, in the sand forest
several-stemmed with upward-growing branches and slightly drooping
foliage. Here the bark is grey, frequently with small raised dots, and
does not peel, although *Flora Zambesiaca* describes it as peeling in
straw-coloured strips.

The leaves are pinnate and are borne on long, smooth, sturdy stalks.
They are composed of from 3 to 4 pairs of leaflets (very occasionally
1 pair) and a terminal leaflet, up to about 9 cm long and 1.9-4 cm wide,
the terminal the biggest, a narrow oblong, the tips narrowed to a point
(which is sometimes jutting), the base rounded or somewhat narrowed,
the margins usually untoothed and sometimes wavy, and the midrib
raised below. They are thin and smooth in texture.

The small 4-petalled flowers, blooming with the leaves, are borne in

a long branched spray in the axils of the leaves about December.

The smooth, cherry-sized fruit is slightly more oval than round, and is borne on a very thick stalk. Within the stout outer shell is a beautiful jet-black seed perched on a bright reddish-pink, cup-shaped aril. The fruits are carried in long heavy bunches on often completely leafless trees.

The common name given here, Jobe's commiphora, refers to Jobe Mafuleka, employee of Ian Garland and a man with a fine knowledge of local plants, near whose home the tree was first found. The locality, "Jobe's Kraal", has of recent times figured frequently in botanical collections.

Unclassed Commiphoras

26. *Commiphora oblanceolata* Schinz

Rhus commiphora

This species from the northern Cape and Namib Desert of South West Africa is a bush or small tree with succulent stems and thick blackish-grey or grey-green bark that generally does not peel.

The leaves are crowded at the ends of the smooth, slender, arching branches. They are distinctive, usually with 3 leaflets which are a very narrow oblong in shape (hence the specific name) with round tips — somewhat like a blunt needle — smooth, with the margins slightly toothed, and are borne on short stalks. Occasionally the terminal leaflet is lobed. They are commonly mistaken for the leaves of a *Rhus*, and usually it is not until a twig is broken that the identity of the tree becomes clear. The sap spurts out and the air is filled with a highly pungent, distinctive perfume. A drop in the eyes is said to cause blindness.

The species is undoubtedly the tree described by the runaway soldier, Wikar, in the 1770's as growing along the Orange River with a "very powerful scent, so different from that of all other trees that one can find it by its scent alone without knowing anything more about it". "In July", he wrote, "the poison worms, which during the time the tree is dry live at the bottom in the grey-brown bark of the stem, begin to appear on the leaves. The Hottentots take only the worms which are tightly tied up in a piece of leather, and kept until they rot. Then they are ground to a fine powder which is rubbed all round the arrows with spit. No one wounded with this mixture, when the gall of the big rock lizard has been added, has any chance of recovery".

Details of flowers and fruit are lacking. The little tree illustrated grew in the rocky hills near Kakamas in company with the kokerboom, and in September was in leaf but without sign of flowers or fruits.

This is probably South Africa's least known commiphora. How fascinating, then, that it should also have been its first-recorded!

(274.1)   27. *Commiphora discolor* E.J.Mendes

Commiphora discolor is a newly described species from northern South West Africa and Angola, a climbing bush or 9 m tree, with papery bark.

OPPOSITE

Above left
Commiphora zanzibarica
The bark

Centre left
The leaves, and the sprays of flowers in their axils, photographed in December

Below left
The fruits

Above right
Commiphora zanzibarica photographed at Jobe's Kraal in the Tongaland sand forest

Below right
Stems of *Commiphora zanzibarica*

Commiphora oblanceolata, with a kokerboom in the background, in the rocky hills near Kakamas

Commiphora oblanceo-lata bark

It is sometimes spiny. The shoots are either long, when the leaves they bear are alternate; or short, when 4 to 6 leaves are crowded in tufts at the end. Those on the long shoots have 3 oval stalkless leaflets with pointed tips and narrowed base, and with toothed margins, the leaf carried on a stalk over 1.3 cm long, while those on the short shoots usually have smaller leaves composed of 1 leaflet and only occasionally 3, borne on stalks under 1.3 cm long. The leaflets may be toothed or almost without teeth, the margins often rolled back, the terminal leaflet often roundish, the side ones oval with a sharp point and narrowed base.

The flowers are in small clusters on the tips of the short shoots, together with the leaves. Details of the fruits are lacking.

28. *Commiphora wildii* Merxm.

Wild's commiphora

Wild's commiphora is a species of northern South West Africa, a shrub or a low spreading tree up to some 2 m high, branching at ground level, with a thick grey-green to brownish trunk sometimes peeling in small papery flakes, at others not peeling at all.

The leaves are made up of 2-4 pairs of opposite leaflets, usually with a terminal leaflet, but sometimes ending with a pair. The leaflets are not divided completely to the midrib, the lower side merging into the common winged midrib. Merxmüller, who described it, first considered the name *querquiloba* for the species and the leaves are indeed oak-like. The terminal leaflet is broadest at the apex and narrows to the base.

The flowers are axillary. The egg-shaped fruits — orange to pale red — have a light yellow cup-shaped and shallowly 4-lobed pseudaril.

The species was named in honour of Professor Hiram Wild of the University College at Rhodesia, editor of the journal *Kirkia* and joint editor of *Flora Zambesiaca*.

48 The Mahogany Family (Meliaceae)

Trees and shrubs, often with scented wood, belong to this large tropical and subtropical family which is famous for its timber trees. Among these are the West Indian Mahogany — *Swietenia* — and the various African mahoganies, *Khaya, Pseudocedrala, Entandrophragma* and *Trichilia* species.

The member best known to most South Africans is not indigenous, It is the seringa from Asia, *Melia azedarach* L., a quick-growing tree with graceful compound leaves and fine, scented, lilac flowers, that now grows wild in many parts of the country. In winter time its bunches of round, shiny, biscuit-coloured drupes — the size of smallish marbles — are a familiar sight from the Transvaal bushveld to the coastal forests of the Cape Province.

In South and South West Africa about 11 species, belonging to 6 genera, grow as trees, while a twelfth, *Turraea obtusifolia* Hochst., although usually a shrub, is occasionally a small tree.

Recently an interesting member of the family was found growing wild in the forest at Hluhluwe in Zululand. It had large pinnate leaves, male flowers in big panicles and female in long spikes, and a fruit that was conspicuous — a fairly large, 3-valved capsule holding oblong seeds with a scarlet aril. At first it was thought this might be a new *Bersama* species, but it was finally identified as an Indo-Malayan species, *Aphanamixis rohituka* Pierre.

Originally the sneezewood, *Ptaeroxylon obliquum* (Thunb.) Radlk., a widely distributed tree in South Africa, was included in this family. The structure of the wood and the pollen grains, among other characters, are different, so that it is now generally considered to belong to the small family Ptaeroxylaceae which, although related to Meliaceae, is even more closely related to Sapindaceae and which is usually placed after it.

The species in the family are mostly characterized by leaves that are alternate, occasionally simple but most often compound, without stipules, and often crowded towards the ends of the branches. The flowers are usually in panicles and occasionally solitary or in close clusters in the axils of the leaves. They are bisexual, or male or female, sometimes borne on different trees. The calyx segments and petals usually number 4-5, a disc is present, the stamens are usually 8-10, often characteristically united in a tube, the ovary superior with 2-5 chambers. The fruit is dry and splits open when mature — a capsule — or fleshy containing a stone with a kernel (when it is a drupe) or with immersed seeds (a berry).

Key to Genera

Large trees; the leaves alternate, big, once compound, terminated by a pair of leaflets; the leaflets untoothed, stalked; the flowers male or female, in panicles in the axils of the leaves; the fruit a *large woody, angled capsule*, splitting into 5 valves, showing a *central column with seed scars*; the seeds winged.

1. Entandrophragma

A small tree or shrub; the leaves simple, alternate or tufted, small, narrow, untoothed; the flowers bisexual, solitary, in the axils of the leaves, bell-shaped; *the fruit an inflated capsule with a papery covering*, 4-angled, 4-celled, the seeds roundish, 1-2 per cell.

2. Nymania

Shrubs or small trees; the leaves simple, alternate or in tufts; the flowers bisexual, solitary, in tufts, or in heads in the axils of the leaves or terminally, tubular, the petals usually 5, *long, narrow, reflexed*, longer than the calyx; the staminal tube cylindric, conspicuous; the fruit *small, often woody,* with *usually 5-10 valves*, splitting open when ripe; the seeds large, roundish, red or black with a bright aril.

3. Turraea

Trees, small to large; the leaves compound with a terminal leaflet, untoothed, the *common midrib often winged*; the flowers male or female borne on different trees in panicles; the fruit a *drupe, more or less succulent*, with 2-5 cells; the seeds usually 1 per cell.

4. Ekebergia

Large trees; the foliage evergreen, heavy, glossy; in the South African species the leaves compound, terminated by a single leaflet; the leaflets untoothed; the flowers male or female in axillary panicles, probably on different trees; the fruit *a capsule with usually 3 valves, splitting open*; the *seeds large, black, with a red aril*.

5. Trichilia

A tree, small to medium-sized; the leaves compound, terminated by a single leaflet; the leaflets untoothed, the midrib often to one side; the flowers male or female probably on different trees; *the fruit a large, rough, woody capsule, usually with 5 valves which curl backwards;* the seeds with *a bright red aril*.

6. Pseudobersama

1. *Entandrophragma* C.DC.

Trees, often large, belong to this small genus, one of which, *Entandrophragma spicatum* (C.DC.) Sprague, grows in northern South West Africa, and a second, *Entandrophragma caudatum* (Sprague) Sprague in northern Zululand and the northern Transvaal.

The leaves are once compound, fairly large and very graceful, with 3-9 pairs of leaflets, terminated by a pair of leaflets. These have untoothed margins and are sometimes unequal-sided. The small male or female flowers are borne in panicles in the axils of the leaves. The calyx is 4-5-lobed, the petals 4-5, the stamens 10, joined into a tube, the

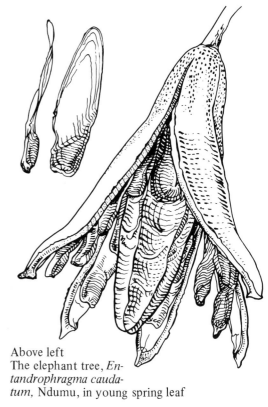

Above left
The elephant tree, *En-tandrophragma cauda-tum,* Ndumu, in young spring leaf

Above right
Entandrophragma caudatum fruit and seeds (50%)

Left below
Entandrophragma caudatum near Chipisi in the northern Transvaal

Opposite
The distinctive bark

1054

ovary 5-celled. The fruit is unique — a very large, woody, angled capsule that splits from the apex, the 5 valves separating, to show within winged seeds and a softly woody, 5-angled central column often conspicuously imprinted with the shape of the seeds.

Under the microscope the lower part of the staminal tube of a flower of *Entandrophragma angolense* C.DC., collected by Welwitsch in Angola and on which the genus was founded, is clearly seen to be divided into small oblong compartments. It was on this character that the genus was named, *Entandrophragma* being based on Greek words meaning "in", "male" (in reference to the stamens), and "compartments".

(294)   *Entandrophragma spicatum* (C.DC.) Sprague

= *Wulfhorstia spicata* C.DC.; = *Wulfhorstia spicata* var. *viridiflora* Schinz; = *Wulfhorstia ekebergioides* Harms; = *Entandrophragma ekebergioides* (Harms) Sprague

Woodland mahogany

This is a species of northern South West Africa, usually growing in mixed woodland, a tall spreading tree up to 18 m high with a crown of light green, graceful foliage and a grey trunk that is smooth and flakes in circular pieces.

The young branches are velvety, becoming smoother with age. The leaves, usually crowded towards the ends of the branches on long hairy stalks, are alternate. They are made up of 3-7 — usually 4 — pairs of leaflets, which are opposite or nearly opposite, shortly stalked, varying in shape from a narrow oblong to egg-shaped or almost round, the apex usually bluntly pointed or sometimes notched, usually 2.5-9 cm long, the uppermost pair the largest, the young leaves softly hairy on both sides, becoming smoother with age. The common midrib is distinctly velvety.

The greenish flowers are borne in long loose heads in the axils of the leaves. The brown, sometimes speckled fruit is 10-15 cm long, spindle-shaped, splitting into 5 long woody segments to show a central column and light brown seeds with large satiny wings.

The name *spicata* means "like a spike".

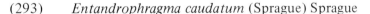

(293)   *Entandrophragma caudatum* (Sprague) Sprague

= *Pseudocedrela caudata* Sprague

Mountain mahogany, berg mahogany; ndjoudjou (Tso); mopumena (Tsw)

This fine mahogany — commonly known as the mountain mahogany because it often grows on rocky hill sides — occurs from Zululand, often in scrub and woodland on sand or on other well-drained soils, to the northern Transvaal, and beyond South Africa to Portuguese East Africa, Botswana, the Caprivi Strip, Rhodesia, Zambia, and Malawi.

In South Africa the mountain mahogany, although never very common, is most often found on the slopes of the Soutpansberg. Several fine specimens grow on the verge of the Rushton road on a hillside not very far from Wyllie's Poort, sometimes dropping their large distinctive

Entandrophragma caudatum: The leaves and inflorescence (100%)

fruits on to the roadside below. A big tree, the only one in the area, grows in the Ndumu Game Reserve in northern Zululand, where it is known locally as "the elephant tree". The seed is reputed to have been deposited there in elephant droppings.

The tree grows up to some 18 m high — in Botswana up to 30 m — and has a spreading, or sometimes rather narrow crown, and a straight clean trunk. The bark may be grey, so light as to appear almost white, or red, yellow, grey and white, smooth and characteristically cracked in a circular pattern, when it is so distinctive that it cannot be confused with that of any other tree. The long, often rather whippy, branches are light coloured and these and the branchlets are knobbly, with the ends, on which the leaves are crowded, turning upwards.

The trees are usually deciduous and in early spring the tufts of tender green leaves appear, together with sprays of green buds on long furry stalks, and these, tipping the bare grey branches, give the big trees a surprisingly light and airy appearance.

The compound leaves are up to 30 cm or more long, with 5-8 pairs of leaflets which are opposite or nearly opposite, 2.5-10 cm long, and 1.3-4 cm wide, broadest at the often unequal-sided base, tapering to a long point, very delicately and neatly formed. They are borne on slender stalks.

At times the leaves may be confused with those of the white seringa, *Kirkia acuminata* Oliv., but they do not have a terminal leaflet, and the leaflets are stalked whereas those of *Kirkia acuminata* have a terminal leaflet and are without stalks, and they taper acutely, while the leaflets of the white seringa are shortly pointed.

Small velvety buds in sprays on long hairy stalks in the axils of the leaves open into greenish flowers a little smaller than a 5 cent coin.

The fruits are capsules like cucumbers in shape, up to about 20 cm long, light brown, hanging downwards on long strong stalks. They split on the tree into 5 woody valves, which open at the tip and curl backwards, exposing the light woody core with 5-angled sides, the long, buff, winged seeds clinging to the outer valves but leaving the marks of their shapes clearly imprinted on the core. In an old fruit the central core is nearly always punctured and if examined is seen to house spiders, or apparently a whole colony of spiders, and these must find such a fruit a remarkably safe refuge. The fruits often remain on a tree for many months.

The scented wood is variously reported as soft or as hard, the heartwood a pale rose, maturing to reddish-brown, working easily and polishing well, and making good furniture. In Botswana it is known as Tati mahogany. Canoes for the Paramount Chief of Barotseland are made from its wood and it is therefore considered there to be a royal tree.

The fruits are eaten by elephants and the seeds by antelopes.

The seed germinates well when absolutely fresh, and the tree is fairly fast-growing.

The specific name *caudatum* is based on the Latin "caudatus" meaning "tailed", and refers to the sharp point of the leaf.

2. *Nymania* Lindb.

Nymania is a small genus of one species which has no close relatives at all. It was placed by Phillips in his second edition of *Genera of South African Flowering Plants* in the family Meliaceae, but it is doubtful

Above left
The klapper, *Nymania capensis,* in
the district of Pearston, in company
with the Karoo cycad, *Encephalartos lehmannii,* and *Maytenus undata.*

Above right
A fruiting branch

Left
Nymania capensis: A flowering and
fruiting twig (50%)

1058

whether this is its rightful place, for today it is recognized that in several points it is a misfit — its pollen, for example, does not match that of other members of Meliaceae. In future it may be removed to another family.

Nymania capensis (Thunb.) Lindb., the single species, has small simple leaves, usually growing in tufts; the flowers solitary in the axils of the leaves, the calyx lobes and petals 4, the stamens 8, the ovary 4-celled, the fruit a large inflated, 4-chambered capsule with 1-2 seeds in each chamber.

The generic name honours a Swedish botanist, Carl Fredrik Nyman, 1820-1893, who published works on European botany and forestry.

(295)   *Nymania capensis* (Thunb.) Lindb.

= *Aitonia capensis* Thunb.; = *Aitonia capensis* var. *microphylla* Schinz

Klapper, Chinese lanterns, brosdoring

Passing through the Karoo in spring after rain, travellers often pause in astonishment at splashes of pure and vivid colour among the dun scrub on koppie slopes. This is the klapper or Chinese lanterns, which grows as a small tree on dry rocky soil, rich in lime, particularly from Oudtshoorn to Graaff-Reinet, Pearston and Somerset East.

It is a common bush species on the hills near Kenhardt and Upington and in Namaqualand, including the Richtersveld, in flower and fruit making a bright splash of colour in these arid and often desert regions. It occurs either as a bush or a small tree in southern South West Africa.

It seldom grows more than 3.6 m high and in the Karoo is typically a low bushy tree with rigid branches and small, narrow, leathery leaves, either alternate or growing in tufts.

If this little tree or bush could be easily cultivated it would be as well known as any of its great timber-producing relatives, not because of its wood but because it is uniquely ornamental. The flowers are comparatively insignificant — pink and bell-shaped — but they develop into inflated, 4-angled fruits (capsules) with a papery covering like that of a large Cape gooseberry, sometimes nearly 5 cm in diameter, in rosy red pink, and green, and every gradation of colour between. These fruits, which are often thickly clustered, remain on the tree for many weeks and such a tree literally glows. The fruits give the tree its common names of klapper and Chinese lanterns. They are 4-chambered with 1-2 roundish seeds per chamber. When the seeds within are ripe the airy, inflated capsules are blown far and wide.

The klapper is drought resistant and withstands extreme heat and cold, so that it should be an ideal cultivated shrub or small tree for the Karoo. It grows from seed and it is said from cuttings. It seldom does well in areas of high rainfall, although initially it may grow quickly and luxuriantly. However, it can sometimes be grown out of the arid country it favours and magnificent specimens grow, for example, in the Caledon wild garden. English gardeners grew it successfully as a greenhouse plant nearly 200 years ago. Masson introduced it from the Cape under the name of *Aitonia capensis* in 1774 and a coloured figure of a beautiful specimen was featured in Curtis's *Botanical Magazine* in the late 18th century.

Klapper is devoured by stock such as goats. In the past it was picked

a good deal for its ornamental fruits but now this is illegal for it is protected in the Cape.

3. *Turraea* L.

About 70 species found in tropical and subtropical countries and centred in east Africa and Madagascar belong to this genus. Two species, *Turraea floribunda* Hochst. and *Turraea nilotica* Kotschy & Peyr., grow as trees in South Africa, while a third, *Turraea obtusi- folia* Hochst., is usually a shrub and only occasionally tree-like. A fourth species, *Turraea zambesica* Styles & White, occurs in the Caprivi Strip, Botswana and Rhodesia.

Members of the family have a thick deep tap-root. The leaves are simple, alternate or in tufts, the flowers somewhat like those of a honeysuckle with usually 5 long, narrow, reflexed petals, and the stamens enclosed in a conspicuous tube from which protrudes the long style tipped with a small knob. The ovary is 5-10-20-celled. The fruit is a capsule, often woody, with 5-10 lobes, splitting to show the roundish, often brightly coloured seeds within.

The genus was named after Giorgio della Turre, Director of the Botanic Garden at Padua (1649-1683) who published a catalogue of the plants in the garden in 1660.

(296)   *Turraea floribunda* Hochst.

Wild honeysuckle tree; uMadlozana, uMadlozane (Z)

"The many-flowered turraea" — commonly known as the wild honey- suckle tree — is a small to medium-sized deciduous tree growing in coastal bush, wooded kloofs, and on stream banks from sea level up to about 760 m, from the eastern Cape, through Natal to Zululand. It grows also northwards to tropical Africa.

This is usually a slender, loosely branched tree, often many stemmed or occasionally with a trunk up to 30 cm in diameter. The bark is pale grey, grey blotched with brown, or a dark red-brown. The young branches are hairy, later becoming smooth and darker in colour. The leaves on long whippy branches tend to grow in a flat plane. They are simple, alternate, soft to the touch, toothed when very young, when mature untoothed, widely lance-shaped to egg-shaped, shortly or blunt- ly pointed, narrowing to the base, 2.5-14 cm long and 1.3-8 cm broad, hairy when young, becoming somewhat smoother, dark green above, lighter below, with the midrib and 7-11 pairs of secondary veins and the network of finer veins prominent below. They are borne on densely hairy stalks. These and the flowers tend to grow at the ends of short side branches.

The long slender green buds open into flowers with 5 long, narrow, ribbon-like petals, a soft greeny-yellow colour, which curve backwards, and with a protruding white staminal tube. They are borne in dense clusters in tufts or singly in great profusion about November when their heavy, sweet, honeysuckle perfume is very noticeable. So penetrating is it, that a few flowers in a sealed plastic bag can scent the air around them.

Surprisingly, considering the abundance of the flowers, very little

OPPOSITE

Above left
Flowers of the wild honeysuckle tree, *Tur- raea floribunda*

Above right
Flowers and leaves (100%)

Below
Turraea floribunda leaves and fruit, and a single fruit which has split to show the seeds within (100%)

fruit is set. What there is, however, is distinctive. The fruits are roundish, shiny, 1.3-2.5 cm in diameter, deeply ribbed, and woody, splitting along the ribs into segments that curl back and show the small, bright orange or red shiny seeds within. When open, these fruits look very like sturdy woody flowers.

The butterfly known as the White-Barred Caraks, *Charaxes brutus natalensis*, breeds on this species.

Zulus use the root and bark of the tree medicinally to treat rheumatism, dropsy, and heart ailments and as a purgative and enema. Gerstner says that the roots are used by Zulu witchdoctors as an emetic to enter the tranced state necessary in their divining dances.

(297)   *Turraea nilotica* Kotschy & Peyr.

= *Turraea randii* Bak.f.; = *Turraea tubulifera* C.DC.

Small mahogany; tshigombo (V)

The small mahogany is a shrub or small tree growing in rocky and gravelly ground in open bushveld and savannah, from the northern Transvaal and Botswana through central Africa to the Sudan.

In South Africa it is usually no more than 3-4.5 m high, a slender tree with a single, rough, fissured pale grey or grey-brown stem and branches that, when young, are covered with tawny hairs and on maturing develop a corky bark.

The leaves are simple, alternate, 5-14 cm long and up to 10 cm broad, oblong to egg-shaped with rounded or notched tips and somewhat narrowed bases, densely velvety when young, particularly on the under-surface, but becoming smoother later, dark green above, paler below, with the thick midrib and secondary veins prominent below. They have somewhat wavy, untoothed margins and are borne on short sturdy stalks.

The flowers, which appear in early spring in tufts on the bare branches in the axils of the fallen leaves, have long narrow, greenish petals which become yellow with age and which curl backwards. From the centre of these protrudes the white staminal tube. The flowers are favourites with bees.

The fruit is an attractive greenish-yellow capsule, slightly wider than long, up to about 1.3 cm in width, splitting into several valves to show black seeds partially covered by the red aril.

The fresh foliage of the small mahogany is eaten by cattle although the dried leaves are said to be poisonous to men and animals.

The specific name means "of the Nile lands".

(297.1)   *Turraea zambesica* Styles & White

Zambesi turraea; motulu (Kol)

Turraea zambesica, as the name implies, is a tree or shrub of the Zambesi valley and of those of its tributaries, where it grows in woodland, bush and forest. It has been collected in the Caprivi Strip, in Botswana, Rhodesia, and Portuguese East Africa.

It is a small, much-branched tree up to about 5 m high, the young branches covered with tawny hairs, the more mature smooth and not

Flower and fruit of *Turraea obtusifolia* photographed at Lake Sibayi

corky as in *Turraea nilotica*, to which it is closely related.

The leaves are very variable — widely lance-shaped to egg-shaped — the apex usually pointed and the base narrowed, up to 10 cm long and 5 cm wide, thin, smooth, with the nerves slightly hairy.

The flowers, 3-7 of which are borne in a cluster in the axils of the leaves or terminally, have narrow whitish-green petals that become yellow with age, and a staminal tube that is shorter than the petals. They are usually borne in great quantities and have a sweet scent.

The fruit is a small, smooth, roundish, shallowly grooved capsule that splits open.

Turraea obtusifolia Hochst.

= *Turraea obtusifolia* var. *microphylla* C.DC.; = *Turraea obtusifolia* var. *matopensis* Bak.f.; = *Turraea oblancifolia* Bremek.

Lesser honeysuckle tree; inKunzi, inKunzi ebomvana, amaZulu (Z)

This shrub or small bushy tree grows in coastal bush and often on dunes, from the eastern Cape northwards to Zululand, and inland in bushveld and woodland through the Transvaal to Botswana, and northwards to Rhodesia and Portuguese East Africa.

The young branches are covered with downy, spreading hairs, but become smoother with age. The leaves are simple and occasionally alternate but are usually borne in tufts. They vary in shape and size. Sometimes they are egg-shaped, at others more slender, tapering to the base, the apex bluntly pointed or notched, the upper half sometimes deeply toothed or lobed, glossy green above and paler below, and almost stalkless. The midrib is raised on the under-surface.

The flowers, 1-3 in a head in the axils of the leaves, are a pure and beautiful white with long narrow petals, and a staminal tube that is not quite as long as the petals. They are among the most striking of the turraea flowers but lack the heavy rich scent of *Turraea floribunda*.

The roundish fruit, about 1.3 cm wide, slightly less in length, and divided into sections, splits to show brilliant red seed within.

The specific name is based on Latin words meaning "rounded at the end" and "leaves" and refers to the often blunt apex of the leaves.

1063

Above
The dog plum or essenhout, *Eke-bergia capensis,* between Butterworth and Wavecrest in the Transkei

Below left
Ekebergia capensis bark

Below right
Ekebergia capensis: A fruiting branch (50%)

4. *Ekebergia* Sparrm.

Ekebergia is a small African genus of about 3 or 4 members, and is represented in South Africa by 2 or possibly 3 species, *Ekebergia capensis* Sparrm. and *Ekebergia pterophylla* (C.DC.) Hofmeyr. The tree formerly known as *Ekebergia meyeri* Presl is now usually included in *Ekebergia capensis*.

These are small to large trees, almost evergreen, with compound leaves composed of 1 to 7 pairs of leaflets and a terminal leaflet, untoothed, the common midrib sometimes winged. The flowers are male or female, usually borne on different trees, in branching heads in the axils of the leaves. They have a saucer-shaped, 4-5-lobed calyx, 4-5 petals, 8-10 stamens, and a 2-5-celled ovary. The fruit is round, more or less succulent, with 2-5 cells, containing 1 to several hard seeds.

The genus was named by the traveller and naturalist, Andrew Sparrman, who first saw the tree he called *Ekebergia capensis* – and on which the genus is based – in 1775. He named it in compliment to a Captain Ekeberg who had made it possible for him to visit the Cape, "who", wrote Sparrman, "by his zeal for natural history and the great pains he has been at in promoting it, is highly deserving of this distinction".

(298)   *Ekebergia capensis* Sparrm.

= *Trichilia ruepelliana* Fresn.; = *Ekebergia ruepelliana* (Fresn.) A.Rich; = *Ekebergia meyeri* Presl; = *Ekebergia buchananii* Harms

Dog plum, essenhout, Cape ash, esseboom; umGwenyezinja (X); umGwenya-wezinja, umNyamathi, uVungu, uSimanaye, uManaye (Z); iNyamati (Sw); mmidibidi (NS); muḍouma, muṯovuma (V)

The dog plum or essenhout is a medium-sized to large tree occurring in most of the forests of the country from the Cape to Swaziland and the Transvaal, although not plentifully in the Amatola mountains. Under good conditions it reaches a height of 21 m, but when standing by itself in the deep soil it favours it is a lower, often magnificently spreading tree with strong horizontal branches, giving good shade. It also occurs in scrub, both along the coast and inland, where it may be stunted or gnarled. The big tree illustrated grew on a river bank near the road between Butterworth and the coast.

Although usually evergreen, it is sometimes semi-deciduous. A leaf turning colour here and there in the crown is a common sight.

The stem varies for it may be tall and fluted in forests, and much shorter and entirely unfluted in the open, with bark that is grey to brown, often mottled, smooth or rough, sometimes flaking in small circles or squares. The branchlets are slender, marked by old circular leaf-scars and with white raised dots or lenticels.

The large compound leaves vary much in size. They may be 10-36 cm long and 8-18 cm broad, with the common midrib sometimes slightly winged. The leaflets are usually in 3-5 pairs, occasionally up to 7, opposite or nearly opposite, with a terminal leaflet, almost stalkless, and smooth. The typical Cape *Ekebergia capensis* has long, rather narrow leaflets tapering to the point, and to the usually unequal-sided base, and this form enters Natal and sometimes the Transvaal. A form from the Transvaal mountains and from Zululand forests, how-

1065

Above
Ekebergia pterophylla growing as a
shapely tree above the Blyde River
Canyon in the eastern Transvaal

Right
Ekebergia pterophylla: Leaves and
flowers (60%)

Below
Ekebergia pterophylla, such as this
specimen in the Ngoye Forest, is
typically a small tree of rocky
slopes

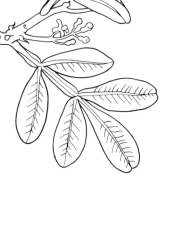

Opposite
Ekebergia pterophylla bark

ever, has leaflets that are much broader in proportion to the length, broadly oval or almost egg-shaped, and this was formerly known as *Ekebergia meyeri* Presl. The leaflets in these two forms are sometimes so different that it is difficult to accept the trees as one species, yet gradations in the shape and size of the leaflets between the two forms are found, as in parts of Natal, so that the two are now generally considered inseparable. Some forest officers, however, still maintain that the two are distinct species, while the Zulus differentiate between the two by the bark, and they and the Vendas give them different names.

The small greenish-yellow, 5-petalled flowers are borne in panicles — long branching heads — in the axils of the leaves, the male and female on different trees. They have a sweet scent rather like that of orange blossom, and are pollinated by bees and ants. Where conditions are favourable the dog plum is covered with flowers every year, although in more unfavourable localities trees may only flower once in several years, and then sparsely.

The fruits are round and dark red, often resembling small apples, and a tree laden with them is a lovely sight. They are up to about 1.9 cm in diameter, succulent — those from the Cape and coastal districts usually fleshier than in the Transvaal form once known as *Ekebergia meyeri* — and taste faintly of onion. They are relished by most fruit-eating birds which sometimes pick off the flesh and leave the seeds still hanging on the stalks. There are 2-4 seeds, or occasionally only 1.

The wood — susceptible to insect attack — is light, soft, the heartwood and sapwood not clearly defined, with an even grain, and easily worked. It is straw-coloured to light brown, polishes well, and makes attractive furniture. It is also used for panelling, beams for boat-building, and for the sides of wagons, and for broom handles. The outside doors and windows of the Anglican Church in Somerset East are of this wood.

The bark was once used for tanning, and Zulus use it as an emetic and cough cure and the root for dysentry. They burn branches in the field to ward off evil spirits.

Farmers may be interested in its fodder value, for although not usually considered a fodder tree, its foliage is eagerly devoured by stock in drought time. In the wild, antelope such as nyala and bushbuck are fond of the fallen leaves.

At least one species of butterfly breeds on the tree. It is the dark butterfly marked with white, known as the White-barred Caraks, *Charaxes brutus natalensis*, found in rain forests from Pondoland to the Transvaal.

The dog plum is easily cultivated and does particularly well in deep sandy soil. Unlike most forest trees it takes only 8-9 weeks to germinate when the seed is fresh, and is fairly fast-growing. Masses of seedlings are often found around birds' drinking places. (Gardeners claim that seeds excreted by birds appear to germinate 100 per cent). The tree is tender to severe frost.

This is a species well worth cultivating for its shade and ornamental fruits.

The specific name means "of the Cape". The common name "dog-plum" is a translation of the Xhosa name, and in the two forms was widely used by settlers and Xhosas in the Cape. "Essenhout", a name used in parts, is derived from the old colonial name "esseboom" recorded by Thunberg in 1773. Essenbosch, near Humansdorp, was named after the *Ekebergia* trees nearby, and some fine old specimens still stand today. Zulus know the *"Ekebergia meyeri"* form of the tree as uSimanaye and uManaye, and the typical *Ekebergia capensis* as uVungu.

This species is easily confused with the kaffir plum or kaffir date, *Harpephyllum caffrum* Bernh. ex Krauss, both in the field and in the herbarium, for the leaves are similar. The stalks of the dog plum leaves, however, are jointed to the stem and leave a scar when falling.

See colour plate facing page 891

(299)   *Ekebergia pterophylla* (C.DC.) Hofmeyr

= *Trichilia pterophylla* C.DC.; = *Trichilia alata* N.E.Br.

Rock essenhout, basternieshout

The rock essenhout is a small tree growing from Pondoland northwards to Natal, Zululand, and Swaziland, to the eastern and northern Transvaal, sometimes on forest edges but most often on rocky, grassed or wooded hill slopes.

Depending on the locality it may be a graceful 5 m tree with a clean trunk and a round crown, or — in rocky exposed situations — squat, bushy, and flat-crowned. It is a common little tree on the rocky outcrops at Ngoye Forest in Zululand, or on the slopes of the western side of the Blyde River Canyon in the eastern Transvaal where — with its backdrop of mountain and rock — it is picturesque.

The crown is dense, evergreen, and usually a rather dark green. The trunk, often short and crooked, occasionally straight and clean, is smooth or rough, a light to dark grey, and often mottled or banded in brown, white, or red.

The leaves are distinctive. They are alternate, once compound, up to about 13 cm long and 8 cm wide, composed of usually 1-3 pairs of opposite leaflets and a terminal one, which are stalkless and vary in shape from lance-shaped to a wide oblong, with bluntly pointed or notched tips, 2.5-6 cm long and 0.6-1.9 cm wide, dark green or sometimes grey, with the midrib plainly visible above and below, with the *common midrib and leaf stalk usually strongly or slightly winged*. This winged midrib is conspicuous and characteristic and an easy aid to identification.

The small white or pale pink 4-petalled flowers are borne in heads in the axils of the leaves or terminally. The fruits are small, round, 2-seeded, green turning red, purple, or black, borne on short stalks, often in quantities.

The botanist, de Candolle, described this in 1894 as a *Trichilia*. Trichilias, however, have fruits that are capsules that split open, and it was not until 1925 when Dr J.D. Keet collected a specimen in fruit that it was assigned to the genus *Ekebergia*.

The name *pterophylla* is based on Greek words meaning "a winged leaf".

5. *Trichilia* Browne

This large genus of trees and shrubs, over 300 of which have been described, occurs in Africa, Madagascar, Asia and America. (When the genus is revised, the number of species is likely to be reduced considerably).

In South Africa 2 species occur, *Trichilia emetica* Vahl and *Trichilia dregeana* Sond. A good deal of confusion exists over these for they resemble one another closely and until fairly recently were both thought to be *Trichilia emetica*. To add to the confusion, they were for a time generally known by the incorrect name of *Trichilia roka* (Forsk.) Chiov.

The genus *Trichilia* has members, which are often large trees, which most often have alternate, imparipinnate leaves (compound leaves terminated by one leaflet) with untoothed leaflets, and male or female flowers in sprays in the axils of the leaves, it is thought borne on separate trees. The calyx lobes and petals number 4-5, the stamens 8-10, and the ovary is 2-4-celled. The fruits are capsules which split open along 2-4 valves, a feature that helps to separate the genus from *Ekebergia*. There are 1 or 2 seeds in each compartment and these have a fleshy aril that is conspicuous.

Trichilia dregeana and *Trichilia emetica* are both large, handsome, evergreen trees with the typical imparipinnate leaves. They grow, however, under different conditions from one another, and the leaves and fruits have small botanical differences. *Trichilia dregeana* is a tree of evergreen forest in high rainfall, its leaflets are usually pointed, the secondary veins are widely spaced, in about 8-9 pairs, and the lower surface is usually smooth or almost hairless. The fruit has a very short sturdy stalk.

Trichilia emetica on the other hand is a tree of lower rainfall areas, of woodland, bush, and river sides, and is one of the common and beautiful trees of the parkland of the northern and eastern Transvaal. It is also common in Zululand. Its leaflets usually have rounded or sometimes notched tips with — according to *Flora Zambesiaca* — about 13-16 pairs of closely spaced secondary nerves, while the lower surface is usually densely hairy. The fruit has a long stalk, divided into two distinct sections, the one at the base of the fruit slightly broader than the true stalk and known as a stipe.

Several species of butterflies are known to breed on trees of this genus, including the White Barred Caraks that breeds, too, on *Ekebergia capensis*.

The name *Trichilia* is based on the Greek "tricho" meaning "in 3 parts", and refers to the often 3-celled fruits.

(300)   *Trichilia dregeana* Sond.

= *Trichilia dregei* E.Mey.; = *Trichilia dregei* var. *oblonga* C.DC.; = *Trichilia chirindensis* Swynnerton & Bak.f.

Forest mahogany, Cape mahogany, thunder tree, Christmas bells, red ash, rooiessenhout, basteressenhout; umKhuhlu (X); umKhuhlu, uMantunzini (Z); nkuhlu (Tso); mmaba (NS); muṭuhu, mutshikili (V)

Trichilia dregeana is a tall tree, reputed to grow up to 30 m high, of evergreen forests in areas of high rainfall, growing from Pondoland through Natal to the eastern and northern Transvaal, up to an altitude of about 1070 m, and beyond to Rhodesia and tropical Africa. It is not clear what its southernmost limit is but it may well be the Gwebe Forest on the north bank of the Bashee River where several big trees occur.

It is common in the coastal forests of Natal and is known to thousands of holiday-makers along the Natal south coast as a tall tree with a

Above left
The forest or Cape mahogany, *Trichilia dregeana*, growing on the edge of the golf course, Umdoni Park, Natal south coast.

Above right
Trichilia dregeana: A flowering twig, the fruits on short stalks and the seed. The leaf to the right is a somewhat unusual form with many veins close together (60%)

Below left
Trichilia dregeana bark

black-green crown growing in small patches of forest still left standing.

The trunk is tall, straight, and sometimes lightly buttressed, up to 1.8 m in diameter, smooth and grey, often beautifully mottled with pink and oyster shades, bearing a crown of heavy, glossy foliage.

The leaves are large, generally up to about 26 cm long when mature but sometimes larger, with 2-5 pairs of leaflets which are opposite or nearly opposite, untoothed, up to about 20 cm long and 9 cm wide, and a narrow or broad oblong in shape. According to *Flora Zambesiaca* they are nearly always broadest towards the tip, but this apparently is not always so in South Africa. The tips are usually pointed, the base rounded or narrowed, the secondary veins in 8-9 — occasionally up to 12 pairs — with the lower surface usually smooth or almost hairless, the upper surface drying dark brown, borne on stalks about 1.3 cm long.

The whitish flowers, with slender velvety petals, are borne in sprays in the axils of the leaves. The fruit is a large somewhat rounded capsule, up to about 3 cm in diameter, usually 3-lobed, splitting to show the black seed which is largely covered with a scarlet aril, a bright and beautiful combination. The capsule is borne on a *short* stout stalk.

The timber is pink turning a darker colour when oiled — it is said then to resemble mahogany — polishes well, and makes good furniture. Africans use it for carvings and dishes.

The seed is very rich in fat which is used to make soap, cosmetics, and for cooking. It is apparently harmless although parts of the seed and bark have poisonous properties. Watt and Brandwijk state that the Tonga boil the oil of this or of *Trichilia emetica* with the fruit pulp of *Strychnos innocua* and store this as a reserve food that lasts well for two years. The Zulus, after soaking the seeds, suck out the milky juice.

The seed, oil, leaves, root, and bark of this species and of *Trichilia emetica* are used medicinally throughout Africa to treat a wide variety of complaints ranging from lumbago to leprosy and sleeplessness. The fruit has emetic and purgative properties.

The seeds are eaten by many birds. They are popular with Purple-crested Loeries and at least one Natal ornithologist claims that their bright pigment passes into the brilliant plumage of the bird!

The specific name of the tree honours the German collector and botanical explorer, Johan Franz Drège, who visited South Africa between 1826 and 1834 and who collected the tree in Natal. In parts of Natal this is known as the Umkomaas tree, a name based on the Zulu word for a cow whale. The whales suckled their young at the mouth of the Umkomaas River where the mahogany trees grow abundantly.

A tree in Mitchell Park in Durban is one of the largest trees in Natal. The trunk measures 5.5 m in circumference; the circumference of the whole tree is 100 m, the diameter 35 m, and the height 18 m. The deep scratches on the trunk are said to have been made a long time ago by the tusks of elephants resting in the shade of the tree.

(301)   *Trichilia emetica* Vahl

Woodland mahogany, Natal mahogany, Christmas bells, thunder tree, red ash, rooiessenhout, basteressenhout; umKhuhlu, uMathunzini, iGwolo (Z); umKhuhlu (Sw); nkuhlu (Tso); mosikiri (Tsw); mmaba (NS); mutshikili, muṭuhu (V)

This is one of the widespread trees of Africa growing, according to

The woodland or Natal mahogany, *Trichilia emetica* — the shade tree of a Tonga kraal

Flora Zambesiaca "from Senegal to the Red Sea and through East and Central Africa to the Congo, Natal, and the Transvaal; also in the Yemen".

In South Africa it occurs in open woodland and on river banks from Natal, Zululand, and Swaziland to the eastern and northern Transvaal in areas of lower rainfall than are associated with *Trichilia dregeana*. It also grows in Botswana to the west and in numbers in Mozambique to the north east. This is one of the most conspicuous trees in the parkland south of the Soutpansberg in the northern Transvaal. It is common in parts of the Kruger National Park and is one of the largest of the magnificent trees along the Pafuri River. Several trees grow within the old Pafuri Camp, now a picnic spot, and at the "look-out" at the junction of the Pafuri and Limpopo rivers.

In the dry sand forest of Tongoland (northern Zululand), it may be found not only growing in the wild but shading African villages, a dark giant spreading its branches over an entire community.

It is usually evergreen, and has a clean, well-formed, smooth or slightly rough, grey or brown trunk, and in the open a wide, often magnificently spreading crown casting what is reputed to be the densest shade of any tree in the Republic.

Stevenson Hamilton writes that in its youth it grows up in the deep shade of its parent tree and is generally found, in the eastern Transvaal, in small groups of various sized individuals, mingled with a few jakkals-bessies.

The deep green, glossy foliage is heavy and somewhat crowded at the ends of the branches. It is composed of large compound leaves up to 30 cm long with 3-5 pairs of leaflets and 1 terminal leaflet. The leaflets, opposite or alternate, are up to about 15 cm long and 5 cm wide, a broad oblong or oval, not as a rule broadest towards the tip, with the apex usually rounded or notched, and a round or narrowed base, the edges sometimes undulating but untoothed, and with usually 13-16 pairs of lateral veins, but occasionally 10 or as many as 19. These closely spaced, numerous veins help to distinguish the tree from *Trichilia dregeana*. *Flora Zambesiaca* says that the upper surface dries olive green or pale brown. The lower surface is hairy with the midrib, the twigs, young growth and flowers covered with small red hairs. The leaves on very young shoots are chestnut-brown and shine as if with varnish.

The leaves on young trees or from coppice shoots are often larger than are the normal ones, sometimes up to 60 cm or more long.

The leaves are borne on short stalks which are densely hairy when young but become smoother with age.

The small bell-shaped flowers, smelling of orange blossom, appear in the spring or summer and are white or yellow, and usually borne in long sprays towards the ends of the branches. These give to the tree one of its common names – Christmas bells.

The fruits are often slightly smaller than are those of the forest mahogany, usually about 1.9 cm in diameter, roundish, hard, pale brown to grey-green, wrinkled, usually 3-lobed, each compartment containing 1-2 bean-like black seeds partially covered with a red aril. Keith Coates Palgrave says these have the vacant expression of dolls' eyes and this is a most excellent likeness.

They are always borne on a long stalk, part of which – the thick portion at the base of the fruit – is known as a stipe. This helps to distinguish the fruit from that of *Trichilia dregeana* which has a short, stout stalk.

1074

The wood of the mahogany is pinkish-brown to brownish-grey but when old darkens considerably: there is little difference between heart-wood and sapwood. It is fairly light and soft and takes glue and polish easily and works well, but, unless treated, is liable to be damaged by insects. C.P. Kromhout says that it may be recognized by its relatively light weight and light red colour, often with blue discoloration. It makes good furniture, shelves and mouldings, and in Zululand is used for fish floats and dug-out canoes. The punts on the pans in the Pongola flood plain are often made of this, as is the single oar the Tongas use when when the pan is deep.

The frame of a traditionally made mbila — African musical instrument — and the beaters are often of this wood. It is used, too, for the small light carvings of crocodiles, fishes, and other animals sold by Africans along the roads in the eastern and north eastern Transvaal, for it is easy to work and seldom cracks when drying.

Like its forest relative, the woodland mahogany is used widely in African medicine and for much the same purposes. The bark is sometimes employed as an emetic — it is this property that gives the tree its specific name. Strangely enough, it is not generally favoured for this purpose, its more common use being as an enema. Zulus soak the bark in warm water and use the infusion as a mild enema, and for a stronger mixture add the roots of *Brachylaena discolor* DC. and the bulb of a small bush lily. A very weak solution is given orally to small children. The leaves are also used.

The oil in the seeds is extracted by grinding and heating them in a pot until the oil exudes. It is used as a body and hair oil and medicinally for it is held to have curative powers. It is believed by the Zulus to hasten healing, in particular in the case of fractures, and is rubbed into cuts around the "break" in a fractured limb. The incisions are then treated with the roasted and ground roots of *Sideroxylon inerme* L.

The seeds are poisonous, the poison apparently being present in the outer covering only for the oil extracted from the seeds is harmless and the skinned seeds are widely eaten by Africans. They are also soaked in warm water and ground, and the milky "juice" is mixed with spinach or pumpkin.

Baboons, monkeys and nyala eat the fruit, while the seeds are taken by many species of birds, such as the Crowned, Grey and Trumpeter Hornbills; Black-collared, White-eared and Black-crowned Tinker Barbets, and Black-bellied Glossy Starlings. Fish such as barbel eat the seeds that fall into the water, and one fisherman at least used them as bait — and caught a barbel.

The flower nectar is taken by Scarlet-breasted Sunbirds, Spotted-backed Weavers, and probably by many more birds, and monkeys eat the flower buds.

Several species of butterflies, including the White-barred Caraks, *Charaxes brutus natalensis*, breed on this species.

The tree is used in Zululand in a burial ritual. When a person dies, the husband (or wife) takes the body to the river in the early morning, girding his loins with the leaves of the tree, and then with the crowds singing mourning songs, the body is carried back to the kraal.

6. *Pseudobersama* Verdc.

This genus of only 1 species, *Pseudobersama mossambicensis* (Sim)

OPPOSITE

Above left
A Natal mahogany, *Trichilia emetica*, at Lake Sibayi

Above right
The trunk of a great Natal mahogany showing scars where the bark had been peeled off for use as medicine

Below
Trichilia emetica: A leaf, flowering and fruiting panicles, and the fruit showing the stipe at the base, and the conspicuous seeds (70%)

Pseudobersama mossam-bicensis: The leaves and fruits (90%)

Verdc., is purely African. Whem Sim first described it in 1909 from Portuguese East Africa he placed it in Sapindaceae calling it *Bersama mossambicensis*, "the Bersama of Mozambique", although he was aware it was not a true *Bersama*. Dr Bernard Verdcourt, while stationed in Kenya, later placed it in the mahogany family calling it *Pseudobersama* – "the false Bersama".

It is closely related to *Trichilia*, but the fruit has 5 valves and not 2-4 and these are very thick and woody.

(302)   *Pseudobersama mossambicensis* (Sim) Verdc.

Opho tree; umOpho (Z)

This small to medium-sized tree occurs down the east coast of Africa from Kenya to Zululand as a common canopy tree in tropical areas. In Zululand it grows in the Mangusi Forest and in the open bush in the north.

The young branchlets are reddish, ridged, and slightly hairy. The leaves are large, up to 30 cm long, composed of about 4-8 pairs of alternate, widely spaced, untoothed leaflets, and a terminal leaflet. These are usually 4-9 cm long and 1.9-4 cm broad, but may be larger (up to 16 by 8 cm) egg-shaped, oblong, or widely lance-shaped, pointed, narrowed to the base, with the midrib often to one side, when the leaves may be mistaken for those of a sneezewood. Very young leaves are densely velvety but become smooth with age.

The small flowers are borne in lax heads, male and female separately and probably on different trees. Few female flowers have ever been collected and this is either because female trees are rare or because the inconspicuous flowers have been overlooked.

The fruit is distinctive. It is 2.5-4.5 cm wide, sometimes roughly the size of a golf ball, round or egg-shaped, rough, knobbly and woody, scarlet, splitting into usually 5 segments which curl backwards, each cell containing 2 brilliant seeds, purple-red with a bright red aril.

The wood is durable and light.

The specific name indicates that this was first collected in Mozambique.

This large, mainly tropical family of roughly 60 genera and 800 species of trees and often climbing shrubs is most numerous in America. Several genera including *Acridocarpus* occur in South Africa.

The family as a whole is characterized by simple leaves, bisexual flowers with petals that are usually clawed, fringed or toothed, and fruits that may be fleshy but which in South Africa break up into 1-seeded winged carpels.

Acridocarpus Guill. & Perr.

Acridocarpus is a genus of about 30 species, several of which occur from the Transvaal to the Transkei. These are mainly shrubs, erect, climbing or sometimes trailing, and only one species in South Africa sometimes grows as a small tree. This is *Acridocarpus natalitius* A.Juss.

The species in the genus have leaves that are simple, alternate, un-toothed, without stipules, and often with glands at the base on the under-surface. The 5-petalled, bisexual flowers are borne in clusters or sprays (cymes or panicles) in the axils of the leaves or at the ends of the branches. Tiny bracts and bracteoles are present. The stamens number 10. The ovary is 3-celled although usually 1 cell fails to develop. The fruit is unusual and decorative, the parts separate and boldly wing-ed.

The generic name is based on Greek words, "akris" meaning "locust" and "karpos" meaning "fruit", and "locust-winged fruit" is a splendidly descriptive name for the genus.

Acridocarpus natalitius A.Juss.

1. var. *natalitius*

= *Acridocarpus reticulatus* Burtt Davy

2. var. *linearifolius* Launert

= *Acridocarpus pondoensis* Engl.

The Binder; uMabophe, inTelezi (Z)

This little tree, scrambling shrub, or twiner, often rambling over other vegetation, is a common and ornamental member of subtropical forest

A little tree widely believed to have magical powers — *Acridocarpus natalitius* var. *linearifolius,* on top of the Lebombo Mountains in northern Zululand

from Pondoland northwards to Zululand and Mozambique, growing in forests, on forest margins, sometimes on rocky outcrops or on wooded hillsides and in open grassland. It also occurs, but not as frequently, in the eastern Transvaal lowveld.

As a tree it can grow up to 6 m in height but is usually smaller with young branchlets covered with red or yellow hairs, becoming smoother later, and simple, dark, in var. *natalitius* often rather large leaves with handsome veining on the under-surface. They are alternate, typically 2.5-13 cm long and 0.6 to nearly 5 cm broad, oblong to lance-shaped, with a pointed, rounded or notched point, and usually a narrowed base, usually smooth on both sides although young leaves may be somewhat hairy, most often with 2 glands at the base on the under-surface, and with the midrib and widely spaced secondary veins much raised below, and often with the fine network of conspicuous.

The form with very narrow leaves is known as var. *linearifolius*. Its distribution and habit, flower and fruit, are much the same as those of var. *natalitius*. The little tree photographed on top of the Lebombo mountains in Zululand was the narrow-leaved variety.

In the summer time, usually from November to February — although occasionally later — long pyramid-shaped sprays (racemes) of round buds on long slender, furry, red-brown stalks are borne, most often at the ends of the branches, and these open into handsome flowers which are 2.5 cm in diameter when open, with bright golden clawed petals.

The fruit occasionally has 3 but most often 2 large, oblique, round-tipped and much veined wings, when it looks remarkably like — not so much a locust — as a brown moth with wings outstretched.

Among the butterflies breeding on this species is the Two Pip Police-man, *Coeliades pisistratus* of the group known as Skippers — dull-coloured butterflies with a jerky flight.

The wood has a faintly peppery smell when cut.

This is a good garden shrub, growing easily from seed and cuttings.

Europeans prize this tree for its ornamental uses, but for Africans it has another and wider significance, for it is used in medicine and magic wherever it grows.

Once Zulu witchdoctors anointed warriors with a medicine made from the roots, which, according to Professor J.M. Watt, made them "slippery" in escaping danger and enemy assagais. Wherever the plant grows the root is a love charm. Sticks are planted in the thatch of huts to ward off lightning, and planted around a home to protect it from sorcerers.

Binding, in a magical sense, seems to be its chief use among Africans, and perhaps this is based on a physical character, such as tough fibres, which is not recorded. Both Pondos and Zulus believe the plant has the power to bind words or actions, and can be used magically to prevent a person performing a certain deed or pronouncing certain words. Naturally it is a splendid weapon in a court of law, a few leaves placed under the tongue of one man rendering his opponent dumb.

The specific name means "of Natal", while *linearifolius* means "narrow-leaved". Zulus often call the tree inTelezi, but this is a general name for all those medicinal charms used to counteract evil, and is given to other species such as *Rapanea melanophloeos* (L.) Mez., *Oncinotis inandensis* Wood & Evans, *Portulacaria afra* Jacq. and *Crassula portulacea* Lam.

The common name, "the binder", is straight from African magic.

Acridocarpus natalitius leaves and fruits

Polygalaceae is a widespread family with over 400 species occurring in most warm and temperate countries of the world. They are most often herbs or small shrubs but occasionally are small to medium-sized trees.

The species have simple leaves without stipules, and bisexual flowers borne in spikes, racemes or heads. In many the lateral sepals are enlarged, growing in the shape of wings and coloured like petals, a characteristic that is apparent in the flowers of the 2 small South African tree members belonging to the genera *Polygala* and *Securidaca*. The fruits are capsules, samaras or drupes.

Polygala L.

E.P. Phillips records 95 described species of *Polygala* in South Africa, most being low-growing. One species, *Polygala myrtifolia* L., can grow into a small tree. Members of the genus have simple leaves and bisexual flowers that are butterfly-shaped with 5 sepals, the 2 lateral ones wing-like and coloured; the petals, 3-5, with the lower one keel-shaped and with a fringed crest, and with smaller side petals, the stamens 8, the ovary 2-celled with 1 ovule in each cell. The fruit is a small flat capsule.

Polygala is an old Greek name and is based on the Greek words "polys" meaning "much", and "gala" meaning "milk", because of the reputation of some members "for promoting secretion of milk".

Polygala myrtifolia L.

= *Polygala pinifolia* Poir.

Augusbossie, Septemberbossie, blouertjieboom, langelier, langelede

The Septemberbossie is most common as a shrub from 0.6-1.8 m high, round-topped, leafy, and luxuriant-looking, but it can sometimes be a small tree up to 4 m high. Sim knew it as a tree near Cathcart with a stem diameter of 15 cm. It grows from the Clanwilliam and Van Rhynsdorp districts eastwards — on Table Mountain itself — through the coastal districts of the eastern Cape and the Transkei to St. Lucia in the north, and inland to such districts as Calvinia, Ladismith, Willowmore and Somerset East. In Natal it has been recorded as far inland as Giant's Castle. It flourishes under a variety of conditions — in the damp forest of the south, in scrub, open grassveld, in gully bush, on stream banks, and on dunes.

It is a dense little tree with upright branches, leafy and fresh-looking, with simple alternate leaves closely crowded up the slender branchlets. Several different forms occur, a large-leaved form — the most

Above left
The violet tree, *Securidaca longipedunculata*, in the Transvaal bushveld

Above right
The violet tree bark

Below left
Securidaca longipedunculata: Fruits and a flowering twig (50%)

Below right
Polygala myrtifolia: a flowering and fruiting twig (60%)

1082

common — growing in the coastal districts, and a form with very narrow leaves from the Little Karoo. This was originally known as *Polygala pinifolia* Poir. The forms tend to grade into one another and are no longer judged separate.

The leaves in coastal forms are usually 2.5-5 cm long and up to 1.3 cm wide, generally oblong or oval, with rounded or almost flat tips, while those further inland are often needle-like with the margins in-rolled.

The flowers grow in short bunches at the ends of the twigs and are often mistaken for those of a legume which they somewhat resemble. They have 3 petals, 2 wings and 1 keel, the keeled petal having a showy crest. The buds are roughly oval, a mauvy pink marked with darker veins, and with a conspicuous light green calyx. As they open, the central petal becomes visible, decorated with a fine, delicate mauve fringe or brush. The petals are usually purple or mauve, beautifully veined in a darker shade, but may occasionally be pink, white or scarlet. At their largest they are nearly 2.5 cm in length and these showy flowers are usually borne on the large-leaved forms of the tree.

Although the tree blooms off and on throughout the year, winter and spring are the main blooming seasons, hence the names Augusbossie and Septemberbossie. A large-flowered tree in full bloom, with its fresh green leaf and purplish flowers, can be ornamental.

The fruit is a small, oval, slightly winged capsule, enclosed between persistent sepals.

In the past this polygala had an unusual use in the Cape. Pappe says that the Cape Malays scraped off the fresh grey bark which they mixed with water and stirred until it frothed. In this they washed their dead before interment.

The tree is easily raised from seed, and is charming in a garden. It makes a satisfactory hedge if clipped several times a year, a treatment to which it responds well.

The specific name means "myrtle-like leaves". The names "langelier" and "langelede" are probably, according to C.A.Smith, a corruption of "lange lede" meaning "long joints".

Securidaca L.

About 80 species of this genus grow in Africa, Asia and America as small to medium-sized, sometimes spiny trees or as shrubs. One species grows in the Transvaal, Botswana, and South West Africa.

They have simple, alternate, untoothed leaves, and bisexual flowers borne terminally and in the axils of the leaves in racemes that are often arranged in a panicle. They have 5 sepals, 2 of which are large and wing-like, and 3 petals, the middle one hooded: the stamens number 8 and the ovary is usually 1-chambered. The fruit is conspicuously winged, is indehiscent, and is known botanically as a samara.

The generic name is based on the Latin "securis" meaning "hatchet", in reference to the shape of the fruit.

(303)   *Securidaca longipedunculata* Fresen.

= *Lophostylis pallida* Klotzsch; = *Securidaca spinosa* Sim.; = *Securidaca longipedunculata* var. *parvifolia* Oliv.

Violet tree, fibre tree, krinkhout; tsatsu (Tso); mmaba (Tsw); mmaba (NS); mpesu (V); mofufu (Sub)

The violet tree is one of the widespread trees of Africa, occurring from the Transvaal and South West Africa northwards through tropical Africa to Senegal (where it was first collected) and to Ethiopia. In South Africa it grows in the central and northern Transvaal, and to the west in Botswana and in northern South West Africa, usually in open bushveld and always in sandy soil.

This is a variable species. In South and South West Africa it is a slender to somewhat spreading, deciduous tree from 3-9 m tall, often graceful, with a smooth pale green or grey trunk frequently banded with light grey or white, and with spine-tipped, often much shortened branchlets.

The leaves, simple, alternate, untoothed, and sometimes with the edges inrolled, are usually 1.3-4 cm long, oval, oblong, or sometimes egg-shaped, with a round apex and narrowed base, carried on short hairy stalks.

The flowers on long slender stalks are borne — in great abundance — in short spreading bunches (racemes), usually at the ends of abbreviated side branches, from about October to December and sometimes as late as February. They are somewhat like those of a sweetpea with 3 frilled petals, purple or wine-coloured, and with a rich sweet scent of pure violets that perfumes the air for far around, and which gives the tree its common name of "violet tree". A sample of the oil expressed from them was well reported on by the Imperial Institute some time ago.

The fruit is a round hard nut bearing a long, light, fibrous, much-veined wing which turns rosy red or brown when mature. The fruits often hang on the tree for many months.

The leaves are said to be browsed by kudu and the roots by elephants.

The wood is a pale buff colour, soft, light and spongy, and when cut shows many circular rings of a soft tissue. It is used only for fuel. The bark, however, yields an excellent fibre which resembles flax and which Africans use to make, among other things, fishing nets and sewing thread.

Medicinally this is an important tree — one African name means "Mother of Medicine" — and Africans use it to treat the most widely differing ailments — coughs, headaches, toothache, sleeping-sickness, malaria, and rheumatism and fibrositis — "which", say Watt and Brandwijk, "is interesting in view of the knowledge that the root contains methyl salicylate". The bark, roots, and seeds all contain poisonous properties and one or the other is used in arrow poisons, in trials by ordeal, to commit suicide — and doubtless murder.

Because of its potency it is a greatly revered tree in Africa. According to Ferreira it is used by many tribes as a charm against witches and wizards, troublesome ancestral spirits, to cleanse those who are ceremonially unclean, and to keep away snakes. In parts it is also thought to have the power to awaken erotic emotions. The anthropologists Edwin M. Loeb and Ella Marie Loeb say that because of this the straight annual shoots are used by boys in Ovamboland in South West Africa to hit the girls before the puberty ceremonies.

This is a decorative tree and many attempts have been made to cultivate it, usually unsuccessfully. It often germinates badly and transplanting is hazardous for the very long taproot is easily damaged. In tins young plants wither away overnight, possibly when the taproot touches the bottom. Fairly good results have been obtained by well soaking the seeds and then sowing them in sandy soil where the plants are to remain. They should be protected from frost when young.

The specific name is based on Latin words meaning "long peduncle" (flower stalk).

Tapura fischeri growing in the open at Lake Sibayi

Three genera with over 300 species in Africa, Asia, and Madagascar belong to this family. The most widely known — and feared — genus is *Dichapetalum*, with a number of species which are highly poisonous to man and stock. Fortunately in view of this only 1 species, the low-growing *Dichapetalum cymosum* Engl., the notorious gifblaar, occurs in South Africa, in the central and northern Transvaal, and also in Botswana and South West Africa.

Until a short while ago this was thought to be the only member of the family in South Africa. Recently, however, a species of a second genus, *Tapura*, was found in Zululand, a discovery of considerable botanical interest.

Nearly all the species are shrubs and only occasionally trees, with simple, alternate leaves, and flowers that are bisexual (or unisexual by abortion), with sepals, petals and stamens usually 5, and the ovary superior or "semi-inferior" of 2-3 carpels. The fruit is drupe-like.

Tapura Aubl.

Tapura — a genus with headquarters in tropical Africa and America — is represented in South Africa by 1 species, *Tapura fischeri* Engl.

The members have simple and alternate leaves with tiny stipules that fall early; and bisexual flowers in small clusters in the axils of the leaves, the flower stalk *united with the leaf stalk*. The sepals and petals number 5, the petals being joined at the base to the stamens to form a tube. The stamens are 2-3, and the ovary 2-3-celled. The fruit is a drupe.

The generic name *Tapura* is of uncertain origin.

(304)   *Tapura fischeri* Engl.

Tapura; uMahlosane (Z)

Tapura fischeri was collected for the first time in Tanzania in 1895 and was originally believed a tropical species not extending southwards into South Africa. It grows, however, in coastal forest in Zululand and is one of the uncommon and fascinating trees in the forests around Lake Sibayi.

It is generally considered a small tree, but in Zululand, in deep forest, it is recorded up to 21 m high. In the open, or on forest margins, it is a small bushy tree from 3-11 m high, many-stemmed, with a grey bark and a leafy, often rather yellow-green crown.

The leaves are simple, alternate, thin, widely lance-shaped to egg-shaped, pointed, 2.5-10 cm long and 1.3 to about 8 cm wide, with

Above
Tapura fischeri leaves
and fruits

Left
Tapura fischeri: A flowering twig and fruits
(50%)

undulating edges. They are almost smooth except for small hairy tufts in the axils of the veins about midway up the leaf.

The minute white, sweet-scented flowers are borne in tiny clusters, not in the axil of the leaf stalk but at the *base of the leafblade*, the flower stalk and the leaf stalk uniting — an interesting character pecu-liar to the genus.

The fruit is a small, smooth, plum-shaped drupe.

The wood is reputed to be hard and tough.

The specific name was given in honour of Dr Gustav Adolf Fischer, German physician, who made the first plant collection from Masailand (East Africa) from 1884-1885.

52 The Euphorbia Family (Euphorbiaceae)

Trees, shrubs and herbs make up this huge, widely distributed and fascinating family of over 4000 species.

In one form or another the family is known to everyone. Various rubber trees are members; so is the castor oil plant, the poinsettia of gardens, the euphorbia succulents of South African veld and bush. In stature, in shape, and character, they differ as widely as plants can do, for they may on one hand be weeds a centimetre high, shorter than the lawn grass they invade, or 18 m trees; grotesque succulents or trees of grace and beauty; plants noted for their poisonous latex; fodder plants; trees, such as *Ricinodendron rautanenii* Schinz, with fruit that is a valued food; medicinal plants; timber trees; trees used in arrow poisons or in witchcraft, or which yield the tapioca of nursery puddings.

In South Africa about 60 trees of 29 genera belong to this family, more than to any other family with the exception of Leguminosae and Rubiaceae. They are widely spread over South and South West Africa, in all types of soil and climate. Those of the genus *Euphorbia* are the best known for their abundance and striking cactus-like appearance. They are not in any way related to the cactus family, however, which is centred in the Americas. South Africa has no member at all of this family with the exception of the little slender-stemmed *Rhipsalis baccifera* Stearn. The succulent and often grotesque forms of South African euphorbias have evolved, like those of the cactus — but separated by an ocean's breadth — to meet their own individual needs in a harsh environment.

Many of the members of the family have an abundant milky latex which is often poisonous. As a rule they have simple, alternate leaves most often with stipules that fall soon, usually small flowers, male and female being separate, on the same or different plants, in various types of inflorescences, the perianth sometimes absent in one or both sexes, when present small, the calyx and corolla often different in the male and female flowers, the petals sometimes absent; the male flowers with a varying number of stamens, the female with a superior usually 3-chambered ovary. A disc is frequently present. The fruit is most often a 3-lobed capsule, but occasionally a berry, or a drupe — a fruit with a single kernel surrounded by a fleshy layer. In South African members, the 3-lobed capsule is characteristic and a clue to family identification.

Key to Genera

Leaves simple, opposite

The leaves in pairs at right angles to one another; the stipules large, sheath-like.

13. *Androstachys*

Leaves simple, alternate

The flowers male or female, borne on the same plant, the male often in fascicles or groups in the axils of the leaves, the female solitary; sepals, petals, and stamens 5-6.

1. *Andrachne*

The bark dark, scaling off in large flakes; the flowers male or female on the same plant, the male in short axillary clusters, the female solitary; the sepals 3, the petals 5.

2. *Heywoodia*

The flowers, male or female, on different trees, in small axillary clusters, sepals, petals and stamens usually 5, the fruit a very small capsule.

3. *Lachnostylis*

The flowers male or female on separate trees, the male in short clusters, the female usually solitary, the petals 0; the fruit often large, 3-chambered, somewhat fleshy, indehiscent.

4. *Pseudolachnostylis*

The flowers male or female on separate plants in axillary clusters, the petals 0, the stamens 5, not joined, protruding; the fruit small, round, slightly fleshy.

5. *Sucurinega*

The leaves often appearing compound; the flowers male or female, usually on the same plant, the males usually in clusters, the female few or solitary, the stamens 2-6, united or free; the fruit a capsule, dry or fleshy.

6. *Phyllanthus*

The leaves often large and toothed; the flowers male or female on different trees in the axils of the leaves or on the trunk and older branches; the stamens few to many, not joined; the fruit often large, plus-minus fleshy, indehiscent.

7. *Drypetes*

The leaves glandular below; the flowers male or female on different trees in spikes or racemes; the ovary 2-celled; the fruit a flat winged capsule splitting into parts from the central axis.

8. *Hymenocardia*

The flowers male or female borne on separate trees, the male in spikes, the female in slender racemes; the ovary usually 1-celled; the fruit a small, colourful, 1-seeded drupe.

9. *Antidesma*

The flowers male or female on separate trees (in South Africa), the petals 5 or absent, the stamens 5; the fruit a small 3-chambered capsule.

11. *Cleistanthus*

The leaves usually with conspicuous parallel secondary veins; the flowers male or female, usually on the same tree, with petals; the male in short dense clusters, the female fewer or singly; the fruit fleshy.

12. *Bridelia*

The leaves often with star-like hairs or small scales below, often with 2 glands at the base of the leaf; the flowers male or female usually borne on the same plant in spikes or racemes; petals often present; the fruit a 3-celled capsule.

14. *Croton*

The leaf stalk with swellings at both ends; the flowers large, yellow, with petals, sweetly scented, the male and female borne terminally on separate trees; the fruit a large, woody, usually 4-lobed capsule.

15. *Cavacoa*

The male flowers in widely spaced roundish heads, the female solitary; the young growth (in South Africa) soft; the buds not scaly.

16. *Micrococca*

The male flowers in widely spaced roundish heads, the female solitary; the young growth woody; the stipules sometimes spiny; the buds scaly.

17. *Erythrococca*

The leaves often with 3 nerves from the base, and glands at the base on the under-surface; the flowers male or female on separate trees; the fruit a small 2-3-celled capsule.

18. *Alchornea*

The leaves usually large, gland-dotted, with 3-7 nerves from the base; the flowers male or female usually on separate trees; the fruit a glandular capsule with usually 2 to several cocci (or parts).

19. *Macaranga*

The leaves often small with 3-7 nerves from the base; the flowers male or female, usually on the same plant, sometimes in the same spike; the fruit a 3-lobed, 3-celled capsule.

20. *Acalypha*

The leaves often lobed, alternate or clustered; the flowers male or female usually in the same flower head, the petals 5, the stamens usually 8; the fruit a capsule breaking up into 2-valved parts.

21. *Jatropha*

The flowers, male or female, usually on different plants, the male in clusters in the axils of the leaves, the female usually solitary, with petals, the stamens 5, joined in a tube; the fruit a small roundish, woody capsule splitting in 2-3 parts.

22. *Clutia*

The leaves gland-dotted; the flowers male or female on separate trees, in clusters *opposite the leaves*, without petals, the stamens few to many, free.

24. *Suregada*

The bark typically thick, black, rough, cracked into rectangular sections; the leaves with 2 small glands at the base; the flowers male or female in the same spike arranged spirally, without petals, the calyx usually 5-lobed, the stamens 3 united into a tube.

25. *Spirostachys*

The leaves often with glands at the base; the flowers male or female in the same spike, without petals, the calyx usually 3-lobed, the stamens 2-3, not joined.

26. *Sapium*

The leaves without glands; the flowers male or female, usually in one spike, the males densely packed above, the few or solitary female below, the stamens 1-3, joined below; bracts present.

27. *Maprounea*

A shrub or tree with abundant milky latex; the leaves fleshy; the flowers male and female grouped in a cup-like structure in branching heads.

29. *Synadenium*

Leaves whorled

The leaves in whorls of 4; the flowers male or female on separate plants; the fruit a large, 8-lobed, 4-celled capsule.

10. *Hyaenanche*

Leaves compound

The leaves digitate with 5-7 leaflets with 2 glands at the base of the stalks; the fruit drupe-like.

23. *Ricinodendron*

Apparently leafless

The branches succulent with abundant milky latex, usually bearing spines; the leaves rudimentary and soon falling; the flowers and fruits on the angles of the branches; the flowers male and female grouped together in a cup-like structure.

28. *Euphorbia*

1. *Andrachne* L.

According to E.P. Phillips about 50 species, herbs, undershrubs, or shrubs, usually occurring in the warmer parts of the northern hemisphere, belong to this genus. Only 1 species enters South Africa and it is fairly widely distributed in the eastern part of the country from the Transvaal to the Knysna district.

Leaves that are simple; monoecious flowers — that is, flowers that

Heywoodia lucens growing alongside the road to Umgazi Mouth, Pondoland

are male or female but borne on the same plant — with sepals that number 5-6, with petals and stamens 5-6, and an ovary that is 3-celled with 2 ovules to a cell, and 3-lobed capsules, are characteristic of the genus.

Andrachne is an old Greek name.

(305)   *Andrachne ovalis* (Sond.) Muell. Arg.

= *Phyllanthus ovalis* Sond.

Andrachne; umMbeza (Z)

This sole member of the genus in South Africa is most often an under-shrub in forest, or a small shrub in bush clumps at forest margins or on bushy slopes, but occasionally grows up to 6 m high, and in one form or the other is found from the northern and eastern Transvaal through Natal to the Knysna district.

It is usually many-branched, with a stem up to 15 cm in diameter, and a smooth, light grey bark. The leaves are simple, alternate, bright green or yellow-green and rather stiff, 1.3-5 cm long, widely lance-shaped to egg-shaped, usually with rounded or sometimes pointed tips, and a narrowed base, untoothed, on short stalks, and with small tri-angular stipules.

The tiny flowers are greenish-yellow, the male usually in short clusters in the axils of the leaves, the female solitary. The fruit is a small 3-lobed capsule which turns yellow with age. The seeds are small, brown, and wrinkled.

Among Africans, the tree is famous for its strong-smelling roots which they hawk widely for their power to kill insects and drive away snakes. Powdered roots mixed with milk kill all flies that drink, and an infusion of the root is used to kill fleas, and as a shampoo to kill lice. Powdered and blown into a snake hole, it is believed to chase away snakes. It is used by the Zulus as a snakebite remedy, as an emetic to treat chest complaints, and when burnt and sniffed, as a headache cure.

The specific name *ovalis* is based on the Latin "ovum" meaning "an egg", and refers to the broadly elliptic shape of the leaves.

2. *Heywoodia* Sim

Heywoodia, a genus of 1 species only, has what at present appears to be a strange distribution, for although it grows in the Transkei and Pondo-land coastal forests, in Natal and Zululand, and in Kenya and Tanzania, it has not yet been collected in Portuguese East Africa, Rhodesia or Zambia.

Heywoodia lucens Sim, the sole member, is a tall forest tree with simple alternate leaves. The flowers, male or female, are borne on separate trees, the male in small dense axillary heads, the female in smaller clusters or singly. Petals, numbering 5 in the male flowers, and a fleshy disc, are present. The stamens are 8-12, the outer free, the inner joined at the base. The fruit is a roundish, lobed capsule.

The genus, founded on a specimen from the Transkei, was named by Sim after A.W. Heywood, Conservator of Forests in the Transkei.

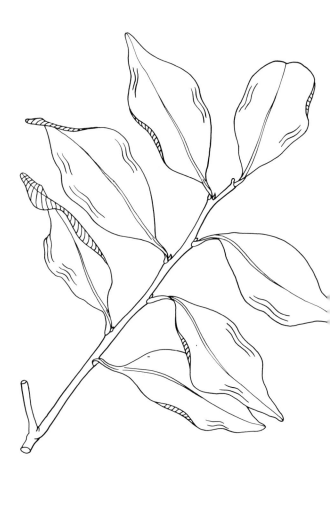

Above left
Heywoodia lucens bark

Above right
Heywoodia lucens leaves (60%)

Left
Heywoodia lucens fruit

(306)   *Heywoodia lucens* Sim

Cape ebony, black ebony, ebbehout, swartebbehout, stinkebbehout;
umNebelele (X); umNebelele, iBeyana (Z)

When Sim first described this tree, which he knew as abundant in the
Transkei in such forests as the Dwessa and Gwebe, and occasional in
east Pondoland, he believed the species was confined to these areas only.
It occurs, however, in southern Natal – a fine specimen grows on the
very edge of the road in the Oribi Gorge Nature Reserve – and in Zululand where trees over 30 m high are reported from the Gwalaweni
Forest. It grows, also, further to the north in Kenya, and Tanzania.

In South Africa it is usually found on fairly dry soils derived from
Table Mountain sandstone, often growing gregariously, as in the Gwebe
forest, where it is dominant in parts.

It is a tall, rather slender evergreen with a clean trunk up to about
1 m in diameter, ashy-grey branches, and a crown of dark green shiny
leaves. The bark is unique – silvery-green to dark brown, scaly, flaking
off in pieces about 5 cm long.

The smooth, stiff, leathery leaves are simple and alternate. Adult
leaves are 4-10 cm long, sometimes widely lance-shaped but most often
in South Africa rather egg-shaped with a rounded or slightly narrowed
base, tapering to the apex, untoothed, with about 4-7 pairs of widely
spaced veins looping along the margin, borne on stalks up to 1.3 cm
long.

Seedling leaves show an interesting variation. They are peltate or
attached to their stalks, not at the margin, as is normal, but by the surface of the blade, slightly inward from the margin.

Male and female flowers are borne on different trees from about
October onwards for several months, the male flowers in greater numbers than the female. They are stalkless and borne in dense clusters,
whereas the tiny female flowers, in the axils of the leaves, are in smaller
clusters or solitary and have short stalks. Although the Cape ebony
has been familiar to botanists and foresters for a long time, the
flowers were not known until this century.

The fruit is a roundish capsule about 1.3 cm wide, 2-lobed, fleshy
and smooth when fresh but wrinkled when dry, with 4-5 ridges on the
surface, splitting explosively into two parts, borne on stalks 1.3 cm
long or shorter. The narrow oblong seeds are light brown, smooth and
shiny. Fruits in various stages of development may often be found at
the same time on one tree.

The wood shows little sapwood, while the heartwood is heavy, hard,
close-grained and strong, dark purple, turning black on exposure, and
very strong-smelling. Africans use it to make sticks.

A professional violin-maker in South Africa successfully used the
wood for the chinrest, fingerboard, frog pegs and tail pieces of a violin
when the traditional imported woods were not available.

The specific name *lucens* is Latin meaning "shining" and refers to
the glossiness of the foliage.

3. *Lachnostylis* Turcz.

Only 2 species, both from the Cape Province, make up this genus. They
are both shrubs or small trees with a limited distribution, with simple,
alternate, leathery, stipulate leaves; male or female flowers borne on

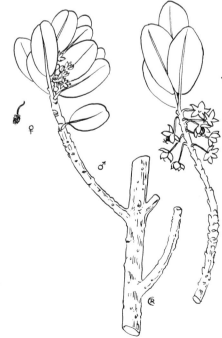

Above left
The klipboom, *Lachnostylis bilocularis,* in Meiringspoort, Cape
Province

Above right
Klipboom bark

Right
Lachnostylis bilocularis: Flowering
twigs (80%)

separate plants, the sepals, petals and stamens 5, the ovary 2-3-chambered, and the fruits small capsules breaking into 2-valved parts.

The generic name is based on the Greek word for "downy", and the Latin for "style", and refers to the hairy style.

(307.1)   *Lachnostylis bilocularis* R.A.Dyer

Klipboom

The klipboom is a many-stemmed shrub, or small tree up to about 6 m high growing among kranses and on rocky slopes in the Little Karoo districts of Oudtshoorn, Ladismith, Uniondale, and Prince Albert. These are all long-settled areas, and it is therefore particularly interesting to note that the tree was collected for the first time as late as 1941 in Meiringspoort by Dr J.D. Keet.

It is conspicuous in this great cutting through the Groot Swartberg, its bright green leafy crown silhouetted against the steep rocky sides of the poort. The stem is up to some 15 or 20 cm in diameter with light brown, corky bark splitting in rectangles. The twiggy crown is composed of many short, knobbly branches and side branchlets with the leaves crowded at their ends. They are simple and alternate, oval or oblong, 1.9-4 cm long and up to 1.3 cm wide, untoothed, velvety when young but the upper side becoming smooth with age, the midrib raised below, carried on short slender stalks.

The flowers, male or female on different trees, are borne on thin stalks in small drooping clusters in the axils of the leaves towards the ends of the twigs. The ovary is 2-celled; the capsule light, roundish, about 6 mm wide, containing small roundish seed.

The specific name means "two-celled" and refers to the 2-celled ovary.

(307)   *Lachnostylis hirta* (L.f.) Muell.Arg.

= *Cluytia hirta* L.f.; = *Lachnostylis capensis* Turcz.

Coalwood, koolhout

The coalwood, which resembles its relative the klipboom in general appearance, has a different distribution and ecology, being a tree of forests, river banks, and rocky wooded slopes in the coastal districts from Swellendam to Port Elizabeth.

It is a small tree up to about 4.5 m high — occasionally up to 9 m — with a much-branched crown, twiggy branches covered with lenticels, and young twigs and stalks which are usually very hairy.

The simple, alternate leaves are egg-shaped to slender, 2.5-5 cm long and up to 1.3 cm wide, bluntly or sharply pointed, narrowed to the base, the margins often undulate, stiff and leathery, the veins conspicuous on both surfaces.

The creamy flowers, male and female borne on separate trees, are in the axils of the leaves, the male in clusters, the female usually singly and on longer stalks than the male. The ovary is 3-celled and not 2-celled as in *Lachnostylis bilocularis*, the capsule 3-celled, roundish, about 8 mm long, containing small wrinkled seeds.

The wood is good fuel and makes excellent charcoal, hence the

Above
The kudu-berry, *Pseudolach-nostylis maprouneifolia,* in the Transvaal bushveld near Groblersdal.

Left
The kudu-berry stem and bark

Right
Pseudolachnostylis maprounei-folia: the leaves and fruits (50%)

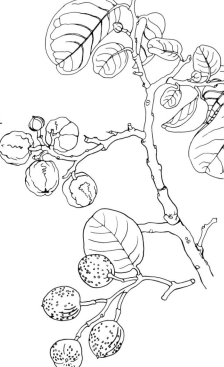

1098

Hibiscus tiliaceus flowers photographed near Kosi Bay

See text page 1449

common names "coalwood" and "koolhout".

The specific name *hirta* means "hairy".

4. *Pseudolachnostylis* Pax

This small genus, native to southern tropical Africa, comprises about 7 species, 1 of which, *Pseudolachnostylis maprouneifolia* Pax, occurs from the Transvaal westwards through Botswana to northern South West Africa.

What was until recently considered a separate species, the tropical *Pseudolachnostylis dekindtii* Pax, which enters northern South West Africa, is now usually included in this species.

Members of the genus have simple alternate leaves, with stipules; male or female flowers borne on different trees, the sepals 5, the petals absent, the stamens 5, the ovary 3-celled; and the fruit round, several seeded, with a thin layer of flesh and indehiscent (in South Africa).

(308) *Pseudolachnostylis maprouneifolia* Pax

= *Pseudolachnostylis dekindtii* Pax; = *Pseudolachnostylis glauca* (Hiern) Hutch.

Kudu-berry, duiker food, duiker tree; nshojowa (Tso); mokonu (Tsw); muṭonḍowa (V); mukunyambambi (Mbuk)

The kudu-berry is widely distributed from tropical Africa southwards to the central and northern Transvaal, Botswana, and northern South West Africa, growing in sandy soil in bushveld, open woodland, and on rocky hill slopes. Trees grow alongside the Great North Road north of Warmbaths in the Transvaal and are common near many of the roads through the Waterberg.

It is usually a small tree up to 6 m high, occasionally reaching 9 m, with a spreading, leafy crown and bark which in a mature tree is brown, yellow or silverish, and rough. The branches are light-coloured and smooth.

The leaves have a particularly fresh, clean appearance. They are simple and alternate, blue-green, and often silvery below, or when young a light, rather yellow green, thin in texture, 2.5-8 cm long, almost round or oval to egg-shaped, with a round base and a round or notched apex, either smooth or softly hairy below, carried on short stalks. Originally only those forms with leaves which were entirely smooth, except for the hairy midrib below, were included in *P. maprouneifolia*, and those with leaves with the under-surface hairy all over were described as *P. dekindtii* Pax. Botanists today tend to regard the two forms as inseparable.

The veining is beautifully distinct with about 4-8 pairs of evenly spaced veins running from the midrib in an upward direction.

The leaves turn bright autumn colours — rich pure yellow, salmon or ruby red — before they fall, and at this time the tree is distinctive.

The small, greenish, inconspicuous male and female flowers are borne on separate trees in the spring, the male in short clusters, the female usually singly on long stalks. They often appear at the same time as the new dark red leaves.

The fruits, with a hard centre and a thin fleshy layer, are round,

Above
The white-berry bush, *Securi-nega virosa*, typically a twiggy shrub or small tree, near Rustenburg, Transvaal

Left
Securinega virosa: A fruiting twig (100%)

1100

about 1.9 cm in diameter with a small jutting point, greenish-yellow speckled with white or yellow, becoming wrinkled with age. When ripe in the autumn they make, with the silvery-green leaves, a particularly soft and subtle colour combination.

They are eaten by antelope — kudu and duiker in particular are very fond of them and give the tree its common names — and by elephant, which also eat the leaves. One African name in the north western Transvaal means "Hyaena-kudu". They are also eaten by birds such as doves.

The wood is a light colour with dark streaks, smooth-grained, and with a strong smell when worked. It is used to make small articles and Africans employ the tree medicinally.

As far as is known all parts of the tree are harmless.

Keith Coates Palgrave says that in Malawi this is a sacred tree, women gathering crops from a field always laying several small bunches of grain at its foot.

It is said to be strongly fire-resistant.

The specific name means "with Maprounea-like leaves", *Maprounea* being another genus of the same family.

5. *Securinega* Comm. ex Juss.

This small genus of temperate and tropical countries takes its name from one of the outstanding characteristics of most of its members — their very hard wood — for *Securinega* is based on the Latin words for "hatchet" and "refuse" because the wood cannot be cut easily.

Only 1 species enters South and South West Africa, *Securinega virosa* (Roxb. ex Willd.) Pax & K.Hoffm., at one time known as *Fluggea virosa* (Roxb. ex Willd.) Baill.

All the members of the genus have simple, alternate, untoothed leaves with stipules, **and m**ale and female flowers borne on different plants, the male in **tufts in** the axils of the leaves, the female few or solitary. They are without petals, with 5 sepals, the male with 5 stamens and a rudimentary ovary, the female with a 3-celled ovary. The fruit is small, round, and in South Africa white and slightly fleshy.

(309)   *Securinega virosa* (Roxb. ex Willd.) Baill.

= *Phyllanthus virosus* Roxb. ex Willd.; = *Fluggea virosa* (Roxb. ex Willd.) Baill.; = *Fluggea microcarpa* Blume

White-berry bush; umYaweyawe (Z); nhlangaume (Tso); muṭangauma (V)

The type specimen of this little tree is from India, for the species ranges widely from Asia, through tropical Africa, to South and South West Africa. In the Republic it grows from the northern, eastern and central Transvaal to Zululand, Natal and Swaziland, and in the Orange Free State — it is particularly abundant in the Willem Pretorius Game Reserve. It occurs, also, to the west in Botswana, northern South West Africa, and the Caprivi Strip. It grows mainly in bush, on forest margins, and on stony koppies.

Most often it is a dense, much-branched shrub, but sometimes a small spreading and rather twiggy tree up to about 3.6 m high, evergreen or deciduous, with smooth, angular, spine-tipped branches and a stem up to about 8 cm in diameter.

Above
Phyllanthus reticulatus and *Hexa-lobus monopetalus* growing together, their branches intertwined, in Punda Milia camp in the Kruger National Park

Left
Phyllanthus reticulatus: Leaves, flowers and fruits (70%)

1102

The leaves are simple and alternate, and crowded up the twigs. They are usually small, 1.3-2.5 cm long, but sometimes up to 6 cm long and 3 cm wide, oval to egg-shaped, with a round, bluntly pointed or notched tip and a round or narrowed base, smooth, and a light green in colour, sometimes with a bluish tinge. They are eaten by impala and kudu.

The tiny green male and female flowers are borne on separate plants in clusters in the axils of the leaves.

The fruits are about 5 mm in diameter, round, slightly lobed, and a waxy white, containing small shiny seed. They are eaten by several species of hornbills.

The wood is white, very strong, tough and elastic, and is used for fencing posts and fish traps. E.E.Galpin says that in the Springbok Flats it is used for whipsticks and other purposes where a thin but strong wood is required. Leafy branches are used as brooms, and occasionally the tree is planted as a hedge.

It is said to be an indicator of underground water.

The specific name *virosa* is Latin meaning "with an unpleasant smell" and refers to the strong smell of the leaves.

6. *Phyllanthus* L.

Phyllanthus, unlike *Securinega* which it resembles, is a huge genus with over 800 described species, spread throughout the tropical countries of the world. About 21 species grow in South and South West Africa, of which 2 or 3 are trees, and one, *Phyllanthus reticulatus* Poir., is usually a shrub but occasionally a tree.

All the species in the genus in South Africa have simple, alternate leaves with stipules, and male or female flowers usually borne on the same plant but sometimes on separate plants, the male in axillary tufts, the female usually singly. They are without petals and have 4-6 sepals and 2-6 stamens, and the females a 3-celled ovary. The fruit is a capsule, dry or fleshy, splitting into 2-valved parts. Botanists note that, unlike those of *Securinega*, the male flowers have no rudimentary ovary.

The name *Phyllanthus* is based on Greek words meaning "leaf-flower", because in some species of the genus the flowers are produced at the edges of leaf-like branches.

(312.1)   *Phyllanthus reticulatus* Poir.

Roast potato plant; inTaba yengwe (Z); thethenya (Tso); makhulu-wa-mutangauma (V)

This is a widespread plant distributed all over tropical Africa and extending southwards to South and South West Africa and Botswana. It is common in the lowveld of the northern and eastern Transvaal, Swaziland and Zululand in dry bushveld and riverine bush, and in northern South West Africa.

Wherever it grows this species is remarkable for its smell of half-cooked potatoes. The whole tree at certain times smells faintly of potatoes, but the strong all-pervading smell is given off by the flowers, and on still mornings and evenings from winter to spring in particular their scent is spread very widely.

This homely smell, known through the world wherever potatoes are

The Egossa red pear, *Phyllanthus discoideus*, growing in coastal forest, Umpambinyoni, near Scottburgh

cooked, suddenly encountered in the bush many miles from any habitation, tantalizes and baffles travellers from the South African lowveld to Central Africa. It is an elusive smell, difficult to track down, for a small plant no more than a few centimetres high scents a large area.

Although the potato plant is usually a shrub from 0.3-1.5 m high, it is sometimes a tree up to 8 m, and in tree form is sometimes found north of the Soutpansberg in the Transvaal, and in the Pongola valley in Zululand. At Punda Milia a small tree, intertwined with a *Hexalobus monopetalus*, grows in the centre of the camp near the office, while a slender tree grows in the grounds of the Letaba Camp in the Kruger National Park.

The stems are grey, hairy when young, becoming smooth with age. Superficially the leaves appear compound, but are in fact simple, the small, soft, neat leaves growing alternately up the slender flexible twigs. They are oval to oblong, 0.8-2.5 cm long, with round or pointed tips, smooth or hairy, and shortly stalked. They are eaten by elephants.

The tiny greenish-yellow or reddish flowers are crowded together up the twigs in the axils of the fallen leaves, 1 female and several male flowers grouped together. The fruits are very small, roundish, green turning red-brown and later purplish-black, and usually densely packed down the twigs. They are eaten by birds such as weavers, and by Livingstone's Antelope, Red and Grey Duiker, and Vervet Monkeys.

Watt and Brandwijk say than in Tanzania the root and fruit are used for criminal poisoning, and that the root is used to dye fishing lines black. They add that the foliage is possibly eaten by stock.

In Zululand the plant has unusual uses, for water, in which the root bark has been soaked, is a magical bath or drink, enabling he who uses it to hide all secrets from the witchdoctor. Such a man then vomits into a hole which he covers with sand, thus burying the "sickness" together with his innermost feelings and secrets, and freeing himself from the witchdoctor's influence.

When mixed with several other ingredients such as the root-bark of *Balanites maughamii* and water, stirred vigorously three times a day and the froth then licked off without the use of the hands, it is believed by Zulus to give clear and penetrating vision.

The specific name *reticulatus* means "netted" and refers to the veining of the leaves.

It should be noted that this species — in spite of its common name — is far removed from the potato family, Solonaceae.

(311)   *Phyllanthus discoideus* (Baill.) Muell.Arg.

= *Cicca discoidea* Baill.; = *Phyllanthus amopondensis* Sim. (*Phyllanthus flacourtioides* Hutch. is included in this species by some botanists).

Egossa red pear, Egossa rooipeer; umPhunzito (X); umDlulamazembe, isiBangamlotha, uMadlozini (Z)

The Egossa red pear, as *Phyllanthus discoideus* is most commonly known in South Africa, is a fairly common and outstandingly beautiful tree of moist areas and deep soil, usually in forested valleys, at the edges of swamps, and on river banks from tropical Africa to the Cape Province. In S. Africa it grows in coastal forest from Pondoland northwards to Zululand, and in the forests of the eastern and northern Transvaal. Fine specimens grow on the Natal south coast in such places as the lovely

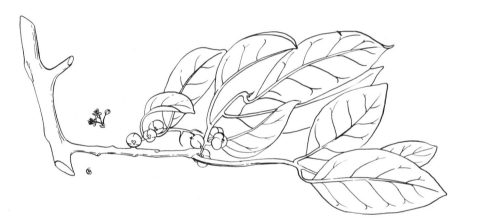

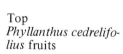

Top
Phyllanthus cedrelifolius fruits

Centre left
Phyllanthus discoideus: male flowers, and a fruiting twig (60%)

Centre right
Phyllanthus cedrelifolius: the neat simple leaves (50%)

Left
The bark of *Phyllanthus discoideus*

forested Umpambimyoni, or Ifafa Lagoon where the trees are labelled and easily accessible.

This is a semi-deciduous tree 6-15 m high, with a spreading crown and a straight, sometimes buttressed trunk, the bark flaky, light brown, greyish-brown or reddish, scaling off in irregular pieces to show a red-brown colour below.

The young branches are a smooth, mottled grey; the small branches grow upwards and the twigs, covered with small white dots, and leaves are held flatly in one plane. The twigs are slightly angled between the leaves.

The leaves are simple, alternate, smooth and untoothed, shortly stalked, with neat parallel herringbone veins running from the midrib towards the margin, these and the midrib being raised below. They are oval, egg-shaped or widely lance-shaped, pointed or with round tips, with a rounded or narrowed base, somewhat like those of *Bridelia micrantha* (Hochst.) Baill, in appearance.

Their size depends on the conditions under which the trees grow. In moist areas the leaves are up to 9 cm long and 5 cm broad, in drier parts often no more than 1.9 cm long.

Male and female flowers are borne on different trees, the male on slender stalks in axillary tufts, the female singly or in pairs in the axils of the leaves. The small dry fruit is a 3-celled capsule, clover-like in outline, about 8 mm in diameter, containing smooth dark seeds with one flat and one rounded side. The seeds are eaten by Crested Guinea-fowl and doves such as the Emerald-spotted Wood Dove.

The sapwood is light grey, the heartwood red-brown or pale red, hard, dense, heavy and durable, and capable of taking a good polish. The punt at Port St. John's, once known to many visitors, was built of it. The ash, bark, leaves and twigs are used medicinally.

The specific name is based on the disc or round platform of the male flower from which the stamens spring.

There is some doubt as to whether *Phyllanthus flacourtioides* Hutch., with somewhat the same distribution, is distinct from this species. *Flora Capensis* separates them mainly on the form of the disc in the male flower, the disc being entire in *Phyllanthus discoideus* and with separate glands in *Phyllanthus flacourtioides*. Botanists today consider it possible that the two species are inseparable.

(310)   *Phyllanthus cedrelifolius* Verdoorn

This small deciduous tree, once thought native only to the forests of the Transkei, is now known to occur in Zululand in the Ngoye Forest. It remains, however, a rare and little known tree.

It has been collected as a small tree only, up to about 9 m high but usually smaller, with a rough bark and very slender leafy branches in a close spiral at the end of the main branches. The slender whippy branchlets with the neat simple leaves arranged alternately along them look like large compound leaves up to 0.6 m long, and have at times been thought compound by their collectors.

The leaves are smooth, untoothed, up to 5 cm long and 2.5 cm broad, widely lance-shaped to egg-shaped, with round or somewhat pointed tips, and the bases rounded or slightly narrowed. Stipules are present.

The tiny flowers are male or female grouped together on the same

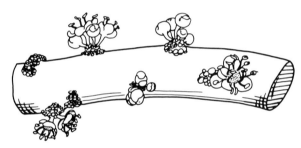

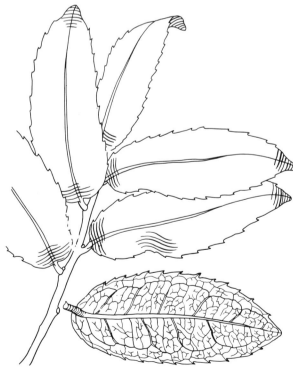

Top
Drypetes natalensis in a Durban
park

Above left
Drypetes natalensis: the flowers
growing on the old wood (50%)

Right
Drypetes natalensis leaves (50%)

1108

tree in long string-like inflorescences which are usually bunched on very short knob-like side branches. They bloom in early spring.

The fruit is a round capsule about 1.9 cm in diameter.

The specific name refers to the fact that the tree resembles a cedrela in general appearance.

7. *Drypetes* Vahl

Drypetes is a large genus of over 150 species distributed mainly in the Old World. Three species occur in South Africa, from the Transkei to the Transvaal, as either trees or shrubs. They are characterized by simple, alternate leaves, often sharply toothed, stipules that fall early, and male or female flowers borne on separate trees, in the axils of the leaves or on the trunk and older branches. They are without petals, the sepals 4-5, a disc present, the stamens 3 to many, the ovary 1-4-celled, the fruit fleshy, sometimes large, and indehiscent.

The name *Drypetes* is Greek and means "ready to fall from the tree", presumably referring to the large heavy fruit of some species.

(316) *Drypetes natalensis* (Harv.) Hutch.

= *Cyclostemon natalense* Harv.

Natal drypetes, stinkbos; iKhushwane elikhulu, umBejiza, umGunguluza (Z)

This shrub to tall tree, mainly of coastal forests in Natal and Zululand, extends northwards through Portuguese East Africa and Rhodesia to central and eastern tropical Africa.

It is a fine evergreen, sometimes with a single smoothish grey trunk, at others many-stemmed, with smooth or almost smooth twigs and sprays of leaves borne in one plane.

The stiff leaves are glossy, sometimes undulating, large and handsome, in South Africa up to about 15 cm long and 7.6 cm broad, oblong to oval, sharply or bluntly pointed, with a base that is somewhat rounded and slightly unequal, usually with sharply and widely toothed margins, dark green above and lighter below, with the midrib and secondary veins dull yellow and raised below. Occasionally the leaves are almost without teeth. They are borne on short strong stalks.

The male and female flowers are borne abundantly in the spring on separate trees in bunches on the older branches or on the trunk, either in small groups or massed densely together. In the dim light of a forest these pale yellow flowers on the bare dark branches are a strange and unreal sight. They have a strong and rather unpleasant smell.

The fruits, from the size of a large cherry to that of a naartjie, are roundish, with 3 compartments, wrinkled, velvety, green turning yellow, without stalks, borne singly or in compact clusters. They ripen about March and are eaten by monkeys.

The wood is used for roofing material, lathes, sticks, and fuel.

The specific name means "of Natal". The common name "stinkbos" refers to the unpleasant smell of the flowers — an unfortunate name for so handsome a species.

Above left
The fruits of *Drypetes gerrardii*

Above right
Bark of *Drypetes gerrardii*

Left
A typical stem of *Drypetes gerrardii*

Below
Drypetes gerrardii: The leaves, and female flowers with
the fruits forming (60%)

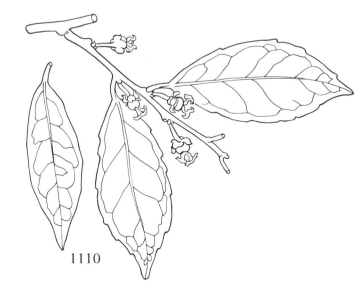

1110

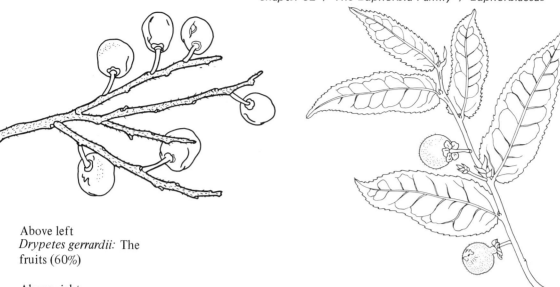

Above left
Drypetes gerrardii: The
fruits (60%)

Above right
Drypetes arguta: A fruiting twig (50%)

(313)   *Drypetes arguta* (Muell.Arg.) Hutch.

= *Cyclostemon argutus* Muell.Arg.

Kushwane tree; bastard white ironwood; umHlagela (X); umKushwane, isiKhwelamfene (Z)

The kushwane tree is an evergreen shrub or tree in coastal forest or bush, often growing on stream banks, from Port St. John's northwards through Natal and Zululand to Portuguese East Africa.
    It has a brown, slightly rough bark cracked in squares, and simple, alternate leaves. These are widely lance-shaped, oblong or egg-shaped, with a round, uneven, notched base, tapering to the pointed apex, sharply toothed, 4-8 cm long, borne on very short leaf stalks. They resemble the leaves of *Drypetes natalensis* but usually have a more tapered apex.
    The yellow, stalked male or female flowers are borne on separate trees in the axils of the leaves of the young growth. The round, apricot-red fruit is about 1.9 cm in diameter and 2-celled. It is edible and Africans make an intoxicating liquor from it.
    Good sticks are made from the wood.
    The specific name *arguta* means "sharp", referring either to the apex or to the sharply toothed margins.

(314)   *Drypetes gerrardii* Hutch.

= *Cyclostemon argutus* Sim

Forest ironwood; umThwakele, umHlwakele (Z)

The forest ironwood is a small to large evergreen tree growing from Port St. John's northward through Natal, Swaziland and Zululand to tropical Africa, usually on well-drained soils, in forest, wooded kloofs, on forest margins, and in bush.
    In forest it may often be identified by its trunk which is mottled grey or light-coloured, fairly slender and much buttressed, fluted, and folded to 6 or 9 m above the ground.
    The twigs are hairy, the leaves variable in shape and size. They are

1111

simple, alternate, stiff, deep green above and lighter below, and usually widely and bluntly toothed, but sometimes with almost entire margins. They are widely lance-shaped to egg-shaped, usually with a long jutting point with a blunt tip, and a somewhat rounded or narrowed, unequal base, 4-9 cm long and up to 5 cm broad, the midrib hairy on both sides, with secondary veins and the network of veins prominent below. They are borne on short, sturdy, furry stalks.

The small, yellow male or female flowers, borne on separate trees, are in the leaf axils, the male in clusters, the female solitary.

The fruits, with a small rim-like calyx, are up to 2.5 cm in diameter and 1.9 cm wide, yellow, softly hairy, with a thin layer of edible pulp which smells when ripe like dried apricots, enclosing 2 large oval seeds about 1.3 cm long. They ripen about March.

The hard white timber is used by Zulus to make sticks.

The specific name commemorates William T.Gerrard, botanical collector in Natal in the 19th century.

(315)   *Drypetes mossambicensis* Hutch.

"The drypetes of Mozambique" — it was from this territory that the species was first described — is a tropical species extending southwards into the Transvaal where it has been collected in the sandveld of the northern Kruger National Park near the Portuguese border.

It is a medium-sized to big tree with a whitish-grey stem, or sometimes several stems, the bark cracked into small squares and sometimes flaking.

The dark green shiny leaves are simple and alternate, oblong to egg-shaped, with the apex usually rounded or notched, and with a conspicuously unequal base, untoothed, up to 9 cm long and 1.3 cm wide, smooth below or with the midrib slightly hairy.

The small lime-green or yellow flowers are in clusters in the axils of the leaves — male and female on different trees. The fruit, up to about 1.3 cm long, is egg-shaped or round, smooth (unlike that of *Drypetes gerrardii*) and crowned with conspicuous persistent paired styles. It has "a pip prized by natives and birds".

8. *Hymenocardia* Wall.

Hymenocardia is a small, mainly African genus of trees and shrubs, with 1 species recorded from Zululand and the Transvaal, extending northwards into tropical Africa.

Members of the genus have simple, alternate leaves and male or female flowers borne on different trees, the male in spikes, the female in short racemes. They have no petals. The calyx lobes number 4-5, the stamens usually 5, and the ovary is 2-celled. The fruit is a distinctive capsule with membraneous wings, splitting into 2 parts from a central axis. The generic name, based on the Greek "hymen" meaning "membrane", and "cardo" meaning "hinge" refers to this fruit.

(317)   *Hymenocardia ulmoides* Oliv.

= *Hymenocardia ulmoides* var. *capensis* Pax; =*Hymenocardia capensis* Hutch.

Hymenocardia; umAndla, iTsatsalathane (Z)

Above left
The bark of *Hymenocardia ulmoides*

Above right
Hymenocardia ulmoides north east of Sibasa

This delicate, fine-leaved tree, "the hymenocardia with the elm-like habit" as the specific name suggests, grows — often in numbers together — from northern Zululand and the northern Transvaal to tropical Africa, in dense coastal forest, in woodland and bush clumps, sometimes bordering swamps, and usually on sandy soil.

Although most often in South Africa a bush or a slender tree, in Zululand it is recorded up to 21 m high with a trunk diameter of 0.6 m. The grey or light brown trunk is rough, often finely and shallowly cracked lengthwise, and the branchlets are slender and smooth.

The shiny neat leaves, red in spring but becoming dark green later, are egg-shaped, oval or lance-shaped, untoothed, bluntly pointed, with a round or narrow base, and usually with tufts of hair in the axils of the secondary nerves. The midrib below is often reddish and hairy, and the leaves are borne on short slender red petioles. Their size varies. In South Africa they are usually small — under 4 cm long — although in tropical Africa they may be larger, much broader, sometimes with a long tapering point.

The small pink male or female flowers are carried on separate trees, the males in spikes on short side branchlets, the female in clusters in the axils of the leaves.

The fruits, about 1.3-1.9 cm in diameter, are roundish flat capsules entirely surrounded — except for a notch at the tip — by a papery wing, yellow turning red or carmine. They are borne in a bunch on a slender stalk. Ripe fruits tinge the trees with colour in late autumn and early winter, and in Zululand, as in the bush around Lake St. Lucia, they are then a common and conspicuous sight.

The wood is strong, straight and elastic, and makes good fencing posts, roofing material for huts, and the framework of the basket traps used in Tongaland for fishing, and for fish kraals. It also provides good fuel.

Stock and game browse the foliage.

Parts of the tree are used medicinally.

This species is sometimes confused with *Pteliopsis myrtifolia* (Laws.) Engl. & Diels of the combretum family. The fruits of the *Pteliopsis*, however, are squarish with 2, 3 or 4 conspicuous wings.

Above
The tassel-berry tree, *Antidesma venosum,* on the golf course Mtunzini

Centre left
Antidesma venosum: A fruiting twig (50%)

Below left
Male flowers of the tassel-berry tree, photographed in December

Below right
The fruits

The wild pear, *Dombeya rotundifolia,* in bloom near Pretoria

See text page 1474

9. *Antidesma* L.

About 245 species, according to E.P. Phillips, belong to this genus and are distributed throughout the warmer regions of the Old World. They are trees or shrubs with large, simple, untoothed leaves with stipules, and with male or female flowers which are borne separately, the male often in spikes and the female in racemes. They have no petals, a calyx that is small with 3-5 segments, the stamens in the male 2-5, the female with an ovary that is usually 1-celled, and fruit that is a drupe.

One species occurs in South Africa from Pondoland to the Transvaal, in Botswana and in northern South West Africa.

The genus takes its name from the Greek words "anti" meaning "for", and "demos" meaning "band", because the bark of one species is used for cordage.

(318)   *Antidesma venosum* E.Mey. ex Tul.

Tassel-berry; isaNgowane, umNangazi, isiBangamlotha (Z); inHlalama-hubulu, umHlalanyoni (Sw); phalakhwari (Tso); moingwe (Tsw); mufhala-khwali, mupala-khwali (V); simai (Kol); muxuva (Sarwa)

The tassel-berry is a common, and in fruit a most beautiful, tree of coastal bush, forest margins and river banks from Port St. John's to Zululand, and inland of open savannah, bush and grassland, in the eastern and northern Transvaal, Swaziland, Botswana, northern South West Africa, and tropical Africa.

It is usually a shrub or a small tree, although in the Ngoye Forest in Zululand it reaches 15 m in height. It may be rounded and spreading or have a slender drooping crown, and is nearly always graceful.

The bark is pale and flaky, and the young twigs are covered with red hairs. The leaves are simple and alternate, untoothed and usually large, 2.5-15 cm long and 1.9-10 cm wide, egg-shaped, oval, oblong or lance-shaped, with a somewhat rounded or bluntly pointed tip, and a rounded or narrowed base, smooth or hairy above, and below thinly or densely covered with hairs which are often rusty red; with about 7 pairs of conspicuous veins, branching and looping along the margin. They are borne on short hairy stalks.

The leaves and shoots are browsed by kudu.

The small greenish flowers are male or female borne on separate trees, the male in spikes, the female in slender racemes. The fruit is a small, 1-seeded drupe borne densely in a long tassel-like bunch, oval, slightly flattened, green turning yellow, pink, red, and black. Fruits at all stages of ripening and of all colours are crowded in a bunch giving a gay and beautiful effect. The fruits are often borne abundantly, the whole tree then being festooned with many-coloured shiny tassels, and at such a time there is little to equal this as a decoration in the forest, on a stream bank, or in a garden.

The mulberry-tasting fruits are favourites with most fruit-eating birds, with impala, with monkey, Africans, and with children of all races (although they are said to be unwholesome and not easily digested by humans).

Both the yellow sapwood and the dark heartwood are dense, hard, and fine, but usually small. The tree is used medicinally by the Bantu, particularly as a dysentry cure. An infusion of the flaked roots, soaked

Above left
The gifboom, *Hyaenanche globosa,* on the farm "Zandkraal" on the slopes of the Gifberg, western Cape

Above right
The gifboom often grows as a bushy tree

Left
Bark of the gifboom

Right
Hyaenanche globasa: A flowering twig and the fruits (80%)

in water, is a bath to ease body aches. It is also used, together
with *Bridelia cathartica* Bertol.f. and the roots of a *Kalanchoe* species,
to ensure fertility, the infusion in which the roots have been boiled
being bottled and a dose being taken three times a day.

According to Watt and Brandwijk the root is toxic and is used in
magic.

This is an exceptionally fine garden tree. Its glory lies in its fruit and
it should be remembered that both a male and a female tree are necessary
to produce this.

The specific name *venosum* is Latin and means "conspicuously veined" in reference to the bold veining of the leaves. The Zulu isiBangamlotha means "makes ash", and the Swazi inHlalamahubulu means
"raven's perch".

10. *Hyaenanche* Lamb.

Hyaenanche is a genus of 1 species confined to the Western Cape.

The single species, *Hyaenanche globosa* (Gaertn.) Lamb. has simple
leathery leaves in whorls of 4, male or female flowers borne on different
trees, the male in small, short, dense, axillary clusters, the female (without stalks) solitary or in groups of up to 3. Petals and disc are absent.
The sepals number 5-6, the stamens in the male are an indefinite
number, and the ovary in the female is 3-4-chambered. The fruit is a
roundish capsule, usually 4-chambered, 8-lobed, splitting open. The
seeds are black and shiny.

The name *Hyaenanche* is Greek, meaning "hyaena poison", and was
given by the botanist Lambert because the fruits were used in bait to
poison hyaenas.

(319)   *Hyaenanche globosa* (Gaertn.) Lamb.

= *Jatrophe globosa* Gaertn.; = *Toxicodendrum capense* Thunb.

Gifboom, hyaena poison, wolwegifboom, boesmansgif, wolweboom,
wolweboontjie

This little tree or shrub from the Van Rhynsdorp and Clanwilliam districts of the western Cape played a part in the early history of South
Africa, for its poisonous seeds are reputed to have made a Bushman
arrow poison, while the early colonists used the pounded seeds in a bait
to kill hyaenas and other wild animals. It was first discovered on the
Van der Stel expedition to Namaqualand in 1685. Colonel Robert
Gordon, the soldier-artist who named the Orange River in the late 18th
century, knew and painted this tree.

The Gifberg range near Van Rhynsdorp is named after the trees
which grow — or once grew — in numbers on it, along streams and in
gullies, at an altitude of 245-365 m above the surrounding country,
forming — according to Marloth — "large shrubs 3 m high very similar
in foliage to another occupant of such situations, the kliphout, *Heeria
argentea*".

Although much of the original vegetation has been destroyed by fire,
these two species may still be found growing side by side, as on the
farm Zandkraal where the accompanying photographs of the gifboom
were taken. They grew together on the lower slopes of the mountain in
company with *Protea laurifolia.*

Above left
Cleistanthus schlechteri near the shores of Lake
St. Lucia, Zululand

Above right
Bark of *Cleistanthus schlechteri*

Below left
Female flowers of *Cleistanthus schlechteri*

Centre right
Cleistanthus schlechteri: A fruiting twig, an individual fruit split open, and the seeds (50%)

Below right
Cleistanthus schlechteri: The leaves (50%)

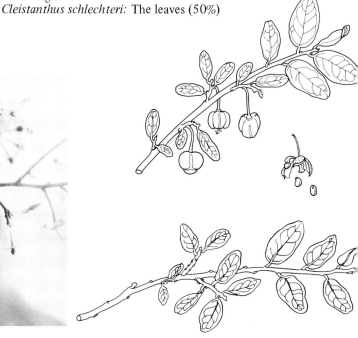

This is a dark bushy erect shrub or small tree up to 4.5 m high with a light grey stem covered with small lenticels, with corky branches, and with grooved hairy twigs becoming smooth with age.

The simple, large, thick leaves, slightly hairy when young, becoming quite smooth with age, are arranged in whorls of 3 to 4. They are usually 4-10 cm long, occasionally up to 20 cm, and 1.3-4 cm broad, lance-shaped, with round, bluntly pointed or notched tips, gradually narrowing to the base, with the yellow midrib conspicuous on the under-surface. They are carried on short stalks.

The shortly stalked wine-coloured male flowers are in dense clusters in the axils of the leaves. The sturdy stalkless female flowers are borne singly or in small groups of up to 3 between each leaf axil.

The fruit is a lobed capsule, green when immature in early spring, brownish-yellow when fully ripe, and this, according to C.A.Smith, "dehisces in sunshine with a crackling noise", into clearly marked segments. It is roughly 2.5 cm in diameter and usually 4-celled, each cell mostly containing 1 roundish, black, shiny seed. These, and to a much lesser degree the leaves and stem, contain toxic principles known as hyaenanchin and isohyaenanchin.Watt and Brandwijk say that although the action of hyaenanchin has been likened to that of strychnine, its action is almost identical to that of picrotoxin and it is about a quarter as powerful as strychnine.

In the past these pounded seeds were used in bait to poison hyaenas and Patterson in 1778 recorded that the Bushmen used the nuts in an arrow poison. It is said that animals have been poisoned by drinking water into which some of the leaves had fallen.

11. *Cleistanthus* Hook.f.

About 50 species, mostly Asian and Malayan, belong to this genus. One tropical African species reaches south into northern Zululand.

The genus is characterized by leaves that are simple and alternate, small flowers that are male or female, either borne on the same tree or separately, the calyx segments 5, the petals, when present, 5, the stamens 5; the ovary 3-celled, the fruits small and often 3-lobed capsules.

The generic name is based on the Greek word "kleio" meaning "closed", and "anthus" meaning "flower", referring to the fact that the flowers remain partially closed.

(320)   *Cleistanthus schlechteri* (Pax) Hutch.

= *Securinega schlechteri* Pax

Umzithi tree; umZithi (Z)

This fine, tall tropical African tree extends southwards into the northern districts of Zululand where it grows in coastal and open forest on sandy soil, and often on the banks of streams.

It is usually more pear-shaped than spreading, with a tall, straight, light or dark grey trunk up to 46 cm or occasionally more in diameter, and a crown of deep green, glossy leaves. These are simple and alternate, 1.3-5 cm long, oval or widely lance-shaped, with a bluntly pointed or rounded tip and a rounded base, shiny green above, duller and paler below, with about 4 pairs of secondary veins, and these, the

Above
Bridelia mollis on the hills close to the Hartebeestpoort
Dam, Transvaal

Left
The leaves and flowers of *Bridelia mollis*

Below
Bridelia mollis: The leaves and fruits (50%)

Opposite
Stem and bark of *Bridelia mollis*

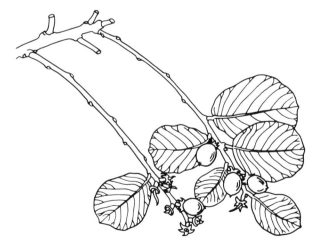

1120

midrib, and netted veins are conspicuous below.

The small, greenish, scented flowers, male or female, are borne on separate trees.

The fruit is a 3-lobed roundish capsule, 0.8-1.9 cm wide, splitting into 3 compartments, each 2-valved, with 1 or more seeds, borne on a long slender stalk in the axils of the leaves. The seeds are eaten by birds such as Turtle Doves, Emerald-spotted Wood Doves, Crested Guinea-fowl and francolins. The leaves are eaten by Red Duiker and Sumi antelope.

The dark brown wood is very hard — in Zululand considered one of the hardest of the local woods. It is used in hut-building, for particularly good sticks, and as fuel.

12. *Bridelia* Willd.

Roughly 40 species of trees and shrubs in tropical Asia, the Malay Archipelago, New Caledonia, Australia, and tropical Africa belong to this genus. Several species grow in South and South West Africa, of which 3 are trees.

All the species have simple, alternate, untoothed leaves; flowers, which are male or female and usually borne on the same tree, the male flowers in short dense clusters, the female fewer or singly, the sepals, petals and stamens 5, the ovary usually 2-chambered, a disc present; the fruits capsules separating into 2 portions or in South Africa drupe-like and fleshy.

The generic name honours the great muscologist, Professor Samuel Elisée Bridel, 1761-1828.

(325)   *Bridelia mollis* Hutch.

Bushveld bridelia; swatima (Tso); mokokwele (Tsw — Kgat); mokoko-kwenana (Tsw — Kwena); mokokonana (Tsw — Ngwak), mokokole (Tsw — Mal), mokamanawe (Tsw — Taw); mukumba-kumba (V); mota-kwabula (Sub); nkumbankumba (Kal)

Bridelia mollis is a small deciduous tree or shrub growing from the central and northern Transvaal westwards to Botswana and northern South West Africa, and northwards to tropical Africa. It often occurs on rocky hills, and is common on the Magaliesberg, the Waterberg and the Soutpansberg in the Transvaal, and sometimes in dry open bushveld.

It seldom grows more than 8 m high, and often is no more than 3 or 4.5 m, an ornamental tree with a thick, leafy, rounded crown and often a drooping habit of growth.

The bark is a rough, greyish-brown. The soft, velvety leaves are simple and alternate, 2.5-13 cm long and 1.3-9 cm broad, round or oval, often widest in the upper portion, with a flattish and sometimes notched tip, with a narrowed or a rounded and sometimes notched base, with the midrib raised both sides and the secondary veins running neatly and regularly, rather steeply upwards from the midrib to the margin. The short leaf stalks, stipules, and young twigs are all densely velvety.

The small green or reddish-yellow male or female flowers, unlike those of many of the family, have petals. They are borne on short stalks in the axils of the leaves in early summer. The round fruits, about

Left
The stem of *Bridelia cathartica* subsp. *cathartica*

Right
Bridelia cathartica subsp. *cathartica:* A fruiting twig (60%)

the size of peas, are green covered with small white dots, turning black when ripe in the autumn, and are borne singly on short stalks. They contain a hard seed, surrounded by a thin layer of pulp of the consistency and flavour of a prune which is edible and relished by children and by birds. The pressed fruits are said to exude a clear gum which is used in country districts to make jam. These shiny dark fruits often remain on the tree after the leaves have fallen.

In parts, Africans believe the tree has magical properties, and will not use it as firewood. If this embargo is broken, their cows — they believe — will never bear heifer calves.

The specific name *mollis* means "soft", and refers to the soft velvety foliage.

(322) *Bridelia cathartica* Bertol.f.
   1. subsp. *cathartica*

= *Bridelia schlechteri* Hutch.

(322.1)   2. subsp. *melanthesoides* (Klotzsch) J.Léon.

umNwangazi, umNangasi (Z)

One or other of the two subspecies of this species is distributed widely from Zululand, Swaziland and the Transvaal westwards to Botswana and northern South West Africa, and northwards into tropical Africa, in bush, on forest edges, and often on river banks. The two subspecies are separated mainly on a small difference in the veining and some botanists consider them inseparable.

This is usually a small tree, many-stemmed or with a clean trunk, light brown or grey, sometimes banded with white, and shallowly furrowed lengthwise. The branches are slender and drooping, the twigs

1122

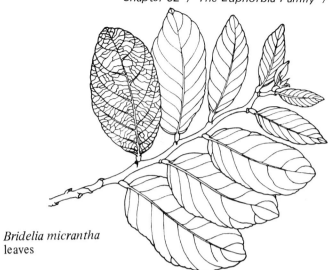

Bridelia micrantha
leaves

brown and knobbly, and the crown small and round with dense, dark green leaves with a dull shine.

The simple alternate leaves are widely lance-shaped, egg-shaped, oval or oblong, often broadest above the middle, with a pointed or round apex, and a narrowed or rounded base, 4-8 cm long and up to 5 cm broad, smooth, deep green above and distinctly blue below, borne on short stalks. In the subspecies *cathartica* the slender lateral veins, clearly marked, extend to the very edge of the margin while in the subspecies *melanthesoides* they branch, forming loops, *before* they reach the edge of the leaf.

The coppice leaves are remarkably like those of *Bridelia micrantha*.

The small greenish flowers are male or female, carried on short stalks. The fruits are small, round, and wine-red, later black, and 1- or 2-seeded, with a thin layer of flesh, borne on short stalks in the axils of the leaves. They crowd the twigs and although small are so abundant and colourful that a fruiting tree is usually decorative. The fruits are favourites with birds such as Tinker-barbets, Black-collared Barbets, and many other species. The wood is not used for building.

This is an easily grown tree and with its small neat shape it is suitable for even a small garden. For bird enthusiasts this, with its many fruits, is a particularly valuable species.

The specific name indicates that the tree has cathartic or purgative properties. It is used medicinally by Africans.

(324)   *Bridelia micrantha* (Hochst.) Baill.

= *Candelabria micrantha* Hochst.

Mitzeerie, coast goldleaf, bruinstinkhout; umHlahla-makwaba (X); umHlahle, umHlalamagwababa, isiHlalamangewibi (Z); motsêrê (NS); munzere (V)

The mitzeerie occurs from the Transkei, through Natal and Zululand to the eastern and northern Transvaal, and northwards into tropical Africa, in open savannah and bush and on forest edges, often on swampy ground or on river banks. A tree, which must have been seen by many thousands of visitors, grows in the temple in the Zimbabwe Ruins in Rhodesia.

Above
The mitzeerie, *Bridelia micrantha,*
used as a shade tree in Hluhluwe
camp, Zululand

Below left
The mitzeerie, *Bridelia micrantha,*
near Sibasa in the north eastern
Transvaal

Below right
Mitzeerie leaves

Opposite
Mitzeerie trunk

At its best, this is a fine and luxuriantly growing, deciduous or semi-deciduous tree up to about 21 m high but usually smaller, with a wide leafy crown, and a trunk that is grey-brown, when young smoothish and covered with small flat knobs, and when older rough; branches that are sometimes spiny, and twigs that are hairy when young but becoming hairless with age, knobbly, and covered with small, scattered, raised, light brown dots.

The slightly undulating leaves are simple and alternate, oval, oblong, or egg-shaped, sharply or bluntly pointed, with a slightly narrowed or rounded base, 4-18 cm long and 2.5-10 cm wide, dark green above and lighter below, usually smooth but sometimes slightly hairy below, with about 8-15 pairs of very clearly marked, slender, lateral veins running upwards and outwards, only occasionally branching near the margin. These and the midrib are slightly raised below. There are small stipules that soon fall off.

The leaves are borne on short, robust, slightly hairy stalks. They are handsome at all times, and in autumn particularly so when they turn bright red and gold.

The inconspicuous greenish male and female flowers are borne in clusters in the axils of the leaves on the same tree, the male with short stalks, the female without any stalks at all.

The fruits are small, oval, and shiny green turning black, and are sweet and edible. Country people eat them, and they are very popular with birds such as Green Pigeons, starlings, doves, louries and bulbuls. A fruiting branch in summer with its neat leaves and fruits crowded abundantly along the twigs is striking and distinctive. Trees do not fruit every year in succession.

The bark and leaves are eaten by Black Rhino.

It has been noted that the Narina Trogan often chooses to rest in the branches of this tree.

The mitzeerie produces a beautiful, lustrous wood, durable and termite resistant, considered by some as fine as stinkwood. The sapwood is a light colour, merging into the brown heartwood. According to C.P. Kromhout no problems are experienced in working it except that the grain is inclined to chip around the many small knots. It makes good flooring, furniture, and fence poles, and has been used for panelling. In Tongaland it is used to make the framework of fish traps, and wherever it occurs it is used in medicine. Zulus boil the roots together with a pinch of roasted and powdered *Dichrostachys* roots, and this is a remedy for lung pains, either drunk or rubbed into incisions in the skin where the pain is felt.

This is one of our fast-growing indigenous trees, beautiful, shady, decorative, and worth planting for its autumn colours alone. It grows easily in deep moist soil and, with some shelter, withstands 5 or 6 degrees of frost. It drops its abundant leaves in late winter or early spring and is usually bare for a few weeks only.

The specific name *micrantha* is based on Greek words meaning "small flower".

Bridelia tenuifolia Muell.Arg.

This tropical *Bridelia*, collected first in Angola, occurs in northern South West Africa as a shrub or a small tree. It has branches which are hairy when young but which become smooth later, leaves which are simple,

Left
The Lebombo ironwood,
Androstachys johnsonii, growing on the northern foothills
of the Soutpansberg

Above
Lebombo ironwood bark

Below
Androstachys johnsonii twig,
showing the velvety hairs on
stems, stalks and the under-
surface of the leaves, and large
stipules enclosing the young
leaves (50%)

alternate and stipulate, 4-11 cm long and up to 6 cm broad, widely lance-shaped or oval, shortly pointed, with a round or narrowed base, smooth above, with the veins slightly hairy below. The 9-11 pairs of slender lateral veins are clearly marked, reaching outwards and upwards.

The flowers are borne in the axils of the leaves.

The fruit is small, egg-shaped, 2-seeded, and drupe-like.

The specific name *tenuifolia* is based on Latin words meaning "thin-leaved".

13. *Androstachys* Prain

The genus *Androstachys* is composed of a single described species native to South Africa, Swaziland, Portuguese East Africa, Rhodesia and Zambia.

This has leaves that are simple and opposite, the stipules large and conspicuous, forming a sheath enclosing the young leaves; the flowers male or female borne on separate trees in the axils of the leaves, the male usually in 3's, and the female singly. They are without petals or disc, the calyx with 2-5 bract-like sepals, the stamens many in the male, the female with a 3-4-celled ovary. The fruit is a capsule breaking up into several 2-valved parts.

The generic name *Androstachys* is based on Greek words meaning "male spike" in reference to the fact that male and female flowers are borne separately.

(327)   *Androstachys johnsonii* Prain

Lebombo ironwood, wild quince, wildekweper; ubuKhunku, um-Bitzani (Z); ubuKhunku (Sw); nsimbitsi (Tso)

This is not a widespread tree in South Africa for it grows only in Zululand, the north eastern Transvaal and Swaziland on the stony sides and in the kloofs of the Lebombo mountains, and also, in the Transvaal, on the northern sandy foothills of the Soutpansberg. On the eastern slopes of the Lebombos it sometimes occurs in neat clear-cut stands and these are easily distinguished from the air for they look like groves of grey pointed Christmas trees on the mountain sides. In the ravines of Swaziland the trees sometimes form solid forest.

This is usually an upright tree 4-8 m high, although it can be tall – in Zululand it is reputed to reach a height of 36 m. It is usually slender with a straight, dark, rough trunk. The twigs are angular. The leaves, simple and opposite, are arranged with one pair at right angles to the next, and are crowded towards the end of the twigs. They are heart or kidney-shaped, with a rounded or notched base, untoothed, 2.5-6 cm long, the upper surface deep green, the lower densely felted with silver or white. The young leaves are palest green, edged with silver hairs, and at such a stage are some of the neatest, softest, and loveliest of all leaves. The leaf stalks are often conspicuously blond and furry, and are sometimes attached to the leaf stalk just *within* the margin.

The outstanding feature of a young twig are the large stipules, up to 4 cm long, round-tipped, pale and velvety, which – sheath-like – enclose the young leaves but which fall off as the leaves mature.

Above left
Croton sylvaticus leaf
and inflorescence (50%)

Above right
Croton sylvaticus: A
fruiting twig (50%)

The small, yellow, inconspicuous male and female flowers are borne on separate trees in late spring or early summer, the male ones in small spikes, the female singly. The fruits are 3-5-celled capsules about 1.3 cm long borne on long, stout, furry stems in the axils of the leaves. They contain several shiny brown seeds.

The tree is deciduous or semi-deciduous, losing its leaves irregularly, and these become yellow, curled and papery before they fall. In tropical Africa it is almost evergreen and the leaves are much bigger than in South Africa.

The timber is much-prized being hard, as the common name suggests, fine-textured, durable and almost completely termite-proof. The narrow sapwood is light-coloured, the broad heartwood brown often with dark markings. It is used for sleepers, fence posts, flooring and joinery. Dr Codd says that the timber used in the huts in the northern camps of the Kruger National Park is mainly from local Lebombo ironwood trees. Africans value it for rafters.

The leaves are browsed by stock and wild animals, and the fruits are eaten by animals such as duiker and squirrels, and by birds.

Honey made from the flowers is said to be poisonous.

This should be a neat easy tree for warm gardens with a sandy soil. In the wild it reproduces itself abundantly, scores of tiny seedlings surrounding a parent tree.

The specific name honours William Henry Johnson, F.L.S., of the Royal Botanic Gardens, Kew, later Curator of the Botanic Station, Aburi, and Director of Agriculture on the Gold Coast, who in 1906 made a botanical collection in Mozambique.

14. *Croton* L.

This large genus of roughly 700 species — mainly trees and shrubs — occurs throughout the tropics of the world, while a few penetrate into cooler areas. In South and South West Africa 3 or 4 species grow as trees, while several more, such as *Croton menyhartii* Pax, *Croton pseudopulchellus* Pax, and *Croton steenkampiana* Gerst., are usually shrubs but occasionally small trees.

Right
Croton sylvaticus, Umdoni Park, the Natal south coast

Below
Croton sylvaticus stem

Members of the genus have simple leaves with star-like hairs or small scales, usually alternate, often with 2 glands at the top of the leaf stalk; male or female flowers usually borne on the same plant in the same spike or raceme, usually with the male above and the few female at the base; the calyx segments usually 5, petals usually present in the male, the stamens 5 to many, a disc present; in the female the petals small or absent, a disc present, the ovary usually 3-celled. The fruit is normally a rounded, 3-celled capsule, breaking up into 2-valved parts. The seeds are smooth and plump. The generic name is based on their appearance, for *Croton* is based on the Greek word for a tick.

A well-known butterfly that breeds on members of the genus is the Green-veined Caraks, *Charaxes candiope,* of forests and bushveld.

=   (330)   *Croton sylvaticus* Hochst.

Woodland croton; umFeze, uMagwaqane (X); umHloshazane, uGebeleweni, umZilanyoni, inDumbahlozi (Z); moêma, moêma-tswetsi (NS); mula-thoho, muima-vanda (V)

This happily named tree — the botanical name means "the woodland croton" — grows in coastal forests and scrub, often on stream banks, from Port St. John's through Natal to Zululand, and inland in forests and on forest margins in parts of Natal, in Swaziland, in the eastern and northern Transvaal, and northwards into tropical Africa.

In autumn, decorated with its strings of brilliant salmon fruits, it is colourful, amongst the most conspicuous trees fringing the main highway of the Natal south coast.

This is a beautiful leafy tree up to 21 m high, or shorter and spreading, usually with a tall straight trunk up to 1 m in diameter, the young trees with pale grey bark becoming darker and rougher with age, and frequently blotched with pink or grey lichen. The branches are smooth and grooved, and the twigs, with prominent leaf scars, usually covered with short rust-coloured hairs.

The dark green, alternate leaves are borne on very long stalks up to

1129

Above
Croton megalobotrys, the lowveld croton, near Chipisi

Left
Croton megalobotrys fruit

Right
Croton megalobotrys: The leaves, flowers and fruit (60%)

Below
Croton megalobotrys bark

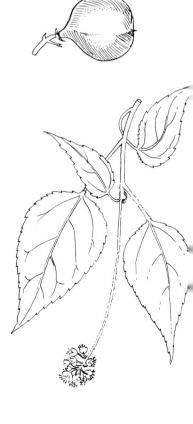

10 cm in length, with 2 small knob-like growths – the glands – where the stalk joins the leaf. The leaves are usually somewhat egg-shaped, often widest towards the base, tapering to a long point, with shortly toothed margins, 5-15 cm long and up to 10 cm wide, with 5 distinct veins from the base, smooth above, and with a few star-shaped hairs below, particularly on the nerves. There are small stipules which fall early.

The small green or creamy flowers are in "strings" up to about 15 cm or more long at the ends of the twigs, the male flowers numerous, the female fewer and borne below the male. An amateur Natal botanist, Captain Leslie Shewell, noted one spring that certain individual trees in flower were predominantly male and others female, and that the flowers of the "minor" sex did not open until those of the "main" sex had fallen, or – if female – had been fertilized by pollen from another tree. On trees bearing spikes containing a number of flowers of both sexes, the same flowering system was apparent, male and female flowers never opening *on the same tree* at the same time, so that cross-fertilization between the different trees – he assumed – seemed to be ensured.

The fruits are roundish, shortly stalked capsules, up to 1.3 cm in diameter, rough, covered with short star-like hairs, a soft salmon or orange colour, with usually 3 roundish smooth seeds. They are poisonous, but are eaten by birds such as Forest Weavers, Cinnamon Doves, Green Pigeons, and hornbills, while Red-eyed Turtle Doves are fond of the fruits that have fallen to the ground.

The wood is a very light colour, often with small dark streaks in it. It is soft, light, and easily worked. Like sneezewood, it burns when it is green.

Parts of the tree are toxic but, as in many other poisonous plants, are used medicinally. The leaves are made into a poultice for pleurisy and the bark is used to treat rheumatism. In Gazaland the bark is utilized as a fish poison.

This would be a decorative and shady garden tree, and it is noteworthy that the Venda name, muima-vanda, means "stand in courtyard".

The Pondo name, umFeze, means "spittle-bug", an insect that often infests the tree.

(329)   *Croton megalobotrys* Muell.Arg.

= *Croton gabouga* S.Moore

Lowveld croton; xunguxungu (Tso); mutsebi (Tsw); motsibi
(Tsw – Taw & Mang); muruthu (V); mutukatuka (Sub); mubwiti (Kol)

The lowveld croton extends southward from tropical Africa into Portuguese East Africa, the northern Transvaal, Botswana – where it is common in the Okavango Swamps – and northern South West Africa, usually as a riverine tree. In the Kruger National Park trees occur on the bank near the junction of the Limpopo and Pafuri Rivers, a spot known to thousands of tourists, and in the Letaba rest camp; and on the road between Louis Trichardt and Chipisi particularly fine specimens grow close to the road in what is normally a stream bed.

This may be a large soft bush or a densely leafy tree, much branched and often rather lax in habit, up to 15 m in height but usually smaller, with a slender, smooth, pale grey trunk, often with longitudinal darker markings, or covered with raised grey dots. The round, smooth branches and older twigs are usually covered with small, raised, light lenticels, while the young twigs are densely hairy.

The large soft leaves are simple and alternate, and usually borne on very long hairy stalks, sometimes as much as 20 cm long but occasionally no more than 1.3 cm. They are roughly triangular in shape, widest at the base which is round, flat or somewhat notched, tapering to the jutting point, 2.5-18 cm long and 1.3-13 cm broad but usually up to 8 cm long and about 5 cm wide at the base, with toothed margins, light green above, when young covered with soft star-like hairs, the underside with long soft white or silver hairs and often somewhat powdery, with 5 conspicuous nerves from the base. Just below the junction of the leaf blade and the stalk are two small wing-like glands. Small, narrow, velvety stipules are present but fall off early.

The tiny greenish-yellow flowers are borne in dense spikes up to 13 cm long at the ends of the twigs. They are male or female, the male more numerous and usually in the upper portion, with the female below. They bloom in late spring and early summer.

The fruits are large hard capsules up to 3 cm long and 2.5 cm wide, somewhat fig-shaped, green, slightly hairy, shortly stalked, containing about 2 large, flat, smooth, grey-brown seeds with oily kernels. They do not appear to be eaten by wild animals — not even by birds. Branches, bark and roots are eaten by elephant.

The clear, golden-yellow oil contained in the seeds is suitable for soap-making, and the timber is white and generally useful.

The seeds and the bark of the tree have purgative properties and are widely used by Africans.

Many years ago when malaria was still the lowveld scourge, a remarkable saga unfolded around this tree. On September 30, 1899, *The Lancet* carried an article by the medical officer in charge of the Klein Letaba Goldfields Hospital, Dr John Maberley, to the effect that some "beans" of an unknown tree had been given him by an old prospector who claimed that they had saved his life.

The old man, who had lain desperately ill with malaria in an African kraal, had exchanged his two greyhounds for a cure by the local witch-doctor who had administered these seeds, whereupon the old man had made a dramatic recovery.

Dr Maberley experimented, and most successfully, with both the beans and bark of the tree. Two grains, mixed into a pill with 0.25 grain of opium, were enough, he found, to cut short his own malaria bouts and those of his patients. For him, this was the answer to malaria. The identity of the tree, however, still remained unknown to him and was to do so for nearly two decades. Of the 8 seeds he could spare to plant, one germinated, only to be demolished by hail. The parent tree from which the seeds and bark had come was destroyed by Africans who believed it to be bewitched.

In 1899 when Dr Maberley's story appeared in *The Lancet* a small piece of bark was his sole clue to the identity of the tree.

Years later during the 1914-1918 war, treating malarial cases from East Africa, he remembered his phenomenal success with the bark and beans of the unknown tree. Taking leave, he set out with his fragment of bark to search the woodlands of the lowveld. He was not successful, but his enthusiasm brought success in the end, for he interested Dr I.B. Pole Evans, who was then Chief of the Division of Botany, who finally tracked down the tree and identified it as *Croton megalobotrys*, a malaria remedy long known to Africans and early pioneers in the lowveld, who used bark and seeds both to treat malaria and as a prophylactic.

No further research into the properties of the tree appears to have been done. Bark and seed probably, however, continue to play an active part in the rural life of the lowveld.

The specific name *megalobotrys* is based on Greek words meaning "large cluster", and refers to the flower head. A North Sotho name for the tree may be translated as "washes itself with water", presumably because it is often found near water.

(328)   *Croton gratissimus* Burch.

= *Croton subgratissimus* Prain; = *Croton gratissimus* Burch. var. *subgratissimus* (Prain) Burtt Davy

Bergboegoe, boog, Kalahari-boegoe, laventelbos, masquassieboom, rekstokbos; uMahlabekufeni, iHubeshane-elikhula (Z); umHuluka (Sw); moologa (Tsw), mologa (Tsw — Hebron), muṯwari

Previously *Croton gratissimus* was considered either as two separate species, *Croton gratissimus* Burch. and *Croton subgratissimus* Prain, or as consisting of two varieties of *Croton gratissimus*, var. *gratissimus* and var. *subgratissimus* (Prain) Burtt Davy. The two forms were separated mainly on the smoothness or hairiness of the upper surface of the leaves, the form known as *subgratissimus* having stellate hairs (which normally can be seen only with the help of a lens or microscope) and which are absent in the typical form.

Today the tendency is to regard the forms as inseparable and *Croton gratissimus* as one variable species.

In addition, another species, *Croton zambesicus* Muell.Arg., is possibly involved, for some botanists think this may not be separable from *Croton gratissimus*.

The bergboegoe is a widespread tree extending from Zululand and Swaziland through the Transvaal, where it is common on the slopes of the Magaliesberg, to South West Africa, and from the north west Cape north west into tropical Africa, growing in particular on stony hills and in rocky places. Burchell collected it near the Langeberg in the north west Cape, and it is the dominant species on the rocky western slopes of the mountains, the soft-coloured foliage tinting the mountain sides silver, gold, mauve and pink.

If the tree is considered as distinct from *Croton zambesicus*, it is a shrub or small tree up to about 8 m high, usually slender, but sometimes spreading as is the lovely old tree below the wall of the Pienaars River Dam outside Pretoria.

It is many-branched, with slender, angled twigs and fine drooping foliage, often with a persimmon-red leaf here and there shining in the crown. The leaves, which glint noticeably in the sun, are simple and alternate, about 2.5-9 cm long and 0.8-4 cm wide, lance-shaped or sometimes broader, pointed or notched, with a narrow notched base, untoothed margins, and with 2 glands where the blade and leaf stalk meet. They are green above and either smooth or covered with star-shaped hairs, and below a bright silver dotted with small cinnamon brown scales which are sometimes so thick that the under-surface appears not silver but red-brown. They are carried on longish silver and red stalks.

1134

They are very fragrant when crushed, with a lavender-like smell, and Bushman girls use them dried and powdered for perfume.

A tree covered in long beaded, drooping strings of reddish-brown buds appears at first glance to be mauve, and at such a stage the crown has an airiness and lightness that is characteristic. The buds open into small creamy-yellow flowers, male or female, borne in spikes at the end of the twigs.

The fruits are small, slightly 3-lobed, densely scaly capsules. They are eaten by Crested Guineafowl, Emerald-spotted Wood Doves, Tambourine Doves, Terrestial Bulbuls, francolins, & probably by many other species.

The wood is used for fencing, roofs, hut posts, and for sticks, and children make catapults of the twigs.

This croton, although reputed to be poisonous, is in parts browsed. It is used medicinally by Africans, in particular to treat fever. Jacob Gerstner, the botanist-missionary from Zululand, wrote tellingly of it: "a famous purgative — kills disease immediately with a death blow! " One of the Zulu names for it is "that which strikes at sickness". It is a famous Zulu love charm.

Zulus use the leaves as a cure for insomnia and restlessness, grinding them with those of two other unspecified species of croton into a paste made with goat fat. This they place on hot coals, inhaling the fumes with a blanket over their heads. Sometimes the leaves are used in a Turkish bath to remove shivers, and as a deodorant.

The specific name *gratissimus* is Latin meaning "very pleasant" or "most pleasant", so that the botanical name of this pretty, scented tree may therefore be translated as "the pleasantest tick of all! "

Several species which are also shrubs or small trees are often confused with *Croton gratissimus. Croton menyhartii* Pax (*C. kwebensis* N.E.Br.) and *Croton pseudopulchellus* Pax range from Zululand to South West Africa, and north to tropical Africa, and their leaves are somewhat similar to those of *Croton gratissimus.*

Croton menyhartii usually has leaves a bright silver below without any rusty dots, the base somewhat rounded and notched, with small glands that usually can only be seen with a strong lens, and mostly with very short stalks. The male and female flowers are in short spikes *at the ends of the side shoots.*

Croton pseudopulchellus has leaves covered with rusty coloured dots below, usually more narrowed to the base than those of *Croton menyhartii,* without any glands at the base of the leaf, and usually with fairly long slender stalks. The small clustered flowers are in short stubby racemes, often less than 1.3 cm long, and when in flower these heads clearly distinguish the species from *Croton gratissimus* and *Croton menyhartii.*

Yet another species, common in the Zululand sand forest (and occurring also in the eastern Transvaal) causes confusion. This is *Croton steenkampiana* Gerst., a low shrub or small tree, with leaves that have glands at the base, and the under-side silvery without rusty dots. They are larger and broader than those of *Croton gratissimus* and *Croton menyhartii,* 5-10 cm in length and 3-6 cm in width. The flowers are in *long terminal* racemes, which distinguish it from *Croton menyhartii.*

(331)   *Croton zambesicus* Muell.Arg.

This tree offers one of the teasing botanical problems that continually

OPPOSITE

Above left
Croton gratissimus in flower on a rocky hillside near Pretoria

Above right
Croton gratissimus stem and bark

Centre left
The long, beaded, drooping strings of buds

Below left
Croton pseudopulchellus: The leaves, and flowers in stubby racemes (50%)

Below right
Croton gratissimus: The leaves and buds (50%)

1136

The much folded trunk of *Cavacoa aurea*

arise, for whether it is indeed a distinct species or inseparable from *Croton gratissimus* is not yet completely clear.

It, too, is widespread from Zululand to South West Africa, but whereas *Croton gratissimus* is a tree of hills and in particular of quartzite ridges, this usually grows in open savannah country, in kloofs, and in the coastal and sand forests of Zululand.

It is a tall tree up to 15 m or more high, with leaves the undersurface of which is a clear silvery-white, usually without rust-coloured dots, and often larger than those of the typical *Croton gratissimus*. To the layman this tall and often imposing tree is very different from the typical small and often shrub-like *Croton gratissimus*. The striking differences in size and habit may, however, be due to environmental factors only. In other respects, the two forms are identical.

15. *Cavacoa* J.Léon.

This comparatively new genus of some 3 species of tropical and subtropical Africa is of considerable botanical interest. The single South African species, *Cavacoa aurea* (Cavaco) J.Léon., a fine and often huge evergreen, was strangely enough for many years mistakenly thought to be *Heywoodia lucens* Sim.

The botanist M.A.Cavaco placed the species in the genus *Grossera*, naming it *Grossera aurea* Cavaco, and in 1955 M.J. Léonard separated *Cavacoa aurea* from *Grossera*, founding a new genus upon it.

The trees have simple, alternate leaves with minute translucent dots, without stipules; and with male or female flowers borne on separate trees in racemes, with sepals and petals 4-5, the male with stamens numbering 15-30, the female with a disc, and the ovary 3-5-celled. The fruit is a 3-5-chambered capsule splitting into 3-5 parts.

The generic name honours M.A. Cavaco, contemporary botanist at the Museum National d'Histoire Naturelle in Paris, who first described the tree.

(332)   *Cavacoa aurea* (Cavaco) J.Léon.

= *Grossera aurea* Cavaco

Cavacoa, South African hickory; umBuku (Z)

OPPOSITE

Above left
Croton zambesicus in coastal forest, Zululand

Above right
Its stem

Below left
Cavacoa aurea: The leaves and fruits (50%)

Below right
A. A twig with female flowers: B. With male flowers (80%)

Cavacoa is a tree of Natal, Zululand, and Portuguese East African forests, where it usually grows on sandy soils. Trees grow close to Durban at Umhlanga Rocks in bush and coastal forest — in the grounds of the Country Club itself — so that is is astonishing that for so long this fine tree should have been mistaken for *Heywoodia lucens*, which it does not greatly resemble.

Its exact distribution is still debatable. Only very recently it was collected by Ian Garland of Zululand at Ntshalala Pan between Ubombo and Ndumu, a locality from where it had never before been known.

It is an evergreen with a dense, heavy crown, and in such areas as the Dukuduku Forest it grows into a huge tree with a much fluted and folded trunk many metres in circumference and with a smoothish bark. Even in smaller trees the fluted stem is characteristic.

The leaves are dull green, leathery and smooth. They are simple and alternate, with stipules, untoothed, widely lance-shaped to egg-shaped, bluntly pointed, narrowing to the base, 4-13 cm long, with the midrib and secondary veins slightly raised on both sides. The secondary veins branch and loop along the margin, and the network of small veins is conspicuous.

The leaves are borne on stalks that have a conspicuous characteristic — a small swelling at both ends of the stalk where it joins the leaf blade and the twig.

The flowers, male or female, are borne in long terminal heads on separate trees, and bloom for several months of the summer. The buds are purple and shiny, and open into small but conspicuous lemon-yellow and very sweetly scented flowers, the male about 1.3 cm in diameter, with 5 petals and a large puff of stamens. The fruit is a large, striking, woody capsule, often 4-lobed but sometimes with 3 or 5 lobes, about 2.5 cm or more in diameter, green turning black, borne on a long sturdy stalk. The seeds are the size of small peas. They are eaten by a species of small shrew.

In the wild, cavoco seeds drop to the ground while still closed, but open after contact with the damp forest soil. Seeds from such fruits can be germinated in moist well-drained soil and plants will flourish in either sun or shade. They are easily cultivated along the Natal coast and have been grown successfully as far inland, and in as cold a spot, as Pretoria.

Zulus drink an infusion of the boiled roots to ease pain and to reduce fever, and inhale the steam to clear the sinus.

The tree yields good sticks.

The specific name *aurea* means "yellow" in allusion to the colour of the flowers.

The tree resembles a species from the Congo, *Cavacoa quintasii* (Pax & K.Hoffm.), with which it is sometimes confused.

16. *Micrococca* Benth.

This fairly small genus of shrubs and herbs belongs mainly to tropical Africa. In South Africa it is represented by one species which occasionally grows as a small tree in forest in the deep shade of larger trees.

The genus is characterized by simple, alternate leaves, and flowers which are male or female, sometimes in the same inflorescence, at others borne on separate trees, the male flowers in small roundish heads far apart on the spike, the female often solitary. The calyx lobes number 2-4, the petals 0, the stamens are few to many, and the ovary in the female is 2-3-chambered. The fruit is a capsule, splitting into 2-valved parts. These are known botanically as "cocci" and are the basis of the generic name which means "fruits with small parts".

Some botanists do not separate the following genus, *Erythrococca*, from *Micrococca*, the difference being minor. Others split them on a few characters such as the non-scaly leaf buds in *Micrococca*, the fewer stamens, and the deeply lobed capsule which opens both along the back and the sides, in contrast to the scaly buds of *Erythrocca*, and the roundish or 2-lobed capsule which splits along the sides.

In South African species three characters may be used to distinguish the genera: the young, soft herbaceous growth and the absence of spines, and the leaf buds without scales, of *Micrococca*, and the hard woody young growth, the spines, and the scaly buds of *Erythrococca*.

1138

(332.2)   *Micrococca capensis* (Baill.) Prain

= *Claoxylon capense* Baill.

Ububu; uBubu (Z)

The ububu is a fairly widely distributed little tree in South Africa occurring in forests from the Transkei through Natal, Zululand, and Swaziland to the Transvaal, usually as a bush or small tree up to about 4.5 m high, brittle-stemmed, with few branches, smooth twigs, and very dark green leaves borne on long stalks.

The young growth is soft and herbaceous. The leaves are thin, smooth, and membranous, lance-shaped, sometimes widely so, with a sharp or blunt point, narrowed to the base, 4-15 cm long, with sharply toothed margins, and small narrow stipules that fall off early.

The tiny greenish male or female flowers are carried on separate plants in long strings in the axils of the leaves. The fruit is a small, yellow, brittle-skinned, 3-celled capsule.

The specific name means "of the Cape".

17. *Erythrococca* Benth.

Erythrococca, largely an African genus based on a plant collected in Sierra Leone, is represented in South and South West Africa by 3 species, one of which, *Erythrococca berberidea* Prain, grows in Natal and Zululand as a small spiny tree.

The genus is very closely related to *Micrococca*, being separated from it on a few characters only, such as the woody nature of the young growth, the often spiny stipules, and the scaly leaf buds.

(332.1)   *Erythrococca berberidea* Prain

= *Micrococca berberidea* (Prain) Phill.

Erythrococca

Erythrococca berberidea:
A fruiting twig (70%)

This is a common shrub or mid-stratum tree of coastal forest and of bush clumps in Natal and Zululand, growing — usually on sand — up to about 6 m high.

It has a smooth grey bark with rough lenticels, smooth twigs, and thin, soft, papery leaves with the stipules modified into short straight spines.

The leaves are simple and alternate, shortly stalked, lance-shaped to egg-shaped, 2.5-8 cm long and 1.3-5 cm broad, often widest above the middle, with pointed tips and narrowed bases, smooth above, with the nerves slightly hairy below.

The small, green or white flowers are male or female, borne on separate trees.

The fruits are small, 3-lobed capsules, bright orange and conspicuous. The specific name, meaning "berberis-like", is based on these.

The dark violet butterfly of Natal coastal forests, the Large Hairtail, *Anthene lemnos,* breeds on this species, laying its eggs on the underside of the leaves.

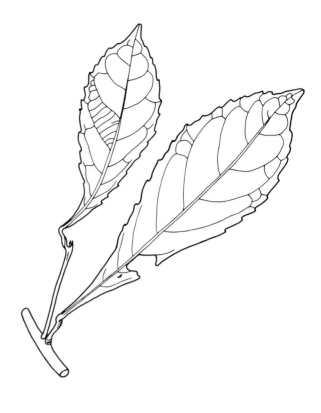

Above left
Alchornea hirtella var. *glabrata* inflorescence

Above right
Alchornea hirtella var. *glabrata* leaves (50%)

Below
Macaranga capensis leaves (45%)

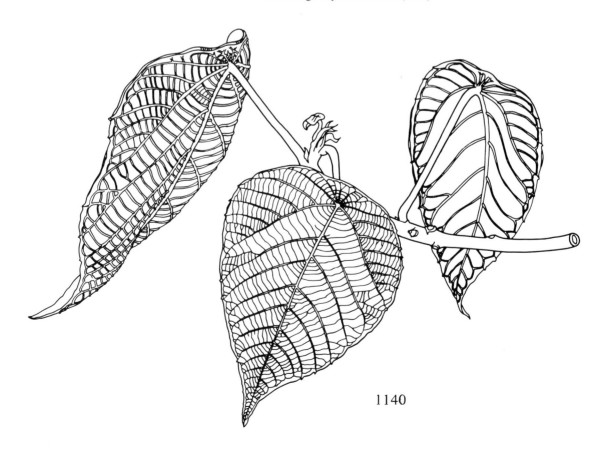

1140

18. *Alchornea* Sw.

Alchornea, a genus of roughly 90 species distributed throughout the tropics, is represented in South Africa by two species.

Members of the genus have simple alternate leaves, often with 3 nerves from the base, and glands between these at the base on the under-surface. The male or female flowers are usually borne on separate trees, the male in a spike, sometimes branched, several to a bract; the female in a spike, or raceme, 1 to a bract. There are no petals; the stamens number 8, and the ovary is 2-3-chambered. The fruit is a roundish capsule with 2-3 parts, each one 2-valved.

The genus was named in honour of Stanesby Alchorne, 1727-1800, honorary demonstrator in the Physic Garden, Chelsea.

(333)   *Alchornea hirtella* Benth.
          var. *glabrata* (Prain) Pax & K.Hoffm.

= *Alchornea glabrata* Prain

Alchornea

A tropical species reaching southwards into the forests of Zululand — it is common in Ngoye — *Alchornea hirtella* var. *glabrata* is a small tree up to 12 m high but usually smaller, with dark grey, smooth bark, drooping branches, hairy twigs, and large, simple, alternate leaves which are thin, papery, and a rather dull, deep green above, and paler below. They are widely lance-shaped, oblong or egg-shaped, pointed, much narrowed to the base, 10-20 cm long and 2.5-8 cm wide, with toothed or untoothed margins, and about 5-8 pairs of lateral veins looping along the margin. These, the net veins, and the midrib, are much raised below. Sometimes 1 or 2 bubble-like glands are present near the base of the leaf on the lower side.

The leaves are shortly stalked.

The small brown or purplish male or female flowers are borne on separate trees in spikes. The fruit is a very small, 3-celled, smooth brown capsule.

The name *hirtella* means "rough", and *glabrata* "without hairs", referring to the rather rough hairless surface of the leaves.

(334)   *Alchornea laxiflora* (Benth.) Pax & K.Hoffm.

= *Lepidotorus laxiflorus* Benth.; = *Alchornea schlechteri* Pax

Transvaal alchornea; murunda-malofha (V)

This small tropical species grows in the north and north eastern Transvaal and is common on rocky wooded hills round Punda Milia in the Kruger National Park. It tends to grow in light shade.

Although a tall tree in tropical Africa, in the Republic it is usually a small, slender, deciduous tree or shrub with a rough, light grey bark and young twigs that are pale and covered with lenticels. The leaves, crowded at the ends of the twigs, are soft in texture, egg-shaped to widely lance-shaped, the apex often with a long jutting point, the base narrowed or round and notched, up to 11 cm long and 8 cm wide, with notched margins. There are 3 or occasionally 5 veins from the base; and the

Jatropha curcas leaves
and fruit

Left
Macaranga capensis growing at the
edge of coastal forest in Pondoland

Below left
The silvery-white, straight stem of a
macaranga growing in a Zululand
swamp

Below right
The slightly buttressed trunk of a
forest macaranga

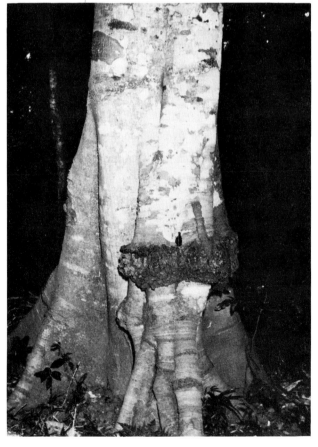

midrib and veins are conspicuously raised below, sometimes slightly hairy, with tiny pockets of hairs in the axils of the veins below. The glands at the base of the leaves are inconspicuous. The twigs and leaf stalks are softly hairy.

The trees are deciduous, with the young leaves a conspicuous reddish-brown and with the autumn leaves a striking red colour.

The small red or yellow flowers are male or female, borne on separate trees, the male in lax spikes. The fruit is a small round, dark brown capsule, with roundish seeds.

The specific name *laxiflora* means "lax-flowered". The Venda name means "blood-exuder".

19. *Macaranga* Thouars.

Macaranga – a large genus of trees and shrubs founded on a Madagascan species – comprises some 230 species distributed throughout the tropics of the Old World. One species occurs in Zululand, Natal, and Pondoland.

All the species have simple, alternate leaves, often large, handsome and gland-dotted, usually with 3-7 prominent nerves from the base. The male or female flowers are usually borne on separate trees in racemes or spikes, lateral or terminal, the male several to a bract, the female solitary. They have no petals. In the male the calyx is 3-4-lobed and the stamens 1-3; in the female the calyx is only sometimes lobed, and the ovary is often 1-3-celled. The fruit is a capsule.

The generic name is the Madagascan name for a species of the genus.

(335)   *Macaranga capensis* (Baill.) Benth.

= *Mappa capensis* Baill.; = *Macaranga bachmannii* Pax; = *Mallotus capensis* (Baill.) Muell.Arg.

Macaranga, swamp poplar; umBengele (X); iPhumela, umPhumeleli, umPhumela, umFongafonga, umFongofongo, umBhongabhonga (Z)

A tree mainly of coastal swamp forests and of stream banks but also of inland swamps and rivers, this striking tree grows from Pondoland northwards through Natal and Zululand to Mozambique.

It is a shrub or a medium-sized to large tree – in the swamp forests of Zululand it reaches a height of 15 m or more – pear-shaped to spreading. The trunk of trees in swamps and on rivers near the coast is usually straight and silvery-white and smooth, but the forest form is often slightly buttressed – in Ngoye forest of great girth and conspicuously buttressed – a brownish-olive mottled with grey, with horizontal cracks and tiny lenticels. The trunks reach up to 0.6 m in diameter and occasionally more.

The twigs are covered with rust-coloured hairs. The large beautiful, usually triangular or rounded leaves are borne on long sturdy stalks which are rose pink or red. The leaves are up to 20 cm long and nearly as much at the base – occasionally 30 by 30 cm – with a wide, flat, or rounded base, narrowing to a long jutting point, and with irregular margins.

This species could be identified by the veining alone of the leaves. The veins, 3-7 in number, radiate from a central point about 2.5 cm (in

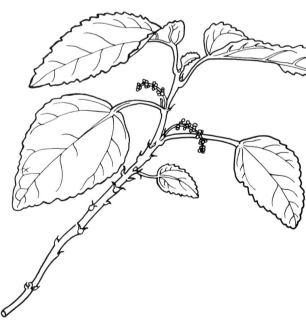

a large leaf) from the bottom of the blade, and the leaf stalk is joined to the under-surface of the leaf at this point. Above these rise another series of veins, usually 7-9 on each side of the midrib, and at right angles to these run fine veins parallel to one another.

The upper side of the leaves is a dark green, smooth or with rust-coloured hairs on the veins, lighter below, at first with reddish hairs but later smooth, gland-dotted throughout, with the secondary veins prominent and yellow, and with the lower parts hairy. The stipules are large and hairy, but soon drop off.

The young growth is reddish and velvety.

The small flowers, yellow, pink or red, are in lax, branching heads in the axils of the leaves, the stalkless male flowers in a tiny cluster in the axil of a bract, the solitary female on a short stalk in the axil of a bract. Male and female flowers are borne on separate trees. They are pollinated by bees.

The fruit is a small, roundish, sticky capsule, shortly stalked, with roundish seeds which are eaten by Delegorgue's Pigeon.

Sim describes the wood as dense, half-hard and strong, pinkish-grey with darker brown parallel lines, closely placed, making handsome furniture and excellent for boxes and light planking.

The tree is fire-resistant and quick-growing.

Tree frogs, which normally are found on plant species with large leaves, favour this tree.

The specific name means "of the Cape". Zulus sometimes call this umBhongabhonga, a name they also bestow on other trees — such as the trema — which grow quickly.

20. *Acalypha* L.

Acalypha is a large genus of over 500 herbs, shrubs and trees found in warm regions throughout the world. A number grow widely in South and South West Africa, of which two are trees.

All the species have simple and alternate leaves, with 3-7 nerves from the base, and male or female flowers, usually borne on the same plant, sometimes in the same spike. According to E.P. Phillips, terminal female spikes and axillary male spikes occasionally occur on separate plants or on distinct branches of the same plant.

The flowers have no petals. The male has a 4-lobed calyx and about 8 stamens; the female a 3-4-lobed calyx and a 3-celled ovary with a single ovule in each chamber. The fruit is a 3-celled, 3-lobed capsule.

Various species are used medicinally in Africa, in particular for treating eye complaints.

The generic name is based on a Greek word for nettle.

(335.1)   *Acalypha glabrata* Thunb.

Uthobothi tree; isiThombothi (X); uThobothi (Z); moharatsweni (Tsw — Ngwak)

This is a widespread and variable species occurring from the eastern Cape through Natal, Zululand, and Swaziland to the central, eastern, and northern Transvaal and Botswana, in coastal forest, on their margins, and in bush, and inland as a forest undershrub, on wooded

OPPOSITE

Above left
A Tonga fish trap made of the tough elastic wands of *Acalypha glabrata*

Above right
Acalypha glabrata, typically many-stemmed

Below left
Its bark

Below right
Acalypha glabrata:
Leaves and spikes of buds (70%)

stream banks, on rocky bushed slopes and in savannah woodland.

It may be a small shrub no more than 1 m high, or a tree up to 12 m, deciduous or evergreen, usually many-stemmed from the base, with flexible branches and grey bark covered with small raised dots.

The papery leaves vary in size, those borne in drought time or in dry localities being very small, often no more than 0.8 to 1.3 cm long, while those in areas with higher rainfall, or borne in rainy seasons, are up to 8 cm long. They are lance-shaped, oval or egg-shaped, sometimes widest at the base and narrowing to the bluntly pointed or rounded apex, with toothed or notched margins, usually smooth, sometimes rough, borne on stalks as much as 8 cm long. The surface of the leaves crinkles soon after picking, and for herbarium work should be pressed at once.

Although usually unarmed, the branches occasionally bear spines.

The small greenish-yellow male or female flowers, appearing in the spring, are usually carried in the same short narrow spike, the males in clusters, the females singly. The fruit is a 3-celled capsule, the seed roundish.

A form with velvety leaves, considered by some botanists to be a distinct variety, *Acalypha glabrata* Thunb. var. *pilosior* (Kuntze) Prain, has much the same distribution.

The plant does not appear toxic for in the northern Transvaal the young twigs are eaten as spinach. The leaves and roots are also used in a purgative medicine.

Nyala, kudu, and bushbuck are known to eat the leaves, and Black Rhino leaves and bark.

The Small Spotted Sailor, *Neptis marpessa*, a little dark butterfly marked with white, breeds on the foliage.

In Zululand and Tongaland the wood is used for fencing for cattle kraals and for the woodwork of the ground ovens in which mkwakwa fruits are dried. Fish traps are often made of the tough elastic wands.

The specific name *glabrata* means "without hairs", while the name of the variety, *pilosior*, means "hairy".

Acalypha sonderiana Muell.Arg.

Sonder's acalypha; imPindisa encane (Z)

Sonder's acalypha is a shrub or small tree growing in coastal bush in Natal and Zululand, often many-stemmed, with smoothish bark covered with small raised dots, with many rigid branches ending in sharp spines, and grey, scaly twigs.

The leaves much resemble those of the tamboti, *Spirostachys africana* Sond., but these have hairy pockets in the axils of the veins, which the tamboti has not, and they lack the 2 small glands at the base, characteristic of tamboti leaves.

They are simple and clustered on slightly hairy stalks at the ends of short side twigs along the branches, and are oval, oblong, or egg-shaped, about 2.5-5 cm long, with the margins scolloped or almost entire and with 3 veins from the base. Small stipules are present.

The male and female flowers are in the same slender spikes, borne – with the leaves – at the ends of the twigs. According to *Flora Capensis* the spikes have a perfect terminal female flower and only male flowers below, whereas *Acalypha glabrata* usually has spikes with a perfect *basal* female flower and only male flowers above.

The fruit is a 3-celled capsule.

The specific name honours Dr O.W. Sonder, 1812-1881, German apothecary and botanist, and joint author with W.H. Harvey of the first three volumes of *Flora Capensis*.

21. *Jatropha* L.

This large genus of over 250 described species occurs in the tropics, in North America, and in warm and temperate parts of South Africa. It is represented by about 11 species in the Republic and South West Africa.

Although not a single indigenous species grows to tree size, one species native to tropical America, which has become naturalized in South Africa, does do so.

This is *Jatropha curcas* L. which is widely cultivated throughout the tropics of the world, somewhat surprisingly in view of its extremely toxic nature.

Species of the genus are herbs, shrubs, or shrub-like trees, often with a large perennial rootstock, with simple, often lobed leaves, alternate or clustered, and with male and female flowers usually on the same plant in a terminal cluster (a cyme). The flowers have 5 sepals and petals, the male 8 stamens, the female a 2-5-celled ovary. The fruit is a capsule, sometimes fairly large, breaking up into 2-valved parts.

Jatropha curcas L.

Physic nut, purging nut, purgeerboontjie; mupfure-wa-tshikhuwa (V)

Meeting this little tree fairly widely in Natal and in remote corners of the Transvaal bush, it is difficult to credit that it is not indigenous. Yet it is not. It is a native of tropical America and found its way to Africa centuries ago.

It is said to have been introduced into the eastern Transvaal by Africans from Mozambique who were accustomed to planting it as a live fence around their cattle kraals. Today it is common planted round Indian and African villages and homes.

It is a thick, sturdy shrub or small tree, seldom more than 3 to 5 m high in the Republic, but up to 8 m in tropical Africa, with thick, upright branches covered with smooth, greeny-yellow or pale brown, papery and often peeling bark.

The twigs are thick and smooth. The leaves — on long stalks — are large and round or heart-shaped, with the margin untoothed or lobed, the base wide and notched, the apex bluntly or sharply pointed, about 18 by 15 cm, 5-9-nerved from the base, smooth, with small stipules.

The small greenish flowers are in clusters which are shorter than, and usually hidden by, the leaves. The fruit is a capsule which is oval, slightly lobed, about 4 cm in diameter, usually splitting in 3 parts, and containing large oblong seeds.

Trees and shrubs are valued for their medicinal properties, and because they grow quickly and easily from cuttings and seeds and are drought resistant, making sturdy hedges with a minimum of care.

The seeds are rich in oil which Africans use to grease their skins, and which in various parts is used for making candles and soap.

Jatropha curcas growing on the outskirts of a kraal in the north eastern Transvaal

The seeds are sweet, tasting like almonds and giving no hint of their poisonous properties. In small quantities they are purgative and used thus as a medicine, but they are also highly toxic, 4-5 being reported as causing death. Cases of poisoning, especially in children, are recorded in South Africa, while twice at least they have caused mass poisoning, once in Ireland when 139 children were poisoned, once in England when 35 people were affected.

The poisoning is due to two irritant substances, one of which affects the blood.

The leaf also is a purgative. The pounded bark is used as a fish poison, and in West Africa the seed forms an ingredient in arrow poison. In view of this it is surprising to find it is also used in dressing wounds.

Watt and Brandwijk say that the stiff hairs of the fruit can cause pain and fever.

A list of the common names given this tree or its nuts in various parts of the world give some indication of their powers — the physic tree, the big-purge nut, the Brazilian stinging nut, the black vomit nut, and the bed bug plant. Its oil is also known as hell oil!

The meaning of the specific name *curcas* is not known. It was first given 400 years ago to "certain seeds" by the Portuguese doctor, Garcia de Orto, who published a work in 1563 on Indian medicinal and drug plants.

22. *Clutia* L.

Clutia is an African genus of roughly 90 species, widespread in South and South West Africa where the members are mainly shrubs or under-shrubs. Two species sometimes grow as small trees.

1148

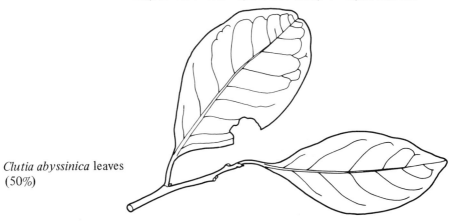

Clutia abyssinica leaves
(50%)

They have simple, alternate, untoothed leaves which are sometimes
very small and erica-like, at others larger; and male or female flowers
usually on separate plants, the male in tufts in the axils of the leaves,
the female usually solitary on longer stalks than the male. They have
4-5 sepals and petals, the male with 5 stamens, the female with a
3-celled ovary with 1 ovule in each cell. The fruit is a roundish, woody
capsule breaking up into 3 parts, and containing shiny black seeds.

The genus was named after a 17th century Dutch botanist, Outgers
Cluyt, whose Latinized name was Angerius Clutius.

(336)   *Clutia abyssinica* Jaub. & Spach.
          var. *abyssinica*

= *Clutia glabrescens* Knauf

Clutia

This clutia is one of the very widely distributed trees of Africa, occurring from the Nile lands in the north southwards to Zululand where it is
a common undershrub or small tree on forest margins, in such forests as
Nkandhla and Ngoye. Near Kosi Bay it is an integral part of the strange
swamp forest vegetation, its old leaves — bright persimmon-red and
gold — glowing among the crotons and ferns in the subdued forest light.

It is seldom more than 6 m high and is usually smaller and slender
with simple, alternate, papery leaves covered with small transparent
dots. They are egg-shaped, widely lance-shaped to oblong, with pointed
or rounded tips, narrowing to the base, 2.5-11 cm long and 1.9-6 cm
wide, with untoothed margins and with the midrib and secondary veins
raised below. They are borne on stalks up to 2.5 cm long. Both sides
are smooth and a dull green, turning bright autumn colours before they
fall.

The small white flowers are male or female, borne on different trees,
the male in small, few-flowered clusters in the axils of the leaves. The
female are in axillary groups of 1-3 on short stalks which lengthen as
the fruit forms. The fruit is a small, smooth capsule containing black
shiny seeds.

The specific name indicates that the species was first described from
Abyssinia.

The wild pepper tree, *Clutia pulchella,* growing on the fringe of Ngoye Forest

Clutia pulchella L.

Wild pepper tree, lightning bush, weerligbos; umSiphane (X); um-Embesa, iKhambi lenkosi (Z); mohlatsoa-mafi (SS)

Clutia pulchella is widespread in South Africa, occurring from the Cape, through the Orange Free State, Natal, Swaziland and Lesotho, to the Transvaal, as an undershrub in forest, or a low shrub or small tree in kloofs, on rocky mountain slopes, in scrub forest, in grassland, and along streams. It is one of the common species on forest margins in Zululand.

It seldom grows more than 4 m high, and is either evergreen or deciduous, its old leaves turning fine reds and pinks. They are possibly the basis of the specific name — meaning "the beautiful small clutia" — for it is not otherwise a particularly beautiful species.

It is reputed to be a troublesome weed in open places in the Knysna forest.

The twigs are often warted and when young are slightly hairy, the leaves simple and alternate, thin, smooth or hairy, covered with raised glandular dots. They are egg-shaped, sometimes nearly round, oblong, or widely lance-shaped, 0.6-6 cm long, carried on leafstalks 0.8-2.5 cm in length.

The small flowers, white to yellow-green, usually bloom in late spring. Male and female are borne on different trees, the males in small tufts in the axils of the leaves, the females singly or in pairs. The fruit is a small, roundish capsule covered with little warts, with a conspicuous calyx.

The common name "pepper tree" is not based on the appearance of the tree but on a caterpillar which often infests it and which stings the skin "like pepper" or — according to Sim — "like an electric shock".

23. *Ricinodendron* Muell.Arg.

Ricinodendron is a very small African genus which is not represented at all in the Republic. One species grows in northern South West Africa and in Botswana.

All the species in the genus are trees, with alternate, compound leaves, divided digitately (like the fingers of a hand), with 5-7 leaflets, and male or female flowers borne separately in panicles. They have 4-5 hairy sepals and 4-5 petals united in a broad tube, the male with 10-18 stamens which are not joined, the female with a 1-3-celled ovary. The fruit is drupe-like and contains one oily seed.

The generic name is based on the Greek words for "tick" and "tree", because the seeds were thought to resemble ticks.

(337) *Ricinodendron rautanenii* Schinz

Manketti nut tree, featherweight tree, wilde akkerneut; mokongwa (Tsw — Mang); mugongo (W. Caprivi); mugongo, ugongo (Deiriku); ugongo (Samb); omungeta (Her); mugongo (Ov)

The manketti nut has not up to date been recorded from South Africa but grows in northern South West Africa, Botswana, Rhodesia and Mozambique, often in groves or forests together on wooded hills and dunes, and always on Kalahari sand.

It was first collected in South West Africa by the botanist, Dinter, in 1885.

Although its usual height is about 7-9 m it is recorded up to 24 m in Ovamboland. It is a spreading tree with a trunk up to 1 m in diameter, a smooth green or golden bark, and stubby branches, when in leaf somewhat like a marula in general appearance, and when bare — according to Story — "resembling a slender baobab".

The robust young twigs are covered with short, soft, white or red hairs which disappear with age.

The graceful leaves on long hairy stalks up to 15 cm long are digitately compound with 3-7 leaflets. These are widely lance-shaped to oval or egg-shaped, bluntly or roundly pointed, with a rounded or flat and rather unequal base, the margin with tiny glandular teeth, occasionally lobed like oak leaves, 5-13 cm long and 2.5-9 cm broad, dark green above and paler below, with star-shaped hairs on both sides, with the midrib and veins covered with rust-coloured hairs. They are borne on sturdy stalks which bear, at the central point from which they spring, 2 small glands. Small stipules are present.

The trees are male or female. The sprays of small, oval, rusty-red velvety buds on long furry stalks open into small whitish flowers, the male in slender loose panicles, the female panicles shorter and few-

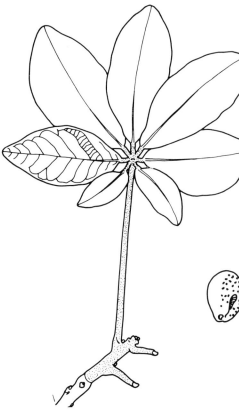

Above left
The manketti nut, *Ricinodendron rautanenii*

Above right
Ricinodendron rautanenii: A leaf and the distinctively pitted seed of the fruit (45%)

Below left
The bark of the manketti nut

Below right
Bowls carved out of the wood

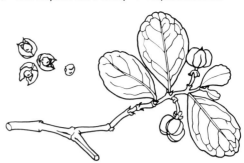

Suregada africana: A fruiting twig, and the fruit and seed (50%)

flowered. They bloom in late spring before the rains.

The fruits are plum-shaped, up to 4 cm long, hairy when young, when mature with a hard, tough, brown shell and a thick layer of pulp surrounding one extremely hard and finely pitted stone which contains one or two light-coloured kernels. The fruits, which ripen about February, are edible and make the tree of great value to the indigenous peoples of the areas where they grow. They are borne in abundance and when they fall sometimes lie knee-deep under the trees.

The pulp, with a sweet fruity flavour, is eaten raw or cooked and keeps well even when shrivelled. A soup and a refreshing and sometimes potent beer are made from it. The nuts or kernels of the seeds — the most popular part of the fruits — have a protein content of 29 per cent and yield up to 63 per cent of a yellow oil. They are dried, cooked, or eaten raw, either whole or pounded to a meal or paste which is often added to meat, roots, or sometimes to baobab pulp.

Dr Margaret Whiting informed Dr A.le R. van der Merwe of the National Nutrition Research Institute of the C.S.I.R. that these fruits formed 50 per cent (by weight) of the vegetable diet of the ! Kung Bushmen of Botswana, and that 100-300 of the nuts were eaten per day by everyone for most months of the year.

The fruits are a staple food not only of the Bushmen but of the Africans. Elephants are also reputed to be very fond of them.

Before the 1914-1918 War the German government granted a concession to a private businessman to exploit forests of the trees near Tsumeb in South West Africa which were said to yield a crop of 50,000 tons of nuts annually. Nothing came of the project.

The timber is yellowish, light, and soft, and is used for floats, dart and drawing boards, packing-cases, boxes, toys, insulating material, and coffins.

The species was named after a Finnish missionary in Damaraland, the Rev Rautanen.

24. *Suregada* Rottl.

Roughly 40 species of trees and shrubs, spread throughout the tropics of the eastern hemisphere, belong to this genus which is represented in South Africa by about 3 species.

Members of the genus have simple gland-dotted leaves which are usually alternate and only occasionally opposite, and flowers in clusters opposite the leaves, male and female being borne on separate trees. They have no petals. The sepals number 5, the stamens in the male are few to many, and the ovary in the female is 2-3-celled. The fruit is roundish and woody, a capsule or drupe, and usually 2-3-celled.

The generic name *Suregada* is based on the Telinga (Indian) name

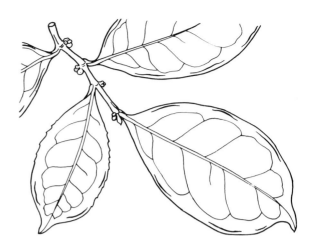

Suregada zanzibariensis:
A leafy twig (50%)

Soora Gada. It is a manuscript name of the botanist, Dr William Rox-burgh, 1751-1815, and was published by J.P. Rottler, Danish missionary and orientalist.

(338)   *Suregada africana* (Sond.) Kuntze

= *Ceratophorus africanus* Sond.; = *Suregada ceratophora* Baill.; = *Gelonium africanum* (Sond.) Muell.Arg.

Isitubi tree; isiThubi, iThambo lempaka (Z)

Suregada africana grows from roughly Uitenhage in the south, through Natal and Zululand to the eastern Transvaal and to Mozambique, as an undershrub in forests, or as a small tree in bushveld, on forest margins, and in dense valley bush, often along streams.

It is usually 4.5-6 m high with a stem diameter up to 15 cm and with a whitish bark. The stiff, glossy leaves are simple and usually alternate, smooth, gland-dotted, 2.5-8 cm long, egg-shaped to widely lance-shaped, narrowed to the base, with the margins untoothed, or toothed towards the often broad, flattish tip. They are dark or yellowish-green.

The tiny whitish flowers — male or female, borne on separate trees — are in small bunches *opposite* the leaves. The fruit is a small 3-lobed capsule carried on a short stalk.

The wood is hard and used for hut-building. It makes a particularly tough and flexible stick. One Zulu name for it is "iThambo lempaka", meaning "wild-cat bone".

(340)   *Suregada zanzibariensis* Baill.

= *Gelonium serratum* Pax & K.Hoffm.

Zanzibar suregada. iKhushwane elikhulu (Z)

The Zanzibar suregada is a tropical species — as the specific and common names suggest — extending southwards into Zululand.

It is a shrub or small tree up to about 4.5 m high, of scrub and riverine forest on sandy soil. The bark is smooth and grey.

The leaves are leathery, egg-shaped to oblong, narrowing to the base, with the apex rounded or with a blunt, jutting point, about 4-9 cm long

1154

and 2.5-5 cm broad, the margins with widely spaced spiny teeth throughout, smooth both sides, with the midrib raised below, dark green above and lighter below, with 4-6 pairs of lateral veins branching and looping along the margin, and with a network of finer veins, with glandular dots clearly visible within the network. The leaves are borne on short stalks.

The tiny cream to apricot-coloured flowers are in small clusters opposite the leaves. The fruits are very small and roundish and are eaten by birds such as Terrestrial Bulbuls. Africans drink the juice.

The wood does not make very good sticks, but is used for lathes for roofing and as firewood. The tree is also used medicinally.

(339)   *Suregada procera* (Prain) Croizat

= *Gelonium procerum* Prain

Tall suregada

Suregada procera is a tropical species which grows as a graceful slender tree up to about 9 m high in forests and in other shaded spots in the northern Transvaal. It has also been recorded from the forests of Howick, Natal, and those in Pondoland.

It has a much-branched crown of light green foliage and a straight trunk, and grey, rough bark.

The twigs are somewhat angular, the leaves simple and alternate with short stalks. They are widely lance-shaped to egg-shaped, narrowing to the base, often unequal-sided, 2.5-10 cm long, sometimes bluntly and broadly toothed, sometimes untoothed – even on the same twig – dark green above, paler below, with 4-6 pairs of secondary veins and a very close, distinct network of finer veins.

The tiny plum-shaped buds in small clusters opposite the leaves open into insignificant yellowish flowers, male or female, carried on separate trees. The fruits are about the size of a small pea, 3-lobed, holding roundish seeds.

The specific name is based on the Latin "procerus", meaning "tall as a tree".

25. *Spirostachys* Sond.

Spirostachys is a genus of 1 species, *Spirostachys africana* Sond., "the African spirostachys", which is widely spread in Central and Southern Africa and which, although never plentiful in South Africa, occurs from Mozambique, Natal, Zululand and Swaziland to the Transvaal, Botswana, northern South West Africa and Angola.

The leaves are simple and alternate with entire or scolloped margins and with 2 glands at the base at the junction of the stalk. Small stipules are present which fall early. The flowers are male or female, borne on the same tree in lateral spikes, the many male flowers above and the few or solitary female below. They have no petals. The calyx lobes number, as a rule, 5. In the male, the stamens are 3 joined in a tube, and the ovary in the female is normally 3-celled with a single ovule in each chamber. The fruit is a smooth capsule of 3 parts.

The generic name is based on Greek words meaning "spiral flower spikes" in reference to the structure of the spikes.

Above
A tamboti, *Spirostachys africana,* in the Transvaal bushveld

Centre left
A tamboti in northern South West Africa

Below left
The spiny branch of a young tamboti

Below right
Spirostachys africana: A. A male flowering twig. B. A fruiting twig (50%)

Opposite
Tamboti bark

1156

(341)   *Spirostachys africana* Sond.

Tamboti, Cape sandalwood, jumping-bean tree, headache tree; um-
Thombothi (X); umThombothi, iJuqu, uBanda (Z); umThombotsi, um-
Thombothi (Sw); ndzopfori (Tso); morukuru (Tsw); morekhure
(Tsw — Kgat); morekuri (NS); muonze (V); orupapa (Her)

The tamboti occurs in lowveld bush, in savannah, on the edges of
kloofs, on rocky hillsides and on river banks in the Transvaal and Zululand, sometimes in the frost-free valleys of southern Natal, and in
Swaziland, westwards to northern South West Africa and northwards
into tropical Africa.

Although usually fairly small, up to about 8 m, it may grow into a
fine tree up to 18 m in height. A well-grown tree usually has a straight
clean bole up to 46 cm in diameter, topped with a dense, rounded, or
pyramid-shaped crown of leaves, with many short woody twigs at the
ends of the branches. Young trees sometimes bear straight grey spines
up to 15 cm long.

The bark is black or almost so, thick, rough, and neatly cracked into
rectangular sections, and often serves to identify the tree.

The tree is sometimes deciduous, sometimes almost evergreen, shedding its old leaves when the new ones appear. The leaves turn colour
before they fall, in a dry cold winter the foliage becoming flushed with
coral or a brilliant deep red.

They are simple and alternate, usually 2.5-5 cm long and 1.9-2.5 cm
wide, firm to leathery, oval, egg-shaped, or widely lance-shaped, with
rounded or bluntly pointed tips and a rounded base; with small round
teeth, or sometimes untoothed; smooth, with the midribs prominent
below. They are borne on short stalks. There are 2 small glands at the
base of the leaf at the junction with the stalk. Small stipules are present.

The tiny flowers are arranged spirally in short, brown, catkin-like
spikes borne in the axils of the leaves, the numerous male flowers
above, and 1-3 shortly stalked female flowers below. They usually
appear before the leaves in late spring or early summer.

The fruit is a 3-lobed capsule, resembling 3 little peas joined together,
splitting into 3 parts, each containing a rounded seed. Seeds split with a
popping sound, and sitting under a tamboti on a warm summer day one
may sometimes hear these small explosions.

The tamboti is widely known for three reasons — its fine wood, its
toxic properties, and its "jumping beans".

The wood is among the most beautiful of all South African native
woods. The sapwood is creamy-white but the heartwood is dark brown
and beautifully figured. It is oily, of very fine texture, very heavy, and
termite-proof. It makes beautiful furniture, although cabinet-makers
complain that it is too oily to take glue readily, rafters, disselbooms,
and formerly it was used for gun stocks. Sometimes ornaments are
carved from it. It does not make good yokes as it "burns" the cattle's
necks.

It has a permanent, pleasant, strong smell and so in parts of the
country has been given the name of sandalwood. In South West Africa
the wood is powdered, mixed with fat, and rubbed into the hair as a
hair oil. Zulu girls use the powdered wood as a perfume; and the hard
black heartwood for scented necklaces. A freshly hewn log placed near
a fire perfumes a room, and sweetly scented torches are sometimes made
of the branches.

Most parts of the tree, however, are toxic. Watt and Brandwijk say that the African is warned against the tamboti from childhood so that in parts his fear of a living specimen amounts practically to a taboo. The sap is acrid raising fearful skin blisters on those sensitive to it. It is dangerous to the eyes causing severe pain and even loss of sight, and sawyers find the sawdust trying to the eyes. (The antidote is said to be cows' milk). An open wound becomes seriously inflamed if infected with the sap. Africans and country people refuse to cook their food on fires made of the wood as they say it poisons the food, and this appears to be true. The smoke is said to cause headache; and the bark is used as a fish poison.

Parts of the tree are used medicinally and in magic by witchdoctors. Boils are treated by rubbing the sap into the boil head. The steam from the boiled roots and bark is believed by the Zulus to cure eye complaints and the infusion is used as an eye-wash, or — in small quantities — as a medicine to cure stomach ulcers. Whether the patient survives the treatment is not recorded. The sap is used to dress cattle sores to stop maggots breeding and to kill live maggots. Slightly burned wood put to the nose relieves headaches. The dry bark is used in an embrocation to cure rash in babies, and it is said that African mothers will travel many miles to get it.

Birds on the whole appear to shun the tree, although the fruits are eaten by Crested Guineafowl, francolins, and doves. Few animals browse it or eat the leaves when fresh, although the Black Rhino will break down a tree in order to feed upon the young branches, porcupines eat the bark, and cane rats nibble the bark near the roots. Kudu, nyala, impala, and Vervet Monkeys eat the dry leaves with impunity.

It is probably for its seeds that the tamboti is best known. These are frequently infested with the larvae of the moth *Emporia melanobasis* which, as they straighten themselves out within the seeds, cause them to jump — sometimes as much as 30 cm — into the air. These fruits are known as "jumping beans" and are a source of delight to children who warm them in the sun or in their hands to make them lively.

They have a potential market value of which South Africans are apparently unaware. Mexican "jumping beans" — not *Spirostachys* but those of another of the euphorbia family — infested by larvae of yet another species of moth, are exported to Europe for their amusement value, and in Mexico and southern California Mexican boys hawk them freely as curiosities. No tourist can resist them.

A species that is often confused with the tamboti is *Excoecaria simii* (Kuntze) Pax (*Sapium simii* Kuntze), of the same family, a small tree-like undershrub in forests from the Transkei to Zululand. The leaves, however, are glossy, the colour of the upper and lower sides distinctly different, and the margins are sharply toothed, unlike *Spirostachys* leaves which are a dull grey-green both sides, and which have margins with rounded teeth.

26. *Sapium* P.Br.

Over 100 species, found widely in the tropics of the world, belong to this genus which is reputed to bear Pliny's name for a pine because the stems of some species exude a pine-like sap.

Three described species, two of which are trees, grow in South Africa from the Cape to the Transvaal lowveld. All have simple alternate leaves, without stipules, and male or female flowers growing in the same terminal spike, the male above the female. They have no petals. The calyx in the male is 3-lobed and the stamens number 2-3; the calyx in the female is 2-3-lobed and the ovary usually 3-celled with 1 ovule in each cell. The fruit is an often woody capsule consisting of 2 or 3 cocci or parts.

It is probable that other species of *Sapium* occur in the Republic. A tree with long, slender, toothed leaves tapering to the point, which may prove to be an undescribed species, has been collected in the swamp forests near Lake Sibayi in Zululand growing in company with *Ficus hippopotami* Gerstn. and *Rauvolfia caffra* Sond., and also in the Duku-duku forest, while the same or a different species comes from the Pondo-land forests. Good flowering and fruiting material are needed to establish their identity.

(342)   *Sapium ellipticum* (Hochst.) Pax

= *Sclerocroton ellipticus* Hochst.; = *Sapium mannianum* Benth.

Jumping seeds; umHongolo (X); umDlampunzi, umHlepa (Z)

Sapium ellipticum ranges from the Transkei, through Natal and Zulu-land to the Transvaal lowveld, to Portuguese East Africa and tropical Africa, in coastal and swamp forests, on forest margins, and on stream banks.

It is a deciduous or semi-deciduous tree up to 12 m or sometimes taller, with a rough bark, smooth branches, and slender drooping twigs, and a milky juice.

The handsome, dark green glossy leaves are simple and alternate, widely lance-shaped, oblong, or egg-shaped, sharply or bluntly pointed, with a narrowed or rounded base, 2.5-15 cm long, the margin usually toothed, with 1-2 glands at each side of the base, the midrib raised both sides, borne on short stalks.

The small male and female flowers are in short spikes at the ends of the twigs, the numerous male flowers above, the 1-3 female flowers below.

The fruit is a small leathery capsule, round and usually 2-lobed, looking like 2 peas joined together, containing roundish pale brown seeds. These are also at times infested with maggots within, which make them jump and which give them the name of "jumping seeds" or "jumping beans".

The tree is used medicinally. The wood is soft, pale coloured, light in weight and tough, but is not durable.

The specific name *ellipticum* refers to the shape of the leaves, which are often elliptic.

(343)   *Sapium integerrimum* (Hochst.) J.Léon.

= *Sclerocroton integerrimus* Hochst.; = *Sapium reticulatum* (Hochst.) Pax

Duiker-berry; umHlepa, umQathampunzi (Z)

This usually small tree up to about 6 m high reaches from Pondoland northwards through Natal and Zululand to the Transvaal, Botswana, and Mozambique, growing on forest margins, in coastal bush, and inland in forest and savannah, often on sandy soil.

1159

Above left
Sapium ellipticum near Port St. John's

Above right
Sapium ellipticum: A fruiting twig (50%)

Centre right
Sapium integerrimum: The leaves and fruit (50%)

Below
The duiker-berry, *Sapium integerrimum,* growing in a street in Amanzimtoti on the Natal south coast

It is usually a graceful tree with a spreading crown, long, slender and often weeping branches, slender, smooth twigs, and a stem either single or branching from the base. The sap is milky-watery.

The leaves are simple and arranged alternately down the long whippy twigs. They are oblong, egg-shaped, or widely lance-shaped, shortly and bluntly pointed, with a round or slightly narrowed base, 2.5-8 cm long and up to 4 cm wide, with the margin toothed or untoothed. They are borne on stalks that are channelled above. The large stipules drop off early.

The small, yellow, male or female flowers are in the same spikes at the ends of the twigs, the numerous male flowers above and the single or paired females below.

The fruit is a large woody capsule up to about 2.5 cm or more wide, usually clearly divided into 3 parts, each bearing 2 roundish, stubby, short horns. The seeds are oval and grey-brown.

The fruits, which often grow in great abundance, hang downwards on long stalks and at this stage the trees are eye-catching. Fruiting trees are conspicuous in Durban parks and gardens and on the Natal south coast, growing on grass verges and in the towns. Striking specimens grow near the car park at Charters Creek on Lake St. Lucia, their fruits weeping onto the cars below them.

The fruits are eaten by cattle and antelope, Red and Grey Duiker eating them whole and belching them up when resting. The seeds are eaten by Turtle Doves and Emerald-spotted Wood Doves.

In the early days of Natal they were used to make ink, and are still sometimes considered a tanning material.

The water in which the root has been boiled makes a wash to ease toothache.

The wood is heavy, hard, and durable, and is used for house- and hut-building, and makes beautiful furniture.

The specific name is based on the Latin "integer", meaning "whole", alluding to the often untoothed leaves. The common name "duiker-berry" refers to the liking of duiker for the fruit, and "jumping seeds" and "jumping beans" to the larvae which often infest the seeds making them — as in the tamboti — wriggle and jump.

27. *Maprounea* Aubl.

This small tropical African and American genus of about 5 members is not represented in South Africa, although one species occurs in the Caprivi Strip.

Members have simple, alternate leaves with small stipules, and male and female flowers usually in one spike, the males densely packed in oval or roundish heads, the solitary or few females below. Small bracts are present. The calyx is 2-3-lobed, the stamens in the male 1-3 and usually protruding, the ovary in the female 3-celled, and the fruit a capsule with 3 parts.

Maprounea is a Guiana name.

(343.1)   *Maprounea africana* Muell.Arg.

"The African maprounea" grows widely in tropical Africa, extending southwards to the Caprivi Strip, growing usually in savannah woodland on sandy soils and often on dunes.

1161

It is a deciduous tree from about 4.5-9 m tall, with pale brown, corky, deeply grooved bark, smooth branches, and smooth reddish twigs. The leaves – papery when young but becoming leathery with age – are simple and alternate, oblong to egg-shaped, with a sharp or round apex, sometimes with a very sharp point, and a rounded base, 1.3-6 cm long, with untoothed margins, dark green above and lighter below, smooth, with distinct secondary and netted veins. They are borne on slender reddish stalks.

The small yellow flowers, male or female, are usually in the same head, borne on short side branches, the male packed into a short dense head, the solitary or few female on long stalks below. The fruit is a small, brown, slightly furrowed capsule on a long stalk.

The tree is used in medicine and magic.

28. *Euphorbia* L.

This remarkable genus, the largest in the euphorbia family, with its 2000 or more species distributed throughout the world, is well represented in South Africa. Roughly 250 species are indigenous to South and South West Africa, and among these the succulent arborescent species are often a picturesque part of the landscape.

About 14 species grow as succulent and usually spiny trees, and these are far more common in the eastern parts of the country than in the west.

Most of them have smoothish trunks, often "seamed" crosswise, crowned with a cluster of succulent and often angled branches, which frequently rebranch. They are usually constricted into segments, and have rudimentary leaves (which soon shrivel and fall) and flowers and fruit borne along the angles.

In all the arborescent species except one – *E. ingens* – the lower branches die off on maturity leaving the stem or stems below the upper branches bare.

The flowers are arranged in a manner peculiar to the genus. They are male and female, without sepals or petals, collected within a cup and surrounded by bracts and glands (which give the impression of a common calyx). The individual male flowers within this cluster consist of single stamens, and the female – of which there is usually 1 in the cup or involucre – consists of a 3-celled ovary. The fruit is a capsule, usually 3-celled, which, when ripe, splits explosively to release the seed.

All the species have a milky latex, containing a resinous substance called Euphorbon, which is a powerful irritant, sometimes with blistering properties, producing intense inflammation and pain in the eyes and in open wounds. Even the vapour near a bleeding plant may cause a burning sensation in the throat and eyes.

Bushmen used the latex of some species, especially of *E. virosa* Willd., in Namaqualand and South West Africa, as one of the ingredients of their arrow poisons. Some species are still used as fish poisons.

Watt and Brandwijk wrote some years back that *Euphorbia* species continually cropped up in the Government Chemical Laboratories in South Africa as the cause of death, "the toxic principle being a resin". As with other toxic species, they are sometimes used medicinally to treat various ailments. The latex of *E. ingens* E.Mey. ex Boiss is reputed to have cured cancer – but on occasions large doses have proved fatal.

1162

Naturally enough, the potency of the latex has been linked with magic. In the Transkei, for instance, two euphorbias are planted near a hut where twins have been born to ward off harmful influences, the life and health of the trees being held to influence those of the children.

Several of the tree euphorbias, such as *E. tirucalli* L., *E. tetragona* Haw. and *E. triangularis* Desf., are known as rubber trees, and at various times in the past factories were set up to process their latex. The high percentage of resin they contain and the poor quality of the rubber, however, prevents their being of commercial value.

The genus is ancient in the history of plants having been named about B.C.25 by Juba 11, King of Mauritania — husband of the daughter of Antony and Cleopatra — in honour of his physician, Euphorbus. It is said that the king enjoyed the play upon words, "euphorbos" being Greek for "well-fed", "a state applicable to both physician and plant".

Tree euphorbias are often known as "naboom", "na" being a corruption of a Hottentot word "gnap", meaning strong or energetic, and emphasizing the vigorous habit of growth of the trees. Laymen often find it difficult to distinguish between them, in particular the common species of the eastern Cape. Africans often do not differentiate at all, and these species are known in both Xhosa and Zulu as umHlonhlo.

The genus in South Africa has been the particular study of Dr R.Allen Dyer. This account of the tree species is based on his help, and the descriptions in *The Succulent Euphorbieae* by Alain White, R. Allen Dyer, and Boyd L. Sloane.

Guide to *Euphorbia* tree species in Southern Africa

Spineless tree

A tree up to about 8 m high, often branched near the base; the crown dense; the branches intertwined, the smaller ones *slender, cylindric*, marked with leaf scars. (Rare in the E. Cape, more common from Natal to tropical Africa)

1. *E. tirucalli*

Spiny trees with trunks that are bare due to the lower branches dying and falling off

A tree 4-6 m tall; *dark green*; the smaller branches *distinctly curved* at the base, *usually 4-angled*, with a *continuous* horny rim along the angles, *deeply constricted* into symmetrical segments; the flower clusters *usually 3 together* from each flowering eye. (Albany, Peddie, Fort Beaufort).

2. *E. curvirama*

A robust tree up to 15 m, often *yellowish-green*; the branches *not distinctly curved* at the base, *3-5-angled, deeply constricted* into segments, the horny rim not always continuous but sometimes separate, *horny shields basing the spines*; the flower clusters usually 3 together.

1163

Euphorbia tirucalli in flower on the Lebombo Mountains

(Eastern Cape, Natal, Zululand, eastern Transvaal).

3. *E. triangularis*

A tree up to 9 m high; *the branches 3-5-angled, constricted into segments*, with horny strips along the angles; the flowers *in 1-3 clusters together*. (Lebombo mountains in South Africa and Mozambique).

4. *E. confinalis*

A tree up to 15 m; the branchlets usually 3-angled, *not constricted into segments*, the angles *deeply warted*, the spine shields separate on the warts, the spines *with a small pair of prickles above them*; the flower clusters *solitary* from each eye. (Eastern Cape to southern Natal).

5. *E. grandidens*

A tree up to about 9 m; the smaller branches 2-4-angled, *not constricted into segments*, the margins gently wavy; the spines *without prickles*; the flowers in *solitary* clusters at each flowering eye. (Muden in Natal to the eastern Transvaal).

6. *E. evansii*

A tree *up to 14 m*; the branches angled, the branchlets *distinctly squared*, with *warty knobs*; the spine-shields *separate* on the angles; the flowers in clusters, *solitary* from each eye. (Uitenhage to the Transkei).

7. *E. tetragona*

A tree up to about 6 m; the branchlets *slender*, angled, slightly constricted; the angles with a *continuous* horny margin; the flowers in a cluster *solitary* at each flowering eye. (Lydenburg, eastern Transvaal).

8. *E. sekukuniensis*

A tree up to 6 m high; the branchlets *3-angled*, constricted into segments with *wing-like angles*, with a *continuous* horny margin along the angles; the flowers in *1-3 clusters* at each flowering eye. (Lebombo mountains in Swaziland).

9. *E. keithii*

A tree up to 15 m; the crown often blue-green; the branches *usually 4-angled*, the branchlets constricted; the angles with a *continuous* horny margin; the flowers in *solitary* clusters at each flowering eye. (Lydenburg, eastern Transvaal).

10. *E. excelsa*

A tree up to about 8 m; the branches *curved near the base, 5-6 angled*, with a continuous horny margin along the angles, *deeply divided into big somewhat egg-shaped segments*; the flowers in *1-3 clusters* at each flowering eye; the capsules *3-angled*. Often confused with *E. ingens*. (Natal northwards to the northern Transvaal and Rhodesia).

12. *E. cooperi*

A tree up to about 4.5 m high; the branches *slender*, usually *6-angled, constricted* into *small* segments; the angles with a usually *continuous* horny margin; the spines in pairs; the flowers in *2-3 clusters* from each flowering eye. (Soutpansberg at the southern entrance to Wyllie's Poort, northern Transvaal).

13. *E. zoutpansbergensis*

1165

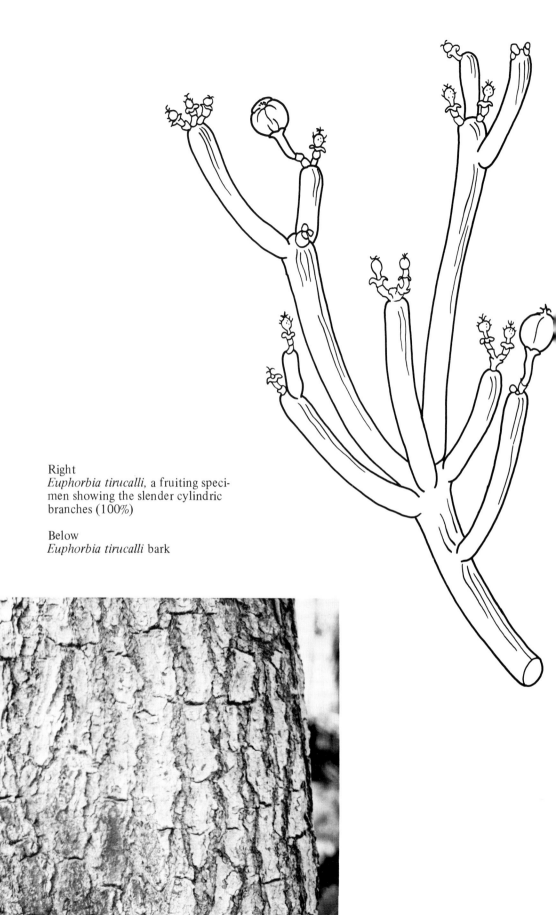

Right
Euphorbia tirucalli, a fruiting specimen showing the slender cylindric branches (100%)

Below
Euphorbia tirucalli bark

1166

A tree up to 10 m high, the trunk sometimes *5- to 6-angled*, the branches curved and upward-growing, the margins slightly wavy, the segments *irregularly and only slightly constricted, unwinged* on the mature parts, the spine shields at *fisst separate* and later *almost continuous*; the flowers in *solitary* clusters above the spine pairs. (Kaokoveld of S.W.A., and Angola).

14. *E. eduardoi*

A much-branched tree not shedding its lower branches

A tree up to 9 m tall, dense, candelabra-like; the branches *straight, erect*, branching and rebranching; the branches with 4 *wing-like angles, not deeply divided* into segments, the segments *broadest towards the middle*; the horny strips along the angles *not* continuous; the flowers in about 3 clusters from each flowering eye; the capsules *roundish*. (South coast of Natal northwards through Zululand to the Transvaal, Rhodesia, Mozambique, and tropical Africa).

11. *E. ingens*

(355)   1. *Euphorbia tirucalli* L.

Kraal naboom, kraalmelkbos; umHlonhlo (X); umuNde, umSululu, umDuze, umuNde wasehlanzeni (Z); mahumbana (Tso)

This is one of the widely distributed and widely travelled euphorbias, for although native to Africa it was first known botanically from India where it had probably been taken by Portuguese navigators. The specific name is based on the Malabar name Tiru-Calli.

In Africa it flourishes from the eastern Cape to central Africa. It is a spineless succulent tree up to about 9 m high with slender, *cylindrical* branches and branchlets which are alternate, opposite, or clustered at the ends of the main branches, appearing to grow without pattern and often making a dense broom-like crown.

The flowers, in the typical cyathia arrangement, are at the tips of the branches. The capsules are small and slightly 3-lobed, and the seeds smooth and brown, marked with white. The fruits are eaten by Crested Guineafowl, francolins, and doves, and by Vervet Monkeys.

This species is sometimes seen in the Cape and more often from Natal northwards to tropical Africa planted as hedges round African huts and villages, for it grows easily and well from cuttings and seed, and is eaten by no animals except the Black Rhino.

At one time its latex was considered commercially as a source of rubber. Gerstner says that is is used for preparing the head-ring of Zulu veterans. Wherever it grows, from Africa to Asia, it is used medicinally, as an insecticide, or to poison fish.

(347)   2. *Euphorbia curvirama* R.A.Dyer

Curved euphorbia

"The euphorbia with the curved branches" is a spiny succulent tree up

1167

Euphorbia triangularis, Umgazi Mouth

to about 4 to 6 m high from the Albany, Peddie, and Fort Beaufort districts of the Cape Province.

It has a single or branched stem, crowned with dark green, upward-growing and curved branches making a round crown. These are usually 4-angled and deeply constricted into segments, with hard horny margins and paired spines along the angles of the branches. The flowers are in clusters, 2 or 3 grouped together at each flowering eye. The capsules are 3-lobed, the seeds egg-shaped, smooth, greyish-brown with — according to the authors of *The Succulent Euphorbieae* — a minute proboscis near the apex, which is unique.

The authors state that **it** differs from *Euphorbia triangularis* in its shorter stature, branches more curved at the base, coarser segments armed with a continuous horny margin, stronger spines, and dark green colour.

(356)   3. *Euphorbia triangularis* Desf.

Three-angled euphorbia, naboom; umHlonhlo (X); inHlonhlwane (Z)

"The three-angled euphorbia" is the most common and abundant of the tree euphorbias in the eastern Cape — it reaches from Uitenhage northwards to Natal, the Transvaal (where it has been collected near Barberton), and to Mozambique, inland in the Cape to Bedford, and in Natal to Muden. The trees often grow densely together, sometimes reaching a height of 15 m.

This drought-loving species often grows on river banks with its roots apparently touching the water. The probable explanation for this surprising fact given by the authors of *The Succulent Euphorbieae* is that the water in the coastal rivers where it grows is brackish and the saltiness prevents the roots absorbing too much moisture — so that in fact it receives as little as if growing under drought conditions. The trees illustrated were photographed near the mouth of the Umgazi River in Pondoland, and further south at the mouth of the Kabonqaba River just north of the Kei. In the latter spot they formed a fascinating association, growing together with *Avicennia marina* (Forsk.) Vierh. (here the southernmost mangrove community in Africa) — the tree of aridity and the mangrove of swamps growing side by side.

It is a spiny succulent tree, green or yellow-green, the trunk slightly 4-angled, with 1 or several thick branches bearing at their top a crown of round, slightly curved branches in whorls. These are 3-5-angled and deeply constricted into segments. The spines are in pairs, the spine shields separate or making a horny margin along the angles of the branches. The flower clusters are in about 2 or 3 groups together.

The specific name is thought to have been based on a Cape species where the branches are usually 3-angled and not 5-angled as in Natal.

The wood is light and useful.

Historically this is an old tree, first cultivated in France, probably about the time of the Napoleonic Wars.

It may be confused with *Euphorbia grandidens* Haw., with which it is often associated on river banks in coastal areas, but which is less robust, and with *Euphorbia curvirama* which is smaller, has more curved branches, and is a darker green.

Euphorbia triangularis, and in the background the mangrove, *Avicennia marina,* at the Kabonqaba River mouth, Transkei

Euphorbia triangularis bearing flowers and fruit and showing the 3-angled branches (70%)

Euphorbia triangularis

(345)   4. *Euphorbia confinalis* R.A.Dyer

Lebombo euphorbia; tshikonde-ngala (V)

Euphorbia confinalis, a rare species in South Africa, which was only recently described, grows near Punda Milia in the northern Kruger National Park, southwards on the Lebombo Mountains, both on the South African and Portuguese side of the border. According to Dr Dyer, "this association with boundaries" suggested the specific name which means "adjacent" or "bordering upon".

It is a tree up to 9 m high, usually with an unbranched trunk and a crown of curved, upward-growing branches. These are 3-5-angled, constricted into segments, with horny strips along the edges of the angles, bearing pairs of spines which are conspicuous in young plants but absent in old, with 1-3 clusters of flowers together, which — according to Dr Dyer — separate it from *E. excelsa* which it resembles but which has single clusters of flowers.

E. triangularis, to which it also bears some likeness, usually has several trunk-like branches, and not a single unbranched trunk as has *E. confinalis*.

(350)   5. *Euphorbia grandidens* Haw.

The warted euphorbia; umHlonhlo (X); umHlonhlo (Z)

This handsome species, growing usually in colonies, occurs in the coastal districts of the eastern Cape, from the Humansdorp district to southern Natal, particularly in dry scrub of river banks and on hill slopes, and is most conspicuous and abundant in the Fish River Valley where it grows in company with the tree euphorbias, *E. triangularis* and *E. tetragona*.

It is a tall, green spiny species, up to about 15 m high, the main trunk cylindric or slightly angled, with 1 or more bare branches growing steeply upwards bearing at their tips a cluster of short branches and branchlets.

These are usually 3-angled and deeply warted, hence the name "the large-toothed euphorbia". They are not constricted into segments. According to the authors of *The Succulent Euphorbieae* it is more graceful than *E. triangularis* and *E. tetragona*, its branches being more drooping, sometimes "with a delicate spiral twist".

The spines, when present, are in pairs, often with a pair of small prickles above them. The clusters of flowers are borne singly and not in groups together.

The type specimen, discovered by James Bowie in 1820 and sent to Kew in that year, is still growing there! This was probably the first tree euphorbia ever seen in England.

It is a hardy and easily cultivated species.

(348)   6. *Euphorbia evansii* Pax

Evans' euphorbia; umHlonhlo (Z)

This near relation of *Euphorbia grandidens* — to the layman almost in-

Above
Euphorbia tetragona in the Eastern Province

Below left
Euphorbia grandidens, Perdepoort, Eastern
Province

Below right
Euphorbia grandidens: The branchlets, 3-angled
and not constricted into segments (70%)

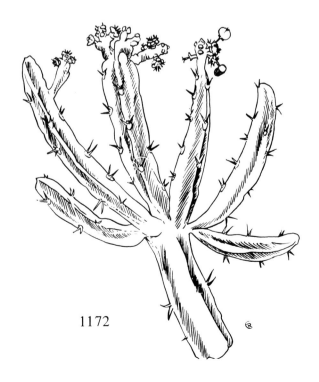

1172

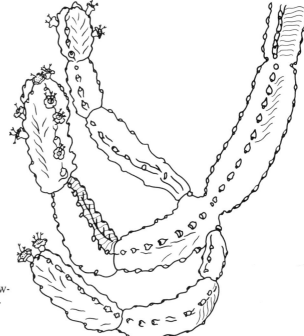

Left
Euphorbia grandidens
stem, with *Azima tetra-cantha* at the base

Right
Euphorbia tetragona, a
flowering specimen show-
ing the 4-angled branch-
es (50%)

distinguishable from it — has a more northerly distribution, from the eastern Transvaal as far south as Muden in Natal, leaving a gap between the two species of over 322 km.

The Succulent Euphorbieae lists these main differences between the 2 species — *Euphorbia grandidens* is taller, up to 15 m high, the branches usually 3-angled, the angles toothed, with prominent warty cushions, and the spines often with 2 minute prickles above them. *Euphorbia evansii* is rarely over 9 m, the branches 3-4-angled, with gently wavy margins, and the spines lack the prickles.

In severe droughts goats and donkeys eat the young shoots.

The specific name honours Dr I.B. Pole Evans, Chief of the Division of Botany, who discovered the species near Barberton in 1907.

(354)   *7. Euphorbia tetragona* Haw.

Square-stemmed euphorbia, naboom; umHlonhlo (X) inHlonhlwane (Z)

"The four-angled euphorbia" is a familiar species in the Cape, growing from Uitenhage through the Albany, Bedford, Queenstown and King William's Town districts, and along the coast to the Transkei, often making small picturesque forests.

Bowie collected this in 1823 and introduced it to Kew so that it has been known botanically for a century and a half.

It is smaller and more compact than *E. grandidens*, up to about 9 m high, with a smooth, slender, 6-8-angled trunk usually with up to 5 branches from near the base, each with a short, often rather flattish crown of branches and branchlets at their ends.

The slender branches appear distinctly squared with flattish sides and 4-5-angled. Young trees are conspicuously spiny with pairs of spines along the warty knobs on the margins. Old trees are less spiny, or some-times quite spineless.

The flower clusters are solitary and not grouped together. They are

Euphorbia sekukuniensis,
Steelpoort valley

Euphorbia sekukuniensis

gay-coloured and, according to *The Succulent Euphorbieae*, so rich in nectar that bees fill their hives from them soon — with dark peppery honey causing indigestion in those who eat freely of it. This at one time (but no longer) was used to cure sore throats. "Presumably", say the authors, "the average patient would consider his sore throat less painful than the remedy".

It is surprising to find that in the past it was used in the confectionery trade in King William's Town.

The latex of this species flows very freely and it is claimed that one large tree can yield over one pound (0.454 kg) of latex in 5 to 10 minutes.

Sim says that the timber is useless, even as fuel, though Africans value it for burning on their mealie lands, believing that its ashes produce a good crop. The forest value of the tree, he states, is as a soil protector and nurse tree for less light-enduring kinds, particularly sneezewood, and "its removal has been followed in some cases by sterility where formerly verdure clothes the slopes".

It transplants easily as a young tree.

(353)   8. *Euphorbia sekukuniensis* R.A.Dyer

Sekukuniland euphorbia

Unlike the familiar euphorbias of the eastern Cape, this is a little known species described fairly recently, growing on rocky hills and precipices in Sekukuniland in the Lydenburg district of the eastern Transvaal, where it was first collected by R. Ross-Frames in 1930. The tree photographed grew in the Steelpoort valley.

It is a small tree, up to about 6 m high, with a single stem, sometimes with 1 or more stout branches, bearing at their ends round, mop-like crowns of slender, angled, slightly constricted branches, and very slender branchlets, with horny margins bearing paired spines. The flower clusters are solitary from each flowering eye. The yellow flowers often bloom in winter.

The tree takes its name from the country where it grows — Sekukuniland — named after a 19th century Bantu chief, Sekukuni.

(352)   9. *Euphorbia keithii* R.A.Dyer

Keith's euphorbia

Keith's euphorbia has a small range of distribution, apparently being confined to the eastern and possibly the western faces of the Lebombo mountains of Swaziland.

It was first collected by Captain D.R. Keith of the farm "Ravelston" near Stegi, and has one of the most unusual associations of any African plant, for it is linked — through its discoverer and specific name — with the lovely Scottish ballad by Sydney Dobell based on the Ravelson family:-

"Oh Keith of Ravelston,

The sorrows of thy line! "

Captain Keith, a member of the famous Scots family, named his Swaziland farm after the Ravelston of the ballad in the country near Edinburgh.

It is a shrub or small tree up to 6 m high, the mature trees with a bare trunk and a crown of dark green branches spreading outward and upward. These are usually 3-angled, constricted into segments, with wing-like angles, with a continuous horny margin along the angles, bearing stout paired spines and clusters of flowers above them.

Dr Dyer says that it has a general likeness to *Euphorbia sekukuniensis* but that its nearer relatives are probably to be found in the mountains between Rhodesia and Mozambique.

(349)   10. *Euphorbia excelsa* White, R.A. Dyer & Sloane

Lydenburg euphorbia

This, like *Euphorbia sekukuniensis*, is a little-known species from the Lydenburg district, growing abundantly on hillsides and valley slopes, and somewhat resembling *Euphorbia tetragona* in habit. It is usually somewhat taller than *E. tetragona* — its specific name means "the lofty euphorbia" and has a tall, clean, usually completely unbranched trunk, bearing at the end a crown of blue-green, upward-growing, slender and usually 4-angled branches.

These have a continuous horny margin, and paired spines which are often absent in old trees. The flower clusters are solitary from each flowering eye. Botanically, these have small differences distinguishing this from other tree euphorbias.

Above
The naboom, *Euphorbia ingens* in the northern Transvaal

Right
Euphorbia ingens, showing the segments not deeply constricted: a portion of two branches. A. with leaves: B. with fruit (50%)

Below
Euphorbia ingens planted along a country road in the northern Transvaal

(351)   11. *Euphorbia ingens* E.Mey. ex Boiss.

Naboom, candelabra tree; umHlonhlo, abaPhaphi (Z); iShupa (Sw); nkonde (Tso); mokgoro, mokgwakgwatha (NS); mukonde (V)

This splendid species grows from the south coast of Natal, inland and northwards to Zululand, Swaziland, the warmer areas of the Transvaal, and from here into Rhodesia, Mozambique, and tropical Africa, in flat bushveld, coastal forest, savannah, and on hills, singly or in communities together, wherever it grows being conspicuous and dramatic. It is the most photographed *Euphorbia* species in South Africa.

Its specific name *ingens*, meaning "huge", refers to its size, for although it seldom exceeds 9 m in height, its dense crown of straight almost erect branches makes it the most solid and compact of all the tree euphorbias. Unlike all the others described, the lower branches do not die down annually, but grow, extend, divide, and multiply every year in a candelabra form, many of the branches reaching to roughly the same level and making a thick succulent crown, the very essence of life and vigour.

The trunk is 3, 4, or 5-angled, the usually leafless flowering branches green with 4 wing-like angles, constricted into segments several inches long, broadest towards the middle, bearing on the edges of the wings separate spine shields or horny strips, and close to them the flowering eyes from which spring about 3 clusters of small, fleshy, red flowers. These and the buds are relished by Vervet Monkeys. They appear in late autumn or winter giving the branches a somewhat reddish appearance. The fruits are roundish in shape. The spines are in short pairs or often in old trees altogether absent.

Birds such as Crested Guineafowl, Purple-crested Loeries, Black-collared Bulbuls, Turtle Doves, Emerald-spotted Wood Doves, and francolins eat the fruits, and porcupines and cane rats eat the roots.

The juice is very acrid and is used medicinally for blistering. Africans use it to kill maggots in sores on cattle. Branches thrown into a stream stupify the fish, and Africans use the dried latex as a poison. It is said that one drop in the eyes can cause blindness.

The wood, like that of many other euphorbias, is light and tough. It is used by Africans for planks, and to make doors and boats. The punts on the pans in the Pongola flood plain in Zululand are often of the wood. In order to stop the milky sap spurting when the wood is cut, Africans pack brushwood round the trunk which they set alight. This "sets" the sap, and the wood can then be hacked in safety. (The same method is used in cutting tamboti wood).

The garden uses of such a species are limited. However, it is easily cultivated in warm areas and cuttings root well.

Euphorbia ingens was first discovered near the present site of the city of Durban in 1831 by the botanist, J.F. Drège. It is believed that Dingaan had his throne built under a specially large tree, and it was near this tree that Piet Retief and his men were murdered in 1838.

No other *Euphorbia* species so merits the name "naboom", meaning "strong tree". The village Naboomspruit north of Pretoria takes its name from this euphorbia which grows abundantly in the country around.

Euphorbia ingens is closely related to *Euphorbia cooperi* which is, however, a smaller tree, its branches are usually 5- or 6-angled, more curved near the base, with a continuous horny margin along the angles of the branches, and deeply divided into big, somewhat egg-shaped seg-

Above left
Euphorbia cooperi near
Jozini, Zululand

Above right
Euphorbia zoutpans-
bergensis at the southern
entrance to Wyllie's
Poort, the type locality

Left
Euphorbia zoutpans-
bergensis

ments, while the lower branches die away annually. The fruit of *E. cooperi* is 3-angled while that of *E. ingens* is roundish.

(346)   12. *Euphorbia cooperi* N.E.Br.

Umphapha euphorbia; umPhapha, umHlonhlo (Z); umHlontlo, umHlohlo (Sw); xihaha (Tso); tshikonde-ngala (V)

Euphorbia cooperi, so often confused with *Euphorbia ingens*, grows from Natal, Zululand and Swaziland to the Transvaal, where it is widely distributed as far north as Messina, in bushveld and on hill slopes. It also extends into Rhodesia.

It is a smaller and fewer branched tree than *Euphorbia ingens*, the lower branches dying away annually, leaving a straight bare trunk topped with a robust crown of ascending branches which are more curved near the base than are those of *Euphorbia ingens*, 5-6-angled, the angles with a continuous horny strip, and the branch segments large and somewhat heart-shaped.

One to 3 clusters of flowers are borne at each flowering eye, and the red capsules are 3-angled.

The tree is used medicinally — the latex placed on pricked warts is said to remove them! — but, like that of most other euphorbias, it is an exceedingly strong skin irritant. Gerstner thought it "the most poisonous euphorbia in Natal". Watt and Brandwijk say that in the Limpopo area Africans soak grass in the latex, wrap it round a stone, and throw it into a pool. This paralyses the fish which then rise to the surface.

It is an easily grown species.

The tree was named after Thomas Cooper who in 1862 introduced it to Kew.

(357)   13. *Euphorbia zoutpansbergensis* R.A.Dyer

Soutpansberg euphorbia

"The euphorbia of the Soutpansberg" has an interesting distribution, for, as far as is known, it is confined to a small area south of the entrance to Wyllie's Poort. Here, against the cliffs and stony sides of this fine pass, it is a splendid sight, with its neat, slender branches clear-cut against its rocky background. Trees can be seen from the main road.

It is a small euphorbia up to about 4.6 m high with a bare trunk crowned with slender branches that spread outwards and upwards, usually 6-angled, and constricted into segments.

The sharp spines on the angles are paired, and the yellow flower clusters are in 2 or 3 groups.

The tree was discovered in 1937 by Dr F.Z. van der Merwe, and a Mr and Mrs van der Vyver.

South West African *Euphorbia* species

The tree and shrubby euphorbias of South West Africa are few and little known compared with those of the Republic. At the time of writing, it is not clear how many species occur. Merxmuller in his work on the South West African flora lists *Euphorbia conspicua* N.E.Br. from the Kaokoveld. The specimen cited, however, was later shown to be a newly described species, *Euphorbia eduardoi* Leach. Botanists have known this tree for some time but appear to have confused it with *Euphorbia conspicua*. Future collections may prove that both — and possibly even more — tree species are represented in the Kaokoveld for botanically the area is little known.

A shrubby *Euphorbia* species which occasionally is a tree is *Euphorbia guerichiana* Pax. It is fairly widely spread in the territory, and also occurs in Namaqualand. *Euphorbia currorii* N.E.Br. has up-to-date been reported as a woody shrub only but perhaps is tree-like on occasions. It was first collected in the 1840's by Dr A.B. Curror of H.M.S. *Water-Witch* who found it at Elephants' Bay in Angola, but it is now known to occur also in the Kaokoveld and Outjo districts.

Other shrubby species include *Euphorbia virosa* Willd. — occurring from Namaqualand to the Karas Mountains — *Euphorbia venenata* Marloth of South West Africa; *Euphorbia avasmontana* Dinter and *Euphorbia volkmannae* Dinter, both of South West Africa, and *Euphorbia hottentota* Marloth of Namaqualand and South West Africa.

14. *Euphorbia eduardoi* Leach

This primarily desert species, collected first in the district of Moça-mades in Angola, extends southwards on dry rocky hills and mountains, and in woodland, into the Kaokoveld of South West Africa. Mr L.C. Leach, who described it only recently, claims that in the past it was confused with other species, in particular *Euphorbia conspicua*.

It is a tall spiny tree up to 10 m high with a bare, sometimes 5- to 6-angled trunk and a crown of whorled curved branches which grow upwards. Mr Leach describes these as having slightly wavy margins, the segments irregularly and only slightly constricted, and as unwinged except on the younger parts, the spine shields reddish-brown, soon degenerating and becoming cracked, grey and corky, at first separate and sometimes enclosing the flowering eye, and later becoming continuous or almost so.

The inflorescence is a single cyme of 3 cyathia, borne above the spine pairs, and the capsule is 3-angled.

Mr Leach named the tree in honour of Dr Eduardo J. Mendes of the Centro de Botânica, Lisbon, "whose gatherings of Euphorbia from Southern Angola included the excellent material from which this was described".

Euphorbia conspicua, with which this species has been confused, is a tree up to 15 m tall with the branches usually 3-angled and distinctly constricted, and the angles wing-like. Welwitsch collected the type specimen in Angola.

29. *Synadenium* Boiss.

Synadenium is a small African genus of shrubs and trees with species occurring in Natal, Zululand, Swaziland, and the Transvaal.

The young branches are fleshy and contain a milky and often poisonous juice, and the leaves are fleshy and arranged alternately. There are

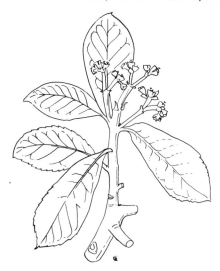

Synadenium cupulare:
The leaves and inflores-
cence (60%)

no stipules. Flowers are male and female. What is apparently the flower
is made up of a number of stamens and sometimes a single ovary (in
fact, a number of male flowers and 1 female) in a cup-like structure
which is entirely surrounded by a gland. There are no petals, and the
calyx is often no more than a shallow rim. The ovary is 3-celled with 1
ovule in each cell.

The inflorescence is a cluster, sometimes branched (a cyme, umbel
or panicle) in the axils of the leaves.

Synadenium means "united gland" in reference to the gland completely surrounding the cup-like structure which encloses the flower.

(357.1)   *Synadenium cupulare* (Boiss.) L.C.Wheeler

= *Euphorbia cupularis* Boiss.; = *Euphorbia arborescens* E.Mey.

Dead man's tree, crying tree; umDlebe, umZilanyoni (Z); mulamba-noni,
muswoswo (V)

The somewhat piratical common name of this little tree or shrub en-
shrines the many superstitions surrounding it: it has an evil reputation
wherever it grows, from Natal, Zululand, and Swaziland to the Transvaal.

Although usually a many-stemmed shrub up to about 1.5 m high, it
can be tree-like, up to 6 m tall, with branches that are green and succulent when young with abundant milky juice, becoming woody with
age, and marked with leaf scars.

The fleshy, rather drooping leaves are simple and alternate, 1.3-10
cm long, up to 6 cm at the widest point just above the middle, with a
round or shortly pointed apex, tapering to the base. They are smooth,
dark green above and bluish or mottled with red below, with a
conspicuous midrib, and they are crowded towards the ends of the
branchlets.

The flowers, 1 female and a number of male, growing from a pair of
green bracts, are contained in a rather cup-shaped, glandular structure
(which is usually and incorrectly thought to be the flower). They grow
in yellow-green branching heads borne on thick green stalks speckled
with white.

Drège discovered this first in 1830 in bush south of Durban. He does not seem to have known the sinister reputation of its latex, but Medley Wood, collecting it later for the Durban botanic gardens, broadcast its toxic qualities. He wrote that, although he had covered his face, kept his distance, and washed his face and hands after he had handled specimens, he could feel their effects in eyes, nose, and lips for hours afterwards.

Zulus believe that the tree cries like the plumed viper umDlondlo (which bleats like a goat) and that it lures people and animals to it in order to kill them. They think it has the power to strike from afar, and that even birds drop down dead when they fly past the tree. The ground beneath it, they claim, is always white with the bones of the animals it has killed.

Recently a Zulu with the traditional fear of the tree, who handled a specimen quite freely and with no ill effects, maintained stoutly that it *could not* be the Crying Tree, but only its "little brother".

The superstitions surrounding the tree are — as in most such cases — founded on solid fact. The latex blisters the skin and causes blindness, being as highly irritant as that of *Euphorbia ingens*. Like the euphorbias, it has its medicinal uses. Africans use it as an embrocation, and to cure (!) toothache and headaches. On occasions they plant it on graves to protect them from animals.

If handled with care, plants are harmless.

The specific name *cupulare* means "cup-like" in reference to the cup-like structure in which the flowers are placed. The Venda name mulamba-ŋoni means "not eaten by birds".

Gerstner says that its Zulu name, umZilanyoni, is also given to a boy who gets no sweetheart.

53 The Box Family (Buxaceae)

Over 30 species of trees, shrubs and herbs belonging to about 7 genera comprise this family. It is widely distributed throughout the temperate countries of the world, with the exception of America and Australia.

Members of the family have simple, evergreen leaves, opposite or alternate, without stipules, and male or female flowers, borne separately on the same or separate trees, in fascicles, or in spikes, racemes or cymes, the female usually borne terminally and the male below, the flowers without petals, the sepals 4-6, and stamens most often 4 or 6; the ovary superior and 3-chambered, the fruit an often 2-horned capsule, or sometimes a drupe.

Buxus L.

Until recently the 2 species of *Buxus* native to South Africa were placed in a separate genus, *Notobuxus* Oliv. Modern botanists, however, feel that *Notobuxus* is not distinct from *Buxus* and include it in this genus.

The European or common box, *Buxus sempervirens* L., is the best known species. It is fairly common as a shrub, hedge, or small, neat, clipped tree and in England it is often seen in one or other of these forms. It is frequently found in the Mediterranean regions and was known in Biblical times.

Various species of box, including the Cape box, yield a timber of value. The wood is typically yellow, very hard, close-grained and fine with an exceptionally even, dense texture and smooth finish. It has been described as the wood most resembling ivory. When the art of wood engraving flourished a great deal of boxwood was used for the blocks of wood-engravers and is still used to a smaller extent for the same purpose.

It is used for tools for clay modelling, for musical and mathematical instruments, for rollers in spinning mills, and for decorative work.

The species are shrubs or trees with simple, opposite, untoothed leaves and flowers that are male or female, borne on the same tree, one to a bract, the terminal ones female, the ones below male or the female borne singly, the sepals 4, the stamens 6 or 4, the female with 6-4 sepals, the ovary 1-chambered; the fruit a horned capsule, the seeds oblong, 3-sided, black and shiny.

Buxus is an ancient Latin name.

(358)   *Buxus macowanii* Oliv.

=*Notobuxus macowanii* (Oliv.) Phillips

Cape box, boxwood, buig-my-nie, Afrikaanse buksboom; iGalagala (X) umGalagala, umNgquzu (Z)

Above left
The Cape box, *Buxus macowanii,* in the forest near the mouth of the Bashee River, Transkei

Above right
The Cape box, fruit and flowers (50%)

Right

Buxus natalensis: leaves and fruit, and a dissected fruit (60%)

Cape box has a limited and strange distribution, erratic and unpredictable. Originally it was thought to occur only from Alexandria to Lusikisiki, seldom more than 32 km and often only 8 or 9 km from the sea. Now it is known to extend to the eastern Transvaal, and has been collected on at least one occasion in the central Transvaal in a wooded kloof in the Waterberg district.

It flourishes on hill slopes, in valleys and in forests, on a variety of soils — in the Alexandria district it grows in one small forest on an old sand dune, and elsewhere on Beaufort shales, on dolerite, and soils derived from Table Mountain sandstone. Wherever it occurs it is usually highly gregarious and forms (or once formed) almost pure forest. It is one of the commonest small trees in forests such as the Gwebe at the mouth of the Bashee River.

It is a small, very slow-growing tree up to about 9 m tall with a clean, slender, greeny-brown stem up to 30 cm in diameter (but usually less) and a crown of shiny green leaves. The twigs are angled, slightly hairy when young and smooth when old. The almost stalkless leaves are simple, opposite and untoothed, and borne in pairs at right angles to one another. They are oval to widely lance-shaped, with a bluntly pointed or rounded apex, narrowed to the base, up to about 2.5 cm or slightly more long, leathery, deep green, smooth both sides, with the lateral nerves scarcely visible.

The flowers, blooming from late winter to spring, are male or female borne on the same tree, the male in short heads in the axils of the leaves, the female usually singly or grouped with a few male flowers. The fruit is a small capsule holding shiny black seeds which ripen from late summer to early winter.

Although much of South Africa's best timber was exploited in the early days of settlement, the Cape box, with a timber very like that of the European box, was strangely enough neglected (except as firewood) until 1883. Even the forest officers believed it to be good for nothing but fuel. From 1886 onwards an export trade with Europe developed.

Sim observes that the wood with finest texture is from the very slow-growing trees on the mountains, those on the plains having much coarser-textured wood.

Cape box makes a very attractive pot plant as well as a low hedge, tolerating deep shade, and deserves to be cultivated far more widely. Much of the seed is parasitized but sound seed germinates easily.

The specific name honours Dr Peter MacOwan, Director of the Cape Town Botanic Gardens, and later Professor of Botany at the South African College, and Government Botanist in charge of the Herbarium until 1905.

(359)　*Buxus natalensis* (Oliv.) Hutch.

=*Notobuxus natalensis* Oliv.

Natal box; iGalagala, ukuXeza (X) umGalagala, umHlulambazo, umPhicamaguma, umMqguzu, isiXeza(Z)

The Natal box grows, often in abundance, from the Transkei to Natal, in coastal forest and in bush, as a low undershrub or as a tree up to 9 m tall, with a stem diameter of 10-30 cm. In Durban it is fairly common in bush on the Bluff. Like the Cape box, it flourishes in dense shade.

The smooth shiny leaves are borne on deeply grooved twigs. They are

Above left
Bark of the Natal box,
Buxus natalensis

Above right
Cape box bark

simple and opposite, untoothed, 2.5–11 cm long and up to 8 cm wide, widely lance-shaped to egg-shaped, with bluntly pointed or notched tips and a narrowed base, the midrib prominent on the under-surface. Young leaves are light green, but darken with age. The leaf stalks are very short or almost absent.

The few-flowered, greenish heads are in the axils of the leaves, the male and female flowers growing together. The capsule is up to 1.9 cm long, 3-valved, with horns, and contains shiny black seed.

The wood resembles that of the Cape box. Sim, quoting a Transkeian forest officer, says that this produces the best wattles for straightness, strength, and resistance against insect borers.

The specific name means "of Natal". Miller says that the general name for this in the Transkei is ukuXeza, meaning "to detach shell-fish from the rocks", because a sharpened stick of this is often used.

1186

The family Anacardiaceae is widespread in the warmer parts of the world. It is a large group with over 60 genera and more than 500 species, among them the pepper tree, *Schinus molle* (L.) DC., which is probably better known in South Africa than most native trees.

Many members of the family have resinous bark. Some have edible fruits such as the mango, the cashew nut, the pistachio nut, and the marula. Japan lacquer is obtained from a Japanese and Chinese species, and China turpentine from another. Some have a highly toxic sap with irritant and blistering properties, such as the notorious poison ivy of America, *Rhus radicans* L. As sinister, with sap as toxic, is its South African relative, *Smodingium argutum* E.Mey. ex Sond.

Many trees, including a number of *Rhus* species, are ornamental with fine autumn colouring.

Over 50 species belonging to 10 genera grow in South and South West Africa as trees. They have simple or compound leaves, without stipules, arranged opposite each other, alternately or in whorls, and flowers usually in branched sprays (panicles), male and female often being separate, and sometimes on different trees, the calyx with 3-7 lobes, the petals 3-7 (occasionally absent), the stamens various, often twice the number of petals, the ovary superior and usually 1-celled, the fruit often a drupe or sometimes hard, dry, and occasionally winged.

Key to Genera

LEAVES COMPOUND

Leaves imparipinnate

A tree; the leaflets usually untoothed, not sickle-shaped; the flowers male or female usually in spikes on separate trees; the fruit *fleshy*, up to 5 cm long, 2-3-seeded.

1. Sclerocarya

A tree; the leaflets *slightly sickle-shaped*, untoothed, the flowers male or female in axillary panicles at the ends of the branches on separate trees; the fruits *plum-like*, about 2.5 cm long, the stone oblong, with 4 cells, 2 usually fertile.

2. Harpephyllum

Trees or shrubs, the leaflets untoothed; the young parts and inflorescences covered with star-shaped hairs; the flowers bisexual; the fruit *a drupe,* often oval and *grape-like,* crowned with the remains of the persistent styles.

3. *Lannea*

A tree; the leaflets untoothed, the common midrib *conspicuously winged;* the flowers male or female borne in terminal panicles on separate trees, the fruit *dry, flattish, 1-seeded.*

5. *Loxostylis*

Leaves with usually 3 leaflets

A small tree or shrub; the leaflets 3, slender, toothed; the fruit *small, dry, winged.*

7. *Smodingium*

Trees or shrubs; the leaflets usually 3 but sometimes 5, toothed or untoothed; the fruit *small, roundish, often slightly flattened drupes,* not *winged.*

10. *Rhus*

LEAVES SIMPLE

A tree, the leaves opposite or nearly so, the fruit a *somewhat flattened drupe.*

4. *Protorhus*

A tree, the leaves alternate; the female inflorescence *woody with flattened branches;* the fruit *hard, dry, slightly winged.*

6. *Laurophyllus*

A tree or shrub, the leaves alternate, the lateral veins neat, parallel, conspicuous; the margins untoothed; the fruit the *size of a small walnut, hard, rough,* 1-celled, 1-seeded.

8. *Heeria*

Trees or shrubs, similar to *Heeria* but the fruits *small, smooth, kidney-bean-shaped or roundish drupes,* becoming *raisin-like* and black.

9. *Ozoroa*

1. *Sclerocarya* Hochst.

Sclerocarya is a small African genus of about 5 species of trees or shrubs, 1 of which grows in South Africa, and 1 or possibly 2 in South West Africa. They all have compound leaves, composed of several to many leaflets and a terminal leaflet (imparipinnate), arranged alternately and crowded towards the end of the branches; the flowers bisexual or male or female flowers borne separately, often on different trees, the sepals and petals 4, the stamens in the male 12-20, the ovary in the female 2-3-celled, the fruit a 2-3-celled fleshy drupe about the size of a walnut.

The generic name is derived from Greek words meaning "hard" and "walnut", referring to the hard kernel.

(360)   *Sclerocarya caffra* Sond.

Marula; umGanu (Z); umGanu (Sw); nkanyi (Tso); morula (Tsw); morula (NS); mufula (V); mfula (Kal); morwa (Yei); uge, muge (Deiriku);
omuongo (Her); omuongo (Ov)

The marula is one of the great trees of Africa, growing from the bushveld and woodlands of Natal, Zululand, Swaziland, the eastern, central
and northern Transvaal into Botswana, South West Africa, Mozambique,
and northwards into tropical Africa, wherever it grows usually being
venerated and preserved by Africans for the abundance of its edible
fruits. It grows in different types of soil — often on sand — usually in
warm frost-free lowveld areas, although trees occur close to the Wonderboom on the outskirts of Pretoria.

 This is a particularly fine tree, in South Africa seldom over 9 m in
height — although recorded up to 18 m — with a shiny much-branched
crown of dense, graceful foliage and a straight trunk up to 1 m in diameter, with light-coloured peeling bark marked with large round, often
smooth depressions. When the tree is bare of leaves the twigs are seen
to be noticeably sturdy with blunt tips, and these and the mottled bark
help to distinguish the tree in winter.

 The leaves are from 15-30 cm long and are composed of from 3 to 6 —
occasionally more — pairs of opposite or nearly opposite leaflets and a
terminal leaflet. These are broadly oval to oblong with a rounded or
narrowed and often lopsided base, the tip usually with a sharp jutting
point, from about 4-9 cm long and 1.3-4 cm wide — occasionally larger —
smooth, a dark shiny green or blue-green above and paler below, usually
with untoothed margins but sometimes toothed on young plants. They
are borne on slender stalks, the side ones up to 3 cm long, the terminal
up to 5 cm.

 The male and female flowers are usually borne on different trees, the
male in spikes terminally or in the axils of the leaves, the female singly
or in small groups towards the ends of the twigs. The male spikes are 5
to nearly 17 cm long, bright red in bud, opening into pinkish-white
flowers, neat and beautiful when examined closely and from a distance
giving the tree a red tinge. They are much frequented by insects which
often, around a large tree in flower, make a humming sound that can be
heard from some distance away. Occasionally bisexual flowers occur on
a tree.

 Usually only the female flowers develop into fruits, but sometimes a
flower in the male spike may also do so. The fruits are oval-shaped,
about the size of large plums — up to nearly 5 cm long — turning yellow
as they ripen, which in South Africa is generally February or March. The
skin is tough and leathery and covered with tiny rough spots, and the
whole fruit smells of turpentine and gives off a strong unpleasant smell
when decaying.

 The white fibrous flesh is juicy, tart, and thirst-quenching, and encloses a large light-coloured stone with 2-3 cells, each cell containing 1
seed. The cells are closed with plugs at one end which are forced out as
the seeds swell in the moist earth, allowing the embryo to grow out.

 The fruit is a great favourite with Africans who eat the flesh raw or
brew an intoxicating drink from it. (The juice is held to have aphrodisiac
properties). Certain tribes have a rule that when the marula tree is in
fruit and it is the season of beer, no man may carry arms for fear of the
violence he may do. Marula beer or wine has probably been brewed for

Above
A marula, *Sclerocarya caffra,* shading a stable and paddock in the eastern Transvaal

Centre
A marula in winter

Below left
A marula in the Transvaal used as a storeroom — bags of monkey nuts are hung for safety in the branches

Below right
Sclerocarya caffra: Leaves, fruit and male flowers (90%)

Opposite above
Bark of a young marula

Opposite below
Bark of a mature marula

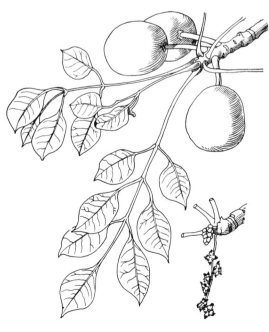

1190

many centuries. The kernels of the fruit have been found by archaeologists on Mapungupwe, the high hill near the banks of the Limpopo, inhabited by a Boskopoid people over 1000 years ago. Because the kernels were unbroken, it was assumed that the flesh only of the fruit was used — and for what better purpose than the making of beer!

A good jelly is also make from the pulp. Sim says that on the west coast of Africa the juice is boiled to a thick black consistency and used for sweetening porridge.

The juice leaves an indelible stain on clothes.

The kernels of the stones are as valuable as the flesh for they are rich in oil and protein, comparing well with an oil seed such as the soya bean. It is claimed that the Vitamin C content is four times as rich as in an ordinary sized orange. The tree recently became of interest to nutrition workers for it solves the puzzle of where Africans of the lowveld get the Vitamin C supply they undoubtedly have. They eat the kernels as nuts, or grind them, using the powder in soups and other foods. The oil from the nut has preservative qualities, and the Vendas use this in preparing meat. They steam this slightly, gradually dripping the oil over it. When dried and stored in a cool place, such meat keeps up to a year.

Naturally the stones are highly prized and are carefully collected and stored by Africans who consider a gift of marula kernels as a mark of great friendship. They have been valued and used since immemorial times. Archaeologists and palaeontologists have for many years been puzzled by small pieces of bone, fashioned to a special pattern, found in Iron Age sites in the Transvaal. Not long ago a scientist, passing a lowveld kraal, saw an old African woman wielding just such an instrument, made to the same age-old pattern. With it she was cracking the hard stones of the marula fruits!

Commercially the nuts are useless. They need to be cracked laboriously and the kernels separated by hand.

The tree is important to a variety of animals for shade, shelter, and above all for food. Stock and wild animals seek the fruits as eagerly as humans. The fruits normally fall before they are fully ripe, maturing upon the ground, and Africans find it necessary to protect them from marauding animals with rough fences. Elephants travel for miles in order to gorge themselves on the fruit, and monkeys and baboons become drunk on the fermenting flesh. Zebra, rhino, antelope of many kinds, squirrels and porcupines all relish it, and warthogs and parrots are known to crack the kernels and eat the nuts. They are also favourites with rats and mice.

The leaves are browsed by kudu, giraffe, elephant, and nyala, and when dry they are eaten by impala and Grey Duiker. Elephant eat bark and roots.

At least 8 species of butterflies breed on the foliage, as does the magnificent green lunar moth, the larvae of which spin large silkworm-like cocoons, which are used by Africans, filled with stones, as ankle rattles for dancing.

An insect that is as intimately linked with the tree is the mosquito. In a recent survey in the Kruger National Park it was found that more mosquitoes bred in holes in the trunk than in any other species examined. The holes held up to 4 pints of water, the run-off from the relatively smooth trunk, and this had been protected from evaporation by the size and density of the crown.

The wood of the marula is pinkish-white to light red, sapwood and heartwood being much alike. It is fairly light and soft with a coarse tex-

The Kaffir Plum, *Harpephyllum caffrum*, in forest at Kranskop in Natal

ture, and according to C.P. Kromhout, is very liable to blue discoloration through fungi and to beetle attacks. He says marulas should be felled in the winter and when necessary dipped in a fungicidal mixture and dried as quickly as possible. The wood turns and glues well, takes nails easily, and when oiled can be handsome. It is used for furniture and panelling, and Africans cut it, usually when the sap is low at the end of winter, to make carved articles, troughs, and dishes. Vendas use the wood to make divining bowls and drums, sometimes carving a whole drum from the soft wood of a single tree.

In parts of the Transvaal the marula and the mobola plum are often the only trees left standing by the Africans. Marulas were, however, cut in large numbers by Europeans until some measure of protection was introduced. It is a bitter thought that many of these lovely trees have been transformed into tomato boxes and lavatory seats!

The tree is used medicinally in many parts, both Europeans and Africans using the bark as a prophylactic and to treat malaria, and the steam for eye disorders. It plays a considerable part in magic practices. In parts the bark is thought able to control the sex of unborn children and the bark of a male tree is administered if a son is desired, of a female tree for a daughter.

Very heavy crops of fruit are often borne — some years ago four trees on the Zebediela Estate in the Transvaal produced an estimated 163,000 fruits — and the tree is naturally important in African fertility rites. Zulus and Tongas call it the "marriage tree" and give a brew of the bark in a cleansing ritual before marriage. When a girl baby is born, Zulus make a fire of marula twigs on which they boil a pot of water in which mother and child are washed. The marula symbolizes fertility, tenderness, softness, and early maturity, and they believe that these qualities will then be transferred to the baby girl.

One of the Shangaan diviners' dice includes a marula nut which, according to Watt and Brandwijk, represents the vegetable kingdom or "medicine".

The marula is easily raised from seed and truncheons planted in the early spring, and is fairly quick-growing but tender to frost.

The specific name *caffra* means "kaffir". The common name, marula, is based on the Tswana and North Sotho name for the tree. Surprisingly, some confusion still exists as to the correct botanical name of the tree. Two forms of the marula are involved, differing mainly in the number of leaflets, the length of their stalks, and in the size of the fruits. Some botanists regard these as 2 distinct species, the tropical form, with up to about 23 almost stalkless leaflets, being *Sclerocarya birrea* (A.Rich.) Hochst. Others see the two as forms of 1 variable species. If in the future the latter is judged correct, the name to be applied will be *Sclerocarya birrea,* an older name than *Sclerocarya caffra,* although our marula may well be given some status as subsp. *caffra.* The specific name *birrea* is based on the common name of the tree "birr" in Senegambia.

2. *Harpephyllum* Bernh.

Harpephyllum is a genus of 1 species only which occurs from South Africa to Rhodesia and Mozambique, and in St Helena, although there it is thought to have been introduced.

It is characterized by alternate compound leaves; leaflets which are

Above left
The Kaffir plum, *Harpephyllum caffrum,* in coastal forest near Port St. John's

Above right
The bark of *Harpephyllum caffrum*

Below
On top of the Lebombos in Zululand. The background bush includes *Diospyros dichrophylla, Cussonia spicata, Bauhinia galpinii, Olea africana, Ziziphus mucronata,* and *Vitex wilmsii*

1194

long, rather sickle-shaped and untoothed, in 4-8 pairs, and with a terminal leaflet; male or female flowers borne on separate trees in terminal panicles; the calyx lobes and petals 4-5, the stamens 8-10, the ovary 1-chambered, and the fruits smooth, plum-like drupes.

The generic name is based on Greek words for "sickle" and "leaf", referring to the shape of the lateral leaflets.

(361)   *Harpephyllum caffrum* Bernh.

Kaffir plum, kaffir date, kafferpruim, suurpruim; umGwenye (X); umGwenya (Z); umGwenye (Sw); mmidibidi (NS)

The Kaffir plum, which so much resembles the dog plum or essenhout, *Ekebergia capensis,* in foliage, is an evergreen tree found in the forests of the Cape Province (but generally not west of Uitenhage) and in the Transvaal and Natal, northwards into Rhodesia and Mozambique. It is a particularly common tree in the Pirie forest in the eastern Cape but may be seen in most forests or forest patches. At Port St John's beautiful specimens grow alongside the river road.

The tree varies from some 6 to 15 m in height, when standing on its own often with a neat, round, smallish, compact crown, at other times more spreading. The trunk is usually clean and straight, the forest form often much buttressed. The bark may be a silvery-white with small, raised, crosswise ridges, or brown and cracking into segments.

The dark green, shiny leaves are alternate and up to about 30 cm long, borne on furrowed leaf-stalks 2.5-5 cm long, crowded towards the end of the branches. They are made up of 4-8 pairs of leaflets which are usually opposite and stalkless or with very shorts stalks and a terminal leaflet, 5-10 cm long and 1.3-2.5 cm wide, the terminal one lance-shaped or broader, pointed, and narrowed to the base, the side ones slender and slightly sickle-shaped, sharply pointed, and narrowed to the base, with the midrib to one side. They are leathery, smooth and hairless, sometimes undulating, with untoothed margins, the midrib slightly raised both sides and the lateral veins conspicuous above.

Seedling or coppice shoots bear longer leaves.

The leaves remain on the tree for about 2 years, turning red before they fall; thus the tree is never bare of leaves. A red leaf here and there in the green shiny crown is characteristic.

Trees are male or female. The small whitish flowers are borne in sprays at the ends of the branches in early winter. The female develop into fruits like long plums in shape, usually about 2.5 cm long and 1.3 cm in diameter, red when ripe, and produced abundantly. In early summer the ground beneath a tree is carpeted with fruit. The rather sour pulp is edible and makes good jelly. It is a great favourite with children who usually strip the fruit from the tree as it ripens. The stone is distinctively pitted.

When the fruit matures, Xhosas know it is time to sow kaffircorn.

Baboons, monkeys and bushbabies love the fruits, and birds such as the Knysna Loerie, Cape Parrots, and toppies relish them. The parrot eats not the flesh but the kernel, ripping off the loose outer skin and opening the tough pip with its bill to extract the sliver of kernel within with its flexible tongue. C.J. Skead says that when a series of nuts was studied in a laboratory it was found difficult to remove the kernels even with the aid of tweezers and sharp tools!

Many insects are probably associated with the tree, among them the

Left
The bakhout, *Lannea discolor,* in the Waterberg

Centre left
Harpephyllum caffrum, leaves and fruit (50%)

Centre right
Lannea stuhlmannii: portion of a fruiting branch (60%)

Below
Lannea stuhlmannii at the northern entrance to Wyllie's Poort

Opposite above
The bakhout stem and bark

Opposite below
Lannea stuhlmannii stem and ba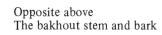

1196

widespread violet-marked butterfly, the Common Hairtail, *Anthene definita,* that breeds on the foliage. Rose Monteiro, in her book on Mozambique, listed another, a greenish-yellow moth, *Lasiocampa kollikerii,* the caterpillars of which — "with short pinkish-grey hair and very pretty faces" — rested in the crevices of the bark by day, and feasted on the foliage by night.

The Kaffir plum yields a pale red timber, fairly heavy and strong, that takes a good polish. It is used for furniture, planking, beams, etc., and Bantu use it for fuel.

It grows easily from seed or truncheons in areas without severe frost.

Sim says that for living fences the truncheons are set as poles and usually strike root forming short, round-headed trees, and these are a common sight in parts of the eastern Cape. It has been used as a decorative street tree in Port Elizabeth, King William's Town, and Grahamstown. The finest cultivated specimens are probably those in the grounds of the House of Assembly in Cape Town.

3. *Lannea* A.Rich.

This is a large genus of about 40 described African and Asian species of which 2 tree species are recorded from South and South West Africa, usually growing in bushveld and savannah.

One of the most interesting species, *Lannea edulis* (Sond.) Engl., is not a tree at all but appears only in the form of large leaves arising from the ground. It has edible fruits that are much liked by game. Another species, *Lannea stuhlmannii* (Engl.) Engl. sometimes produces a wool on its roots. Dale and Greenway say that this is like the wool on the roots of the tropical *Lannea alata* (Engl.) Engl. — a wool probably derived from cork cambium — which was once marketed as "Floatite" and used to float the British Expeditionary Force over the Juba River in the last war.

All the species have young parts and flowering heads covered with star-shaped hairs; leaves that are alternate and imparipinnate, or sometimes with 3 leaflets, the leaflets opposite, and untoothed; and usually small bisexual flowers in racemes, which are sometimes arranged in panicles, in the axils of the leaves or terminally. The calyx lobes and petals number 4, the stamens 8, and the ovary is usually 1-chambered. The fruit is a somewhat oval drupe, crowned with the remains of the persistent styles.

The generic name is based on the Latin "lana" meaning "wool" and refers to the woolly hairs on the young parts, or possibly to the wool on the roots of some species.

(362)   *Lannea discolor* (Sond.) Engl.

= *Odina discolor* Sond.

Bakhout, tree grape, live-long, boomdruif, dikbas; isiGanganyane, isi-Gaganja (Z); siGanganyane, isiKhanganyane (Sw); molebatsi (Tsw), moopyane (Tsw — Kgat); morula-moôpyane, mokgôkgôthwane (NS); muṇii, muvhumbu (V); ngamba (Kal)

This little deciduous tree is common in open grassland, bush, and woodland, often on rocky hill slopes, from Swaziland and the central and northern Transvaal, westwards to northern South West Africa and northwards to Rhodesia, Mozambique, and the Congo.

It is a graceful little tree, usually no more than 6 m high but reaching 12 m on occasion, with a rounded crown, a single upright or forked trunk, which is grey or reddish-grey and smooth, thick bark, smooth greyish branches, and sturdy, blunt, wrinkled twigs, sometimes densely hairy.

The leaves are compound, 11-33 cm long with 3-6 pairs of opposite leaflets and a terminal one, oval, oblong to egg-shaped or almost round, the point sharp, blunt or somewhat rounded, the base narrowed or round and notched, the lateral leaflets with an unequal base — usually 2.5-6 cm long and 1.3-4 m wide but sometimes almost twice as big. The young leaves are soft, pink, and furry, the adult leaflets green above, and below white or grey, densely or slightly velvety, with the midrib and veins conspicuous. They are striking both in colour and texture. The leaves are borne on long furry stalks.

Kudu, giraffe and elephant browse the foliage, elephant and bush pigs eat the bark, and elephant the roots.

The greenish-yellow, sweet-scented flowers, blooming in early spring when the tree is leafless, are in spikes grouped together and crowded at the ends of short, densely hairy branches, male and female often on different trees. The fruit is smooth, roundish to egg-shaped, somewhat flattened, about 0.8-1.3 cm long, crowned with short horns — the remains of the styles — making it, says Pardy, "rather like a very miniature sea mine" — when ripe with a purple-black skin, enclosing a thin layer of grape-like flesh and 1 stone. The fruit is edible, popular with children, Africans, monkeys, baboons, elephant and kudu, and birds such as starlings.

The wood is soft and does not crack easily. Africans carve plates and bowls and brake blocks from it and use it as floats for fishing nets. Coates Palgrave says that country children in Rhodesia know the tree well for the bark, carefully removed, makes good popguns.

The fibrous bark of young twigs is stripped by Africans and made into twine. Africans use the tree medicinally.

This shares, with the commiphoras, the common name "never die" or "live long" and for the same reason — poles planted in the ground strike easily. This is therefore a quick and easy tree for warm areas.

The specific name *discolor* is a Latin word meaning "of different colours", in reference to the different colour of the upper and lower surface of the leaflets.

(363)   *Lannea stuhlmannii* (Engl.) Engl.

= *Odina stuhlmannii* Engl.; = *Lannea kirkii* Burtt Davy

Tree grape, boomdruif, bastard marula, baster-marula; uLibasi, umGanunkomo (Z); umGanunkomo (Sw); ndivata (Tso)

The tree grape is one of the most graceful trees of the open dry bushveld and woodland from Zululand, Swaziland, the northern and eastern Transvaal to Botswana, South West Africa, and Mozambique, northwards to tropical Africa, often growing on flat, gravelly, gritty or sandy soil. Fine trees grow close to the national road at the northern entrance to Wyllie's Poort, the deep cutting through the Soutpansberg.

Above left
Lannea discolor: fruit
and leaves (90%)

Above right
Lannea stuhlmannii:
a leaf (50%)

This rather marula-like tree may grow up to 12m high with a trunk diameter of over 30 cm, but as a rule it is a smaller tree, spreading, leafy and drooping, with a straight grey or light brown, mottled trunk, the bark flaking off in rectangular pieces showing a creamy-orange colour below.

The branches are grey, slightly hairy at first but becoming smooth, and the large shiny compound leaves are carried on long stalks, smooth or hairy, at the ends of the small branchlets. They usually consist of 1-4 pairs of opposite leaflets and a terminal leaflet, which are oval, egg-shaped or almost round, usually bluntly pointed, the side leaflets somewhat lopsided, usually 4-6 cm long by 1.3-4 cm wide, but sometimes larger, borne on short stalks. They are untoothed, hairy when young and occasionally when mature, sometimes with tufts of hairs in the axils of the nerves below. They often turn bright yellow in late autumn.

Giraffe and kudu are known to browse them.

The flowers, which bloom from October to November, are usually in long string-like racemes in the axils of the leaves. The fruits are oval to oblong, slightly flattened, 0.8-2.5 cm long, with 3 small knobs at the apex — conspicuous when the fruits are fresh — green turning purple, borne in handsome sprays. The skin slips off the fruit exposing the bright orange, slimy flesh. They ripen in late summer and autumn and are edible and quite well-flavoured. Birds such as the Grey Hornbill, monkeys, baboons, and kudu are especially fond of them.

Africans use the tree medicinally.

In Tongaland fish nets are boiled in water to which bits of the bark have been added, for the tannin in it has preservative properties. It dyes them a dull mauve.

The specific name honours Franz Ernest Stuhlmann, a German colonial senior official, Acting Governor in Tanzania, who made a collection of plants between 1883 and 1894.

The red beech, *Protorhus longifolia*, near Oribi Gorge, Natal

4. *Protorhus* Engl.

Protorhus is a small African and Madagascan genus of about 12 species. One tree species grows in South Africa.

The leaves are simple, opposite or nearly opposite. The small flowers may be bisexual, but male and female are usually borne on separate trees in axillary or terminal panicles. The calyx segments and petals are 5, the stamens 5, the ovary 1-3-celled, and the fruit is usually a 1-celled, 1-seeded drupe.

The generic name is based on the Greek "protos" meaning "first," and *"Rhus"*, another genus of the family and possibly meant in the sense of "approaching the *Rhus* genus".

(364)   *Protorhus longifolia* (Bernh.) Engl.

= *Anaphrenium longifolium* Bernh.; = *Rhus longifolia* Sond.

Red beech, rooibeukehout, harpuisboom; umKomiso, umKupati, iKhubalo (X); umHluthi, umHluthi wehlathi, isiFico, isiFico sehlathi, uNhlangothi, umHlangothi (Z); umHlangothi, imFuce (Sw)

The evergreen, heavy, shiny foliage, typically with a red leaf here and there, and round dense crown, makes this tree conspicuous from the eastern Cape, through Natal, Zululand, and Swaziland to the northern Transvaal, growing in forest, on forest margins, in kloofs and on river sides, from sea level to an altitude of 1220 m.

As a forest tree it may reach 18 m in height with a trunk diameter of 1 m, but in the open and on forest fringes it is usually shorter with a compact, round or dome-shaped crown.

The bark is thin, red-brown to brown, rough and often fissured, and when injured exudes a white juice. The shiny, smooth, leathery leaves are simple and opposite or nearly so, dark green above, paler below, a slender oblong, narrowing both ends, bluntly pointed, 10-15 cm long and 1.9-4 cm wide, with conspicuous wavy, thickened, and slightly inrolled margins, the midrib slightly prominent above and conspicuously so below, and the neat, bold, parallel secondary veins branching outwards almost at right angles and forking near the margin. They are borne on sturdy stalks 1.3-2.5 cm long.

The bark and leaves are eaten by Black Rhino.

The pale mauvy-pink to greenish-white flowers, about 6 mm in diameter, are borne in sprays up to 15 cm long in the axils of the leaves or terminally, usually male and female flowers being borne on different trees. The fruits are drupes like small kidney beans up to 1.3 cm long, smooth, purple, and somewhat fleshy. Vervet and Samango Monkeys eat them, as do Plum-coloured Starlings.

Fourcade described the wood as moderately heavy and hard, strong, elastic and compact, fine-grained, purplish or grey tinged with red, the heartwood dark, not durable in water or in contact with the ground. It has been used for rafters, beams, planks and handsome furniture, for which purposes it is satisfactory if cut in the winter. In summer the wood is apt to decay.

The milky, gummy liquid exuding from the bark has an unusual use. Sim says that Africans use it as a depilatory, smearing it on their fingers to give them a grip and then pulling out the hairs by the roots. African women use the strong-smelling fruits as a perfume.

Left
Protorhus flowers

Centre
Protorhus longifolia: a portion
of a branch (50%)

Below
Protorhus fruits, photographed at Port Edward in November

1202

The tree is reputed to be poisonous, and Gerstner says that African witches use it to cause paralysis of one side of the body. (The bark is used for making a vaccination powder to cure it).

The specific name is derived from Latin words meaning "long leaves". Xhosas sometimes speak of this as iKhubalo, a generic term for various plants with roots used as charms to ward off evil and attract good luck.

5. *Loxostylis* Spreng.f. ex Reich.

Loxostylis is a genus with but a single species, growing from the eastern Cape to Natal. Its most noteworthy character is the form of the compound leaf, the common midrib of which is boldly winged. The leaves are alternate and imparipinnate and the flowers male or female in a terminal panicle borne on separate trees. The calyx lobes and petals number 5, the stamens 5, and the ovary is 1-chambered. The fruit is a dry, rather flat, 1-seeded drupe.

The generic name is based on the Greek words for "oblique" and "style" in reference to the oblique carpels.

(365) *Loxostylis alata* Spreng.f. ex Reichb.

Tierhout, teerhout, wild pepper tree, wildepeperboom

The tierhout — the tiger-wood — is a small, dense, often rather spreading and ornamental little tree usually up to 6 m high, but higher in forest, growing in bush, in forest, on forest margins, in kloofs, and along rivers from about Uitenhage northwards to Natal and Zululand.

The tree photographed grew on the slopes of the Suurberg where it was fairly common.

The bark is grey, showing bright red when injured, and is often corky and fissured lengthwise; the branches are grey and furrowed. Young growth is red. The leaves, dark green when adult, are alternate with 2-6 pairs of opposite stalkless leaflets and a terminal leaflet, borne on a broadly winged common midrib. The leaflets are usually 1.3-6 cm long and 0.6-1.3 cm wide, lance-shaped, pointed, sometimes bluntly so, sometimes with a short thorn-like point, with recurved margins, the leaf being carried on a stalk 1.3-2.5 cm long.

The flowers, in terminal sprays, are male or female, borne on different trees, the male white, the female green. When the female flower has been fertilized the greenish-white sepals — the segments of the calyx — grow longer and turn red, and these — surrounding the small, oval, hard fruit in the centre — are bright and distinctive.

The seed germinates easily but seedlings transplant badly.

The specific name is based on the Latin "alatus" meaning "winged". Two reasons are sometimes given for the common name tierhout. One is that leopards — the name "tier" is often given erroneously to them — sharpen their claws on the corky, damp, mossy trunks, and in the kloofs of the remote Cape mountains this is a possibility. C.A. Smith says the name may refer to the strength of the wood. The common name "wild pepper tree" refers to its likeness to the pepper tree, *Schinus molle.*

Above
The tierhout, *Loxostylis alata*, on the slopes of the Suurberg

Right
Loxostylis alata: A flowering twig (50%)

Below left
Tierhout bark

Below right
Loxostylis alata fruit (90%)

Above left
Laurophyllus capensis:
The leaves and striking
female inflorescence
50%
Above right
Smodingium argutum
leaf 80%

6. *Laurophyllus* Thunb.

Like *Loxostylis,* this is a genus of 1 species only, occurring from Swellendam to Uitenhage. The solitary member, *Laurophyllus capensis* Thunb., is a tree or shrub with simple, alternate, serrated leaves; male or female flowers borne on different trees, the male in a terminal panicle, the female in a dense, woody bracteate inflorescence; the male flowers with the calyx segments, the petals and the stamens 4-5; the female with petals narrow and coloured, the ovary 1-celled, the fruit an achene — a small, hard, dry fruit, slightly winged along the margin and not bursting open.

The generic name is based on the Latin word for "laurel" and the Greek word for "leaf" so that this is "the laurel leaf".

(366)   *Laurophyllus capensis* Thunb.

= *Botryceras laurinum* Willd.

Filabossie, vlakwitels, ystermartiens.

This dense leafy shrub or small tree up to 6 m tall grows on wooded hills and on stream banks from Van Stadens Pass westwards to Swellendam.

The bark is smooth and brown. The leaves are simple, alternate, smooth, resinous, lance-shaped to somewhat egg-shaped, 2.5-13 cm long and 1.9-3 cm wide, pointed, narrowing to the base, roughly and conspicuously toothed.

Trees are male or female. The flowers are small, the male ones in lax terminal sprays, the female in an extraordinary bracteate inflorescence with dense, flattened, woody branches, the whole, says Phillips, "resembling a cluster of much-branched antlers". The generic name in synonymy, *Botryceras,* meaning "clustered horns", was singularly applicable.

The fruit is small, light, and narrowly winged.

The seeds germinate easily but the young plants are tender to frost.

The specific name means "of the Cape".

1205

7. *Smodingium* E.Mey. ex Sond.

Smodingium is a genus of 1 species, a small tree or shrub confined to the eastern parts of the country from East Griqualand and the Transkei through Natal and Zululand to the eastern Transvaal.

It is characterized by alternate leaves with 3 toothed leaflets; small flowers which are male or female borne on different trees in dense terminal panicles; the calyx segments, petals and stamens 5, the ovary 1-celled, the fruit roundish, hard, dry, resinous, appearing somewhat winged, enclosing a single seed.

The tree is noteworthy as being extremely toxic, its sap, or even its pollen, causing swelling, blisters and rash similar to that of the poison ivy of America, *Rhus radicans* L.

In view of this, the derivation of the name is surprising. "Smoding" is the Greek for a swelling or weal and the meaning of the generic name would appear clear. But no — the name, apparently, means "an indurated mark" and refers to the calloused fruit.

(367)   *Smodingium argutum* E.Mey. ex Sond.

Tovane; uTovani (X); inTovane (Z); tshilabele e kgolo (SS)

This graceful little tree or spreading shrub with its gentle rounded lines and drooping leaves gives no idea of its frightful properties which, indeed, are unknown to most Europeans. Yet, wherever it grows, from the Transkei, Lesotho, and the eastern Orange Free State to Natal and the eastern Transvaal lowveld, it is familiar to Africans, who hold it in dread.

It occurs mainly in kloofs, on forest edges and on stony stream banks, as a small tree up to 6 m in height or more usually as a rounded shrub with branches and foliage drooping to the ground. It is very *Rhus*-like in form and leaf and is separated mainly on its fruit which is not a round drupe but hard, flattish, and winged.

The stem or stems are often crooked and up to 23 cm in diameter. The pale green leaves are composed of 3 long, lance-shaped leaflets about 7-13 cm long and 2.5 cm wide, narrowed at both ends, coarsely toothed, smooth, hairless, and shortly stalked or without stalks. They turn red in autumn.

The tiny flowers are usually male or female, borne on separate trees in large terminal sprays. The fruit is small, hard, oblique and winged, reddish when ripe in autumn, when it tints the tree a warm colour.

The wood does not appear to be used and the chief use for the tree has been its decorative qualities — its grace, luxuriance, and the bright red colour of its autumn foliage.

It is an extremely dangerous plant in a garden. Its sap contains a toxic principle which appears to be akin to that of the poison ivy, causing similar swollen blisters. A touch can cause this dermatitis in sensitive persons, while others — at first immune to its toxin — often develop a sensitivity to it if they handle the tree over a long period. The rash produced is no ordinary one but accompanied by agonizing burning and irritation which sometimes persist for several weeks in spite of all treatment. Both Europeans and Africans may be sensitive to the plant and many cases are recorded of its causing acute dermatitis in both races.

The irritation may occur without actual contact with the tree. The pollen itself is dangerous and persons walking to the windward of a flowering tree have been affected without touching the tree at all.

Naturally "the terrible Tovana plant of Pondoland" has been known to Africans and used in magic and for charms. The Zulus today believe the tree has magic properties and that all who meet it should greet it deferentially. If they do not, they say, violent skin irritation follows. Europeans learned of its toxic qualities much later. Sim, who knew that poison ivy had "the curious property of seriously affecting some people when seen without even being touched" thought that no South African species held similar dangers. The knowledge has been built up — painfully — over the years.

The toxic properties of *Smodingium* are now recognized by the medical profession. A full account of the plant by Dr G.H. Findlay is included in the *South African Medical Journal,* Volume 37, August 1963.

The tree was first discovered by Drège in 1832. Strangely, no common name for it in English or Afrikaans appears to have arisen spontaneously, although Sima Eliovson calls it the Rainbow Leaf because of its bright autumn colouring. Perhaps the African "tovana" is as good a name as any. The specific name *arguta* means "sharp" in reference to the serrated leaves.

8. *Heeria* Meisn.

Heeria is an African genus of 1 (or possibly more) species which included, until very recently, all the South and South West African species now known as *Ozoroa.*

Many field observers regret the separation into two genera for the leaves of *Heeria* and *Ozoroa* species have a strong resemblance. Often silvery on the under-side, they have pronounced midribs and strongly marked, clean-cut veins running from the midribs almost at right angles to the thickened, untoothed margins. These lateral veins are evenly spaced, giving an effect of extreme neatness and precision. An observer, knowing one species of *Heeria* or *Ozoroa,* may often correctly identify an unfamiliar species as a member of the same group.

The genera have been separated largely on their fruits, *Heeria* having large fruits sometimes the size of walnuts with a smooth woody covering, and *Ozoroa* small fruits with a fleshy covering, becoming black and wrinkled with age and looking much like raisins. *Heeria* is confined to the south west Cape while the genus *Ozoroa* is widespread from the eastern Cape and Natal westwards to South West Africa.

The latex is milky and resinous. The leaves are simple and alternate; the flowers small and creamy, male and female being borne on separate trees in terminal panicles; the calyx segments and petals 5, the stamens 3, the ovary 1-celled, the fruit a drupe.

The generic name *Heeria* honours Oswald Heer, 1809-1883, Director of the Botanic Gardens in Zurich.

(368)   *Heeria argentea* (Thunb.) Meisn.

= *Sideroxylon argenteum* Thunb.; = *Roemeria argentea* (Thunb.) Thunb.; = *Anaphrenium argenteum* (Thunb.) E.Mey.; = *Rhus thunbergii* Hook.

Kliphout, klipesse, rock ash, wild apricot.

A small, sturdy, bushy shrub or tree of the Western Province, often

Above
Heeria argentea growing in the Gifberg — a
typical bushy specimen among rocks

Right
Heeria argentea: A fruiting twig, the underside
of a leaf, and dissected fruit (45%)

Below
Heeria argentea: A female flowering twig (70%)

branching near ground level, the kliphout grows — as the common name suggests — among rocks and boulders on hillsides and mountains, from Worcester northwards to Clanwilliam. It is abundant on the mountain slopes in Viljoen's Pass, although here mostly of small size, and in the Pakhuis Pass where, under a sheltering rock ledge near Louis Leipoldt's grave, it grows and blooms magnificently. On the slopes of the Gifberg it often grows in company with the gifboom, *Hyaenanche globosa.*

The bark is rough, resinous, mottled grey and brown, and often almost indistinguishable from the lichened rock among which the tree frequently grows.

The leaves are simple and alternate, shortly stalked, dark green above, bluish or silver below, from 2.5-5 cm or more long, egg-shaped to oval, often with a round notched apex, narrowed or somewhat rounded at the base; with the typical precise veining of the *Heeria* and *Ozoroa* groups. When crushed, they have a spicy smell.

The sweet-scented flowers, male and female on different trees, appear in autumn in handsome sprays at the ends of the branches, often on the sides of the tree away from the prevailing wind. They are small, cream-coloured, with orange centres, and smell of sweet marmalade.

The fruits, about the size of smallish walnuts, are hard, yellow-green, rough, and ripen about midsummer. Marloth says they are eaten by dassies which distribute the seed.

Since early times the bark and leaves have been used for tanning hides and skins — the bark often being stripped from living trees — and were once the chief local source of tannin in the Clanwilliam and neighbouring districts.

Pappe described the wood as resinous, fine-grained, hard, heavy, and handsome when polished, useful to the turner and maker of musical instruments. It is still used for general carpentry. The gum exuding from the bark is employed in country districts as an ointment to draw boils and abscesses.

The specific name is Latin, meaning "silvery" in reference to the foliage.

9. *Ozoroa* Del.

About 40 species of trees, shrubs, or perennials belong to this African and Arabian genus. It is characterized by a milky, resinous latex, leaves with numerous neat, parallel veins and untoothed margins, and other characters as in *Heeria.* The fruits, however, are small, smooth, fleshy, kidney-shaped or roundish, green becoming black and wrinkled like raisins. It is in the latter character that this genus is separated from *Heeria*, in which the fruits are larger and woody.

About 15 described species in South and South West Africa grow as trees — although whether all these are indeed entitled to specific rank is doubted by some botanists.

The plants which were until recently known in South Africa as *Ozoroa insignis* Del. are now, following *Flora Zambesiaca,* considered as two species, *Ozoroa engleri* R.&A. Fernandes, and *Ozoroa obovata* (Oliv.) R.&A. Fernandes, which are separated from each other largely on the shape of their leaves. *Ozoroa engleri* has slender leaves narrowing at both ends and *Ozoroa obovata* wider leaves with a rounded apex.

Because of their resinous bark nearly all the species bear the common name of "resin tree" or "harpuisboom".

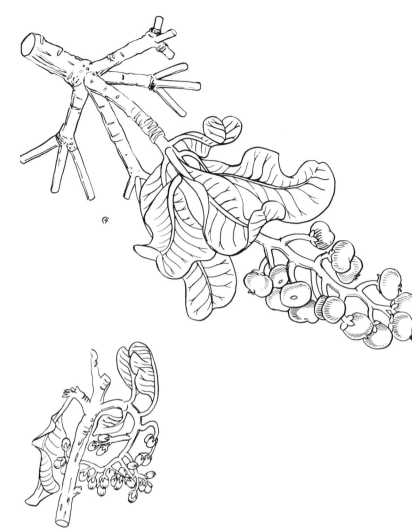

Above left
Ozoroa crassinervia near Tsaris, South West Africa

Above right
Ozoroa concolor: The leaves and fruit, and a twig with buds (80%)

Left
Ozoroa crassinervia bark

1210

Key to species

The leaves up to 5 cm long, *spoon-shaped, concolorous,* bright dark green both sides, markedly wavy; the fruit *under 1 cm wide,* not shiny. (Northern Namaqualand and southern South West Africa)

2. *O. concolor*

The leaves up to 8 cm or more long, oblong to egg-shaped, *markedly 2-coloured,* green above, below covered with greyish-yellow felted hairs, the *fruits 1 cm and more wide,* shiny, *covered with "pore" marks.* (Namaqualand, Gordonia, southern South West Africa, Botswana)

3. *O. dispar*

The leaves up to 10 cm long, egg-shaped, the tips round or notched, *velvety;* below somewhat grey-felted, with the *fine network of veins very conspicuous.* (South West Africa)

1. *O. crassinervia*

The leaves up to 9 cm long, egg-shaped to *round, shiny green above,* below with *silvery* hairs, the netted veins *not very conspicuous,* borne on long slender stalks. (North eastern South West Africa)

5. *O. longipes*

The leaves up to 4 cm long (often smaller), a narrow oval, slightly discolorous, blue-green, *velvety.* (Southern South West Africa).

4. *O. namaensis*

The leaves oblong, *smooth above,* below with thick silver or grey hairs. (North eastern S.W.A.)

10. *O.* insignis
subsp. *latifolia*

The leaves variable, the tips round, blunt or pointed, discolorous, the upper surface dark green, smooth or velvety, the lower paler and densely velvety, with the midrib and veins much raised and *the netted veins conspicuous, the leaf stalks usually over 1 cm long.* (Natal, Zululand, Swaziland, eastern and northern Transvaal, Botswana, north-east S.W.A., northwards).

6. *O. reticulata*

The leaves with round or blunt tips, the margins wavy; discolorous, above green, below lighter and densely velvety, the leaf stalks *usually under 1 cm.* (Eastern Transvaal, Swaziland, Mozambique)

7. *O. sphaerocarpa*

The leaves variable, *egg-shaped or oval,* the tips usually *rounded;* sometimes concolorous; at others green above and below silver, white or grey, and shortly velvety; the lateral veins *hardly raised,* borne on short stalks. (Zululand, in coastal bush and forest, northwards into tropical Africa).

8. *O. obovata*

Above
Ozoroa concolor in a rocky defile
beyond the Wondergat, Richtersveld

Left
The bark of a young tree

Below
The bark of an old tree

The leaves a slender oblong, *narrowing both ends; markedly 2-coloured,* above green or grey, below light green, grey or silver, often densely velvety; the netted veins *almost invisible.* (Zululand, Swaziland, eastern and northern Transvaal, Mozambique, in bushveld, grassveld and woodland).

9. *O. engleri*

The leaves usually a *narrow oblong,* the tips often *roundish or flat,* the margin wavy; discolorous, above grey-green, often shortly silky, below pale, with grey or yellow hairs and the midrib and lateral veins *raised and very conspicuous.* (Natal, Zululand, Swaziland, Transvaal, Botswana, S.W.A., Mozambique).

11. *O. paniculosa*

The leaves *lance-shaped to oblong,* the tips round, blunt or notched, usually with a pronounced tail-like point at the tips; markedly discolorous, above dark green and smooth, below silver-grey and slightly velvety, the veining *not very conspicuous.* (Eastern Cape)

12. *O. mucronata*

(369)   1. *Ozoroa crassinervia* (Engl.) R.&A. Fernandes

= *Anaphrenium crassinervium* Engl.; = *Heeria crassinervia* (Engl.) Engl.; = *Heeria dinteri* Schinz

Ozoroa crassinervia grows in Namaqualand and is widespread in South West Africa from north to south, often growing on granite hills where it is conspicuous, sometimes with a short, wide, leafy crown spread luxuriantly against the rocks, at others sparser in habit.

The leaves are egg-shaped with a rounded and sometimes notched apex, narrowing to the base, 2.5-10 cm long and 1.9-8 cm wide, velvety, somewhat grey-felted below, the midrib and veins clearly marked above, and thick and heavy below, with the fine network of veins very conspicuous. These give the tree its specific name, meaning "thick-veined". They have short stout stalks and are clustered towards the ends of the twigs.

The small white flowers are borne in terminal sprays, male and female separately. The fruits are small, roundish, becoming dark and wrinkled with age, and are borne on longish stalks.

(369.1)   2. *Ozoroa concolor* (Presl ex Sond.) De Wint.

= *Rhus concolor* Presl. ex Sond.; = *Anaphrenium concolor* E.Mey.; = *Heeria concolor* (Presl) Meisn.

Richtersveld ozoroa

Until late 1970 it was not clear whether this species belonged to the genus *Heeria* or to *Ozoroa,* because no mature fruiting specimens had ever been collected. Good rains, however, fell in that year in the north western parts of the country, with the result that the trees fruited abundantly, collections were made, and it was possible to assign the species to *Ozoroa.*

Above
Ozoroa dispar growing on a rocky
hillside south of Springbok

Below left
Ozoroa dispar bark

Below right
Ozoroa dispar: A fruiting branchlet (80%)

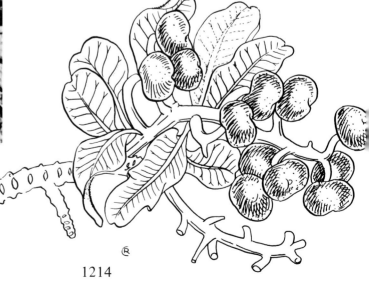

1214

This is a small sturdy tree up to about 4.5 m high, recorded from the desert country in the Richtersveld of northern Namaqualand and in southern South West Africa as far north as Luderitz, growing in dry stream beds and on arid rocky hill and mountain slopes.

The tree photographed grew in a rocky defile bare of all other trees, east of the farm "Beauvallon" and close to the Alexander Bay-Sendelings-drif road. It was several-stemmed from the base — as were other specimens seen — the main stem 15 cm in diameter, grey and fairly smooth (cracked into segments in older trees) with a crown of fairly dense foliage, making a luxuriant and unexpected splash of green among the rocks on the desert slope.

The short, dark green twigs were most often arranged in whorls of about 5, bearing towards their tips tufts of leaves (although sometimes the leaves were alternate). These were firm and leathery in texture, a bright dark green both sides, with the midrib and veins clearly outlined in yellow when seen against the light, spoon-shaped, 2.5-5 cm long, tapered to the base, and so much undulate as to appear frilled.

In September the trees seen were both in flower and fruit, the terminal sprays of these on strong yellow-green stalks arising from the centre of the clustered leaves. The panicles were up to some 8 cm long, the female flowers tiny, creamy-white, 5-petalled, with a faint sweet scent; the individual fruits kidney-shaped, slightly fleshy, up to 1 cm wide and slightly less in length, the small calyx brown, the fruits green turning russet-red, borne on short stalks.

The specific name *concolor* means "of one colour" referring to the leaves, the upper and lower surface of which are almost the same shade.

The better known and more widespread *Ozoroa* species in Namaqualand is *Ozoroa dispar* (Presl) R.&A. Fernandes, which occurs, too, in the Richtersveld, and which in general habit resembles *Ozoroa concolor*. The latter may be distinguished from it by its concolorous leaves which are usually shorter and more undulate and a glossier green, and by its fruits which are smaller, generally less than 1 cm wide, smooth, with a somewhat dull surface, and borne on slender stalks, in comparison with those of *Ozoroa dispar* which are usually 1 cm or more in width and shiny, marked with small but conspicuous "pores", and which are borne on sturdy stalks. In the field these differences are very clear; less so in dried material in the herbarium.

(370)   3. *Ozoroa dispar* (Presl) R.&A. Fernandes

= *Rhus dispar* Presl; = *Anaphrenium dispar* (Presl) E.Mey.; = *Heeria dispar* (Presl) Kuntze; *Ozoroa rangeana* (Engl.) R.&A. Fernandes

Namaqualand ozoroa

Ozoroa dispar occurs in the north western Cape, in southern South West Africa and in Botswana. It is one of the common trees of Namaqualand, where its luxuriant crown of strong, leathery leaves is a familiar sight hugging rocks and stony hillsides round Springbok and in the hills to the south. It occurs, also, in the Richtersveld in the north, and as far east as the islands in the Orange River near the Augrabies Falls.

It is a small, compact, wide-crowned tree up to 4.5 m tall or a spreading bush, with grey, cracked bark and leaves clustered at the ends of the twigs. They are simple and alternate, somewhat undulate, smooth and bright green above, with the netted veins conspicuous, below covered

Above
Ozoroa namaensis on the hills near
Aroab, South West Africa

Left
Ozoroa longipes leaves and flowers

Below
Ozoroa reticulata: A fruiting twig
and flowers (70%)

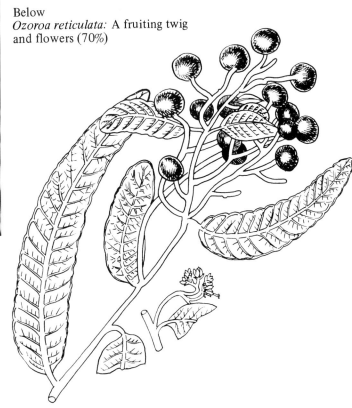

with short greyish-yellow felt, the veins often somewhat reddish; oval, oblong or egg-shaped, 2.5-7 cm long and 1.9-3 cm wide, with the usual *Ozoroa* veining, borne on stalks up to 1.9 cm long.

The small white or yellow flowers are carried in sprays at the ends of the branches. The fruits are kidney-shaped, 1 cm or more in width, and slightly less in length, at first plump, shiny, and covered with conspicuous "pores" but with age becoming wrinkled like raisins. They are borne in heavy pendulous bunches and ripen in late spring.

The specific name is Latin meaning "dissimilar" in reference to the two-coloured leaves.

4. *Ozoroa namaensis* (Schinz & Dinter) R. Fernandes

Nama ozoroa

The Nama ozoroa appears to be confined to rocky situations in southern South West Africa. It is a small tree up to about 4.2 m in height, often with a single trunk and very rough brown bark cracked into knobbly segments. It is strong-smelling, the scent described by one collector as "like distant goat".

The leaves are simple, small, 1.3-4 cm long and 0.8-1.3 cm wide, a narrow oval with round or bluntly pointed tips, velvety, blue-green, with the usual *Ozoroa* veining, crowded towards the ends of the twigs.

The small flowers are in long terminal sprays.

Parts of the tree are used medicinally.

5. *Ozoroa longipes* (Engl. & Gilg) R.&A. Fernandes

= *Heeria longipes* Engl. & Gilg

This is most often a shrub or sometimes a small tree up to about 3 m high occurring in woodland in north-eastern South West Africa and the Caprivi Strip.

The leaves may be alternate, crowded together or whorled, a shiny green above with silvery hairs below, egg-shaped to almost round, 2.5-9 cm long by 1.3-6 cm wide, sometimes with a short thorn-like point, the midrib and slender secondary veins conspicuous and the midrib much raised below, the netted veins not conspicuous. They are borne on long slender stalks. The small whitish flowers are in terminal and axillary sprays, and the fruits are small, kidney-shaped, a shiny black becoming wrinkled.

(376)   6. *Ozoroa reticulata* (Bak.f.) R.&A. Fernandes

= *Heeria insignis* var. *reticulata* Bak.f.; = *Heeria reticulata* (Bak.f.) Engl.

Isifico, isiFico (Z); shinungu (Tso)

Ozoroa reticulata is widespread in parts of Natal, Zululand, Swaziland, the eastern and northern Transvaal, Botswana and north east South West Africa, northwards into tropical Africa, as a shrub or as a slender or many-branched, spreading tree up to 10 m. It grows in open bush and savannah, often among rocks.

Above
Ozoroa obovata, Charters Creek,
Zululand

Left
Ozoroa reticulata near Piet Retief

Below
Ozoroa reticulata stem

1218

The bark is rough and brown, the young branches with lenticels and with reddish-yellow hairs, becoming hairless with age. The leaves are simple and borne alternately or in whorls of 3. They are very variable in shape and size, 4-15 cm long, usually oblong, with a round, blunt or pointed apex, often with a small thorn-like point, the base round or narrow, the upper surface velvety, smooth, or sometimes with hairs on the veins only, the lower side densely velvety, dark green above and paler below, the margins untoothed, thickened and often wavy. The veining is not conspicuous above — the midrib is slightly sunken — but below the midrib and veins are much raised, and sometimes these and the thickened margins are all a warm gold. The netted veins are conspicuous. Twigs and leaf stalks are often velvety. The latter are fairly long, usually over 1 cm.

The small white or yellow flowers are borne abundantly in many-branched sprays in the axils of the leaves and at the ends of the branches and are much visited by butterflies and bees. Trees are male or female.

The small oblique, oval fruits are black, shiny, and more or less compressed, becoming wrinkled with age. They are eaten by Africans and are particularly popular with birds.

Africans use the wood to build huts. Coates Palgrave says it was once used for arrowheads, smelting and ironwork because its addition made the metal malleable. The tree is widely used in medicine in Africa.

Flora Zambesiaca divides this into 3 subspecies and a number of varieties.

The specific name is based on the reticulated veins.

(377)   *7. Ozoroa sphaerocarpa* R.&A. Fernandes

Usually a small, spreading tree of rocky slopes, bush and woodlands in the eastern Transvaal, Portuguese East Africa and Swaziland, this much resembles *Ozoroa reticulata.*

The leaves are alternate, 4-11 cm long and 1.3-4 cm wide, a narrow oblong to egg-shaped, with a round or blunt apex, often with a thorn-like point, the base rounded or slightly narrowed, soft when young, leathery and stiff when old, dull or shiny above, densely velvety below — young leaves look as if cut out of velvet — the margins thickened and wavy, the midrib and veins raised below, the leaf stalks short (under 1 cm) and hairy.

The flowers are in terminal and axillary sprays, the male more compact than the female. The fruit is small, roundish, shiny, and black.

The specific name is based on Greek words meaning "round fruit".

(374)   *8. Ozoroa obovata* (Oliv.) R.&A. Fernandes

= *Rhus insignis* var. *obovata* Oliv.; = *Anaphrenium abyssinicum* var. *obovatum* (Oliv.) Engl.; = *Anaphrenium abyssinicum* var. *mucronatum* (Bernh.) Engl.; = *Heeria mucronata* Bernh. var. *obovata* (Oliv.) Engl. (Formerly erroneously known in South Africa as *Ozoroa insignis* Del.)

Resin tree, harpuisboom; isiFica, isiFico (Z); shinungumafi (Tso); mochudi (Tsw); munungu-mafhi (V)

Sometimes a shrub, at others a luxuriantly spreading evergreen tree up to 9 m high, this species is common in Zululand coastal bush and forest,

Above
Ozoroa engleri on the Makatini
Flats, a picturesque and graceful
species

Below left
Ozoroa engleri in full bloom in
February — female flowers

Below right
Ozoroa engleri: A fruiting twig
(70%)

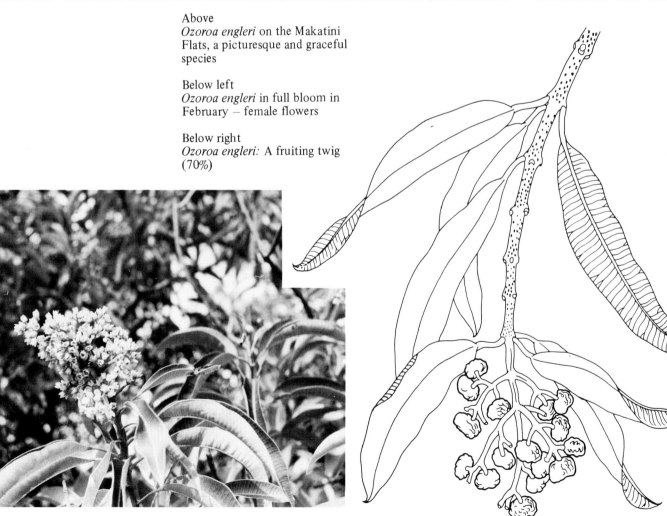

Left
Ozoroa obovata: a fruiting twig (60%)

Above right
Ozoroa engleri: the bark of an old tree

reaching northward into Rhodesia, Portuguese East Africa, and tropical Africa.

The grey or rusty yellow twigs, smooth or hairy, are covered with small raised dots. The leaves, alternate or whorled, are sometimes of one colour, at others dark or olive green above and silver below, the upper surface sometimes slightly hairy or with hairs on the midrib and nerves only, the lower surface smooth or covered with white, grey, or silver hairs. They are oblong to egg-shaped, 2.5-12 cm long and 1.5-4 cm wide, the apex usually rounded and with a tiny curled point, or sometimes notched, the base usually narrowed, the margins slightly thickened, not wavy, the midrib raised below but the secondary veins hardly raised at all, borne on short stalks that are slender or broad and flat, and hairy.

The flowers are in sprays at the ends of the branches. The fruits are at first light green with darker green dots, looking like beans made out of smooth, green, mottled marble, turning black, wrinkled and raisin-like with age.

The fruits are eaten by Grey Hornbills, the bark by elephant, the young shoots by steenbuck and eland, and by impala and kudu which also eat the leaves.

Until recently this species and *Ozoroa engleri* R.&A. Fernandes were included in a broad concept of *Ozoroa insignis* Del., which is essentially a north African species. *Ozoroa engleri* is separated from *Ozoroa obovata* largely on the shape of its leaves which are slender and narrowed at both ends.

Ozoroa engleri:
the bark of a younger tree

(371)   9. *Ozoroa engleri* R.&A. Fernandes

Makatini ozoroa; isiFica, isiFico (Z); shinungumafi (Tso)

Ozoroa engleri, now regarded as distinct from the more northern *Ozoroa insignis* Del., is a common little tree in grassveld, bushveld and in woodland in Zululand — in particular on the Makatini Flats — in Swaziland

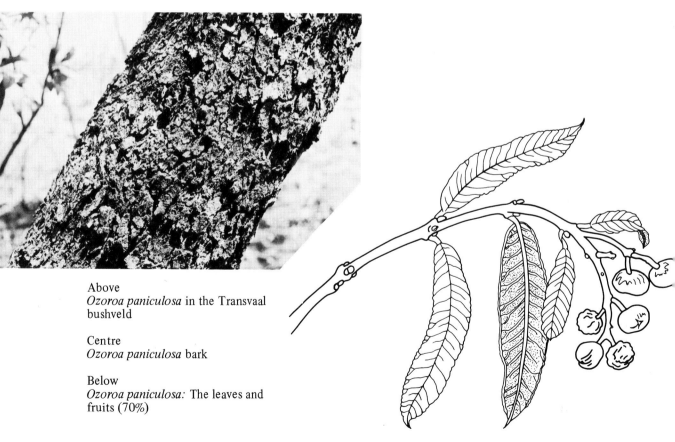

Above
Ozoroa paniculosa in the Transvaal
bushveld

Centre
Ozoroa paniculosa bark

Below
Ozoroa paniculosa: The leaves and
fruits (70%)

and the eastern and northern Transvaal, northwards into Portuguese East Africa. The tree photographed grew on the Makatini Flats where it was flowering profusely in late summer.

It may be a spreading bush, or a tree 8 m high, and has a rough grey trunk, the bark cracked into small squares, light-coloured branches, and upward-pointing, yellow-brown twigs, smooth or covered with fine hairs.

The leaves are simple, alternate or in whorls of 3, borne on stalks that are pinky-grey to brown and often softly hairy. The leaves are variable, from dark green to grey above, smooth or hairy and light green to ashy-grey or silver below, a narrow oblong, narrowing to both ends, often with a thorn-like point, usually 4-13 cm long and 1-3 cm wide, or sometimes larger; the margin thickened and sometimes wavy, the fine parallel veins conspicuous, the midrib raised below, and the netted veins invisible. They are borne on slender stalks, often noticeably flattened near the base, which are yellow, reddish or dark brown.

The small, creamy, sweet-scented flowers are in handsome sprays at the end of the branches and are favourites with bees. The fruits are small, kidney-shaped to roundish, somewhat flattened, reddish turning black and raisin-like. When gound up, they are used as a scent with which Zulu women anoint their hair.

The wood is hard and tough, and the tree is used medicinally.

All the ozoroas are handsome shrubs or trees for a garden. If the form of this species, with silvery velvet leaves borne on yellow velvet stalks, were to be cultivated it would be among the best of all silver-grey shrubs so loved by landscape gardeners. It is probably tender to frost.

The tree was called after Adolf Engler, 1844-1930, distinguished German botanist, traveller and author, who was Professor of Botany and Director of the Botanic Garden at Berlin Dahlem.

10. *Ozoroa insignis* Del.
subsp. *latifolia* (Engl.) R. Fernandes
= *Anaphrenium abyssinicum* var. *latifolium* Engl.

Ozoroa insignis is a north and west African species, one subspecies of which has been collected in the Grootfontein district of South West Africa.

It is a bush or tree with hairy twigs and leaves that are usually arranged in whorls of three. They are oblong or widely lance-shaped, sharply or bluntly pointed, with a small thorn-like point at the tip, smooth above and below covered with thick silver or grey hairs, 5-13 cm long, 1.9-4 cm broad, with the usual neat ozoroa veining.

The flowers are in sprays at the ends of the branches and the fruit is up to 1.3 cm long, black becoming wrinkled.

The specific name is Latin, meaning "conspicuous".

(375)   11. *Ozoroa paniculosa* (Sond.) R.&A. Fernandes

= *Rhus paniculosa* Sond.; = *Anaphrenium paniculosum* (Sond.) Engl.;
= *Heeria paniculosa* (Sond.) Kuntze

Bushveld ozoroa; isiFico sehlanze, isiFica (Z); monokane (Tws-Hebron); monoko (NS)

This graceful species, which varies from a shrub to a 12 m tree, is fairly common in hilly country in bush and savannah from Natal, Zululand and Swaziland, through the Transvaal — it is common in bushveld close to Pretoria and Joahnnesburg — and Botswana to South West Africa, where it is widely spread, and in Portuguese East Africa. It is probable that the South West African shrub formerly known as *Heeria hereroensis* Schinz, with leaves velvety on both sides, and *Heeria salicina* (Sond.) Burtt Davy with very narrow leaves — from the Transvaal, Botswana and South West Africa — are no more than forms of this species.

The trunk, although usually slender, occasionally reaches 1.5 m in diameter.

The bark is smooth and grey in young trees, becoming dark grey to brown, rough and scaly. The reddish-brown branches, velvety or smooth, are inclined to droop. The evergreen foliage is composed of slender, silvery-green leaves on short stalks arranged alternately or sometimes whorled. They are variable in size, at times no more than 2.5 cm long and 6 mm wide, at others up to 13 cm long and 4 cm wide, usually a narrow oblong but sometimes wider, the apex usually roundish or flat with a short, thorn-like point, the base slightly narrowed, the margin thickened and slightly wavy, above with the veins hairy or the whole surface shortly silky, below covered with pale silky hairs, the midrib raised below, and this and the parallel secondary veins conspicuous.

The creamy-coloured, strongly scented flowers are in long sprays, terminally and in the axils of the leaves — male and female on separate trees — and the ripe fruits are small, slightly oblong, broader than long, flattened, green and spotted becoming black and wrinkled. They are often carried in heavy bunches at the ends of drooping branches making characteristic silhouettes. The fruits are used as a perfume by Africans, and to make a dye for the leather aprons of Zulu women.

Black Rhino eat the bark and leaves.

In country districts the sap from the trunk is sometimes tapped, dried, and used for mending cracks in pottery, while Africans sometimes paint it on the strings of their musical instruments.

The wood, according to Galpin, is reddish-brown, fine-grained, soft, brittle, of poor quality, and not used. The tree, however, is decorative, is fairly hardy, and should be neat and graceful in a garden.

The specific name is Latin meaning "with a loose flower cluster".

(373)   12. *Ozoroa mucronata* (Bernh.) R.&A. Fernandes

= *Heeria mucronata* Bernh.

Cape ozoroa

Ozoroa mucronata is a small tree or bush from the eastern Cape, recorded in the Kei River valley, and the East London, Albany and Alexandria districts, growing in forests and on river banks.

The leaves are simple and alternate, 2.5-8 cm long, narrowly or widely lance-shaped to oblong, the apex round or bluntly pointed, with a sharp point, dark and smooth above, paler below and slightly velvety. The veining is not conspicuous. The flowers are in long sprays terminally and in the axils of the leaves. The fruits are small, kidney-bean-shaped and shiny, becoming raisin-like.

The specific name is the Latin mucronatus meaning "with a short and straight point" in reference to the leaves.

10. *Rhus* L.

This largely tropical and subtropical genus of roughly 250 species is well represented in South and South West Africa with over 60 described species. The majority of these occur in the eastern parts of the country although all four provinces of the Republic are rich in them, whether shrubs or trees, and they flourish from high forest to bushveld and to arid areas, on hills, on plains, on river banks, in kloofs and valleys and around pans.

Rhus is an exceedingly difficult genus, even for botanists, and full of surprises, for new species are still being discovered. The last authoritative work on the genus was that of Dr S. Schonland 30 years ago. He arranged the South African species in 12 groups, dividing the species into numerous varieties and forms, depending on leaflet size and shape, type of leaf stalk and margins, degree of hairiness, etc., noting at the same time that the species hybridized easily.

The most recent work on these by Mme Rosette Fernandes in *Boletim da Sociedada Broteriana* Vol. XLI (2nd Series) 1967, deals only with new combinations of names and does nothing to dispel the confusion existing around these interminable subdivisions. Modern botanists tend to ignore them, and when the genus is revised it will probably be much simplified. Nevertheless, Schonland's account of the genus is still the basis of all work done on the *Rhus* group — including the following descriptions.

Most of the *Rhus* are shrubs of fair size, and at one time or another these are nearly all found as bushy trees. It is possible that species such as *Rhus ciliata* Licht. and *Rhus populifolia* E.Mey. from the arid west, or *Rhus nebulosa* Schonl. from the east, are on occasions trees, but they are not included here because no record of them as anything but shrubs exist. Some are clearly trees up to 9 m high, and one, *Rhus chirindensis* Bak.f. forma *legatii* (Schonl.) R.&A. Fernandes, is a forest tree up to 25 m.

The leaves are the distinguishing feature, nearly always being composed of 3 leaflets and occasionally of up to 5 or 7, the central leaflet being usually the biggest. The leaves are usually alternate and stalked, the stalks usually being furrowed and sometimes winged, while the leaflets are usually without any stalks at all. Some *Rhus* are spineless, others always or occasionally with spines.

Many have glands secreting a resinous varnish which makes the leaves shiny as if polished, but — even in the same species — this is not always constant. Marloth remarked that the leaves of *Rhus laevigata* and *Rhus lucida*, growing near Cape Town, had little resin, while those in dry areas were constantly covered in resin. The varnish appears to be a protection against excessive transpiration.

The flowers are small and usually greenish-yellow, in loose branching heads (panicles), terminally or in the axils of the leaves. Plants are nearly always male or female, although occasionally bisexual flowers do occur. The calyx segments and petals number 5, the stamens in the male 5, the staminodes in the female usually 5, and the ovary is 1-celled.

The fruits are small drupes, roundish, often somewhat lopsided and flattened, smooth, green or white, brown or red when mature. They are edible although of very poor flavour and give the common names rosyntjiebos (raisin bush) or rosyntjieboom (raisin tree), korentebessie (currant) or kraaibessies (crow berries) to the species. The fruits were once, and in parts still are, an important part of the diet of Bushmen and Bantu peoples.

Above
The fruits of the widespread karee, *Rhus lancea,* eaten by
people and by birds

Left
Jan Jafta, a Hottentot basket-maker, on the farm "Cranemere" in the Pearston district, and his baskets made of
rushes and the young wands of *Rhus lancea*

In lean times they are taken by most fruit-eating birds.

A number of butterflies breed on *Rhus* species. These include the
beautiful Pearl Carax, *Charaxes varanes;* The Foxtrot Copper, *Phasis
thero* – widespread in the Cape – the Samba Copper, *Phasis clavum,* a
small dark butterfly marked with orange-red; *Phasis braueri* (known to
breed on *Rhus longispina*); the Burnished Copper, *Poecilmitis chrysoar,*
and the Common Hairtail, *Anthene difinita.*

The bark of several species was once used extensively for tanning,
and to make rope, hence – according to Schonland – the common name
taaibos. The wood is usually tough and red and used to make fencing
posts, strong kerries and handles, the branches of some for thatching
and for wagon tents, and the pliable young branches to make baskets
and whips. Once they made the strong flexible bows of the Bushmen.
The species from arid areas have a particular value as shade trees. A few
are browsed.

When used as fuel, the wood often sparks, and thus Xhosas think
that the burning wood can attract lightning. Africans use *Rhus* species
widely in medicine and in magic.

Schonland suggests that this interesting and diverse race has, as its
parent, the group he terms Mucronata (which includes what is now
Rhus laevigata Thunb.) and that this group spread from Northern to
Southern Africa. The majority of the South African species, he thinks,
evolved here – how, why, and in response to what stimuli remaining
unknown.

The generic name *Rhus* is based on a Greek word meaning "red" and
probably refers to the often red autumn leaves of many species.

Key to species

(*Rhus* leaves are notoriously variable. This "key" is therefore no more than a rough guide).

LEAFLETS OFTEN BROAD OR FAIRLY BROAD IN PROPORTION TO THEIR LENGTH

Not toothed or scolloped or only slightly so

A shrub or small tree, spiny or unarmed; the leaf stalks sometimes *winged;* the leaflets variable, the central one generally up to 4 x 2.5 cm. (South West Cape to Natal, often in dunes).

1. *R. laevigata*

A bush to a 9 m tree, often spreading and drooping, spineless; the leaflets occasionally 5, usually egg-shaped, up to 6 x 4 cm, soft, velvety or smooth, sometimes slightly toothed, *the network of fine veins often conspicuous.* (Cape, Natal, Swaziland, Transvaal).

2. *R. macowanii*

A shrub or a small tree resembling the above species but the central leaflet with a *round or flat, toothed apex.* (Natal, Swaziland, Transvaal).

3. *R. rehmanniana*

A shrub or tree, *usually spiny;* the leaflets lance-shaped to oblong, often broad, the central one up to 6 x 3 cm, *the network of veins conspicuous;* smooth or velvety; the leafstalk up to 1.9 cm long. (Cape, O.F.S., Natal, Transvaal, Botswana, northern S.W.A.)

4. *R. pyroides*

A shrub or small tree, often with *a fastigiate habit,* very closely related to *Rhus pyroides,* separated mainly on the absence of reticulate venation in the adult leaves. (E. Cape, Natal, Transvaal).

9. *R. fastigiata*

A shrub or small tree; the leaf stalks *somewhat winged;* the leaflets oblong to egg-shaped, untoothed, the central one up to 6 x 4 cm, the midrib and veins prominent.

5. *R. krebsiana*

A shrub to a 14 m tree; the leaves leathery, usually egg-shaped and untoothed, the central one up to 6 x 3 cm; the midrib, lateral veins and network of fine veins *conspicuous both sides;* shiny above, duller below. (Transvaal, Swaziland).

6. *R. dura*

A shrub or small tree, *sometimes spiny;* the leaf stalk often *winged;* the leaflets bright green above, paler below, egg-shaped to widely lance-shaped, usually untoothed or with about 3 rounded teeth, slightly hairy, the terminal (the middle) leaflet up to 3 x 1.3 cm. (Pondoland, Natal, O.F.S., Transvaal, Mozambique).

10. *R. pentheri*

Rhus leaves: 1 *R. lucida.* 2 *R. undulata* var *celastroides.* 3 *R. undulata* var *undulata* 4 *R. glauca.* 5 *R. pentheri.* 6 *R. transvaalensis.* 7 *R. laevigata* 8 *R. krebsiana.* 9 *R. dentata.* 10 *R. fastigiata.* 11 *R. dura.* 12 *R. engleri.* 13 *R. carnosula* (100%)

A forest tree up to 25 m tall; the leaf stalk *slender, long, reddish;* the leaflets usually *large,* egg-shaped to oblong, smooth, the central one up to 13 x 6 cm (occasionally larger) and shortly stalked. (Forests of the Cape, Natal, Swaziland, Transvaal).

11. *R. chirindensis* forma *legatii*

Usually a shrub; the leaves *blue-green,* leathery, usually untoothed, egg-shaped to oblong; the central one usually up to 9 x 1.9 cm. (Transvaal).

13. *R. zeyheri*

A shrub or tree; the twigs often hairy and resinous; the leafstalk frequently short and *slightly winged;* the leaflets leathery, glossy, egg-shaped to oblong, usually untoothed, the central one up to 8 x 2.5 cm; the flowers often *bisexual.* (Cape, Natal, and possibly the Transvaal).

14. *R. lucida*

A shrub or small tree; the branches and leaves covered with resin, drying to a grey powder, the stalks often *winged;* the leaves green to *blue- or grey-green, shiny,* the leaflets usually 3 but sometimes 1-4; the central leaflet up to about 1.9 x 1.3 cm with the apex wide, flat, and often notched. (Western to eastern Cape).

15. *R. glauca*

A shrub to 6 m tree, usually spineless (the arid forms spiny); the leaf stalks *often winged;* the leaflets often *shiny and sticky;* oblong, egg-shaped, to lance-shaped, usually untoothed, *wavy,* the central leaflet up to about 5 x 1.3 cm. (Cape, Natal, O.F.S., Transvaal, South West Africa, Botswana).

16. *R. undulata*

A drooping, willow-like shrub or small tree; the leaves with 3-7 usually 3, leaflets; the leaflets lance-shaped to egg-shaped; deeply or slightly toothed or not at all, smooth or hairy, the size variable. (Pondoland, Natal, eastern O.F.S., Transvaal, Swaziland).

24. *R. montana*

A low shrub or small tree, the leaflets oval, untoothed, slightly to densely hairy, the midrib and veins prominent, the central leaflet up to 6 x 1.9 cm. (Inland forests of Natal, Zululand and the Transvaal.)

26. *R. microcarpa*

A shrub or small bushy tree, *very spiny;* the leaves usually *in tufts;* the leaflets and flower sprays covered with small reddish glands; the leaflets egg-shaped or narrower, untoothed, the central one up to 5 x 2.5 cm; the leaf stalk *often winged.* (Cape)

29. *R. longispina*

A shrub to 6 m tree, the leaflets distinctly *two-coloured,* dark green and smooth above, grey or tawny and densely hairy below; egg-shaped, toothed or untoothed, stalked; the leaf stalks usually over 1.3 cm; the

Rhus leaves: 14 *R. montana* 15 *R. incisa.* 16 *R. quartiniana.* 17 *R. tomentosa.* 18 *R. tenuinervis.* 19 *R. crispa.* 20 *R. marlothii.* 21 *R. microcarpa.* 22 *R. natalensis* 23 *R. gueinzii.* (100%)

fruits *hairy*. (S.W.Cape, George, Transkei, Natal, Transvaal).

30. *R. tomentosa*

A shrub to a 6 m tree, *sometimes spiny;* the leaflets resinous, dark green above, below *yellowish and scurfy,* oval to lance-shaped, the central one up to 8 x 2.5 cm, the margins usually untoothed. (South West Africa, Botswana, Caprivi Strip).

33. *R. quartiniana*

Conspicuously toothed, scolloped, or lobed

A shrub or tree, sometimes slightly spiny; the leaflets usually egg-shaped, with the upper parts *boldly toothed;* the central leaflet usually up to 5 x 2.5 cm, smooth or *hairy*. (E. Cape, O.F.S., Natal, Transvaal, Rhodesia, Mozambique).

7. *R. dentata*

A shrub or tree; the leaves slightly *fleshy;* the leaflets oblong to egg-shaped, untoothed or boldly toothed, *hairless,* the midrib and lateral veins conspicuous, the central leaflet up to 8 x 1.9 cm. (Eastern Cape, Pondoland)

8. *E. carnosula*

A shrub to 6 m tree; the leaves leathery, hairless, dark to light green above, paler below, oblong or lance-shaped, the central one up to 9 x 4 cm, the margins *scolloped* or entire. (E. Cape, Natal, to tropical Africa).

18. *R. natalensis*

A shrub to small tree, the leaflets lance-shaped to egg-shaped, the margins in the upper part often scolloped, the central leaflet 5 x 2.5 cm, *velvety*. (Transvaal, Botswana, South West Africa).

20. *R. marlothii*

A shrub to 6 m tree, *sometimes spiny;* the leaflets hairy, egg-shaped to oblong, the margins in the upper parts scolloped, the central leaflet up to 10 x 5 cm, dark or grey-green above, *yellowish below*. (Transvaal, Cape, South West Africa, Caprivi Strip, Botswana).

21. *R. tenuinervis*

A shrub to small tree; the leaflets small, oblong, the apex flat or round, the margins untoothed or *deeply toothed,* dark green above, below *velvety-white;* the leaflets up to 1.9 x 1.3 cm; the fruit *grey with shaggy hairs, often splitting open*. (Namaqualand, south west and eastern Cape).

32. *R. incisa*

LEAFLETS OFTEN SLENDER

Not — or scarcely — toothed or scolloped

A low shrub to small tree; the young twigs furry, the leaf stalks *often very hairy;* the leaflets lance-shaped to oblong, smooth or hairy, *un-*

toothed, sometimes wavy, the central one up to 5 x 1.3 cm. (Transvaal and Natal highveld).

12. *R. transvaal-ensis*

A small tree, *sometimes spiny;* the twigs *softly hairy;* the leaves usually small, oblong to lance-shaped, *velvety,* dull green above, grey below, untoothed or slightly toothed, the central one up to 4 x 0.8 cm. (Transvaal bushveld).

17. *R. engleri*

A shrub to 6 m tree, usually spineless; the leaf stalks *winged;* the leaflets often *shiny and sticky;* oblong, egg-shaped to lance-shaped, usually untoothed, *wavy,* the central leaflet up to about 5 x 1.3 cm — but often much smaller. (Cape, Natal, O.F.S., Transvaal, South West Africa, Botswana).

16. *R. undulata*

A shrub to 6 m tree, unarmed or *spiny;* the leaflets usually 3, lance-shaped to oblong, the central one up to 6.5 cm long, the apex round or bluntly pointed and notched, sometimes toothed, dark green above, paler below. (E. Cape, Natal, Zululand, Swaziland, Transvaal, Rhodesia).

19. *R. gueinzii*

A tree up to 9 m; the leaflets narrow, stiff, smooth, dark green above, *pale below,* usually untoothed; the central one usually up to 13 x 1.3 cm; the venation *usually clearest on the upper surface, flowering autumn.* (Transvaal, O.F.S., Cape, Botswana, South West Africa).

22. *R. lancea*

A tree up to 9 m, closely resembling *R. lancea* except that the leaflets are slightly broader, the central one up to 8 x 1.9 cm and a *fairly uniform green* above and below, *flowering spring.* (Cape midlands, north west Cape, Namaqualand, South West Africa).

23. *R. viminalis*

A drooping willow-like shrub or tree; the leaflets smooth green above, *densely hairy-white below,* stalked, narrow, the central one up to 5 x 1.3 cm, untoothed, the leafstalks 1.3 cm long, the fruit hairy. (Western Cape)

31. *R. angustifolia*

Conspicuously toothed, scolloped or lobed

A shrub to small tree; the leaves with 3-7, usually 3, leaflets; the leaflets lance-shaped to egg-shaped; deeply or slightly toothed for part of, or the whole length (or occasionally not at all), smooth or hairy, the size variable. (Pondoland, Natal, eastern O.F.S., Transvaal, Swaziland).

24. *R. montana*

A tree up to 6 m; often confused with *R. lancea;* the leaflets fairly light green, soft, narrowly lance-shaped, the central leaflet generally up to 10 x 1.9 cm, the margins sometimes untoothed, usually *shallowly toothed the whole length;* the venation usually more conspicuous *on the undersurface; flowering late spring.* (O.F.S., northern Cape, Transvaal, Swaziland, Botswana, Rhodesia).

25. *R. leptodictya*

A shrub to small tree, the leaflets thin, smooth, wavy or flat, deep green above, lighter below, toothed or untoothed, the central leaflet up to 9 x 2.5 cm. (Cape, Transkei, Natal).

27. *R. crispa*

A shrub, large and rounded, very occasionally a tree, up to 3 x 9 m, spineless; the leaflets very *long, narrow, and pointed,* leathery, hairless, *sticky,* the margins usually *deeply jagged;* the central leaflet up to 13 x 0.3 cm. (O.F.S., Cape, Lesotho)

28. *R. erosa*

1. *Rhus laevigata* L.

= *Rhus mucronata* Thunb.

Dune taaibos, duinetaaibos, korentebos; umHlakothi (X)

Rhus laevigata, although commonly a large shrub, can grow into a short spreading tree, and is found in one or the other form in the coastal districts from the south west Cape to Natal. It often grows on dunes, and in the dwarf macchia on the granite and limestone hills of the south west.

It may be spiny or without spines, the leaves – with 3 leaflets – with sturdy, sometimes narrowly winged stalks, the leaflets leathery, varying in shape from lance- to egg-shaped, narrowing to the base, with a bluntly pointed, round, or notched tip, the margins usually untoothed, with the midrib, lateral veins and small network of veins often conspicuous; smooth or hairy; the terminal leaflet – the biggest – generally up to 4 cm long and 2.5 cm wide.

The small greenish flowers are in lax branching heads, those in the axils of the leaves shorter than the leaves, those borne terminally usually longer, the fruit a small roundish drupe about 6 mm in circumference.

The wood is red, yielding a red dye.

Schonland called this *Rhus mucronata* (splitting it into 5 varieties) and until recently it was known by this name.

The specific name is the Latin "laevigatus" meaning "smooth". The common name "korentebos" is derived from the likeness of the fruits to currants, and according to C.A. Smith the name still survives in the name "Korenterivier" in the Riversdale district where many trees of this species grow along its banks.

(389)   2. *Rhus macowanii* Schonl.

Macowan's taaibos; inTlokolotshane ephakathi (X); inHlokoshiyane (Z); inHlangutshane (Sw)

This well-known *Rhus* species grows from the Cape, through Natal and

Rhus macowanii: A fruiting twig (90%)

Rhus macowanii on a hillside near Estcourt

Zululand to Swaziland and the Transvaal, from sea level to 900 m or just over, in scrub, in bush, on forest margins, and on stream banks.

It may be either a shrub or a tree — when it can reach 9 m in height — but is always beautiful, as a tree inclined to be drooping, with dark, very rough, furrowed bark and leaves that are soft and usually velvety.

The leaves, usually with 3 leaflets but occasionally with 4 or 5, are egg-shaped to widely lance-shaped, bluntly or sharply pointed or rounded, narrowing to the base, up to nearly 8 cm long and 4 cm wide but usually smaller, dull green, soft-textured, velvety or smooth, untoothed or slightly toothed, the midrib and secondary veins prominent below, with the network of fine veins often conspicuous.

The tiny yellow flowers are in softly hairy, much-branched sprays, the lateral sprays as long as, or longer, than the leaves, the terminal bunches much longer. The fruits are small, round, slightly flattened drupes, on short stalks, green and pink turning red, and a tree loaded with these long, luxuriant bunches is not only graceful but colourful. The fruits usually ripen in autumn.

This is a beautiful species, particularly when overhanging a stream, as it often is, and is outstanding in a garden.

The specific name honours Dr Peter MacOwan, Professor of Botany at the South African College and Government Botanist in charge of the Herbarium until 1905.

Rhus macowanii is easily confused with *Rhus pyroides* Burch. Schonland distinguishes between them thus: *Rhus macowanii* has leaf stalks relatively shorter and thicker, panicles which are longer and denser, flowers slightly smaller, its pubescence neither as flat nor silky, and more often deciduous on older plants.

A species that may possibly be confused with this is *Rhus refracta* Eckl. & Zeyh. which Schonland describes as looking like a small-leaved *Rhus macowanii,* and which grows from Knysna eastwards to possibly Natal. He says that its leaflets lack the netted veining of *Rhus macowanii,* the flowers are in greyish, hairy, loose heads, longer than the leaves, and the small roundish fruit is "blackish with a greyish bloom".

A tree occurring on the edges of Natal and Transvaal forests, *Rhus intermedia* Schonl., with a large, oblong, leathery leaflets, is possibly a cross between this species, *Rhus macowanii,* and *Rhus chirindensis* Bak.f. forma *legatii* (Schonl.) R.&A. Fernandes.

(393.1)   3. *Rhus rehmanniana* Engl.

= *Rhus macowanii* Schonl. forma *rehmanniana* (Engl.) Schonl.

Rehmann's taaibos; inHlokoshiyane (Z); inHlangutshane (Sw)

Rhus rehmanniana is a graceful little tree occurring from Natal, Zululand, and Swaziland to the eastern and northern Transvaal, in bushveld and grassveld, on forest margins and on stony hillsides. It is a common tree along the roads round Tzaneen and Duivelskloof in the northern Transvaal, and over the wooded hills in parts of Natal, as on the lovely road overlooking the Wagondrift Dam near Estcourt.

Its relationship to *Rhus macowanii* is clear — Schonland considered it no more than a form of this species — and in its graceful drooping habit, spreading crown, and rough dark bark it resembles it closely. The leaflets, however, separate it. Typically the middle leaflet has a wide, round or flat and toothed apex, narrowing to the base, the two side

Above left
Rhus pyroides growing at a picnic spot on the Vaal River at Parys

Above right
Rhus pyroides fruiting

Below
Rhus rehmanniana near the Wagondrift Dam outside Estcourt

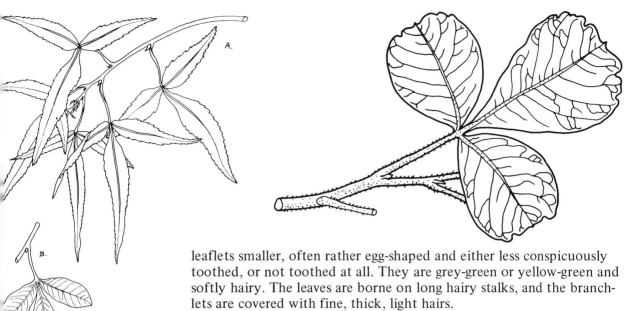

Above left
A. *Rhus leptodictaya:*
The leaves. B. *Rhus pyroides:* A leaf (90%)

Above right
Rhus rehmanniana leaf (80%)

leaflets smaller, often rather egg-shaped and either less conspicuously toothed, or not toothed at all. They are grey-green or yellow-green and softly hairy. The leaves are borne on long hairy stalks, and the branchlets are covered with fine, thick, light hairs.

The small fruits turn a rich red in autumn and are carried in delicate branching sprays terminally and in the axils of the leaves.

The tree was named after a Polish plant collector and geographer, Anton Rehmann, who collected in South Africa in the 1870's.

(392)   4. *Rhus pyroides* Burch.

Fire thorn, brandtaaibos, rooi kareeboom, taaibos; inHlokoshiyane (Z); koditshane (SS), mogodiri (Tsw – Hebron), mogodiri, mogwediri (Tsw– Ngwak), modupaphiri (Tws – Taw); mogodiri, mogweriri (NS)

Rhus pyroides, in its various forms, is very widely distributed for it grows in every province of the Republic under widely differing conditions – as it does beyond its borders – along the Orange River and around pans in the north west Cape, on ironstone hills in the Orange Free State, in open bush in the Transvaal and Natal, on forest verges, in valleys, and in open grassland, from Kosi Bay in the east to Botswana and northern South West Africa in the west.

It is a common species on the Witwatersrand and around Pretoria, and beautiful specimens grow around the famous Sterkfontein Caves near Krugersdorp, one overhanging one of the entrances to the cave.

It was first collected by Burchell on the Asbestos Mountains in the north west Cape, and his specimen is still preserved at Kew. He described it as a large bush "in the habit, ramification, and broad deciduous foliage of which there was a character that reminded me of the common wild pear tree of Europe". It also grows as a sprawling shrub or as a 12 m tree, although usually much shorter, with a spreading crown, an often crooked trunk or trunks, and rough grey bark.

It bears very stout thorns – which Burchell noted – and leaves composed of 3 leaflets, the leaves borne on slender stalks which are furrowed above. The leaflets are somewhat oval-shaped, narrowing both ends, sometimes with a short thorn-like tip or the terminal one – the largest and up to 7 x 3 cm – with a round or flat tip. They are smooth or velvety above, the lower surface usually slightly hairy, the midrib and secondary veins often conspicuous, and raised below.

The small greenish flowers are in lax branched bunches in the axils of the leaves and at the end of the branches. The white and red fruits – ripe summer to late autumn – are small, roundish, and often borne in quantities when the branches are bent down with their weight. Birds are particularly fond of them, as Burchell noted. Wattled Starlings and Red-eyed Bulbuls have been seen gorging them.

Elephant, impala and kudu eat shoots and young leaves.

The branches are very tough and the reddish, sweet-scented wood is used for hoe handles. A slash shows a bright red colour, hence the common name "rooikaree".

This is a wonderfully decorative little species in a garden, either as a tree or hedge. It is sometimes deciduous, at others evergreen.

The specific name is based on the Greek "pyros" meaning "fire" and refers to the burning sensation caused by a prick from the thorns.

Very closely related to this species is *Rhus baurii* Schonl. (number 378), from the Midlands of the Cape, Kimberley and the eastern Cape around Albany, where it grows on rocky ridges and stream banks. Schonland separates it from *Rhus pyroides* on its thinner leaflets, longer and more slender stalks, and the shape of the middle leaflet which is much narrowed to the base. The two may prove to be inseparable.

The specific name honours the Rev L.P. Baur, 1825-1899, a Moravian missionary who, when stationed in the Transkei, made a large botanical collection.

(385.1)   5. *Rhus krebsiana* Presl ex Engl.

Kreb's taaibos

A 3 m shrub or small tree, this grows from Griqualand East to the Pearston district, in bush and on forest fringes, often at an altitude of over 900 m.

The twigs are reddish and the leaves are borne on stalks that are furrowed and somewhat winged. They are oblong to egg-shaped, round or bluntly pointed, slightly notched or with a small thorn-like point, narrowing to the base, the middle the biggest – up to about 6 cm long and 4 cm wide – the lateral ones often slightly lopsided, untoothed, with the midrib and secondary veins prominent below, and the fine network of veins prominent both sides. The flowers are in short lax bunches in the axils of the leaves.

The species was named after L. Krebs, 1791-1844, a German apothecary, naturalist and botanical collector at the Cape.

(381.2)   6. *Rhus dura* Schonl.

The hard taaibos

When Schonland described *Rhus dura* it was known only from Graskop in the eastern Transvaal, at an altitude of roughly 1400 m. Now it is known to occur fairly widely, if rather rarely, from the eastern to the northern Transvaal and in Swaziland, in forest and on mountain sides. A group of trees stands near the top of Kowyns Pass near Graskop, and the type specimen may well have come from one of these.

Typically a shrubby tree up to about 3.6 m high, it is reported as

Rhus dura in the Long
Tom Pass

reaching 14 m in forest, while on the other hand it may make not a
bush but a perfect miniature tree 0.6 m high with a gnarled trunk and
spreading branches, and may be seen thus on the mountain side near
Sabie.

The leaves are usually egg-shaped, narrowing to the base, the central
one — the biggest — up to 6 cm long and 3 cm broad, bluntly pointed,
rounded, or with a flattish tip, often with a tiny thorn-like point. The
midrib and numerous neat, parallel secondary veins are raised below and
the network of fine veins is clear on both sides. The leaves are
shiny above, duller below, and are carried on stout channelled hairy
stalks. They are noticeably leathery.

The small flowers are in lax heads in the axils of the leaves and terminally. The fruit is a tiny roundish drupe.

The wood is reputed to be very tough, and possibly this, or the
leathery leaves, are the basis of the specific name, derived from a Latin
word meaning "hard".

(381.1)   7. *Rhus dentata* Thunb.

Nanabessie, inHlokoshiyane (Z); lebelebele (SS)

The nanabessie is a widespread species occurring in every province, in
the Republic reaching from roughly Humansdorp in the south to the
central Transvaal, and northwards into Rhodesia and Portuguese East
Africa, in forest, on forest margins, in kloofs, in thick bush, and on dry
scrubby hillsides. It is equally at home on an Orange Free State koppie,
overhanging a stream in the Natal Drakensberg, in coastal bush, or on a
Karoo mountain.

Naturally enough, it is an extremely variable species, the shape and
size of the leaflets and their smoothness or hairiness differing greatly.
Schonland divides the species into 3 varieties and a number of forms.
When the genus is revised many of these will probably fall away.

Rhus dentata grows as a shrub or as a graceful small tree, sometimes slightly spiny, with grey branches and soft foliage which turns bright autumn colours.

The twigs are red or yellowish, hairy or smooth. The leaves, borne on slender stalks, have the typical 3 leaflets of the *Rhus* group. They are thin, deep green above and lighter below, the central leaflet 2.5-5 cm long — occasionally 8 cm — usually egg-shaped, narrowing to the base, with a sharply pointed or rounded apex, and with the upper parts boldly toothed, sometimes so much so as to appear lobed, but occasionally almost untoothed. The midrib and veins are prominent below. The leaflets may be smooth, slightly hairy, or sometimes covered with long, silky hairs looking as if fashioned out of fine fur. The stalks are smooth or hairy.

The small yellow-green, sweet-smelling flowers bloom in spring in loose branched heads, those in the axils shorter than the leaves, those borne terminally being longer. The fruit is a small shiny roundish drupe, turning brown, red or orange, often borne abundantly. In December this is often particularly colourful with the new leaves copper shades and the fruit just beginning to turn colour.

The Zulus eat the fruits in time of famine, raw or mixed with milk, while other African peoples eat them regularly. Black Rhino eat the bark and leaves, and kudu and nyala the leaves.

Possibly the best use for the tree is in a garden, for it is small, graceful, the foliage is charming, and it grows easily from seed or cuttings.

This species hybridizes freely with other species, such as *Rhus pyroides* and *Rhus chirindensis* forma *legatii*.

The specific name *dentata*, meaning "toothed", refers to the toothed margins of the leaflets.

(379)   8. *Rhus carnosula* Schonl.

Rhus carnosula grows as a shrub or small tree from about Grahamstown to Pondoland, in coastal bush and forests, on grassy slopes and in wooded gullies.

It is a branched, rounded tree up to about 4.5 m high, with slightly fleshy leaves — which give the tree its specific name — and leaflets that are oblong to egg-shaped, the middle one up to nearly 8 cm long, with a narrowed base and sharply pointed apex, sometimes with a thorn-like point, untoothed or boldly toothed, with midrib and secondary veins conspicuous.

Schonland says that near Grahamstown this merges into some forms of *Rhus dentata* in the shape of the leaflets.

The flowers are in loose bunches terminally and in the axils of the upper leaves. The fruit is small, round, smooth, often with a persistant style.

(383.1)   9. *Rhus fastigiata* Eckl. & Zeyh.

inTlokolotshane yedobo, inTlokolotshane encinane (X)

This species is distributed in coastal districts from Uitenhage to Natal and Zululand and inland to the mountains of the eastern Cape and to the Transvaal.

It is a large shrub or a small tree up to 3 m high, much branched,

Right
Rhus pentheri, Kranskop

Below
Rhus pentheri stem and bark

with slender hairy twigs and dark green leaves. Schonland says that this is not clearly separated from the hairy form of *Rhus pyroides*, the main difference being in the absence of reticulate venation in the adult leaves.

The tree often has a fastigiate habit of growth, that is, the branches are more or less parallel to the main stem, although Schonland says this should not be taken as a distinguishing character.

(391)   10. *Rhus pentheri* Zahlbr.

Thornveld taaibos, inHlokoshiyane (Z), muṭasiri (V)

Rhus pentheri occurs from Pondoland northwards to Natal and Zululand, and inland to the eastern Orange Free State, the eastern Transvaal and Portuguese East Africa, growing in bushveld, on forest edges, wooded mountain slopes and rocky hills, often on stream banks. It is a common shrub or small tree in the thornveld of Natal.

It grows up to about 4.5 m high, either as a spreading tree or, in closely wooded areas, with a bare trunk and small, often rather drooping crown. The bark of the trunk and branches in an old tree is characteristic — dark brown, corky, and much fissured, the segments standing out in deep ridges. The twigs are sometimes spiny.

The leaflets are usually fairly small — the middle one 0.8-3 cm long — egg-shaped to widely lance-shaped, the tips bluntly pointed, notched or with a few teeth, the margin slightly inrolled, the midrib prominent both sides, the network of veins not clearly seen, when young slightly hairy, later becoming smooth, glossy bright green above, paler below, the whole leaf borne on a slightly hairy, flattened and winged stalk.

The tiny flowers are in short, loosely branched, hairy sprays borne in the axils of the leaves or at the ends of the branches, the fruit small, brown, roundish, slightly flattened, and a shiny light brown when ripe.

The roots of the tree are eaten by Vervet Monkeys, the bark by Black Rhino, and the leaves by Black Rhino, impala, nyala, and kudu.

The wood is a reddish colour.

The tree was named after Dr A. Penther, a Viennese botanist who collected in South Africa at the beginning of the 20th century.

Above left
A red currant *Rhus chirindensis* forma *legatii* in "Cranemere" garde
in the Karoo. It was planted as a fence post, took root, and grew.

Above right
A red currant in forest on the southern slopes of the Soutpansberg

Below left
The red currant, on the Suurberg, Eastern Province

Below right
Rhus chirindensis forma *legatii:* a fruiting twig (90%)

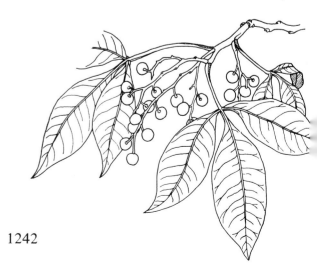

1242

(380)   11. *Rhus chirindensis* Bak.f.
         forma *legatii* (Schonl.) R.&A. Fernandes

= *Rhus legatii* Schonl.

Red currant, bush jarrah, bloedhout, westelike essenhout,
bostaaibos, bosganna; umHlakothi omkhulu, inTlokolotshane enkulu
(X); isiBanda, umHlabamvubu (Z), monaatlou (NS); muvhadela-
phanga (V)

This tall forest species is widespread in South Africa from Swellendam,
through the eastern Cape, Natal, Zululand, and Swaziland to the eastern and northern Transvaal, growing in forests, in kloofs, in scrub, and
on wooded stream banks.

It has probably been seen by most people for it often grows at the
edge of forest roads from Knysna to the Suurberg and Hog's Back in
the Amatola Mountains, and from the mountain drive around the Bosberg near Somerset East to the Soutpansberg in the northern Transvaal
where some fine trees grow alongside the road just beyond the Mountain Inn.

In one Karoo garden a tree flourishes that was planted more than
half a century ago as a stout corner post in a fence. It took root and
grew.

The red currant is the tallest South African tree of the genus *Rhus*.
It grows up to 25 m in height and has a stem diameter of 0.6-1.3 m,
and – when growing in the open – a spreading crown. It is variable,
however, and is sometimes found as a small straggling shrub very
unlike the beautiful forest tree.

The stems of young plants and of coppice shoots are often thorny,
but the mature tree is spineless. The bark is rough brown, and the stem
when cut exudes a blood-red sap. The young leaves are reddish, the
mature a dark glossy green, making a dense and luxuriant crown.

The tree is usually completely hairless, and this separates it from the
typical *Rhus chirindensis* of tropical Africa. The leaflets are usually
large – the central up to 13 cm long and 6 cm wide – and the side
leaflets slightly smaller, egg-shaped to oblong, narrowing both ends,
sharply pointed, the central leaflet often shortly stalked, the lateral
leaflets usually without stalks, the margin usually untoothed and the
edges slightly wavy, the midrib and lateral veins slightly raised below.
The whole leaf is borne on a slender, often reddish and very long stalk.

Leaves and bark are eaten by Black Rhino.

The tree is usually deciduous.

The flowers are borne in sprays that, according to Schonland, are
"richly and delicately branched", the male being mainly long and borne
at the ends of the branches, and the shorter female mostly in the axils
of the leaves. Although the flowers are tiny, they are borne in such
masses that they are conspicuous.

The fruits are small, roundish, red, shiny drupes borne abundantly.
A tree with twigs and young branches weighed down with fruit is a
lovely sight. The fruits are sweetish – although the local name at Kei
Road is "sour berry" – and are edible. Monkeys are fond of them as are
birds such as bulbuls, barbets, white-eyes, and parrots.

The sapwood is yellowish, the heartwood red, heavy, and strong, and
makes attractive furniture with a lovely sheen. It was formerly used for
wagon wood and for turning. Sim says that Africans made pipes of it,
"carving a single pipe out of a considerable log". The Venda name,

Above left
A big red currant in the Suurberg

Above right
Rhus lucida bark

Below left
Rhus lucida on the edge of the lagoon at Knysna

Below right
Rhus zeyheri: A fruiting twig (80%)

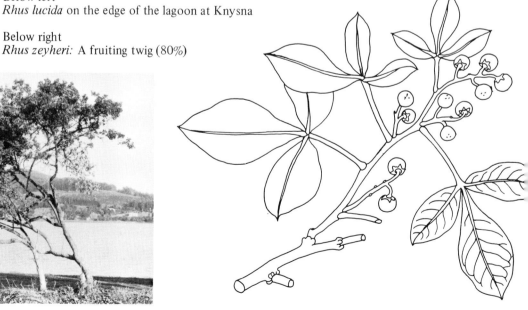

1244

muvhaḍela-phanga, means "wood for knife handles".

Africans use the tree medicinally. Gerstner says that it furnishes the Zulu herbalists' medicine "to cure the heart".

This species hybridizes freely with species such as *Rhus dentata* and *Rhus laevigata*. Schonland describes a "species" which he names *R. intermedia* Schonl., which is possibly a hybrid between this and *Rhus macowanii.*

The specific name indicates that the typical form of the tree was first collected near the Chirinda forest in south east Rhodesia near the Portuguese border. The name of the form *legatii* honours C.E. Legat, formerly Chief Conservator of Forests.

(394.1)   12. *Rhus transvaalensis* Engl.

Transvaal rhus; muṭzhaku-ṭzhaku, muthaku-thaku, muṭasiri, tshiṭasiri (V)

"The Transvaal rhus" is common in parts of the northern and eastern Transvaal and the Natal highveld growing along streams, in low forest, in bush clumps, and in wooded kloofs at altitudes from roughly 600 to 1200 m above sea level.

Although frequently a low shrub it can grow into a small tree up to 4.5 m with twigs so hairy as to appear furry, becoming smooth with age, and leaves composed of 3 slender leaflets, oblong to lance-shaped, narrowing both ends, the central one up to about 5 cm long and 1.3 cm wide, the lateral ones smaller, untoothed and sometimes slightly wavy, the young ones hairy, the older smooth, borne on stalks that are often densely hairy.

The tiny grey flowers are in short lateral bunches, the fruits roundish, shiny, and white and yellow to red. They appear with the new leaves.

Kudu are known to browse the leaves.

13. *Rhus zeyheri* Sond.

Bloublaar taaibos

Schonland knew this only as a shrub from stream banks and koppies near Pretoria and from the Drakensberg, but it can occasionally be tree-like, and then is conspicuous because of its blue-green colour and waxy bloom.

It is quite smooth, with rather leathery leaves, the leaflets egg-shaped to oblong, the apex rounded or bluntly pointed, often with a small thorn-like point, narrowing to the base, the margins usually untoothed.

The small yellow flowers are in short loose heads, in the axils of the leaves or terminally. The fruit is a small, brown, shiny drupe.

This is a particularly good specimen in a garden where its blue-green colour is an asset. It may sometimes be seen, carefully preserved, in Pretoria gardens.

The specific name honours K.L.P. Zeyher, famous German botanist and collector in South Africa.

(388.1)   14. *Rhus lucida* L.

Shiny rhus, korentebos; inTlakotshan 'ebomvu (X)

This variable species grows in the coastal districts from the western
Cape to Natal, and penetrates inland possibly to the eastern and northern Transvaal and Rhodesia, on wooded hill slopes, mountain sides, in
gully bush, scrub, and on forest margins, from sea level to an altitude of
over 2100 m.

It is a common species round Knysna, growing to the edge of the
lagoon, sometimes as a dense shrub, at others as a small tree up to 4.5 m
high. The bark is rough and the twigs often hairy, with a resinous excre-
tion. The leaf stalk is often slightly winged and short. The glossy,
rather leathery leaflets are egg-shaped to oblong, usually widest at the
tip and bluntly pointed, or occasionally notched, narrowed to the base,
with the midrib slightly raised, usually untoothed or occasionally slightly toothed at the tip, with a resinous gloss. The central one is up to
about 8 cm long.

The flowers are unusual botanically for those of a *Rhus* as they are
often bisexual. They are carried in loose bunches, which are hairy or
covered with resin, in the axils of the leaves and terminally and are so
abundant from June to September that they colour the trees yellow. The
fruit is a small, roundish, shiny brown drupe.

Marloth says that the leaves of this species are often infested with
galls formed by the larvae of a moth.

The wood makes particularly good fence posts, being hard, tough,
dense and durable, with a thin sapwood and large heartwood, and is
much used around Knysna. The bark of the roots and branches was
once used for tanning.

Schonland divides this into 4 varieties, largely on the size of leaflets
and fruits.

The specific name *lucida* means "shining", referring to the gloss of
the leaves.

A species very close to the small-leaved form of this is *Rhus schlechteri* Diels, found on the sand dunes from Bredasdorp to Port Alfred.
Schonland says that its relatively broader and stalkless leaves distinguish
it from *Rhus lucida*.

15. *Rhus glauca* Desf.

Grey-green taaibos, blinkblaar, korentebessie, rosyntjiebos, suurbessie,
taaibos

Rhus glauca grows on sand dunes, hills and mountain slopes, and in
riverine bush, from Cape Town eastwards to East London and as far
inland as Queenstown. It is one of the trees on the Cape Flats, and
along the coast helps to bind the sand, for which purpose it is considered very useful.

It is a spineless shrub or tree up to about 4.5 m high with branches
and leaves covered with resin which dries to a grey powder. The leaf
stalks are often slightly winged. The leaves are distinctive. The middle
leaflet, usually up to about 1.9 cm long, has a wide, flat tip, often dent-
ed in the centre, narrowing to the base, the lateral leaflets shaped much
the same or oval and narrower, but considerably smaller. The midrib
and veins are slightly raised below. Young leaves are green, more mature

ones blue- or grey-green and often shining as if with varnish.

The small flowers are in much-branched bunches in the axils of the leaves and terminally, and usually bloom in the winter. The fruits — ripe in the spring — are round, shiny, and reddish.

The specific name is Latin meaning "sea green" or "covered with bloom" in reference to the leaves.

(395)   16. *Rhus undulata* Jacq.
         1. var. *undulata*

= *Rhus excisa* Thunb.

         2. var. *celastroides* (Sond.) Schonl.

= *R. celastroides* Sond.

         3. var. *tricrenata* (Engl.) R.Fernandes

= *R. burchellii* Sond. ex Engl.; = *R. rangeana* Engl.

Kunibos, blinkblaar taaibos

This widely spread and variable species extends from central and southern South West Africa round the coast to the eastern Cape and Natal, and inland through the Cape, the Orange Free State, the Transvaal, and Botswana, growing — often on limestone formations — in scrub on hills and mountain slopes, in kloofs, and along dry river beds in the interior.

This is a common species in the hills bordering the Orange River near the site of the Verwoerd Dam, and on the mountains in the Karoo districts of Pearston and Graaff-Reinet, spreading rapidly and a cause of anxiety to farmers who regard it as an inedible weed. Locally it is known there as "blinkblaar". The variety *celastroides*, most often a dense rounded shrub, is abundant on the hills of Namaqualand, in spring time making dark islands in the sea of daisy flowers that flows over the plains and hills.

Schonland divides the species into several varieties and a bewildering number of forms, separating these largely on the shape, size and texture of the leaves, and the degree to which they are resinous and shiny. Mme Fernandes recently altered the names of varieties and forms, although the specific name still stands. Var. *undulata* is widespread and includes big-leaved forms — Natal specimens are included in this. Mme Fernandes sees 3 separate forms of this variety, but whether these should be upheld is doubtful. Var. *celastroides* and var. *tricrenata* are from arid areas, the former from Namaqualand and South West Africa and usually a low-growing rounded shrub, and the latter from dry parts of the Cape, Lesotho, the Orange Free State and South West Africa, and often tree-like. They are both apt to be thorny, and their leaves are frequently smaller and more leathery than those of var. *undulata*, often somewhat triangular in shape, and very resinous.

Rhus undulata may be a shrub or a 6 m tree, many-branched, with slender rough brown trunks, sometimes up to 23 cm in diameter. The leaves vary greatly from area to area. The leaflets may be 0.8 cm to 6 cm long, oblong, egg-shaped or lance-shaped, narrowing to the base, often conspicuously so, with the apex pointed, rounded, or flat with a pronounced dent in the middle, often with a thorn-like point, sometimes

Above
Rhus undulata var.
undulata — a well-grown
tree near Colesberg

Centre
Rhus undulata var.
celastroides in its typical
bushy form in the hills
near Concordia, Nama-
qualand

Left
Rhus undulata var.
tricrenata on the heights
above the Verwoerd
Dam on the Orange
River

growing on stout spiny twigs, sometimes on spineless branches, the margins usually (but not always) untoothed, at times not conspicuously resinous, at others shiny as if lacquered and sticky to the touch. They are a yellow-green to dark green, leathery, and usually much undulate or wavy, a character on which the specific name is based. The leaf stalk is sometimes slightly winged.

The small, creamy, sweetly-scented flowers bloom in autumn in lax bunches borne in the axils of the leaves or more often terminally. The fruits are small, roundish, somewhat flattened, and green, sometimes turning red. They are edible and were once eaten by Bushmen and Hottentots. Birds favour them.

The young leaves are browsed by goats but generally farmers regard this as a useless species. The early Hottentots used it medicinally, and in Namaqualand the leaves are used to cure chest complaints. The first colonists made from it a remedy for heart disease.

The Bushmen once made bows from its springy wood.

Swanepoel in his *Butterflies of South Africa* describes the attraction the variety *celastroides* has for two common butterflies of Namaqualand, the Namaqua Bar, *Spindasis namaqua,* and the Samba Copper, *Phasis clavum.* The males and females of both species, he says, flutter about the bushes, the female sometimes looking for a spot on which a lay her eggs, the male Namaqua Bar defending his territory — his bush — and chasing away all intruders.

C.A.Smith says that the common name "kunibos" is derived from the original Hottentot name for the small-leaved form of the tree which is found only in arid parts.

This is not usually a decorative species but, grouped with rocks or against a stony mountain side, it has great character.

(382)   17. *Rhus engleri* Britt.

= *Rhus incana* Engl.

Karaa

The karaa, as the tree is known locally on the Springbok Flats, is a small tree of the Transvaal bushveld, growing in the districts of Potgietersrust, Naboomspruit, Wakkerstroom, and Waterberg, usually on red loamy soil.

It is a much-branched, bushy little tree up to about 4 m in height with spreading and sometimes thorny branches and softly hairy young twigs.

The leaves are usually small — the terminal leaflet may be up to 4 cm long but is usually smaller — oblong to lance-shaped, usually bluntly or sharply pointed, velvety and soft, dull green above, grey below, with the margins untoothed or slightly toothed.

The small yellow flowers are in loose velvety heads, often longer than the leaves, borne in the axils of the leaves or terminally. The fruit is small, slightly flattened and lopsided, often with a small swelling to one side of the tip, smooth, brown and shiny.

The wood is reddish-brown and tough, and is used sometimes to make pick handles, although according to Schonland it is not nearly as good as that of *Rhus pyroides*.

This species is often attacked and sometimes the leaves almost entirely destroyed by hairy caterpillars.

The tree was called after H.G. Adolf Engler, 1844-1930, distinguished traveller and author, Professor of Botany and Director of the Botanic Gardens at Berlin Dahlem.

(390) 18. *Rhus natalensis* Bernh.

= *Rhus glaucescens* A.Rich.; = *R. crenulata* A.Rich.

Natal taaibos; inHlokoshiyane (Z)

The Natal taaibos is a tropical species reaching from Ethiopia southwards through Zululand and Natal to about East London in the south. In South Africa it is common in scrub along the beaches — it is a familiar little tree along the Transkei coast — in coastal bush, and in coastal forest, growing as a shrub to a 6 m tree.

The branches are rough and grey. The rather leathery leaves are dark to light green above and paler below, the leaflets oblong, egg-shaped, or lance-shaped, narrowing to the base with round, bluntly pointed or notched tips, the central leaflet up to about 9 cm long and up to nearly 4 cm wide, the margins scolloped or entire, with the midrib prominent on both surfaces or on the upper alone. The young leaves are a beautiful red.

The small greeny-white flowers are in short, lax, branched bunches in the axils of the leaves. The fruit is small, roundish, somewhat flattened, smooth, and yellow-brown when ripe.

(384) 19. *Rhus gueinzii* Sond.

= *Rhus spinescens* Diels; = *Rhus simii* Schonl.; = *Rhus simii* Schonl. var. *lydenburgensis* Schonl.

Thorny taaibos, taaibosdoring; umPhondo (Z); inHlangutshane (Sw); motshotlho (Tsw); nsasane (Kal)

This widespread and fairly common species grows from the eastern Cape, through Natal, Zululand and Swaziland to the eastern and northern Transvaal and Botswana, and beyond into Rhodesia, in scrub forest, gully bush, kloofs, and on stony slopes.

It is a variable species, sometimes a shrub, at others a 6 m spreading tree, many-stemmed, with a light brown, much fissured bark, and slender whippy, grey or reddish, often arching branches, which may be either smooth or hairy. It may be completely unarmed or spiny, while the spines may be smooth or hairy, short or long, and stout, bearing leaves upon them. Some botanists see the spiny form as a separate variety — var. *spinescens* (Diels) R.&A. Fernandes.

The leaves themselves are variable. They usually have 3 leaflets — occasionally 4 — lance-shaped or a narrow oblong to oval, the central one up to 7 cm long, with a round or bluntly pointed apex — neatly notched — narrowing to the base, the margins sometimes toothed, dark green above, paler below, the midrib usually prominent on both sides, the leaf stalks usually slender and often reddish.

The small yellow flowers, blooming from summer to late autumn, are in loose heads which are sometimes densely velvety, borne in the axils of the leaves and terminally. The fruits are roundish, often slightly flattened or lopsided, smooth, and brown. They are eaten by people,

OPPOSITE

Above
Rhus gueinzii at Evangelina in the northern Transvaal

Below
Rhus gueinzii, many-stemmed

A karee, *Rhus lancea,* in the Transvaal bushveld

and by birds such as doves, toppies, Yellow-breasted Bulbuls, Crested and Black-collared Barbets, and Redwing Starlings. Goats relish the leaves.

The hard red wood is used to make sticks which are exceptionally tough, and for fuel.

Africans use parts of the tree in treating eye complaints. The water in which branches have been boiled is a popular eye-wash, while the smoke from a burning stick is believed to help eye injuries.

The specific name honours Wilhelm Guienzius, German apothecary and naturalist, who lived in Natal from 1841 until his death about 30 years later.

20. *Rhus marlothii* Engl.

Bitter karee

The bitter karee has a more northern distribution than most of the South African *Rhus* species, growing in the central Transvaal, in central and northern South West Africa, and in Botswana. Visitors to Namutoni Camp in the Etosha Game Reserve may remember these little trees growing in the camp grounds.

Although most often a shrub, it can grow into a 3 m tree with slightly hairy, spineless branches and velvety leaves. The leaflets are widely lance-shaped to egg-shaped, the tips pointed or narrowly rounded, narrowing to the base, the margins in the upper part usually scolloped, with the midrib raised on both sides. The central leaflet is 2.5-5 cm long and 1.3-2.5 cm wide.

The flowers, blooming in summer, are in velvety branching heads in the axils of the leaves or terminally. The fruits are small, lopsided, somewhat flattened, often crowned by the persistent styles, shiny and yellow-brown when ripe.

C.A. Smith says that the plant is held to be an indication of good grassveld and that it is not grazed by stock owing to the bitterness of the leaves. These give the tree its common name.

Engler named this species after the noted Cape botanist, Rudolf Marloth.

(393.2)   21. *Rhus tenuinervis* Engl. & Gilg

= *Rhus commiphoroides* Engl. & Gilg; = *Rhus kwebensis* N.E.Br.

Hyaena taaibos; modupaphiri, morupapiri (Tsw)

This species, literally "the thin-nerved rhus", has, like *Rhus marlothii,* a western distribution, growing in the western Transvaal, the northern Cape, central and northern South West Africa, the Caprivi Strip, and Botswana (where it is the dominant *Rhus* in parts), northwards into Rhodesia and tropical Africa. It is a common little species in the Gemsbok National Park. It favours sandveld, woodland, and also grows on rocky kranses and ironstone koppies.

Although usually a low-growing shrub it can reach 6 m in height. The crown is dense and many-branched, and the twigs, leaves, and leaf stalks hairy. The leaves are borne on short and sometimes spiny branchlets.

Above left
The widespread karee, *Rhus lancea*, has many forms. Here it is growing in the Orange Free State alongside the national road

Above right
A karee trunk

Centre left
A karee, often associated with water, on the banks of a Karoo dam

Below left
Rhus lancea fruits are often borne in abundance and ripen as a rule in spring

Below right
Rhus lancea, the karee: A fruiting twig (90%)

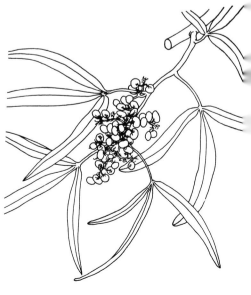

1254

The leaflets are egg-shaped to oblong, bluntly pointed or flattish, narrowed to the base, the margin in the upper parts usually coarsely scolloped, the midrib and secondary veins raised below, the leaflets 1.3-10 cm long and 0.8-5 cm wide, the middle one being the largest. They are dark or grey-green above and lighter and often yellowish below, and sometimes wavy. They turn red in autumn.

The foliage is apparently browsed.

The greenish-white flowers are in loose many-branched hairy sprays, borne in the axils of the leaves and terminally, towards the end of summer. The fruits are small, pea-sized, roundish, and flattened, whitish to purplish-brown when ripe in the late autumn, with a conspicuous bloom. They are eaten by Bushmen.

No common English or Afrikaans name for this species seems to have been recorded, so that a name – the hyaena taaibos – based on the Tswana, is here used. The Tswana "modupaphiri" means literally "scented by hyaena".

(386)   22. *Rhus lancea* L.f.

Karee, bastard willow, Karoo tree, rooikaree, taaibos; iQunguwe (X); inHlokoshiyane (Z); inHlangutshane (Sw); mosilabele, mosilabelo (SS); motlhotlho, mohlwehlwe, mokalabata (NS); mosilabele (Tsw); moshabela (Tsw – Mal), moshilabele (Tsw-Tlokwa); oruso (Her); / garas (Nama)

The full rounded shape of the karee and its evergreen, drooping willow-like foliage, give a soft note to what is often otherwise a bleak landscape, for the karee flourishes along river banks or near underground water in the arid and bleak regions of the country. It is most conspicuous in these parts – the Orange Free State, the Cape, South West Africa and Botswana – although also widely distributed through the Transvaal. It does not appear to grow in Natal although Sim recorded it there.

It occurs not only on river banks but on flats away from surface water, on mountains and koppies, and is often associated with lime soils. Farmers consider it as an indicator of underground water.

It may be no more than a small, rather scrubby bush, or a tree 9 m high, with a gnarled, dark brown, rough and often twisted trunk. The slender reddish branchlets are horizontal or hang downwards, and the leaves on slender stalks with their 3 long, narrow, pointed leaflets droop gracefully.

The leaflets are usually fairly stiff, smooth, dark green and shiny above, pale green below, very narrowly lance-shaped, narrowing to both ends, usually pointed and completely untoothed, 6 cm to 13 cm long (sometimes longer), the central leaflet being the longest, and up to 1.3 cm wide. The midrib is raised both sides. The secondary veins are usually slightly raised on the upper surface, and these and the fine network of veins are usually conspicuous on this side only. In this they differ from the leaves of a close relative, *Rhus leptodictya* Diels, with somewhat similar leaves but with the venation usually (but not always) clearer below.

Although almost evergreen, the karee often sheds its old leaves in late spring when the new leaves are forming.

The minute yellow-green flowers are in smooth, loose, much-branched sprays in the axils of the leaves or terminally. They usually flower from late summer to early winter when the trees have a yellowish tinge.

The fruit is roundish and slightly flattened and lopsided, with a large seed, a thin layer of flesh, and a shiny brown outer skin. To sophisticated palates these are very poor fare but they are eaten by primitive peoples. Pounded with water and fermented, they make a beer popular with the Magaliesberg Africans. Birds eat them and they make an excellent poultry food.

The wood is hard, tough, durable, close-grained, rather splintery, and red-brown in colour, works and polishes well, and has a pleasant smell when fresh. According to Galpin, big trees are often hollow and it is difficult to get straight pieces of fair length. In the Karoo it was once used a great deal for fence poles — which probably explains why farms bearing such names as Kareefontein or Kareehoek are today bare of the trees. Pick handles, disselbooms and other wagon parts were often made of the wood and Pappe says that the younger and longer branches were used as spars in thatching houses and for wagon tents. Supple branchlets were used by the early Bushmen and Hottentots to make bows, which were strung with fibres made of the dorsal muscles of the springbuck, twisted into a cord. Sometimes in country districts baskets are still made of them. In Graaff-Reinet the wood was once used for making pipe bowls.

In some areas the foliage is browsed but not, apparently, in all. The bark was once used for tanning.

The kareeboom is a drought and frost-resistant tree and grows on chalky or sandy soil, as well as in deep rich earth. It is termite resistant, evergreen, shady, and one of the most beautiful trees of the drier areas. It is extraordinary that so little use is made of it by gardeners and farmers for it grows easily from seed, cuttings, truncheons, or by layering, and it is fairly fast-growing. An avenue or hedge of karees gives permanent shade in summer and shelter in winter. Towns in the dry west, in particular, might with advantage follow the example of Kimberley, Lichtenburg, and a few such other centres, where the karee has been used as a beautiful and suitable street tree.

The karee features frequently in the early journals of travellers in the Cape. In 1811 Burchell, when passing through Karoo Poort north east of Ceres, camped under two large bushy trees of "karee-hout" near a small stream of water. The trees still stand and 120 years later Dr John Hutchinson of Kew, another famous botanist, camped under the selfsame trees.

The specific name is based on the lance-shaped leaves. The common name "karee" is derived from the Hottentot name, on which the name "karoo" is based, and was first recorded in 1778 as "care-boom".

Rhus lancea is easily confused with *Rhus viminalis* Vahl which both in habit and foliage bears a strong resemblance to it.

(396)   23. *Rhus viminalis* Vahl

Western karee, witkareeboom, wilderosyntjieboom; / garas (Nama)

Rhus viminalis — literally "the rhus with the twiggy crown" — is a tree of rivers and vleis of the western districts of the country, from the districts of Graaff-Reinet, Beaufort West, Sutherland and Prieska to Clanwilliam, and of the country along the Orange River from Griqualand

Above left
Rhus viminalis: A twig
(90%)

Above right
Rhus viminalis in a dry
stream bed near
Groblershoop in the
north west Cape

Below
Rhus viminalis stem
and bark

West to Namaqualand and southern South West Africa. It is a common tree along the banks of the river, growing together with *Salix capensis* almost to its very mouth. In the Transvaal and to a large extent in the Orange Free State, its place is taken by *Rhus lancea* (although their areas of distribution overlap). The two species are often confused.

Rhus viminalis is a sturdy tree up to some 9 m in height, with a rough brown bark, smooth pliable branchlets, reddish twigs, and leaves borne on slender stalks. The leaflets are widely lance-shaped, slightly broader in proportion to their length than are those of *Rhus lancea*, usually up to about 8 cm long and 1.9 cm wide, the apex pointed, sometimes with a thorn-like point, the margin untoothed and sometimes wavy, the midrib raised both sides, and the secondary veins distinct. Whereas the leaflets of *Rhus lancea* are dark green above and much lighter below, there is little colour difference in the leaflets of this species.

The small flowers are in hairy, diffuse sprays, both terminally and in the axils of the leaves. All the fruits examined in the field have been round and not conspicuously flattened as are those of *Rhus lancea*. Unlike this species, *Rhus viminalis* flowers most often in early summer and the fruits ripen in the autumn.

Once the tribes living along the Orange River used the pliable wands to make fish traps.

(384.1)   24. *Rhus montana* Diels

= *Rhus gerrardii* (Harv. ex Engl.) Schonl.

Mountain taaibos; inHlokoshiyane (Z)

This most graceful and often willow-like little tree occurs in the eastern districts of the country in Pondoland, in Natal above 900 m, in Lesotho, the eastern Orange Free State around Harrismith, in Swaziland, and in the eastern Transvaal.

It is a variable species. Schonland knew it as *Rhus gerrardii* Harv. and separated it into 4 varieties but these are now recognized as forms of *Rhus montana* Diels and are separated on the size, shape and number of the leaflets, the form of the margins, and the degree of hairiness.

Above
The Assegai River in the eastern Transvaal with
Rhus montana, a form of *Diospyros lycioides,*
and *Combretum erythrophyllum* growing on
the hill slopes

Right
Rhus leptodictya bark

Below
Rhus leptodictya in the Transvaal bushveld near
Pienaar's River Dam

Rhus montana grows up to about 3 or 4 m high, and is leafy and many-branched. The leaves are borne on slender stalks which are smooth or hairy. The leaflets are lance-shaped, sometimes widely so, and may be almost egg-shaped, narrowed both ends, of variable size, deeply toothed in the upper portion, or almost entirely toothed, or sometimes not toothed at all. They are smooth or hairy. The leaflets number from 3 to 7.

The flowers are in compact sprays which are smooth or hairy, borne in the axils of the leaves or terminally. The fruits are roundish, green turning red.

The wood is used in Lesotho for building huts, and the trees have been planted in the eastern Transvaal as hedges. They should be excellent in a garden, either as specimen trees or as a hedge, and in landscape gardening wherever a drooping, willow-like tree is required.

The specific name is the Latin "montanus", meaning "of mountains", in reference to the fact that this species often occurs on mountain sides.

(387)   25. *Rhus leptodictya* Diels

= *Rhus amerina* Meikle; = *Rhus gueinzii* (of various authors)

Mountain karee, false karee, bergkaree, basterkaree, plat kareebessie-boom, taaibos; mohlwehlwe (NS); mushakaladza (V)

The mountain karee, as the common name indicates, is often found on rocky hillsides, although it occurs also on flats, in bushveld and open savannah, and sometimes in grassveld, from the central Orange Free State and northern Cape, throughout the Transvaal and Swaziland to Botswana, Rhodesia and Malawi. It is a tree known to most of the people of Johannesburg and Pretoria for it is common on the hills around the cities. In Pretoria it may still be seen in the steep suburban streets and has sometimes been preserved in gardens here.

It is a beautiful species with a rounded, drooping, leafy crown, a rough, deeply furrowed, dark brown or grey trunk, and reddish branches, in its general habit and foliage much resembling the karee, *Rhus lancea*, although usually not as big, seldom reaching more than 6 m in height. The long, smooth, slender, lance-shaped leaflets are usually a lighter green than those of the karee, softer in texture, broader in proportion to the length, and with the whole length of the margin toothed. Occasionally completely untoothed forms are found and these are particularly difficult to distinguish from those of *Rhus lancea*. Often the venation, however, is clearer on the under than the upper surface and this is a quick, rough-and-ready — although not foolproof — aid to identification. The leaves are borne on slender and sometimes reddish stalks.

The tiny creamy flowers are borne in long, graceful, loosely branched heads in the axils of the leaves or terminally in spring. The fruits are small, brown, or yellow-brown, very smooth and shiny, distinctly flattened and ripening in late summer or autumn. They are eaten by doves and probably by other birds as well, and Africans brew an intoxicating liquor from them.

The tree has medicinal properties.

The timber is sometimes said to be twisted and of poor quality, at others to be hard, durable and termite-resistant.

This makes a particularly good garden tree being decorative, hardy,

Above
The besembos, *Rhus erosa*, covering the hills in the eastern Orange Free State

Below
A besembos near Colesberg

(it usually tolerates at least 7 or 8 degrees of frost) flourishing in most soils, in either sun or shade, fairly quick-growing, and almost evergreen. It grows easily from seed or cuttings, and probably from truncheons.

The specific name is based on Greek words meaning "delicate net" and probably refers to the fine venation of the leaves.

In the past this was often incorrectly identified as *Rhus gueinzii*.

26. *Rhus microcarpa* Schonl.

Although Schonland, who described the species, knew it as a shrub of 0.9-1.8 m in height, it may be a small tree up to 5 m, growing on grassy mountain slopes, on forest edges, on rocky outcrops, in forest, or as a forest undershrub in the inland forests of Natal, Zululand, and the northern Transvaal.

The leaflets are widely lance-shaped, oval to egg-shaped, the terminal 4-6 cm long and 1.3-1.9 cm wide, the lateral ones slightly smaller, the tips pointed, the base narrowed, densely to slightly hairy, the margins untoothed, the midrib and veins prominent.

The tiny flowers are in velvety heads, those in the axils shorter than the leaves, those at the ends of the branches longer. The fruits are very small, slightly flattened, and orange-brown in colour. They give the tree its specific name based on Greek words meaning "small fruit".

(381)   27. *Rhus crispa* (Engl.) Harv. ex Schonl.

= *Rhus gueinzii* Sond. var. *crispa* Engl.

Rhus crispa is a small tree up to about 6 m high occurring from the eastern Cape to the Transkei and Natal, often growing along streams or in scrub forest.

The leaflets are long and slender, the central leaflet up to nearly 9 cm long and 2.5 cm wide, the lateral ones shorter and sometimes wider, bluntly pointed, narrowing to the base, thin, often crisped — hence the specific name — wavy or flat, toothed or untoothed, smooth, thin, a deep green above and lighter below.

The tiny flowers are borne in masses in short, loose sprays in the axils of the leaves and terminally in late summer. The fruit is small and roundish.

(383)   28. *Rhus erosa* Thunb.

Besembos, soettaaibos, rosyntjiebos; tshilabele (SS)

The besembos is one of the outstanding features of dry stony hill and koppie slopes in parts of the Orange Free State, the Cape Midlands, and of Lesotho, and travellers along the national road from Bloemfontein over the Orange River to Graaff-Reinet cannot fail to observe its large, soft, green or yellow-green form clothing slopes otherwise bare of shrubs or trees.

This is nearly always a shrub up to some 3 m high and as much as 9 m across, but occasionally tree-like, always densely branched and a light green or yellow-green colour. The leaves distinguish it at once for

On the wide Karoo plains of the Midlands, *Rhus longispina* is often a common species

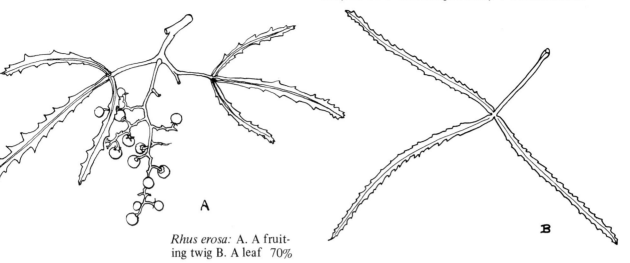

Rhus erosa: A. A fruit-
ing twig B. A leaf 70%

the leaflets are unique — long and very narrow and pointed, often up to
13 cm long and no more than 3 mm wide, occasionally with untoothed
margins but usually with jagged edges looking as if they have been
gnawed — "the gnawed rhus" is the meaning of the descriptive botanical
name. They are leathery, hairless, and sticky, the upper surface looking
as if varnished, with the midrib usually conspicuous on both sides.

The small white or greenish-yellow flowers are in lax, slender sprays
which are usually shorter than the leaves. The fruit is a small, yellow,
smooth, shiny drupe.

The tree is not grazed and its main use is as a soil protector, its removal having often caused soil to erode on bare hill slopes. It has been
cut in quantities over the years, mainly for fuel, for the country where
it grows is often notoriously lacking in firewood; for making kraals, for
crude thatching, for brooms — hence the common name "besembos" or
"broom-bush" — for hair brushes, for snuff, for medicine and magic.
African witchdoctors use it in rain-making ceremonies and it is easy to
understand why its luxuriant, spreading form should suggest abundance.

It is sometimes used to make a dense, soft, evergreen hedge in
gardens, where its airy foliage is decorative.

(388)   29. *Rhus longispina* Eckl. & Zeyh.

Karoo thorny taaibos, buffalsdoring

Rhus longispina — literally "the long-spined rhus" — is a common little
tree in dry areas from about Swellendam to East London, and inland to
Oudtshoorn, Graaff-Reinet and Pearston, often many-stemmed, with a
dense, round crown, sometimes shapely, sometimes reaching to the
ground in an untidy dense mass. The "candles" of children, *Loranthus
elegans* Cham. & Schlecht. are often found in the crown, in autumn
their glowing orange flowers making brilliant patches.

It grows up to about 3 to 4.5 m in height and has a stem diameter in
old trees of up to 0.6 m. It is usually a dark shiny green with grey
twigs, these, the leaves and flower sprays being covered with small reddish glands, and with shortened branchlets ending in a sharp point or
bearing stout spines.

The leaflets are variable, the central one up to 5 cm long, the side

1263

Right
Rhus longispina: A portion of a flowering and
fruiting branch showing the robust spines 90%

Below left
It frequently grows close to water. The little
tree on the left, on the edge of a Karoo dam,
was covered with richly scented flowers in May

Below right
The multiple stems of *Rhus longispina*

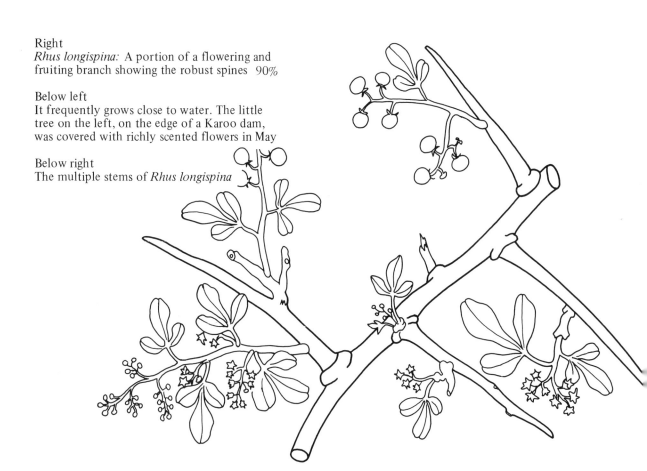

ones shorter, from widely lance-shaped to egg-shaped, often with round tips, the base narrowed, untoothed, borne on stalks that are often winged, not alternately but usually in tufts together.

The small greeny-yellow flowers with a sweet citrus scent are in small, short sprays, covered with red glands, borne abundantly in the axils of the leaves in the autumn. The fruits are small, green turning red-brown, smooth, shiny, and roundish, becoming slightly flattened with age. They have a strong aromatic smell, something between pine and pepper.

Sometimes this species is confused with *Rhus undulata*. In the Cape Midlands where they both grow they are easily distinguished, this being a dense, spiny tree common on the plains and often near pools or dams (where it is most decorative), with foliage that is browsed, flat leaflets, and flowers usually in short bunches in the axils of the leaves. *Rhus undulata* is most often a tree of dry mountain sides, often spineless and seldom as dense, with foliage that is seldom browsed, wavy leaves that often have flat and indented tips, and flowers that are usually borne in terminal sprays. Botanists note that *Rhus longispina* has rather diffuse branching veins and *Rhus undulata* clear-cut secondary veins.

In the Karoo wild creatures of all kinds use the tree as shelter, its low dense branches giving cover to leguaans, snakes, sometimes birds, and many small mammals. At least one butterfly, the brown and red *Phasis braueri,* breeds on the tree, laying its eggs on the stems of young shoots.

C.A.Smith says that once this was used as a spiny hedge to keep buffaloes out of gardens and "wolves" from kraals, hence the common names "buffelsdoring" and "wolwedoring". Gardeners today, wishing to plant a thick hedge, might bear in mind this dense, neat, shiny little tree, hardy and drought-resistant.

(394)   30. *Rhus tomentosa* L.

= *Rhus ellipticum* Thunb.

Hairy taaibos, korentebessie, wild currant, umHlakothi (Z)

Rhus tomentosa is a shrub to a 6 m tree growing on mountains and hills, in river bush and on forest margins from Namaqualand, through the south west Cape to George, and then — according to Schonland — in isolated groups in the Transkei, Natal, and the Transvaal.

It has angular twigs which are hairy and red when young, becoming smooth later, and striking leathery bi-coloured leaflets, the central one up to 9 cm long. Mature leaflets are smooth and dark green or grey-green above, and below densely hairy and grey or tawny. They are egg-shaped to broadly lance-shaped, sharply or bluntly pointed, sometimes with a thorn-like point, narrowing to the base, the margins untoothed or toothed, sometimes deeply so, above the middle, the midrib promi-nent below, generally borne on short stalks — an unusual character in *Rhus* leaflets which are usually stalkless. The leaves are carried on slender rather furrowed and often reddish stalks.

The small flowers, with a strong unpleasant smell, are in long, delicate, branching heads which are velvety and grey or yellowish, and borne at the ends of the branches and in the axils of the leaves from winter to spring. The fruit is small, grey and hairy, roundish or lopsided and flattened.

Top
Rhus incisa near Garies in Namaqualand

Above left
Rhus incisa: A fruiting twig (70%)

Right
Rhus angustifolia leaves (60%)

1266

The leaves, twigs and bark were once used in tanning and the bark for rough rope.

31. *Rhus angustifolia* L.

Willow taaibos

This little tree or shrub looks remarkably like a willow in habit and foliage as it overhangs the clear mountain streams of the western Cape, often in company with the smalblad, *Metrosideros angustifolia* Smith.

It is most often a shrub, but sometimes a little 4 m tree, with brown branches, smooth or softly hairy twigs, and long narrow graceful leaflets. These are lance-shaped, sometimes widely so, pointed, narrowed to the base, untoothed, above a shiny green and smooth, below densely covered with short whitish-grey hairs, the thick, hairy, yellowish midrib being conspicuous. Like *Rhus tomentosa,* they are shortly stalked. The leaf stalks are usually about 1.2 cm long, shorter than in *Rhus tomentosa.*

The small flowers, blooming in spring, are in long, lax sprays which are smooth or hairy, in the axils of the leaves or borne terminally. The grey velvety fruit is about 6 mm in diameter — larger than those of many *Rhus* species — flattened and often lopsided.

This resembles *Rhus tomentosa* but the leaflets are always narrower and the leaf stalks shorter.

The specific name is Latin meaning "narrow-leaved".

(385)   32. *Rhus incisa* L.f.

= *Rhus obovata* Sond.

This is a large, rigidly branched shrub to small tree scattered in open scrub on hillsides and often on river banks, growing from Namaqualand through the south west to the eastern Cape, usually in the coastal districts, but inland as far as Oudtshoorn and King William's Town.

The leaflets are oblong or oval, narrowing to the base, with a round or flat apex, the margins flat or inrolled, untoothed or slightly toothed or sometimes so deeply lobed as to appear like miniature oak leaves, or each lobe like a separate leaflet, dark green and shiny above, often somewhat hairy, and white and densely velvety below. They are usually very small, sometimes no more than 8 mm long, and stalkless. The leaves are borne on hairy stalks.

The small greenish-yellow flowers are in hairy sprays at the ends of short side branches. The fruit is roundish, up to about 8 mm in diameter, grey, covered with shaggy hairs, often splitting open.

In parts the foliage is browsed.

Schonland included *Rhus obovata* in this species, making it a separate variety, *Rhus incisa* var. *obovata* (Sond.) Schonl. This variety now becomes var. *effusa* (Presl) R.Fernandes.

The specific name is the Latin "incisus" meaning "with a sharply cut margin" referring to the lobed leaflets.

This little tropical species, growing as far north as Ethiopia, is not native to South Africa but occurs in northern South West Africa, the Caprivi Strip and Botswana, as a shrub to a 6 m tree, sometimes spiny, usually growing in bush on river banks.

The branches are brown and furrowed, the twigs covered with dense yellow or white hairs. The leaflets are oval to lance-shaped, sharply or bluntly pointed, and narrowed to the base, the central leaflet up to nearly 8 cm long and 2.5 cm wide, the margins untoothed or slightly toothed, dark green and smooth or slightly hairy above, yellowish and scurfy below, covered with resin. The leaf stalks are hairy.

The small flowers are in short sprays in the axils of the leaves, blooming in late summer, and the small, smooth, round to egg-shaped, red and yellow fruits ripen about May.

The tree was named after Richard Quartin-Dillon, medical doctor and naturalist, who made an expedition to Ethiopia from 1839-1843.

Rhus angustifolia in the right foreground near a stream in the Hex River valley

The holly family is a fairly large one with over 400 species, occurring mainly in Asia and tropical America and poorly represented in Africa and Australia. The most famous member of the family is the holly, *Ilex aquifolium* L., with its glossy evergreen foliage and bright fruits, which has played a part in European mythology since the earliest times.

Members of the family are trees or shrubs which are usually evergreen, with simple, alternate leaves, the stipules very small or absent, and bisexual or unisexual flowers, the calyx segments 3-6 or with 4 teeth, the petals usually 4-5, the stamens most often as many as the petals, the ovary superior, usually 2-5-chambered, and the fruit a drupe.

One genus and 1 species occur in South Africa.

Ilex L.

Over 200 species of evergreen trees and shrubs, growing mainly in the warm regions of the world, belong to this genus. They all have simple, alternate, and often glossy leaves. The flowers are usually male or female in the axils of the leaves. The calyx is 4-6-toothed and persistent, the corolla lobes 4-6, the stamens as many, the male flowers with a rudimentary ovary, the female ovary with 3-6 chambers. The fruit is a round, often bright-coloured drupe, crowned with the persistent stigmas.

The name *Ilex* is the Latin name for the Holm oak.

See colour plate facing page 986

(397)   *Ilex mitis* (L.) Radlk.

= *Sideroxylon mite* L.; = *Ilex capensis* Sond. & Harv.

Cape holly, wild holly, watertree, waterboom, waterhout, without; umDuma (X); iPhuphuma (Z); liBota (Sw); phukgu, phukgile (SS); mutanzwa-khamelo (V)

The Cape holly, a fine, shining-leafed tree of woods and forests, growing in moist spots and on the banks of streams, is widely distributed in Africa, occurring from Table Mountain to Ethiopia, and from Natal in the east to Angola in the west. In South Africa it grows in every province and in Lesotho and Swaziland, from almost sea level to inland mountain slopes. It is a common tree in the Natal National Park overhanging the mountain streams.

It is variable in size. Although sometimes it is small, in the Knysna forest and eastwards it reaches a height of 18 m with a trunk diameter of 0.6 m. It is nearly always a graceful tree. The bark is almost white, the young twigs are red. The shiny dark leaves are simple and alternate,

Above
Ilex mitis growing on a stream bank in Pondoland in company with
the tree fern, *Cyathea dregei*

Left
Ilex mitis bark

lance-shaped, sometimes widely so, 7-10 cm long and 1.9-2.5 cm wide,
with pointed, often curled tips, and a narrowed base, and wavy, sometimes slightly toothed edges. The midrib is slightly sunken. Small stipules
are present. The leaves are carried on short leaf stalks that are usually
conspicuously plum-coloured. These often help to identify the tree.

The bunches of small, white, sweet-scented male or female flowers
are borne in spring or early summer in the axils of the leaves. In autumn
the fruits, small, round, with a short point, and shortly stalked, ripen and
when these bright red fruits are packed densely up the stems they are a
brilliant and gay sight, matching in colour the fruits of the more famous
holly. A tree is then particularly lovely, and is visited by flocks of birds
of all kinds. Each fruit has several seeds.

The tree yields a whitish, light, easily worked wood which is used for
furniture and for fuel.

The leaves, when rubbed together in water, give a lather and with this
the Knysna woodcutters once washed themselves in forest streams.
Zulus use the lather to wash those suffering from influenza, and the bark
is in parts considered a purgative.

This is one of our faster-growing indigenous trees. It germinates and
transplants well, and is semi-hardy although it needs protection while
young. It could be used with great effect in landscape gardening where
there is running water. Visitors to Kirstenbosch may remember the fine
pair growing over Lady Anne Barnard's pool.

The specific name *mitis* means "soft". The Zulu name "iPhuphuma"
means "it foams out", and the Venda name is translated as "milkpail-
washer".

56 The Pendoring Family (Celastraceae)

This baffling and fascinating family, spread throughout the warmer parts of the world, is represented in South Africa, according to the Botanical Research Institute in Pretoria, by 12 genera — *Maytenus, Putterlickia, Catha, Pterocelastrus, Cassine, Allocassine, Maurocenia, Hartogia, Pleurostylia, Salacia, Hippocratea,* and *Pseudosalacia.*

The number of genera, however, differs according to the views of different botanists. Dr N.K.B. Robson — who dealt with the family in *Flora Zambesiaca* — splits the genus *Cassine* into several different genera, such as *Mystroxylon, Elaeodendron,* and *Crocoxylon,* while one of his new genera, *Lydenburgia,* is included in *Catha* by the Botanical Research Institute.

A genus such as *Maytenus* is particularly difficult. Although some of the species are common and widespread and have been known botanically for a long time, they are still not fully understood. What forms does the common pendoring, *Maytenus heterophylla* (Eckl. & Zeyh.) N. Robson encompass? Are the various pendorings which cover such large areas of the Cape Midlands — and differ considerably according to their proximity to water — all forms of *Maytenus heterophylla?* Is *Maytenus polyacantha* (Sond.) Marais separate from them? Are *Maytenus lucida* (L.) Loes. and *Maytenus procumbens* (L.f.) Loes. seperable from *Maytenus undata* (Thunb.) Blakelock? These, and other such questions, remain teasing problems for the present.

The family is a large one with about 60 to 70 genera, composed of trees, shrubs, and climbers, which are sometimes spiny. Members all have simple leaves and bisexual or unisexual flowers, the calyx with 3-5 segments, the petals and stamens usually 3-5, a fleshy disc present, and the ovary superior and 1-5-chambered with usually 2 ovules to each chamber. The fruit is a capsule, berry or drupe.

The cosmopolitan nature of the family may be guessed from some of the generic names. *Maytenus* is based on a Chilean common name and *Catha* on an Arabian name.

In South and South West Africa the family is distributed widely and represented in almost every forest, in nearly every large bush clump, on dunes, in desert, on mountains, in kloofs, and on streams, from sea level to an altitude of at least 1500 m.

In terms of money it is not a very important group in South Africa. In terms of life its value is considerable. Men use the trees to make huts and boats, furniture and rough utensils, for fuel, for medicinal and magic properties, and sometimes for food. One member, *Catha edulis* (Vahl) Forsk. ex Endl., has an ancient history. It has been used from time immemorial as a stimulant and maker of dreams from the Cape to Arabia. Wild animals and stock sometimes eat the fruit and leaves of various species, and birds feast on the more succulent fruits, often leaving the bare pips decorating the twigs. Many species are evergreen, giving shade and shelter in a harsh climate.

The common pendoring,
Maytenus heterophylla,
a confusing species

Key to genera

Fruit a dehiscent capsule

The fruit fairly small, round to oval, not winged; the seeds with an aril.
The ovary with 2 ovules per chamber.

1. *Maytenus*

The ovary with 3-6 ovules per chamber.

2. *Putterlickia*

The fruit winged or with horns; the seeds with an aril.

4. *Pterocelastrus*

The fruit oblong, narrow, without wings or horns; the seeds winged or
with a small aril.

3. *Catha*

The fruit somewhat walnut-sized and shaped, hard, leathery; the seeds
large, angled, hard, smooth, not winged.

11. *Pseudosalacia*

Fruit an indehiscent drupe

The fruit fleshy or dry, the seeds endospermous, without an aril, (the
ovary 2-3-chambered, the ovules erect).

5. *Cassine*

1272

The fruit fleshy; the seed 1, without an aril (the ovary 2-chambered, the ovules pendulous).

7. *Maurocenia*

The fruit fleshy becoming dry; the seed without endosperm.

8 *Hartogia*

The fruit dry, 1-chambered, bearing on one side the persistent style; the seeds usually 1, without an aril.

9. *Pleurostylia*

The fruit a fleshy drupe, the seeds without endosperm.

10. *Salacia*

Fruit a berry

The fruit fleshy; the seeds long, narrow, 2-4, without an aril.

6. *Allocassine*

1. *Maytenus* Molina

This large genus of about 200 species is common in the warm regions of the world, particularly in Brazil. About 15 species of trees and shrubs occur in South and South West Africa both in areas of high rainfall and in arid regions.

The genus now includes the species formerly placed in *Gymnosporia,* while the number of species upheld has been considerably reduced.

In spite of work done on *Maytenus* in recent years it remains, at any rate in South Africa, a difficult genus, the exact number of species, subspecies, and forms uncertain. Extensive field work is necessary for a fuller understanding of some species such as *Maytenus heterophylla,* a very common and widespread species which has numerous groups within it. The difficulties past and present botanists have experienced over this one species are indicated by the number of names now included in synonymy. *Flora Zambesiaca* lists over 40!

All the species have simple leaves, alternate or tufted, toothed or untoothed, with or without stipules; bisexual or unisexual flowers in tufts, cymes, or singly in the axils of the leaves or in bunches on shortened shoots, the flowers often borne on jointed stalks, the sepals, petals, and stamens 5, the ovary 2-4-chambered, the fruits roundish or 2-3-lobed capsules that split open to show 1-8 seeds with an aril partly or entirely covering them.

Some species are spiny, the spines often being stout and conspicuous.

The somewhat rare butterfly, the Giant Caraks — *Charaxes castor* — is associated with the genus, breeding on the foliage of various species.

The name *Maytenus* is based on a Chilean common name "Mayten".

For complete lists of synonyms of *Maytenus* species, readers are referred to *Flora Zambesiaca,* Vol. 2, 1963-1966, or to W. Marais's work on the *Maytenus* species of Southern Africa in *Bothalia,* Vol. 7, 1958-1962.

Key to species

A low shrub to bushy tree; spineless; the leaves up to 4 x 4 cm, oval to round, the base usually rounded; the margins recurved and *untoothed;* the fruit a 3-celled capsule. (Cape Peninsula to Caledon).

a. *M. lucida*

A tree; spineless; the leaves 1.3-10 cm long, round to lance-shaped, the base often narrowed, the margins rarely inrolled, frequently with *numerous bold spiny teeth;* the fruit a 3-lobed capsule; the seeds with a *yellow* aril. (Widespread)

b. *M. undata*

A procumbent or climbing shrub to small tree; spineless; the leaves 2.5-6 cm x 1.3-3 cm, oblong to round, the base narrowed, the margins recurved, thickened slightly toothed or *with 3-5 spiny teeth on each side;* the fruit a 3-celled capsule; the seeds with an *orange* aril. (Knysna to Zululand)

c. *M. procumbens*

A tree; spineless; the *twigs hairy;* the leaves 1.3-9 cm x 1.3-4.5 cm, widely lance-shaped to egg-shaped, the base narrowed, the margins toothed or almost untoothed, *velvety* below; the fruit a small yellow, *2-valved capsule,* the seed with a white or yellow aril. (Knysna and the eastern Cape to Swaziland, Zululand, and the eastern Transvaal)

d. *M. peduncularis*

A small to medium-sized tree; spineless; without hairs, the leaves 4-6 x 0.6-3 cm, usually small, egg-shaped to oval, the base narrowed, the margins *untoothed* and recurved; the capsule oval, yellow; the seed with a yellow aril. (South west Cape)

e. *M. oleoides*

Usually a small tree; spineless; the leaves 1.3-10 x 0.6-4 cm, often fairly small, egg-shaped to lance-shaped, the base round or narrowed or notched, the margins toothed or untoothed, *showing elastic threads when torn;* the fruit an orange-yellow 2-3-lobed capsule, the seeds 1-3 with a yellow aril. (In all the provinces)

f. *M. acuminata*

A shrub to small tree, sometimes weeping; spiny; the leaves alternate or in tufts, smooth 2.5-8 cm x 1.3-4 cm, egg-shaped, the base narrowed, *thick* in texture; the capsule *reddish, 3-lobed.* (Knysna to Zululand)

g. *M. nemorosa*

An undershrub or small tree; *with slender spines,* the leaves smooth, 1.3-6 cm x 0.8-4 cm, roundish to lance-shaped, the base rounded or narrowed, the margins toothed, *papery,* the stipules *threadlike;* the fruit a *round or pear-shaped* capsule, *white to red,* the seeds about 3 with an orange to red aril. (Eastern Cape, Natal, Transvaal, Swaziland)

l. *M. mossambicensis*

A shrub or tree; usually with *long, straight, often robust spines;* the branches often *shortened into knobs;* the young shoots green; the leaves usually 1.3-6 cm x 0.6-2.5 cm, egg-shaped to oblong, the base narrowed, the margins usually *finely and irregularly toothed;* the flowers with a strong carrion smell; the fruits *2-3-chambered,* yellow to bright red; the seeds 1-4 with a yellow aril. (Widespread in South and South West Africa)

i. *M. heterophylla*

A shrub or tree; spiny; the young shoots often *reddish;* the foliage frequently glaucous; the leaves 1.9-10 cm long, oblong to egg-shaped, the base narrowed, the margins usually *densely and finely serrated;* the fruit usually *2-chambered;* the seeds with a pink or yellow aril. (Natal, Zululand, Swaziland, Transvaal, South West Africa)

j. *M. senegalensis*

A bush to small tree; glabrous, spiny, grey-green; the leaves *very narrow,* 2.5-6 cm x 0.3-0.8 cm, untoothed or slightly toothed; the capsule usually 2-valved, the seeds chestnut-coloured. (Dry eastern Cape, north west Cape, South West Africa)

k. *M. linearis*

Leaves in tufts

A shrub to small tree; the spines long and stout; the branches often abbreviated; the leaves usually up to 2.5 cm long, a narrow oblong, the tips frequently notched; the margins *untoothed or slightly toothed;* the fruit a *3-chambered capsule;* the seeds with a yellow aril. (Eastern Cape to possibly the Transvaal).

h. *M. polyacantha*

A shrub to tree; the spines long and straight; the branches *often shortened into knobs,* the young shoots *green;* the leaves usually 1.3-6 cm x 0.6-2.5 cm, egg-shaped to oblong, the base narrowed, the margins usually *finely and irregularly toothed,* the flowers *with a strong carrion smell;* the fruits 2-3-chambered, yellow to bright red, lobed or unlobed; the seeds usually 1-4 with a yellow aril. (Widespread in South and South West Africa)

i. *M. heterophylla*

A shrub or tree; the young shoots often *reddish;* the leaves smooth, 1.9-10 cm long, oblong to egg-shaped, the base narrowed, the margins usually *densely and finely serrated;* the fruit *usually 2-valved;* the seeds with a pink or yellow aril. (Natal, Zululand, Swaziland, Transvaal, South West Africa)

j. *M. senegalensis*

An undershrub or small tree with *slender spines;* the leaves smooth, *papery,* 1.3-6 cm x 0.8-4 cm, roundish to lance-shaped, the margins toothed, *the stipules threadlike;* the fruit a round or pear-shaped capsule, white to red; the seeds about 3 with an orange to red aril. (Eastern Cape, Natal, Transvaal, Swaziland)

L. *M. mossambi-censis*

Maytenus undata on a rocky hillside near Rustenburg

a. *Maytenus lucida* (L.) Loes

= *Celastrus lucidus* L.; = *Gymnosporia lucida* (L.) Loes

This Cape coastal species occurring from the Cape Peninsula westwards to about Caledon is commonly a low shrub, but occasionally a small bushy tree with many stiff, erect branches.

It has alternate, leathery, smooth leaves, 1.3-4 cm long and 0.8-4 cm wide, egg-shaped, oval, or round, bluntly pointed, often with a sharp thorn-like point, the base usually rounded, the margins recurved and untoothed, the veins distinct, borne on short stalks.

The small flowers are in tufts in the axils of the leaves and the fruit is a small, usually 3-celled brown capsule containing angular seeds with a thin aril.

The name *lucida* means "bright".

(403)   b. *Maytenus undata* (Thunb.) Blakelock

= *Celastrus undatus* Thunb.; = *Celastrus ilicinus* Burch.; = *Catha fasciculata* Tul.; = *Celastrus zeyheri* Sond.; = *Celastrus albatus* N.E.Br.; = *Gymnosporia rehmannii* Szyszyl.; = *Gymnosporia undata* (Thunb.) Szyszyl.; = *Gymnosporia zeyheri* (Sond.) Szyszyl.; = *Gymnosporia fasciculata* Loes.; = *Gymnosporia albata* (N.E.Br.) Sim; = *Gymnosporia deflexa* Sprague; = *Gymnosporia peglerae* Davison; = *Maytenus zeyheri* (Sond.) Loes.

Koko tree, kokoboom, South African holly, iGqwabali, iKhukhuze, iNqayielibomvu (Z)

The koko tree is a very widely distributed species growing in all the provinces of South Africa, in Swaziland and Botswana, northwards through tropical Africa to Ethiopia, and in Madagascar and the Comoro Islands, occasionally in high forest, more often on forest fringes, in dry forest, bushveld and karoo, on wooded hillsides and rocky koppies, along streams, often on shale formations, from the coast to an altitude of 1500 m.

Naturally it is an extremely variable species, in the forests of tropical Africa having large leaves and pink to white fruits, and at the other extreme in arid parts of South Africa small leaves and palish yellow-green fruits. *Flora Zambesiaca* sees the South African species, *Maytenus lucida* and *Maytenus procumbens* (L.f.) Loes., as two extreme forms of this, although treating them as distinct species.

This is a shrub to 6 m tree, occasionally up to 12 m high, evergreen, spineless, much-branched, often bushy, branching from the base or with a rounded crown and single trunk up to 40 cm in diameter, the bark thin, smooth when young, rougher later, varying from almost white to light or dark grey, and pink within. The angular twigs are often a purplish colour.

The handsome, leathery, holly-like leaves are simple and alternate, dark green to grey or silvery green, sometimes both sides of the same colour, at others the lower side whitish; egg-shaped, round, oblong or lance-shaped, the tips round to pointed, the base usually narrowed, the size very variable, 1.3-5 cm long in dry areas, and in forest or moister regions up to 10 x 8 cm, the margin seldom thickened or recurved, slightly to boldly toothed, the teeth numerous — usually more than 4 on each side of the margin — and sometimes sharp and spiny. They are borne on short stalks.

1278

The small white to greenish, sweet-smelling flowers bloom irregularly from spring to winter. They are borne on slender often maroon-coloured stalks in dense clusters in the axils of the leaves.

The fruit is a small, often 3-lobed capsule, the size of a large pea or smaller, pale yellow, green or orange, splitting to show reddish-brown seeds completely or partly enclosed by a shiny yellow aril.

The timber is red, dense, heavy and close-grained, and was once used for making wagons and farm tools. It is particularly good fuel.

This is a handsome tree or shrub with ornamental leaves and fruits, easily grown from seed or cuttings, and tolerating sun, shade, drought and frost. It should make a particularly good evergreen for enterprising gardeners.

The name *undata* means "undulate", and refers to the often slightly wavy margins. The common name "koko" is Hottentot.

It is noteworthy that Burchell, one of the greatest collectors of all time, collected this near the Asbestos Mountains in Griqualand West, He called it *Celastrus ilicinus*.

(401.1)   c. *Maytenus procumbens* (L.f.) Loes.

= *Celastrus procumbens* L.f.; = *Gymnosporia procumbens* (L.f.) Loes

Coast maytenus; umPhophonono (Z)

Maytenus procumbens, closely related to the low-growing *Maytenus lucida* of the western Cape, has a wider distribution for it grows from Knysna eastwards and northwards along the coast through the eastern Cape to the Transkei, Natal and Zululand to Mozambique.

The specific name indicates that this species is procumbent, lying flat upon the ground. This is misleading for although it does grow in this form it is also sometimes a shrub or a tree. It is common around Port Alfred as a low shrub sprawling among the undergrowth or further north as a drooping or climbing shrub or tree up to 6 m high, on sand dunes, in dune forest, in wooded dune valleys, and in sandy riverine bush. A tree grows at Ifafa Lagoon on the Natal south coast where the trees, usually clearly labelled, are familiar to many visitors.

The bark is greyish-brown and smooth, sometimes — when mature — with fine cracks and often lichen-covered. The tree is spineless, the twigs angular, the young stems often pink, and the leaves without latex.

The rather pale green or blue-green leathery leaves, shiny above, are simple and alternate, oblong, oval, or round, 2.5-6 cm long and 1.3-3 cm wide, the tips rounded or pointed, the base narrowed, with the 4-6 pairs of nerves conspicuous, the margins recurved and thickened, slightly toothed or with 3-5 conspicuous spiny teeth on each side. They have short stalks.

The small white, yellow or greenish flowers are in dense tufts in the axils of the leaves, blooming in the late summer and autumn. The fruit is a yellow-orange, roundish to oval, 3-celled capsule which splits to show the seeds within completely covered in a bright orange aril. They ripen from late autumn to winter.

This species is closely related to the more common and widespread *Maytenus undata* (Thunb.) Blakelock. It has been suggested that the two should not be separated as distinct species but as subspecies only.

OPPOSITE

Above left
Maytenus procumbens,
Bashee River mouth

Above right
Maytenus undata trunk

Centre left
Maytenus procumbens
bark

Below left
Maytenus undata: Capsules and seeds (80%)

Below right
Maytenus undata leaves
(80%)

Above left
The slender stem of a young blackwood, *Maytenus peduncularis*

Above right
The blackwood, *Maytenus peduncularis,* in the Royal Natal National Park

Below left
Maytenus polyacantha: a portion of a fruiting branch (90%)

Below right
Maytenus peduncularis: a leafy twig with flowers and capsules (60%)

1280

Maytenus peduncularis
leaves, a large-leaved
form. 100%

(401)   d. *Maytenus peduncularis* (Sond.) Loes.

= *Celastrus peduncularis* Sond.; = *Gymnosporia peduncularis* (Sond.)
Loes.

Blackwood, swarthout; umNgqi (X); umNqayi omyama, iNqayi, iNqayi
elimnyama (Z); makhulu-wa-mukwatule (V)

The blackwood is an evergreen tree of forests and forest margins, most
often growing on stream banks, from Knysna through the eastern Cape,
the eastern Orange Free State and the Transkei to Natal, Zululand,
Swaziland and the eastern Transvaal, from sea level to an altitude of
about 1500 m. It is a common and beautiful tree in the Royal Natal
National Park, with slender weeping branches overhanging the streams.

It grows up to 15 m in height but is usually from 6-9 m, erect, the
main branches growing upwards and outwards, the slender ones and the
softly hairy twigs hanging downwards like a willow; the trunk clean,
grey and smooth becoming darker and rougher with age, the bark on old
branches sometimes almost black. An old trunk may reach 0.6 m in diameter.

It is spineless. The simple, alternate leaves differ greatly in shape
and size from area to area. They are from 1.3-9 cm long and 1.3-4 cm
wide, widely lance-shaped to egg-shaped, bluntly pointed, narrowed
slightly towards the base, the margins toothed or almost untoothed,
green above, below paler and often velvety, when young covered with

The mountain maytenus, *Maytenus oleoides*, growing in Van Rhyn's Pass in the western Cape

1282

Above left
Maytenus oleoides leaves,
flowers and capsules 100%

Above right
Maytenus oleoides bark

soft brown hairs, with the veins distinct. They are carried on hairy stalks.

The tiny yellow flowers on slender stalks are in lax clusters in the axils of the leaves. The fruit is a small, yellow, shiny, 2-valved capsule, oval to egg-shaped, splitting to show the seed, covered with a pearly-white to yellow aril.

The timber is heavy, hard, tough, elastic, with white sapwood and dark grey heartwood, almost black when mature — as the common name suggests — used for handles, and once for making wagons. Sim says that the bark on the branches changes to nearly black when dry, sticking to the wood, and that in this state is much used by Africans for knobkerries. This is reputed to yield one of the best of all fighting sticks.

The specific name refers to the slender peduncle or flower stalk.

(400)   e. *Maytenus oleoides* (Lam.) Loes.

= *Celastrus oleoides* Lam.; = *Gymnosporia laurina* (Thunb.) Szyzsyl.;
= *Gymnosporia monococca* Davison; = *Maytenus angustifolius* Loes.

Mountain maytenus; klipkersbos

This native of the south west and western Cape occurs from Namaqualand and the Calvinia district to about Caledon and Uniondale, mainly on mountains where it is conspicuous. It grows, among other well known spots, on Paarl Mountain where it is conspicuously associated with isolated granite boulders, in the Swartboskloof Nature Reserve in the Jonkershoek valley near Stellenbosch, and in Van Rhyn's Pass where trees grow alongside the road.

The fact that it usually occurs among protecting rocks and coppices readily from stumps and unburnt parts, has helped this tree to survive the fires that often devastate the countryside where it grows.

This is held by some to be one of the most decorative trees of South Africa. It is often a low spreading tree up to 6 m high with ash-grey bark that is smooth when young but becomes rough and cracked with age, contrasting with the dense crown of neat, delicate, dark green foliage.

The leaves are simple and alternate, usually small, 4-6 cm long and

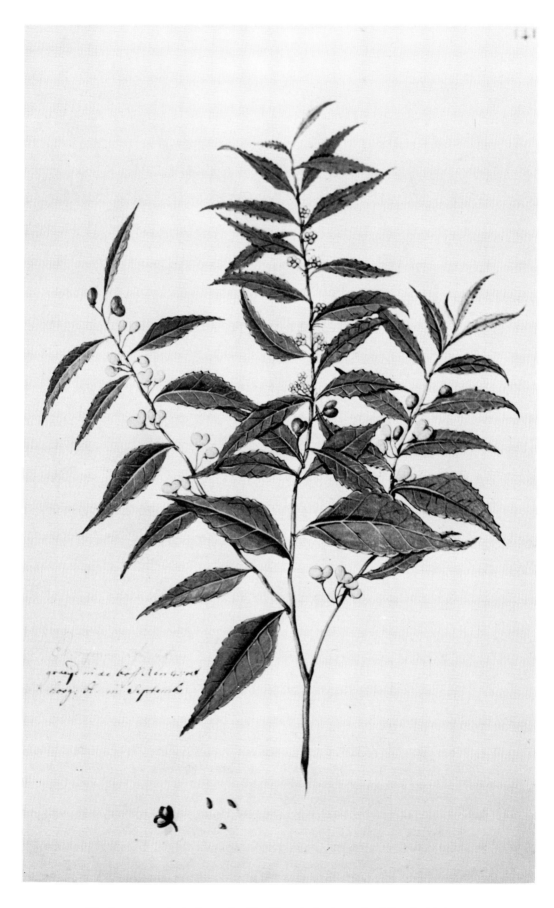

Maytenus acuminata drawn by Claudius. A photograph of the sketch in
Icones Plantarum et Animalium

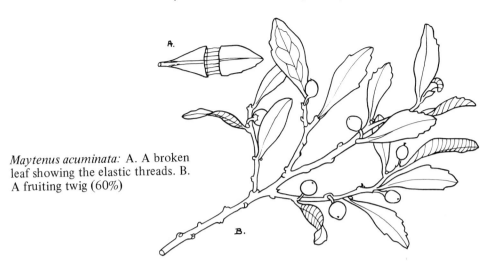

Maytenus acuminata: A. A broken leaf showing the elastic threads. B. A fruiting twig (60%)

0.6-3 cm wide, egg-shaped to oval, the tips round or pointed, the base narrowed, the margins untoothed and rolled back, carried on short leaf stalks. The twigs are often reddish, and the young foliage is a bright, russet red.

The small, greenish, insignificant flowers grow in clusters in the axils of the leaves. The fruits are small, round to oval, yellow capsules splitting along the two lobes to scatter small, oblong seeds covered with a yellow aril.

The specific name *oleoides* means "resembling the olive" — and the tree does look like it, both in general appearance and in its mountain setting. This must have been one of the first trees the early colonists knew for it grew, and still grows, on Table Mountain, yet strangely enough the common names of mountain maytenus and klipkersbos are little known.

(398)   f. *Maytenus acuminata* (L.f.) Loes.

= *Celastrus acuminatus* L.f.; = *Celastrus cordatus* E.Mey.; = *Gymnosporia acuminata* (L.f.) Szyszyl.; = *Gymnosporia acuminata* var. *microphylla* (Sond.) Davison

Silkbark, sybas; umZungulwa, umNama (X); umNama, iNama elimhlophe (Z); umNama (Sw); tshikane (SS)

The silkbark or sybas has a wide distribution, occurring from eastern tropical Africa to the Cape, in South Africa growing in every province, in forests, on forest margins, and in scrub, from sea level to an altitude of 1500 m, sometimes as a 15 m tree but more often as a small spineless tree 3 to 6 m high, or as a shrub. Small and picturesque trees grow at the edge of the cliffs overlooking the Blyde River Canyon in the north eastern Transvaal, at Kranskop in Natal, at Fraser's Falls in Pondoland, and in many other such high rocky places.

The foliage is evergreen and dense, the trunk a mottled grey to dark red-brown, the mature branches furrowed, the twigs angular, slender, brown to purplish, sometimes knobbly, bearing many often drooping, alternate leaves. These are variable in shape and size, often small but ranging from 1.3 to about 10 cm long and 0.6 to about 4 cm wide, egg-shaped or oval to narrowly lance-shaped, the tips acutely or bluntly pointed, sometimes with a thorn-like point, the base round or narrowed, some-

Above
The silkbark, *Maytenus acuminata,*
at Fraser's Falls, Pondoland

Left
The stem of the silkbark

Below right
Maytenus nemorosa: A fruiting twig
and a dissected fruit (60%)

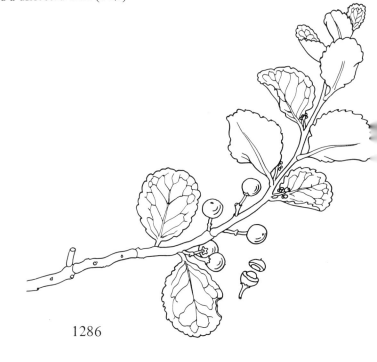

1286

times notched, the margins toothed or untoothed, a deep green above, lighter below, the netted veins conspicuous below, borne on often reddish stalks. One feature is constant — the silky elastic threads in the leaf which show clearly when a leaf is torn across and which join the broken parts like strands of finest silken chewing-gum. Even an old dried leaf retains this fascinating characteristic.

The bark also shows silky threads when broken.

The minute flowers, cream-coloured, yellow-green or reddish, bloom in clusters in the axils of the leaves in summer. The fruit is a 2-3-lobed capsule, sometimes round, usually yellow to orange, holding 1-3 seeds enclosed in a bright yellow or orange, fatty aril, popular with the birds. The fruits are borne in quantities when, in spite of their small size, they tinge the tree with colour.

The wood is a fine pale pink tinged with brown, hard, heavy, strong and close-grained, showing beautiful shades when polished and used in joinery and formerly by wheelwrights to make screws. Africans use it for building huts and to make sticks.

The leaves are sometimes browsed. Pappe noted that the Knysna elephants were very partial to the foliage and pulled down many trees.

The gutta-percha-like properties of twigs and leaves have been investigated commercially and found promising — some types of gutta-percha are used for making golf balls.

The specific name is the Latin "acuminatus" meaning "with a gradually diminishing point", in reference to the shape of the leaves.

(399.3)   g. *Maytenus nemorosa* (Eckl. & Zeyh.) Marais

= *Celastrus nemorosus* Eckl. & Zeyh.; = *Gymnosporia nemorosa* (Eckl. &Zeyh.) Szyszyl

Forest maytenus; umHlangwe (X); inGqwangane (Z)

The forest maytenus grows from about Knysna eastwards and northwards through the Transkei to Zululand and Swaziland, in forest, on forest margins, in bush, and on wooded hill slopes.

It may be a spiny shrub, sometimes climbing into surrounding vegetation, or a small tree, often with drooping branches. The branches are long, greyish, and warted, or much shortened when they often bear tufts of leaves, flowers and fruits. The strong spines are up to 5 cm long.

The smooth, grey or blue-green leaves are simple, alternate, or borne in tufts, 2.5-8 cm long and 1.3-4 cm wide, rather egg-shaped, the tips rounded or widely pointed, the base narrowed, the netted veins distinct, the margins toothed, borne on short or long stalks.

The small white flowers are bisexual and are borne singly or in clusters on slender stalks. The fruit is a small reddish, 3-lobed capsule splitting to release dark seeds.

The leaves and bark are eaten by Black Rhino.

The specific name *nemorosa* is Latin and means "inhabiting woods" in reference to its forest setting.

Above left
The robust, umbrella-shaped pendoring *Maytenus heterophylla*, common in parts of the Karoo - photographed in the Pearston district

Above right
The pendoring, *Maytenus heterophylla*, in the bushveld near Pretoria

Below left
The thick stem and bark of the Karoo form

Below right
Maytenus heterophylla, the small umbrella-shaped form common on the Karoo flats: A portion of a flowering and fruiting branch, and a dissected fruit (60%)

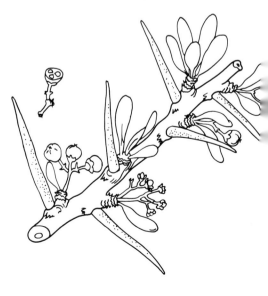

h. *Maytenus polyacantha* (Sond.) Marais

= *Celastrus polyacanthus* Sond; = *Gymnosporia polyacantha* (Sond.)
Szyszyl.; = *Gymnosporia vaccinifolia* Conrath

Pendoring

What is *Maytenus polyacantha?* The answer is exceedingly confused.

At present it is generally considered to be a spiny shrub or small tree
growing from Uitenhage — and inland from Graaff-Reinet and Somerset
East — to the Orange Free State and the Transvaal. The typical *Maytenus polyacantha* came from near Swartkops in the Eastern Province and
was described as a rigid grey shrub up to about 2 or 3 m with long robust
spines and branches that were either long or much shortened (when they
bore the leaves in tufts at the ends). The Transvaal and Orange Free State
forms are shorter and less sturdy with tiny clustered leaves and slender
spines. This, in the Warmbaths area, makes dense thickets no more than
1.5 m high.

Both forms have small white flowers in compact clusters, round, 3-
celled capsules, and seeds covered with a yellow aril.

The southern form may indeed be *Maytenus polyacantha,* a distinct
species, although it shows affinities with the arid form of *Maytenus
heterophylla.* The forms from the Transvaal and Orange Free State, on
the other hand, may prove to be separate from it.

(399)   i. *Maytenus heterophylla* (Eckl.&Zeyh.) N.Robson

= *Celastrus heterophyllus* Eckl. & Zeyh.; = *Catha heterophylla* (Eckl. &
Zeyh.) Presl; = *Gymnosporia buxifolia* of various authors; = *Gymnospo-
ria woodii* Szyszyl.; = *Gymnosporia heterophylla* (Eckl. & Zeyh.) Loes.;
= *Gymnosporia condensata* Sprague; = *Gymnosporia angularis* (Sond.)
Sim; = *Gymnosporia elliptica* (Thunb.) Schonl.; = *Gymnosporia uniflora*
Davison; = *Gymnosporia crataegiflora* Davison; = *Maytenus cymosa*
(Soland.) Exell

Pendoring, lemoendoring, gifdoring; umQaqoba (X); inGqwangane, in-
Gqwangane yehlanze, uSolo (Z); isiHlangu (Sw); shihlangwa (Tso);
sefeamaeba se senyenyane (SS); motlhono, mothono (Tsw); mopasu (NS);
tshipandwa (V); murowanyero (Mbuk)

The pendoring, one of the commonest and most widespread trees or
shrubs of South and South West Africa, first described over 200 years
ago, remains an incompletely known species. In its history it has borne
over 40 names and today no finality has been reached for in its huge
range from Northern to Southern Africa it assumes many forms. Botanists
recognise many groups within it.

It grows from Ethiopia through the Sudan and the Congo, Zambia
and Rhodesia to South Africa, Lesotho and Botswana, east to Madagascar and west to Angola and South West Africa. It is widespread in South
Africa, north, south, east, and west, growing under the most widely
differing conditions, in forest, on forest fringes, in woodland and bushveld, in karoo and semi-desert, on plains, on koppies, on mountains and
on river banks, from sea level to an altitude of about 1500 m, often associated with limestone. Although it is frequently scattered, as in the
Transvaal bushveld, it can grow in colonies as in parts of the eastern

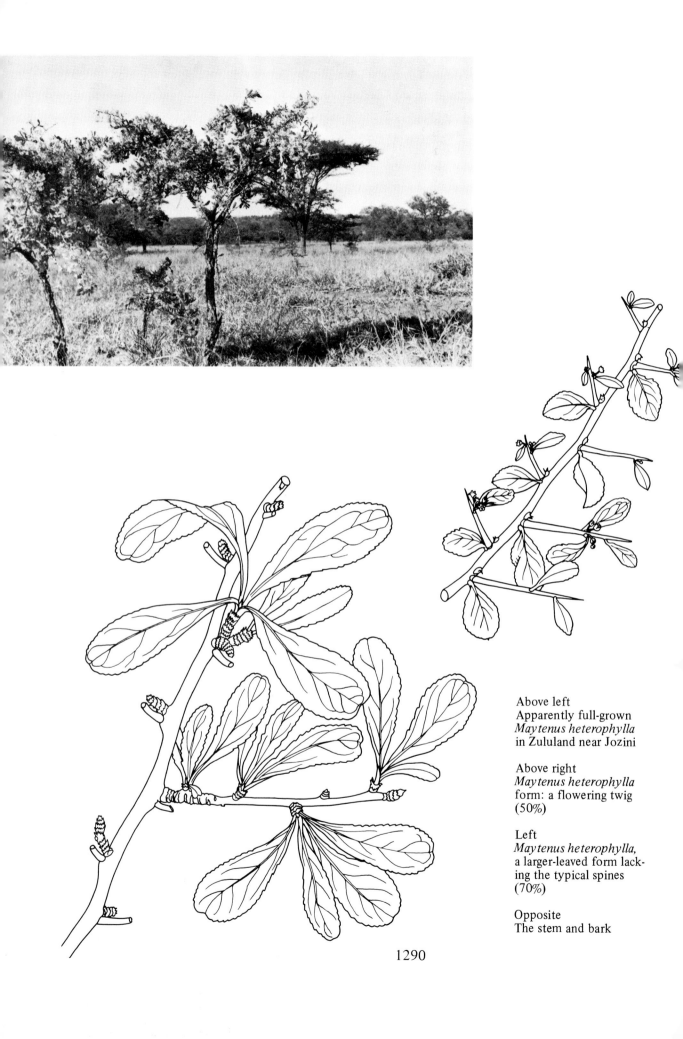

Above left
Apparently full-grown
Maytenus heterophylla
in Zululand near Jozini

Above right
Maytenus heterophylla
form: a flowering twig
(50%)

Left
Maytenus heterophylla,
a larger-leaved form lacking the typical spines
(70%)

Opposite
The stem and bark

1290

Karoo where for miles on end these little trees, like three-quarters-open umbrellas, cover the great plains.

The pendoring may be either a straggling bush or a tree up to 6 m high, sometimes unarmed but frequently spiny. A common form is a rugged little tree with spreading, drooping branches, mature trees no more than 3.6 or 4.5 m high, sometimes having a trunk at ground level measuring 46 cm, this and the older branches being grey and deeply furrowed. Sometimes it is many-stemmed from the base. In dry parts in particular the crown bristles with stout spines, and sometimes with dead wood, while old dead branches often trail untidily to the ground. At its best — and its most formidable — with its seamed trunk and spiky crown it is a tree of great character.

It is noteworthy that in parts of the Karoo the dwarf form common on the plains, short, robust and often umbrella-shaped, may grow within a few feet of a stream-side *Maytenus* three times as tall with weeping and more flexible branches, narrower in shape, and with thinner and longer leaves, flowering and fruiting at different times, and whether these differences are due entirely to the position of the trees and their proximity to water is not yet clear.

The branches may be either long and often arching, robust or slender, or so short and abbreviated as often to appear as knobs or cushions. Mature branches may be deeply or shallowly fissured. The spines may be absent, short, or long, from 1.3-20 cm in length, often immensely stout and strong, grey, brown, or almost black, sometimes bearing leaves upon them.

The leaves, deep green, pale or grey-green, are either arranged alternately or in tufts at the ends of the abbreviated shoots. They are generally 1.3-5 cm long and 0.6-2.5 cm broad, usually egg-shaped to oblong, occasionally rounded, the tips pointed or broadly rounded, sometimes notched, the base usually narrowed — often much tapered — the margins sometimes untoothed but usually finely toothed, the midrib usually conspicuous but the lateral veins only sometimes so, thin or tough and leathery, borne on stalks which are sometimes short, sometimes up to 1.3 cm long.

The male and female flowers are usually on separate plants. They are small and white, creamy or green, usually in much-branched clusters on short shoots in masses up the branches. In full bloom they are airy and beautiful, spoilt only by their often strong unpleasant smell of decayed meat. Occasionally they are without scent or are sweet-smelling, but generally the carrion odour is characteristic and conspicuous. It attracts insects of many kinds, and bluebottle flies in particular, which fertilize the flowers. The crown of a tree in bloom may be not white but metallic blue with its blanket of bluebottles and the air around filled with the sound of their buzzing.

The fruits are usually 3-celled capsules (sometimes 2-4-celled) the size of peas or sometimes up to 1.9 cm in diameter, smooth or marked into segments, yellow to bright red, thin-walled or woody, usually with 1-4 red-brown seeds, partly covered with a thin yellow aril. The red fruits can sometimes be a particularly fine bright colour and then a fruiting tree is a lovely sight.

This little tree has many and varied uses. In parts the fruits are eaten by Bantu, and by birds such as the Cape White-eye. The leaves are browsed by impala, nyala, kudu and giraffe, and the bark and leaves are eaten by Black Rhino.

It is widely used in medicine and African magic. The bark is a remedy for dysenteryand the roots and thorns for colds and coughs, while a decoction of the plant together with parts of snakes is a snake-bite remedy.

Used in an embrocation, it is held to be a love charm, and the thorns are used in a picturesque ritual to cure pain near the heart. The heart of a goat, pierced by a pendoring thorn, is cooked, the thorn removed and the heart then eaten by the patient, the disease, it is believed, being plucked from the human heart as is the thorn from that of the goat.

The wood is heavy, strong, hard and tough, varying from reddish-brown and pink to yellow or almost white, resembling boxwood and once used like it for such purposes as wood engraving and musical instruments. Bantu use it for making stools, spoons, knobkerries, and for carving and fuel. Farmers and Bantu sometimes use the spiny branches, like those of *Acacia karroo,* for kraals, and in country districts the spines are still sometimes used as needles.

The specific name is based on Greek words meaning "different leaves". Pricks given by the thorns are said to become inflamed hence the common name "gifdoring". "Pendoring" means literally "quill thorn" and is a descriptive name given this and several other species of *Maytenus* with robust spines.

A shrub growing in the mopane scrub of the northern Transvaal and Rhodesia, *Maytenus pubescens* N.Robson, appears — according to Robson — to be a derivative of *Maytenus heterophylla.* It has hairy leaves, inflorescence, and capsule.

(402)   j. *Maytenus senegalensis* (Lam.) Exell

= *Celastrus senegalensis* Lam.; = *Gymnosporia crenulata* Engl.; = *Gymnosporia senegalensis* (Lam.) Loes.; = *Gymnosporia dinteri* Loes.

Isihlangu; isiHlangu (Z); isiHlangu (Sw); shihlangwa (Tso); muthone, mothono (Tsw); tshibavhe, tshipandwa (V); mukutema tembuze (Sub)

This species, literally the "maytenus of Senegal", is one of the very few species common to Africa, Europe and Asia.

It is distributed from Natal, Zululand, Swaziland, the eastern, western, central and northern Transvaal, Botswana and South West Africa — where it is widespread — northwards through tropical Africa, Egypt and Morocco, to southern Spain, and eastwards through Arabia to India and Pakistan. It grows in bushveld, woodland and grassveld, in coastal bush on dunes, on the edge of swamps, and along streams, sometimes forming dense thickets.

This is a bushy tree in the Letaba rest camp in the Kruger National Park in the east of the country, and in the west it grows in Namutoni and Okaukuejo camps in the Etosha Game Reserve, often attracting butterflies which flutter around its crown.

It is a shrub or small tree up to 6 m high, sometimes weeping, at others low and bushy, spiny or unarmed, with a trunk up to about 15 cm in diameter and grey-brown bark which may be smooth, finely fissured, or rough.

The branches are somewhat flattened, a dark reddish colour or grey-green when young, becoming grey later. They often droop. The spines, which are in the axils of the leaves or at the end of short branches, are usually up to about 5 cm long but may be as much as 10 cm, sometimes bearing leaves.

The leaves are simple, alternate or in tufts, and usually grey-green,

Maytenus senegalensis
in the north eastern
Transvaal

often with a reddish midrib, smooth, thick, 1.9 to about 10 cm long, oblong, widely lance-shaped to egg-shaped, often broadest above the middle, the apex bluntly pointed, round, and often notched, the base narrowed, the margins sometimes untoothed or slightly toothed, but usually densely and finely serrated the whole length. They are borne on stalks that are often reddish.

The small creamy to greenish-white or pink flowers are in clusters — cymes or panicles — in the axils of the leaves and are crowded up the stalks. They have a brief blooming period, the petals falling when still apparently quite fresh, and thus — according to Keith Coates Palgrave — giving it the name of confetti tree in Rhodesia. Male and female flowers are usually borne on separate plants. The blooming season is irregular.

The fruits are small, smooth, usually 2-valved capsules, round to pear-shaped, pink to red, holding 1 or 2 smooth red-brown seeds, partially covered with a pink or yellow aril.

Birds of various kinds, particularly pigeons, eat the fruits. Zebra, giraffe, and buck such as impala, nyala, bushbuck, kudu, and Grey Duiker, and — it is claimed — monkeys, eat the leaves, and Black Rhino eat the bark. Butcher birds use the spines as larders, impaling their prey upon them, and Africans use the spines as pegs and the trees medicinally — to cure snake bite among other things, and the roots as an aphrodisiac.

The tree yields good quality sticks which are popular with Africans, and they sometimes use these to make fire by friction. The hard, durable, yellowish-white wood, according to Coates Palgrave, saws and planes well but splits during seasoning.

In the Okavango Native Territory the tree is known by a name meaning "Bush of the Tigerfish", perhaps because of its Tigerfish-teeth-like spines.

The species is easily confused with *Maytenus heterophylla*. The young shoots are, however, reddish to grey-green while those of *Maytenus heterophylla* are greenish, the leaves usually have the margins neatly and beautifully scolloped or bluntly toothed, unlike those of *Maytenus heterophylla* which are usually irregularly and sometimes sharply toothed, and the capsules are usually 2- and not 3-valved as in *Maytenus heterophylla.*

Above left
Maytenus linearis in the Karoo,
Pearston district

Centre left
Maytenus senegalensis: A fruiting
twig (70%)

Below left
Maytenus linearis: a branch

Below right
Maytenus linearis: A fruiting twig
(90%)

Opposite
Maytenus linearis stem and bark

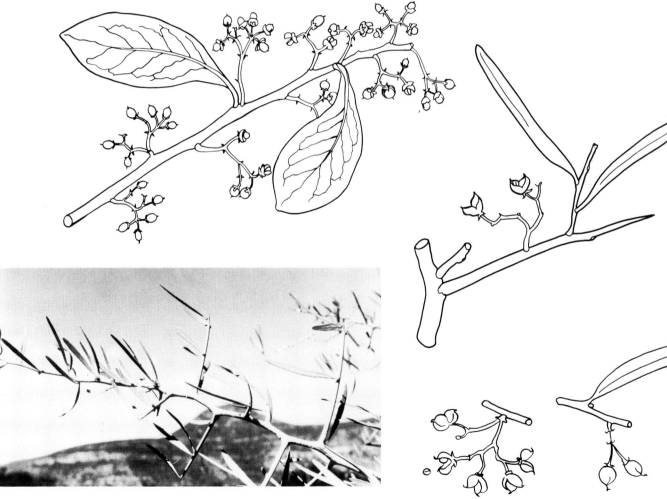

1294

(399.1)   k. *Maytenus linearis* (L.f.) Marais

= *Celastrus linearis* L.f.; = *Celastrus lanceolatus* E.Mey. ex Sond.; = *Gym nosporia linearis* (L.f.) Loes.; = *Gymnosporia lanceolata* (E.Mey. ex Sond.) Loes.

Western pendoring

Maytenus linearis is a pendoring of the dry western areas, growing from Albany and Uitenhage inland to Somerset East and Graaff-Reinet, in the north-west Cape, and in southern South West Africa, in dry bushveld, karoo scrub, and along often dry stream banks. It also occurs in southern Madagascar.

Robson says that this is a derivative of the very widespread *Maytenus senegalensis* and where their areas of distribution meet in South West Africa a few intermediate specimens occur.

It is a bush or small tree up to about 5 m high, sometimes willow-like, sometimes dense and bushy, at others with a round dense crown and a clean stem. This is a grey colour, and in old trees is deeply ribbed.

It has smooth grey branches and long sharp spines which often bear leaves. The greyish-green leathery leaves are simple and alternate, 2.5-6 cm long and 0.3-0.8 cm wide, pointed, untoothed or slightly toothed, with the midrib conspicuous but the veins not visible. They are borne on short stalks.

The tiny creamy flowers, blooming in spring and summer, are in branching bunches in the axils of the leaves. The fruits are small oval or round capsules the size of a pea crowned with a small sharp point, usually 2-valved, and splitting to show small, roundish, shiny, chestnut seeds within.

The specific name *linearis* is a Latin word meaning "narrow and several times longer than wide", and is based on the shape of the leaves. The common name is an old one. Burchell, who collected the tree in the Sneeuberg near Graaff-Reinet in 1812, knew it as "pendoring".

(399.2)   L. *Maytenus mossambicensis* (Klotzsch) Blakelock
            1. var. *mossambicensis*

= *Celastrus mossambicensis* Klotzsch; = *Gymnosporia mossambicensis* (Klotzsch) Loes.; = *Gymnosporia harveyana* Loes.; = *Celastrus concinnus* N.E.Br.

2. var. *rubra* (Harv.) Blakelock

= *Celastrus ruber* Harv.; = *Gymnosporia rubra* Harv. Loes.

Mozambique maytenus; inGqwangane yehlathi (Z)

The "maytenus of Mozambique" is, in its various forms, a widely distributed species growing from Kenya, Tanzania and Zanzibar, to the Transvaal, Natal, Swaziland, and the eastern Cape.

It is a common undershrub in inland mountain forests, or grows as a shrub or small tree on forest fringes and in woodland, often on streams, tolerating dense shade.

Two varieties occur in South Africa, the typical form var. *mossambicensis,* which is a shrub or tree with a smooth stem, leaves and white

Putterlickia pyracantha drawn by Claudius, in *Icones Plantarum et Animalium*

1296

flowers, and var. *rubra* which is low-growing with smaller leaves and with hairy pink or red flowers. This has in parts, as in the forests near King William's Town, made impenetrable thickets.

The typical variety grows up to about 9 m high, sometimes drooping, at others semi-climbing, with reddish-grey bark and slender spines up to about 8 m long in the axils of the leaves or at the end of short branches. Sometimes the spines are absent.

The darkish green leaves, alternate or in tufts, are 1.3-6 cm long and 0.8-4 cm broad, roundish, egg-shaped to lance-shaped, the tips pointed, bluntly pointed or rounded, the base rounded or narrowed, sometimes slightly notched, the margins roundly or sharply toothed They are often rather papery in texture, with the midrib sometimes prominent and light-coloured, and the fine thread-like stipules often conspicuous. They are borne on stalks which are usually short. The leaves much resemble those of *Maytenus nemorosa* which, however, are thicker and lack the fine stipules.

The small, white, bisexual flowers on slender stalks are in delicate clusters in the axils of the leaves or on short shoots. They bloom from summer to autumn. The fruit is a small, smooth, pear-shaped or roundish capsule, white turning brown to bright red when ripe, holding 3 seeds covered with a bright orange to brick-red aril.

2. *Putterlickia* Endl.

This small Southern African genus of only 2 species is almost indistinguishable from *Maytenus*. The genera are separated mainly on the number of ovules – the young seed before fertilization – in each cavity of the ovary. In *Maytenus* there are 2 ovules per cavity, in *Putterlickia* usually 6, although *Putterlickia pyracantha* Endl., growing in dry areas, often has only 2-5.

The two species are spiny shrubs or small trees with simple leaves, alternate or tufted; bisexual flowers in clusters, the flower stalks often jointed, the fruit a 3-angled capsule, splitting to show 6-18 shiny, reddish-brown seeds covered completely or partly by a thin aril.

The generic name honours A. Putterlick, 1810-1845, who was assistant in the Botanical Museum in Vienna.

Putterlickia pyracantha (L.) Endl.

= *Celastrus pyracanthus* L.; = *Celastrus saxatilis* Burch.; = *Gymnosporia integrifolia* (L.f.) Glover, = *Gymnosporia saxatilis* (Burch.) Davison

Fire-thorn putterlickia

Although usually a low shrub, this may be a 6 m tree, and in one form or another is widely distributed around the coast from Saldanha Bay, Cape Town, Port Elizabeth, northwards to Zululand, inland across the eastern Karoo to Kuruman and north to the Transvaal, in forests, kloofs, and scrub.

The branches are often arching. The spines are straight, up to 5 cm long, bare or bearing small tufts of leaves. The branches are *not* warted, a character that helps to separate this species from *Putterlickia verrucosa* Szyszyl.

The leaves are borne in tufts on small knobs or alternately. They are

Left
Catha edulis, Duivels-
kloof, northern Trans-
vaal

Below
Catha edulis flowers

egg-shaped or oblong to widely lance-shaped, often broadest at the top, tapering to the base, the tips round and sometimes notched, or pointed, 1.3-8 cm long and 0.6-3 cm wide, the margins sometimes inrolled, toothed or untoothed, smooth and glossy.

The small star-like flowers, scarlet and cream-coloured, are borne on slender jointed stalks in lax bunches in the axils of the leaves or at the ends of short shoots. The fruit is a capsule from the size of a pea to that of a cherry, red, roundish, with 3 woody lobes.

This on the whole rather humble little species has one claim to fame. Burchell found it near Postmasburg in the north west Cape in 1812 and described it in his journal as "an exceedingly pretty sort of *Celastrus* with red branches and very small leaves" decorating the rocks.

The name *pyracantha* is based on Greek words meaning "fire-thorn" and refers either to the colour of the thorns or to the burning sensation of a thorn prick.

Putterlickia verrucosa (E.Mey. ex Sond.) Szyszyl

= *Celastrus verrucosus* E.Mey. ex Sond.

Warted putterlickia

This small thorny shrub or tree grows from the eastern Cape Province to Mozambique, often scrambling, or as an undershrub in woods, on the fringes of swamp forest, in dune bush, and in forest.

It much resembles *Putterlickia pyracantha* with its strong, straight, robust spines, tufted leathery leaves, and brownish-red, woody capsules, but the branches are warted — the name *verrucosa* means "warted" — and the flower stalks are not jointed as in *Putterlickia pyracantha,* nor as long. It appears always to have 6 ovules — young, unfertilized seed — in each ovary cavity, while *Putterlickia pyracantha* may have from 2 to 6.

To the layman the two species are almost indistinguishable, while they are both easily mistaken for species of *Maytenus.*

3. *Catha* Forsk. ex Scop.

Until recently *Catha* was considered to be (in S.A.) a genus of 1 species, *Catha edulis* (Vahl) Forsk. ex Endl., a species widespread from Arabia and eastern tropical Africa to the Cape. Recently, however, another species, *Catha transvaalensis* Codd, was described from the north eastern Transvaal. This was originally placed by Robson in *Lydenburgia,* a new genus created for it, but this is not upheld by the Botanical Research Institute in Pretoria.

The species are spineless, with simple, opposite or alternate leaves, bisexual flowers in 2-branched cymes, the sepals, petals and stamens 5, the ovary 3-chambered; the fruit a narrow, 3-valved capsule with 1-3 seeds with a basal wing or with a small aril.

The name *Catha* is based on an Arabian word.

(404)   *Catha edulis* (Vahl) Forsk. ex Endl.

= *Celastrus edulis* Vahl, = *Methyscophyllum glaucum* Eckl. & Zeyh.

Bushman's tea, Boesmanstee; iGqwaka (X); umHlawazi (Z); lwani, luthadzi (V)

This remarkable tree reaches from Arabia — where it is cultivated — down the eastern side of Africa from Ethiopia to the Cape. In South Africa it grows from Knysna along the coast to Natal and Zululand, and inland to Swaziland and the eastern and northern Transvaal, in forest, on forest margins, in kloofs, on stream banks and on hill sides, often among dolerite rocks. It is particularly common on the southern and eastern slopes of the Soutpansberg in the northern Transvaal.

It can grow up to 15 m high but is more common as a smaller tree or shrub, usually slender and upright, with smooth foliage. The young trees have light grey bark which becomes darker with age. The twigs are grey, smooth, and ridged, the young twigs sometimes pink, the leaves firm, glossy green above and paler and duller below, 4-10 cm long and 1.3-5 cm broad, egg-shaped to widely lance-shaped, tapering to the apex, sharply or bluntly pointed, the base narrowed, the margin serrated, borne on short, pinkish stalks. They are arranged opposite one another on flowering shoots, and alternately on flowerless ones. The stipules are "free" or often united making a ridge between the leaf stalks.

The small, light, round, cream buds are borne in dense 2-branched heads which are much shorter than the leaves. The flowers are bisexual, small, 5-petalled, white or green, blooming irregularly, and develop into small, red, oblong, 3-sided, 3-chambered capsules, splitting to release 1-3 seeds which are winged at one end.

This species is noteworthy not for its appearance but for its intoxicating and narcotic properties. These are due to an alkaloid in the leaf known as cathine which has a reaction somewhat similar to that of cocaine and caffeine. From the Cape to Arabia leaves and twigs are, or have been, used either in the form of a tea, or chewed, occasionally smoked or eaten with honey, as a stimulant, relieving fatigue, trouble and hunger and inducing a feeling of happiness and alertness. "Immoderate use if persisted in", write Watt and Brandwijk, "produce a condition in which the habitué lives in a dream world", and "excessive chewing can apparently end in insanity". It is still used as an "exciter" in parts of tropical Africa where it is sold in native markets.

In small doses it has medicinal value being used by country people and Bantu for coughs and asthma, and as a mild stimulant. It was said to be a favourite with the Bushmen, hence the common name "Bushman's tea". In other parts it is known as Abyssinian tea or Arabian tea.

A small twig of 8 to 12 leaves is a dose usually sufficient to produce a feeling of well-being.

The wood is golden to brown, glossy, hard and fairly strong, sawing, planing and polishing well. It is borer-proof and is used for building posts and rafters.

The tree is fast-growing and suckers readily.

Specimens from South Africa were once placed in a separate genus, *Methyscophyllum*, a name based on Greek words meaning "intoxicating leaf", a most fitting generic name. The specific name *edulis* means "edible".

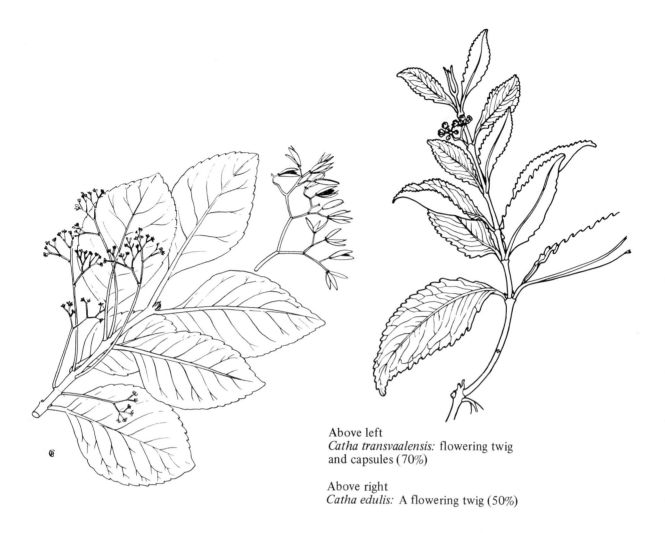

Above left
Catha transvaalensis: flowering twig
and capsules (70%)

Above right
Catha edulis: A flowering twig (50%)

(404.1) *Catha transvaalensis* Codd

= *Lydenburgia cassinoides* Robson

Transvaal catha; mohlolodi (NS)

"The Transvaal catha" from Sekukuniland in the north eastern Transvaal, has only recently been described. It differs from the other member of the genus *Catha, Catha edulis,* mainly in its seeds. These are longer, 3-sided, and with a small and not a winged aril.

It is an unarmed, robust shrub or tree, evergreen or deciduous, up to about 9 m high, often growing in pure stands, in kloofs and in bushveld, often on stony slopes, in Sekukuniland, and in the Lulu Mountains in particular.

The trunk is up to about 46 cm in diameter and is rough and corky, the branches are brittle, the twigs red. The leathery leaves are simple and usually opposite with stipules that soon fall off. They much resemble those of *Catha edulis,* being about 2.5-8 cm long and 1.3-5 cm wide, lance-shaped, oval, or egg-shaped, the tips pointed or rounded, the base round or narrowed, the margins serrated, and shortly stalked.

The small white, 5-petalled flowers are in lax bunches in the axils of the leaves. The fruit is a small capsule, pale greenish-brown, splitting into

Above left
Catha transvaalensis in the north eastern Transvaal

Above right
The bark of *Pterocelastrus echinatus*

Centre left
Pterocelastrus echinatus at the head of Kowyn's Pass

Below left
The bark of *Catha transvaalensis*

Below right
The bark after having been nibbled by goats

usually 3 valves, exposing 3-4 elongated, 3-sided seeds, sometimes with a small white aril at the base.

The wood is used by Africans to make door posts and window frames, and the foliage is eaten by cattle. Goats nibble the trunk bark.

The specific name means "of the Transvaal". Originally the tree was known in South Africa as *Catha cassinoides* (Robson) Codd, but as the name *cassinoides* had already been given to another species of the genus, it could not be upheld in this case. The North Sotho mohlolodi is the basis of the name of the Mohluluding valley in Sekukuniland.

4. *Pterocelastrus* Meissn.

This genus of about 4 species is confined to south eastern Africa.

The species are spineless trees or shrubs with simple, alternate, leathery leaves, small thick stipules that are deciduous, the inflorescence a cyme in the axils of the leaves or bracts, the flowers small, with 5 sepals, petals and stamens, and the ovary usually 3-celled. The fruit is a distinctive capsule with characteristic horns or wings, often remarkably hedgehog-like, the seeds 1-3, red-brown, almost covered with a thin yellow aril.

Flora Zambesiaca says that the genus is allied to *Maytenus oleoides,* but that the fruit is distinctive.

All the *Pterocelastrus* species resemble one another. The leaves are often much alike and the species are separated largely on the type of inflorescence and fruit. These differences are not always clear-cut. Nevertheless, 3 forms do appear to emerge in South Africa.

A coastal shrub, thick bushy tree, or tall tree reaching from Saldanha Bay round the coast to Natal and inland to about Somerset East in the Cape and the Royal National Park in Natal, growing in forest, in scrub, often on dunes, in grassland, on wooded and grassed hills and along rivers, is *Pterocelastrus tricuspidatus* Sond. It has a short dense inflorescence and the protruberances on the capsule are more winged than horn-like.

An often graceful tree in coastal forest and in nearby mountains from Swellendam northwards to the Natal and Zululand mountains with the inflorescence a loose, many-branched cyme, and a many-horned capsule, is *Pterocelastrus rostratus* Walp.

A shrub or tree of evergreen forests and rocky slopes from Maclear, through Natal, Zululand, Swaziland, and the east, central, and northern Transvaal, northwards to Malawi and Mozambique, is *Pterocelastrus echinatus* N.E.Br. It has flowers in a short cyme and a capsule with few to many short horns. Two forms formerly believed separate species, *Pterocelastrus galpinii* Loes., and *Pterocelastrus rehmannii* Davison, are now generally included in this.

The name *Pterocelastrus* means "winged Celastrus". Celastrus is the Greek name for an evergreen tree.

(405)   *Pterocelastrus echinatus* N.E.Br.

= *Pterocelastrus galpinii* Loes.; = *Pterocelastrus rehmannii* Davison; = *Gymnosporoa nyasica* Burtt Davy & Hutch.

Hedgehog pterocelastrus; isiHlulamanye, uGobandlovu (Z); mutongola (V)

A very widely distributed species, *Pterocelastrus echinatus* extends from Maclear in the Transkei through Natal, Zululand, and Swaziland to the

Right
Pterocelastrus echinatus: A fruiting
twig (50%)

Above left
Pterocelastrus rostratus: A fruiting
twig (50%)

central, eastern and northern Transvaal, and northwards through Rhodesia to Malawi and Mozambique.

It grows in forest, on forest fringes, in kloofs, in scrub forest, or on rocky hillsides, often in cliff scrub or on stream banks, sometimes on grassy slopes, suiting its form to its habitat. In high forest, as in the Ngome Forest in Zululand, it is a tall straight tree 9-22 m tall with a trunk diameter of 0.6 m, and in this form it is common in the forests of Swaziland and the eastern Transvaal. On mountain slopes and rocky koppies from Mont-aux-Sources to the Blyde River Canyon in the eastern Transvaal it is a small evergreen tree or shrub, stocky and round-crowned or spreading, sometimes slender and many-stemmed, sometimes no more than a dense shrub. It is fairly common as a bush or low tree in the Magaliesberg and mountains to the north, and is thus known to many of the people of Pretoria and Johannesburg. On the Blouberg in the north western Transvaal, at an altitude of over 1800 m, it is often only a 0.6 m shrub.

The trunk is rough and grey, tall and straight in forests, short and straight in the open, sometimes many-stemmed, the branches grey-brown becoming reddish with age, the twigs angular and often a bright plum-red.

The thick, rather leathery leaves are simple and alternate, glossy, dark green or mid-green to yellowish green above, paler and duller below, 1.3-9 cm long and 0.8-3 cm wide, lance-shaped to egg-shaped, the apex sometimes round or more often bluntly or sharply pointed, the base narrowed, the margins untoothed and sometimes inrolled, the midrib often red, the lateral veins slightly prominent below, borne on stalks that are frequently red or purple. Dry leaves are noticeably wrinkled.

The tiny, creamy, scented flowers are in small stalked clusters in the axils of the leaves. They are bisexual and develop into small yellow to reddish capsules bearing 2 to many protruberances like short thick horns or sometimes like slender whiskers, a fruit often looking like a miniature hedgehog.

The specific name is a happy one. It is the Latin word for a hedgehog or sea-urchin.

(408)   *Pterocelastrus rostratus* (Thunb.) Walp.

= *Celastrus rostratus* Thunb.; = *Asterocarpus rostratus* (Thunb.) Eckl. &
Zeyh.

Beaked pterocelastrus; rooikershout; uGobandlovu (Z)

The beaked pterocelastrus, common in the mountains around Swellendam, reaches to George, apparently reappearing again in the mountains
of Natal and Zululand.

It can be a graceful tree up to 6 m high, occasionally much taller, with
a trunk diameter of up to 0.6 m, grey-barked, the twigs often red or
plum-coloured. The simple, alternate, leathery leaves are widely lance-
shaped, the tips pointed and often notched, narrowed to the base, a
glossy green above, paler and duller below, usually only the midrib clearly visible, borne on stalks about 6 mm long.

The white or greenish flowers are in conspicuous many-flowered lax
clusters. The fruits, on long stalks, are 0.8-1.2 cm in diameter, studded
with few to many protruberances, like small, pointed, rather curly horns,
brilliant orange when ripe, hanging downwards and splitting open on the
tree into 3 lobes to show small egg-shaped, silvery-brown seed. The fruits
are often borne in quantities when the tree appears a shower of brilliant
orange.

The bark contains tannin. Gerstner says it was once sold all over Zululand as a love charm emetic and sprinkling medicine to ward off evil.

The Zulus, according to Watt and Brandwijk, use the roots mixed
with other plants, and the dried carcase of the fruit bat, to treat spinal
diseases.

It is doubtful if this species has ever been cultivated. It should make a
particularly graceful, medium-sized tree giving bright colour when in
fruit.

The specific name is the Latin word "rostratus", meaning "beaked"
or "with a slender point", in reference to the spiky fruit.

(409)   *Pterocelastrus tricuspidatus* (Lam.) Sond.

= *Celastrus tricuspidatus* Lam; = *Pterocelastrus variabilis* Sond. = *Pterocelastrus stenopterus* Walp.; = *Pterocelastrus litoralis* Walp.

Kershout, candlewood, cherrywood; iBholo, iTywina (X)

The kershout is one of the common trees or shrubs growing along the
coast from north of Saldanha Bay to the eastern Cape, often dominant
in the dune scrub. It also grows inland to areas such as Willowmore and
Somerset East, the Royal Natal National Park, Swaziland, and the eastern Transvaal, sometimes as an 18 m tree in forests but often as a low
spreading tree on forest margins, or a big bush on wooded hillsides, on
rocky koppies, and in grassland where it often occurs among boulders.
It is a common tree on the old mountain road across the Suurberg from
Addo to Somerset East and along many of the roads in Port Elizabeth's
mountainous hinterland.

It is a variable species with a blue-green to yellow-green or dark glossy
crown, often many-branched, with a short sturdy bole up to 0.6 m in
diameter, covered with light grey to reddish mottled bark, and with greyish-brown furrowed branches.

The leaves are alternate, long and slender to short, broad and egg-

Above left
The kershout, *Pterocelastrus tricuspidatus,* on the slopes of the Suurberg

Above right
The kershout growing in forest at Storms River mouth

Below left
Pterocelastrus tricuspidatus: a fruiting twig and individual fruits (60%)

Below right
Kershout bark

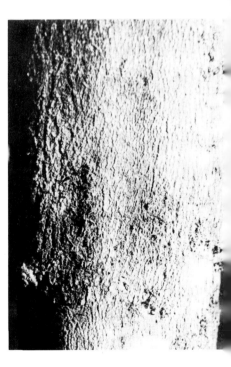

shaped, 1.9-9 cm long and 1.3-5 cm wide, the tips usually rounded and sometimes notched, but also pointed or blunt, hard, leathery, the margins inrolled on the under-surface and thickened, the midrib and veins more prominent below than above, carried on stalks that are very short or of medium length.

The small, creamy-white, sweet-scented flowers grow in short, dense-flowered heads, blooming in early summer, and develop into orange-yellow capsules, usually with 3 horn-like wings which are toothed or untoothed and often split into further prongs, the fruit frequently appearing frilled, when ripe splitting open and the lobes spreading backward, at which stage the fruits look like wide open fleshy flowers. The tree is usually undistinguished and may be passed a dozen times without being noted until fruiting time, when its many brilliant orange fruits clustered up the stems in masses make it memorable.

White-backed Mousebirds are sometimes observed flying around trees in fruiting time, and it is therefore assumed they take the fruit.

The wood is pink to red, heavy, hard and compact, beautifully marked and planing and polishing well. The leaves and bark contain tannic acid and in the past were widely used in tanning, especially in the district of Clanwilliam where an industry grew up around them.

The tree has a little-known historical significance. Xhosa warriors are said to have fixed their assegai blades to the handles with the resin from the heated roots, and Bushmen to have used wax obtained from the tree to fix their glass flakes as arrow heads.

The specific name means "tipped with 3 cusps" in reference to the fruit. C.A.Smith says that the common name "kershout" means "cherrywood" because the wood resembles that of the cherry. Other authorities consider cherrywood a misnomer, giving the translation as "candlewood", a fairly widely used name, the reason for which is, however, not clear.

5. *Cassine* L.

This difficult and interesting genus, occurring in Africa, Madagascar, Australia and tropical America, has given rise of late to certain differences of opinion.

The latest detailed work done on it in Southern Africa is that by Dr N.K.B. Robson working on species in the *Flora Zambesiaca* area in which he restricts the genus to 2 Cape species, *Cassine peragua* L. and *Cassine parvifolia* Sond., placing the other species, formerly included in it, in various other genera.

This view is not at present upheld by the Botanical Research Institute in Pretoria which considers *Cassine* as a large variable genus including the genera *Elaeodendron, Lauridia, Crocoxylon,* and *Pseudocassine*. Following this broad concept of the genus, 8 tree species of *Cassine* are here dealt with and 2 species – *Cassine tetragona* Loes. and *Cassine barbara* L., which, although normally low shrubs, scramblers or climbers, are sometimes trees. A further tree species from the savannah woodland of Botswana is the tropical *Cassine matabelica* (Loes.) Steedman, the *Elaeodendron matabelicum* Loes. of *Flora Zambesiaca*, a small tree with leathery, somewhat oval leaves, abundant yellow-green flowers, and roundish, oval or pear-shaped fruits, yellow drying red or brown. This is O.B. Miller's *Elaeodendron capense*.

All these species of *Cassine* are trees or shrubs with leathery leaves, opposite or alternate, flowers in cymes or panicles, bisexual, or male or female, sometimes borne on separate trees, the sepals and petals 4-5, the stamens 5, the ovary usually 3-5-celled, and the fruit a hard or fleshy drupe which does not burst open. The seeds have no aril.

The generic name *Cassine* is based on a Florida Indian name.

Key to species

Leaves alternate

A bush or tree; the leaves 2.5-5 x 1.3-2.5 cm; dark green, opaque, lance-shaped to egg-shaped, the tips round or blunt, the margins slightly wavy, often inrolled, untoothed to slightly toothed, *showing elastic threads when broken;* the fruit 2-celled, fleshy, pea-like, *yellow or white.* (Cape to Transvaal)

a. *Cassine eucleae-formis*

A bushy, twiggy tree; the leaves short, 1.3-5 cm long, egg-shaped to oblong, the margins toothed or untoothed; the fruits fleshy, *up to 1.3 cm long,* egg-shaped, *pinkish to salmon.* (Pretoria to Rustenburg)

b. *C. burkeana*

A tree, smooth or hairy, the leaves 1.3-13 cm x 0.8-6 cm, round, oblong, or lance-shaped, narrowed to the base, the margins toothed or untoothed, *the fruit up to 2.5 cm long,* oval to round, *pink to red,* the seed solitary. (Cape, Natal, Zululand, Transvaal, Swaziland, South West Africa)

c. *C. aethiopica*

A tree, glabrous, the young branches whippy; the leaves opposite, alternate or tufted, 1.9-8 cm x 0.8-3 cm, oval to lance-shaped, toothed or untoothed; *the flowers with 3 petals and stamens;* the fruit *hard-shelled,* smooth, roundish, *yellow to red-brown,* up to about 1.9 cm in diameter. (Natal, Zululand, Swaziland, Transvaal, often in bushveld)

j. *C. transvaalensis*

Leaves opposite

A shrub or small forest tree; the leaves 1.3-6 cm x 0.3-2.5 cm, lance-shaped to egg-shaped, the margins inrolled, *untoothed,* the fruit small, round, purple-black. (Cape)

d. *C. parvifolia*

Usually a climber, occasionally a tree; the *twigs 4-angled;* the leaves 1.3-8 cm x 0.6-5 cm, narrow oblong to egg-shaped, the margins inrolled, usually with *spiny teeth;* the fruits pea-like, red and purple to black. (Cape to Zululand and Swaziland)

e. *C. tetragona*

A shrub to small tree; glabrous; the leaves 1.3-4 cm long, round to oblong the margins inrolled, the *upper part toothed;* the fruit small, round, purplish. (South west Cape)

f. *C. barbara*

A tree; glabrous; the leaves 2.5-5 cm x 1.3-4 cm, lance-shaped to round, the tips bluntly pointed and often *notched;* the margins inrolled and *toothed;* dark green, the fruit small, oval, dark purple. (Table Mountain to Zululand)

g. *C. peragua*

A tall tree; the mature leaves 2.5-5 cm long, oval to egg-shaped, the tips bluntly or sharply pointed or notched; the margins *closely toothed;* the veining *very heavy below;* the fruit a round to oval *white* drupe. (Swellendam to Natal)

h. *C. crocea*

A tree; the twigs with *conspicuous lenticels;* the leaves usually opposite, 2.5-10 cm x 1.9-6 cm, oblong to egg-shaped, the tips pointed, *toothed,* the fruit up to 2.5 cm long, oval, *yellow to pink.* (Cape to Natal, Zululand, Transvaal)

i. *C. papillosa*

A tree; the young branches whippy; the leaves opposite, alternate, or tufted, 1.9-8 cm x 0.8-3 cm, oval to lance-shaped, toothed or untoothed; the flowers with *3 petals and 3 stamens;* the fruit *hard-shelled,* roundish, *yellow to red-brown,* up to about 1.9 cm in diameter. (Natal, Zululand, Swaziland, Transvaal, mostly in bushveld)

j. *C. transvaalensis*

Leaves in tufts

A tree, the young branches whippy, the leaves 1.9-8 cm x 0.8-3 cm, oval to lance-shaped, toothed or untoothed; the flowers with *3 petals and 3 stamens;* the fruit *hard-shelled,* roundish, *yellow to red-brown,* up to about 1.9 cm in diameter. (Natal, Zululand, Swaziland, Transvaal, mainly in bushveld)

j. *C. transvaalensis*

(413)   a. *Cassine eucleaeformis* (Eckl. & Zeyh.) Kuntze

= *Mystroxylon eucleaeforme* Eckl. & Zeyh.

Witsybasboom; iHlalamanzini, iNama elimbomvane (Z); uSasatye (Sw)

This evergreen species is confined to South Africa and Swaziland, growing in forest, in kloofs, and on wooded hill slopes, from George and Knysna, through the eastern Cape, the Transkei, to Natal, Zululand, Swaziland, and the central, northern and eastern Transvaal, from sea level to at least 1500 m.

In forest it may be a 12 tree with a single trunk up to about 20 cm

Above left
The witsybasboom, *Cassine eucleaeformis,* in Ngoye forest

Above right
Its stem and bark

Below left
Growing as a dense shrub on the edge of forest, Oribi Gorge, Natal

Opposite
Cassine eucleaeformis: Flowering and fruiting twigs (90%)

diameter or many-stemmed, on forest fringes and mountain slopes a low tree, often dense and bushy with shiny and frequently blackish-green foliage.

The bark is light to brownish-grey, often mottled grey and white, smooth in youth, becoming slightly furrowed with age, and the twigs are angular. The simple, alternate leaves are dark green and shiny above, duller, lighter and sometimes wrinkled below, leathery, lance-shaped, oval or egg-shaped, the tips round or bluntly pointed, the base narrowed, the margins slightly wavy, often rolled back, slightly toothed, or untoothed, 2.5-5 cm long and 1.3-2.5 cm wide, borne on short stalks. The leaves, like those of the sybas, *Maytenus acuminata,* have silky elastic threads which show when the leaves are broken, the leaves of the maytenus, however, usually being a lighter green and more translucent.

The small greenish-white, scented flowers are in short clusters. The fruits are 2-chambered, fleshy drupes about the size of a small pea, yellow or white when ripe.

The timber is of good quality, when polished showing beautiful markings. It was once used for making wagons and for joinery, and is still used to make spokes and handles.

This species is the *Mystroxylon eucleaeforme* Eckl. & Zeyh. of Robson in volumes 39-40 of *Boletim da Sociedade Broteriana,* 1965-66.

(411)   b. *Cassine burkeana* (Sond.) Kuntze

= *Mystroxylon burkeanum* Sond.

Transvaal lepelhout

The Transvaal lepelhout is a small evergreen tree up to 6 m high, common in clumps of bush or on rocky outcrops around Pretoria and Johannesburg, extending to the bushveld of the Rustenburg district.

It is often a bushy tree with a dense crown, rough, dark bark and many short knobbly twigs. The leaves are alternate, 1.3-5 cm long and up to 1.9 cm wide, egg-shaped to oblong, the tips usually round and notched, the base rounded, the margins finely toothed or untoothed, leathery, dark green above and paler below. Branches, twigs and leaves, particularly the under-side of the leaves, are sometimes covered with hairs.

The small insignificant flowers are 5-petalled, a greenish-yellow, and appear about January in small bunches. The fruits are small drupes, the mature ones about 1.3 cm long, green and pale pink, turning a bright salmon colour, shiny and very decorative, borne singly or in small bunches. They have a thickish, sweet flesh and are great favourites with birds which eat the ripe ones on the tree, often leaving only the single seed clinging to the stalk by a wisp of skin.

This species is seldom cultivated yet could look very good in a garden where evergreen trees play an important part. In the veld a clump of lepelhouts with their thick darkish foliage and dark brown, often lichen-covered trunks, is decorative, and also gives good shelter.

This species closely resembles the more widespread *Cassine aethiopica* Thunb. and may be no more than a bushy, small-leaved and few-flowered form of it. *Flora Zambesiaca* groups the two together under the name *Mystroxylon aethiopicum* (Thunb.) Loes. For the present the Botanical Research Institute regards it as a separate species, upholding the name *Cassine burkeana.*

The species was named after the botanist, Joseph Burke, who collected plants on and around the Magaliesberg in the 1840's.

Above left
Cassine burkeana in the bushveld near Hartebeestpoort Dam

Above right
Cassine burkeana bark

Below left
Cassine aethiopica: fruiting and flowering twigs (50%)

Below right
Cassine burkeana: A twig with immature fruits, a flowering twig, individual flowers, and a mature fruit half-eaten by birds (50%)

1312

(410)   c. *Cassine aethiopica* Thunb.

= *Mystroxylon aethiopicum* (Thunb.) Loes.; = *Mystroxylon schlechteri* (Davison) Loes.; = *Cassine velutinum* (Harv.) Loes.; = *Cassine pubescens* (Eckl. & Zeyh.) Kuntze; = *Cassine schlechteri* (Loes.) Davison; = *Cassine sphaerophylla* Kuntze; = *Elaeodendron aethiopicum* (Thunb.) Oliv.; = *Elaeodendrum velutinum* Harv.; = *Elaeodendron sphaerophyllum* Presl;

Cape cherry, kooboo-berry, kaboebessie, kaboehout, lepelboom, lepelhout; umNqayi (X); umGunguluzampunzi, umNqayi obomvu (Z); inGulutane (Sw); nqayi (Tso)

The Cape cherry is one of the widely distributed trees of Africa occurring from George and Knysna through the eastern Cape, Natal, Zululand, Swaziland, and the Transvaal, northwards to Ethiopia, east to Mozambique, and west to Botswana, South West Africa and Angola, growing under widely differing conditions, in dune bush, in thornveld, bushveld, forest and swamp forest, along streams, on hillsides, and in arid scrubby flats.

Four species, hitherto held to be distinct, *Cassine velutinum, Cassine pubescens, Cassine schlechteri* and *Cassine sphaerophylla,* have now been included in it, and this gives some indication of how the species differs under varying conditions. It may be a much-branched or slender tree up to about 12 m high, with a trunk diameter up to 0.6 m, or with a clean bole and a spreading, densely leafy crown, or at other times a bush, in which form it is common on the dunes along the coast of the eastern Cape.

The trunk is usually rough and grey to almost black, the branches smooth grey or greyish-brown, the twigs smooth or softly hairy. The leaves are simple, alternate, and leathery, about 1.3-13 cm long, 0.8-6 cm wide, round, oblong, egg-shaped or lance-shaped, the tips usually rounded or bluntly pointed, occasionally acute, sometimes notched, the base narrowed or notched, the margins with round or pointed teeth or untoothed, dark green to grey-green above, the secondary and netted veins often conspicuous, smooth and glossy to slightly hairy or with the midrib and nerves only hairy, below duller and paler and smooth to densely velvety. They are borne on often yellowish stalks up to about 6 mm long.

On the whole the forms from Natal and the Transvaal have larger leaves than those from the Cape, although a form with large, thick, fleshy leaves and large red fruits comes from the dune forests of the eastern Cape and Transkei. In the swamp forests of Zululand this grows as a shrub with large leaves up to 10 cm or more long and 8 cm wide.

The large-leaved forest form was formerly known as *Cassine velutinum;* the slender-leaved, almost smooth form as *Cassine schlechteri;* the hairy coastal form from the Cape as *Cassine pubescens,* and the round, smooth-leaved form as *Cassine sphaerophylla.*

The small yellowish flowers are borne in clusters in the axils of the leaves, often crowded up the stems, and smell of mignonette. The fruit is a fleshy drupe, 0.8-2.5 cm long, oval to round, deep rose pink, red or purple when ripe, smooth, hairy, or wrinkled, at its most decorative the size and shape of a crabapple, shiny and a deep glowing red. This is edible and known in parts as kooboo-berry or kaboebessie. It is a favourite with baboons, monkeys and such animals as nyala, Grey and Red Duiker and Livingstone's Antelope, and birds such as Purple-crested Loeries, Green Pigeons, and toppies. Duiker eat the leaves and Black Rhino eat both leaves and bark.

Parts of the tree are used medicinally by Africans.

The wood is of good quality, tough, close-grained and hard, used for wagon parts and rough utensils, for sticks and particularly for sharpened sticks. The pointed fighting stick the Xhosas use in single combat, and the stick they hold above their heads in dancing, are traditionally from this tree. The wood is also good fuel. A brown dye is obtained from the bark.

The specific name *aethiopica* means "from the country of the black people".

In *Flora Zambesiaca* this is dealt with as *Mystroxylon aethiopicum* (Thunb.) Loes.

d. *Cassine parvifolia* Sond.

This species, literally "the small-leaved cassine", is usually a small shrub of the fynbos often growing in hard rocky soil, from Ceres and Piquetberg through Worcester to the George and Humansdorp districts. Occasionally, in forest openings, it is a small tree up to about 4.5 m high.

The leaves are simple and opposite, 1.3-6 cm long and 0.3-2.5 cm wide, lance-shaped to oval or egg-shaped, the tips pointed to round, sometimes notched, the base narrowed, the margins inrolled but untoothed, the midrib thick and prominent below.

The small, dull white flowers are in sparse clusters. The fruit is a roundish juicy drupe, purplish-black when ripe.

(411.1)   e. *Cassine tetragona* (L.f.) Loes.

= *Rhamnus tetragonus* L.f.; = *Celastrus tetragonus* Thunb.; = *Cassine scandens* Eckl. & Zeyh.; = *Cassine latifolia* Eckl. & Zeyh.; = *Cassine latifolia* var. *heterophylla* Sond.; = *Allocassine tetragona* (L.f.) N. Robson

Bob-cherry, droëlewer

The bob-cherry grows from the Knysna district through the eastern Cape, the Transkei and Natal to Zululand and Swaziland and to the eastern and northern Transvaal, in forests, on forest margins, in bush and scrub, along streams in grass veld, and on wooded sand dunes where it is common.

It is best known as an evergreen climber or scrambling shrub, or as a shrub from 0.6-2.5 m high, but occasionally is a tree.

The branches are grey and flexible, the twigs usually 4-angled. A characteristic is that the flowering shoots tend to grow backwards. The almost stalkless leaves are simple and opposite, leathery, 1.3-8 cm long and 0.6-5 cm wide – the upper leaves usually the smallest – a narrow oblong to egg-shaped, the tips pointed or rounded and often notched, the base round and notched or narrowed, the margins inrolled, wavy and usually with spiny teeth, occasionally untoothed, the veins raised above.

The small white flowers are in loose or dense clusters. The fruits are greenish drupes about the size of a pea turning red, purple or black as they ripen about May. They are eaten by children, who call them bob-cherries, and by birds.

The foliage is sometimes eaten by sheep.

OPPOSITE

Above Left
Cassine aethiopica growing in the open, Mkuze

Above right
Its bark

Below left
Cassine aethiopica growing in a forested kloof of the Suurberg

Below right
Its bark

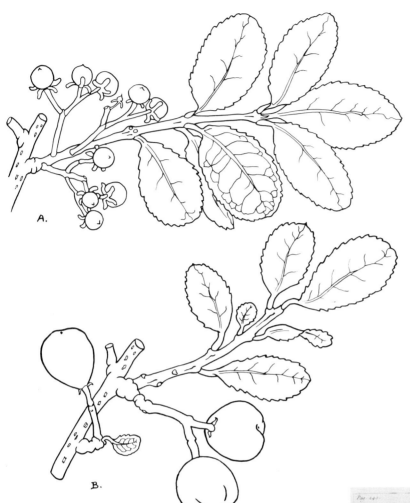

Left
Cassine peragua: A. A twig with young fruit. B. A twig with mature fruits (70%)

Below left
Cassine crocea: a fruiting twig (50%)

Below right
Cassine peragua — a photograph of an illustration in *Decades Plantarum Africanum* by Jan Burman, 1738

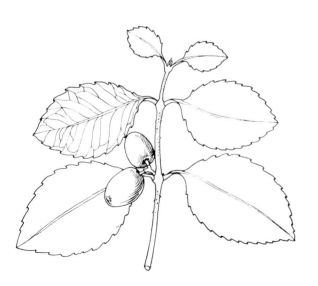

1316

The specific name *tetragona* means "four-angled" and is based on the shape of the twigs. The common name droëlewer means "dry-liver" and is said to describe the taste of the fruits.

This species is the *Allocassine tetragona* (L.f.) N. Robson of *Boletin da Sociedade Broteriana,* vols. 39-40, 1965-1966. The name is not accepted by the Botanical Research Institute in Pretoria.

(411.2)   f. *Cassine barbara* L.

= *Cassine capensis* in the sense of Davison in *Bothalia,* Vol. 2, 1932.

Barsbessie, lepelhout

Cassine barbara is a western Cape species occurring from the Clanwilliam district to Bredasdorp as one of the principal species in dune scrub. It grows on Table Mountain.

Although this is usually a small bushy shrub with dark stiff, upward-growing branches, it can grow as a tree up to 6 m high with purple, angular twigs and dull, dark green, leathery leaves arranged in opposite pairs. These are 1.3-4 cm long and as wide, round to egg-shaped or oblong, the tips often notched, the base round, the slightly inrolled margins bluntly toothed in the upper part, with netted veins raised below. They are borne on short stalks.

The white flowers bloom in winter in loose, many-flowered, branching heads in the axils of the leaves. The fruit is a small round, purplish berry which is said to cause "bursting" in cattle that eat it, hence the common name "barsbessie" or "bursting berry".

This species is believed to hybridize with *Cassine peragua* L. The two are often confused, partly because Davison in *Bothalia,* Vol. 2 (1932) dealt with specimens of *C. barbara* under the name *C. capensis,* (a synonym of *C. peragua* L.). The two species were correctly separated in the *Flora of the Cape Peninsula.*

The specific name *barbara* means "foreign".

(414)   g. *Cassine peragua* L.

= *Cassine capensis* L., = *Cassine kraussiana* Bernh.; = *Elaeodendron kraussianum* (Bernh.) Sim

Bastard saffron, bastersaffron, lepelhout; iKhukhuzi, umBofanyamagone (Z)

The bastard or false saffron occurs from the Cape Peninsula — it grows on Table Mountain — through the eastern Cape and Natal to Zululand and Swaziland. It is a handsome evergreen species of forests, forest margins and kloofs, a small to a large, branching tree 12 m high, with a trunk diameter up to 1 m, and bark that varies from yellow to dark brown.

The tough, leathery, dark green leaves are opposite, 2.5-5 cm long and 1.3-4 cm wide, lance-shaped to almost round, the tips bluntly pointed and often notched, the base narrowed, the margins slightly inrolled and coarsely toothed, the netted veining conspicuous, borne on stalks up to nearly 6 mm long.

The small, white, fragrant flowers are in loose branching clusters. The fruit is a small, oval, dark purple drupe, which is eaten by Speckled Mousebirds.

Cassine papillosa on a hillside between Butterworth and the sea

Pappe described the wood as hard, tough, very handsome when varnished, and used by cabinet-makers and wheelwrights. It makes good sticks.

The specific name is inappropriate but interesting. It was given in error by Linnaeus who confused the species growing at the Cape with one in Carolina, called Cassena by the natives. The Carolina species was in turn thought identical to a Paraguay plant known as Paraguay tea or South Sea tea, a noted medicinal plant used by both the Indians and the Spanish. Linnaeus based his specific name on this common name. He later renamed the Cape plant *Cassine capensis,* a procedure not acceptable according to the present rules of nomenclature, the older name being the legitimate one. Thus our Cape species is, in fact, named "the cassine of Paraguay".

(412)   h. *Cassine crocea* (Thunb.) Kuntze

= *Ilex crocea* Thunb.; = *Elaeodendron croceum* (Thunb.) DC. = *Crocoxylon excelsum* Eckl. & Zeyh., = *Crocoxylon croceum* (Thunb.) N. Robson

Saffron cassine, saffraan; umBomvane (X); umBomvane (Z)

The large, spreading saffron cassine occurs in coastal forests from Swellendam eastwards and northwards to Natal, often as a gnarled tree with a stout trunk up to 1.2 m in diameter at breast height.

The bark is smooth and whitish, sometimes with a yellow or yellowish-red crust. If the bark is scraped, a deep yellow colour is visible. Uncovered roots are also yellow.

The branches are grey, the twigs warted. The foliage is usually evergreen. The smooth leathery leaves vary according to locality. They are simple and most often opposite. Those from mature trees are usually from 2.5-5 cm long, oval to egg-shaped, the tips bluntly pointed and sometimes notched, or sometimes more sharply pointed, the base round or narrowed, the margins closely toothed, the veining heavy and conspicuous, particularly on the lower side. The shaded leaves of seedlings are often holly-like and up to 13 cm long.

The flowers are greenish and borne abundantly in small bunches which – when the tree is deciduous – appear just before the leaves. The fruit, ripening April to May, is a round to oval white drupe, up to about 2.5 cm in diameter, enclosing a large hard stone. It does not appear to be eaten by people but wild pigs grow fat on it.

The sapwood is white, the heartwood from a pinkish-purple to brown tinged with red, hard, close, tough and fine-grained, taking a fine polish and generally useful. It has been used for beams, planks, wagons, and for all kinds of furniture, for carving, engraving, and the crooked trunks for boat knees. Pappe recorded that butter casks were made from it.

The bark was once used for tanning and dyeing and the leaves also contain a small amount of tannin.

The root is poisonous and on occasion is believed to have caused death. Witchdoctors once used it for trial by ordeal, and perhaps still do. Watt and Brandwijk say "the plant has been found to have a digitalis action", while the bark is known to have purgative properties.

Both the specific name and the common names of the tree refer to the yellow or reddish colour of the bark – *crocea* means "saffron-yellow", while the Xhosa and Zulu name "umBomvane" means "red". The Xhosa

1320

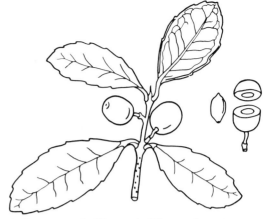

Left
Cassine papillosa bark

Right
Cassine papillosa: A fruiting twig and a dissected fruit (100%)

give this name, too, to *Pleurostylia capensis* (Turcz.) Oliv. and to *Olinia radiata* J. Hofmeyr & Phill.

(415)   i. *Cassine papillosa* (Hochst.) Kuntze

= *Elaeodendron papillosum* Hochst.; = *Elaeodendron capense* Eckl. & Zeyh.

Saffron-red cassine; iKhukhuze, isiThuntu, uMaqunda (Z); inGulutane (Sw)

The saffron-red cassine is an evergreen shrub, sometimes growing into an 11 m tree, occurring from George, through the eastern Cape and Transkei to Natal, Zululand, and the Transvaal to Rhodesia, in high forest, in dune forest, and on wooded hill slopes.

It is often a much-branched tree, with a leafy neat crown, the trunk bark grey to yellow, reddish below the surface, that on the branches greenish-grey to grey-brown or red with conspicuous dark raised markings. The stiff, smooth, leathery leaves are opposite or nearly opposite, grey-green to dark glossy green, about 2.5-10 cm long and 1.9-6 cm broad, oblong, oval to egg-shaped, the tips sharply or bluntly pointed, the base narrowed, toothed — the teeth often spiny — the netted veins prominent both sides. They are borne on stalks 6-12 mm long.

The flowers are small, green, white or yellow, 4-petalled, and bisexual. They are borne in clusters at the base of the current year's shoots or sometimes in the axils of the lower leaves, on stalks 2-12 mm long.

The fruit is a drupe, 1.3-2.5 m long, oval to egg-shaped, fairly smooth, pale yellow to pink, drying red, and shortly stalked. The seed is solitary and hard.

The tree is reputed among the Zulus to have powerful magic qualities. They believe it has the ability to blunt evil influences, and that it is a species liked both by girls and by ancestor spirits.

The wood is white to yellowish, hard, and generally useful, especially in wagon-making. The bark is used for tanning.

This is a "rain-tree", for it acts as host to the spittle bugs which suck the sap from the branches, ejecting it as moisture which runs down the branches to make pools of "water" below.

The specific name *papillosa* means "with nipples", and refers presumably to the small raised knobs on the twigs. This species is the *Elaeodendron capense* Eckl. & Zeyh. of *Flora Zambesiaca.* The Zulu names isiThuntu and uMaqunda are based on words meaning "to blunt", because of the tree's reputed power to blunt evil.

OPPOSITE

Above left
Cassine transvaalensis near the foot of the Wolkberg, northern Transvaal

Above right
Cassine transvaalensis stem

Below left
Cassine papillosa: A leafy twig with flower buds (60%)

Below right
Cassine transvaalensis: A flowering twig and fruits (80%)

(416)   j. *Cassine transvaalensis* (Burtt Davy) Codd

= *Salacia transvaalensis* Burtt Davy; = *Elaeodendron croceum* var. *triandrum* Dinter; = *Elaeodendron croceum* var. *heterophyllum* Loes.; = *Pseudocassine transvaalensis* (Burtt Davy) Bredell; = *Crocoxylon transvaalense* (Burtt Davy) N. Robson

Oupitjie, lepelhout; inGwavuma (Z); shimapana (Tso); monomani (Tsw – Mang); monamane (NS), dikulukhazi (Mbuk)

The oupitjie grows from Natal, Zululand and Swaziland, through the eastern, central and northern Transvaal, westwards to Botswana and South West Africa, and northwards to Mozambique, Rhodesia, Zambia, and Angola, in various soils – often favouring those rich in lime – in woodland, bushveld, thornveld, and scrub, sometimes growing on termite mounds.

It is one of the conspicuous trees of the Natal bushveld, common in both the Hluhluwe and Mkuze game reserves.

It may be a bush or a tall tree, deciduous or evergreen, up to 18 m high with a trunk diameter up to 1 m, but is more common as a 6-9 m tree with a straight stem and wide-spreading crown, and with rigid, often drooping branches, stiff, light-coloured twigs which are sometimes like sturdy blunt spines growing at right angles to the stem, and smooth or slightly cracked ash-grey bark. Arching branches and whippy twigs are characteristic of young trees.

The leaves may be alternate, opposite, or in tufts on knobs up the stems. They are simple, hard, leathery, smooth, both sides a clear green to grey-green, on mature shoots 1.9-4 cm long and 0.8-3 cm wide and on young shoots bigger; oval, egg-shaped or widely lance-shaped, the tips rounded to bluntly pointed, the base rounded or narrowed, the veins prominent on both sides, particularly on the lower side, the margins usually entire but sometimes toothed. The leaf stalks are short.

The small green or white 3-petalled flowers are in branched heads on long stalks in the axils of the leaves. The fruit is a hard-shelled drupe, roundish, oval or egg-shaped, white to yellow, drying red, up to 1.5 cm in diameter or just over. It ripens from summer to autumn and is eaten by birds such as loeries and by monkeys.

The leaves and branches are browsed by giraffe.

The wood, according to Galpin, is whitish-pink, cross-grained, and of medium weight and hardness. Africans use it to make cattle troughs, spoons – as the name lepelhout suggests – sticks and tobacco pipes, and it is suitable for turners' work.

The bark is used for tanning.

Africans regard the bark as one of the best medicines for stomach troubles and fever, using it to make emetics or enemas. It is sold by all African herbalists as "umGugudo" or "inGwavuma". Tea made from it is said to have a pleasant flavour. Father Gerstner, the Zululand botanist, left this recipe for it.

"Take 1 teaspoonful of the powdered bark and cook it in 1 quart of water. Strain and allow to cool to 37 degrees Centigrade and drink it as quickly as possible. It will return again . . . . . but will leave one feeling better with a large appetite".

Zulus believe that a small piece of the bark placed in a gourd of curdled milk improves the quality of the milk.

This species, with its 3-petalled, 3-stamened flowers, is unusual in the *Cassine* group – in which 4-5 petals and 5 stamens are typical – and it

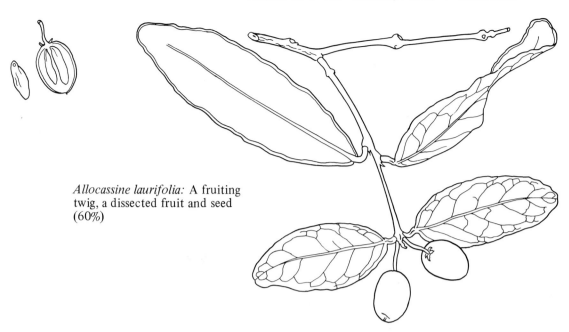

Allocassine laurifolia: A fruiting twig, a dissected fruit and seed (60%)

was until recently known as *Pseudocassine transvaalensis* (Burtt Davy) Bredell. Dr Codd, however, who grouped it among the cassines, sees the reduction of the flower parts merely as an evolutionary stage within the group.

The specific name means "of the Transvaal". The Zululand district, Ingwavuma, is named after the tree.

6. *Allocassine* N. Robson

In *Flora Zambesiaca* this is treated as a genus of 2 species in south east Africa. At present the Botanical Research Institute in Pretoria retains only 1 of these, *Allocassine laurifolia* (Harv.) N. Robson, placing the other in *Cassine.*

The genus is characterized by flowering shoots that tend to grow backwards; by leaves that are alternate or opposite, by small, triangular, deciduous stipules; and by flowers that are bisexual, greenish or yellow, and 4-5-petalled, borne in cymes. The bracts are persistent. The fruit is a succulent berry, and the long narrow seeds number 2-4.

The name *Allocassine* means "the diverse cassine".

(416.1)   *Allocassine laurifolia* (Harv.) N. Robson

= *Elaeodendron laurifolium* Harv.; = *Cassine laurifolia* (Harv.) Davison

Allocassine; iGobandlovu (Z)

Allocassine laurifolia, rare in South Africa, is a forest shrub, often scrambling or climbing, or a tree, growing from Natal and Zululand northwards into Rhodesia and Mozambique.

The branches are a smooth purple-brown. The leaves are simple and usually opposite, alternate on young plants and on climbing shoots — stiff, leathery, blue-green and shiny on both sides — 4-13 cm long (usually shorter) and 2.5-6 cm wide, oblong to egg-shaped, the tips round or broadly pointed, the base round or narrowed, the margins entire or slightly toothed with 5-7 pairs of secondary veins branching and looping along the margin, these, the midrib, and the netted veins prominent both sides.

The greenish-yellow flowers are in clusters and develop into smooth, red, fleshy berries, oval, egg-shaped or roundish, up to 2.5 cm long, enclosing about 4 long, narrow, black seeds 0.8-1.3 cm long, embedded in a pithy pulp.

The specific name *laurifolia* means "with laurel-like leaves".

7. *Maurocenia* L.

Maurocenia is a genus of only 1 species, confined to the south west Cape and occurring mainly along the coast from Saldanha Bay to Caledon.

It has opposite leaves; flowers that are usually bisexual, in cymes, the sepals 4-5, the petals 5, the stamens 5, the ovary 2-chambered, the fruit a fleshy drupe.

The genus was named after a Venetian politician, G.F. Morocini, 1658-1739, who was a patron of botany.

(417)   *Maurocenia frangularia* (L.) Mill.

= *Cassine maurocenia* L.; = *Maurocenia capensis* Sond.

Hottentot's cherry, Hottentotskersbos, aasvoëlbessie

The Hottentot's cherry is a small tree or shrub of the mountains, coastal hills and the stream beds of the Western Province (reaching down to the sea shore itself), and occurring from about Saldanha Bay to Caledon. It grows on Table Mountain.

Although often a shrub, it can make a small spreading tree up to 4.5 m high. The mature foliage is dark green and shiny, the young foliage chestnut brown, and the young twigs purple. The short stem is up to about 10 cm in diameter, and the bark is grey and rough.

The leaves are simple, opposite and leathery, the margins conspicuously thickened on the under-surface, usually roundish to oblong, 2.5-8 cm long and often nearly as wide, the apex rounded and sometimes notched, the base narrowed and often heart-shaped, the midrib raised on the under-surface. They are carried on short, thick stalks.

The white, sweet-scented flowers, attractive to bees and other insects, bloom in clusters in the axils of the leaves from autumn to winter. They are usually bisexual. The fruit is a drupe about the size of a cherry, somewhat fleshy, red to plum-coloured, containing 1 seed.

The fruit is edible and was once eaten by Hottentots, hence the common name.

The wood, according to Pappe, is fine, hard and tough, yellow with brownish veins, polishing well, and suitable for the manufacture of musical instruments.

This pretty, hardy little tree is occasionally cultivated, but on the whole is little known.

The specific name means "like *Frangula*", a generic name derived from the Latin "frango", meaning "to break", because the wood of some species of the genus was supposed to be very brittle.

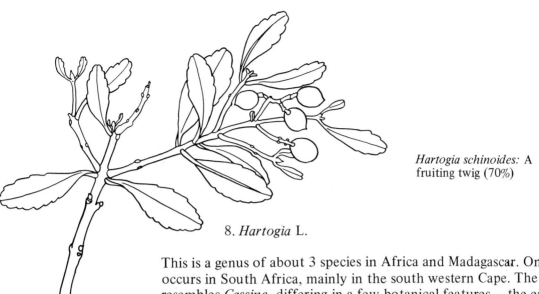

Hartogia schinoides: A
fruiting twig (70%)

8. *Hartogia* L.

This is a genus of about 3 species in Africa and Madagascar. One species occurs in South Africa, mainly in the south western Cape. The genus resembles *Cassine,* differing in a few botanical features — the endosperm, for example, is scanty whereas that in *Cassine* is abundant.

The leaves are opposite; the flowers in loose cymes; the sepals, petals, and stamens 4, the ovary 2-chambered; the fruit, although fleshy when young, becoming dry. It does not burst open.

The genus was named after John Hartog, plant collector and gardener in the Cape in the latter part of the 17th and the beginning of the 18th century.

(418)   *Hartogia schinoides* C.A.Sm.

= *Hartogia capensis* L.f.; = *Hartogia riparis* Eckl. & Zeyh.; = *Hartogia multiflora* Eckl. & Zeyh.

Smalblad, ladle wood, spoon wood

The smalblad is a species principally of the south west Cape, and is common round Clanwilliam, Cape Town, and Caledon, but extends eastwards through Knysna to Albany, usually growing on the edge of forest, in patches of bush, on rocky mountain slopes and in ravines, often associated with *Olinia, Heeria,* and *Halleria.* A small tree grows at Louis Leipoldt's grave in the Pakhuis Pass.

It may be a small spineless bush or a 9 m tree, single-stemmed, with a trunk up to 46 cm in diameter, or with many slender erect stems, a smooth, mottled, dark or ash-grey bark, the branches grey and somewhat wrinkled, and the crown much-branched and often spreading.

The leathery leaves, copper-coloured when young, becoming green with maturity, are simple, opposite, and variable in size and shape, 2.5-6 cm long and 0.8-1.9 cm wide, widely lance-shaped to egg-shaped, the tips pointed, bluntly pointed or round and often notched, narrowing to the base, smooth, the upper three quarters deeply or slightly toothed, the midrib raised above, the stalks reddish and up to about 0.6 cm long. When broken, the leaves show slight elastic strands in the midribs.

The small, white, scented flowers bloom in summer in lax clusters on slender stalks in the axils of the leaves. The fruit is about the size of a pea, roundish to egg-shaped, yellow, fleshy when young but becoming dry, borne on slender stalks 0.8-1.3 cm long.

Above left
A young *Pleurostylia capensis* on a stream bank near the Butterworth-Wavecrest road, Transkei

Above right
Pleurostylia capensis growing as a tall forest tree in a kloof of the Suurberg

Left
Hartogia schinoides, Pakhuis Pass

Opposite above
Pleurostylia capensis: Flowering and fruiting twigs 80%

Opposite below
The bark of *Pleurostylia capensis*

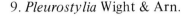

The wood is fine-grained, hard and tough, and was once used for wagons and farm utensils. It makes handsome furniture and is said, when polished, to surpass mahogany in beauty of colour and texture.

The common name "smalblad" or "small leaf" is an old one and was recorded by Thunberg in 1772.

9. *Pleurostylia* Wight & Arn.

Pleurostylia, a small genus of 3-4 species of the tropics of Africa and Asia, and of Queensland and New Caledonia, is represented in South Africa by 1 species.

All are trees or shrubs with simple, opposite leaves, small stipules that soon fall off, flowers that are most often bisexual, in branching cymes, the sepals, petals and stamens 4-5, the ovary 1-celled, the bracts persistent, and the fruit usually a dry drupe with a thin shell and 1 cavity, enclosing usually 1 seed without any aril.

The generic name means literally "lateral style", referring to the fact that as the ovary matures the style is borne laterally, its position in mature fruits being marked by a scar about half way up one side of the fruit.

(419)   *Pleurostylia capensis* (Turcz.) Oliv.

= *Cathastrum capense* Turcz.

Umkwankwa, bastard saffron, mountain hard pear, bastersaffraanhout, berg hardepeer; umNgqangqa (X); umThunyelelwa (Z)

This somewhat rare species occurs from the eastern Cape, northwards through the Transkei to Natal, Zululand and Swaziland, in mountain and coastal forests, in scrub, in wooded kloofs, and along streams.

In high forest it may be a straight tree up to 15 m tall with a trunk up to 1 m in diameter, but in scrub forest it is a shorter and more spreading tree. The bark is light grey to grey-brown, often with a reddish tinge, smooth when young but when mature cracked into small squares or rectangles. The small tree in the accompanying photographs, growing on a stream bank near the Butterworth-Wavecrest road, was slender, neat and decorative, with a smooth, light grey bark, while the tall tree in a kloof of the Suurberg had the typically fissured bark of age.

Both the twigs and leaves are opposite. The leaves, on short red stalks, are leathery, dark to yellow-green, glossy above, paler below, usually slender, lance-shaped to a narrow oblong, about 2.5-8 cm long and 0.8-2.5 cm wide, pointed or bluntly pointed, the tips sometimes notched, narrowed to the base, the margins wavy and usually untoothed but sometimes very faintly toothed, and the veins distinct.

The tiny white flowers in small clusters in the axils of the leaves bloom abundantly in summer time. The fruits, usually ripening in early winter, are dry, curved, oval drupes, 1-celled and 1-seeded, with a scar half way up one side marking the site of the style.

The wood is white or yellow with a pink tinge, and is heavy, hard, and compact, with wavy bands of softer tissue. It was once used for wagon wood.

The specific name means "of the Cape".

The tree is commonly known as the bastard saffron, a name also borne

The stem and bark of a young *Pleurostylia capensis*

by *Cassine peragua;* or sometimes as the mountain hard pear, which is likewise confusing, the name hard pear being used for several other trees, notably those of *Olinia* and *Strychnos* species. It is suggested that a common name such as Umkwankwa — based on the Xhosa umNgqangqa — would be appropriate.

This species is closely related to the more northern *Pleurostylia africana* Loes. They are separated largely on the number of ovules in each ovary cavity, *Pleurostylia capensis* having 6-8 and *Pleurostylia africana* 2-3.

10. *Salacia* L.

Salacia, a large genus of about 150 species, fairly common in the tropical and subtropical countries of the world, is represented in South and South West Africa by several species, only about 1 of which is tree-like. Most of the species are climbing, others are "underground trees" with a large rootstock and only a small part growing above the ground. Such a one is *Salacia rehmannii* Schinz from the central Transvaal.

The leaves are simple, opposite or alternate, with or without stipules, the flowers bisexual or male or female, borne in various types of inflorescences, the bracts persistent. The flowers usually have 5 sepals and petals, 3 stamens, and a superior 3-chambered ovary. The fruit is a juicy, usually edible drupe, often with many seeds.

The genus is named after Salacia, the wife of Neptune, and the Roman goddess of the sea.

Formerly the Hippocrateaceae, in which this genus was included, were upheld as a distinct family, but the tendency is now to include the family in Celastraceae.

Salacia leptoclada Tul.

= *Salacia baumannii* Loes.; = *Salacia wardii* Verdoorn

Ward's salacia; inGobandlovu, inSontwane (Z)

A shrub, a climber or a small tree, *Salacia leptoclada* grows from Zululand, where it occurs in low-lying sand forest, northwards to tropical Africa. It also occurs in Madagascar.

It was first collected in South Africa by the Natal botanist, C.J. Ward, who described it as a small, slender tree or shrub up to about 2.7 m high, often dominant in the shrub layer, in short forest on sandy soil being a single-stemmed shrub, and in taller forest often a climber.

When scandent it climbs by means of hooked or twining side branches. The stems are smooth or with raised lenticels, green or purple-brown. The leaves are simple and opposite or alternate, fairly thin, glossy, dark green above and paler below, usually 5-10 cm long and 2-3 cm wide, lance-shaped to egg-shaped, sharply or bluntly pointed, narrowed to the base, the margins untoothed or slightly toothed, borne on fairly short stalks.

The green to yellow, bisexual flowers are in clusters in the axils of the leaves. They develop into roundish fruits, about 1.3 cm in diameter, smooth, reddish-brown when ripe, and 1-3-seeded.

Zulus use the roots as an aphrodisiac.

This species closely resembles another Natal species of the genus,

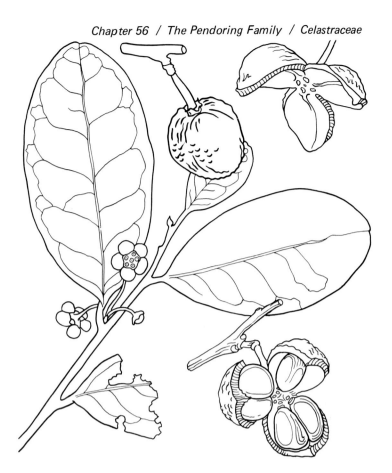

Pseudosalacia streyi: A flowering twig, a fruit, and fruits after bursting open showing the seeds and the empty shell (60%)

Salacia gerrardii Harv. ex Sprague, which is a climber at higher altitudes, and which has thicker and more oblong leaves.

When *Salacia leptoclada* was first collected in South Africa, it was thought a new species and was named *Salacia wardii* Verdoorn, but was later included in the tropical African species, *Salacia leptoclada.* The specific name is based on Greek words meaning "slender-branched".

11. *Pseudosalacia* Codd

If the finding of a new tree species in an area well known to botanists and collectors is a botanical event, how much more so is that of a new genus! *Pseudosalacia,* founded on a species from southern Natal, was described only within the last year by Dr L.E.W. Codd.

The genus, composed as far as is known of 1 species only, is intermediate between *Cassine* and *Salacia,* having characters of both. The floral characters could be those of *Cassine,* but it differs from that genus in its dehiscent, several-seeded fruits. From *Salacia* it is separated by the number of stamens — 5 instead of 3 or 4 — and by their arrangement, for they are situated in the fleshy part of the disc and do not spring from the base of the ovary as in *Salacia.*

1329

(419.1) *Pseudosalacia streyi* Codd

Although Gerrard in 1843 collected a specimen of a tree that may well be this interesting species, excellent flowering and fruiting material was collected only recently by an amateur botanist, Mr Hugh Nicholson of Natal, and by Mr R.G. Strey of the Durban Herbarium, in coastal forest along the Uvongo River and its tributaries, close to the sea in southern Natal.

It is a medium-sized tree with simple alternate leaves which are hard and leathery, oblong or oval, the apex round and often notched, the base slightly narrowed or round, 6-10 cm long and 4-6.5 cm wide, deep green above and lighter below, the underside with the 5-8 pairs of lateral veins and the midrib conspicuous. They are borne on short sturdy stalks.

The yellow bisexual flowers, blooming about October and November, measure about 1.3 cm in diameter. They have a small calyx and 5 broad petals surrounding a fleshy disc, through the surface of which the 5 stamens grow. They are borne on long green stalks.

The fruit, large as a walnut, is a hard, leathery capsule, oval and sometimes slightly pointed, with a sturdy "neck", greenish and covered with rough dots, bursting open along three thick valves and disclosing 3 or 4 large seeds. These are hard, smooth and angled, milky white when the capsule opens but soon turning red, and finally a bright chestnut brown.

The tree was named after Mr Strey, Curator of the Natal Herbarium.

The white pear, *Apodytes dimidiata,* growing in the Waterberg of the Transvaal

Icacinaceae is mainly a tropical and subtropical family of some 48 genera, 3 of which are represented in South Africa. Of these, 2 genera, *Cassinopsis* and *Apodytes,* contain tree species, 1 of which, *Apodytes dimidiata* E.Mey. ex Arn., grows from Ethiopia to the Cape.

All the members have simple leaves without stipules, and regular, bisexual flowers, the calyx with usually 4-5 segments and the petals and stamens as many as the sepals; the ovary superior and usually 1-celled, and fruit that is a drupe.

Cassinopsis Sond.

This small genus of 4 species, native to tropical and Southern Africa and Madagascar, is represented in South Africa by 2 species of small trees or shrubs, reaching from the Transvaal to the Cape.

They have simple opposite leaves, toothed or untoothed, without stipules; small, bisexual flowers arranged in panicles, the calyx small and 5-lobed, the petals and stamens 5, the ovary 1-chambered, and fruit that is a dryish, somewhat rounded drupe, 1-celled and 1-seeded.

The generic name means "resembling *Cassine*'.

(420) *Cassinopsis ilicifolia* (Hochst.) Kuntze

= *Hartogia ilicifolia* Hochst.; = *Cassinopsis capensis* Sond.

Holly cassinopsis, lemoendoring; iCegceya (X); iHlazane, iKhumalo, isiHloko, isaNhloko (Z)

The holly cassinopsis, although not a very striking species, has an impressive distribution in South Africa — from the Cape, through the eastern Orange Free State, Lesotho, Natal and Zululand, to the Transvaal and northward from there to Rhodesia.

It grows on forest edges, in kloofs and on stream banks in shady places and often near rocks, as an undershrub, a wide spreading bush, or as a small tree with slender drooping branches, often with a tendency to scramble or climb.

It reaches a height of about 4.5 m, and has flexible branches, bright, glossy green foliage, and straight sharp spines up to about 5 cm long that spring from between the opposite leaf stalks. The leaves are opposite, 1.3-6 cm long, egg-shaped, pointed, sometimes narrowed to the base, the margins sometimes inrolled, with spiny teeth or untoothed, rather leathery, a bright glossy green above and paler and duller below. They are borne on short stalks. The twigs are conspicuously zig-zag and the leaves tend to be borne in one plane.

The small, white or greenish, inconspicuous flowers bloom in spring

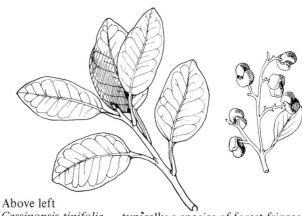

Above left
Cassinopsis tinifolia — typically a species of forest fringes — to the left, to the right *Schlefflera umbellifera,* Ngoye Forest

Above right
Apodytes dimidiata, the white pear: leaves and a fruiting twig

Below left
Cassinopsis tinifolia twig (70%)

Below right
Apodytes dimidiata, the white pear, near Kosi Bay on the northern Zululand coast

Opposite
Its stem and bark

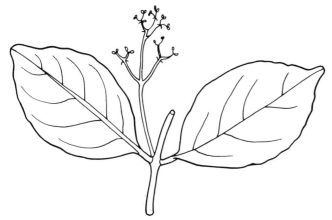

1332

in small branching clusters, not in the axils of the leaves but from a point between them. The fruit is a slightly fleshy, orange-yellow drupe nearly 1.3 cm long, plum-shaped or round, crowned with a small wisp, the remains of the persistent style. It contains 1 seed.

Zulus wear the seeds as ornaments.

The foliage is browsed by goats and is reputed to taint their milk.

This is a good garden shrub, germinating easily and hardy to frost, and flourishing in shade or in full sun. It is somewhat slow-growing.

The specific name means "leaves of Ilex" in the sense that they are holly-like. The common name lemoendoring suggests the likeness of the spines to those of the orange tree.

(421)   *Cassinopsis tinifolia* Harv.

Green snake, spineless cassinopsis; luHlaza (X); iNyoka eluhlaza, iMamba eluhlaza, iSolemamba (Z)

Cassinopsis tinifolia, native to the eastern regions of the country from the Transkei and Natal to Zululand and Swaziland, and northwards into Mozambique and Rhodesia, is a small evergreen, spineless tree or shrub, sometimes straggling, at others bushy, up to about 4.5 m high, growing on the edges of mountain forest, in wooded kloofs, and in river vegetation.

The bark is smooth and grey, the branches often flexible and drooping, with the young ones a conspicuous bright green. The leaves are simple and opposite, egg-shaped to widely lance-shaped, bluntly pointed, the tips sometimes notched, the base slightly narrowed or rounded, 2.5-9 cm long and 1.9-5 cm wide, the margins untoothed and inrolled, sometimes slightly wavy, a dark glossy green above. The midrib is prominent below. They are borne on short stalks.

The small white flowers are in many-branched heads on long stalks in the axils of the leaves. The fruit is a small, purple, ribbed drupe about 8 mm long, tipped with the persistent style.

The specific name means "with Tinus-like leaves". Miller gives the Xhosa name as luHlaza, meaning "green", possibly because of the distinctive green bark on the young branches. The Zulu name iNoka eluhlaza means "green snake".

Apodytes E.Mey. ex Arn.

Apodytes is a small genus of about 15 species, mainly African or occurring in the islands off the African coast — Madagascar, Réunion and Mauritius — although a few are native to Indo-Malaysia, China and Australia. One species grows in South Africa and is widespread.

They are all trees or shrubs with simple, alternate, untoothed leaves, and small flowers that are bisexual and borne in terminal panicles. The calyx is small and 5-toothed, the petals and stamens 5, the ovary 1-celled, and the fruit is a drupe, often with a fleshy "heel", and a tail-like growth, the remains of the style, to one side.

The generic name *Apodytes* is based on the Greek "apodyns", meaning "to strip off" in reference to the uncovered corolla.

(422) *Apodytes dimidiata* E.Mey. ex Arn.

White pear, witpeer; umDakane (X); umDakane (Z); umDzakane (Sw); kgalagangwê, mmêtla-kgamêlô (NS)

From the Cape to Ethiopia this is a common and often a lovely tree. In South Africa it occurs from the Cape Peninsula — it grows on Table Mountain — eastwards to the forests of George and Knysna and the eastern Cape, and northwards to Natal, Zululand, Swaziland and the Transvaal, in coastal and inland forests, in bushveld, and on grassy mountains slopes.

It earned early fame in the first days of colonization on account of its strong elastic wood, much valued and sought by wagon builders. So many white pears, indeed, were cut out for timber that most of the finest specimens have disappeared from forests. This is a pity as it is an ornamental tree, and under good conditions it grows to roughly 20 m in height with a girth up to 2.5 m. Outside forest it is usually a smaller tree with a more compact crown, often outstandingly graceful, while in the Transvaal bushveld it may be a luxuriant bush, on rocky hill tops a stunted tree, or on sand dunes close to the sea it often grows as a small twisted shrub a metre or less high.

The bark is white or pale grey or green, often so covered with green or orange lichens that it appears a totally different colour. It frequently peels off in patches. The stem in forest trees is seldom round but is usually fluted irregularly, in which it differs from other trees with light-coloured bark, such as *Ilex mitis,* in which the stem is normally round. Older branches are grey marked with lenticels, while the younger ones are often purple or red.

The ornamental evergreen foliage is composed of dark, glossy green leaves, often no more than 2.5 to 3.5 cm long and 1.3 to 2.5 cm wide, but occasionally up to 13 cm long and 8 cm in width. They are egg-shaped or oval, the tip bluntly or sharply pointed or rounded and sometimes notched, at times tapering, the base usually narrowed, the margins untoothed but sometimes wavy with the margins inrolled, smooth or hairy on one or both sides. The midrib (which is not visible towards the tip) is slightly sunken above and prominent below, and the secondary veins are usually inconspicuous. The leaves vary from area to area, those — for example — from the Natal Drakensberg tending to be small and hairy and those from nearer the coast large and smooth. A very small-leaved form grows in the Transvaal bushveld.

The leaves have the peculiarity of drying black and of falling off the stem while they are being pressed.

The leaf stalks are reddish and often from below give a reddish tinge to the foliage.

A white pear either in flower or in fruit is a pretty sight. The small white flowers with a heavy sweet scent are borne abundantly in loose bunches at the ends of the twigs and stand out above the leaves. The fruit is a small black drupe which when young has a bright red, succulent heel which becomes grey with age. When in full fruit the tree is draped in shiny scarlet and black and can be identified at a glance. The fruits are devoured by birds such as spreeus, by Bush and Rameron Pigeons, by Layard's Bulbul, and by various white-eyes.

The "aril" or heel is said to leave a permanent blue stain on clothing. Both leaves and bark are eaten by Black Rhino.

The timber is light-coloured with a fine uniform grain and is very solid, strong, and elastic. It takes a high polish. Although it has been used chiefly for wagon making it has proved useful for furniture, agricultural implements and for engraving. Scott says that in printing work it is preferred to any other wood for "cutting sticks" — the piece of wood placed between the paper being cut on the printer's guillotine and the metal surface — and that it is the most suitable of all woods for cart and wagon felloes.

In northern Zululand Africans use the wood to make baskets for trapping fish and for "fish-kraals".

This species can easily be raised in a nursery although germination may take up to one year. Seed should be sown in winter, lightly covered, and screened. Young transplants, which should be protected, grow slowly for the first year and thereafter are fast. They make graceful garden trees, and in cold districts might with profit be used as a handsome hedge.

58 The Litchi Family (Sapindaceae)

The litchi, *Litchi chinensis* Sonner., an exotic and cultivated species, is probably the member of Sapindaceae that is best known in South Africa.

There are, however, a number of native trees and shrubs worthy of attention for the beauty of their fruits, occasionally for the wonderful colour of the young foliage, and often for their botanical interest.

This is a family that has made many experiments, showing today a diversity of flowers and fruits, and also sometimes a strange distribution. Botanists speculate on the trend of evolution in the family, "Whether", in the words of Dr R.A. Dyer, "these unique forms are recently evolved or relics of a bygone abundance". He inclines towards the latter view.

The distribution of a genus such as *Atalaya* is of particular interest. At one time it was believed indigenous only to Australia and the Malay Archipelago. The discovery just over 30 years ago that it was represented in South Africa was a fascinating fact to botanists and to those who believe in a former land link with Australia.

Erythrophysa, one of the most interesting of all the genera, is represented by 2 species in South Africa, one from Namaqualand and the other from a limited area in the western Transvaal. The nearest relative of the genus within the family is thought to be in north China!

Two genera from tropical Africa, *Pancovia* and *Blighia*, have only within the last decade been known to occur in South Africa. They are found in the forests of Zululand, which even today — botanically speaking — are only partially known.

Over 120 genera and 1000 species belong to the family. They are usually trees and shrubs with leaves of various kinds, often with lopsided leaflets with the midrib to one side, the common midrib often winged, and usually without stipules; male or female and bisexual flowers on the same or different plants, the flowers taking many different forms. The inflorescence is a raceme, panicle or cluster, or sometimes the flowers are borne singly. The calyx lobes and petals usually number 5, the latter often with an appendage on the inner face, a disc is usually present, the stamens are often 8 (but sometimes less or more), the ovary superior and usually 3-celled. The fruit is a capsule, a berry, a drupe, or composed of 1 or more cocci or lobes which are often reduced to 1, or sometimes it is winged or bladder-like. The seed is usually solitary, often with an aril-like structure. Some species have a soapy or saponaceous covering on which the name of the family is based.

Key to Genera (in South Africa)

Leaves Compound

Leaves with usually 3 leaflets

The leaflets often toothed; the fruits small drupes of 1-3 cocci, often bright-coloured. (Widespread from the Cape to the Transvaal in forests or on their edges)

1. *Allophylus*

Leaves terminated by 2 leaflets

The leaflets toothed or untoothed, often *conspicuously unequal-sided* and sometimes half-moon-shaped; the *fruit a samara* with *large wings.* (The Cape to the eastern Transvaal)

2. *Atalaya*

The leaflets untoothed, *not* conspicuously unequal-sided, the fruit with 2-5 *berry-like cocci* in axillary and terminal racemes. (Natal, Zululand, the eastern Transvaal)

3. *Deinbollia*

The leaflets untoothed, not unequal-sided; with *short swollen stalks;* the fruit *fleshy* with 1-3 cocci, 1-2 often not developing fully, *borne on the old wood.* (Zululand)

4. *Pancovia*

The leaflets unequal-sided, untoothed, the common midrib *slightly winged;* the fruit *a fleshy drupe.* (Zululand)

6. *Haplocoelum*

The leaflets slightly *unequal at the base,* untoothed; the fruit 1-3-lobed, *splitting* to show large roundish seed covered with an aril. (Kruger National Park)

8. *Stadmania*

The leaflets untoothed; the young leaves salmon-pink; the mature fruit a *top-shaped, lobed capsule, splitting to show woody lobes, crimson within, and a pendulous, black, oval seed.* (Zululand)

9. *Blighia*

Resinous, the leaflets *unequal-sided,* toothed or untoothed, the common midrib *winged;* the fruit *pulpy, pea-sized, black.* (Port Elizabeth and Humansdorp to the Transvaal)

12. *Hippobromus*

Leaves terminated by 1 leaflet

The *rachis terminating in a point with a single leaflet to one side;* the leaflets *boldly toothed,* the midrib often *slightly to one side,* the common midrib not winged; the fruit *fleshy, usually 2-lobed.* (Port Elizabeth to Uniondale)

5. *Smelophyllum*

The common midrib *winged;* the fruit *membranous and balloon-like.* (Namaqualand and the western Transvaal)

10. *Erythrophysa*

The leaflets *untoothed,* not conspicuously unequal-sided, the common midrib not winged; the fruit with 2-5 *berry-like cocci.* (Zululand and the eastern Transvaal)

3. *Deinbollia*

Leaves simple

The leaves *alternate;* the fruit a capsule, the shell splitting to show the seed with *a red, fleshy aril-like covering.* (Widespread in South and South West Africa)

7. *Pappea*

The leaves *spirally arranged, sticky, shiny;* the fruit a capsule with 2-3 *thin wings.* (Widespread)

11. *Dodonoea*

1. *Allophylus* L.

Phillips lists about 260 species in this genus but it is a notoriously difficult one, not yet fully understood and with many possible hybrids. They are trees or shrubs found in most of the warm countries of the world and especially in America.

In South Africa about 7 species are commonly supposed to occur, *Allophylus melanocarpus* (Sond.) Radlk.; *Allophylus transvaalensis* Burtt Davy, *Allophylus rubifolius* (Hochst. ex A.Rich.) Engl., *Allophylus natalensis* (Sond.) De Winter, *Allophylus decipiens* (Sond.) Radlk., *Allophylus dregeanus* (Sond.) De Winter, and *Allophylus chaunostachys* Gilg, a tropical species which has been collected in the eastern Transvaal.

A further 2 species, *Allophylus africanus* Beauv. and *Allophylus welwitschii* Gilg, enter the Caprivi Strip.

Of the South African species only 3, *Allophylus dregeanus, Allophylus chaunostachys,* and *Allophylus natalensis,* are in any way clear-cut. The others, together with *Allophylus africanus* and *Allophylus welwitschii,* make a closely-knit group. It is possible further to separate *Allophylus decipiens* from the rest on the basis of its usually smaller leaves and shorter inflorescence, but all the characters by which the remainder of the South African species are separated are apt to break down.

Of these, the more glabrous-leaved forms are termed *Allophylus melanocarpus.* This is supposed to have black and white fruits but this may be an unreliable character. *Allophylus welwitschii* is possibly identical to this.

The hairy-leaved forms make an even tighter group. *Allophylus trans-*

1338

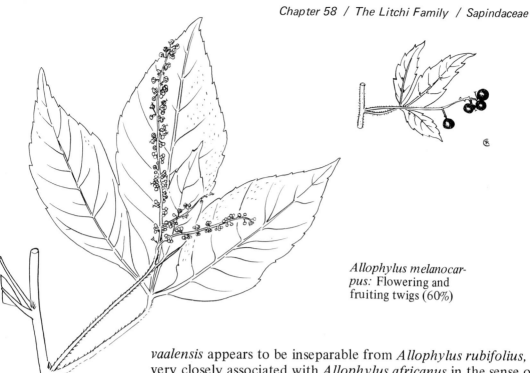

Allophylus melanocar-pus: Flowering and fruiting twigs (60%)

vaalensis appears to be inseparable from *Allophylus rubifolius,* which is very closely associated with *Allophylus africanus* in the sense of A.W. Exell in *Flora Zambesiaca.*

Some botanists see all these latter forms as one variable species. If this is upheld, then the oldest name, *Allophylus africanus,* is the correct one, but extensive work is needed before this is established.

In South Africa the species occur from the Cape to the Transvaal, growing generally in forest, on forest edges, and in bush, in the moister eastern areas.

In South and South West Africa the species have alternate leaves, usually with 3 leaflets reminiscent of those of a *Rhus* — with the exception of 1 species in South Africa which has simple leaves — tufts of hairs in the axils of the veins; tiny greenish-yellow flowers that are male or female in the same inflorescence or sometimes on separate plants, borne in racemes or panicles. They have usually 4 calyx segments and petals, a disc, 8 stamens, and the female has a 2-chambered ovary. The fruits are drupes of up to 3 cocci or lobes, only 1 of which often develops. These round fruits are frequently bright-coloured and distinctive.

Two butterflies known to breed on members of the genus are the Mirza Blue, *Azanus mirza,* and the widespread Common Hairtail, *Anthene definita,* a smallish violet butterfly that breeds also on the buds and flowers of *Bersama* species and of *Pappea capensis.*

The name *Allophylus* means "diverse leaves". Most of the species at one time or another have probably been known as "red berry tree" or "rooibessieboom".

(425)   *Allophylus melanocarpus* (Sond.) Radlk.

= *Schmidelia melanocarpa* Sond.

Black-fruited allophylus, kieriehout; inQala (X), isiHlohlela, umNcanda-thambo, umHloshazana (Z); sudzungwane (V)

This, literally "the allophylus with the black fruit", grows from the

Transkei through Natal, Zululand, Swaziland, and the eastern and northern Transvaal to north eastern South West Africa and the Caprivi Strip. It is a tree of forests and forest margins – it is particularly common along the edges of coastal forest in Zululand – wooded kloofs, scrub, bush and thornveld, growing from sea level to an altitude of at least 1500 m.

It may be a bush, sometimes with rambling branches, or a small tree with a spreading crown, a smooth, light grey-brown stem, and smooth or softly hairy branches. The leaves have 3 leaflets which are oval, pointed and boldly toothed, 7-10 x 1.9-5 cm, usually smooth or slightly velvety on the under-surface, dark green above, paler below, with the veins raised, with tufts of hairs in the axils of the veins on the lower surface. The leaflets are stalkless or shortly stalked, and the common leaf stalks are 4-5 cm long and are often hairy.

The small white or pale yellow, scented flowers are borne in summer in string-like, branching racemes. They attract many insects. The small roundish fruits are often black as the specific name indicates.

The possibility exists that the tropical African *Allophylus rubifolius* (Hochst. ex A.Rich.) Engl. may prove inseparable from *Allophylus melanocarpus.* If this is so the older name *rubifolius* will have priority. If, however, this in its turn is found inseparable from *Allophylus africanus* this name, being the oldest, will stand.

Allophylus rubifolius (Hochst. ex A.Rich.) Engl.

= *Schmidelia rubifolia* Hochst. ex A. Rich.; = *Allophylus transvaalensis* Burtt Davy

Red-fruited allophylus, rooibessieboom

Allophylus rubifolius is a tropical African shrub or small tree which extends southwards to the Transvaal and Natal in woodland and in bush.

It closely resembles *Allophylus melanocarpus* except that the twigs, leaf stalks and leaves are often densely hairy, and the fruit is red or orange. The inflorescence may be branched or unbranched.

Botanists now tend to include *Allophylus transvaalensis* in this species.

If this eventually proves inseparable from *Allophylus melanocarpus,* the name *rubifolius,* being the older, will be the correct one. It means "with Rubus-like leaves".

(423.1)   *Allophylus africanus* Beauv.

= *Schmidelia africana* (Beauv.) DC.; = *Allophylus cataractarum* Bak.f.; = *Allophylus holubii* Bak.f., = *Allophylus spragueanus Burtt* Davy

African allophylus

Although this is a common and widespread species in tropical Africa it is not – if it is considered separate from *Allophylus melanocarpus* and *Allophylus rubifolius* – represented at all in South Africa, although it does enter the Caprivi Strip and occurs also in Botswana.

It is a shrub or tree up to about 9 m high with strong branches which are smooth or covered with tawny hairs. The leaves are made up of 3

Allophylus natalensis on the golf course at Port St. John's

leaflets, oblong to egg-shaped, the terminal — the largest — up to about 15 cm long and 8 cm wide (although those specimens from the Caprivi Strip and Botswana are smaller and narrower), the tips pointed or rounded, the base wedge-shaped, the upper part of the leaves toothed, smooth or hairy, often with tufts of hairs in the axils of the nerves below, stalked or without stalks. The common petiole of the leaf is up to nearly 8 cm long, smooth or densely hairy.

The tiny cream or green flowers are in small, crowded clusters borne in long branched hairy "strings". The fruits are small, usually only 1 coccus or lobe developing, roundish or shaped like a top, red or orange, smooth or hairy.

At least 4 species of butterflies are known to breed on this, including the lovely Pearl Caraks which, when it folds its wings, appears to be a dry leaf.

The specific name means "of Africa".

(426)   *Allophylus natalensis* (Sond.) De Winter

= *Schmidelia natalensis* Sond.; = *Allophylus erosus* Radlk.

Natal allophylus; umHlohlela (Z)

Unlike *Allophylus melanocarpus,* this does not grow inland but is one of the common species along the coast from Port Alfred in the eastern Cape northwards through Natal and Zululand to Mozambique. It occurs on the edge of forest and bush, often on the dunes themselves.

This is a shrub or sometimes a fairly large tree with a dense crown, a fairly smooth brown trunk, and light-coloured, usually smooth twigs. The leaves are composed of 3 leaflets. They are slender oblong, narrowing both ends, the tips rounded or bluntly pointed, the middle leaflet, which is slightly the largest, 3-8 cm long and 1-2.5 cm wide, the margins rolled back, regularly and shortly toothed, dark green above and below duller and glandular, quite smooth or covered with tiny flat hairs. The midrib, 5-8 pairs of lateral nerves, and netted veins are usually distinct. The leaflets are usually without stalks, while the whole leaf is borne on a stalk 1.3-3 cm long, which is smooth or hairy.

1341

Allophylus natalensis: A
fruiting branchlet (80%)

The small white or green flowers with a strong sweet scent are borne
in inflorescences like branched strings, a few flowers being grouped together in small round bunches along a central stem or axis.

The fruits are small, round and pea-like — only one coccus or lobe usually
developing — a brilliant pillar-box red and glossy. They are often borne
in enormous quantities, their weight making the branches droop, and
are immensely gay among the handsome foliage. They ripen from autumn
into winter.

The wood is said to be soft and is little used. The greatest value of the
tree is its decorative character combined with its toughness. Sim half a
century ago remarked that it withstood salt winds and spray and should
make a good hedge in difficult positions close to the sea. It is doubtful
whether — in 50 years — a single gardener has followed his advice!

This species is sometimes confused with *Allophylus melanocarpus*
which often occurs in the same areas but the leaflets are narrower in
proportion to the length and the leaves usually have shorter stalks.

The specific name means "of Natal".

1342

Right
Allophylus decipiens: A.
A fruiting twig B. A leaf
showing the tufts of
hairs in the axils of the
nerves below (60%)

Below
Allophylus dregeanus
stem and bark

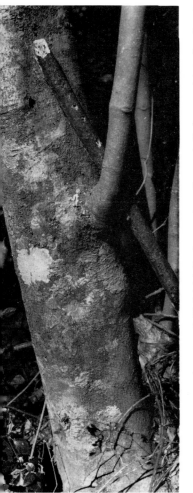

(423)   *Allophylus decipiens* (Sond.) Radlk.

= *Schmidelia decipiens* Sond.; = *Rhus spicata* Thunb.; = *Allophylus spicatus* (Thunb.) Fourcade

Red berry tree, rooibessieboom, umCandathambo (X); umNcandathambo, uMaquanda (Z)

Allophylus decipiens reaches from Knysna in the south, through the eastern Cape, the Transkei, Natal, Zululand and Swaziland to the Transvaal and Mozambique, growing from coast level to an altitude of about 1500 m. Trees grow alongside the national road between the Grootrivier and Knysna.

In the Cape it is usually a species of forest margins or stream banks but in Zululand it may also grow in short dense forest.

This may be either a shrub or a small and very graceful tree with light-coloured stem or stems, silver-white branches which are downy or smooth, and whitish twigs. The leaves are made up of 3 leaflets, the terminal the largest, 1.3-5 cm long, the lateral leaflets shorter, egg-shaped to widely lance-shaped, the tips rounded or pointed, the base narrowed, sometimes almost untoothed, at others the upper half broadly and often roundly toothed, the margins slightly inrolled, smooth or the midrib and nerves hairy, sometimes with tufts of hairs in the axils of the nerves below. The midrib and 3-6 pairs of nerves are conspicuous below. The leaflets have very short stalks or none at all. The common leaf stalk is up to 3 cm long and often finely hairy.

The Transvaal and Zululand forms tend to have leaflets softer and with larger crenulations than those from the Cape, which are often longer in proportion to the width and sometimes almost untoothed, but there is a full range of gradations between these two forms.

The small, white, sweet-scented flowers are in spike-like inflorescences. The fruits are somewhat larger than those of the other *Allophylus* spe-

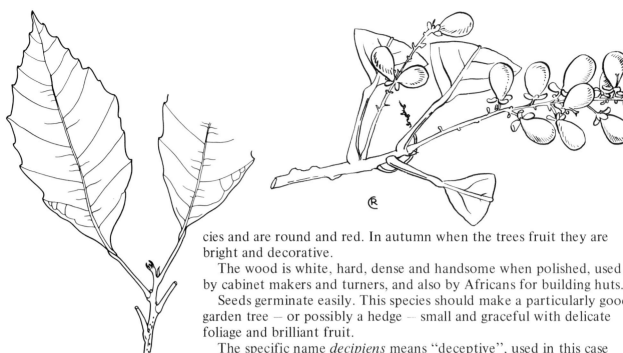

Above left
Allophylus dregeanus
leaf (100%)

Above right
A fruiting twig

cies and are round and red. In autumn when the trees fruit they are bright and decorative.

The wood is white, hard, dense and handsome when polished, used by cabinet makers and turners, and also by Africans for building huts.

Seeds germinate easily. This species should make a particularly good garden tree – or possibly a hedge – small and graceful with delicate foliage and brilliant fruit.

The specific name *decipiens* means "deceptive", used in this case because of a resemblance to a *Rhus*. Gerstner says that the general Zulu name, uMaqunda, is based on a word meaning "to blunt", because the tree is thought to have the ability to blunt the sharp power of a witch. This name, he says, is also given to *Cassine papillosa* for the same reason.

(424)   *Allophylus dregeanus* (Sond.) De Winter

= *Schmidelia dregeana* Sond.; = *Rhus monophylla* E.Mey.; *Allophylus monophyllus* (E.Mey.) Radlk.

One-leaf allophylus

The one-leaf allophylus, a tree of forests, forest margins and bush, grows from the Transkei to Zululand, from sea level to an altitude of over 1500 m. It is a common species round Port St. John's and in the Egossa Forest. Sim stated that it grew in Mozambique but this is a doubtful record.

This is usually a small tree up to 6 m high but may grow up to 9 m with a stem diameter of 30 cm. It is the only member of the genus in South Africa to have simple leaves. These are fairly thin, dull or shiny green above and paler below, in adult trees usually up to 8 x 5 cm or slightly larger, but in younger trees up to 23 x 11 cm, egg-shaped to oval or widely lance-shaped, pointed, narrowed to the base, usually toothed, wavy, and sometimes with tufts and hairs in the axils of the nerves. The netted veins are usually conspicuous. The leaves are carried on slightly hairy stalks about 2.5 cm long.

The small white, sweet-scented flowers are in spike-like racemes. The fruit is composed of 2 or often only 1 cocci, ripening in late winter.

The wood is white, hard and dense.

The specific name honours Johann Franz (Jean Francois) Drège, 1794-1881, a German of Huguenot descent and an outstanding collector in Southern Africa from 1826-1834. He collected about 200,000 specimens of 8000 species.

Allophylus chaunostachys Gilg

= *Allophylus gazensis* Bak.f.

A shrub or small tree, this grows from Malawi, Mozambique and Zambia to Rhodesia. It has been collected in the eastern Transvaal near Barberton but is a rare tree in South Africa.

The twigs are hairy when young becoming smoother with age, pale and covered with small raised dots. The leaves, on stalks up to nearly 8 cm long, are composed of 3 rather large leaflets, the terminal one up to 15 x 6 cm and larger than the lateral leaflets, a narrow oval in shape, tapering to the point, the base wedge-shaped; smooth, sometimes with tufts of hairs in the axils of the leaves below.

The white or green flowers are in unbranched inflorescences up to 23 cm long. The fruit is composed of 1 to 2 roundish cocci.

The specific name is based on Greek words, "chaunos" meaning "soft", and and "stachys" meaning "spike".

2. *Atalaya* Blume

This small genus was originally thought to be native only to Australia and Timor at the southern end of the Malay Archipelago. In the 1930's specimens of an unknown species of tree were collected independently by forest officers W.E.Dix and F.S.Laughton in various parts of the wooded country not far from Port Elizabeth. It was established at Kew that this was a member of the genus *Atalaya* and in 1937 was named by Dr R.A.Dyer, *Atalaya capensis*.

Its discovery caused much surprise and excitement, firstly because a member of the genus was a most unexpected find in South Africa, and secondly because it had been found in such a locality – long-inhabited, well-populated, and the hunting ground of many noted botanists from early times.

Since then 2 more species of *Atalaya* have been found in South Africa, *Atalaya alata* (Sim) H.Forbes from Zululand, Swaziland, the eastern Transvaal and Mozambique, and *Atalaya natalensis* R.A.Dyer from Ngome and other forests in Natal.

Members of the genus are trees or shrubs with leaves that are usually paripinnate – pinnate or once compound, terminated by a pair of leaflets – small flowers that are often polygymous, that is, with bisexual or male or female flowers on the same or on different plants, borne in a terminal panicle, the sepals and petals 5, the disc fleshy, the stamens 8, the ovary 3-chambered and 3-lobed. The fruit – botanically a samara – has 1-3 conspicuous, stiff wings, the seed making a round bulge at the base. It does not burst open when mature. When ripe the fruit falls, the wings making it gyrate in its descent.

The origin of the name *Atalaya* is not certain. It is possible that it is based on the word "talaria", the winged sandals of Roman mythology, and if this is so it is a charming interpretation of the light, airborne, winged fruits.

(428)   *Atalaya capensis* R.A.Dyer

Cape atalaya

This, the first of the genus *Atalaya* to be described in South Africa,

The tree that caused a botanical sensation — *Atalaya capensis* — growing on a valley slope in the Suurberg

Above
Atalaya capensis: A
fruiting twig and indivi-
dual fruits (60%)

Below
Atalaya capensis stem
and bark

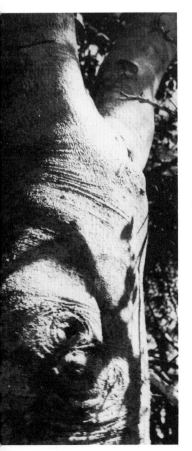

grows in the Eastern Province of the Cape, in forests and in bush, often
on steep wooded hill slopes. One of the first specimens to be collected
was from the Longmore Settlement near Port Elizabeth and today it
still grows in the Van Staden's Nature Reserve close to the city where it,
and *Sterculia alexandri* Harv., are considered two curiosities. It also
occurs in the mountains of the Baviaan's Kloof and in the Suurberg,
where its light green foliage is conspicuous in kloofs and on mountain
slopes.

It is most often a fairly small tree but in the forest at Van Staden's
reaches 12 m in height. The tree photographed — some 9 m high — was
a shapely specimen growing on a valley slope in the Suurberg in company with *Aloe ferox,* and clustered about its base *Apodytes dimidiata,
Cussonia spicata, Pterocelastrus tricuspidatus,* and *Diospyros dichrophylla.* In the background was a group of cycads, *Encephalartos longi-
folius.*

This is a very leafy species with abundant green foliage. The smooth
trunk, up to 46 cm in diameter, is often conspicuous among the surrounding vegetation for it is light-coloured — that in the photograph was a
milky white. The branches are pale grey with scattered, raised, corky
dots.

The dark green, compound, wavy leaves are made up of 3-5 pairs of
usually opposite leaflets, lance-shaped or wider, sharply or sometimes
bluntly pointed, the margins usually entire but sometimes lobed, the
midrib often slightly to one side, the netted veins usually conspicuous
both sides, stalkless or borne on short stalks.

The small cream-coloured flowers are in branched heads at the ends
of the branches or in the axils of the upper leaves. The fruit is 1-3-wing-
ed — the wings with conspicuous veins — and the seed is round and hard.
The fruits do not split open. Sound seed is difficult to collect for the
fruits do not remain long on the tree and fallen fruits are often parasitized.

The seed germinates easily and small seedlings are frequent in the forests where the tree grows.

The specific name *capensis* means "of the Cape".

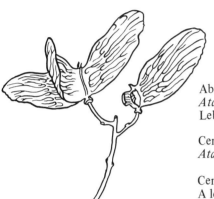

Above
Atalaya alata in young leaf on the
Lebombo Mountains near Ubombo

Centre left
Atalaya alata: The fruits (70%)

Centre right
A leaf (50%)

Below
The same species in full leaf

(427)   *Atalaya alata* (Sim) H.Forbes

= *Diacarpa alata* Sim

Winged atalaya; umZondo, umNondo(Z)

The winged atalaya, from stream banks or wooded and densely bushed hill slopes of Zululand, Swaziland, and the eastern Transvaal, was originally known as *Diacarpa alata* Sim and is described under this name in his *Forest Flora of Portuguese East Africa.* Small trees of this species are a feature of the slopes of the Lebombo Mountains between Mkuze and Ubombo in Zululand, often growing alongside the main road.

This is a small, spreading, many-branched and graceful tree up to about 9 m in height but often no more than 4.5 m, with light grey or whitish bark which is smooth, warty, or seamed crosswise, and with slender grey branches.

The large compound leaves are made up of 5-7 pairs of neat leaflets which are alternate or nearly opposite and shortly stalked. They are up to 6 cm long and 2 cm wide, and may be long, straight and slender, narrowed both ends, or curved somewhat like a new moon, with the midrib towards the lower margin. The tips are rounded or bluntly pointed. The lower margin is usually untoothed or sparsely toothed while the upper is usually toothed. The common leaf stalk is slightly hairy.

The tree is deciduous and in spring the small, tender green leaves at the ends of the twigs give it an air of great delicacy, in contrast to the rugged mountain sides where it often grows.

The small white flowers in loose terminal sprays or panicles bloom about September. The fruit, ripening in autumn, is 1-3-winged, 1 or 2 of the wings often being only partially developed. The veined wings are up to 2.5 cm or more long, green flushed with rosy red, and when paired much resemble the wings of a butterfly or moth.

This species can be distinguished from *Atalaya capensis* by its leaflets which are more halfmoon-shaped and toothed, whereas those of *Atalaya capensis* are usually untoothed.

The specific name is the Latin "alatus" meaning "winged".

(429)   *Atalaya natalensis* R.A.Dyer

Natal atalaya; umHlambila (Z)

Atalaya natalensis, often the largest of the three South African atalayas, was originally believed to occur only in the Ngome forest in Natal in rocky and stony soil, growing in numbers together with few other species intermixed. It has now been collected in Ngoye and Nkandhla forests and is possibly more widespread than is realized even now.

It is a leafy tree up to about 12 m high with a trunk diameter at breast height of roughly 30 cm. The compound leaves are composed of 3-5 pairs of leaflets — occasionally of only 2 pairs — which are usually opposite. They are lance-shaped to oblong, pointed, narrowed to the often slightly lopsided base, the midrib sometimes very slightly to one side, the margins untoothed and usually slightly wavy, the veins fairly prominent both sides.

The flowers are in dense sprays — panicles — at the ends of the branches or in the axils of the upper leaves. The fruit is 1-3-winged, the wings roughly half-moon-shaped and stiff.

A Zulu name for this species is umHlambila meaning "dassie-food".

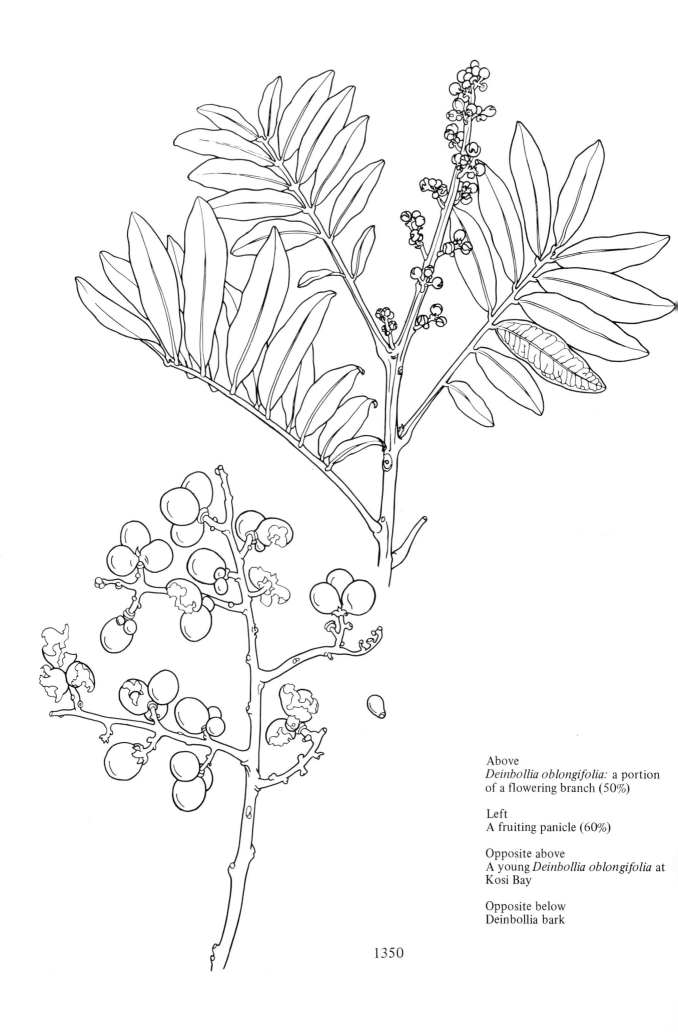

Above
Deinbollia oblongifolia: a portion
of a flowering branch (50%)

Left
A fruiting panicle (60%)

Opposite above
A young *Deinbollia oblongifolia* at
Kosi Bay

Opposite below
Deinbollia bark

1350

3. *Deinbollia* Schum.

This genus of 30-40 species — mainly African but also occurring in the Mascarene Islands near Madagascar and in Madagascar itself — is represented in South Africa by 2 species, 1 of which grows from Zululand to the eastern Cape, and another which occurs in the north eastern Transvaal.

The species are usually trees or shrubs with alternate, compound leaves, either abruptly pinnate or imparipinnate, the leaflets alternate or nearly opposite; the flowers usually in branched racemes terminally or in the axils of the leaves, male and female usually on separate plants; the sepals and petals 5, a disc present, the stamens 12-20, the ovary 2-3-lobed (or with 2-3 parts), each part with 1 cell. The fruit consists of generally 2-5 cocci or parts of which 1-4 often fail to mature. These cocci are roundish and berry-like, leathery or sometimes fleshy, each coccus containing 1 seed.

The generic name honours Peter Vogelius Deinboll, a Danish botanist and collector who was born in Copenhagen in 1783 and died in Norway in 1876.

(430)   *Deinbollia oblongifolia* (E.Mey. ex Arn.) Radlk.

= *Rhus oblongifolia* E.Mey. ex Arn.; = *Hippobromus oblongifolius* (E.Mey.) Drège; = *Sapindus oblongifolius* (E.Mey. ex Arn.) Sond.

Soap berry, uMasibele (X); iGolo-lenkama (Z)

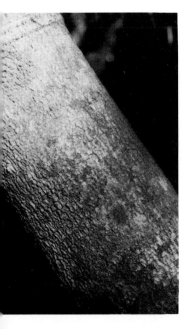

The soap berry occurs from the East London district northwards through Natal and Zululand to Mozambique, in dune bush and forest, open forest and scrub. It grows in such familiar spots as the Bluff at Durban and in Hluhluwe camp in Zululand.

Although occasionally reaching 9 m or more in height, it is usually a smaller tree 3-6 m high, sometimes sprawling, at others small, slender and upright, with a clean unbranched stem. It is interesting to note that in *Flora Zambesiaca* it is described as a low shrub only.

It is a deep-rooting species, the main root, according to Medley Wood, penetrating the ground to a depth of 1.8 m or more. The trunk is a fairly smooth grey-brown, often splashed grey and green with lichen, and marked horizontally with small raised seams. It reaches a diameter of about 30 cm.

The large compound leaves are crowded at the ends of the branches. They are from 15-46 cm long, borne on slightly hairy stalks up to about 9 cm in length, the smooth, thin leaflets usually in about 5-10 pairs, with or without a terminal leaflet, alternate or opposite, 5-13 cm (occasionally 20) long and 2.5-5 cm (occasionally 9) wide, somewhat oblong but narrowing both ends, the tips usually rounded or bluntly pointed, the base rounded or wedge-shaped, the margins untoothed and sometimes wavy, the midrib sometimes slightly to one side, the lateral nerves in 12-15 pairs and the netted veins yellow and conspicuous both sides, the leaflets sometimes without stalks, at others with short *twisted* stalks. They may overlap one another or be widely spaced.

The pale to greeny-brown or red-brown, round, furry buds in upright panicles open into white, flask-shaped flowers which do not open wide and are largely hidden by the calyx. They are packed tightly together in small clusters along the flowering stalk, the conspicuous calyx, often

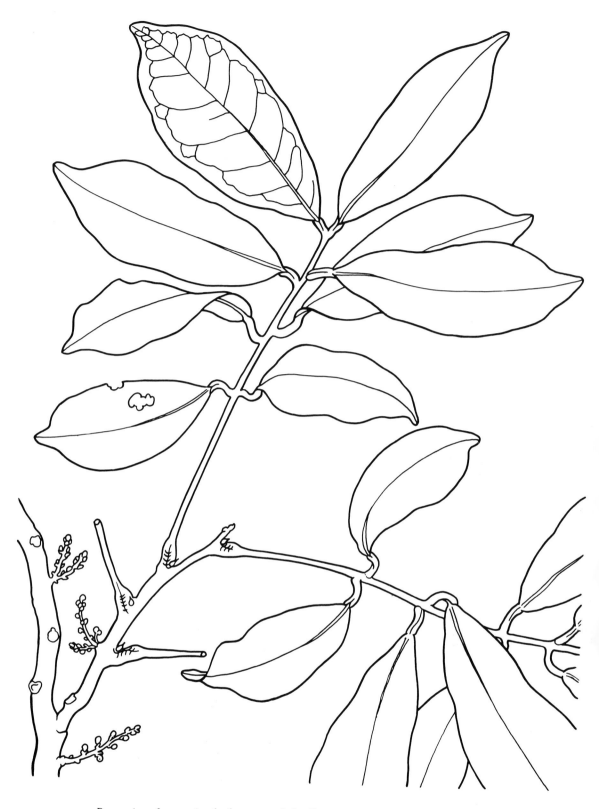

Pancovia golungensis: the leaves, and the flowers growing upon the old wood (70%)

covered with soft reddish hairs, making a bright colour contrast. In the very early morning the flowers are often covered with small mauve moths feasting upon them, and later in the day with butterflies.

It is noteworthy that although this species has been described as dioecious, that is male and female flowers being borne on separate trees, plants may bear bisexual flowers one season and mainly unisexual in another.

The fruits consist of up to 3 cocci or parts, appearing like separate fruits, grape-like in shape, rounded or oval, sometimes the oval seed within clearly outlined, about 1.3 cm or more in diameter, woolly when young but on maturing becoming smooth and yellow. They are borne in large clusters, sometimes on plants no more than 1.2 m high but perfect little trees in form. Children and monkeys eat them, and they are popular with white-eyes, Layard's Bulbul, the Speckled Coly, the Cape Glossy Starling, and the Masked Weaver.

The single seed is coated in a white material used as a soap substitute.

Zulus never make fighting sticks from the wood because it breaks easily.

Formerly the tree was known as *Sapindus oblongifolius,* the name *Sapindus* being based on the botanical name of Indian soap, *Sapo indicus,* in reference to the soapy covering of the seed. The name *oblongifolia* means "oblong leaves".

Pancovia golungensis flowers growing on the old wood

(430.1)   *Deinbollia xanthocarpa* (Klotzsch) Radlk.

= *Sapindus xanthocarpa* Klotzsch; = *Deinbollia marginata* Radlk.

In *Flora Zambesiaca* this species is kept separate from *Deinbollia oblongifolia* which it closely resembles, and in the opinion of the Botanical Research Institute there may be grounds for this separation.

If this is upheld, the *Deinbollia* occurring in the north western Transvaal is *Deinbollia xanthocarpa* -- "the deinbollia with the yellow fruit".

The leaflets are smaller than those of *Deinbollia oblongifolia,* usually up to 8 x 3 cm, and in South Africa more perfectly oblong in shape. According to *Flora Zambesiaca* they are more numerous – from 3-9 pairs – the leaf-rachis usually narrowly winged (although this is not apparent in the South African material collected) and the whole leaf is usually borne on a very short stalk, often with a small pair of leaflets at the base of the rachis. The inflorescence is said to be shorter, up to 20 cm long instead of up to 36 cm, the fruit with 1-2 egg-shaped to roundish cocci or parts, yellow, hairy, becoming smoother, and edible.

4. *Pancovia* Willd.

Pancovia is a small genus of about 10-12 species of trees and shrubs native to tropical and subtropical Africa. One species occurs in South Africa in the forests of Zululand.

All have leaves that are paripinnate – once compound, terminated by a pair of leaflets – flowers that are male or female on the same or different plants, in panicles or groups in the axils of the leaves or on the old wood, the sepals 4-5, the petals 3-4, the stamens 6-9, the ovary 3-chambered, each with 1 ovule or unfertilized fruit, and the fruit fleshy with 1-3 cocci or parts that are completely united or joined at the base, 1-2 ften failing to develop. The seed is oval and flattish, without an aril.

The genus was named after Thomas Panckow, a 17th century botanist who died in Berlin in 1665.

(430.2) *Pancovia golungensis* (Hiern) Exell & Mendonça

= *Aphania golungensis* Hiern

Pancovia, umuThionzima (Z)

This little known tree from Zululand forests, often growing on stream banks, may be a 2 m shrub in bush, as fringing the Hluhluwe River, a scrambler, or a slender tree, often an understorey but sometimes reaching 12m height. It grows as a shrub or tree in Mozambique, Malawi, and in Angola where it was first collected at Golungo, a locality from which the tree takes its specific name.

The slender trunk is brownish, often blotched with lichen, and the branches are brown covered with small, raised, reddish dots. The young twigs are covered with tawny hairs but become smoother with age.

The leaves of seedlings are simple. Those on adult trees are compound and large, up to 30 cm long. They are composed of 2-5 pairs of leaflets which are opposite or nearly opposite and are borne on short and conspicuously swollen stalks, a character that helps to identify the species. They are up to 15 x 4 cm long, oblong to egg-shaped or widely lance-shaped, the tips bluntly or sharply pointed, rounded or notched, often with a jutting point, the base narrowed, the margin untoothed, the midrib raised below, and the netted veins below with swollen glands (not visible to the naked eye). The lateral veins are in 10-13 pairs. The young leaves are almost white, the veins showing red, but they become dark green with age.

The male and female flowers are on separate trees. They are borne on the old wood in an inflorescence — botanically a racemoid thyrse — up to 10 cm long. The ovary is 3-lobed and the fruit is formed of 1-3 cocci or parts, each one oval, up to about 1.5 cm long, orange when mature and either smooth or hairy. They hang in clusters from the old branches — and are among the least-known of all the wild fruits of South Africa.

5. *Smelophyllum* Radlk.

Only 1 species belongs to this genus of the Port Elizabeth, Humansdorp and Uniondale districts of the Cape Province.

It is a tree with alternate leaves, abruptly pinnate, — that is, the rachis terminating in a point with a single leaflet to one side; bisexual flowers in a short axillary panicle, the calyx saucer-shaped, the petals 5, a disc present, the stamens 6-10, the ovary 2-3-celled, the fruit 2-lobed and fleshy.

The origin of the generic name is uncertain. It may possibly mean "with leaves like *Smelowskia*", an Asian and north American genus with pinnate leaves.

Above
Smelophyllum capense:
A portion of a fruiting
branchlet (30%)

Below
Its stem

(431)   *Smelophyllum capense* Radlk.

= *Sapindus capensis* Sond.

Buig-my-nie

The buig-my-nie, a small to medium-sized tree, grows from Port Elizabeth to Uniondale in forest and bush. It is common in the kloofs of the
Great Winterberg and Elandsberg and is one of the trees, together with
Atalaya capensis and *Sterculia alexandri,* with a particularly interesting
distribution, which are found in the Van Staden's Nature Reserve close
to Port Elizabeth.

The trunk is fairly smooth and is grey blotched with white. The branches are smooth and ash-grey, the leaves alternate and once compound
with 3-4 pairs of leathery leaflets which are opposite or alternate, terminated by a point with a leaflet to one side. They are 2.5-8 cm long,
oblong, narrowed both ends, bluntly pointed, the upper part boldly
toothed, wavy, the midrib often slightly to one side, with netted veins
and tiny transparent dots. They are stalkless or with very short stalks.

The flowers are in short branching heads in the axils of the leaves.
The ovary is 2-3-celled and the fruits are fleshy, usually 2-lobed, each
lobe being round and up to 1.3 cm in diameter, apparently separate but
in fact joined at the base, each one containing a large, smooth, purplish-
brown seed.

When cultivated, this is very slow-growing.

The branches are brittle, hence the common name "buig-my-nie"
or "bend-me-not". The specific name means "of the Cape".

6. *Haplocoelum* Radlk.

Haplocoelum is a small genus of about 7 species native to tropical and
subtropical Africa, and to Madagascar.

They are trees or shrubs with paripinnate and imparipinnate leaves,
the leaf rachis or common midrib slightly winged; the flowers bisexual
or unisexual, in axillary clusters, the sepals 5-6, the petals absent, the
stamens 5-6, inserted in the middle of the disc, the ovary 3-locular with
1 ovule per chamber, the fruit fleshy and 1-seeded (by abortion).

The name *Haplocoelum* is based on the Greek words "haploos" and
"coelum" meaning "single ceiling" in reference to the single perianth.

(432)   *Haplocoelum gallense* (Engl.) Radlk.

= *Pistaciopsis gallensis* Engl.

Umtambo tree; umThambo (Z)

The umtambo tree is a small, much-branched, twiggy species of Zululand, growing up to about 6 m high in such parts as the sand forest in
False Bay Park, and in short forest and bush in Mkuze and Ndumu
Game Reserves. It was first recorded from Somaliland "in highlands and
rocky hollows" and its occurrence in Zululand is interesting.

It is easily confused with the sneezewood, *Ptaeroxylon obliquum*
(Thunb.) Radlk., for the leaves, like those of the sneezewood, have
several pairs of untoothed leaflets often conspicuously unequal-sided
(with the midrib to one side), terminated by a pair of leaflets. They,

however, tend to be shorter and wider in proportion to their length than those of the sneezewood and are often oblong or egg-shaped, or sometimes almost round, with blunt, notched tips, the uppermost being the largest and decreasing in size towards the base of the leaf. They are shortly stalked or without stalks. The common midrib is slightly winged. The leaves are borne at the end of the branchlets.

The tiny brownish flowers are in short dense clusters in the axils of the leaves, male and female on separate trees. The fruits, ripe about February, are most handsome, rose pink to claret, round, 1.3-1.9 cm in diameter, borne on short stalks. They are edible and are great favourites with monkeys, baboons and bushbabies. Livingstone's Antelope, Red and Grey Duiker, and birds such as loeries also eat them.

The hard wood is very strong and is used by the Zulus to make pointed fighting sticks and for hut and roof poles. It is excellent fuel.

Zulus use the roots medicinally.

The specific name indicates that the tree was first collected in the Galla highlands in Somaliland.

7. *Pappea* Eckl. & Zeyh.

Various species and varieties have in the past been included in this genus, but botanists now tend to consider it a genus of 1 variable species only, *Pappea capensis* Eckl. & Zeyh.

The species is widely distributed in eastern tropical Africa and in South and South West Africa.

It has simple, alternate leaves without stipules; male or female flowers in racemes or panicles in the axils of the leaves, borne on separate trees, the calyx saucer-shaped, the petals 4-6, the disc small, the stamens in the male 8-10, the ovary in the female 2-3-lobed and 2-3-celled. The fruit is a capsule, sometimes 3-lobed but often reduced to 1.

The name honours Dr Ludwig Pappe, who was Colonial Botanist at the Cape and died in Cape Town in 1862.

(433)   *Pappea capensis* Eckl. & Zeyh.

= *Sapindus capensis* (Eckl. & Zeyh.) Hochst.; = *Sapindus pappea* Sond. = *Pappea radlkoferi* Schweinf. ex Radlk.; = *Pappea ugandensis* Bak.f.; = *Pappea fulva* Conrath; = *Pappea capensis* Eckl. & Zeyh. var. *radlkoferi* (Schweinf. ex Radlk.) Schinz; = *Pappea radlkoferi* var. *angolensis* Schlecht.; = *Pappea schumanniana* Schinz

Wild plum, oliepit, bushveld cherry, wildepruim, bergpruim, pruimbessie, noupit, doppruim, iliTye (X); umGqogqo, umKhokhwane (Z); liLatsa (Sw); gulaswimbi (Tso); mothata (Tsw), mopennweng (Tsw- Kgat & Kwena); mongatane, morôba-diêpê (NS)

Two well-known forms of this widespread tree occur in South Africa, that growing in woodland and bush of the moister eastern and northern parts of the country — Natal, Zululand, Swaziland, and the Transvaal — and in tropical Africa, being typically a medium-sized and often luxuriant looking tree. That from the more arid areas — parts of the eastern Cape, the Karoo, Namaqualand, Botswana, and South West Africa — having evolved in a harsher climate, is a smaller tree with smaller leaves, shorter inflorescences, and smaller fruits. The more northern form was

Above
A. *Pappea capensis,* the arid form: fruiting and flowering twigs
B. The leaves of the form from moister woodland and bushveld (50%)

until recently known in South Africa as *Pappea capensis* var. *radlkoferi.* Today this form, and that from South West Africa often known as *Pappea schumanniana,* are generally considered inseparable from *Pappea capensis.*

The wild plum grows from 3-9 m high. The arid form is a small tree with a clean, grey, often lichen-covered stem or stems and a dense, twiggy crown, round or somewhat flat on top, browsed into a neat shape with never an untidy or hanging branch. In the Karoo it often grows in association with the witgat, *Boscia oleoides,* or on koppie slopes with the spekboom, *Portulacaria afra,* and the gwarri, *Euclea undulata.*

In areas of heavier rainfall it is a taller, and generally a much lusher tree, the branches sometimes slightly drooping, the trunk thicker than that of the arid form, graceful and densely leafy, when not in flower or fruit frequently mistaken for a species of wild fig tree.

The branches are a light grey and spreading, with the leaves towards the ends of the twigs, arranged alternately or so crowded that they appear to grow in tufts. They are stiff, rough, simple, and vary much in size, those in arid forms often being no more than 2.5-4 cm long and 8 mm wide and hairless, and those from moister areas being almost three times as big and hairier. They are usually oblong, sometimes widely so, the tips round or slightly pointed, the base usually rounded or slightly heart-shaped and sometimes slightly unequal, the margins untoothed or toothed, often wavy, the midrib and 10-12 pairs of lateral veins conspicuous both sides and raised below. The leaves are usually green above, paler below, and the midrib and veins yellow. They are browsed by giraffe and elephant, and sometimes by domestic stock.

The small greenish-yellow flowers — the male usually in a branched inflorescence or panicle, the female in racemes or "strings" — are scented and popular with bees. The inflorescences differ a good deal in length, those in arid forms often being no longer than 2.5-5 cm and those in forms in higher rainfall areas being up to 15 cm.

The fruit, with 3 cocci or parts, is usually reduced to 1 coccus, from 0.8-1.9 cm in diameter, round or oval, with a hard, brittle, brown shell which splits in two to show the thin, bright red, translucent flesh within. In the bushveld of the Transvaal a tree in autumn or winter is often a wonderful sight, the branches loaded with brilliant, red, shiny fruit making a flush of colour. The fruits in arid forms, although individually bright, are often too sparse to make a good show.

Enclosed in the flesh is a brown shiny stone rich in oil.

The dark shells of the fruits sometimes hang on the tree for many months after the fruiting time is past giving it a rather untidy appearance.

The wood is white, sometimes tinged with brown, fairly easily worked, hard, heavy, tough, and used for poles, yokes, furniture, spoons, and for sticks. The North Sotho name, morôba-diêpê, means "axe-breaker".

The fruit is pleasantly tart and juicy and a great favourite with children, monkeys and baboons, elephant, bushbuck, domesticated stock, and all manner of birds. Red-faced Mousebirds, Green Pigeons and Black-collared Barbets are particularly fond of them.

Country people still make a good vinegar and jelly from the flesh. At one time they crushed the stones to extract the oil and with this they oiled their guns, made soap, and treated baldness and ringworm. The oil is slightly purgative.

An interesting little insect, *Leptocoris hexophtalma,* is associated with the tree. It is a sucking bug, small, wingless when immature, and a brilliant red, and it sucks the oil from the fallen seeds. The ground beneath a tree in the fruiting season is sometimes a moving mass — a very brilliant one — of these little creatures.

The widespread butterfly *Anthene definita* breeds on the buds and flowers.

The wild plum was one of the best known trees in early colonial days. Pappe considered its presence "as a criterion of excellent pasturage for wool-bearing flocks", and its shade, fruit, and foliage, browsed eagerly by animals, made it of great value.

It has a place in early history. Wikar, the Swedish runaway soldier who was the first white man to journey along the Orange River and left an account of his adventures here from 1775-1778, noted that the tribes along the river used the berries from the tree, called the Koouw-tree, as food and drink, "indeed a delicious fruit", and the seeds roasted under the coals to make a sweetly scented oil with which they anointed themselves.

A male wild plum is what is termed Lobengula's "indaba tree" in the grounds of Government House, Bulawayo.

The specific name means "of the Cape".

This is the *Sapindus pappea* Sond. of *Flora capensis.*

Above
The crown of *Blighia unijugata* overtopping the dense coastal
vegetation at Lake Sibayi

Below left
Young blighia fruits

Below right
Male flowers

Opposite
Blighia stem and bark

8. *Stadmania* Lam.

Stadmania is a genus of 1 tree species of tropical east Africa, Madagascar, and Reunion. It has been collected in South Africa in the Kruger National Park.

It has paripinnate leaves and flowers that are functionally male or female, in single or branched racemes terminally or in the axils of the leaves, the sepals with 5 segments (sometimes joined), petals absent, the stamens usually 8, the ovary 3-chambered, the fruit sometimes with 1 but usually with 2-3 cocci, splitting to reveal the seed within. The seed has an aril-like covering.

The genus was founded by Lamarck in 1793 and named in honour of M. Stadman, a German botanical traveller.

(435)   *Stadmania oppositifolia* Poir.
         subsp. *rhodesica* Exell

= *Stadmania sideroxylon* DC.; = *Melanodiscus venulosus* Bullock ex Dale & Greenway

Although reported in tropical Africa as up to 18 m high, in South Africa, in the Kruger National Park which is the only locality where it has been collected, this species is known as a small to medium-sized tree up to 6 m high, with grey bark flaking off and leaving lighter mottled patches.

The branches are a light grey, hairy or smooth. The leaves are up to 15 cm long and are composed of usually 2-3 pairs of oval leaflets, or occasionally 1 pair, which are usually opposite or nearly so. These are up to nearly 9 x 2 cm, the apex round and often notched, the base rounded or triangular, the margin untoothed and recurved, smooth above, sometimes hairy below, often unequal-sided with the midrib to one side, the midrib raised both sides, without stalks or with very short ones. The midrib and very young leaves are densely velvety.

The yellowish flowers, without petals, are in racemes, sometimes branched, in the axils of the leaves. The fruit is 1-3-lobed, each lobe being roundish or pear-shaped, covered with silky hairs, and up to 1.3 cm in diameter. They split to show large, brown, roundish seed covered with an aril, looking rather like the fruits of *Pappea capensis*. Hornbills are fond of the fruits.

The wood is tough and hard.

The specific name indicates that the leaflets are opposite, while the subspecific name means "of Rhodesia" — where the type was collected in the Umtali district.

9. *Blighia* Konig

About 6-7 species of trees or shrubs belong to this tropical African genus, 1 of which occurs in Zululand.

They have paripinnate leaves with 1-5 pairs of leaflets, 5-petalled flowers that are usually male or female on separate trees, the calyx small and 4-5-lobed, the stamens 7-10, and the ovary 3-celled, and fruit that is a 3-lobed capsule, 1 or 2 lobes of which often do not develop fully,

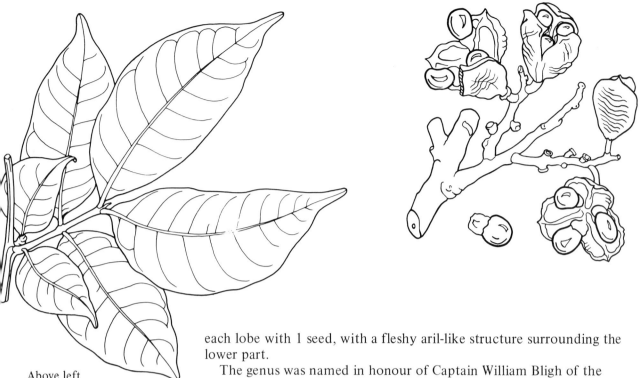

Above left
Blighia unijugata: A leaf
(50%)

Above right
The curiously shaped
fruits (70%)

Below
The inflated, bladder-
like fruits of *Erythrophysa transvaalensis*

each lobe with 1 seed, with a fleshy aril-like structure surrounding the lower part.

The genus was named in honour of Captain William Bligh of the Bounty who is said, in 1793 while in H.M.S. *Providence,* to have introduced a plant to the Royal Botanic Gardens, Kew. It is one of the romances of botanical nomenclature that a Zululand tree should bear a generic name so closely associated with one of the world's great sea adventures.

(436)   *Blighia unijugata* Bak.

= *Blighia zambesiaca* Bak.; = *Phialodiscus unijugatus* (Bak.) Radlk.;
= *Phialodiscus zambesiacus* (Bak.) Radlk.; = *Phialodiscus plurijugatus* Radlk.

Blighia

This species, with its curious and beautiful fruits, was collected in South Africa for the first time in 1958 by the Natal Parks Board ranger, Ken Tinley, who found it in the coastal forest at Lake Sibayi in northern Zululand.

It grows from Zululand northwards to Kenya, Tanzania, and Malawi, and north west to Nigeria.

This is a fairly common tree in swamp forests, and in the forests around Lake Sibayi which have in recent years yielded several new records for South Africa, and is also found in riverine forest in the Ubombo district and in the Mkuze Game Reserve. Sim, who wrote of this in the *Forest Flora of Portuguese East Africa* under the name *Blighia sapinda,* knew it as common in bush or around cultivated lands in Mozambique.

In South Africa it reaches a height of about 17 m, although in tropical Africa it is reported up to 30 m high. It has a grey trunk, often with a red tinge, smooth, ridged or warted, sometimes fluted, and grooved hairy branches that are spreading and sometimes drooping.

1362

The dark green leaves on hairy stalks consist of usually 2-4 but sometimes 1-5 pairs of leaflets that are opposite or nearly opposite, arranged along an often hairy common midrib. They are oblong, egg-shaped to widely lance-shaped, untoothed, sharply or bluntly pointed, often with a long-drawn-out point, the base narrowed or rounded, 4-15 cm long, the uppermost the biggest, the midrib and 6-12 pairs of veins conspicuous and raised below. Young leafy shoots bear leaves that appear to form a rosette. The young leaflets are very thin, shiny, and salmon pink, and these — against the darker foliage — are exquisite.

The fragrant white flowers are in axillary racemes up to about 8 cm long. They are small and insignificant but, arranged together with the new leaves, make a fine combination.

The capsular fruits are as colourful as the young foliage. They are shaped like triangular, 3-sided tops up to 2.5 cm wide, salmon-coloured and softly leathery when young, when mature harder, splitting to show somewhat woody lobes lined with rich crimson from which protrudes the pendulous, shiny, black, oval seed about 1.3 cm long, an extraordinary and splendid mixture of colours. They are borne on sturdy stalks, clustered towards the base of the branches.

One seed only is usually fully developed in a fruit. It has a soft, velvety, aril-like base, which is often riddled with small insects. The fruit ripens from about December to February. When old, the seed hangs below the woody lobes like a long wrinkled raisin. It is said to be edible.

In Mozambique the flowers are used in distilled water to make a fragrant cosmetic.

The sapwood is light-coloured and fine, the heartwood reddish and durable. It is used to make furniture, and in building.

The colour of the new foliage and of the fruits would make this an attractive garden tree for warm areas. Little is known of its cultivation. Under good conditions it germinates readily. In the light, sandy forest patches round Lake Sibayi, cleared by Africans for mealie lands, *Blighia* seedlings grow almost as thickly as the mealies, and this gives some hope that they will never be entirely eradicated.

The name *unijugata,* meaning "with 1 pair of leaflets" is not appropriate as the leaf usually has several pairs.

10. *Erythrophysa* E.Mey.

About 4 species, 2 in South Africa, 1 in Ethiopia, and 1 in Madagascar, make up this interesting genus. It is an fascinating fact that — as far as can be ascertained — the genus which is the nearest relative, *Koelreuteria,* is not in Africa at all but in northern China!

The plants are small trees or shrubs, the leaves alternate, imparipinnate and crowded towards the ends of the branches, the common midrib winged; the flowers bisexual, red, in a panicle or cluster of racemes. The calyx is bell-shaped or lobed, the petals 4, clawed or crested, the stamens 8 — in Phillip's words "inserted in a bundle beneath a fleshy gland at one side of the flower where the fifth petal is deficient". The ovary is 3-celled. The fruit is inflated, bladder-like, membranous, 3-angled, with 3 carpels or parts joined by their inner faces, and the seed is round, pea-like, purple or black.

The generic name *Erythrophysa* is based on Greek words for "red" and "bag" in reference to the red, bladder-like fruits. In the past the

1364

name was published as *Erythrophila* and *Erythrophyla*, but it is considered that the name intended was *Erythrophysa*.

The genus was founded on a Namaqualand species. Its name was proposed by E.Meyer while working on Drège specimens collected in Namaqualand, but he did not validly publish it. This was done by Arnott in 1841, who attributed the name of the species *E. undulata* to E.Meyer. However, the same species had also been found by Ecklon and Zeyher who had described it in 1835 as *Fagara alata* Eckl. & Zeyh.

It was not until 90 years later that Dr John Hutchinson discovered that the two names described the same plant. As Ecklon and Zeyher's specific name was earlier, and the plant was obviously wrongly placed in *Fagara*, he made the transfer to the genus *Erythrophysa* as *E. alata* (Eckl. & Zeyh.) Hutch. which, in accordance with the international rules, replaced *E. undulata* E.Mey ex Arn.

But the story does not end here because, while a revision of *Schotia* was being undertaken a few years ago, it was found that Thunberg had already described the same species in 1823 as *Schotia alata* Thunb. An original specimen of Thunberg's in the Uppsala Herbarium is unmistakably the same species as the plants collected later by Drège, Ecklon and Zeyher. Due to the fact that there is already a combination *Erythrophysa alata* (Eckl. & Zeyh.) Hutch., Thunberg's epithet *alata*, although the older, cannot now be taken up in *Erythrophysa*. This is one of those tangles which delight botanists but which also waste a great deal of their time.

(436.1)   *Erythrophysa alata* (Eckl. & Zeyh.) Hutch.

= *Schotia alata* Thunb.; = *Fagara alata* Eckl. & Zeyh.; = *Erythrophysa undulata* E.Mey. ex Arn.

Namaqualand red balloon, klapperbos, sumoë

This shrub or small tree of Namaqualand with its stiff, light grey branches and bunched leaves at the ends of the twigs, is a little known species, interesting mainly because of its striking fruits, reminiscent of those of the klapper, *Nymania capensis*.

The little tree photographed grew on a rocky hillside not far from Springbok close to the Springbok-Spektakelberg road. In general appearance and in leaf it resembled a *Schotia*, but in September its bright balloon fruits, conspicuous from afar, established its identity. Simon van der Stel's party saw this on their Namaqualand expedition from 1685-1686, and Claudius, the artist, must have noted its exotic appearance for he made a drawing of it.

It does not appear to exceed about 3 m in height, but is a tree in form with a slender grey trunk up to some 12 or 15 cm in diameter and a flat-topped crown.

The small compound leaves are composed of several pairs of tiny, sometimes minute, leaflets and a terminal leaflet, arranged along a common midrib that is winged. The leaflets are dark green, egg-shaped, wavy and untoothed, and are borne in bunches at the ends of short side branchlets.

The red flowers have a cup-like calyx covered — as can be seen under the microscope — with small, stalked black glands, and 4 petals about 8 mm long which turn back to expose tiny crested outgrowths on the inner side and long, straight, delicate stamens. They are bisexual and

OPPOSITE

Above
Erythrophysa alata, a 3 m tree on a hillside close to Springbok

Below left
The leaves and balloon-like fruits 100%

Below right
Erythrophysa alata bark

Above left
Erythrophysa transvaalensis near the Bospoort Dam, western Transvaal

Above right
Erythrophysa transvaalensis stem

Below left
Erythrophysa transvaalensis: The leaves and a flowering twig (60%)

Below right
The balloon-like fruits, and seeds (40%)

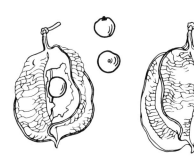

1366

give rise to large, membranous, inflated fruits with a wispy point at the ends, about 4 x 5 cm (sometimes larger), bright red, sometimes with a purple sheen, the netted veins conspicuous. They hold large round purplish seed.

The name *alata* means "winged", no doubt in reference to the winged leaf-rhachis.

This was the *Erythrophysa undulata* E.Mey. of *Flora capensis.*

(436.2) *Erythrophysa transvaalensis* Verdoorn

Transvaal red balloon, klapperbos, wild jacaranda

The Transvaal red balloon is known to grow in a few places only in the western Transvaal — on the slope of a hill near the Bospoort Dam in the Rustenburg district, near Thabazimbi, and in the western Waterberg. A tree grows just behind the Bospoort Dam wall among boulders on a steep slope, and this type of country appears to be its normal habitat.

The species was first sent to the Botanical Research Institute in 1933 by the engineer in charge of the building of the Bospoort Dam, Mr V.K. Hands, who had noted that the African women used the seeds as beads. He left the neighbourhood before the site of his find was established and for 8 years Dr Inez Verdoorn hunted fruitlessly for what she realized was a unique species. In 1941 she and Dr H.H. Curson of the Department of Native Affairs found trees on the slope behind the dam. Botanically, it was a moment of great excitement!

Dr Verdoorn describes the tree as the most striking species in this unusual genus. It is a deciduous shrub or small tree up to about 4 or 5 m high with many slender stems branching from ground level or just above the base, crowned with what Dr Verdoorn calls "a plume of graceful compound leaves or an erect panicle of red and green flowers". The stems grow up to about 20 cm in diameter. The bark is grey to reddish-brown, and covered with small raised dots. The branches are smooth and shiny with the leaves crowded towards the ends on the young growths.

The leaves are imparipinnate — with several pairs of leaflets terminated by a single leaflet — and the common midrib is conspicuously winged. There are about 9-15 pairs of leaflets, 2-7 cm long and 5-10 mm wide, which are opposite or nearly opposite, a slender lance-shape, untoothed or sometimes lobed near the base, with the midribs raised below. If these are examined closely, they are often found to be slightly to one side of the leaflets. The size and shape of the leaflets distinguish this from *Erythrophysa alata.*

The flowers, with 4 clawed petals and straight protruding stamens, are in an upright panicle or branching head, leafless or borne with a few leaves. They are green suffused with red or pink and bisexual or male or female borne on the same or different trees.

The large, balloon-like fruits are 3-angled and 3-chambered, the persistent style usually making a wispy point, with 1-2 large round, smooth, black seeds in each chamber. The fruits are a rich splendid red and very decorative.

The leaves appear at the same time as the flowers, about October, and the fruit is borne soon after, although dry fruits may be found on the tree as late as midwinter.

It is not clear why the distribution of this species should be so limited for the seeds germinate well and plants grow easily in cultivation. Several trees grow in Pretoria gardens.

Above left
Dodonaea viscosa var. *angustifolia,* the typical form in the scrub on Karoo mountains

Above right
The same variety on the farm "St. Olives" in the Graaff-Reinet district

Below left
The stem and bark

Below centre
Dodonaea viscosa var. *viscosa:* a fruiting twig (50%)

Below right
Dodonaea viscosa: A. var. *angustifolia* fruiting twig. B. var. *viscosa* leaf. C. var. *angustifolia* leaf (50%)

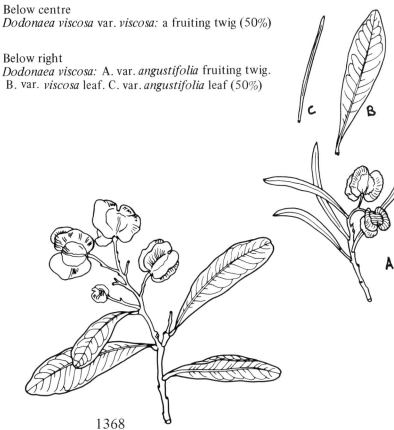

1368

grow in Pretoria gardens.

The specific name means "of the Transvaal".

11. *Dodonaea* Mill.

This largely Australian genus of about 50 species is represented in South Africa by 1 species which occurs from the Cape to the Transvaal, from Natal to South West Africa, northwards through tropical Africa and throughout many tropical countries of the world. One or 2 species occur in Madagascar.

All the species are trees or shrubs, the leaves usually simple, alternate, and often sticky, without stipules, the flowers usually male or female, borne on separate trees in axillary or terminal racemes, corymbs or panicles, the sepals 2-5, the petals absent, the stamens in the male 5-8, the ovary in the female 3-chambered and 3-angled. The fruit is a 2-6-locular papery capsule, the angles often winged, with 1 or 2 seeds in each chamber.

The genus was named in honour of Rambert Dodoens, or Dodonaeus, a famous physician and author of a book on plants of the Middle Ages who died in 1585.

(437)   *Dodonaea viscosa* Jacq.
          1. var. *viscosa*

= *Ptelea viscosa* L.

(437.1)   2. var. *angustifolia* Benth.

= *Dodonaea thunbergiana* Eckl. & Zeyh.

Sand olive, sandolien, sandolyf, bosysterhout, ysterhoutbos, gansiebos

The sand olive is a tree with a vast distribution growing throughout the tropics of the world. In Africa it occurs from South West Africa, Namaqualand and the south western Cape to the eastern Cape, Natal, Zululand and the Transvaal, northwards to the tropics.

The typical variety grows on rocky wooded hill slopes — it is common on the northern slopes of the hills in the Wonderboom Reserve near Pretoria — on the edge of subtropical forest, in bush, and on wooded sand dunes, particularly in parts of the Zululand coast.

It is a small tree up to about 8 m in height in South Africa. In the Transkei it is common as a shrub growing on old forest land, cultivated and then abandoned, where it serves as shelter for young forest trees.

It is evergreen and usually rather slender, when small leafy, when older often sparse, with a rough, grey, ribbed trunk and glossy leaves borne towards the ends of the branches. The branches are reddish-grey, the twigs smooth, angular, and resinous. The leaves, alternately or spirally arranged, are simple, lance-shaped, often widely so, or a wide oblong, up to 10 cm long and 1.9 cm wide, the tips round or pointed, the base sometimes so narrowed as to appear stalk-like, the midrib prominent both sides and the numerous neat, straight, parallel veins conspicuous, with usually untoothed margins. They secrete a gummy substance which makes them shine, and this is often an aid to indentification.

The small green flowers – stated to be often bisexual – are in branched heads terminally or on the axils of the leaves. The fruits, on slender stalks, are roundish capsules up to 1.9 cm in diameter with 2 or sometimes 3 thin, glistening, pale yellow wings, becoming a purplish red as they mature. They remain on the tree for a long time. The seed is small, black and smooth.

The variety *angustifolia* has often shorter and always narrower leaves, about 4-7 cm long and 4-8 mm wide. These, often somewhat yellowish and shining as if varnished, are a common sight in the scrub on Karoo mountains, on mountains of the south west Cape, and in rocky places in Namaqualand.

The tree is often infested with a white scale.

The foliage does not usually appear to be grazed, probably because of the resinous quality of the leaves. A few cases of possible poisoning when stock have eaten the leaves have been recorded.

Both the varieties are used medicinally to cure a number of ailments – skin diseases, fever, sore throats, influenza, chest complaints, stomach disorders, and cancer. This must be one of South Africa's oldest remedies for the common cold for a decoction of the roots was used as a cold cure by the Hottentots and later by the first colonists. The leaves are supposed to have anaesthetic properties and when chewed to act as a stimulant.

The wood is said to be hard.

The sand olive is one of the few native trees to have been cultivated from early times. It was once used fairly extensively as a hedge plant and may sometimes still be found in old gardens, frequently only a relic and often a decorative one. It germinates easily and is drought and fire resistant. It would probably lend itself to landscape gardening for in nature – against piled rocks or on rocky slopes – it can be picturesque. In the United States it is considered a decorative pot plant.

In various parts of the world this adaptable species is used to bind sand or reclaim marshes.

The specific name is the Latin "viscosus" meaning "sticky" in reference to the gummy leaves. The name of the narrow-leaved variety is a combination of the Latin "angustus' and "folium" meaning "narrow-leaved". The common name of var. *angustifolia,* "ysterhout", originates from the hardness of the wood, while the name "sand olive" or "sand-olyf" is very old. Thunberg recorded it in 1774.

12. *Hippobromus* Eckl. & Zeyh.

Hippobromus is a genus of 1 species only, *Hippobromus pauciflorus* (L.f.) Radlk., which is apparently confined to South Africa and ranges from Port Elizabeth and Humansdorp to the Transvaal.

It is resin-secreting, the leaves alternate, pinnate, ending with a pair of leaflets, the leaflets opposite or alternate; the flowers bisexual or male, in short axillary panicles; the sepals and petals 5, the disc thick, the stamens 8, the ovary roundish and 3-celled. The fruit is roundish, somewhat 3-lobed and 3-celled, the seed flattened on two sides.

According to C.A.Smith, *Hippobromus* is, in a sense, a misnomer. It was given by Ecklon and Zeyher to a plant which they recorded as "paardepis' but in error, for this name belonged to a completely different species, but with similar foliage which possibly led to the confusion.

Hippobromus paucifloros on the Suurberg

This was *Clausena anisata*. They translated the name "paardepis" or "perdepis" into the generic name *Hippobromus,* based on Greek words meaning "horse stench" which would have been a most fitting name for *Clausena anisata,* but is less so for this species which has strong, but not unpleasantly scented leaves.

(438)   *Hippobromus pauciflorus* (L.f.) Radlk.

= *Rhus pauciflora* L.f.; = *Hippobromus alatus* (L.f.) Eckl. & Zeyh.

Horsewood, baster perdepis, isiFutha, ulwAthile (X); u(lu)Qhume (Z)
luTwile (Sw)

A small to medium-sized tree, the horsewood grows from the Uitenhage district through the eastern Cape, Swaziland, Natal, and Zululand to the Transvaal, from sea level to an altitude of at least 1 200 m, in dune bush, in forests, on forest margins, in kloofs — it is common in the kloofs of the Transvaal lowveld — in riverine bush, in scrub, and along streams. Sim says that it is abundant in all forests and scrubs, often forming on the shale formation a large proportion of the tree growth. It is particularly common around Grahamstown.

It is usually 3-9 m tall, slender, the trunk up to about 15 or 20 cm in diameter, or sometimes a densely branched shrub with a rough, grey-brown bark with yellow often showing through, and forming light-coloured strands when broken, and with upright branches which are grey or reddish and finely downy.

It may be evergreen, or sometimes deciduous when the leaves are often a fine yellow colour before they fall. They are alternate, compound, with 3-6 pairs of oval to egg-shaped leaflets 0.8-5 cm long, which

Hippobromus pauciflo-rus: A fruiting branch-let (50%)

are opposite or nearly opposite, arranged about a winged common mid-rib. They are usually unequal-sided and narrowed to the base, and are lobed, toothed, or untoothed, and smooth, except for the midrib which may be hairy and is conspicuous above and below. They are stalked, or more generally without any stalks at all.

The small yellow, cream or reddish, fragrant flowers are in short, dense, velvety panicles in the axils of the leaves. They are produced irregularly throughout the year, although often there is a heavy blooming period in late summer. They are attractive to bees which frequent them throughout the day.

The fruit is round and pea-sized, sometimes slightly lobed, with a small point at the tip, pulpy and black with a rusty-brown calyx. It is said to be inedible.

The seed is black and flattened on two sides.

The timber, although fairly small, is valuable. The sapwood is white with a brown tinge and the heartwood brown. It is heavy and hard and very strong, and is used for a variety of purposes such as wagon-building, hut wattles, and for walking sticks. It contains a resinous substance which makes it burn readily and perhaps because of this, and its scent, it is used by Africans in preparing love charms.

The tree has some unusual uses. The leaves and fruits when beaten in water make a froth like whipped cream which is relished by children. It is said, however, to result in vomiting. Witchdoctors sniff it to produce the necessary foaming of the mouth and nose before falling into a trance.

Bark, leaves and roots are used medicinally by Africans as an emetic, for coughs, diarrhoea and dysentery, the vapour from crushed leaves to ease headaches, the bark to cure hysteria, and for eye inflammation in men and animals. It is said that the liquid from crushed leaves removes the film from calves' eyes.

Watt and Brandwijk say that the leaves are highly poisonous, yet this apparently is not always so for in parts the tree is browsed. Nyala and Black Rhino eat the leaves and rhino eat the bark.

The caterpillar of the butterfly known as the Orange Dog or Christmas butterfly, *Papilio demodocus,* sometimes feeds on the foliage.

In Zululand this is occasionally used as a hedge.

The specific name is based on Latin words meaning "few-flowered".

1372

59 The Sneezewood Family (Ptaeroxylaceae)

This small family of only 2 genera, *Ptaeroxylon* from the southern half of Africa, and *Cedrelopsis* from Madagascar, has in the past been included by some botanists in Sapindaceae, and by others – including Phillips in *The Genera of South African Flowering Plants* – in Meliaceae. It differs from the latter, however, in the arrangement of the stamens which are free and not united in a tube, a characteristic of the flowers in Meliaceae, in the structure of the pollen grains, and in the anatomy of the wood. Modern botanists tend to recognise the group as a separate family, placing it after Sapindaceae.

The family is an aromatic one, the young parts of the trees and shrubs having oil-cavities.

Ptaeroxylon Eckl. & Zeyh.

A genus of 1 species only, this grows across Southern Africa in forest, in bush and in scrub.

It is characterized by leaves that are opposite, compound, and pari-pinnate – pinnate leaves, terminated by a pair of leaflets – flowers that are dioecious (male and female borne on different trees), the calyx small with 4 segments, the petals 4, the disc fleshy, the male with 4 stamens (the filaments free), the female with a 2-chambered ovary. The fruits are capsules, 2-lobed at the tips, splitting into 2 valves, and the seed is winged.

The generic name is based on Greek words meaning "sneezewood", which is the common name of *Ptaeroxylon obliquum* in South Africa, where the tree was first collected.

See colour plate facing page 1003

(292) *Ptaeroxylon obliquum* (Thunb.) Radlk.

= *Rhus obliqua* Thunb.; = *Ptaeroxylon utile* Eckl. & Zeyh.

Sneezewood; umThathi (X); umThathe, uBhaqa (Z); umThathi (Sw) tati (Tsw); munukha-vhaloi (V)

Harvey and Sonder, in *Flora capensis,* knew the sneezewood only as a common tree of the Eastern Province. Now it is recognized as reaching not only Natal, Zululand, Swaziland, and the eastern and northern Transvaal, but Tanzania in the north and Botswana, South West Africa and Angola in the west.

In South Africa it does not occur in the Cape Peninsula or in the Midland forests but it is one of the commonest species in the eastern Cape districts. It seldom occurs in the rain forests of the higher hills and mountains of the interior but when it does – as in East Griqualand,

A sneezewood, *Ptaeroxylon obliquum,* on the Suurberg

Natal, Zululand, and the Transvaal — it is often a very fine tree indeed, hardly recognizable as the same species as the smaller form of dry forests, woodland, bush and scrub, so common, for instance, around Grahamstown, the upper reaches of the Fish River, or in the Natal thornveld. In the Kruger National Park it is usually a shrub only. Apparently it flourishes best on shale and lime.

In the Cape Province it is seldom found growing together with the black stinkwood, *Ocotea bullata.*

As a small tree of scrub forests sneezewood is usually shaped like a slender inverted cone with smooth stems blotched with white and grey or a pale grey-green. In deep forest it grows into a fine tree with a tall clean bole, a trunk 1.2 m in diameter, and smooth whitish-grey bark which becomes slightly fissured with age.

It is sometimes deciduous although not always so. In the Eastern Province it is apt to lose its leaves after a very dry summer and in June and July the colours of the foliage are then remarkable. Yellow, rusty-red and bronze, they are conspicuous among the other vegetation from the mountains round Somerset East towards the coast, yet, strangely, these colours have seldom been recorded.

The leaves are compound and 8-15 cm long, made up of 3-8 pairs of almost stalkless and often opposite leaflets which are usually terminated by a pair of leaflets, the uppermost the biggest, decreasing in size towards the base, conspicuously unequal-sided, the tips rounded or bluntly pointed, the base narrowed, the margins untoothed. As a rule they are small, from 1.3-2.5 cm long and 0.6-1.3 cm wide, although the size depends on the locality, and they may be much bigger. They have close, rather prominent veins and are hairy when young, becoming smooth with age, the common midrib sometimes remaining hairy. They are very bitter to the taste.

The flowers are male or female borne on different trees. They are small, 4-petalled, pale yellow and sweet-smelling, in branched heads in the axils of the leaves or of the fallen leaves. They are often borne in great abundance from spring to early summer turning the whole crown of the tree a pale yellow, as striking against a green background as are the winter colours.

The fruit is a small, light, oblong, 2-lobed capsule, reddish-brown and much-veined, holding 2 light, winged seeds. Sometimes on a hot day the capsules on a tree will all burst open, the 2 lobes parting, and set free the seeds, but the capsules remain on the tree long afterwards. They ripen from early to late summer.

The timber is dark red when freshly cut but changes to brown or golden-brown on exposure. The wood from the coastal districts is reputed to be darker and of better quality than that from the interior. It has a good surface and a satiny lustre and is extremely fine-grained, strong and durable. While alive the tree is, however, subject to heart rot, and young sapwood is apt to decay. Sim remarks that farmers always prefer trees which have been lying dead in the forest for centuries for splitting into fence posts as these are "indestructible".

The wood is now in short supply but in the past was used a great deal in building of all kinds and was widely known for its almost imperishable properties. It was once used for marine works — for the piles through the tidal flats in the construction of the Port Elizabeth-Uitenhage railway, for the early Natal harbour works, and for bridges in Griqualand East.

It makes handsome furniture, understructure poles in house building,

Above
A sneezewood in the Tongaland sand forest

Left
Sneezewood leaves and capsules (50%)

Opposite above
A young sneezewood stem and bark

Opposite below
Bark of an old sneezewood

1376

beams, shoes for perishable timber, and is very popular with farmers for fence poles for these are reputed to resist decay "like a piece of stone". In former times farmers would import sneezewood posts from a long distance away, and in the sheep farming districts of Pearston and Graaff-Reinet many of the first fences were of sneezewood. Some of the posts still stand after 90 years.

The wood, imbued with a pungent oil, is highly inflammable even when green and this is sometimes a drawback for fencing purposes. Wood-cutters used to say that it burnt "like paraffin'. Today farmers sometimes salt away old sneezewood posts to use on special occasions when a particularly bright hot fire is needed. Africans use the wood as tinder and to make fires by friction.

Sim remarks that machine bearings of sneezewood wear longer than those of brass or iron.

There was enormous wastage of sneezewood in the past. Thousands of trees, often perishable sapwood, were cut for sleepers and for telephone posts before the introduction of iron telephone posts. Conservator Hutchins in 1884 reported that a few years before 50,000 immature sneezewood saplings worth many pounds each to the Stutterheim forests, were cut to make worthless telegraph poles. Great quantities of sneezewood were felled for fuel. For years, it is said, on Bathurst commonage alone five lime kilns burned sneezewood and other valuable woods as fuel and one contractor for years supplied 30 loads of sneezewood every month to steam tugs at the Kowie.

When cut, the pungent irritating dust from the wood causes violent sneezing among the workmen using it, giving the tree its common name.

The sawdust and pieces of wood are used to keep moths out of clothes. Thomas Pringle in the last century wrote that sneezewood was said to possess the property of repelling all noxious vermin from its neighbourhood. "On this account it is now much in request for bedsteads throughout the colony", he wrote.

The foliage is sometimes eaten and antelope in particular browse, and often destroy, young plants.

The tree is popular both in medicine and in magic. The powdered wood is used by the Xhosa people to relieve headaches, and it is reputed to be good for sinus and heart complaints, and for rheumatism. The resinous juice which exudes from the heated wood is often applied to warts. It is also used as a wash to kill cattle ticks.

Watt and Brandwijk say that both the Xhosa and Zulu peoples use it as a charm, and that a torch, made of its bark and python fat, is used to discover an evil-doer in a household, the innocent being impervious to the flame and the guilty alone being burnt!

The specific name *obliquum* refers to the oblique, lopsided leaflets. Umtata in the Transkei and Umtati in the Peddie district take their names from the Xhosa and Zulu name "umThathi". *Flora Zambesiaca* suggests that the name of the district Tati in Botswana may be based on the same Zulu name — given by Matabele impis when they found the tree here, far from their Zululand home.

The Zulu name ' uBhaqa" means "torch", because branches are used as torches. The Venda name means "Tree Smelling Evilly of Witches".

The best known members of this family are the plants widely known as kruidjie-roer-my-nie (little-herb-do-not-touch-me), *Melianthus* species, with strong-smelling, often poisonous foliage and flowers with copious nectar attracting bees and sunbirds.

Three genera, all African, belong to the family — *Melianthus* L., a genus of shrubs only; *Bersama* Fresen., and *Greyia* Hook. & Harv. At present the Botanical Research Institute still includes *Greyia* in the family but it is possible that in the future it will recognize the genus as having family rank, when the family will be known as Greyiaceae.

Melianthaceae is characterized by simple or compound leaves with or without stipules; flowers that are usually bisexual, in a terminal or axillary raceme, the calyx segments and petals usually 5, a disc present, the stamens 4-10 placed inside the disc, the ovary superior and 1-4-5-chambered, and the fruit a capsule.

Bersama Fresen.

About 10 species of trees and shrubs are now recognized in this genus which in tropical Africa has proved a difficult group. *Flora Zambesiaca* says that 54 species described from tropical Africa have mostly been united in 1 species, *Bersama abyssinica* Fresen. Five species occur in South Africa and of these, 2 species, *Bersama swinnyi* Phill. and *Bersama stayneri* Phill. were until fairly recently confused with *Bersama tysoniana* Oliv.

A former member of the genus, *Bersama mossambicensis* Sim, has now been placed in a new genus, *Pseudobersama* Verdcourt, in the family Meliaceae.

The genus is characterized by leaves that are imparipinnate — pinnate terminated by 1 leaflet — the stipules intrapetiolar; the flowers male or female, bisexual, in a dense raceme; the sepals and petals 5, a disc present, the stamens usually 4, the ovary 4-5-celled, and the fruit a striking capsule, 4-5-chambered and 4-5 valved, woody or leathery and often covered with protruberances. The seeds are large, often with a waxy aril.

The butterfly popularly known as the Common Hairtail, *Anthene definita,* breeds on members of the genus.

The name *Bersama* is Ethiopian.

Key to Species

A big tree; the leaflets often oblong; untoothed, *smooth;* the flowers in the axils of *silky bracts in a thick, stalkless raceme up to about 5 cm long;* the fruit *a knobbly,* woody capsule about 2.5 cm in diameter (Transkei to Zululand)

a. *B. swinnyi*

A shrub to medium-sized tree; the leaflets often oblong, toothed or untoothed, the lower sides, leaflet stalks, and common midrib *densely hairy;* the flowers in a *dense raceme up to 8 cm long,* borne on a *thick velvety stalk.* The fruit *a knobbly,* woody capsule 2.5-3 cm long. (Transkei to Zululand)

b. *B. stayneri*

A shrub or small tree, the leaflets often egg-shaped, toothed or untoothed, the margins thickened, *smooth, shiny;* the flowers on slender stalks in a *rather lax raceme up to 23 cm long,* on a hairy stalk; the fruit a *rough, hairy capsule,* 1.9 cm long. (Eastern Cape, Natal, Zululand, Swaziland, eastern Transvaal)

c. *B. lucens*

A medium-sized tree; the leaflets often oblong or oval, toothed or untoothed, *smooth both sides;* the flowers in a *shaggy dense* raceme 5-15 cm long borne on a hairy stalk (or nearly stalkless), the fruit *a knobbly woody* capsule about 2.5 cm long. (Eastern Cape, Natal, Zululand, Swaziland, eastern Transvaal)

d. *B. tysoniana*

A shrub to medium-sized tree; the leaflets widely lance-shaped to egg-shaped, toothed or untoothed, *velvety below* and sometimes with *small hairy tufts* in the axils of the veins; the common midrib and leaf stalk velvety, the flowers in *lax racemes* up to 15 cm long; the fruit *a knobbly* capsule, about 1.9 cm long. (Mistbelt forests of the eastern and northern Transvaal).

e. *B. transvaalensis*

(441)   a. *Bersama swinnyi* Phill.

Swinny's bersama; isiNdiyandiya, umHlakaza (Z)

This often tall tree grows, somewhat sparingly, from the Transkei to Zululand, in forests and on forest margins.

Forester H.H. Swinny, after whom the tree was named, claimed that there were two forms of the species, one up to 27 m tall with a stem diameter up to 1 m, and a second which when fully grown had a trunk diameter of only 0.3-0.45 m. The bark is rough and furrowed, the branches velvety when young but becoming smooth with age, the leaves compound — made up of 4-7 pairs of leaflets and a terminal leaflet — crowded towards the ends of the branches.

The leaflets, opposite or nearly opposite, are about 2.5-8 cm long, oblong, egg-shaped to lance-shaped, the tips rounded or pointed, and sometimes notched, the base rounded or slightly narrowed, untoothed, the midrib and lateral veins distinct; smooth; the common leaf stalk hairy when young and smooth when mature.

The flowers, 5-petalled and bisexual, are in a thick, stalkless raceme

Above
Bersama swinnyi: A leaf and the thick stalkless raceme, the flowers in the axils of the bracts, and the knobbly fruit splitting to show the seed (70%)

Left
Bersama stayneri: The leaves, and dense raceme borne on a thick velvety stalk (50%)

1380

up to about 5 cm long, often like a tail or an elongated cone in shape, the individual flowers borne in the axils of silky-haired bracts. They are so closely packed together that their short stalks are not visible. They bloom about January.

The fruits are 4-valved capsules, knobbly, brown, and woody, which split open when mature in late autumn or winter. Within are several oval, red-brown seeds.

This species has in the past been confused with *Bersama tysoniana*. E.P. Phillips, who described the species, noted that its bark had a burning taste lacking in that of both *Bersama tysoniana* and *Bersama stayneri*. This burning is characteristic and very strong and said to dull the taste for hours after the bark has been placed in the mouth. It is used medicinally in the Transkei.

(440)   b. *Bersama stayneri* Phill.

Stayner's bersama

Bersama stayneri grows from the Transkei to Zululand and is fairly common as a small tree or undershrub of upland forest. It grows to about 9 m height and sometimes more.

The bark is thick and rough, the branches smooth or furrowed lengthwise. The foliage is often somewhat grey-green, and young shoots are reddish. The compound leaves have 4-6 pairs of opposite or alternate leaflets and a terminal one, 1.3-10 cm long, lance-shaped to egg-shaped, the tips pointed or rounded, the base slightly narrowed or rounded, the margins untoothed or often toothed in the upper half. Sapling leaves are up to 25 cm long and strongly toothed. The upper surface of the leaflets is smooth, while the lower and the common midrib and leaf stalk are densely hairy. In this they differ from *Bersama tysoniana* which has hairless leaves and petioles.

The shortly stalked flowers are in dense racemes, or spike-like heads, up to 8 cm long, carried on thick, velvety stems, in this differing from *Bersama swinnyi,* the racemes of which are stalkless or nearly so. They bloom about April and May.

The knobbly fruit, up to 2.5 cm or more long, splits to show 4 woody valves. The seeds are oval and reddish, with a waxy yellow aril-like covering at the base.

The bark, with a pronounced bitter but not a burning taste, is used in African medicine. Many trees have been injured through the bark being stripped.

The tree was named after a district forest officer in Natal, F.J. Stayner.

(439)   c. *Bersama lucens* (Hochst.) Szyszyl.

= *Natalia lucens* Hochst.

Shiny-leaf bersama; uNdiyaza (Z)

This is "the shining bersama", a fitting name for this glossy-leaved species which occurs from the north eastern Cape to Natal, Zululand, Swaziland and the eastern Transvaal. It grows in swamp and coastal forest and high inland forest of the interior, on forest margins, in kloofs

Above left
Bersama tysoniana: The leaves, the dense shaggy raceme of flowers, and knobbly fruit (60%)

Above right
Bersama lucens stem

Left
Bersama lucens: A flowering and fruiting branchlet (60%)

1382

and in dune bush — it is found on Durban Bluff — from sea level to an altitude of about 1200 m.

It is not a tall species, seldom exceeding 9 m in height, and usually a shrub or small tree up to 4 m, with grey wrinkled branches, a grey blotched trunk, and handsome dark green, shiny foliage.

The leaves have about 2-4 pairs of leaflets and a terminal leaflet. These are a wide oval or egg-shaped, often wider in proportion to their length than are those of the other bersamas, the tips round or occasionally pointed, the base slightly narrowed, 2.5-9 cm long and 1.3-5 cm wide, the margins thickened and wavy and toothed or untoothed, smooth, the yellow midrib distinct and raised both sides, the lateral veins distinct and branching near the margin. They are shortly stalked.

The small, pale, oval buds with an olive-green calyx, open into greenish-white or dull yellow flowers in a long lax raceme, 8 to about 23 cm in length, borne on a furry stalk terminally or in the axils of the leaves. The individual flowers are carried on distinct slender stalks, very different from the flower stalks of all the other species, and are usually well spaced. They bloom over a long period from about November to June. Flowers and fruit are often borne at the same time.

The fruit is a roundish or oval capsule about the size of a cherry, pale green or brown and rough and hairy, splitting into 4 segments to release the scarlet seed with a white or yellow aril-like covering at one end. They ripen from late summer to winter and are eaten by Vervet Monkeys.

Zulus use the tree medicinally although the leaf and root are reported in Natal to have caused death.

(443)   d. *Bersama tysoniana* Oliv.

Bitter-bark, bastard sneezewood; isiNdiyandiya (Z)

The bitter-bark is usually a medium-sized tree growing from the eastern Cape and the Transkei through Natal, Zululand and Swaziland to the eastern Transvaal, in forest and on forest margins, in coastal and mountain forests, up to an altitude of at least 1500 m.

It grows up to about 9 m high, sometimes — it is reported — larger, with a girth of over 1 m and greyish-brown bark. The compound leaves are borne mainly at the ends of the branches. They have 3-6 pairs of oblong, egg-shaped or widely lance-shaped leaflets and a terminal leaflet, 1.3-6 cm long with the tips rounded or pointed and the base narrowed or rounded, smooth both sides, the margins usually untoothed but sometimes toothed in the upper half, the midrib prominent below. The common leaf stalk is up to 5 cm long and is smooth or hairy.

The creamy-white, strong-smelling flowers on short velvety stalks are in a dense, fat, shaggy, spike-like inflorescence 5-15 cm long which is borne on a hairy stalk or is sometimes almost stalkless. The fruit, ripe about August, is up to about 2.5 cm in diameter, round, woody, knobbly, splitting to release the seeds which are red with a yellow aril-like covering at the base. The thick bunches of fruit are unusual and striking. The tree is said to fruit abundantly.

The bark, which is bitter but without a burning taste, is used in African medicine to cure fever and hysteria and also for gallsickness in cattle. Africans usually cut the bark from the living tree.

The species was named after William Tyson, F.L.S. a schoolmaster and an indefatigable botanical collector, who was born in Jamaica in 1851 and died in Grahamstown in 1920.

Above
Bersama transvaalensis: a leaf, the lax, spike-like inflorescence, and the spiky fruits (100%)

Below left
Greyia sutherlandii, the Natal bottlebrush: flowers and young leaves (50%)

1384

(442)   e. *Bersama transvaalensis* Turrill

White essenwood, witessenhout

The white essenwood is a tree of the mistbelt forests of the eastern and northern Transvaal, growing to an altitude of about 1800 m.

It is an evergreen shrub to medium-sized tree with a shady dense crown, fairly frequent in forest undergrowth, on forest margins, in wooded kloofs, and on mountain slopes.

The leaves usually have 2-4 pairs of widely lance-shaped to egg-shaped leaflets and a terminal one, 1.3-10 cm long and 0.8-5 cm wide, bluntly or sharply pointed, narrowed to the base, the midrib and lateral veins conspicuous, the latter forking and looping along the margin, the margins generally untoothed although the upper part of the leaf is occasionally toothed, the leaflets on young growth toothed (and large), the underside of the leaves velvety, sometimes with small hairy tufts in the axils of the veins. The common midrib and stalk are velvety.

The creamy-green, stalked flowers with a silky calyx are in lax, spike-like inflorescences, up to 15 cm long, and bloom about November.

The fruit, ripe from late summer to autumn, is a roundish capsule, up to about 1.9 cm long, spiky or knobbly, splitting to release orange seeds. They are borne in long bunches and are curious and handsome.

The specific name means "of the Transvaal".

Greyia Hook. & Harv.

This small and bright-flowered genus of 3 described species from the eastern parts of South Africa is not very closely related to the other genera in the family Melianthaceae, and is considered by some botanists to be a separate family, Greyiaceae.

The members are shrubs or small trees with simple, alternate, roundish leaves crowded towards the ends of the branches, the margins roundly toothed and often lobed, without stipules; the flowers bisexual, red, showy, in racemes; the calyx with 5 segments, the petals 5, the disc fleshy and 10-lobed, and the stamens 10 and long and protruding. The fruit is a 5-grooved capsule.

An undescribed species with rough hairy leaves and long slender racemes of flowers comes from Haenertsberg in the north eastern Transvaal.

The genus was named in honour of Sir George Grey, 1812-1898, Governor of the Cape Colony in the second part of the 19th century, a great patron of botany and of Africana generally.

Key to species

The leaves *smooth or minutely glandular;* the flowers in *dense terminal* racemes. (Transvaal, eastern Orange Free State, Natal, Swaziland, eastern Cape)

a. *G. sutherlandii*

The leaves smooth or hairy above, and below covered with a *dense white felt;* the flowers in a *dense terminal* raceme. (Eastern Transvaal, Zululand, Swaziland)

b. *G. radlkoferi*

The leaves *smooth or slightly hairy or glandular;* the flowers in *lax, few-flowered* racemes *below the young growth.* (Transkei and eastern Cape)

c. *G. flanaganii*

Above
Greyia radlkoferi

OPPOSITE

Above left
Greyia flanaganii, an illustration from *Icones
Plantarum,* published in
1895

Above right
Greyia sutherlandii bark

Below
Greyia sutherlandii,
Oliviershoek, the Dra-
kensberg

(446)   a. *Greyia sutherlandii* Hook. & Harv.

Natal bottlebrush, mountain bottlebrush, baakhout; isiDwadwa, inDalu, uBande, umBunge (Z)

The Natal bottlebrush grows as a shrub or a small tree mainly on the slopes and rocky ridges of the Drakensberg up to an altitude of about 1800 m, from the eastern Cape, through the eastern Orange Free State, Natal and Swaziland to the eastern Transvaal. It is a common tree on the mountain sides over Oliviershoek, the steep pass between Harrismith in the Orange Free State and Natal, and on the steep slopes in the Royal Natal National Park.

Young trees are compact and leafy but old trees, although never tall, are rugged with a spread of up to 11 m and with rough dark trunks. They are deciduous and in late autumn the leaves turn shades of bright red.

The leaves are simple, alternate, rather leathery, the surface hairless and minutely glandular, somewhat heart-shaped, oval, or with a flat base, up to 8-13 in diameter, slightly lobed and coarsely toothed, the veins radiating from the base, borne on long straight stalks. They are often mistaken for *Pelagonium* leaves.

This is a gay and beautiful little tree in spring, when its brilliant red flowers, with oblong petals and long protruding stamens, open in closely packed racemes at the ends of the branches, which are then bare, or bearing the first young green leaves. The flowers are rich in nectar, attracting many insects. Africans are said to make beer from it.

The fruit is a somewhat cylindrical capsule.

The wood is a pale pink and generally light and soft, used by Africans to make dishes and for carving. Some farmers — surprisingly — maintain they make good and lasting fencing posts, durable above and below ground.

The Natal bottlebrush is sometimes cultivated and the demand for it is slowly increasing. Once it is well known it is sure of popularity for it is hardy, fairly drought resistant, under suitable conditions quick-grow-ing, never becoming too big for even a small garden, seldom — in cultiva-tion — exceeding 3m. A well-drained soil is essential. It can be grown from seed, cuttings, or suckers. Suckers, potted one year, have been known to flower the next.

The specific name honours Peter Cormack Sutherland, M.D. (Aber-deen) — 1822 to 1900 — who was appointed Surveyor-General of Natal in 1855 and made many plant collections during his term of office. He was the first to send specimens of the tree to England.

The common name "bottlebrush" suggests the resemblance of the flowers to those of the common cultivated bottlebrush of the Australian genus *Callistemon.* The Zulu name isiDwadwe means "the apron leaf". In Zululand the flowers, as apart from the tree, are called inDluze.

The species is often confused with a close relative, *Greyia radlkoferi,* or the Transvaal bottlebrush, which has leaves with the under-surface densely felted and petals that are narrowed to the base, whereas the leaves of the Natal bottlebrush are smooth and the petals oblong.

(445)   b. *Greyia radlkoferi* Szyszyl.

Transvaal bottlebrush, wild bottlebrush, baakhout; inDlebelembila (Sw)

The Transvaal bottlebrush grows mainly in the mist-belt mountains — often on mountain tops — of the eastern Transvaal and also in Zululand near Ngome, and in Swaziland.

It is a shrubby tree 3-4.6 m high, usually with several crooked stems, thick dark brown bark, and leaves crowded towards the ends of the sturdy branches.

The leaves are simple and alternate, heart-shaped to oval, with a notched base, usually up to about 13 cm long, coarsely toothed and somewhat lobed, veined from the base, above hairy when young and later almost smooth, and below silver-white and densely velvety, especially when young. This dense felt may be used as a character to separate the Transvaal from the Natal bottlebrush, *Greyia sutherlandii*, which has smooth leaves. Occasionally intermediates occur.

In early spring the handsome scarlet flowers bloom in upright racemes at the ends of the bare branches. They are up to 2.5 cm or more long and have petals slightly narrowed to the base and long protruding stamens. The fruit is a cylindrical capsule up to 1.3 cm in length which splits open at one end to release the small seed.

Aphids sometimes infest the tree. Dudley D'Ewes once watched white-eyes methodically working over the flowers and young green shoots to find these.

The tree can be raised from seed or from cuttings.

The specific name honours Ludwig Radlkofer (1829-1927), Professor of Botany and Director of the Botanical Museum in Munich, who published papers covering a period of 70 years. The Swazi name means "dassie's ear".

(444)   c. *Greyia flanaganii* H.Bol.

Flanagan's bottlebrush, uSinga lwamaxhegokazi (X)

This is a shrub or small branching tree growing on grassy, rocky slopes in the eastern Cape and the Transkei.

The leaves much resemble those of the other species of *Greyia*. They are roundish, lobed, usually toothed, 5-10 cm long, smooth or slightly hairy or glandular, the veins spreading from the base.

The bright red, stalked flowers up to about 2.5 cm long, in racemes, are few and hang downwards and never make the fine, dense, upright inflorescences so typical of the other wild bottlebrushes. The capsule resembles those of the other species of the genus.

The species was named after Henry George Flanagan, 1861-1919, South African born collector and traveller, and owner of Prospect Farm in the Transkei Territory where he developed a noted garden containing rare exotics as well as South African trees and shrubs.

The Xhosa name means "the thread of the old women".

61 The Blinkblaar Family (Rhamnaceae)

Rhamnaceae is a large family with 51 genera and, according to Phillips, over 600 species, spread throughout the warm countries of the world.

Nine genera occur in South Africa and of these 7 include species that are trees. One species, *Ziziphus mucronata* Willd., is one of the commonest and best-known trees of South and South West Africa, while another, *Lasiodiscus mildbraedii* Engl., which has been collected a few times in the forests of Zululand, is one of the rarest.

This is an important family biologically for the edible fruits of *Ziziphus, Berchemia,* and *Scutia* species, in particular, are often borne in abundance and are eaten by birds, wild animals, domestic stock, sometimes by country people, and always by children. The rather insignificant flowers are nectar-bearing and often yield a good honey. Many species are used in medicine and magic.

The family is characterized by simple leaves which are usually alternate, and with stipules; and by small flowers that are most often bisexual, in cymes, umbels, spikes or heads, the calyx with 4-5 lobes, the petals 4-5 (or absent), a disc usually present, the stamens 4-5, the ovary superior or more or less inferior, usually 4-5-chambered, and fruit that may be a drupe or a capsule which is sometimes situated within the calyx tube.

Key to Genera

Fruit a drupe

Stipular spines usually present; the leaves alternate, with 3 conspicuous veins from the base.

1. *Ziziphus*

Spines (not stipular) usually present; the leaves opposite, pinnately veined.

3. *Scutia*

Spines absent; the leaves usually alternate, pinnately veined, the margins not toothed, the fruit 2-chambered.

2. *Berchemia*

Spines absent; the leaves alternate or nearly opposite; the margins usually closely and finely (if sometimes inconspicuously) toothed; the fruit 2-4-chambered.

4. *Rhamnus*

Above
The blinkblaar-wag-'n-bietjie, *Ziziphus mucronata*, at Leeubron near Okaukuejo, South West Africa

Below left
A tall blinkblaar on the Vaal River at Parys

Below right
Flowering and fruiting twigs (50%)

Opposite
Ziziphus mucronata trunk and bark

Fruit a capsule

The leaves alternate, 5-7 cm long, fairly thin, oval-shaped or oblong, the tips blunt or round, the margins not inrolled, stipules absent; the capsule marked towards the *base* with the remains of the calyx.

5. *Noltia*

The leaves alternate, usually small, hard, pointed, sometimes needle-like, with the margins often deeply inrolled, the stipules usually absent; the capsule *crowned* with the base of the old calyx tube.

6. *Phylica*

The leaves opposite, thin, papery (in South Africa), the stipules *between* the leaf stalks, the capsule velvety, the base of the calyx tube showing as a line *in the middle* but not very conspicuous.

7. *Lasiodiscus*

1. *Ziziphus* Mill.

This large genus of — according to Phillips — about 138 species native to Africa, tropical America, Australia, and the Mediterranean countries, is represented in South and South West Africa by about 3 species, the widespread *Ziziphus mucronata* Willd., the dwarf *Ziziphus zeyheriana* Sond. of the Transvaal grassveld, and by the rather rare *Ziziphus rivularis* Codd of the northern and eastern Transvaal.

The species most widely — if indirectly — known is *Ziziphus jujuba* Lam., the fruit of which makes the jujube of commerce.

Historically the genus is of interest. Christ's crown of thorns is supposed to have been made of the branches of *Ziziphus spina-christi* Willd., a species resembling our native *Ziziphus mucronata* but which grows from central Africa northwards.

The species are trees or shrubs, often spiny, with simple, usually alternate leaves, often 3-5-veined from the base, small, bisexual flowers in short axillary cymes, the calyx lobes and petals 5, a disc present, the stamens 5, the ovary superior and usually 2-celled. The fruit is a drupe.

The generic name is based on the Arabic "zizouf", the name of the lotus, *Ziziphus lotus* Lam.

(447) *Ziziphus mucronata* Willd.

Blinkblaar-wag-'n-bietjie, buffalo-thorn, buffelsdoring; umPhafa (X); umPhafa, umLahlankosi, isiLahla, umKhobonga (Z); umLahlabantu (Sw); mphasamhala (Tso); mokgalo (Tsw); mokgalô, moonaona (NS); mukhalu, mutshetshete (V); monganga (Kol); omukaru (Her); omukekete (Ov), /aros (Nama)

The buffalo-thorn, or as it is more frequently known, the blinkblaar-wag-'n-bietjie, is a familiar tree or shrub is many parts of South Africa, often with mistletoe or "matches" in its rather drooping crown, In late winter and early spring when the foliage is sparse the dark mounds of mistletoe in the branches are very obvious, giving the crowns a distinctive appearance in the bush.

The tree does not usually grow in dense forest but is widely distributed in open scrub, on rocky koppies, in grassveld, bushveld and woodland, on forest margins and on stream banks, growing in a variety of soils across most of South Africa with the exception of the central and south western Cape, and in South West Africa and Botswana, and from there occurring northwards across Africa to Ethiopia and Arabia.

In parts its presence is believed to indicate underground water.

It is usually a shrub or a medium-sized tree up to 9 m tall, and sometimes bigger in Natal and Zululand, with spreading, often drooping branches and a trunk that is frequently crooked, branching either well above ground or near the base. The bark is grey-brown and smooth when young (and often spiny), but becomes darker brown and fissured with age.

The glossy, shiny, rather drooping foliage is irregularly deciduous, and the leaves are easily identified for they are characteristically and conspicuously 3-nerved from the base, and the edges are more or less serrated (and often badly eaten by insects). They are simple and alternate, egg-shaped, oval or widely lance-shaped, the tips bluntly or sharply pointed, the base often heart-shaped and sometimes unequal-sided, 2.5-8 cm long and 1.9 cm to nearly 8 cm broad, shiny, densely hairy to quite smooth. The twigs, leaf stalks and veins are often covered with fine hairs, especially when young.

A form with leaves covered with coarse brown hairs occurs in the Caprivi Strip and in Botswana. This is subspecies *rhodesica* R.B.Drummond.

The stipules take the form of small thorns at the nodes, one straight and one hooked, but one or both of these may be missing. For all their smallness, these thorns are strong and extremely sharp and when arming the long, flexible, whippy branches they are found to have diabolic powers. They give the tree its common name of "wait-a-little". Completely thornless trees are sometimes, although rarely, found and more often an almost thornless tree will have an occasional thorny branch.

The small, greenish, bisexual flowers bloom irregularly from late spring until autumn, the heaviest blooming often being in spring and summer. They are borne in short, smooth or hairy clusters in the axils of the leaves and are attractive to insects of all kinds — bees, wasps, beetles and flies. Beekeepers consider this a valuable tree.

When in fruit in late summer or autumn this is conspicuous for its branches are loaded with round fruits, sometimes no bigger than peas, at others as big as cherries, red-brown or deep red, smooth and shiny, with a leathery skin and a thin layer of slightly sweetish, mealy pulp surrounding a large solitary seed. They often remain on the tree after the leaves have fallen.

Although this cannot be counted a very palatable fruit, it plays an important role ecologically. It is eaten by all the primitive peoples of Africa, and has been since time immemorial, either fresh or dried, in meal and in porridge. During the Anglo-Boer War the stones were roasted and ground by Europeans as a coffee substitute, and it is said that such coffee is still made in parts.

Birds of many species eat the fruits, as do wild animals such as monkeys, warthogs, impala, nyala, Black Rhino, rats and mice. The leaves are browsed by domestic stock and by wild animals from impala, nyala, and kudu to giraffe and rhino. Giraffes are reputed to be especially fond of them. According to Ranger N.N. Deane, a branch was customarily used in the Hluhluwe Game Reserve to entice a young bottle-reared giraffe away from the buildings into his own quarters.

Butterflies of several species breed on the tree, including the Hintza Blue, *Castalius hintza*, which is often to be seen in wooded places in the eastern parts of the country, usually near a blinkblaar-wag-'n-bietjie tree. Two other members of the genus, the White Pie, *Castalius calice*, and Black Pie, *Castalius melaena*, a bushveld species, also breed on the tree, as does the Dotted Blue, *Tarucus sybaris*, common in the eastern parts of the country.

The wood is yellow or, according to Galpin, pinkish-white, light, of medium strength, tough and elastic with a twisted grain, warping badly and not very durable. It is sometimes used for wagon parts and for fencing posts. Today whips are made from saplings and from the flexible shoots, and once bows were made from them. The wood is good fuel.

Thorny branches are sometimes used to make kraals.

The medicinal and magic uses of the tree are many and varied. The bark, leaves and roots are used to treat, among other things, chest troubles, dysentery, swollen glands, infectious diseases such as measles, and for lumbago. Watt and Brandwijk say that for pain of any sort Africans frequently apply a poultice of meal made with a root decoction, or powdered baked root, "the poultice being eaten thereafter".

The roots make a Zulu toothache cure of interest. "Dig around the roots", says the recipe. "Tie the selected root with string. Carry the piece which is tied to a pot. Make an infusion. Do not at any time touch with the hand. Soak the tooth in the infusion three times a day".

Zulus also use the pounded leaves as a poultice on a boil, and the bark in a steam bath to purify the complextion, or as an emetic.

Zulus use the branches to attract the ancestral spirits from an old dwelling site to a new one. They call it umLahlankosi, "that buries the chief", as it was once customary to put branches on a chief's grave. In other parts, Africans drag a branch round a village to protect it from harm (its thorns having power to hold evil at bay). In Griqualand West the African people will not cut the blinkblaar during the summer as they believe that drought, hail, or lightning would follow such an action. The vaalboom and swarthaak are sometimes preserved for the same reason.

There it is also believed that the blinkblaar wards off lightning and that anyone standing under one in a storm will be safe.

This is a species very easily raised from seed. It is adaptable, growing in all types of soil, and standing intense heat and cold equally well. It is drought-resistant, and under good conditions will reach a height of 4-6 m in four or five years. Although one of our loveliest and most ornamental trees, it is so common that it is usually scorned, yet, particularly if the thornless form is planted, it is an unusually good garden tree and branches can easily be pruned into shape.

In the wide landscapes it often favours in the wild, this tree is as evocative as the sweet-thorn. The artist, Walter Battiss, remembering a blinkblaar of his childhood near Koffiefontein in the Orange Free State, wrote that it was the only tree along 24 km of road, so exciting that he longed to count and feel each glossy leaf.

The specific name *mucronata* is Latin meaning "pointed", probably in reference to the sharp thorns. The origin of the common name "blinkblaar-wag-'n-bietjie" or "shiny-leaved-wait-a-bit" is obvious to all who have been grasped by its ferocious thorns.

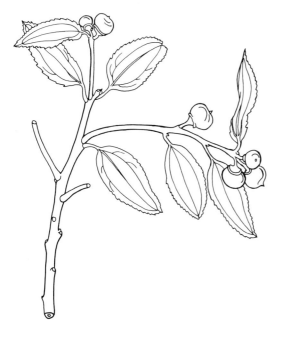

Above left
The bird plum, *Berchemia discolor,* near Waterpoort, northern Transvaal

Above right
Berchemia discolor: A fruiting twig (60%)

Below left
Ziziphus rivularis: A fruiting twig (60%)

Opposite
The bird plum bark

1394

(448)   *Ziziphus rivularis* Codd

River blinkblaar

"The ziziphus of the stream" is aptly named for this little tree of the northern and eastern Transvaal and Mozambique usually occurs on river banks, often among rocks. The most accessible trees are probably the group growing on the rocky slopes above the stream bed in Wyllie's Poort in the northern Transvaal.

This is usually a shrub or a small tree up to about 6 m high with a slender trunk or trunks and many wide-spreading, slender, drooping, velvety branches covered at intervals with knobs. The stem bark is grey and smooth, becoming brown and rough with age.

The leaves are crowded towards the ends of the branches. They are simple, 2.5-6 cm long and 0.6-4 cm wide, lance-shaped (sometimes widely so), pointed, the base rounded and often unequal-sided, finely toothed, conspicuously 3-veined from the base, the upper side deep glossy green, the lower side lighter, the nerves below and the margin slightly hairy when young but becoming smooth with age.

The tree is without any thorns at all.

The small flowers are in short clusters of 1-5 in the axils of the leaves. The ovary is 3-celled, an unusual feature in the genus, and the fruit is small, round, the size of a large pea, and usually 3-celled and 3-seeded.

This little tree has probably never been cultivated, but — if seed becomes available — might be easy and should be decorative.

2. *Berchemia* Neck. ex DC.

Phillips records over 40 species as belonging to this genus, occurring in Japan, China, the Philippine Islands, and in Southern Africa. Two species grow in South Africa and 1 in South West Africa. Until recently these species were included in the genus *Phyllogeiton*. Modern botanists, however, do not support their separation from *Berchemia*.

All these are shrubs or trees without thorns and with simple, alternate leaves, with small stipules; bisexual flowers, the calyx lobes and petals 5, a disc present, the stamens 5, the ovary usually 2-chambered, and the fruit a 2-celled drupe.

The genus was named after a French botanist, M. Berchem.

(449)   *Berchemia discolor* (Klotzsch) Hemsl.

= *Scutia discolor* Klotzsch; = *Phyllogeiton discolor* (Klotzsch) Herzog

Bird plum, wild almond, mountain date, wilde dadel; umMumu, uBalatsheni likulu (Z), nyiyi (Tso); mutsintsila (Tsw); muhukhuma (V); mozinzila (Sub); omuve (Her); omuve (Ov)

This tropical species, occurring in Arabia and widely spread from Ethiopia to South Africa, extends in Southern Africa from the northern and eastern Transvaal and Zululand to South West Africa, growing in dry forest, open bushveld and woodland, on wooded hillsides and on stream banks. It is not a very common species. It is, however, one of the trees marked in the Kruger National Park and a tree grows in the Skukuza Rest Camp so that thousands of people must have at least a slight acquaintance with it.

Although it can grow into a big tree 18 m tall, it is more often in South Africa a medium-sized tree up to 9 to 12 m, with spreading branches and a dense round crown of shiny green foliage.

The bark varies from a light grey cracked into small segments to dark brown and rough, cracked into large segments and sometimes peeling in pieces. The twigs are smooth or hairy.

The leaves are simple and usually opposite or nearly so, although those towards the bottom of the shoots are inclined to be alternate. They are distinctive and handsome, dark green above and paler below, 2.5-10 cm long and up to 8 cm broad, oval, sometimes broadly so, the tips pointed, bluntly pointed or flattish, the base round or narrowed, the margins untoothed, smooth or with the veins slightly hairy. The 5-8 pairs of lateral veins run fairly steeply upwards from the midrib to the very edge of the leaf, parallel to one another, these and the midrib raised below and beautifully neat and even. They resemble those of the red ivory, *Berchemia zeyheri* (Sond.) Grubov., but are larger.

Giraffe browse the leaves and shoots.

This is usually a deciduous tree, the new leaves appearing in the spring at about the same time as the inconspicuous flowers. These are borne in small stalked clusters in the axils of the leaves from about October to December. They are bisexual and give rise to fruits — ripe from March to May — like small pointed plums, about 1.3-1.9 cm long, yellow to reddish, consisting of a sweet yellow pulp and a kernel holding 2 seeds.

The sugar content of the pulp of these is high — about 30 per cent when fresh and probably higher when dry — and so is often used by Africans in place of sugar. They eat the fruits raw or dried. When dry — according to Dr. A.le R. van der Merwe — they resemble sultanas and can be stored for a long time. The Venda, he says, pound the dried flesh to make a meal which, mixed with the seeds of the wild grasses, *Eleusine coracan* Asch. & Gr., (wild millet), and *Pennisitum typhoides* Stapf. & C.E.Hubb (Kaffir manna), is kneaded into a biscuit dough and baked or steamed. The meal is reputed to keep well even when raw.

The Vitamin C content of the pulp is 65 mb/100 gr.

The fruits are popular also with monkeys, and birds which give the tree its common name "bird plum". Loeries and Green Pigeons, in particular, are fond of them.

The wood is resinous, yellow-brown and close-grained, hard and strong, and made by country people into furniture — excellent furniture it is said. Africans use it for sharpened sticks and knobkerries, knife handles, poles for huts and grain stores, and for fuel. In Ngamiland tobacco pipes are fashioned from it.

The wood and bark yield a brown or purple dye which in South West Africa is used for dyeing baskets. There, too, the fruits are used by young girls as hair ornaments.

Zulu herbalists use the bark extensively and in parts a decoction of the leaves forms a poultice.

It is not known how the tree thrives in cultivation.

The name *discolor* means "of different colours", indicating that the colours of the two sides of the leaves are unalike. Although the Herero know the tree as omuve, they call the fruits ozombe.

(450)   *Berchemia zeyheri* (Sond.) Grubov.

= *Rhamnus zeyheri* Sond.; = *Phyllogeiton zeyheri* (Sond.) Suesseng.

Red ivory, rooi ivoor, rooihout; umNini (X); umNini, umNcaka, um-

Neyi, umGologolo (Z); umNeyi (Sw); moye (Tsw — Mal); monee (NS)
muniane, munia-niane, muhukhuma (V)

Unlike its tropical relative, the bird plum, *Berchemia discolor*, the red
ivory is a species of Southern Africa only, growing from the Transvaal,
Natal, Zululand and Swaziland to Mozambique, Rhodesia and westwards to Botswana.

It is a tree of bushveld, woodland and rocky hillsides, stony ridges
and bushy stream banks. Particularly beautiful specimens grow near the
Pienaars River Dam and the Haartebeestpoort Dam close to Pretoria,
and at least one tree has been preserved in a Pretoria garden.

Although the red ivory is usually a fairly small bushy tree it can grow
up to 12 m in height with a stem up to 36 cm in diameter and with a
round, leafy crown. The bark is grey to light brown, when young smooth
but later rough and cracked into longitudinal segments.

The foliage is luxuriant and delicate. The leaves are simple and opposite or nearly opposite and resemble those of the bird plum except that
they are much smaller, in South Africa usually only 2.5-4 cm long although occasionally up to 6 cm. They are a neat oval or oblong, or
sometimes widest at the base, the tips round or bluntly pointed, the
base round or narrowed, the lateral nerves parallel and reaching to the
very edge of the leaf, these and the midrib being prominent below. They
are bright green when young and grey-green when mature. The veins on
the under-sides, the leaf stalks and young twigs are often a reddish-purple
colour. The leaf stalks are short and slightly twisted.

The tree is sometimes evergreen but usually deciduous, and in winter
the leaves often turn a clear golden colour.

The small pale green flowers are borne singly or a few grouped together on long slender stalks in the axils of the leaves. They give rise to
smooth fruits very much like those of *Berchemia discolor*, usually 0.6-
1.3 cm long, oval, or widest at the base, pointed, smooth, green turning
yellow or red when mature, with a thin layer of flesh surrounding a
2-seeded kernel. They are edible, with a pleasant flavour and much
sought after.

Galpin in *Native Timber Trees of the Springbok Flats* says that in
Spelonken, near Munnik in the north eastern Transvaal, where red ivory
trees grow in profusion, their drupes are larger and sweeter than the
usual fruits. Africans collect and store the surplus fruits in grain-storing
baskets where they form a solid brown, sugary mass. They are a great
delicacy and a concentrated ration on a long journey. Fruits are also
stored and dried in the sun for stamping and mixing with porridge. They
are said to make a good jam.

Animals such as monkeys, bushbabies and goats relish the fruits, as
do many species of birds, including toppies, barbets, starlings, loeries,
doves and Green Pigeons. Impala and nyala eat both fruit and leaves
and porcupines eat the bark.

Red ivory timber is famous for quality and colour. The sapwood is
yellow and the heartwood pink to bright red becoming duller on exposure. It has a particularly fine texture and a curly grain, polishes well
and is extremely hard, strong, durable, and resistent to insect attack and
to decay. C.P. Kromhout says that turning is easy and that it saws well
but is difficult to plane. The wood being heavy and dense, he writes,
takes an exceptionally long time to become air-dried.

Africans use it for knobkerries, sharpened sticks, and hut poles. In
parts of Zululand this is considered a royal tree, chiefs alone carrying

Above
Red ivory bark — Zulu-
land

Below
Red ivory bark — the
Transvaal

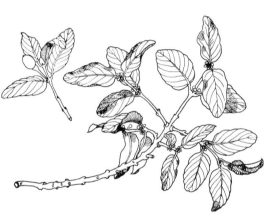

Above
Red ivory trees, *Berchemia zeyheri,* near Hartebeestpoort Dam

Centre left
Flowering and fruiting twigs (50%)

Centre right
Scutia myrtina: A fruiting branch (40%)

Below left
Scutia myrtina near Hankey, Eastern Province

1398

knobkerries made of it. The wood is much sought after for carving.

The leaves have an unusual use. When carrying buckets of water Zulus will sometimes place the leaves on the surface of the water to keep it from spilling.

The tree is used medicinally. Africans smoke the powdered root as a headache cure and the powdered bark as an enema. The bark is said to be poisonous.

The specific name honours K.L.P. Zeyher, famous German botanist and collector in South Africa. In Rhodesia the tree is often known as "pink ebony".

3. *Scutia* Comm. ex Brongn.

Scutia is a small genus of about 14 species which are native to Africa, Madagascar and Brazil. One species occurs fairly widely in South Africa.

The species may be small trees, shrubs or climbers, spiny or spineless; the leaves are simple and usually opposite, the stipules small and deciduous; the flowers are bisexual, in a group or umbel in the axils of the leaves; the calyx lobes, petals and stamens 5, a disc present, the ovary superior, 2-4-chambered, the fruit an oval or roundish 2-celled drupe, the seeds 1-4.

The generic name is based on the Latin "scutum" meaning "shield".

(451) *Scutia myrtina* (Burm.f.) Kurz

= *Rhamnus myrtina* Burm.f.; = *Scutia commersonii* Brongn.

Droog-my-keel, drogies, spingle, cat-thorn, katdoring, katnael, isiPhingo, umSondezo, umQapuna, umQaphula, umQokwane (X); isiPinga, uSondela, uSondeza, uSondelangange (Z)

The droog-my-keel may be a small tree, a sprawling shrub, or a robust climber, and in one form or another has a tremendously wide distribution from Africa to India. In South Africa it occurs from Cape Town eastwards through Swellendam and Knysna to the eastern Cape — where it is abundant — and northwards through the Transkei and the Orange Free State, Natal and Zululand to the central and northern Transvaal. It extends from here through Rhodesia and Mozambique to Malawi, Kenya and Uganda.

In South Africa it grows from sea level to an altitude of at least 1200 m, on coastal sand dunes, where it is often only a low sprawling shrub, in thick evergreen coastal and inland bush — it is particularly common in parts of the eastern Cape and is dominant in the bush around Grahamstown, often making a very dense, thick bush — in scrub, on steep wooded hillsides, in mountain forest where it may be a spindly tree or a robust woody climber scrambling over tall trees which are often killed by the dense foliage. It is common in Natal as a creeper.

As a tree it is usually small or medium-sized, seldom above 6 m high — often eaten down or trimmed by stock — spreading and usually many-stemmed, the trunk with rough, brown, corky bark, the branches slender, the twigs smooth. Its most outstanding characteristic is its thorniness. Although sometimes the spines or prickles are absent, usually the branches are armed with small, strong, curved thorns, rather like rose thorns in shape, in the axils of the leaves.

The smooth, shiny, leathery leaves are in nearly opposite pairs. They

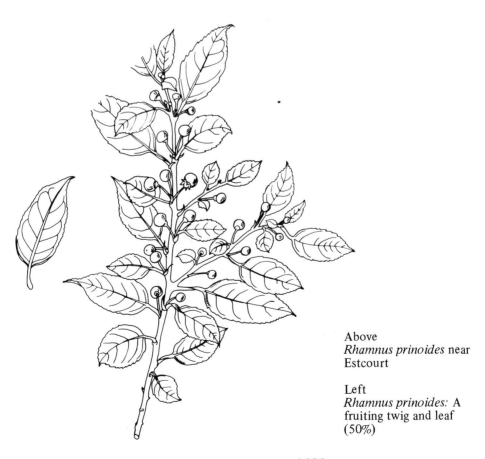

Above
Rhamnus prinoides near
Estcourt

Left
Rhamnus prinoides: A
fruiting twig and leaf
(50%)

1400

are often small, 0.8-2.5 cm long, but sometimes up to 7 cm in length, oblong, oval, or egg-shaped, the tips pointed, rounded, flat, or notched, the base rounded or narrowed, the margin untoothed or sometimes slightly toothed, the margins often rolled backwards making a pronounced rim on the lower side, the secondary veins in about 5-8 pairs. The leaves are shiny above and duller below and are shortly stalked.

The small, greenish-white, sweet-scented flowers are borne — from late spring to about January — in small, short bunches in the axils of the leaves and are often visited by wasps and flies, and by white-eyes which apparently much enjoy the nectar. They are bisexual and develop into small egg-shaped fruits, usually about the size of a pea but sometimes smaller or larger, with a broad, saucer-like calyx, borne singly or in a small, long-stalked bunch. These ripen in late summer and in autumn. They are green and turn red and later purple, or bluish-black, often with a waxy bloom, and have a thin layer of flesh and 2 stones. These fruits are the "drogies" — the little dry ones — of children and beloved by them. They dry the throat very noticeably, hence the most widely used common name "droog-my-keel" or "dry-my-throat". They are also eaten by many species of birds such as Green Pigeons, toppies, barbets and guineafowl.

This is an important fodder plant, the foliage being devoured by stock and wild animals such as kudu, which browse the tree heavily. In drought time farmers often cut branches as feed for their domestic stock.

The wood is usually too small to be of much use. It is a lustrous light brown colour, dense, fine-grained and strong.

Like many thorny species, this is used by Africans as a protective charm.

The specific name means "myrtle-like". The common names "cat-thorn" and "katdoring" refer to the sharp, hooked thorns. The name "spingle" or "spindle", used by English-speaking people along the coast of the Eastern Province, is a corruption of the Xhosa isiPhingo.

The Xhosa and Zulu name "umSondezo" means, according to Ferreira, "that which is brought near", denoting a form of offering to the ancestral spirits "to keep them near and in sympathy with the affairs of their living descendants". A Zulu name "uSondelangange" has both humour and point in view of the thorny branches. It means "Approach and let me kiss".

4. *Rhamnus* L.

About 260 species, spread throughout all the continents of the world and the Pacific Islands, belong to this genus. One tree species grows widely in South Africa.

Members of the genus are small trees or shrubs with simple leaves that are alternate, opposite, or in tufts, and with small stipules, usually early deciduous; and flowers that are usually bisexual in a raceme or cyme in the axils of the leaves, the calyx lobes, petals and stamens 4-5, the ovary superior and 2-4-chambered, and fruit that is an often fleshy, roundish or oval drupe.

Rhamnus is an ancient Greek name signifying "a tuft of branches".

(452)   *Rhamnus prinoides* L'Hérit.

Mofifi, dark blinkblaar, dogwood, hondepishout; umGlindi (X);
umGilindi, uNyenye, umHlinye (Z); liNyenye (Sw); mofifi (SS)

This widespread species reaches from about Swellendam through the
eastern Cape, Orange Free State and Lesotho to the Transkei, Natal,
Swaziland, and the eastern and north eastern Transvaal, and northwards
through tropical Africa to Ethiopia, growing from sea level to an altitude
of about 2100 m, on mountain and wooded hill slopes, in forests, on
forest fringes and on stream banks, frequently among rocks.

Often, in the high, grassy, cold country of the north eastern Cape
this little tree is conspicuous. It grows, among other places, in numbers
between Mount Fletcher and Maclear, and in Natal between Estcourt
and Giants Castle where it is dominant over a section of the countryside.

Flora Capensis calls it "a moderate tree". It is, however, most often
a shrub or a small tree up to about 4.5 m high, often bushy, with a slender trunk or trunks covered with dark bark and with grey twigs. It is
usually a very dense, thick, bushy tree, quite spineless, and although the
young leaves are light green, the mature foliage is very dark and shiny.
On grassy hillsides the tree often appears quite black, or at times it
glitters in the sun so conspicuously that it can then be distinguished at a
distance by this alone. It shares this character with two other trees, the
wild olive, *Olea africana* Mill., and the stamvrug, *Bequaertiodendron
magalismontanum* Heine and Hemsl., which, however, have very differently shaped leaves and habit.

It casts so deep a shade that it often prevents other growth around it.

The leaves are simple and alternate or sometimes nearly opposite,
2.5-8 cm long, egg-shaped, oblong, oval, or lance-shaped, sharply or
bluntly pointed, the base wedge-shaped or round, the margins closely
and finely toothed, a dark shiny green above, and paler below, the
nerves — sunken above and below, — conspicuous and covered with hairs.
They are shortly stalked.

The small greenish flowers, blooming almost throughout the year in
small clusters in the axils of the leaves, are popular with bees. The fruits
are about the size of a pea, roundish, clearly divided into usually 3 compartments, fleshy, green turning red and later purple, with a small saucer-
shaped calyx and with usually 3 seeds. They are borne on thin stalks.
Strangely, these do not seem very popular with birds, although fowls
eat them.

The wood is white to yellow, often streaked with brown, pink, red or
green, and is hard and heavy. It is too small to be generally useful, although sticks are made of it.

The chief use of the tree is magical. It is widely used as a protective
charm to ward off lightning and evil influences from homes and crops
and to bring luck in hunting. The South Sotho name is "mofifi" meaning
"darkness", and in Lesotho they say "darkness overcomes witchcraft".

It is also used medicinally by Africans to cleanse the blood, to treat
pneumonia, rheumatism, sprains, and stomach ache, and as a gargle.

Mofifi is easily grown from seed and plants can be obtained from
many nurseries. It is tough and fairly frost resistant, growing readily in
most soils, is evergreen and suitable for small gardens. It never grows
very big and its shiny, handsome foliage, and fruits which at various
stages are green, yellow, red and purple on the same tree are attractive.

In the wild, along stream banks in particular, it is often beautiful and

1402

it might be used with effect in landscape gardening.

When cut and placed in water the foliage keeps fresh for a long time.

The name *prinoides* means "resembling *Prinos*", which is an evergreen oak. The tree is probably most often known as "blinkblaar", a name which is borne by several other species of trees, including its relative *Ziziphus mucronata*. A more fitting common name would be the South Sotho "mofifi", easily pronounced, simple, descriptive, and redolent of the lore that surrounds the tree.

5. *Noltia* Reichb.

Noltia is a purely South African genus of 1 species which reaches from Natal to the Cape.

It has simple alternate leaves without stipules, and small bisexual flowers in a lax panicle terminally or in the axils of the leaves. The flowers have 5 sepals, petals and stamens (the disc is not evident), and a 3-chambered ovary, the lower portion of which is joined to the calyx tube. The fruit is a round, 3-celled capsule with a saucer-shaped calyx.

The genus was named after Ernst Ferdinand Nolte, 1791-1875, Professor of Botany and Director of the Botanical Garden at Kiel.

(453)   *Noltia africana* (L.) Reichb.f.

= *Ceonothus africana* L.

Noltia, soap bush, seepbos; umGlindi, iPhalode, maKutula, amaLuleka (X); uMahlahlakwa (Z)

Noltia is a shrub or small tree up to about 6 m high, growing from the Cape Peninsula eastwards and northwards to Natal, in scrub, in valley bush and on forest edges, usually along streams.

It is often a bushy tree with a slender stem, erect brown branches, reddish twigs, and simple, alternate leaves. These are oblong to lance-shaped, the tips sharply or bluntly pointed, the margins toothed, 5-7 cm long, smooth, green above and paler below. The stalks are red. The red buds open into small white flowers in few-flowered short clusters in the axils of the leaves or terminally. They bloom in spring.

The fruit, the size of a large pea, is a dry 3-celled capsule.

The whole plant is soapy and Xhosas use water mixed with crushed leaves and twigs when washing clothes. C.A.Smith says that a decoction of the tree, which probably contains saponin, is used by Africans as a prophylactic against, as well as a remedy for sponssiekte in cattle.

The specific name means "of Africa".

6. *Phylica* L.

Phylica is a genus of about 150 species of shrubs and small trees with an interesting distribution. It is confined to Southern Africa — most species occurring in the extreme south west corner of South Africa — to Madagascar, Mauritius and St. Helena, and to the little known islands of Tristan da Cunha, Gough, Nightingale and Inaccessible where trees grow even in the most exposed places.

Only 2 species in South Africa are usually considered trees, *Phylica*

Phylica paniculata, Nkhandhla Forest, Zululand

paniculata Willd., widely distributed from the Cape to Rhodesia, and *Phylica buxifolia* L., which is confined to the south west Cape. Nevertheless, species such as *Phylica oleifolia* Vent. and *Phylica villosa* Thunb. have been recorded as small trees, while *Phylica purpurea* Sond. occasionally reaches tree height. There may be others.

The species are small trees, shrubs or undershrubs, with simple, alternate leaves, usually without stipules, that are egg-shaped to very narrow, with conspicuously inrolled margins which often almost cover the lower surface; bisexual flowers in a spike, raceme or a close head or solitary, usually with bracts; the calyx with lobes, petals, and stamens 5, the disc usually distinct, the ovary inferior and 3-chambered. The fruit is usually a capsule, most often crowned with a raised ring — the base of the persistent calyx — a characteristic and distinguishing feature. The seed is smooth and usually 3-sided.

The generic name is based on the Greek "phyllikos" meaning "leafy", in reference to the abundant leaves.

Key to species

The leaves fairly broad in relation to their length

The leaves crowded, egg-shaped to lance-shaped, the margins inrolled; *the flowers often in terminal panicles.* (Widespread on mountains from the south west Cape to the Transvaal)

1. *P. paniculata*

The leaves often widest at the base, tapering to the tips, the margins slightly inrolled; *the flowers in short heads in the axils of the leaves.* (South west Cape eastwards to about Caledon)

2. *P. buxifolia*

The leaves widely-spaced, egg-shaped to lance-shaped, the margins slightly inrolled; the flowers *in loose racemes at the ends of the branches.* (The mountains of the south west Cape to Namaqualand)

3. *P. oleifolia*

The leaves narrow

The leaves needle-like (with the margins so much inrolled that the surface is cylindrical), the upper ones often very hairy; the flowers in *round or oblong racemes at the ends of the branches.* (Coastal and mountain fynbos of the south west Cape)

4. *P. villosa*

The leaves short, very narrow, the base the broadest, much inrolled; the flowers *in dense, round, woolly heads, borne terminally.* (From about Knysna to Port Elizabeth in fynbos)

5. *P. purpurea*

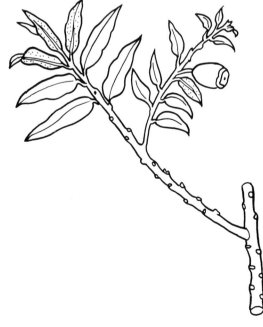

(453.2)   *Phylica paniculata* Willd.

Umdidi tree, luisboom; umDidi (Z)

The umdidi tree or luisboom — a particularly unfortunate name for this decorative little tree — is the most widely distributed member of the genus in South Africa growing along a fairly wide belt of mountainous and hilly country from about Worcester in the south west Cape, through the eastern Cape, the Transkei, Natal, Zululand, and the central and eastern Transvaal to the Chimanimani mountains in Rhodesia.

It grows on forest edges, the margins of bush, in mountain grassland, and on stream banks, usually at a high altitude, forming — according to Sim — part of the smaller fynbos on most of the eastern mountain tops and upper slopes.

It is a much-branched shrub or a small tree — strongly fire-resistant — up to 6 m in height, spreading or drooping, with a trunk often mottled brown and white, up to 25 cm in diameter, and with slender branchlets covered with short grey hairs.

The small hard leaves are crowded up the slender twigs, often over-lapping. They are 0.8-1.3 cm long and often about 3 mm wide, narrowly oval, egg-shaped or needle-like, pointed, the base rounded, dark green above, whitish below, untoothed, the margin often so much inrolled that the leaf appears folded, and without stipules.

The tiny white or creamy-green, bisexual flowers with a strong scent are borne in panicles in the axils of the leaves and at the ends of the branchlets in autumn and winter. The fruits are small, oval, oblong or pear-shaped capsules, purple-black, with flat tips crowned with small points which are the base of the calyx. They contain 3 flattish seeds. The fruits, supposed to resemble ticks, give the tree the common name of "luisboom" or "tick-tree".

The small blue butterfly known as Bowker's Blue, *Tarucus bowkeri,* breeds on the tree.

This hardy species has probably never been cultivated. It might prove a valuable garden evergreen.

The specific name *paniculata* refers to the fact that the flowers are borne in a panicle or loose cluster.

OPPOSITE

Above left
Phylica villosa, Pakhuis Pass

Above right
Phylica oleifolia, Pak-huis Pass

Below left
Lasiodiscus mildbraedii flowers

Below right
Phylica paniculata: leaves, and fruit showing the characteristic flat-tened tip (100%)

(453.1)   *2. Phylica buxifolia* L.

Box phylica

Phylica buxifolia — "the phylica with box-like leaves" — grows as a shrub or small tree up to about 4 m high in rocky places from Table Mountain to the Caledon district.

It is sturdy and many-branched with hairy, buff-coloured twigs and small leaves well spaced up the branchlets. They are oval or often widest at the base, tapering to the point, most often 1.3-2.5 cm long, with the margins inrolled, the upper surface dark green and rough, the lower covered with light-coloured felt and with the secondary nerves conspi-cuous.

The white velvety flowers are usually in small branched heads in the axils of the leaves at the ends of the branches. The fruit is a velvety capsule up to nearly 1.3 cm long with the tip flattened.

(453.3)   3. *Phylica oleifolia* Vent.

Hardebos

Travellers through the Pakhuis Pass and Van Rhyn's Pass, or in other rocky parts of the south west Cape and Namaqualand, note this little *Phylica* species growing abundantly, often as a bush and sometimes as a small tree, occasionally in company with *Phylica villosa*.

Its maximum height appears to be about 3 m, and it may be either sturdy or slender, the stems grey and fairly smooth, up to some 10 cm in diameter. The many, thin, twiggy branches are stiff, and the branchlets, covered with short grey hairs, are set with small, hard, decorative leaves. These are a shiny dark green above – if examined closely tiny warts upon their surface are apparent – and below hairy and white, sometimes with a golden flush. They seldom exceed 3 cm in length and are often no more than half that length, oval, egg-shaped or lance-shaped, most often with the base broad and the tips pointed. The edges are inrolled.

The small white flowers, covered with white hairs, are borne about March in short racemes at the ends of the branches or in the axils of the leaves. The fruit, ripening about September, is red, about the size of a small cherry, round or somewhat top-shaped, encircled just above the middle with a distinct ridge, the remains of the calyx, with the round tip – cushion-like – protruding.

In spite of its humble appearance, this little tree has an honourable history, for the botanists who collected it are among the illustrious. Burchell found it at "Roode zand kloof" and "Witsenberg" and Drège in Tulbagh Kloof, and they were followed by others such as MacOwan, Zeyher, Ecklon, Bolus, Marloth, and Pillans.

The specific name means "with *Olea*-like leaves".

(453.4)   4. *Phylica villosa* Thunb.

"The shaggy-haired phylica" – like *Phylica oleifolia* – is a species of coastal and mountain fynbos of the south west Cape, and is particularly common on the mountains of the Clanwilliam district. It grows in the Pakhuis Pass, where the accompanying photograph was taken, in company with the waboom, *Protea arborea*, an association that has been noted by several collectors.

Although most often a shrub, it can grow into a little tree some 3 or 4 m high, with upward-growing branches, a twiggy crown, and slender grey stem.

The long thin branchlets, covered with flat grey hairs, are clothed with abundant, closely-set green leaves which are short – plus-minus 1-1.5 cm long – and needle-like with the margins much rolled under. The lower ones are often almost smooth, and the upper densely covered with grey hairs.

The small, white, grey or reddish, hairy flowers – blooming about May and June – are borne in dense, round or oblong racemes at the ends of the branches. The fruit, just under 1 cm long, is roundish or oval, with a ridged ring towards the tip – the remains of the calyx. It is chestnut-brown and smooth or hairy, even when smooth often with a few tufts of grey hairs at the base.

Above
Phylica oleifolia : a twig and the fruit with the characteristic ridge just above the middle
100%
Below
Phylica *oleifolia* bark

1408

5. *Phylica purpurea* Sond.

"The purple phylica" has a more eastern distribution than the preceding two species, being frequent in the fynbos in stony places from about Knysna and Riversdale to Oudtshoorn, Humansdorp and Port Elizabeth.

It, too, is a dense shrub or small tree with upward-growing branches covered with grey hairs. The slender branchelets are closely set with short, narrow, broad-based leaves from 0.5-1 cm long with the edges conspicuously rolled under. The twigs rebranch towards the tips bearing at the ends the small, white, woolly flowers in dense round heads resembling balls of silky cotton wool. They bloom about April.

The small, oval fruits, the tips marked with a ring, are some 6 mm long, and are covered with spreading, silky-white hairs.

7. *Lasiodiscus* Hook.f.

Lasiodiscus is a small tropical genus of trees and shrubs represented in South Africa by 1 species, which occurs in Zululand.

The leaves are opposite or nearly opposite, the stipules large and interpetiolar, that is situated not in the axils of a leaf but on the twig between the two leaf stalks. The flowers are bisexual in axillary cymes or clusters, the sepals and petals 5, the stamens 3, the disc fleshy, the ovary "half-superior" and 3-chambered. The fruit is a 3-lobed capsule.

The generic name is based on Latin words meaning "woolly disc".

(453.5) *Lasiodiscus mildbraedii* Engl.

= *Lasiodiscus ferrugeneus* Verdc.

Lasiodiscus

This is a rare tree in South Africa. It is a species widely distributed in tropical Africa, extending into Zululand where it has been collected in the Hlabisa district and in the forests round Lake Sibayi, a fascinating area botanically where several rare tropical species have lately been discovered.

It is usually a short shrubby tree growing in dense forest shade, but may reach 9 m in height. The bark is thin, rough, and ash grey, often with raised corky spots, and the young branches are covered with rusty red hairs.

The rather papery leaves are simple and opposite, 5-19 cm long and 2.5-8 cm wide, although in South Africa often no more than 9 cm long; oval, oblong or lance-shaped, the tips rounded, shortly pointed or with a long-drawn-out point, the base rounded or somewhat heart-shaped and lopsided, the margins toothed, the lateral veins in about 6-10 pairs, prominent below. These and the midrib are covered on the under-surface with silky red hairs. The leaves are borne on short hairy stalks, grooved on the upper surface.

The stipules are situated between the leaf stalks.

The small, white, bisexual flowers are borne in branched heads on long hairy stalks in the axils of the leaves. The young inflorescences are covered with soft white hairs. The fruit is a 3-lobed capsule the size of a very large pea, the base of the calyx tube showing as a line around the middle, and the style as a small wisp at the tip. It is golden-brown and

Lasiodiscus mildbraedii:
The leaves and fruits
(80%)

densely velvety, borne on a slender stalk, and ripens in late summer. The seed is somewhat triangular, with one side rounded.

The species was named after Professor Johannes Mildbraed, 1879-1954, German botanist at Berlin-Dahlem, who took part in several German expeditions to central Africa and to the Cameroons.

This little group of 2 or 3 species is now usually placed in a family of its own, Heteropyxidaceae, but various botanists have in the past assigned it to the families Lythraceae and Myrtaceae, while others have suggested an affinity with the citrus family, Rutaceae, the members of which, like those of this group, have gland-dotted and often deliciously scented leaves.

One species grows in South Africa from Natal, Zululand, Swaziland and the Transvaal to Rhodesia, while the other is confined to a small area in the eastern Transvaal and Swaziland.

The characters of the family are the same as those of the genus.

Heteropyxis Harv.

This small genus is represented in South Africa by 2 species, *Heteropxis natalensis* Harv. which is fairly widely distributed from Natal, Zululand and Swaziland to the Transvaal, and *Heteropxis canescens* Oliv. which is confined to a limited area in the mountains of the eastern Transvaal and Swaziland.

They have simple, alternate, gland-dotted leaves, no stipules; small flowers that are bisexual, borne in terminal panicles, the cup-shaped, gland-dotted calyx with 5 lobes, the petals 5, gland-dotted, the stamens 5, the ovary superior and 2-3-chambered, the fruit a small 2-3-locular capsule, the seed brown and 3-angled.

The name *Heteropyxis* is based on the Greek word "heteros" meaning "other" or "distinct", and on the Latin "pyxidatus" meaning "a capsule with a box-like lid".

(455)   *Heteropyxis natalensis* Harv.

Lavender tree, laventelboom; umKhuswa, inKunzi, inKuzwa (Z); inKunzi, umHlosheni (Sw); thathasane (Tso); mudedede, munukha-vhaloi (V)

The lavender tree is fairly plentiful in parts of Natal, Zululand, Swaziland, and in the central, eastern and northern Transvaal, growing on rocky slopes, and in woodland and riverine bush, from almost sea level to an altitude of at least 1300 m.

It is usually a shrub or a small tree 3.6-6 m high, although reported up to 15 m in Rhodesia, with a slender trunk which is white or grey, often marked with cream and orange, sometimes smooth, at others flaking or with sections raised and depressed and a rather small crown of evergreen, glossy green leaves.

These are simple and alternate, usually long, narrow and wavy,

The lavender tree, *Heteropyxis natalensis*, in the Waterberg, Transvaal

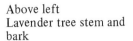
Above left
Lavender tree stem and
bark

Below left
The stem and bark of
another tree of the same
species

Right
Heteropyxis natalensis:
A portion of a flowering
branch (60%)

smooth, 2.5-10 cm in length, lance-shaped or wider, pointed, the base
narrowed, the margins usually untoothed and *not* inrolled, the midrib
clearly defined below, with 1 pair of rather steeply ascending veins
which are often conspicuous, and with pits in the axils of the veins. They
are a glossy green above and paler below, carried on slender stalks —
the base of which is often red — and when crushed have a strong,
pleasant, aromatic smell which gives the tree its common name. The
scent persists even when the leaves are dried.

The tiny, tight, greenish buds in branched clusters at the ends of the
twigs open into small, creamy, 5-petalled flowers blooming in early
summer, which attract bees, wasps and butterflies. They are bisexual
and develop into small, oval, dark capsules on short stalks which split
open on the tree to shed tiny dark seeds. They are often borne in
dense sprays.

The wood is a brownish-purple colour and tough although reputed to
be somewhat soft. It is used for fence posts and charcoal.

The tree is used to make a medicinal tea, the leaves to scent tobacco
and in Zululand as a perfume. According to Watt and Brandwijk, medicine for goats, donkeys and cattle is obtained from them. The Venda
treat bleeding of the nose and gums by steaming the face in the vapour
obtained from a decoction of the roots. Both bark and leaves are eaten
by Black Rhino, and kudu browse the foliage.

This is often a rather ragged-looking little tree, its most memorable
character being the fragrance of the bruised twigs and leaves. When well
grown, however, with its graceful form, glossy foliage, and light trunk,
it can be charming. Plants are obtainable from some nurseries and are
easy and satisfactory trees for even small gardens.

It is not generally known that its autumn colours can be splendid. In
the bitter June of 1968 the lavender trees of the Transvaal bushveld
turned a glowing ruby-red, and these — together with the tamboti and
kudu berry in winter foliage — were wonderful from the hills near the
Pienaars River Dam outside Pretoria northwards. Trees may find a place
in landscape gardening if only for their red winter foliage.

The specific name means "of Natal".

1413

(454)   *Heteropyxis canescens* Oliv.

This, literally "the hoary heteropyxis", grows only in forest and wooded ravines, often along streams, in the mountains from Barberton in the eastern Transvaal to Swaziland.

It may be a small to medium-sized tree up to 12 m high, with a straight or crooked stem and smooth, brown, flaking bark.

Although it resembles the lavender tree, *Heteropyxis natalensis,* in many respects, there are certain differences. The leaves are usually larger, firmer, hairy on the lower surface, with the margins inrolled, and the secondary veins prominent below, and the capsule round and almost stalkless.

63 The Grape Vine Family (Vitaceae)

This large family of over 500 species, spread throughout the warm countries of the world, has been famous since ancient times for the beauty and pleasure its most celebrated member, the grape vine, *Vitis vinefera* L., has conferred upon the world.

The grape vine, although widely cultivated in South Africa, is not indigenous nor is the genus *Vitis,* to which it belongs. Several genera, however, of the 51 belonging to the family, are native to South and South West Africa and contain a number of species, some grotesque, some unusually beautiful, and all of interest. Most are climbers.

Two genera in South and South West Africa contain species that are trees or species which, although often shrubs or climbers, can be tree-like under certain circumstances. These belong to the genera *Rhoicissus* and *Cyphostemma.*

A number of species of *Rhoicissus* grow in South Africa, all with grape-like fruits that are sometimes edible, and often with swollen underground roots. Most of them are climbers, some of them occasionally growing as small trees or shrubs. These are *Rhoicissus tridentata* (L.f.) Wild & Drummond, and *Rhoicissus digitata* (L.f.) Gilg & Brandt.

The best known and most widespread member is the wild grape, *Rhoicissus tomentosa* (Lam.) Wild & Drummond [*R. capensis* (Burm.f.) Planch.], a high climber of forests from the Cape to Malawi, which, with its simple, deep green, vine-like leaves and bunches of purple grapes, is a most handsome species with tart fruits that make a fine jelly and a sour wine with a pleasant fragrance.

Rhoicissus revoilii Planch. is a strong-growing creeper with broad leaflets, the margins untoothed or slightly lobed, that is widespread in forest and woodland.

Rhoicissus rhomboidea (E.Mey. ex Harv.) Planch. is another tall forest climber or monkey rope used in Zululand to pull the light rafts made of raphia palm over the streams. Neither this species, nor *Rhoicissus tomentosa,* are recorded as trees, but it is possible that under exceptional circumstances they are.

The genus *Cyphostemma* is well represented in South and South West Africa. Three species, *Cyphostemma currorii* (Hook.f.) Desc., *Cyphostemma juttae* (Dinter & Gilg) Descoings, and *Cyphostemma bainesii* (Hook.f.) Descoings, may become tree-like. They are all interesting-looking plants with thick, succulent stems and bunches of grape-like but poisonous fruits.

The genera *Ampelocissus* and *Cissus,* occurring in South Africa and sometimes in Botswana and the Caprivi Strip, include no tree species.

In the past species now known as *Rhoicissus* and *Cyphostemma* were placed in the genus *Cissus,* but are now separated on a number of points, such as the form of leaves and flowers.

Members of the family may be woody or succulent, sometimes with tendrils, with leaves that are simple or compound, with or without stipules; and with small flowers that are usually bisexual, borne in spikes, racemes, panicles or cymes, often *opposite* the leaves; the calyx sometimes with 4-5 teeth, the petals and stamens usually 4-5, a disc present, the ovary superior and 2-8-celled; the fruit a berry.

Key to Genera

Mostly climbers, but sometimes shrubs or small trees; the leaves usually with 3 leaflets.

1. *Rhoicissus*

Climbers; the leaves usually simple; the inflorescence often opposite the leaf stalks (no tree species).

2. *Cissus*

Often short succulent trees or plants, the leaves usually compound; the inflorescence often axillary.

3. *Cyphostemma*

1. *Rhoicissus* Planch.

A number of species of this genus occur in South Africa all of which are commonly strong woody climbers, but 3 of which are sometimes trees.

They usually have tendrils by which they climb, and these grow opposite the leaves; leaves which are usually composed of 3 leaflets, but sometimes 5, or which occasionally are simple, usually with stipules; bisexual, 4-6-petalled flowers, the calyx usually small, the stamens 5, the ovary 2-chambered, borne in tight cymes growing opposite the leaves; and grape-like, fleshy fruits, usually with 1-2 seeds.

It is easy to mistake the shrubby forms of *Rhoicissus* for *Rhus* species, as the leaves are very similar, and early botanists often included them in *Rhus.*

While the fruit of some species is edible that of others causes pain to the lips, mouth, and throat when they are chewed.

The name *Rhoicissus* is based on two Greek words, "rhoia", meaning "pomegranate" — perhaps in allusion to the appearance or taste of the fruits — and "kissos", meaning "ivy", in reference to the climbing habit of a number of the species.

Guide to *Rhoicissus* tree species

The leaflets usually under 3.5 cm long

The leaflets 3, a narrow oblong, spathulate or oval, untoothed or slightly lobed. (Common in arid parts, especially the eastern Cape)

a. *R. tridentata*

The leaflets usually over 3.5 cm long

The leaflets 3, green above, the central one often roughly triangular, the lateral ones conspicuously unequal-sided, the tips often flat, boldly toothed. (Cape, Natal, Transvaal, on forest edges and in woodland)

a. *R. tridentata*
var.

The leaflets 3-5 (usually both forms borne on the same tree), green above, typically a narrow oblong or oval, the margins untoothed or slightly toothed. (From about Knysna northwards through Natal to the Transvaal in forest, bush and on dunes)

b. *R. digitata*

A small tree, the leaflets 3, above grey- or silver-green, narrow, untoothed. (The Waterberg and the Soutpansberg of the Transvaal, on grassy and wooded slopes).

c. *R. digitata*
Waterberg form

(456.6)   a. *Rhoicissus tridentata* (L.f.) Wild & Drummond

= *Rhus tridentata* L.f., = *Cissus cuneifolia* Eckl. & Zeyh.; = *Rhoicissus cuneifolia* (Eckl. & Zeyh.) Planch.; = *Rhoicissus erythrodes* (Fresen.) Planch.

Droog-my-keel grape, bobbejaantou, wild grape, wildedruiwe; murum-bula-mbudzana (V)

Rhoicissus tridentata has a wide distribution in South Africa, from about Knysna through the eastern Cape, the eastern Orange Free State, Natal, Zululand and Swaziland to the eastern and northern Transvaal, and northwards throughout tropical Africa to the Middle East.

It is a very variable species indeed growing in the most diverse positions and under widely differing climatic conditions — on forest edges, in woodland, on rocky wooded hillsides, in coastal grassveld, in arid scrub — it is common in the Fish River valley scrub of the eastern Cape — on Karoo koppies, from sea level to an altitude of at least 1200 m. On forest fringes it may be a high climber, in Karoo scrub a pretty twining shrub (most often growing in company with, and twining through, *Grewia robusta* Harv.), or — as at Mkuze in the Zululand bushveld or on the northern slopes of the Soutpansberg in the Transvaal — a small neat tree up to about 3.6 m in height.

It may be many-stemmed or occasionally with a simple clean trunk, which is often smooth and light grey; many-branched, with young branches and twigs covered with rust-coloured, tawny, or greyish hairs, and with tendrils that are either hairy or smooth.

The leaves vary so much in shape and size that it is often difficult to credit that they belong to the same species. They are composed of 3 rigid leaflets. The true *R. tridentata* has small leaves some 1.3-3.5 cm long, a narrow oblong or oval, unlobed or only slightly lobed, a form apparently adapted to the arid conditions of parts of the eastern Cape where it is common. Towards the coast and in the north, in Natal and the Transvaal, this grades into a big-leaved form (which is probably worthy of varietal rank). In this the leaflets are up to some 10 cm long

Above
Rhoicissus tridentata on the northern foothills of the Soutpansberg

Right
Rhoicissus digitata: A fruiting twig (60%)

Below
Rhoicissus tridentata growing — together with *Aloe marlothii* — on the Lebombo Mountains near Jozini

Opposite
Rhoicissus tridentata : Two forms of stem and bark

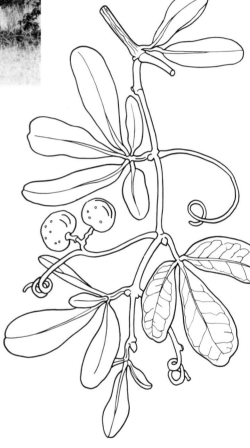

1418

and 7 cm wide, egg-shaped, rounded, or oblong, the central one often roughly triangular and narrowed to the base, the side leaflets conspicuously unequal-sided, the tips often flat and boldly toothed. They are glossy green above and paler below, the veins running steeply upwards, on the under surface often rusty red and raised. The leaflets are borne on short sturdy stalks.

Black Rhino eat the stems and leaves.

The small greenish flowers with a velvety calyx are borne in clusters opposite the leaves on velvety, rust-coloured or tawny stalks. The fruit is up to nearly 1.3 cm in diameter, smooth, roundish, slightly wider than long and black when mature, with 1-2 seeds which are marked with a furrow lengthwise and have one rounded side. The fruit is edible but very sour and constricts the throat, hence the common name "droog-my-keel".

The most notable feature of this species is its large, thickened tuberous rootstock which is said to be edible and easily digested. It is popular with porcupines and baboons and probably with other animals as well. A small plant no more than a few centimetres high may have an underground rooting system more than 18 m long, the tuberous swellings being produced at intervals below the surface of the ground. It is not surprising that — armed thus against drought — this is a common species of many arid areas. The tuberous roots were known to the Bushmen and were figured in rock paintings.

The specific name, meaning "with 3 teeth", is misleading, for the leaflets may have more teeth or none at all. The Venda name "murumbula-mbudzana" means "pricks the kid '.

(456.2)   b. *Rhoicissus digitata* (L.f.) Gilg & Brandt

= *Rhus digitata* L.f.; = *Cissus thunbergii* Eckl. & Zeyh.; = *Rhoicissus schlechteri* Gilg & Brandt

Baboon grape, wild grape, bobbejaandruif, bobbejaanbolle, Boesmansdruif

(456.3)   c. *Rhoicissus digitata* (L.f.) Gilg & Brandt
           Waterberg form

Rhoicissus digitata appears to be a southern species which has extended northwards from the Cape through Natal and the Transvaal to Mozambique.

In form it may be a strong woody climber up to 15 m high, a low shrub, or a small, bushy tree, and its habitat may be high forest, forest margins, coastal bush, sand dunes, bare rocks fringing the sea, or open grassy slopes from sea level to an altitude of at least 900 m.

It is uncommon as a tree, but when it does grow in this form it is remarkably attractive, neat, spreading, with firm yet delicate foliage. Young branches and twigs are covered with bright reddish-brown hairs, a contrast to the dark foliage. The leaves are composed of 3-5 leaflets up to 9 cm long and 3 cm wide, the middle the largest, a narrow oblong or oval, or widely lance-shaped, the tips plus-minus round, the base narrowed and often unequal, the margins untoothed or slightly toothed, sometimes inrolled, smooth above, and below the midrib or nerves on the whole surface covered with reddish hairs, often with little pits at the junction of the midrib and veins. The leaflets are usually shortly stalked,

Above left
Cyphostemma currorii leaf (50%)

Below left
Rhoicissus digitata, Waterberg form
A twig with immature fruit (60%)

Below right
Cyphostemma juttae leaf and fruit
(60%)

1420

Above
A form of *Rhoicissus digitata* near Palala in the Waterberg

Below
The bark

and the leaf is borne on a reddish petiole up to just over 2.5 cm long. Stipules are present.

The small yellow-green flowers are borne in rather lax, hairy, branching clusters. The fruits are roundish, somewhat fleshy, green turning reddish-brown, purple, or black.

Africans use this species in making mats.

The name *digitata* is based on the Latin "digitatus" or "fingered", meaning that all the leaflets, finger-like, spring from the same point at the apex of the leaf stalk.

A *Rhoicissus* that grows as a tree on the grassy slopes of the Waterberg and the Soutpansberg in the Transvaal and in Rhodesia may prove to be a form of *Rhoicissus digitata* and is here included as the Waterberg form of this species. It should be noted that Wild (who revised the genus for *Flora Zambesiaca*) included this in *Rhoicissus revoilii,* but this view is not upheld by the Botanical Research Institute.

It is a small tree usually growing to about 3.5 m in height, with a single trunk which in old trees is covered with dark deeply fissured bark, and a wide crown with often somewhat drooping branches. The young branches and twigs are covered with tawny hairs and red raised dots. Tendrils, when present, are opposite the leaves and may be hairy or smooth. The leaves are composed of narrow, glaucous, untoothed leaflets, and are borne on hairy stalks. The leaflets are usually up to about 4-5 cm long, a narrow oblong, and are grey or silver-green with the midrib on the under-surface conspicuously hairy-red. The stalks are reddish.

The small flowers are in often dense and many-flowered, reddish-hairy clusters. The fruits are roundish, up to about 1.3 cm in diameter, smooth and black when ripe, enclosing 1-2 seeds which are seamed lengthwise. They are relished by Crested Guineafowl.

Cyphostemna currorii photographed in July near Tsumeb

3. *Cyphostemma* (Planch.) Alston

A number of *Cyphostemma* species occur in South and South West
Africa, but in South Africa these are usually herbs, climbers, or shrubs.
In South West Africa 3 species grow normally or occasionally as trees,
and all are noteworthy for their thick succulent stems which make them
an outstanding feature of the countryside where they grow. They are
all deciduous.

The species have leaves, (with stipules) with 3-9 leaflets springing from
the same point, or which occasionally are simple, sometimes with tendrils opposite them; the flowers bisexual, in cymes opposite the leaves
or in the leaf axils; the calyx with 4 teeth (or none at all) the petals 4,
a disc of 4 fleshy glands present. *Flora Zambesiaca* lists as a key character
the shape of the bud which is cylindric or flask-shaped, the tips rounded
and often inflated, and more or less constricted near the middle (in contrast to the buds of *Cissus* species which are conical and not constricted
in the middle). The fruit is grape-like and usually 1-seeded and the seeds
are often crested and rough.

The origin and allusion of the generic name are not clear. It is probably
based on Greek words meaning "curved" or "humped garland", or perhaps "humped crown".

Key to species

A succulent tree *up to 6 m high;* the trunk bark yellow or light brown
and papery; the leaves with 3 leaflets, *not winged.*

a. *C. currorii*

A *dwarf* succulent tree rarely reaching 3.6 m; the bark creamy and
papery; the leaves in young plant *simple* and lobed, in older with 3 leaflets, *winged.*

b. *C. juttae*

A *dwarf* succulent tree; the bark yellowish-orange and papery; the leaves
with 3 leaflets, often rimmed with red, *not winged.*

c. *C. bainesii*

(456)   a. *Cyphostemma currorii* (Hook.f.) Desc.

= *Vitis currori* Hook.f.; = *Cissus crameriana* Schinz; = *Cyphostemma
crameriana* (Schinz) Descoings

Kobas, botterboom

The kobas, as it is known to the native peoples of South West Africa, is
a succulent tree of remarkable appearance, somewhat baobab-like, with
a thick swollen stem, a round crown of large, compound, fleshy leaves,
and grape-like fruits, growing in the northern districts of South West
Africa. It is particularly plentiful in the district of Karibib.

It grows up to about 8 m high, the trunk, often 2 m across at the base,
sometimes dividing into a number of stems. The bark is yellow to light
brown and shiny, peeling in small papery pieces, and when the tree is
without leaves in winter this thick bare trunk and robust interlacing
branches are distinctive against the rocky hillsides where it usually grows.

Above
The bark of *Cyphostemma currorii*

Right
Cyphostemma juttae flowers

Below
Cyphostemma juttae bark

The leaves are compound and are made up of 3 often huge leaflets up to about 30 cm long and 18 cm broad, the lateral usually sessile and the middle one with a short, thick stalk. They are oval, egg-shaped or oblong, not winged as in *Cyphostemma juttae,* bluntly pointed with a broad unequal base, the margins toothed, thick, fleshy, light green, when young covered with short, soft, white or reddish hairs; on the upper surface the midrib, and the lateral veins, which are upward-pointing, visible only towards the base, on the underside conspicuous over the whole surface. They are often folded together so that their breadth is not easily seen. They are borne on long, very thick leaf stalks.

The yellow-green, rather inconspicuous, 4-petalled flowers are in flat, spreading, branched heads, the whole inflorescence on a long stout stalk growing at the ends of the branches. The fruits are grape-like, juicy, red, containing oxalic acid which damages the mouth and throat. Baboons and monkeys eat the ripe fruit, and so – according to Dinter – do the indigenous peoples, swallowing them whole!

Watt and Brandwijk say that the fresh leaf also contains oxalic acid and that an amount no larger than a sixpence, chewed, has produced difficulty in swallowing and a burning in the throat, gullet and stomach persisting for a period of 2 weeks. The leaves are not, apparently, browsed by any animals.

The species was named after Dr A.B. Curror of *H.M.S. Water-Witch* who collected the tree at Elephant's Bay in Angola in the 1840's. Kobas is a native name.

(456.1)   b. *Cyphostemma juttae* (Dinter & Gilg) Desc.

= *Cissus juttae* Dinter & Gilg

Jutta's botterboom

Jutta's botterboom, from the Namib Desert of central and northern South West Africa, is a stocky, succulent tree, often no more than 2 m high but sometimes up to 3.6 m, with an often rather barrel-like, thick trunk, short, stubby, smooth branches – the young ones sometimes with small spines – and large fleshy leaves.

The trunk is covered with creamy, papery bark which peels off to show a creamy-green colour below. The leaves have the interesting characteristic of being simple, although often deeply lobed, in young plants, and compound in older ones, a character noted in the earliest descriptions of the species. They are alternate, large – up to nearly 30 cm long – roughly oblong in shape, the tips rounded or sharply pointed, fleshy, blue-green, either deeply lobed or with 3 leaflets, the terminal the largest, the lateral ones uneven-sided at the base, conspicuously winged, the margins coarsely toothed, the common midrib and those of the leaflets with small spines below, and the veins below sometimes with reddish hairs; the stipules long, lance-shaped and conspicuous. The leaves usually fall about May or June, the young foliage appearing in the spring.

The small flowers are in branched heads carried on a long thick stalk armed with small prickles, borne at the ends of the branches. The grape-like fruits are green, usually – about March – becoming light scarlet and purple, and these bright sprays are exceedingly handsome. The fruits have been reported as sweet and edible, although this is generally considered incorrect as they constrict the throat in somewhat the same way as do those of the kobas.

The stem sap is said to be poisonous and to have formed as ingredient in Bushman arrow poison.

The species was named after Jutta Dinter, the wife of the noted South West African botanist and collector.

c. *Cyphostemma bainesii* (Hook.f.) Descoings

= *Vitis bainesii* Hook.f.; = *Cissus bainesii* (Hook.f.) Gilg & Brandt

Above
Cyphostemma bainesii
leaves and flowers

Below
Cyphostemma bainesii
bark

Baines' gouty vine, botterboom

"Baines' gouty vine" was the first popular name this dwarf, succulent tree of central and western South West Africa — of the Namib Desert itself — ever received. This was based on its outstanding characteristic, its thick, swollen, barrel- or turnip-like trunk, smooth yellow-green or silver-white with yellowish-orange, papery, peeling bark.

The trunk bears several branches and large, thick, succulent, compound leaves up to 30 cm long. These have 3 stiff leaflets, blue-green and often rimmed with red, the veins yellow, when young covered with silver-white, velvety hairs, oval to oblong in shape, the margins toothed and often crinkly. Sometimes the lower leaves may be simple. Stipules are present.

The small, fat, fleshy, greenish-yellow flowers are borne terminally in flat, branching sprays on stiff, upright stalks often marked with red. They bloom about December. The fruits are grape-like and orange when ripe in the autumn. These, as well as the fruits of the other tree species, are — according to Dinter — swallowed whole by the native peoples.

The plant was named after Thomas Baines, traveller and artist, who sent it to England from South West Africa. It was illustrated in Curtis's *Botanical Magazine* in 1864, in which year it flowered for the first time in cultivation. Sir William Hooker, who described it as *Vitis bainesii*, gave it the curious but appropriate name of "Baines' gouty vine" which, with its aptness and historical associations, it would be pleasant to resurrect, especially as the name it now commonly bears, "botterboom", is shared by at least 3 other different species of succulent trees.

Tiliaceae is a large family with about 44 genera and 500 species of small trees, shrubs, climbers or herbs, spread throughout the warmer parts of the world. Jute is the most famous member.

Two genera in South or South West Africa include species which are trees. These are *Sparrmannia,* with 1 tree species, and *Grewia,* an important genus, with a number of small trees or bushy shrubs that are often tree-like. Some of these yield a good fibre, although none are as valuable as jute.

The family is characterized by leaves — with stipules — that are alternate and most often simple (always so in the South African tree species); the flowers usually bisexual, the sepals and petals often 5, the stamens 4 to many, the ovary superior with 2-10 chambers, and the fruit a drupe or capsule with 2-10 chambers, or by abortion, one. Star-shaped hairs are a feature of the family.

Sparrmannia L.f.

This small genus of Africa and Madagascar is represented in South Africa by 1 tree species, *Sparrmannia africana* L.f.

All the species are shrubs or trees with simple, alternate, hairy leaves which are angled or lobed, with palmate veins; with stipules; and with white bisexual flowers in umbels which are terminal or opposite the leaves, the sepals and petals 4, the stamens numerous, the ovary 4-5-celled, and the fruit a prickly capsule, 4-5-celled and 4-5-valved, with numerous seeds in each cell.

The genus was named after Anders (Andrew) Sparrmann, 1748-1820, famous Swedish naturalist and traveller in South Africa who introduced *Sparrmannia africana* into cultivation in Europe.

There has been confusion in the past over the spelling of the generic name. *Sparrmannia* is now judged correct.

(457)   *Sparrmannia africana* L.f.

Stock-rose, stokroos

The stock-rose is common in the Cape Province, principally in the districts of George, Knysna, Uniondale and Humansdorp, as a shrub or a bushy soft-wooded tree up to 8 m in height, growing in damp places on forest edges, on hill slopes, and along streams. It is a common species alongside the road through the Montagu Pass and near other mountain roads close to George, its large white and golden flowers making it conspicuous in winter and early spring.

Above
Sparrmannia leaves

Below
The flower

Sim describes it as a weed in the Knysna area.

The branches are spongy and covered with soft hairs. The pale green leaves, borne on long stalks, are 5-7-angled, or roughly heart-shaped, the base round and notched, narrowing to a slender point, up to 15 cm long and 10 cm wide at the base, toothed, the veins radiating from the base, softly hairy both sides. Young leaves are densely velvety. The stipules are awl-shaped.

The oval furry buds open into moderately sized, showy, white flowers, occasionally with a pink tinge, 4-petalled, with numerous yellow stamens, borne in a long-stalked, many-flowered umbel (a cluster of flowers springing from the same point), at the ends of the branches. They bloom from June to September.

The fruit is a roundish, 4-5-celled capsule covered with thin spikes, giving the effect of an untidy mop.

The timber is too soft to be much value, but it yields a good fibre which was once known as African hemp. About 80 years ago this became locally famous when the Kama Fibre Syndicate was formed to exploit its fibre possibilities, and plantations of the tree were made in the Storms River forests. The Syndicate lasted only a few years. The fibre is not of top quality.

The stock-rose is sometimes cultivated, and is easy, handsome, and very quick-growing. Gardeners should note that contact with the hairy leaves is apt to produce a skin irritation.

The tree is used medicinally.

The specific name means "of Africa '.

Grewia L.

More than 400 species of *Grewia* occur in Africa, Asia and Australia. Over 20 species grow in South and South West Africa and of these perhaps 14 or 15 species are known to grow as trees, or as shrubs which occasionally are tree-like. Others, such as *Grewia tenax* (Forsk.) Fiori, *Grewia avellaria* Hiern, or *Grewia hispida* Harv. may possibly be trees in certain circumstances, but if so, there are no records of this.

They all have simple, alternate leaves, 3-7-nerved from the base, with stipules; starry flowers that are usually bisexual, medium-sized, borne in panicles or cymes or singly terminally or in the axils of or opposite to the leaves, the sepals 5 and petal-like, the petals 5, shorter than the sepals, the stamens many, the ovary 2-4-chambered, the fruit round or 2-4-lobed, slightly fleshy, containing a hard stone. It does not split open.

This is a confusing genus, the various species often resembling one another closely.

None of the native species are very outstanding trees. Yet they play a part in the lives of men and animals out of all proportion to their appearance, or to their small, rather unappetising fruits. A species such as *Grewia flava* DC., which is widespread in the north western parts of the country and in South West Africa, is a little tree or shrub or inestimable value. Almost every part of the tree is used by men, or eaten by mammals and birds — bark, wood, leaves, roots, fruits — and for Bushmen and Bantu peoples it is one of the most generally useful of all species.

The small dryish fruits of many species are a basic food of primitive peoples, animals and birds, the foliage of some is browsed, the wood makes sticks which are used for weapons and tools, and for bows and arrows, the pliable branchlets for baskets, the bark for cordage and string, and parts are used in medicine and magic. The sap is widely used by Africans as a germicide, and also to kill insects.

The genus was named after Nehemiah Grew, M.D., of London, who wrote a work on the anatomy of plants in 1682. The common names borne by the various species depend largely on the types of fruits. Sometimes they are known as rosyntjiebossie (raisin bush) or those with 4-lobed fruits are commonly called "kruisbessie", the 4 lobes forming a rough cross.

Guide to *Grewia* tree species

The characters on which this guide is based are not absolutely constant. These are the lop-sidedness or equal-sidedness of the leaf bases, and the colour of the flowers — conspicuous features and often the first to be noted in the field

Leaves with an equal or almost equal base

The flowers yellow

The leaves usually *hairless,* the margins untoothed or toothed in the upper part; the inflorescences *terminal;* the fruit *never lobed, pendulous.* (Zululand, Transvaal, in short forest, bushveld and woodland)

a. *G. microthyrsa*

Usually a shrub, the leaves often *finely velvety,* somewhat discolorous, often silver-grey, slightly paler below, fairly coarse-textured; the flowers *axillary,* the fruit *round or 2-lobed, not pendulous.* (Dry bushveld from Natal — where it is rare — Swaziland and the Transvaal to O.F.S., north west Cape, Botswana, South West Africa)

h. *G. flava*

The stems *4-angled;* the leaves *roughly and harshly hairy,* the veins on the upper surface *not* conspicuous; the inflorescence axillary; the fruit 1 *or slightly 2-4-lobed,* hairy. (Transvaal, Swaziland, Botswana, South West Africa, in woodland and bush)

b. *G. flavescens*

The stems *round,* the leaves *smooth or nearly smooth,* the net veins on the upper surface *conspicuous;* the inflorescence axillary, the fruit *never lobed.* (Transvaal, north west Cape, Botswana, South West Africa, Caprivi, in bush and open woodland)

c. *G. retinervis*

Most often a climber or rambling shrub, sometimes with branch thorns, the older stems square, the leaves up to 5 cm long, thin, *concolorous,* smooth, or *slightly hairy below,* the base sometimes slightly lopsided, the inflorescence axillary, the fruit round, *never lobed.* (Natal, Zululand, Transvaal, in bush and on forest margins).

d. *G. caffra*

The leaves up to 8 cm long, oval to lance-shaped, *discolorous,* green above and smooth or velvety, below covered with *dense, white or grey-blue felt;* the inflorescence axillary; the fruit round or deeply 2-lobed. (Zululand, Swaziland, O.F.S., Transvaal, Botswana, in open bushveld)

g. *G. bicolor*

Usually a much-branched shrub, the leaves up to 14 cm in diameter, round or heart-shaped, discolorous, above green, *hairy, rough;* below grey and velvety, the veins conspicuous; the inflorescence *opposite* the leaf stalk; the fruit round and *slightly 4-lobed* with hairs based on small warts. (Zululand Swaziland, Natal, Transvaal, Botswana, South West Africa, in bush or woodland)

L. *G. villosa*

The flowers usually pink or lilac

A shrub or many-stemmed tree; the leaves *alternate, up to 7 cm long,* oval to lance-shaped, smooth or slightly hairy, *not noticeably discolorous,* the fruit 4-lobed. (Moist eastern areas of South Africa, rare in South West Africa)

n. *G. occidentalis*

Usually a sturdy, many-branched shrub, the twigs rigid and sometimes spiny; the leaves *often in tufts* on short side shoots, *frequently only up to 1.3 cm long,* oval to egg-shaped, the adult leaves *somewhat discolorous,* shiny green above, below with blue-green velvety hairs; the fruit 4-lobed. (Eastern Cape and Cape Midlands in dry scrub)

o. *G. robusta*

A shrub or tree; the leaves *large,* up to 10 cm and sometimes more in length, often round, somewhat discolorous, above green and *very rough,* below lighter and velvety, the midrib and 3 veins conspicuous; with reddish hairs, the netted veins distinct; the fruit 4-lobed but often with lobes missing. (Eastern Cape to Natal on forest margins)

p. *G. lasiocarpa*

Leaves with an often pronounced lopsided base

The branches *often drooping;* the leaves large, up to 10 cm long, and leathery, discolorous, the upper side grey-green, hairless or slightly hairy, the lower covered with dense bluish-white hairs, *the veins often with rust-coloured hairs, the margins coarsely and irregularly toothed;* the inflorescence axillary, the flowers yellow or orange, the fruit round or 2-lobed, *covered with bristly hairs.* (Natal, Zululand, Swaziland, Transvaal, Botswana, South West Africa, in bush and open woodland)

f. *G. monticola*

The leaves discolorous, green and often velvety above, below grey and shortly velvety, fairly thin, the *margins finely and regularly toothed;* the inflorescence axillary, the flowers yellow, less than 1 cm in diameter; the fruit round or 2-lobed. (Zululand, Swaziland, Transvaal, Botswana, South West Africa, Caprivi Strip, in bush and woodland)

g. *G. subspathulata*

A leafy tree; the young growth *with reddish hairs;* the leaves leathery, large, discolorous, the upper side shiny green, the lower with a whitish-grey or *golden felt,* the veins with *long reddish-brown hairs;* the inflorescence axillary, the flowers yellow, *large,* often over 1 cm in diameter; the fruit round or 2-lobed, *each lobe up to 2 cm in diameter.* (Swaziland, Transvaal, in lowveld bush)

i. *G. hexamita*

Often a scrambler; the leaves oblong to ovate, up to 18 cm long, discolorous, green and hairless above, below with velvety white or grey hairs; the veins *without long brownish hairs* but clearly marked; the inflorescence axillary; the flowers yellow; *the fruit up to 13 mm in diameter,* round or 2-lobed. (North eastern Transvaal, Botswana, northern South West Africa, in vleis or river valleys)

j. *G. inaequilatera*

A shrub to small tree, the leaves large, up to 14 cm long, discolorous, green and shortly hairy above, below covered with *dense grey or brown hairs, the veins of the same colour;* the inflorescence axillary; the flowers yellow, the fruit round or deeply 2-lobed, slightly hairy. (Northern South West Africa and Botswana, in bush and woodland)

k. *G. schinzii*

A shrub or small tree, the leaves up to 8 cm long, above slightly hairy or smooth, below with *dense, light-coloured hairs, the veins brownish;* the inflorescence in the axil of the leaves; the flowers yellow; the fruit 2-lobed or with 1 lobe missing. (Natal, Swaziland, eastern Transvaal)

m. *G. micrantha* form

Grewia microthyrsa: leaves and fruit (100%)

(461.1)   a. *Grewia microthyrsa* K.Schum. ex Burret

Tongaland grewia, isaNywane (Z); nsihana, nsihani (Tso); mufuka (V)

Grewia microthyrsa is a shrub or small tree occurring in the eastern and northern Transvaal, Zululand, Tongaland, and southern Mozambique, in short sandy forest, bushveld, and in woodland, often on rocky hillsides, and usually at a low altitude.

It is a dense shrub or slender tree with light grey bark. The leaves are simple and alternate, oval or oblong, 2 to 6 cm long and 1.3-2.5 cm wide, bluntly pointed, the base rounded and sometimes lopsided, the lateral veins in 4-5 pairs looping along the margin, these and the midrib prominent and conspicuous below, the margins untoothed or slightly toothed

1432

in the upper portion, both surfaces usually hairless or nearly so, borne on stalks covered with star-like hairs. The stipules fall off early.

The flower buds are covered with grey or brown hairs. They open into cream or yellow, velvety flowers in small branching heads — panicles — at the ends of the branches.

The fruit is oval, up to about 1.3 cm long, never lobed, smooth and pendulous. It is eaten by duiker and bushbuck.

In Tongaland the wood is sometimes used to make hunting spears. The tree is thought to have magic qualities, and Gerstner says that if placed "over a man's heart", he will be disliked.

The specific name is based on a Greek word meaning "small" and a botanical word for a mixed inflorescence.

b. *Grewia flavescens* Juss.

= *Grewia rautanenii* Schinz

Grewia flavescens has a very wide distribution, growing from Africa to Arabia and India. It is interesting to note that the type specimen came from India. In Southern Africa it occurs from the eastern, central and northern Transvaal and Swaziland westwards to Botswana, in open woodland and bush, often on the banks of dry watercourses, in areas of low and medium rainfall, often on soils rich in lime. It also grows in the northern and north eastern parts of South West Africa.

It is a small, shrubby, evergreen tree rarely growing higher than 3 to 5 m, sometimes partially climbing, with typically somewhat square and fluted stems. The mature branches are 4-angled and smooth, the younger ones covered with coarse hairs. The leaves are 2.5-10 cm long, egg-shaped, oblong or widely lance-shaped, the tips pointed, the base rounded or slightly notched, the margins irregularly toothed, roughly and harshly hairy, in particular on the lower side, the midrib and veins conspicuous below only. They are borne on short velvety stalks. The stipules are up to 1 cm long and hairy.

Klipspringer and impala eat the leaves.

The small oblong buds open into starry flowers with 5 slender gold petals in small bunches in the axils of the leaves.

The fruit is usually slightly 2-lobed but sometimes roundish or 4-lobed, yellow-brown or brown, shiny, and covered with both short and long, star-shaped hairs. They are edible, the dry skin usually being rubbed off before the flesh is eaten.

The foliage is browsed and the strong, tough wood is used to make bows, sticks, and knobkerries. The young branchlets are woven into baskets.

Parts of the tree are believed to have the power to stop bleeding of the nose, and in South West Africa the chewed root, thought to have disinfective qualities, is placed on wounds. Sprigs of a *Grewia* species possibly this one — are used by the Herero for sprinkling medicine on animals about to be sacrificed.

The specific name is Latin, meaning "yellowish".

Below
Grewia retinervis: Leaves and fruits
(70%)

Above right
The abundant fruits

c. *Grewia retinervis* Burret

Kalahari grewia; mokankele (Tsw – Ngwak); nya-muzwila (V)

This sometimes scrambling shrub or small bushy tree, which resembles *Grewia flavescens,* is typically a species of dry Kalahari sand and grows in sandy bush and open woodland in the Transvaal, the north west Cape, Botswana, and in central and northern South West Africa, including the Caprivi Strip. It also occurs in Angola, Rhodesia, and Zambia.

In the past this has sometimes been considered as a form of *Grewia flavescens.* It is, however, usually smaller, the branches are not 4-angled but rounded, the leaves are smooth, or nearly so, with the net veins, including those on the upper surface, conspicuous, and the fruit – red-brown, shiny, and round – never lobed. They are sweet and pleasant-tasting, and are the staple food, eaten either raw or dried, of several African tribes.

Story says that the dry stems usually have tunnellings of grubs which are full of their brown, pithy excreta. This is a Bushman tinder, the stems being split and a small depression made which serves as a socket for a fire-drill.

The specific name is Latin and means "net-veined".

(459)　　d. *Grewia caffra* Meisn.

Spiny grewia, doringtou; umLalanyathi (Z); liKholo (Sw); nsihana, nsihani (Tso)

Although this is often a many-stemmed and somewhat rambling shrub, or sometimes a climber, it may be a small tree up to 4.5 m high, or occasionally a 9 m tree with a trunk up to 30 cm in diameter.

It grows from Natal, Zululand, Swaziland, and the eastern and north-

1434

ern Transvaal, northwards into Rhodesia and Mozambique, in mixed tree veld, bush, on forest margins and on sand dunes, often on river banks, sometimes making dense thickets.

Sometimes the side branches become stout spines, described by collectors as "horrible branch thorns of awful size".

The older stems are square. The young twigs are hairy but become smooth with age. The thin, bright green leaves are 2-5 cm long and 0.8-2.5 cm wide, egg-shaped, oblong and lance-shaped, tapering to the point, the base broadly wedge-shaped to rounded, sometimes slightly lopsided, finely toothed, smooth or slightly hairy both sides, the stalk slightly hairy, the stipules bristle-like.

Good sticks are made from the wood.

The oblong, stalked flower buds open into cream or yellow, starry flowers borne in the axils of the leaves. The fruit is round, never lobed, up to 1 cm in diameter, smooth or slightly hairy. It is edible and popular with Vervet Monkeys.

(458)   e. *Grewia bicolor* Juss.

= *Grewia grisea* N.E.Br.; = *G. kwebensis* N.E.Br.; = *G. mossambicensis* Burret, = *G. miniata* Mast. ex Hiern

Two-coloured grewia, basterrosyntjiebos; umHlabampunzi (Z)

Grewia bicolor is one of the widely distributed species growing from South Africa and Swaziland to Ethiopia in the north, west to South West Africa and Angola, and east to Arabia and India. In South Africa it occurs in Zululand, the Orange Free State, and from the central Transvaal westwards to Botswana, in open bushveld, frequently associated with mopane, often in soil rich in lime, on stony hill or along stream banks.

It is a bush, a tree up to about 9 m tall, or more often a small, shrubby, several-stemmed tree, the trunk in old trees with grey, cracked, sometimes peeling bark, and in young trees smooth, and the branches covered with soft hairs.

Grewia bicolor: A fruiting twig (80%)

The leaves are variable. They are 1-8 cm long, widely lance-shaped to oval, the tips rounded or pointed, the base narrowed, rounded or notched, and sometimes slightly unequal, the margins finely toothed, or sometimes almost untoothed, above green and either smooth or velvety, below white or grey-blue and densely velvety, rather thin in texture, borne on short stalks. The stipules are needle-like or awl-shaped. Leaves and shoots are eaten by impala.

The bunches of small stalked buds open into bright yellow flowers with 5 narrow petals and a puff of stamens, usually 3 being borne on the common flower stalk in the axils of the leaves. The fruit is about 5 mm in diameter, round, single or deeply 2-lobed, purple-black or brownish when ripe, somewhat fleshy, and edible. The fruits of most grewias are an important item of diet of fruit-eating birds, and those of this species are no exception. Hornbills are particularly fond of them — and so are baboons and monkeys.

In parts the bark is stripped and used for cordage, and the wood of large trees is used for sticks and axe handles.

Some of the variation in this species is probably due to hybridization with *Grewia monticola* Sond.

The specific name *bicolor* means "two-coloured" and is based on the appearance of the leaves.

Above
Grewia bicolor near Chipisi

Below left
Grewia monticola near Jozini

Below right
Grewia monticola bark

(462)   f. *Grewia monticola* Sond.

= *Grewia cordata* N.E.Br.; = *G. obliqua* Weim.

Mountain grewia, vaalrosyntjiebos; umSipane (Sw); nsihana, nsihani (Tso); motuu (Tsw), moretlwa (Tsw-Hebron), mogwana kgomo (Tsw – Ngwak)

The mountain grewia is widespread in South Africa from Natal, Zululand and Swaziland through the eastern, central, and northern Transvaal to Botswana and South West Africa. Its distribution extends further to Mozambique, Rhodesia, Zambia and Tanzania.

It is a variable species of bush and open woodland, growing in many types of soil and often on rocky hill slopes. While it is sometimes a shrub, it is often a graceful small tree up to 4 to 6 m tall with a crown of spreading, weeping branches, the stems – single or several – round, with grey rough bark, and with the young flexible branches covered densely with reddish hairs.

The leaves are generally fairly large and leathery, 2.5-10 cm long and up to 5 cm wide, egg-shaped, oblong, oval, heart-shaped or lance-shaped, the tips rounded or occasionally pointed, the base round or notched and usually conspicuously unequal-sided, the margins sharply and irregularly toothed, the upper side grey-green, hairless or slightly hairy and somewhat rough, the lower covered with dense white or bluish-white hairs, marked with strong, often rust-coloured veins. They are borne on short, red, furry stalks. The young leaves are reddish. The stipules are narrow and pointed.

The small, oval, velvety buds in small heads borne on long stalks in the axils of the leaves, open into bright yellow or orange, starry flowers 0.8-1.3 cm in diameter with a conspicuous calyx. The fruit is 1-lobed, or sometimes so deeply 2-lobed that it appears to be twin-fruited, yellow covered with bristly hairs, borne on a robust stalk. It is edible. Galling of the fruit sometimes makes it appear brown and woolly.

The leaves are browsed by stock and wild animals, and the bark is relished by elephants which are said – after they have feasted – to leave "only a neat pile of leaves". The leaves are sometimes used to make a tea and the fruits are eaten by Bushmen.

The wood is very hard, strong and borer- and termite-proof, and is used to make sticks, assegai handles and whips, and in building huts, and the bark is used as thread in sewing baskets.

An ornithologist, Captain Leslie Shewell, notes that the Red-headed Weaver uses the tree for nest-building, stripping the leaves off the last 15 cm of a twig, which it then snaps off. Occasionally, he says, it uses the bark only.

This species, which is often associated with *Grewia bicolor,* appears to hybridize with it.

The specific name *monticola* is Latin, meaning "dweller in the mountains".

A species sometimes confused with *Grewia monticola* is *Grewia rogersii* Burtt Davy & Greenway, a spreading bush or tall shrub which appears to be confined to rocky hillsides in the central Transvaal near Warmbaths and Naboomspruit. In fruit this is easily distinguished for the fruit is 4-lobed and covered with long brown hairs. The species was named after Archdeacon Frederick Arundel Rogers, an amateur botanical collector, 1876-1944, who – while attached to the South African Railways – collected largely towards the beginning of the century in South Africa, Mozambique, and Rhodesia.

Grewia subspathulata in the bushveld near Beestekraal in the western Transvaal

(See detailed drawing on page 1444)

g. *Grewia subspathulata* N.E.Br.

Botanists are uncertain as to whether this is a species in its own right or a hybrid between *Grewia monticola* and *Grewia bicolor*. It grows within the range of these two species and is intermediate between them.

It is a lax shrub or small spreading tree growing from Zululand and Swaziland westwards through the Transvaal to Botswana, South West Africa and the Caprivi Strip, and northwards to Malawi, in bush and woodland, often on sandy soil.

The leaves are 1.3-10 cm long, oblong, oval or egg-shaped, the tips rounded or pointed, the base rounded and somewhat lopsided — in shape rather like those of *Grewia monticola* — the margins finely and regularly toothed, the surface 2-coloured, darkish green or grey-green and shortly velvety above and below greyish-velvety (somewhat similar in colour to *Grewia bicolor*). They differ from *Grewia monticola* mainly in the finely and regularly toothed margins, in the texture which is thinner, and in the smoother upper surface of the leaf.

The small, roundish, velvety, stalked buds — 2 or 3 in a bunch in the axils of the leaves — open into yellow, starry flowers. The fruit is 1- to 2-lobed and edible.

The bark is used as a cordage in building huts.

(459.1)   h. *Grewia flava* DC.

= *Grewia cana* Sond.; = *G. hermannioides* Harv.

Brandy-bush, raisin bush, brandewynbessie, bessiebos, kafferbessie, wilderosyntjie, rostyntjiebos; umHlalampunzi (Z); moretlhwa (Tsw), murapfa, muredwa (V); morezwa (Kal); omuvapu, omundjendjere (Her), ╪ŏub (Nama)

Few of the grewias are striking-looking and this is one of the most insignificant. It is a spreading, branched, twiggy and deciduous shrub or a

1438

small bushy tree seldom exceeding 4 m in height, yet in the areas where it grows — and it is widespread — it is one of the most generally valuable of all plants.

It grows in dry bushveld from Natal (where it is rare), and Swaziland, through the Orange Free State, north west Cape, and the Transvaal to Botswana, South West Africa and Rhodesia. Acocks terms a portion of the arid sweet bushveld in the northern Transvaal "*Grewia flava* veld" because of the dense growth there of this species. Here it grows in company with various acacias, *Commiphora pyracanthoides,* and the witgat, *Boscia albitrunca.* It often favours limestone and red Kalahari sand. This is also one of the commonest shrubs in parts of the grassland of Botswana.

The young branches are grey and hairy, the older ones darker. Trees or bushes often have a silver-grey appearance due to the colour of the foliage. The leaves are 1.3-8 cm long and up to 2.5 cm wide, oblong or oval, the tips rounded, the base narrowed and equal-sided (and in this it differs from *Grewia bicolor*), the margins finely toothed or almost entire, finely velvety both sides, the lower side paler than the upper, with the veins fairly prominent. They are rather coarser in texture than the leaves of *Grewia bicolor.* The small stipules are hairy.

The small, sweet-smelling, starry flowers with narrow yellow petals are usually borne singly in the axils of the leaves in summer.

The fruit is round, or 2-lobed, pea-sized, sometimes with bristly hairs, yellow turning red when ripe, edible, with a high percentage of sugar and some protein value, and important to primitive peoples because of its abundance and high sugar content. They eat it raw, fresh or dried, sometimes stamped and made into a meal, sometimes eaten with dried locusts. In parts of South West Africa it is considered the "most sought-after veldkos".

Farmers in the Transvaal once made (and perhaps in parts continue to make) a brandy known as mampoer from the fermented fruits, and here the species is widely known as "brandy-bush". This is considered the best local brand of liquor. Africans in South and South West Africa make beer from them and the Hottentots of the north western Cape distil a spirit from them.

The fruit is devoured by many species of birds, particularly guinea-fowl and korhaans, and by domestic poultry and stock. Duikers are reputed to be particularly fond of it.

Stock and wild animals browse the palatable leaves and young shoots. In South West Africa, where this species is common in dry bush, it is considered a particularly important fodder plant in late spring and early summer when other food is scarce, as it always has some leaf.

Old trees have a handsome brown heartwood, fine-grained and hard, but it is too small for most purposes. It is, however, very important to the indigenous peoples who make excellent sticks, bows, and arrows from it. Silberbauer says that the usual Bushman bow in Botswana is made from a straight stick of it, cut while still green and rubbed with the fat of the roasted seed of the sour plum, *Ximenia caffra,* and that the link-shaft and main shaft of the arrows are usually made from the flexible branches of the tree.

Dingaan's sticks are reputed to have been fashioned from the wood of this species.

Africans use the wands and sometimes the bark to make bowls and baskets. An old African woman on the farm "Somerset" in the Springbok Flats of the Transvaal, still makes woven bowls using *Grewia flava*

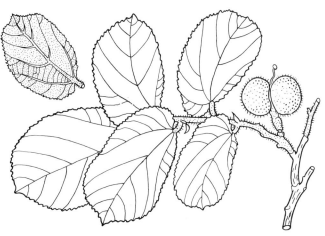

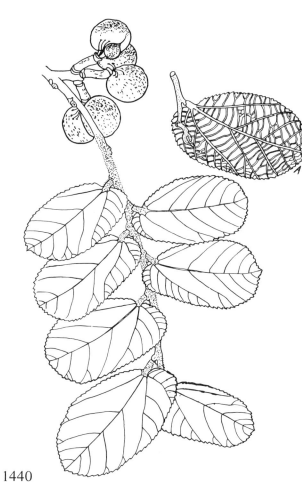

1440

Grewia hexamita: a
flower (100%)

wands for the framework, with the white, supple roots of the common
wild asparagus woven through them. This makes a delicate, light, and
waterproof bowl, beautifully and finely patterned.

The bark fibre is sometimes used for sewing.

Ferreira says that the Bushmen called this plant "ou" and used the
thin twigs to tune their reed flutes and to make the bows of their
stringed musical instruments.

The plant has medicinal and magic uses. The pounded roots, mixed
with ostrich egg, are used as a plaster on burns — said to be an effective
one — and the sticks, planted in the roofs of huts, are believed to ward
off lightning.

The specific name is the Latin "flavus" meaning "a bright clear yellow", presumably in reference to the flowers.

(460)   i. *Grewia hexamita* Burret

= *Grewia messinica* Burtt Davy & Greenway; = *Grewia schweickerdtii*
Burret

Lowveld grewia, umSipane (Sw); nsihana, nsihani (Tso)

The type specimen of this species came from the Transvaal. It is one of
the handsomest of the grewias here, a shrub or moderately sized tree up
to 8 m tall, with a leafy and glossy crown and rough grey bark,
growing from Swaziland to the eastern and northern Transvaal, and in
Mozambique and Rhodesia, in lowveld bush, on rocky hill slopes and on
river banks. It occurs in numbers between the Soutpansberg and the
Limpopo and is common in the valleys of the Limpopo and the Komati
rivers.

It may be a shrub or a fairly tall, spreading, and luxuriant-looking
tree, widely branched and leafy, the shine of its large leaves usually
being conspicuous. The young branches and twigs are covered with conspicuous red hairs. The leaves are leathery, 2.5-13 cm long and up to
9 cm broad, oval, egg-shaped or oblong, the tips rounded, pointed, or
occasionally flat, the base round, notched, and conspicuously lopsided,
the upper surface a shiny green and rough, the lower side a whitish-grey
and felted or sometimes a striking velvety red-gold with the veins covered with long reddish-brown hairs, and with dark, inrolled, serrated
margins looking remarkably like a fancy border. The network of veins
is often conspicuous below. The leaves are borne on short, furry stalks.

The buds, oval and reddish velvety, open into handsome yellow,
honey-scented flowers up to 2.5 cm in diameter with a conspicuous
calyx, yellow within and green and hairy without, borne in the axils of
the leaves.

The fruit is like a small cherry in shape and size, or more often 2-lobed,
appearing then like paired fruits, each lobe up to 2 cm in diameter, at
first hairy, later smooth, green turning yellow or red-brown, and shiny.

The wood is said to be generally useful.

j. *Grewia inaequilatera* Garcke

Grewia inaequilatera is primarily a tropical species which has been collected at Pafuri in the north eastern Transvaal, in Botswana, and in
northern South West Africa, usually in vleis or in low-lying river valleys.

OPPOSITE

Above left
Grewia hexamita near
Chipisi

Above right
The fruits and leaves

Centre left
Grewia hexamita: A
fruiting twig (60%)

Below left
The flowers

Below right
Grewia hexamita: A
fruiting twig. A. The
under-surface of a leaf
(60%)

It may be a scrambler, a dense shrub forming thickets, or a 3-7 m tree with a round stem, spreading or rambling, grey branches, and hairy twigs. The large green leaves are 5-18 cm long and 2.5-8 cm broad, oblong or oval, the tips flat or more often with a jutting point, the base round and very lopsided, the margins toothed, particularly in the upper portion, green and hairless above, and below covered with velvety white or grey hairs, the veins without the long brownish hairs of *Grewia monticola*. They are borne on hairy stalks. The roundish, hairy-grey stipules fall off early.

The flowers, borne in small groups in the axils of the leaves on sturdy, white-dotted stalks, are yellow. They have numerous stamens. The fruit is round or more often 2-lobed, when it appears like paired fruits, somewhat hairy, yellow when ripe, and edible.

The specific name is Latin meaning "unequal-sided", in reference to the shape of the leaves.

k. *Grewia schinzii* K. Schum.

= *Grewia velutinissima* Dunkley

Notu grewia, notuu, mokgompatha (Tsw)

This is not a South African species but occurs in northern South West Africa, Botswana, Angola, and Zambia in bush and woodland, often near rivers.

It is a shrub or small tree with a round crown and many branches from the base, and with young branches covered with reddish hairs. The leaves are large, 5-14 cm long and 2.5-9 cm broad, oblong to egg-shaped, the tips round or bluntly or sharply pointed, the base rounded or heart-shaped and notched, the margin coarsely and irregularly toothed, green above and covered with short, star-shaped hairs, below covered with dense grey or brown hairs.

The flowers, with roundish yellow petals, are borne 2-3 together on a reddish, very hairy stalk in the axils of the leaves. The fruit is round or deeply 2-lobed, usually about 7 mm wide, yellow, hairy, and edible.

The species was named after Prof Dr Hans Schinz, 1858 to about 1941, Swiss botanist and Director of the Botanic Garden and Botanical Museum at the University of Zurich, who collected in South West Africa from 1884-1887.

l. *Grewia villosa* Willd.

Round-leaf grewia; iKholo (Z); murapfa (V)

The type specimen of this species came from India and it grows in Arabia and the Cape Verde Islands, as well as in the drier areas of Africa, where it is widespread. In Southern Africa it grows in Mozambique, Zululand, Natal, Swaziland, the Transvaal, Botswana and South West Africa, in bush or woodland, often as an undershrub.

It is usually a much-branched shrub up to about 3 m high, with large leaves, 2.5-14 cm in diameter, round or heart-shaped, the tips round, the base sometimes lopsided, the margins toothed, the upper surface green, hairy and rough, the lower grey and velvety, with the veins conspicuous. The young leaves are prettily wrinkled.

The roundish or oblong, silky flower buds open into yellow flowers on hairy stalks borne opposite or away from the leaf. The slightly 4-lobed fruits are up to 1.5 cm in diameter, reddish and warted, the warts bearing long hairs. They are eaten by Bushmen.

The specific name is Latin meaning "bearing long weak hairs".

m. *Grewia micrantha* Boj.

The typical *Grewia micrantha* is purely a tropical species. What is possibly a form of it occurs in Natal, Swaziland, and the eastern Transvaal. It is a shrub or a small tree, often somewhat drooping, with leaves up to about 8 cm long, egg-shaped or roundish, the tips rounded or pointed, the base rounded, heart-shaped, and lopsided, the margins toothed, above slightly hairy or smooth, below covered with dense, light-coloured hairs, the veins almost hairless.

The yellow flowers are borne in the axils of the leaves. The fruit is 2-lobed but 1 lobe may be missing.

The species is browsed by animals.

The specific name is based on Greek words meaning "small flower".

(463)   n. *Grewia occidentalis* L.

= *Grewia chirindae* Bak.f.; = *G. microphylla* Weim.

Kruisbessie, four-corners, star-flower, button-wood, bow-wood, assegai wood; umNqabaza, umVilani (X); umHlalanyathi, iLalanyathi, iKlolo (Z); umSipane (Sw); mokukutu, mogwana, motswetsweyane (Tsw); mulembu (V)

This, the first-known of the grewias in South Africa, has a place in the history of botany and gardening. In 1768 Miller, in his *Garden Dictionary,* described this as "the Grewia with oval, crenated leaves — an Ethiopian shrub with the appearance of an elm". It had, he said, been grown for long in "many curious gardens both in England and Holland" and he himself had raised it from seed sent him from the Cape.

It is a widespread species in South Africa. Whereas most grewias grow in the drier areas of the country, this species occurs more often in the southern, eastern and northern areas which have a moderate or heavy rainfall, in all four provinces and in Swaziland and Lesoto, along forest margins, in dense coastal bush, on wooded hillsides, in open woodland, in scrub, sometimes on dunes — where it is often almost prostrate — from sea level to an altitude of at least 1500 m above the sea. It grows on Table Mountain itself — it was in this countryside that it was first collected — and it is one of the common shrubs along the eastern reaches of the Orange River. Its distribution extends to Rhodesia, Mozambique, and Malawi, and to South West Africa, where, however, it is rare.

It may be a low straggly shrub on sand dunes, a semi-climber, a slender bush, or a much-branched, many stemmed tree up to 5 or 6 m high. The variety *litoralis* Wild from dunes in Mozambique is no more than a semi-prostrate shrub.

The flexible stems are smooth grey, becoming somewhat 4-angled with age. The leaves are from 2-8 cm long and 1.3-4 cm wide, oval, pear-shaped, quadrangular, or lance-shaped, the tips rounded or broad, or pointed, the base slightly narrowed, or rounded, sometimes slightly

Above
Grewia occidentalis on mountain side, "St. Olives", Graaff-Reinet district

Centre left
Grewia subspathulata: A fruiting twig (80%)

Below left
Grewia occidentalis: A flowering and fruiting twig and an individual flower (80%)

Below right
Grewia occidentalis, often many-stemmed

heart-shaped, the margins with irregular blunt teeth, smooth or very slightly hairy on both surfaces, dull or shiny green above, somewhat paler below, thin in texture. They are borne on smooth stalks. The narrow hairy stipules fall off early.

Although the kruisbessie flowers irregularly throughout the year, the heaviest blooming is in spring and early summer. The flowers are starry, pink, mauve, violet, claret, or occasionally white, the petals and inside of the sepals being of the same colour; with a conspicuous puff of stamens; up to 2.5 cm in diameter. One to 3 are borne on slender stalks in a stalked cluster at a point opposite the leaf stalk.

The 4-lobed fruit, up to about 2.5 cm in diameter, appears to be composed of 4 small, pea-like balls linked together roughly in the form of a cross. These give the tree its most common popular names of "kruisbessie" or "cross-berry", and "four-corners". They are usually bristly, purple when ripe in the autumn, and somewhat fleshy. Each lobe contains 1 seed.

The fruit is edible and Speckled Mousebirds, and probably many other species, devour it. The foliage is browsed by cattle and by wild animals.

Black Rhino eat both stem and leaves.

Buffaloes are said to show a preference for standing in the shade of this species.

This is much used in African medicine, the bruised and soaked bark as a dressing for wounds, parts of the plant in midwifery, and for impotence and barrenness.

The wood is moderately heavy and fine-grained, generally light in colour but sometimes with a dark heart. It was used by Bushmen because of its toughness and flexibility to make bows, it yields good sticks, and the Pondos use it for spear shafts. O.B. Miller says that its Pondo name, umVilani, means "assegais of an army".

This is a satisfactory garden tree. The seed germinates easily and the young seedlings transplant readily and thrive in sun or in partial shade. The flowers are delicate and charming and the tree has a long blooming period. Miller in his *Garden Dictionary,* wrote that it could be reproduced easily from seed, cuttings, or by layering. It may be questioned how many gardeners, in the two centuries since he cultivated it in a London garden, have grown this species in its native land.

The name *occidentalis* means "of the west".

This species together with two others, *Grewia robusta* Burch. and *Grewia lasiocarpa* E.Mey. ex Harv., make up a small group in Southern Africa which have flowers in shades of pink, lilac and purple and not the usual yellow. A species, probably undescribed, from the forests of Pondoland and Natal with thick leaves and lilac flowers resembling those of *Grewia occidentalis,* but very much larger, clearly falls within this group. It awaits investigation.

o. *Grewia robusta* Burch.

= *Grewia krebsiana* Kuntze

Karoo kruisbessie

The Karoo kruisbessie is easily confused with *Grewia occidentalis* for the leaves, flowers, and fruits are somewhat similar.

It is, however, nearly always a shrub and only very occasionally a tree up to about 3 m high, and it is confined to the Cape Province where it

Left
Grewia robusta fruit

Right
Grewia robusta flower

grows — often on shale and on hill slopes — in parts of the Midlands and the eastern Cape, from about Prince Albert, Beaufort West, Graaff-Reinet, Pearston, and Cradock to Bedford, Grahamstown and Alexandria. It is particularly common in the scrub of the Fish River valley and in the catchment of the Sundays River.

It is usually a dense, rounded, sturdy, many-branched shrub up to about 3 m high with hard, rigid, grey twigs which are often spiny, and leaves which are frequently clustered in tufts on short side-shoots.

The leaves are small, 1.3-2.5 cm long, oval or egg-shaped, the tips bluntly pointed, the base rounded or sometimes notched, with the margins usually finely toothed, adult leaves a shiny green above and below covered with a blue-green mat of hairs, and with the veins clearly marked.

The buds, like small fat figs in shape, are mauve flushed with ruby. The flowers have 5 petals but appear, like many grewias, to have 10, for the sepals, although slightly longer than the petals, are remarkably petal-like. The flowers bloom irregularly from spring to autumn and are star-like, up to 2.5 cm in diameter, pink, mauve and ruby, or occasionally white, with a puff of stamens, sweet-scented, and attractive to bees, flies, and butterflies. Usually only 1 flower is borne opposite a leaf, but often it is in a tuft with the leaves so that its position is not easy to see.

The fruit is deeply 4-lobed, 1 or more lobes sometimes failing to develop, shiny and covered with small stiff bristles.

It is an excellent fodder plant for the leaves and fruits are readily eaten by stock.

The karoo kruisbessie might make a good garden shrub, compact, hardy and undemanding, worthy of cultivation for its charming flowers.

(461)   p. *Grewia lasiocarpa* E.Mey. ex Harv.

Shaggy-fruited grewia, elephant's ear grewia; umHlolo (X); iKlolo (Z)

The shaggy-fruited grewia is a small tree, a bush, or a climber of forest, forest margins, and kloofs, occurring from about Kei Mouth northwards through the Transkei to roughly Lower Tugela in Natal. It is a common species in the forests round Port St. John's.

The bark is smooth and grey, and the twigs brown and very rough. The leaves are larger than those of most grewias, normally up to about 9 cm long and 8 cm broad, but sometimes larger — the common name "elephant's ear" is apt– egg-shaped, oval, or almost round, the tips

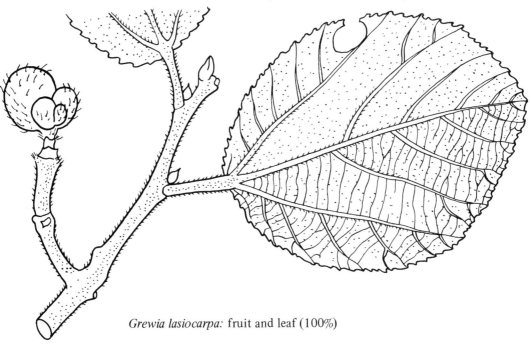

Grewia lasiocarpa: fruit and leaf (100%)

rounded or occasionally bluntly pointed, the base sometimes narrowed but usually rounded, the margins roundly toothed, conspicuously 3-veined from the base, the upper surface rough to the touch, the lower lighter and velvety, the midribs and veins raised, conspicuous, and covered with reddish hairs, and the netted veins between distinct. They are borne on sturdy, hairy stalks.

The reddish, oval, velvety buds open into large pinkish or lilac flowers nearly 5 cm in diameter, about 2-4 usually being borne in robust stalked clusters opposite the leaves. They usually bloom in summer.

The fruit is large, up to about 2.5 cm in diameter, 4-lobed, although 1 or more lobes may be missing, and hairy.

The specific name is based on Greek words meaning "shaggy fruit".

This grewia, when not in flower or fruit, is often confused — even by botanists — with *Trimeria grandifolia* (Hochst.) Warb., for the leaves are very similar. The grewia, however, has only 3 veins from the base and the trimeria has 5 or 7.

1447

65 The Hibiscus Family (Malvaceae)

This is a well-known and well-loved family for the big, bright flowers which characterize it have a place in many South African gardens. Its most famous member economically is the cotton plant, *Gossypium herbaceum* L.

It is a large and cosmopolitan group with about 43 genera and 1700 species of small trees, shrubs and herbs spread throughout the warm parts of the world. In South Africa trees occur in 3 genera, *Hibiscus, Thespesia,* and *Azanza,* which have species usually with simple, often lobed leaves arranged alternately, and big handsome flowers which are regular and most often bisexual; the sepals 5, characteristically with an epicalyx – a ring of bracts resembling a second calyx – below the calyx proper; the petals 5, the stamens typically united into a tubular column, with the style protruding through the tube, the ovary superior, of 2 to many carpels, free or joined, and the fruit usually dry and splitting open into many parts.

Some of the species produce a useful fibre which can be spun and woven.

Key to Genera

The fruit splitting open

The leaves not scaly; the epicalyx cup-shaped with 10 teeth; the calyx usually lobed, the sepals often long and hairy; the fruit splitting along the lobes.

1. Hibiscus

The leaves with star-shaped hairs, not scaly; no separate epicalyx; the calyx cup-shaped; the fruit splitting along the valves.

3. Azanza

The fruit not splitting open

The leaves scaly; the epicalyx of 3 segments; the calyx cup-shaped; the fruit somewhat fleshy.

2. Thespesia

1. *Hibiscus* L.

Hibiscus is a large genus of nearly 600 species widely spread throughout the warm countries of the world. It is well represented in South Africa with about 40 species which are mainly shrubs or herbs. One species, *Hibiscus tiliaceus* L., from the shores of the eastern Cape, Natal, and Zululand is a tree.

All the species have alternate leaves which are usually simple and often lobed, or occasionally digitately compound, bisexual flowers that are usually solitary, borne in the axils of the leaves but sometimes, when the leaves are much reduced, appearing to be in terminal inflorescences. They are often large and showy, red, pink, white, or yellow with a dark centre and a particularly beautiful, soft texture. The calyx lobes and petals are 5, and the staminal tube is composed of stamens which are free almost to the base. An epicalyx, or ring of bracts below the calyx, is usually present. The ovary is 4-5-locular, and the fruit is a 4-5-valved capsule surrounded by the persistent calyx, the valves bursting open on maturity.

An interesting character in some species is the rapid change of colour of the flowers after opening. To one such species, *Hibiscus mutabilis* L., the Chinese gave a name meaning Civil Servant, "obviously uncomplimentary in intention", says Alice M. Coats in her history of garden shrubs. Our native tree hibiscus has flowers which open a clear yellow or sometimes pink and which change within a day to rich apricot and red.

The inner bark of many species yields strong, tough fibre used for making rope and string.

The generic name is derived from the Greek "Hibiskos", the name given to the marshmallow. It is said to be derived from "Ibis", meaning "stork", which was supposed to feed on some of the marshmallow species.

See colour plate facing page 1098

(464)   *Hibiscus tiliaceus* L.

= *Paritium tiliaceum* (L.) St. Hil.

Lagoon hibiscus, Linden hibiscus, wild hibiscus, katoenboom; umLolwa (X), uLola (Z)

The lagoon hibiscus is one of the most cosmopolitan of all our trees for it grows, usually along sea shores, lagoons, and coastal rivers, from South Africa, the islands of the Indian Ocean — Mauritius, Madagascar and the Seychelles — to India and Java in the east and America and the islands of the Pacific in the west.

In South Africa it is common from the eastern Cape northwards to Zululand — extending northwards into eastern tropical Africa — growing on the sea shore, fringing lagoons, swamps, and river mouths, often near mangroves.

It is a striking bush, or tree 3-12 m high, often branching from ground level, with a big, rounded, leafy crown, big heart-shaped leaves, and bright yellow or apricot flowers, and in this form is often seen at the edge of lagoons. At the edge of swamp forest, growing closely together in dense shade, it is apt to be more slender.

The stem, up to about 46 cm in diameter, is grey to grey-brown, sometimes smooth or with small raised dots, becoming slightly rough with age. The young branches are covered with star-shaped hairs. The leaves,

Above
The lagoon hibiscus, *Hibiscus tiliaceus*, Umdoni Park. Its large leaves identify it from afar.

Right
Hibiscus tiliaceus: The leaves, buds and flowers (50%)

Below left
Hibiscus tiliaceus overhanging the lagoon at "Twinstreams", Zululand. In the background are *Mimusops caffra, Canthium obovatum,* and *Brachylaena discolor*

Below right
The bark of an old tree

Opposite
The bark of a young hibiscus

1450

borne on long and often hairy stalks, are big — 4-26 cm in diameter — roundish or heart-shaped, often broader than long, with a pronounced jutting tip and a deeply notched base, untoothed or minutely toothed, smooth and green above, covered with dense white hairs below, with 5-9 veins from the base which on the under-surface are silver-green, pink or yellow, raised and conspicuous. Above they often have a red or pink patch at their point of junction at the leaf base. The netted veins are conspicuous both sides.

The young growth is protected by large stipules which soon fall off.

The leaf stalks are noticeably thickened at their junction with the stem.

The flowers, blooming from spring to autumn, are borne in the axils of the leaves but when these are reduced they often appear to be growing terminally. They are handsome, up to about 8 cm across, with a cup-shaped epicalyx and a conspicuous lobed calyx, and with 5 large petals, usually a clear lemon yellow with a maroon or purple centre when they open, but soon turning a rich apricot-red or orange. The change in colour is quick and the flowers have a brief life.

The fruits are round or oval capsules, pointed, about 2.5 cm long, and hairy. They split into 5 parts to show small, dark, smooth seeds.

The sapwood is whitish, the heartwood a dullish green marked with black. It is fibrous, coarse-grained, fairly hard, durable, and has been used for planks. The bark yields a good fibre. In Zululand the tree is used to make fish traps.

The lagoon hibiscus makes a beautiful and shady tree in frost-free areas and has been used as a street tree in Durban, and as a handsome hedge on the Natal south coast. It is particularly good near water, and its large leaves and rich flowers are at their best contrasted, as in the wild, with pools or running streams. In grows easily from seed, cuttings, or truncheons and transplants readily. For at least 200 years it has been cultivated in many parts of the world.

The specific name *tiliaceus* refers to the likeness of the plant to the genus *Tilia.* "Tilia" was an ancient name for the lime or linden tree.

2. *Thespesia* Soland. ex Corr.

Thespesia is a small genus of about 11 species occurring in all tropical countries. One tree species, *Thespesia acutiloba* (Bak.f.) Exell & Mendonça, grows in South Africa. A somewhat similar and very widespread species with larger leaves, flowers and fruits — with which our native species is sometimes confused — is *Thespesia populnea* (L.) Soland ex Corr. This grows in Mozambique and does not appear to extend into South Africa.

The species are trees or shrubs with alternate leaves covered with small scales, flowers that are showy, bisexual, and solitary, borne in the axils of the leaves, the epicalyx with 3 segments, the calyx cup-like sometimes with 5 teeth, the petals 5, the stamens united in a tube, the ovary 5-locular, the fruit somewhat fleshy.

The generic name is based on the Greek word "thespesios" meaning "divine", supposedly because *Thespesia populnea* was frequently planted round temples in the tropics.

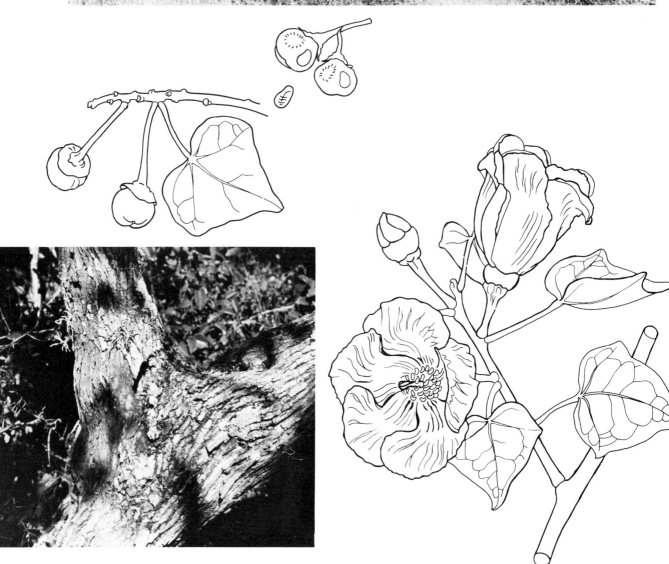

1452

OPPOSITE

Above
Thespesia acutiloba,
False Bay, Zululand

Centre left
A fruiting twig of *Thespesia acutiloba,* individual fruits showing the position of the seeds, and a seed (60%)

Below left
The bark

Below right
A flowering twig (80%)

(465)   *Thespesia acutiloba* (Bak.f.) Exell & Mendonça

= *Thespesia populnea* (L.) Soland ex Corr. var *acutiloba* Bak.f.

Thespesia, tulip tree; iBhicongo, iPhuphuma (Z)

Like the lagoon hibiscus, this is a cosmopolitan species growing from South and tropical Africa through the tropics of the world. In South Africa it grows along the coast from Zululand as far south as the Umfolozi River, on the edges of swamp, sometimes up river valleys, in bush and thickets. It grows in both the Hluhluwe and Umfolozi Game Reserves.

It is a spreading evergreen bush, or tree up to about 9 m high, often branched from the base, with a grey, furrowed trunk, and grey branches and twigs covered with scaly dots.

The green, shiny leaves are simple and alternate, much resembling ivy or poplar leaves. They are up to 8 cm long and nearly as much wide, and are usually 3-lobed, the tips pointed, the base flat or somewhat heart-shaped, 5-nerved, untoothed, both sides scaly, borne on long slender, scaly stalks. Occasionally they are egg- or heart-shaped and not lobed.

The flowers, blooming in the autumn, are borne singly in the axils of the leaves and sometimes appear to make terminal sprays. They are up to 4 cm in diameter, red in bud but opening a clear yellow with maroon centres. The flowers open for only a short time at midday, closing again in the afternoon. Only the upper portion of the petals spread outwards and the flowers do not appear ever to open fully. The epicalyx is soon deciduous.

The fruit is slightly fleshy, roundish or sometimes slightly flattened, up to 1.9 cm in width, perched on a cup-like calyx, and carried on a long, strong stalk. It is shiny, vermilion to deep plum red, turning finally black, and is striking among the handsome ivy-like leaves. It is eaten by birds such as coucals and loeries.

The heartwood is black, at first soft when cut but becoming hard. It is durable and is used in Zululand for carving and to make spears, sticks, and strikers for chest-bows, the musical instruments known as makwelane.

The medicinal uses of the tree are many, both roots and fruits all being used. In Zululand a bath to refresh the body and to dispel troublesome spirits is made by soaking the roots in water.

The seeds are rich in oil and the flower petals yield a dye.

The tree is easily cultivated.

The specific name means "acutely lobed" in reference to the shape of the leaves.

3. *Azanza* Alef.

This tropical genus of shrubs or small trees is represented in South Africa by 1 tree species.

All have alternate, hairy leaves; solitary, bisexual flowers in the axils of the leaves with a conspicuous cup-like calyx, with which the epicalyx is fused; the petals 5, the stamens many, the ovary 5-chambered, the fruit 5-valved and splitting open along the valves. The dehiscent fruit is one of the main differences between this genus and *Thespesia.*

The derivation of the generic name is obscure. The strips of desert coast extending below the equator in Africa were once known as the "courses of Azania", the name Azania being based on a word meaning

The young thespesia fruit forming

Above
A snot apple, *Azanza garckeana*, at
Modjadje's Kraal, northern Transvaal

Below left
The leaves

Below right
Azanza garckeana: A portion of a
fruiting branchlet (60%)

Opposite above
Snot apple bark

Opposite below
A snot apple flower that has opened
and closed

black and surviving in Zanzibar — and it is possible that *Azanza* is derived from this.

(466)   *Azanza garckeana* (F.Hoffm.) Exell & Hillcoat

= *Thespesia garckeana* F.Hoffm.; = *Thespesia triloba* Bak.f.; = *Thespesia rogersii* S.Moore; = *Shantzia garckeana* (F.Hoffm.) Lewton

Snot apple, snotappel, wild hibiscus; morajwa (Tsw — Mang); muthowa, muthowa (V); moneko (Kol)

Unlike the other tree members of the hibiscus family in South Africa, the snot apple has not a world-wide distribution but is confined to eastern and southern tropical Africa, growing in the eastern and north eastern Transvaal, Botswana, northern South West Africa including the Caprivi Strip, northwards to Malawi and Tanzania, in open woodland.

It is a shrub or a graceful, spreading, usually evergreen tree up to 9 m tall with a grey or dark brown trunk cracked lengthwise, and twigs that are hairy when young but that become smooth with age.

The leaves are alternate, simple, roundish, and 3-5-lobed, the tip usually bluntly pointed or rounded, the base heart-shaped and 5-7-nerved, the margins untoothed, often large — 5-20 cm in diameter — hairless or hairy and rather rough above, and below hairy with the veins raised. The midrib usually has a small fissure lengthwise, which appears on the lower surface as a short dark line.

The young leaves are a bronze colour and velvety.

The leaf stalks are up to 13 cm long and are hairy. Stipules are present but fall off early.

The rather bell-shaped, crinkled flowers, up to 6 cm across, are creamy-yellow, changing to red or purple, with a dark centre. They usually bloom in summer.

The fruit is a hard capsule up to nearly 5 cm long, roundish or oval, covered densely with hairs and splitting open along 5 valves. It is perched on a conspicuous, saucer-like calyx. Green fruits are glutinous within and are eaten by Africans who peel off the outside rind and suck the fleshy inner surface. This results in a great flow of saliva and is the basis of the common name "snot apple" or "snotappel", from the Afrikaans "snotter", meaning "to snivel". The dried fruits, soaked in a small amount of water, make a stiff jelly. The seeds are brown.

The long shoots of the snot apple are used as whips and the wood for axe handles and sheaths. A fibre is made of the inner bark.

In the wild the tree suckers very freely so might be unsuitable for a small garden. It is the host of the red and black beetle known as the cotton stainer and is unpopular in cotton producing areas.

The species was named in honour of Prof August Garcke, 1819-1904, a German professor of botany.

66 The Baobab Family (Bombacaceae)

About 21 genera and 150 species, according to Phillips, belong to this family and are distributed through Africa, Madagascar, India, Australia, the Malay Archipelago, and America. Some of these are very large trees and many, such as our indigenous species, have big and handsome flowers.

Only 1 tree species occurs in South and South West Africa, *Adansonia digitata* L., and this is the most famous member of the family. In Mozambique the genera *Bombax* and *Ceiba* are represented by several tree species but these do not penetrate into South Africa.

Many have the strangely swollen trunks typical of the baobab; all have alternate leaves, simple or digitately compound, with stipules, and bisexual flowers. These have a leathery calyx, sometimes with 5 lobes, 5 petals, the stamens free or joined in a tube, the ovary superior and 2-5-chambered, and fruit that is usually a capsule or nut.

Adansonia L.

This remarkable genus is widely distributed in the hot dry parts of Africa from Ethiopia to the northern Transvaal and northern South West Africa, in Madagascar and in northern Australia, while species are cultivated in Ceylon and the East Indies where they are believed to have been taken by Arab traders.

All the baobabs of Africa, distributed over a vast area, are believed to be one and the same variable species, *Adansonia digitata* L. (It should be noted that some botanists see in this not one but several species.) Yet in the comparatively small country of Madagascar at least 4 — and possibly more — species occur, and 2 in a fairly small area in Australia.

All are trees, often of tremendous girth, with alternate leaves that are digitately 3-9-foliolate; flowers that are large, bisexual, often handsome, with a deeply 5-lobed calyx, 5 petals, and numerous stamens joined at the base in a tube; the ovary 5-10-chambered, the fruit woody, roundish or oval, *not* bursting open, containing numerous seeds in a powdery pulp. They are borne singly in the axils of the leaves.

The genus was named by Linnaeus after a French surgeon, Michel Adanson, who saw *Adansonia digitata* when travelling in Senegal between 1749 and 1753, and wrote an account of it.

(467)   *Adansonia digitata* L.

Baobab, cream-of-tartar tree, monkey-bread tree, lemonade tree, kremetartboom; isiMuku, umShimulu, isiMuhu (Z); ximuwu (Tso); mowana (Tsw), moana (Tsw — Taw); muvhuyu (V); ibozu (Sub); mobuyu (Kol); dovuyu (Mbuk), omukura (Ov)

A monarch, a monster, a carrot growing up-side-down?

Of all the many strange forms of plant life in Africa there is none more strange and grotesque than the baobab. This oddly shaped tree with its enormous and tapering branches fascinates all who see it. It has been likened to a monarch, a monster, a vegetable elephant, a carrot growing up-side-down — yet, superb or ridiculous, according to the beholder — it is always a curiosity of the first order.

It has probably been more often described than any other tree in Africa. An account of it appeared in Prospero Alpini's *Natural History of Egypt* in 1592. The first person to give an exact account of it was Michel Adanson who actually brought seed of it to Paris in 1754, and who left beautiful drawings of the tree, flower and fruit. In 1768 Miller, who called it "the Ethiopian Sour Gourd", described it in his famous *Garden Dictionary*. Since then many travellers and explorers have written of it, including Chapman, Livingstone, and the artist-explorer, Thomas Baines.

In South Africa the baobab grows in numbers as far south as the Soutpansberg in the northern Transvaal, and the Olifants River in the east. A few stragglers grow south of this, including some big trees on the southern banks of the Nwaswitsontswe River some 50 miles south of the Olifants River, a few in the Waterberg, and one in the Rustenberg district. The baobab, however, seldom grows out of the dry, hot, sandy country, where it is so conspicuously at home. This is usually some 450-600 m above sea level with a rainfall of from 300-500 mm a year. The baobab is at its best in deep, well-drained soil, although it is often seen on the sides of koppies or hills. It grows in large numbers on the northern slopes of the Soutpansberg, giving this country in winter time something of a prehistoric air. The mining town of Messina has grown around some fine specimens which still stand in the streets. Its distribution extends further to Botswana, northern South West Africa, the Caprivi Strip, Rhodesia, and to tropical Africa.

The baobab is not remarkable for its height, which is usually from 14-23 m, but for its enormous girth and unusual shape. Livingstone camped under a baobab the trunk of which, 1 metre from the ground, measured 26 m in circumference. The main trunk, which is usually cylindrical in shape, suddenly tapers into comparatively small thin spreading branches, looking rather like roots. (Many Africans, indeed,

Pl. 1.

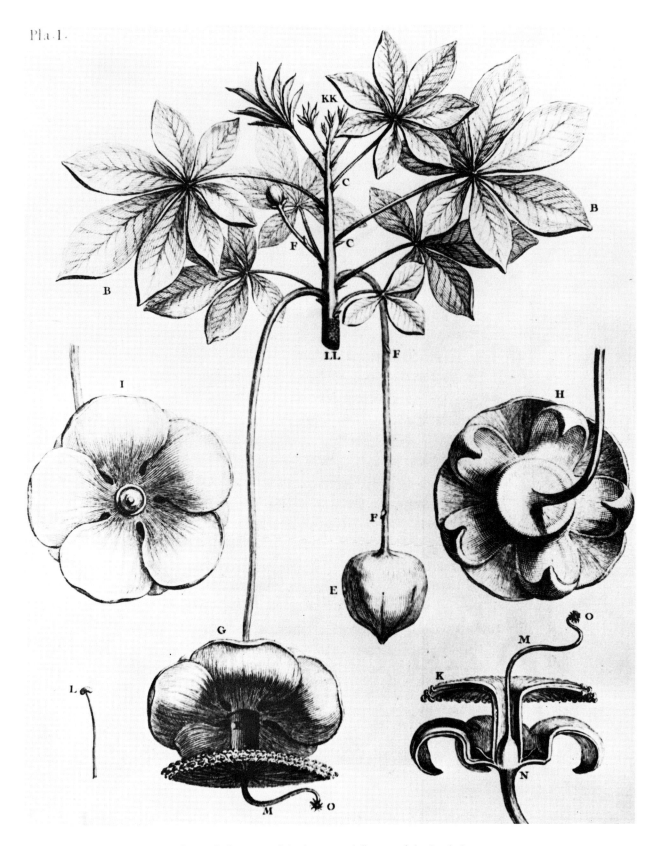

Adanson's drawing of the leaves and flower of the baobab

believe that the baobab grows up-side-down). The thick shiny trunk is covered with bark 5-10 cm thick, sometimes smooth but often folded and seamed, greyish-brown but sometimes with a red or mauve tinge. Some fine specimens grow near the famous archeological site of Mapungupwe in the northern Transvaal and these have a memorable purple sheen.

A very young baobab is smooth, slender, and tapering, very unlike the mature tree. Baines described young baobabs in Australia "before age had made their stems gouty", as "smooth and round and long-necked, as a champagne bottle, which, with a branching twig stuck in its cork, would be no bad representation of them", and this is an excellent description of young African plants as well.

The tree is deciduous and the new foliage usually appears in late spring or early summer, or after rains, at the ends of the branches. The leaves are digitate, that is, divided into leaflets diverging from the same point like the fingers of a hand. There are usually 5-7 leaflets which are large — 4 to 15 cm long — and glossy, oblong, oval, or widely lance-shaped, narrowed both ends, the tips pointed, untoothed, when young covered with star-shaped hairs below but later becoming smooth. Stipules are present but soon fall off. The leaves on young plants are simple.

The big round buds open into large, sweet-scented, drooping flowers, 13-18 cm wide, on long stalks. The velvety sepals curl back to show the spreading crisped and snow-shite petals with a big puff of stamens in the centre. Dr Inez Verdoorn of the Botanical Research Institute, who has made a special study of the baobab, has wondered for years what insect, bird, or animal pollinates these handsome blooms. Now she suggests it may be the bat, *Eidolon helvum*, which is known to pollinate them in North Africa and which is found in South Africa as well. Small mammals, birds, reptiles, and insects are all attracted in numbers to the tree.

The flowers turn brown soon after they are picked. This makes them difficult to photograph or paint.

The fruits are usually somewhat egg-shaped and large, 10-26 cm long, with a woody shell. They are suspended from the under-side of the branches and are covered with "a very rich, deep-sea green, downy substance", becoming greyish-brown with age. The thick shell encloses numerous black seeds, edible and nourishing, embedded in a white pulp which has a pleasant tart flavour and is rich in Vitamin C, calcium and thiamine. When dry, this pulp becomes powdery, and mixed with water makes a refreshing drink. It is this powder which has given the names "cream-of-tartar tree" and "lemonade tree" to the baobab. Baboons and monkeys tear open the fruits to reach this pulp.

The leaves are said to have a high vitamin and calcium content, and in parts are boiled and eaten by Africans as a vegetable. The shoot of the germinating seed can be used in place of asparagus; and the root of the very young baobab is reputed to be edible. The caterpillars which feed on the leaves in the northern Transvaal and in South West Africa are collected by Africans as an important source of food. The fallen leaves are eaten by animals, and cattle are said to "love the flowers like pudding".

The wood contains a high proportion of water — it is estimated that a tree with a volume of 210 cubic metres contains about 136,400 litres of water. When chewed, it relieves thirst, and is eaten by humans, elephants, antelope and cattle in times of need.

The tree has been employed medicinally for centuries. At one time the bark was used in Europe to treat fevers and as a substitute for cinchona bark. The leaves and fruit pulp are still used in parts of Africa as a remedy for malaria.

Above
The "Baines Tree" north of Ghanzi, painted by Baines on December 7, 1861

Below left
The Big Tree south of Gootsa Pan in Botswana, recorded by both Chapman and Livingstone

Below right
The "Baines Tree" – photographed by G.L. Guy – as it is now

The bark is the most generally useful part of the tree. Africans in various areas obtain an excellent fibre by stripping it from the tree, pounding it, and soaking it in water. The fibre is then used for rope, fishing nets, sacks, and even woven into material for clothing. There have been repeated unsuccessful attempts by Europeans to make artificial silk and string from the tree. A sample of wood and bark, sent to London, was made into a fairly strong paper but this could not be bleached by ordinary methods.

The wood is light yellow, spongy and soft, and an axe driven into the trunk with a good blow is extricated with difficulty. In parts Africans make boxes of it but this does not seem a very general practice.

Old baobabs often have hollow trunks, or are deliberately hollowed out by Africans, who then use the tree for storing grain or as a temporary home for themselves. Sometimes they construct a ladder up the side of a baobab which they then use as a look-out or a place of safety out of reach of prowling lions.

In the Sudan a baobab is often hollowed out and used as a water tank, which is filled by Africans during the rainy season. Hollow baobab trunks collect rain water naturally which they retain for a long time. A hole is often drilled in the trunk and a bung inserted, and many hunters and early settlers in the lowveld and the Kalahari have had cause to bless these natural water reservoirs. Such a reservoir may hold about 4546 litres (1000 gallons) of water. Bushmen often reach the stored water by fitting hollow grass stalks, one end into the other, to form a tube, and sucking it out. Unfortunately mosquitoes breed in these hollow trees.

Early writers on the baobab in tropical Africa recorded a sinister use. The bodies of those considered not worthy of decent burial were, they said, hung within the hollow trunks.

A big tree in the Transvaal was once used as a dairy. Many of the old prospectors of the Transvaal must have remembered the baobab with affection, for a hollow tree near Leydsdorp was turned into a bar, known as the Murchison Club, and was frequented by miners and prospectors who flocked to the Murchison Range when gold was discovered there in the last century. The tree still stands although doors and windows are overgrown with new bark and tissue.

One of the most famous trees in Central Africa is a baobab in the Caprivi Strip which grows close to the house of the Administrator. A whole lavatory, complete with water flush, is installed inside the tree!

The mature baobab is remarkably tough. Although its bark is often completely stripped from the trunk as far as a man can reach — treatment that would destroy an ordinary tree — the baobab merely grows another bark and continues to flourish.

Livingstone wrote: "No external injury, not even a fire, can destroy this tree from without; nor can any injury be done from within as it is quite common to find it hollow, and I have seen one in which twenty or thirty men could lie down and sleep as in a hut. Nor does cutting down exterminate it, for I saw instances in Angola in which it continued to grow in length after it was lying on the ground . . . . . The roots, which may often be observed extending along the surface of the ground 40 or 50 yards from the trunk, also retain their vitality after the tree is laid low".

Baines also recorded the vitality of the tree in his diary on May 21, 1862 . . . . . "Five full-sized trees and two or three younger ones were standing . . . . . One gigantic trunk had fallen and lay prostrate, but still losing none of its vitality, sent forth branches and young leaves like the

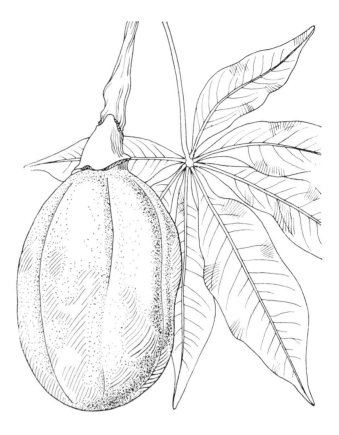

Above left
The flower of the
baobab , *Adansonia
digitata*

Above right
Adansonia digitata, the
baobab: A fruit and
leaf (80%)

Below
Stem, roots, and bark o
a baobab in the north-
ern Transvaal

1462

rest". In the painting of this group, which he did on the spot, a herd of wildebeest are shown in the bottom right corner. Roughly 100 years later, Mr G.L.Guy, formerly Conservator of Forests in Matabeleland, and later curator of the National Museum in Bulawayo, photographed the same clump, noting its likeness to the painting — and the fact that a troop of gemsbok had superseded the wildebeest.

Modern research endorses the remarkable vitality of the baobab. Yet, strangely enough, when it dies there is no majestic downfall like that of a great strong forest tree; it subsides into a huge fibrous mass. So swift is its disappearance that the story has arisen that the baobab catches fire spontaneously and burns itself away. Such a spectacular end would be fitting but is probably untrue.

How old is a baobab? Livingstone, although he doubted that it existed before the Flood, nevertheless remarked that he would back a baobab against a dozen inundations — provided it was not boiled in hot sea water. He estimated the age of one dead tree at 1400 years. Mr P.C. de Villiers of the Forestry Department worked out the age of one baobab at 4000 years, basing his estimate on the number of rings, which he took to be annual, found to the inch (2.5 cm) in a transverse section of the stem. There is a good deal of doubt, however, as to whether the baobab does form annual rings from which age can be deduced, the general opinion being that the rings form irregularly, being affected by even a heavy storm.

Recently Mr Guy determined to settle the matter by taking and studying core specimens of baobabs of a known age. In the first core rings were easily visible, giving the tree an age which was almost accurate. Several other experiments with other trees yielded a like result. Now laboratory confirmation that these were indeed annual rings is awaited from the Laboratory of Tree Ring Research at the University of Arizona.

The age of at least one baobab is definitely known through radio-carbon dating.

Dr E.R. Swart, who did the dating at the University College of Rhodesia recently, established that a sample from the heart of a baobab with a diameter of 4.6 m gave a radiocarbon dating of plus-minus 1010 years, indicating an age several times as much for really large specimens.

How fast does a baobab grow and what conditions govern growth? It is fairly well established that some young trees put on about 30 cm in diameter in 10 years, but that older trees grow more slowly.

Livingstone's tree, which had a circumference of 25.9 m in 1853 and has now been located by Mr Guy near the Ntwetwe Pan in Botswana, had a circumference in 1966 of only about 24.4 m, nearly 1.6 m (or 5 feet) *less* than in Livingstone's day. Guy further located the big hollow baobab at Shiramba, measured by Livingstone in 1858 and by Kirk in 1860, and noted that in 100 years it had increased at most 0.6 m in circumference.

What is possibly a tree measured by Emil Holub in 1875 at the south east corner of the Makarikari Pan in Botswana as having a circumference of nearly 15.8 m is found today to have a circumference of about 16.6 m, a small increase in over 90 years.

From the various radiocarbon tests on wood taken from different parts of Swart's baobab it can be deduced that in its first 270 years the baobab grew fast reaching a diameter of 2.1 m, and that the remaining 2.4 m took some 750 years. The average annual increase in radius was thus just over 2.5 mm!

Various measurements indicate that the baobab is very sensitive, not

Above
Baines's painting of a clump of baobabs near the Ntwetwe Pan in Botswana

Below
The same clump — now a national monument — photographed by G.L. Guy in July 1967

The Livingstone tree at Shiramba

only to prolonged drought, but even to a short dry season, and that at such times its girth may actually diminish in size.

It might be noted that in the Limpopo valley many trees died during the drought years from 1959-1967. This is thought to be due to lack of moisture in the soil, the twin causes being low rainfall and the destruction of the ground cover due to overgrazing.

Seeds apparently keep their viability for years. They germinate well in a nursery where plenty of moisture can be regularly provided. In their natural conditions they are believed to germinate only in exceptionally good rainy seasons. Young trees soon develop a swollen underground organ for storing water, from which the tap and side roots develop, and thereafter they withstand drought fairly well. Truncheons planted near Messina by officials of the Department of Forestry all failed to make roots, so that planting by seed is possibly the only way of propagating the baobab.

When the natives of tropical Africa move from one area to another, they often take baobab seed with them which they plant at once in their new home. Few Europeans have ever planted baobabs although mature trees are sometimes a focal point in Rhodesian gardens. Several are reported to have been cultivated in Natal gardens, and one in the Transkei, protected from frost and wind by encircling trees. This grew, apparently quite happily, to 6 m in 20 years. It is unusual to find a baobab in such a locality so that the record is of particular interest.

An unusual garden of baobabs was once made in Messina by Mr C.D.J. Scholz. He recorded that his trees flowered at about 16 years of age, that his 17-year-old trees were roughly 5.4-6m high, and that in winter his young trees decreased about 1.3 cm in girth.

South African gardeners, hesitant to experiment with this species, should note that baobabs were successfully grown in England 250 years ago. Plants flourished in several gardens, reaching 5.4 m in height, but were lost in the severe frost of 1740. Further plants were again — successfully — grown from seed Adanson sent to Europe. In 1768 Miller gave exact directions for their cultivation in England.

It is not surprising that legend and superstition surround the baobab. Common beliefs are that spirits inhabit the big white flowers; that he who plucks one will be eaten by a lion, that the maternal ancestor of the baobab was frightened by an elephant; that the tree grows up-side-down.

In the Transvaal it is thought by Africans that a boy baby should be washed in water in which the bark has been soaked, so that — like the tree — he would grow mighty and strong. (They are careful not to overdo this lest the child become obese, nor to let the water touch his head which would then swell up).

In parts the baobab is worshipped as a fertility tree. Professor Watt says that it has magical and symbolic value to the indigenous peoples of the Limpopo valley, where the vast majority of rock paintings of women have life-size fruits of baobabs instead of breasts.

The specific name *digitata* is based on the digitate leaves shaped like the fingers of a hand.

In 1941 the baobab was protected under the Forestry Act. It was the only tree in South Africa to be given universal state protection.

67 The Wild Pear Family (Sterculiaceae)

Sterculiaceae is a family of particular interest in South Africa, for the spring or autumn pear-like bloom of some members, for the oddness and rarity of others, or for the abundance of a genus such as *Hermannia* which has about 240 species in South Africa alone.

Commercially this is a large and important family with over 50 genera and well over 1000 species. The cacoa tree of tropical America, the source of cocoa and chocolate, is a member, and so, too, is the cola nut of tropical west Africa with a caffeine content so great that it is eaten by Africans on long and difficult journeys to give them energy.

Trees are found in 3 genera in South or South West Africa, *Dombeya, Sterculia,* and *Cola.*

This is an extremely diversified family, showing many different habits of growth, form and botanical detail. Nearly every member, however, has one character in common — star-shaped hairs — and these are sometimes intermixed with simple ones. The nature of these can usually be seen only under the microscope.

The leaves are simple or digitately compound and arranged alternately. The flowers are bisexual, or male or female borne on the same tree, sometimes with an epicalyx, the calyx with 3-5 segments, the petals 5, the stamens various, the ovary usually of about 2-5 free carpels with 1 or many ovules in each chamber, the fruit dry or fleshy, and often dividing into separate parts.

Dombeya Cav.

Dombeya is a large genus of more or less 190 species, which are native to Africa, Madagascar, and the Mascarene Islands. Seven species are recognized in South Africa and 1 species and 2 varieties in South West Africa.

They are all shrubs or trees with simple, alternate leaves that may be lobed or unlobed and are usually somewhat heart-shaped with — in all the African species — 3 or more main veins arising from the base. They are covered with hairs that under the microscope are seen to be star-shaped and which are often mixed with simple hairs. Stipules are present.

The flowers are bisexual, in cymes or umbels in the axils of the leaves and terminally, and are usually white or pink, the 5 petals persistent, although turning colour and becoming papery with age, with the fruit developing in the centre. *Dombeya* flowers, which appear in the spring or autumn, are individually delicate but massed together provide a characteristic burst of colour. The fertile stamens number 10-15, the calyx is 5-lobed, and there are often 3 bracts, the epicalyx, arising from below the calyx. The ovary is 3-5-locular. The fruit is a roundish capsule, splitting to release the small rough seed which is ridged or pitted, 1 to several being contained in each chamber.

Butterflies of several species breed on members of the genus. These include the reddish-brown butterfly of coastal forests, *Eagris nottoana*, and the Buff-tipped Skipper, *Netrobalane canopus* of woodland and forest.

The genus was named in honour of Joseph Dombey, 1742-1793, botanist and traveller in Peru and Chili.

The genus in South and South West Africa has recently been revised by Dr Inez Verdoorn of the Botanical Research Institute, on whose help much of this work has been based.

Key to *Dombeya* species

Flowers large (about 2.5 cm or more in diameter)

A shrub or small weak tree; the trunk *dark and rough;* the leaves often elongated *towards the tips,* lobed or angled, hairy or almost smooth, up to 9 cm long; the flowers usually white, 2.5 cm or more in diameter, blooming late summer and autumn. (Uitenhage to Zululand)

a. *D. tiliacea*

A shrub or tree; the leaves large, roundish or triangular, the upper half sometimes lobed, pointed, the upper surface green and velvety, the lower *silver and felted,* up to 20 cm long, the flowers white or pink, blooming late summer and autumn. (Eastern Transvaal and Swaziland)

b. *D. pulchra*

Usually a sturdy rounded shrub; the leaves egg-shaped, usually 3-5-lobed, pointed, velvety, the hairs *obvious and spreading, not conspicuously 2-coloured* as is *D. pulchra,* up to 20 cm long; the flowers pink or white, blooming summer to autumn. (Natal, Zululand, Swaziland, tropical Africa)

c. *D. burgessiae*

Flowers medium-sized (1.3-2 cm in diameter)

A small tree; the stem dark *and fissured;* the leaves *roundish,* thick, 2.5-15 cm long, hairy; the flowers usually pure white, in dense clusters *on the bare branches, blooming in spring.* (Natal, Zululand, Swaziland, Transvaal, South West Africa, tropical Africa).

f. *D. rotundifolia*

Flowers small (less than 1.3 cm in diameter)

A bush or slender tree, *the bark light and smoothish;* the leaves up to 8 cm long, widest at the base, often tapering to the tips, roughly hairy or

1468

smoothish, *the hairs flat;* the flowers white, slightly less than 1.3 cm wide, the calyx *not conspicuous,* blooming autumn to winter. (Eastern Cape, Natal, Zululand, Swaziland, eastern Transvaal, Mozambique)

d. *D. cymosa*

A shrub or tree; the leaves egg-shaped, sometimes 3-lobed, tapering to the tip, broadest at the base, up to 13 cm long, roughly hairy, the hairs *obvious and spreading, long and short;* the flowers small, white, *the calyx large and hairy,* the flower stalks conspicuously hairy, blooming autumn. (North east Transvaal)

e. *D. kirkii*

A shrub or small tree, usually several-stemmed; the bark *smooth grey;* the leaves *roundish* and thinnish, 1.3-5 cm in diameter; the flowers white, sometimes slightly over 1.3 cm in diameter, *blooming late summer and autumn.* (Eastern Transvaal)

g. *D. autumnalis*

(472) a. *Dombeya tiliacea* (Endl.) Planch.

= *Xeropetalum tiliaceum* Endl.; = *Dombeya dregeana* Sond.; = *Dombeya natalensis* Sond.; = *Dombeya gracilis* K.Schum

Forest dombeya; forest dog rose, little dog rose; iTyibo (X); iBunda, umBovu (Z)

The forest dombeya is a prettily-flowered species growing from about Uitenhage and Port Alfred in the south, through the Transkei to Natal and Zululand, from sea level to about 1500 m above the sea, in coastal forest, on forest margins, in gully bush, in thorn veld, in hillside scrub, often along streams. It may be a half-climbing shrub or small weak tree — such a one grows along the main road in Oribi Gorge in southern Natal and is conspicuous when in flower — or a tree up to 9m high with a stem up to about 30 cm in diameter, and with a dark, fissured trunk.

The branchlets are slender, scarred, with small, pale, raised dots. The lobed or angled leaves, simple and alternate, are rather like small vine leaves in shape — *Flora Capensis* calls them aspen-like — up to about 9 cm long and 8 cm broad, thin, heart-shaped, often much elongated towards the tips, the base round or deeply indented, the margins toothed, covered with minute, star-shaped hairs, or with age becoming almost hairless, with 5-7 nerves from the base. They are borne on long hairy stalks.

The flowers, usually appearing in late summer or autumn, are 2.5 cm or more in diameter, pure white or occasionally pink, with age becoming red-brown. The smooth veined petals are unequal-sided and persistent. They are borne in heads, arising from the axils of the upper leaves, standing well above these to make a cloud of bloom. They are sweet-scented and popular with bees which make a good honey from them.

The fruit is a roundish, hairy capsule and the seed is small, rough, and 3-sided.

1469

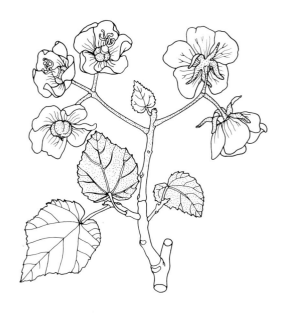

Above left
Dombeya cymosa on a
hillside near Estcourt

Above right
Dombeya tiliacea: a
leafy twig, with the
fruits in the heart of the
persistent petals (50%)

Left
Dombeya burgessiae: A
flowering twig (80%)

Opposite
Dombeya cymosa bark

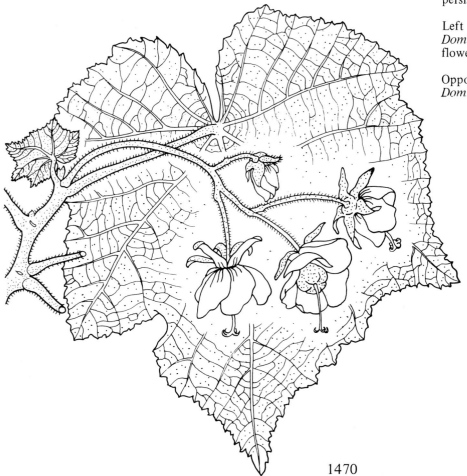

1470

This pretty little species is sometimes cultivated, and then its blooms are noticeably larger than in the wild.

The specific name means "like Tilia". The common name "little dog rose" refers to its flowers which are somewhat like small, single roses.

This species is both the *Dombeya natalensis* Sond. and *Dombeya dregeana* Sond. of *Flora Capensis,* forms that were separated on the shape of the bracts and the buds but are now held to be inseparable.

(470.1)   b. *Dombeya pulchra* N.E.Br.

Blombos

Dombeya pulchra has a somewhat restricted distribution for it grows in the cool, moist parts of the eastern Transvaal and Swaziland, on rocky hillsides and mountains, in wooded kloofs and on stream banks, often as a shrub but sometimes as a tree up to about 7 m tall.

The slender branches are smoothish, wrinkled, and often covered with glandular hairs. The large velvety leaves are from 4-20 cm in diameter, and are roundish or roughly triangular, sometimes the upper half lobed, the tips pointed, the base deeply indented, the margins roundly toothed, with 5-7 veins from the base which are prominent below, the upper surface green and covered with short dense hairs, the lower side felted with velvety, silver hairs, the two sides making a fine colour contrast.

In spring the velvety buds open into flowers that are white or pink, often with a darker eye at the base of the petals, turning reddish with age. They are borne on hairy stalks in long-stalked bunches in the axils of the upper leaves. The capsule is covered with dense hairs and the seeds are small, brown, and pitted.

This resembles *Dombeya burgessiae* Gerr. ex Harv. which has a much wider and slightly overlapping area of distribution.

The specific name *pulchra* is the Latin for "beautiful".

(468.1)   c. *Dombeya burgessiae* Gerr. ex Harv.

= *Assonia burgessiae* (Gerr. ex Harv.) Kuntze; = *Dombeya elegans* K.Schum.; = *Dombeya rosea* Bak.f.

Pink dombeya; iBunda (Z); mufulwi, mupfulwi (V)

This beautiful and variable species is widespread, growing from Natal, Zululand and Swaziland, through the eastern and northern Transvaal, to Mozambique, Rhodesia, Zambia, and northwards to Malawi, Kenya, and Tanzania, on forest margins, in bush and kloofs, on wooded hillsides and grassy slopes, frequently on stream banks, usually as a many-stemmed, rounded shrub up to 3 m high, but sometimes as a slender tree.

The stems are covered with brown bark. The sturdy branches are more or less hairy, the younger, slender ones, like the leaf and flower stalks, being densely so. The large, soft, often roughly triangular leaves up to 20 cm long, are usually 3-5-lobed, the lobes blunt or sharp, the base deeply notched, 5-9-nerved from the base, the margins untoothed or roundly toothed, more or less velvety both sides, the hairs spreading, the lower side often much lighter than the upper, the veins raised and often reddish. The network of veins is usually clearly seen. The leaves are borne on long, densely hairy stalks.

The wild pear, *Dombeya rotundifolia,* in flower near Pretoria

The oval, pointed, pinky-green buds open into white or soft pink flowers, often marked with a deeper colour at the base, about 2.5 cm in diameter, with a light, green, velvety, lobed calyx. The petals turn a papery brown and the calyx becomes reddish with age. They are borne — in abundance — in branched heads on long hairy stalks in the axils of the leaves, the clusters drooping, each with a leaf usually making a small umbrella above it, and are particularly graceful and charming. The trees flower from autumn to winter.

The fruits are small, round, furry capsules.

The bark is exceptionally strong, and baskets are made from it. Black Rhino eat both bark and leaves.

Dombeya burgessiae is occasionally cultivated and makes a good garden shrub. Cultivated forms, differing in small botanical details, are sometimes found in Natal and their origin is obscure.

The species was named by Gerrard in honour of "Miss Burgess of Birkenhead". It would be pleasant to know more of her, but the details appear to have been lost in time.

The artist, Marianne North, noted in the last century that this shrub was sometimes called "Zulu cherry".

(469)   d. *Dombeya cymosa* Harv.

Small-flowered dombeya; uZingati (X); iGcibo, iBunda, umXaba (Z)

Dombeya cymosa — readily distinguished from most of the other dombeyas when in bloom because of the smallness of its flowers — grows from the eastern Cape, through Natal, Zululand and Swaziland, to the eastern Transvaal and Mozambique. It is very common in parts of Natal, and round Weenen, Estcourt, Richmond and Ixopo, for example, it is one of the most conspicuous trees in autumn when its delicate blooms whiten the hillsides. It grows on forest and bush margins, in valley scrub and on stony hills, and sometimes on stream banks.

Although it may be a straggling bush or a fairly dense shrub, it often grows as a slender tree up to about 6 m high with gracefully arching branches, a leafy drooping crown, and a smooth, light grey bark which immediately distinguishes it from *Dombeya rotundifolia* (Hochst.) Planch. or *Dombeya tiliacea* which have rough dark trunks.

The branchlets are slender and marked with leaf scars and small raised dots. The leaves are often small, 1.3-8 cm long, widest at the round or heart-shaped base or in the middle, sometimes the upper half much tapered, bluntly pointed, the margins roundly toothed, 3-7-nerved from the base, coarsely and rather roughly hairy on both sides or almost smooth, on long, slender stalks. They are light green, in autumn touched with red.

The small white flowers, slightly less than 1.3 cm wide, in branched sprays in the axils of the leaves, are borne most abundantly in autumn. As the petals age they turn a rich red-brown, and then the tree has a second period of bright colour. The bracts below the calyx are scattered along the flower stalks. The round fruit matures in the heart of the petals and is covered with short hairs. It is usually 1-seeded.

At least 8 species of butterflies are known to breed on the tree.

This should make a decorative small garden tree. It has, as well, two practical uses — excellent honey is made from its flowers, and the timber makes good shafts for spears.

Dombeya cymosa: a leaf, and the fruits maturing in the heart of the petals (50%)

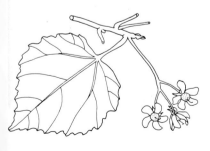

The specific name indicates that the flowers are borne in cymes.

This may be confused with *Dombeya kirkii*, another small-flowered species. The leaves of *Dombeya cymosa*, however, are smoother with a short pubescence and no long hairs, the flowering spray is almost hairless, and the calyx is much smaller than in *Dombeya kirkii*.

(470)   e. *Dombeya kirkii* Mast.

= *Dombeya gilgiana* K.Schum.

Kirk's dombeya

Dombeya kirkii is a rare species in South Africa occurring only in the Kruger National Park in the north eastern Transvaal. It extends northwards through Mozambique into tropical Africa, growing mainly in thickets on river banks.

In South Africa it is usually a shrub up to about 4.5 m high but it may be tree-like and in tropical Africa is sometimes over 9 m tall.

The leaves are egg-shaped, occasionally somewhat 3-lobed, tapering to the pointed tip, broadest at the round or heart-shaped base, 5-7-nerved from the base, up to about 13 cm long and 10 cm broad, roughly hairy above, softly hairy below, borne on long, robust, and often hairy stalks. The leaves and young shoots are eaten by elephant.

The rather small white flowers are borne in many-flowered, branched sprays in the axils of the leaves and at the ends of the branchlets from late summer to autumn. Like the other species of *Dombeya*, the petals do not fall but are persistent and turn light brown with age. The fruit is a small, roundish, sometimes slightly 3-lobed capsule.

This species could possibly be confused with the more widely distributed *Dombeya cymosa*. The leaves, however, are often larger and always more hairy — botanists note that the pubescence consists of short and long hairs — the calyx is larger and very hairy, while the flower stalks are quite clearly hairier than those of *Dombeya cymosa*.

In Kenya the wood is said to be used for bows.

The species was named after Sir John Kirk, traveller and naturalist, and companion of Dr David Livingstone.

Dombeya rotundifolia:
the flowers and young
leaves (50%)

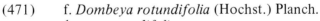

(471)   f. *Dombeya rotundifolia* (Hochst.) Planch.
          1. var. *rotundifolia*

= *Xeropetalum rotundifolium* Hochst.; = *Dombeya densiflora* Planch. ex Harv.; = *Dombeya damarana* K.Schum.; = *Dombeya dinteri* Schinz

Wild pear, wild plum, blossom tree, round leaf dombeya, blombos, blomhout, dikbas, drolpeer; inHliziyonkulu, uNhliziyonkulu, isAdlulambazo (Z); umBikanyaka, umWane (Sw); nsihaphukuma, xiluvarhi (Tso); motubane (Tsw), molobare (Tsw — Mal); mohlaba-phala, mokgoba (NS); tshiluvhari (V); ntogwinzane (Kal)

2. var. *velutina* Verdoorn

See colour plate facing page 1115

Dombeya rotundifolia — with its splendid, snowy, pear-like blossom appearing in the spring — is generally known as the wild pear wherever it grows from Natal and Zululand, through Swaziland to the Transvaal

Above
Dombeya rotundifolia
in the Khomas Hoch-
land, South West Africa

Below
Dombeya rotundifolia
bark

and to South West Africa. The Vendas know it as "tshiluvhari" — the blossom tree. It is a widely distributed species growing also in Botswana and northwards to tropical east Africa, in open woodland and bushveld, in clumps or singly, in areas often with a moderate to low rainfall.

In South Africa 1 variety, the typical, occurs, but in South West Africa another, var. *velutina*, is recognized and this is restricted to that territory alone.

The typical form, var. *rotundifolia*, occurs in both South and South West Africa. It is a very common tree in the middleveld and bushveld of the Transvaal, growing in numbers on the hills and in the bush close to Pretoria and Johannesburg, and sometimes in the streets of Pretoria.

It is usually a small to medium-sized, deciduous tree up to about 9 m high with a many-branched round crown and a single stem 20-30 cm in diameter, covered with a very dark brown, corky bark, fissured lengthwise. In the dry central areas of South West Africa and in Bots-wana, however, it is most often a many-stemmed tree or shrub. The leaves are simple, alternate, thick, and roundish, 2.5-15 cm in diameter, the tips usually rounded, the base notched and 5-7-nerved, the margins almost untoothed or irregularly and roundly toothed, rough, with many short star-shaped hairs above and below, and with the secondary and netted veins prominent below. They are carried on hairy stalks. The narrow stipules fall off early.

The flowers may be pink but are usually pure white, and are borne in masses in branched clusters at the ends of the bare branches in early spring. The tree often, in the wild, occurs near a kafferboom and as the trees blossom about the same time the brilliant white and scarlet are splendid together. Like the flowers of the other dombeyas, these do not drop but remain on the tree, the petals later acting as wings to the ripe fruits. With age they fade to brown. The clustered coffee-coloured flowers against the tracery of black branches are almost as fine as the snowy bloom and make the tree of unique ornamental value.

This is one of the first trees to flower in the spring and the Swazi

1475

name — umBikanyaka — refers to this. It means "the tree that heralds the new season".

The bushy form of this variety from South West Africa flowers irregularly through the year. The shrubby tree from the Gamsberg Pass in the Komas Hochland illustrated here was in bloom in July bearing bunches of pale pink flowers with a sweet almond scent.

The tree plays a part in the lives of many animals. Kudu browse the leaves and young shoots. Many insects, including butterflies, are associated with it. At least 3 species of butterflies breed on the foliage, and many more are attracted to the flowers. The pollen is taken by a small, slender, blue-green beetle, *Melyris interstitalis*, of the family Melyridae, a relative of the small black and yellow pollen beetles of gardens. These brilliant little insects, flashing about in numbers in the wide open white flowers add to the beauty and attraction of the tree in spring. Very different is an insect even more typical of this dombeya — the small, white, immobile scale, *Lecanodiaspis tarsalis*.

The tree is widely used medicinally, and its magical uses are in relation to the youth and vigour of its bloom. The first spring blossoms, mixed with honey, the hearts of Namaqua Doves, and "portions of a mole", make a love potion that is surely potent.

The bark fibre is very strong and is used to make rope. The wood, bluish-grey, heavy, tough and strong, is — according to Galpin — first class, and excellent for any purpose for which a timber is required that does not split and has great strength, such as for wagon work. It is also used for mine props, yoke-skeys, and for general work.

The tree appears slow-growing in the veld but in a garden grows well and quickly when it has good depth of soil and adequate moisture. It is easily raised from seed and stands light frost. It is fire-resistant.

The specific name means "round-leaved".

Var. *velutina* is recorded only from the Naukluft Mountains west of Mariental in South West Africa. It differs from the typical form in its habit — it is a shrub only with tall, slender, wand-shaped stems — and in the velvety texture of the leaves. Dr Verdoorn, who described the variety, notes further that the hairs on the ovary are short, dense, and star-shaped, whereas those on the ovary of the typical variety are bristly.

The name *velutina* means "velvety".

(468)   g. *Dombeya autumnalis* Verdoorn

Autumn dombeya

Dombeya autumnalis is a pretty little species occurring in the eastern Transvaal on wooded hill slopes and in bush on stream banks. It is particularly numerous on the hillsides near the Abel Erasmus Pass, growing among rocks on the steep mountain side.

It may be a shrub or a small tree up to about 4.5 m high, differing from *Dombeya rotundifolia* — as can be seen at a glance — in its several to many stems and in the smoothness of the grey bark which never becomes rough, fissured and corky.

The leaves are roundish and thinnish, 1.3-5 cm in diameter, with star-shaped hairs both sides, the margins with round teeth, mostly 5-veined from the base, borne on slender hairy stalks.

The flowers appear in late summer and autumn in loose bunches on

Dombeya autumnalis in
the Abel Erasmus Pass

slender stalks in the axils of the upper leaves. They are small, white and
sweet-scented, becoming cinnamon-red with age. The fruit is a small
capsule covered with star-like hairs.

In habit this resembles *Dombeya cymosa* but the leaves are round and
do not taper to a point. In shape they are much like those of *Dombeya
rotundifolia*, from which species it can easily be separated by its habit,
its autumn blooming, and the fact that its flowers are borne together
with the leaves and not on the bare branches.

The specific name indicates that the tree flowers in the autumn.

Sterculia L.

About 300 species belong to this fascinating African and Asian genus, 3
of which occur in South Africa and 2 in South West Africa. All these
are of particular interest, either for their rarity, or for their unusual
appearance.

They are trees with alternate leaves that are simple and often lobed,
or digitately compound — the leaflets arranged like the fingers of a
hand; the stipules deciduous; the flowers usually male or female, on the
same or separate trees, without petals, but the calyx often coloured,
petal-like and usually 4-5-lobed, the stamens 10-15, the ovary with 4-5

1477

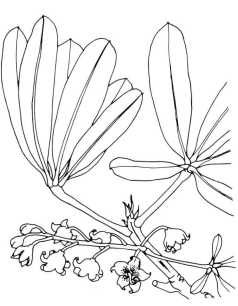

Above
Sterculia alexandri, Van
Staden's Wild Flower
Reserve

Below left
The flowers and leaves
(50%)

Below right
The fruit (50%)

Opposite
Sterculia alexandri stem

carpels which on maturity separate into distinct woody or leathery and pod-like parts which open down the side to expose the often large seeds, 1 to many in each part.

Most of the species have soft, pithy and rather useless wood, but the bark — like that of others of the family — yields a good fibre.

The generic name is based on the Latin "stercus", meaning "manure", in reference to the smell of the flowers and leaves of some species.

The genus has recently been revised by Mr J. Landman, formerly of the Botanical Research Institute.

Key to species

Leaves digitate (finger-like)

The leaflets *oblong, stiff, leathery*; the fruits with 1-5 separate, pod-like carpels, boat-shaped, woody, horned or knobbly, up to about 8 cm long. (The Van Stadens and Winterhoek mountains of the Cape Province)

a. *S. alexandri*

The leaflets widely *lance-shaped, velvety, soft*; the fruits with 1-5 separate pod-like carpels, large, woody, spiny, hairy, splitting to form big, shallow, boat-shaped shells, up to about 18 or 20 cm by 10 to 13 cm. (Eastern Transvaal lowveld, Swaziland)

b. *S. murex*

Leaves simple and usually lobed

The leaves large, up to 40 x 40 cm, *widely egg-shaped*, usually 3-5-lobed, the fruit usually with 3-5 pod-like carpels, up to about 5 cm long, shortly hairy, *borne erect on a hairy stipe*. (Northern South West Africa, and tropical Africa)

c. *S. quinqueloba*

The leaves small, 2.5-6 cm long, often 3-5-lobed (ivy-like), dark green above, below grey-green and hairy; the fruits with 1-5 *almost stalkless*, separate carpels, up to about 8 cm long, roughly oblong; soft and plum-coloured when young, harder and golden-brown later, hairy. (North and eastern Transvaal, Zululand, Swaziland, Rhodesia, Mozambique)

d. *S. rogersii*

The leaves 5-15 cm long, broadly egg-shaped or 3-5-lobed, hairy, rough; the fruits with 1-5 separate carpels, oblong or oval with a *strong, tail-like point*, hairy, splitting wide like walnut shells. (South West Africa, Caprivi Strip, Botswana, tropical Africa)

e. *S. africana*

(473)   a. *Sterculia alexandri* Harv.

Cape sterculia

Sterculia alexandri is one of the very rare trees of South Africa, hitherto known only from several isolated areas of the Cape Province, the Elandsberg close to Hankey and Van Staden's Pass (near Port Elizabeth), and in the Winterhoek mountains not far from Uitenhage. Now the tree has been found near the Kouga Dam, so that possibly it thrives unrecognized in the Kouga mountains and those of the Baviaanskloof.

It is most easily seen in the Van Staden's Wild Flower Reserve growing on steep northern slopes with good sun and drainage, but even here is accessible only by the active. It seems always to be associated with Table Mountain sandstone.

The species was discovered in 1848 by Dr Alexander Prior who found a solitary tree in a narrow kloof somewhere in the Van Staden's mountains, "a locality probably still concealing other novelties", according to *Flora Capensis*. It was so little known that botanists were not able, until fairly recently, to complete their knowledge of it. The fruit was found by a Port Elizabeth botanist, Dr E.A.A. Archibald, who was led to the tree by an African child who had eaten the sweet seeds.

It is usually a small to medium-sized tree up to about 4.5 m tall on the steep scrubby hillsides, but up to 8 m or more in forested kloofs, with a stem diameter up to 30 cm. It may be upright, or frequently sprawling at an angle when it suckers freely, one tree then tending to make a small colony. When injured, it coppices readily.

The slender, silvery-grey trunk is smooth, blotched with white and covered with small raised dots, and often with lichen. The leaves grow only at the tips of the branches and are alternate and digitately compound, that is, finger-like and springing from one point, borne on strong yellow stalks. All the 2-7 stiff, leathery leaflets point upwards. They are oblong, usually about 8-13 cm long and 1.9-2.5 cm broad, the tips rounded or bluntly pointed, with a small, thorn-like point, the base narrowed, dark green above and slightly shiny, with the midrib, secondary veins which branch near the margin, and netted veins all very distinct, below grey-green with the veining less conspicuous. They are stalkless. The trees seem to come into new leaf after rain, and these are a bright red.

The tree flowers summer and winter – February and March are often the main blooming season – with odd flowers in between.

The flowers in sprays (botanically compound cymes) are mostly male but sometimes, and usually in the younger part of the spray, bisexual. They have no petals but the 5-7 lobes of the calyx are petal-like in appearance, pale yellow or a creamy green, the outside covered with long star-shaped hairs, the centre of the flower often claret-coloured. The flowers on the trees in the deep shade of the kloofs do not have the maroon markings of those growing in the sun. All the flowers hang downwards, and at the height of the blooming season cover the tree.

The fruits are conspicuous and strange. Each carpel develops into a pod-like structure, 1-5 carpels in all, quite separate but joined at the base, forming the fruit. These are up to about 8 cm long, rather boat-shaped, woody and horned or knobbly, covered with yellow-brown, star-shaped hairs. They split down one side to release the 4-8 fairly large, oval seeds. These have a sweet nutty flavour and are great favourites with baboons and with children. Trees on the hillsides fruit more heavily than those in the valleys.

This is not a difficult tree to cultivate if certain precautions are observed. Mrs Gwen Skinner of Port Elizabeth, who has probably raised more seedlings of this tree than any other person in South Africa, makes three points – the seeds must be placed *on top* of the soil; this should be damp and not wet; and the seeds should be protected from

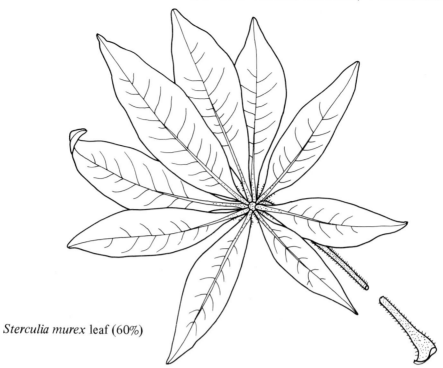

Sterculia murex leaf (60%)

rats and mice. She has noted that in the wild a seed sends out a root-like feeler which — when it finds a crevice in a rock — stops short and forms a little tuber. From this the tap-root grows.

The tree was named after its discoverer, Dr Richard Chandler Alexander, F.R.C.P., who made plant collections in the southern Cape districts between 1846 and 1848. In 1849 he inherited a large estate in Somerset, England, and added the name Prior to his patronymic name.

(475)   b. *Sterculia murex* Hemsl.

Lowveld chestnut, laeveldkastaiing; umBhaba (Sw)

The lowveld chestnut is a handsome leafy tree growing only in a limited area in the eastern Transvaal lowveld, most often on wooded, rocky hills, and in Swaziland. Fine trees grow on the hills near the old Pretorius Kop entrance to the Kruger Park — in the grounds of one of the hotels nearby — and on the turn-off between the main road and the Park gates.

It is a 6-12 m tree with wide, spreading branches and 1 or 2 stems up to 30 cm in diameter, covered with thick, ribbed, grey-brown bark which in old trees becomes almost black and is cracked into rectangular segments.

The leaves, borne on long hairy stalks, are alternate and composed of 5-10 stalkless leaflets radiating, finger-like, from one point. They are oblong to widely lance-shaped, narrowed to both ends, pointed, usually up to 10 cm long and 5 cm wide, velvety both sides, the midrib, secondary veins and netted veins conspicuous on the lower surface. They may be evergreen or deciduous.

The flowers are borne in sprays at the ends of the usually bare branches from August to October. They are waxy and yellow, marked with brown or crimson, and as in all the sterculias, the petals are absent while the sepals are petal-like.

Above
Sterculia murex in the Transvaal lowveld near the main entrance to
Pretorius Kop

Below left
The flowers

Below right
The fruit

Opposite
Sterculia murex bark

The fruits are of unique appearance. The 5-lobed ovary enlarges and separates into distinct segments, 1-5 developing, and these appear to be separate pods radiating from one point. They are large, woody and covered thickly with hard spines and dense star-like hairs, and split to form big, shallow, boat-shaped shells, each one lined within with long stinging hairs, holding a number of large oval seeds. When every one of the 5 lobes develops this is an enormous fruit, often more than 30 cm in diameter, and even when only one or 2 develop it is large. It is seldom that a very big and complete fruit is collected for they grow high on the trees and shatter as they fall. Baboons and monkeys, moreover, pluck them for the sweet oily nuts. Single empty shells are often picked up under the trees, but never a nut for these are devoured before or immediately after they fall. The shells are often used as unusual ashtrays.

The trees are the breeding place of the "cotton-stainer" and are therefore unpopular with farmers who grow cotton.

The wood is soft and of little use. Probably the main use of the tree is decorative for it is shapely and the foliage is handsome.

The specific name is the Latin "murex", meaning "having rough points" or "prickly", in reference to the spiky fruits.

(476)   c. *Sterculia quinqueloba* (Garcke) K.Schum.

= *Cola quinqueloba* Garcke; = *Sterculia zastrowiana* Engl.

"The five-lobed sterculia" is not a South African species but a tropical one that extends into northern South West Africa, growing in dry bush and woodland and on rocky hills. It is common on rocky outcrops and on hillsides in the districts of Outjo and Omaruru.

It is a small to large tree 18 m high with a trunk up to 60 cm in diameter covered with distinctive white, smooth bark which often peels in small pieces to show a silvery colour below. The spreading branches are thick and stiff, bearing at their ends large, simple lobed leaves. These may be up to 40 cm long and broad, widely egg-shaped, usually with 3-5 pointed lobes, but occasionally unlobed, the base deeply indented, the margins untoothed, velvety both sides, particularly below, several-veined from the base, the veins very conspicuous below, borne on long hairy stalks.

The flowers bloom with the young leaves at the ends of the branches in long, many-flowered sprays. They are male or female, borne on the same tree, without petals, but with 5 petal-like, green calyx lobes, and are small and insignificant.

The fruits are composed of 3-5 pod-like sections or lobes (follicles), up to about 5 cm long, covered with short golden-brown hairs, each one held more or less erect on a hairy stipe or stalk. Each contains a circle of stinging hairs and several oblong, black seeds. When the pods burst open, from May to September, they look remarkably like miniature canoes in shape.

The specific name means "five-lobed", in reference to the leaves. Coates Palgrave says that in Rhodesia one African name means "the tree the dassies find hard to climb", a good name in view of the smoothness and slipperiness of the trunks.

1483

1484

Above
Sterculia rogersii in the
dry bushveld of the
northern Transvaal

Below left
The stem and the bark

Below right
Sterculia rogersii: a leaf
and flowers and the
fruit and seeds (70%)

Below
Sterculia rogersii an-
other form of the bark

(477)   d. *Sterculia rogersii* N.E.Br.

Ulumbu tree; uLumbu, inKuphenkuphe, umuMbu (Z); uLumba (Sw);
samani (Tso); mokakata (Tsw — Mang)

This species apparently has no common name in South Africa in either
English or Afrikaans, and this is inexplicable in view of its unusual
appearance and its wide distribution in the dry northern parts of the
country. It is at its most common in the arid bush between the Soutpansberg and the Limpopo River — specimens grow along many of the
country roads here. It occurs, too, in the eastern Transvaal, Zululand — where fine specimens grow in the Ndumu Game Reserve — and
in Swaziland, and northwards to Mozambique and Rhodesia.

This is most often a squat, dumpy tree resembling a *Commiphora* in
habit or a baobab in the swollen shape, colour and shininess of its trunk.
It is often no more than 3 m but may reach 8 m in height, usually
branching near the base, the trunk stout and shiny, the principal
branches robust and grey. It is noteworthy that the outer bark on old
trees is rough and dark brown but this peels off and is only seldom
seen, and it is the smooth, creamy-grey, red or purple-mauve, occasionally peeling, surface that is typical.

The leaves are borne alternately on long, buff, wand-like branches, or
in tufts together at the ends of knob-like side shoots. They are beautifully
neat, 2.5-6 cm long, often 3-5-lobed, with the lobes bluntly or fairly
sharply pointed (when they resemble ivy leaves) or egg-shaped, with the
bases usually indented, 3-5-nerved from the base, dark green above and
slightly hairy, and below greyish-green and hairy. They are carried on
slender stalks.

Stipules are present but fall off early.

The flowers are male or female borne on the same tree. They appear
before or with the young leaves at the ends of the side branches from
about August to November and are about 1.5 cm in diameter, yellow-
green streaked with red. The calyx lobes are petal-like and no petals are
present. Although small, they are interesting, and striking against the
bare branches.

The fruit consists of 1-5 almost stalkless lobes or separate parts, roughly oblong in shape, up to nearly 8 cm long. When young these are the
texture of foam rubber but become hard with age. They are plum-
coloured at first and later golden-brown, covered with hairs that glisten
noticeably in the sun. Mature fruits may be 15 cm in diameter and
remain on the tree for months after the "pods" have split. Within are
numerous oval seeds about the size of peas surrounded by dense, stinging hairs.

The seeds are eaten by birds, wild animals, cattle and goats, and the
young shoots and leaves by elephant. In times of need, Africans sometimes eat the heartwood.

The wood is light-coloured, soft and brittle. Rope and string "for
cows' noses", for fishing nets, to tie thatch to the framework of a roof,
and to sew sleeping mats and grain baskets, are made from the bark.

The tree was named after Archdeacon Frederick Arundel Rogers, an
amateur botanical collector, 1876-1944, who collected largely in South
Africa, Mozambique, and Rhodesia towards the beginning of the
century. The common name "ulumbu tree" suggested here is an adaptation of the Zulu and Swazi name.

Sterculia africana growing in a valley of the Brandberg, South West Africa

(474)   e. *Sterculia africana* (Lour.) Fiori

= *Triphaca africana* Lour.; = *Sterculia triphaca* R.Br.; = *S. ipomoeifolia* Garcke; = *S. guerichii* K.Schum.; = *S. tomentosa* of various authors.

Mopopoja tree: mopopoja (Sub); mokokobuyu (Kol); omumbambahako (Her)

Sterculia africana is a tropical species which enters northern South West Africa, the Caprivi Strip and Botswana, growing mainly in hot dry areas and often on mountain sides. Many grow on the hill slopes of the valley leading to the rock painting, "The White Lady of the Brandberg", and one fine tree stands at the side of the road at the point where it descends into the valley.

It is a medium to tall tree with a thick trunk, single or forked, up to 2.5 m in diameter, the bark somewhat peeling, shiny grey, brown, or silver marked with purple. In the Brandberg valley, in particular, the silver trunks and stiff, thick branches, almost leafless in winter time, shine wonderfully against the black piled rocks.

The light green leaves are crowded at the ends of the branches. They are 5-15 cm long and 4-13 cm wide, broadly egg-shaped or 3-5-lobed, the lobes pointed, the base indented, 7-veined from the base, hairy and often rough to the touch, borne on long hairy stalks.

The small, velvety buds in sprays at the ends of the rough twigs open into sweet-scented flowers about 1.9 cm in diameter with 5 or 6 petal-like lobes which are yellow striped heavily with red. The flowers are male or female and they bloom before the leaves appear. The tree in the accompanying photograph was in bloom in July, but the normal blooming time is from October to November.

The fruits have 1-5 follicles or lobes, which are thick, hard, oblong or oval "pods" with a strong tail-like point, covered with golden hairs, looking exactly like elfin-caps in a child's fairy story. They open wide along a seam like walnut shells to show an interior covered with minute stinging hairs that prick like thorns, and numerous large, oblong, blue-grey or black seeds with a small white aril. In South West Africa these are roasted in ash and eaten.

The wood is very soft and light.

The specific name means "of Africa".

Until recently the South West African form of this species was known as *Sterculia guerichii* K.Schum., but this is now generally included in *Sterculia africana*.

Cola Schott & Endl.

This purely African genus is represented in South Africa by 2 species, one or other of which occurs from Pondoland to Zululand. No species grow in South West Africa.

Until recently only 1 species, the common *Cola natalensis* Oliv., was believed to grow in South Africa. Recently a second species, now known to be fairly common in the short sand forests of Zululand and in the high forest round Lake Sibayi, *Cola microcarpa* Brenan, was collected.

The species have simple, alternate leaves, often lance-shaped, flowers that are either male or female, probably borne on separate plants, without petals, but with petal-like calyx lobes, the stamens 10-12, often united into a column, the ovary with 4-10 carpels, the fruit with 1-5 woody or leathery carpels.

Above left
Cola natalensis growing in a
Durban park

Above right
Cola natalensis: A fruiting
twig, a fruit, and a
follicle torn open to
show the seeds (70%)

Below left
The handle of a stick, carefully carved out of *Cola natalen-sis*

Below right
Cola natalensis female flower

Opposite
Cola natalensis bark

The name *Cola* is based on an African common name.

The genus has recently been revised by Dr Inez Verdoorn, whose work has formed the basis of these descriptions

Key to species

The swelling at the junction of the leaf stalk and blade dark and *smooth*; the fruits with 1-5 carpels, *large*, up to 4 cm long, *hard, warted, green to orange-yellow*. (Eastern Cape to southern Zululand)

a. *C. natalensis*

The swelling at the junction of the leaf stalk and blade dark and *velvety*; the fruits with 1-5 carpels, *small, cherry-sized*, the "shell" *soft and brittle, usually a brilliant orange-vermilion*. (Zululand from about Mtunzini northwards)

b. *C. microcarpa*

(478)   a. *Cola natalensis* Oliv.

Natal cola, wild mango; umTenenenda (X); umThenenende, iThenenende, umQhosho (Z)

Cola natalensis was until recently believed the only species of the genus in South Africa, occurring widely from the north east Cape, through Natal, to Zululand. Now it is known to grow only as far as about Mtunzini from where, northwards, its place is taken by *Cola microcarpa*.

It is a common evergreen tree of dense coastal forest — it may be seen in Durban parks and on the Bluff — growing up to 15 m high.

The bark is grey, smooth, and often shallowly dimpled, flaking off in small patches. The dark green leaves are simple and alternate, widely lance-shaped, broadly narrowed to the tips, sharply or bluntly pointed, gradually narrowed to the base, 6-20 cm long and 1.3-6 cm wide, the mature leaves smooth, on the under-side the midrib raised and the secondary veins conspicuous, borne on long slender stalks with a slight swelling at their junction with the leaf blades. This swelling is black and *smooth*, whereas in *Cola microcarpa* it is velvety, a character that appears to be constant and is a quick and easy means of distinguishing between the two species when they are not in fruit.

The small, yellow, star-like flowers are male or female on the same tree or possibly on different trees, a point still in doubt, 2 to several in a cluster in the axils of, or below, the leaves, at the base of twigs, or often on short shoots. They have no petals but the calyx lobes are petal-like.

As the fruit develops the carpels enlarge into 1-5 separate pod-like, woody follicles and these look like a cluster of separate fruits. Each follicle is up to 4 cm long, and is round, oval or fig-shaped, hard-shelled, with a blunt point — the remains of the style — and is covered with small warts. It is green turning orange or yellow when ripe. Within, each one is creamy-white with a pink tinge and sticky. The seeds number 2-4.

The fruits are not generally considered as edible, although cicadas eat the flesh. Black Rhino eat both bark and leaves.

The rather sombre little butterfly with a quick, jerky flight, the

Above left
Cola microcarpa, Lake Sibayi

Top right
    Cola microcarpa leaves, showing the hairy swelling at the base, and female flowers (50%)

Above right
    Cola microcarpa: A male flowering twig (60%)

Left
Cola microcarpa: A fruiting twig (50%)

Below left
    Cola microcarpa leaf (60%)

Opposite above
Cola microcarpa male flower

Opposite below
Cola microcarpa bark

1490

Paradise Skipper, *Abantis paradisea*, breeds on the tree.

The wood is hard and durable and, although straight pieces are rare, it is sometimes used for disselbooms. Saplings make excellent sticks, and these are very popular from Zululand to the Transkei, and sometimes are beautifully carved and treasured by their owners.

The specific name means "of Natal".

(478.1)   b. *Cola microcarpa* Brenan

Vanquisher; umQosho, umNgqosho (Z)

This species differs from *Cola natalensis* in its distribution which is more northerly, and also in certain botanical details.

It is common in parts of northern Zululand and is one of the interesting tree species in the short, dense sand forest near False Bay and in the high forest round Lake Sibayi. Until recently the tall forest form at Sibayi was something of a mystery for flowers and fruits, needed for a positive identification, had never been seen. In November 1968 these were collected for the first time by Mr Ian Garland and the identity of the trees established.

Whereas *Cola microcarpa* in short forest usually grows up to about 6 or 8 m, the high forest form grows into a 15 m tree. It has a light brown, flaking bark, and — characteristically — very young leaves which are straw and copper-coloured or palest green, and which hang downwards in contrast to the mature leaves which grow outwards. A forest tree in young leaf is thus deep green boldly splashed with pale colours.

The leaves somewhat resemble those of *Cola natalensis*, but are often slightly shorter and wider in proportion to their length, and, like those of *Cola natalensis*, are smooth when mature with the midrib and secondary veins conspicuous below. The leaf stalks show one characteristic difference. The small swellings at the junction of the stalks and leaf blades are not smooth but densely hairy, like small velvet spats.

The flowers, male or female — probably on different trees — are borne singly in the axils of the leaves or massed between them, and bloom about October.

The fruit is unique and beautiful. One to 5 carpels develop and these are the size of small cherries, round with a slight neck, the necks united, sometimes green when mature but more often a rich orange-vermilion, making — in the case of fruit with 5 carpels — a brilliantly coloured ring. The rind is rather brittle although not hard as in *Cola natalensis*, and is covered with hairs that rub off easily. Each carpel is a browny-pink within and holds 1 to 2 flattish seeds. The inside is not sticky as in *Cola natalensis*.

The fruits are sometimes chewed by the Zulus, but never swallowed. They are eaten by Livingstone's Antelope, Red Duiker, and rodents.

Zulus use the tree medicinally. They value it most for its wood which — together with that of *Cola natalensis* — makes the best of all sticks. (Hence the name umQosho, meaning "the Vanquisher"). It is also used for upright hut poles.

The specific name is based on Greek words meaning "small fruit".

IAN GARLAND   House among *Albizia forbesii,* 714. *Albizia forbesii* flowers, 716. *Albizia anthelmintica* pods, 724. *Cordyla africana,* 890. *Millettia sutherlandii* pods, 924. *Craibia zimmermannii,* 926. *Craibia zimmermannii* stem and bark, 926. *Craibia zimmermannii* stem and bark, 927. *Dalbergia melanoxylon* bark, 934. *Balanites pedicellaris,* Jobe's Kraal, 972. *Fagara* sp. foliage, 982. *Oricia bachmannii* flowers, 988. *Vepris reflexa* stem, 992. *Commiphora woodii* (habit), 1036. *Commiphora zanzibarica* bark, 1048. *Commiphora zanzibarica* flowers, 1048. *Commiphora zanzibarica* fruits, 1048. *Tapura fischeri* leaves and fruits, 1087. *Phyllanthus cedrelifolius* fruits, 1106. *Drypetes gerrardii* bark, 1110. *Drypetes gerrardii* fruit, 1110. *Cleistanthus schlechteri* flowers, 1118. *Cavacoa aurea* trunk, 1137. *Alchornea hirtella* var. *glabrata,* 1140. *Acalypha glabrata* fish trap, 1144. *Euphorbia tirucalli,* Lebombos, 1164. *Protorhus longifolia* flowers, 1202. *Pancovia golungensis* flowers, 1353. *Blighia unijugata* trunk, 1361. *Blighia unijugata* fruits, 1360. *Blighia unijugata* flowers, 1360. *Lasiodiscus milkbraedii* flowers, 1406. *Cola microcarpa* stem and bark, 1491.

THE DIRECTOR, BOTANICAL RESEARCH INSTITUTE   *Albizia versicolor* flowers, 718. *Greyia flanaganii* drawing, 1386. Drawing of baobab leaves and flowers, 1458. *Dombeya rotundifolia* (habit), 1472. *Sterculia murex* flowers, 1482. *Sterculia murex* fruit, 1482.

G. VELCICH   Baskets made of *Acacia ataxacantha,* 746. Kiaat carvings from the Okavango, 938. *Ricinodendron* bowls, 1152. Bags hung in a marula, 1190.

ROSEMARY ZENZINGER   *Acacia montis-usti* bark, 757. Camelthorn on farm "Oasis", 770. *Acacia reficiens* near the Petrified Forest, 810. *Commiphora glaucescens* in leaf, 1038. *Commiphora dinteri,* 1040. Violet tree (habit), 1082. *Euphorbia sekukuniensis* (habit), 1174. *Ozoroa crassinervia* (habit), 1210. *Catha transvaalensis,* 1302. *Catha transvaalensis* bark, 1302. *Catha transvaalensis* bark, 1302.

DR. R. A. DYER   *Acacia tortilis* subsp. *heteracantha,* 782. and *Euphorbia ingens.*Fever trees, Weipe Farm, 812. Baobab flower, 1462.

D. HARDY   *Acacia nebrownii* in South West Africa, 792.

CHRISTOPHER NICHOLSON   *Acacia Kirkii,* 786, 787. *Acacia reficiens* stem, 810. Amblygonocarpus trunk, 822. *Erythrophleum africanum,* Caprivi, 832. *Erythrophleum africanum,* stem, 832. *Pterocarpus antunesii* stems, 940, 941. *Commiphora edulis* (habit), 1036. *Ozoroa crassinervia* bark, 1210.

G. S. DUDLEY   *Amblygonocarpus andongensis* (habit), 822. *Guibourtia coleosperma,* 838. *Brachystegia boehmii* trunk, 845. *Baikiaea plurijuga,* 860. *Baikiaea plurijuga,* 860. *Baikiaea plurijuga* bark, 860. *Dialium engleranum,* 874. *Dialium engleranum* bark, 874. *Ricinodendron rautananii* 1152. *Ricinodendron rautananii* bark, 1152.

EVELYN RUSHMORE   *Guibourtia coleosperma* stem, 838. *Brachystegia boehmii* (habit), 844. *Brachystegia spiciformis,* 848. *Brachystegia spiciformis* bark, 848.

DR. COURTENAY LATIMER   *Umtiza listerana,* 858. Umtiza stem, 858.

DEPARTMENT OF INFORMATION   Xhosa pipe, 764.

KEITH COOPER   *Baphia racemosa* trunk, 909. *Heywoodia lucens* fruit, 1094. *Antidesma venosum* flowers, 1114. *Buxus natalensis* stem, 1186. *Protorhus longifolia* fruits, 1202.

C. J. SKEAD   *Erythrina caffra* at a waterhole, 954. *Erythrina caffra* stem, 955. *Erythrina caffra* stem, 955. *Commiphora woodii* fruits, 1010. *Commiphora woodii* fruits, 1936,

GEOFFREY JENKINS   *Millettia Sutherlandii* trunk, 924. *Macaranga capensis* buttressed trunk, 1142. *Smelophyllum capense* trunk, 1355.

THE AFRICANA MUSEUM   Burchell's sketch of *Acacia hebeclada* pods, 778. Burchell's sketch of *Psoralea pinnata,* 920. Claudius' *Maytenus acuminata,* 1284. Claudius' *Putterlickia puracantha,* 1296.

EUGENE MOLL   *Oricia bachmannii* fruits, 988.

G. L. GUY   The Big Tree south of Gootsa Pan, 1460. Baines tree north of Ghanzi – Baines picture, 1460. The Baines tree today, 1460. Baines's painting of baobabs near Ntwetwe Pan, 1464. The same clump photographed recently, 1464. The Livingstone tree at Shiramba, 1465.

C. J. J. VAN RENSBURG   *Euphorbia ingens,* 1176.